INTERNATIONAL SEX TRAFFICKING
of Women & Children

UNDERSTANDING
THE GLOBAL EPIDEMIC

An Anthology by

LEONARD TERRITO
Saint Leo University

and

GEORGE KIRKHAM
Florida State University

43-08 162nd Street
Flushing, NY 11358
www.LooseleafLaw.com
800-647-5547

Library of Congress Cataloging-In-Publication Data

International sex trafficking of women and children : understanding the global epidemic / edited by Leonard Territo and George Kirkham.
    p. cm.
  Includes index.
  ISBN 978-1-932777-86-4
  1. Human trafficking. 2. Child trafficking. I. Territo, Leonard. II. Kirkham, George.
  HQ281.I69 2010
  364.15--dc22

                                                     2009045046

Cover design by *Sans Serif, Inc.* Saline, Michigan

Dedication

To the thousands of women and men throughout the world who have devoted their professional and personal lives to combating the sex trafficking of women and children.

Table of Contents

ABOUT THE EDITORS

Dr. Leonard Territo is presently a Distinguished Visiting Professor in the Department of Criminal Justice at Saint Leo University, Saint Leo, Florida as well as Professor Emeritus in the Department of Criminology, at the University of South Florida, Tampa, Florida. He has previously served first as a Major and then as Chief Deputy (Undersheriff) with the Leon County Sheriff's Office, Tallahassee, Florida. As Chief Deputy he was responsible for the daily operation of the Leon County Sheriff's Department. While serving with the Leon County Sheriff's Office he was a major homicide investigative advisor on the Chi Omega murders committed by Theodore Robert (Ted) Bundy on the Florida State University campus in Tallahassee, Florida. This investigation eventually led to the arrest, conviction and execution of Ted Bundy. He also served for almost nine years with the Tampa Florida Police Department and had assignments as a patrol officer, motorcycle officer, homicide, rape, and robbery detective, internal affairs detective, and member of the police academy training staff. Dr. Territo is the former chairman of the Department of Police Administration and Director of the Florida Institute for Law Enforcement at St. Petersburg Junior College (now St. Petersburg College), St. Petersburg, Florida.

He is a graduate of the United States Secret Service "Dignitary Protection Seminar," the nationally recognized University of Louisville, "National Crime Prevention Institute" and the Saint Leo University Institute for Excellence in Criminal Justice Administration "Non-Verbal Communications/Detecting Deception."

He has coauthored some of the leading books in the law enforcement profession including: *Criminal Investigation*, 10th edition which is by far the best-selling book of its kind in the United States and has recently been translated into Chinese for use by Chinese law enforcement and Chinese criminal justice students; *Police Administration*, 7th edition; *Crime and Justice in America*, which is in its 6th edition; *Stress Management in Law Enforcement*, 2nd edition; *Stress and Police Personnel*; *The Police Personnel Selection Process; Police Civil Liability; Hospital and College Security Liability;* and *College Crime Prevention and Personal Safety Awareness* were coauthored by Dr. Territo. His books have been used in over one thousand colleges and universities in all 50 states and he has had numerous articles published in nationally recognized law enforcement and legal journals. His books have been used and referenced by both academic and police departments in sixteen countries which are: Australia; Barbados; Belarus; Canada; Chile; China; Czechoslovakia; England; France; Germany; Israel; The Netherlands; Poland; Saudi Arabia; South Korea; and Spain.

He was selected for inclusion in "Who's Who" in American Law Enforcement, selected as Florida's "Outstanding Criminal Justice

Educator" by the Florida Criminal Justice Educators Association, cited for ten years of "Meritorious Service" by the Florida Police Chiefs Association, given the "Outstanding Teacher Award" by the College of Social and Behavioral Sciences, University of South Florida, Tampa, Florida, and cited for twenty-five years of teaching and meritorious service to the Tampa Police Academy and awarded the Saint Leo University, Saint Leo, Florida Outstanding Publication Award.

As a Police Policies and Procedures Expert, he has been qualified in both state and federal courts in the following states: Alaska; Arizona; District of Columbia; Florida; Georgia; Illinois; Iowa; Kansas; Kentucky; Louisiana; Michigan; New Jersey; Ohio; Oregon; Pennsylvania; Tennessee; Virginia; Washington; Wisconsin.

Dr. Territo has served as a lecturer throughout the United States and has instructed a wide variety of police subjects to thousands of law enforcement officials.

Dr. George Kirkham (Doctorate in Criminology, University of California, Berkeley), in 1991, at age 49, was awarded title of Professor Emeritus at the Florida State University School of Criminology and Criminal Justice, making him one of the youngest faculty members in the history of the university to receive the status as a result of outstanding contributions to a field of knowledge.

Characterized by syndicated columnist William F. Buckley Jr. as "... an honor to his profession," Dr. Kirkham has been the recipient of numerous awards for service to the law enforcement profession nationwide, including The Distinguished Service Award, The J. Edgar Hoover Award and the Freedom's Foundation at Valley Forge Award.

He is nationally and internationally known as "the professor who became a cop." In 1973, Dr. Kirkham took leave of his university post in order to study the police and the problems of crime in a way that no criminology professor had before. He personally went through a police academy as a recruit and spent six months working as a uniformed patrol officer on the streets of a high crime beat in a major American city.

This pioneering research project earned Dr. Kirkham widespread respect in both the law enforcement profession and the field of criminology. Over the years, his observations on the police have appeared in research and law enforcement journals in many other countries, including England, Canada, Germany, India, Australia and Russia. He has authored to date some 23 law enforcement training films and video tapes which are used to instruct police officers and administrators throughout the nation. Under grants from the U.S. Department of Justice, Dr. Kirkham's award winning film series, "Police, The Human Dimension" was distributed to the law enforcement training directors of all 50 states and the F.B.I. Academy. This series is also used at the Peel Centre in London to train the British Metropolitan Police.

Dr. Kirkham has served as a consultant to more than 50 American law enforcement agencies at the federal, state and local levels. He has been called upon more often than any other criminologist in the nation to serve as a case consultant and expert witness in civil and criminal actions involving police, jail and private security issues. His experience as a consultant to both plaintiffs and defendants throughout his professional career encompasses over 1,500 cases in 50 states.

In addition to receiving widespread professional recognition, Dr. Kirkham's work has also been the subject of considerable attention by the mass media and the American public: he was the subject of a CBS 60 MINUTES segment entitled "Ivory Tower Cop," and has made numerous national television appearances to discuss the subjects of crime and the police, including ABC's GOOD MORNING AMERICA and NBC's TOMORROW SHOW. His 1974 article, "A Professor's Street Lesson," was serialized in newspapers throughout the nation and has been read by more police worldwide than any article ever published by the F.B.I. during the fifty-seven-year history of its LAW ENFORCEMENT BULLETIN.

Dr. Kirkham's personal autobiography, SIGNAL ZERO, was selected by Book-of-the-Month Club as one of its alternates and his views on the police have appeared in publications ranging from NEWSWEEK, TIME, U.S. NEWS & WORLD REPORT, READER'S DIGEST and PEOPLE MAGAZINE, to the UNITED STATES CONGRESSIONAL RECORD and INTERPOL.

Throughout his twenty years as a university criminologist, Dr. Kirkham's "hands on" research on the subjects of crime and the police has led him to work as an officer with four different law enforcement agencies and in assignments as diverse as uniformed patrol, crisis intervention, vice, criminal investigation, and undercover duty as part of an organized crime strike force.

ACKNOWLEDGMENTS

We wish to express our thanks and indebtedness to the following distinguished scholars who allowed us to use their research papers in this book. Without their dedicated efforts this book could have never come to fruition: Osita Agbu, Michigan State University; Alexis A. Aronowitz, United Nations, Interregional Crime and Justice Research Institute; Andrea Marie Bertone, University of Maryland; Kerry Carrington, University of New England; Katherine Y. Chon, Polaris Project; Terry Coonan, Florida State University; Melina Czmoniewicz-Klippel, Pennsylvania State University; Fiona David, Australian Institute of Criminology; Julia O'Connell Davidson, University of Nottingham; Moshoula Capous Desyllas, Portland State University; Jo Doezema, University of Sussex; Derek P. Ellerman, Polaris Project; David W. Engstrom, San Diego State University; Monica Espinoza; Cornelius Friesendorf, Ludwig-Maximillians-University; Olga Gajic-Veljanoski, University of Toronto; Glenda L. Giron; Eglantina Gjermeni, University of Tirana; David E. Guinn, Administrative Judicial Institute, New York City; Edlira Haxhiymeri, University of Tirana; Jane Hearn, Australian National University; Elizabeth Hoban, Deakin University; Donna M. Hughes, University of Rhode Island; Kevin Ireland, The Save the Children Fund; Sheila Jeffreys, University of Melbourne; Loring Jones, San Diego State University; Erica Kotnik; Mark Logan, Department of State; Victor Malarek; Sarah A. Minas, San Diego State University; Anupriya Sethi, Labour Program of the Human Resources and Social Development Canada; Padam Simkhada, University of Aberdeen; Louise Shelley, Transnational Crime and Corruption Center; Sarah Stephen-Smith, POPPY Project; Donna E. Stewart, University of Toronto; Mary P. Van Hook, University of Central Florida; Sallie Yea, Charles Sturt University.

We wish to thank Autumn Frei, doctoral candidate in the Department of Criminology at the University of South Florida, Tampa, Florida, for her many hours of hard work in obtaining copies of more than 150 research papers from which we selected the final 27 research papers. She also obtained the addresses, e-mails, fax numbers and phone numbers of all the publishers and authors we had to contact so we would be able to most efficiently get permission to reprint these research papers. We feel confident that in the not-too-distant future we will be able to call our colleague Dr. Frei.

Typing and other numerous clerical and research services were also provided by our hard-working secretary, Sharon Ostermann, whose constructive comments and long hours of work are very much appreciated. She has a wonderful attitude and it is always a pleasure working with her. We also want to thank her trusty assistant, Shari Allen, for her numerous hours of typing. She, too, was a pleasure to work with.

Lastly, we want to thank our publisher, Mary Loughrey, for sharing our conviction that this book will make a significant contribution toward the understanding and prevention of the international sex trafficking of women and children.

PREFACE

The U.S. State Department has estimated that between 700,000 and two million women are trafficked each year worldwide and that as many as 50,000 women and children are trafficked into the United States annually, primarily from Latin American countries and the former Soviet Union and Southeast Asia. Beyond this it is estimated that between 100,000 and 300,000 children are exploited annually by the sex industry within the United States alone. The U.S. Congress has recently reported that the sex trafficking of women and children was the 3rd largest source of revenue for organized crime worldwide, following closely behind drug and firearm trafficking.

International Sex Trafficking of Women and Children has been designed so that it will be of value and interest to the following audiences: first, academicians who have a scholarly research interest in the sex trafficking of women and children and who may want to teach the subject as a college seminar; second, law enforcement trainers who teach the subject of sex trafficking to both recruit officers as well as veteran officers; third, law enforcement administrators who must deal with the problem of sex trafficking within their local jurisdictions and need to formulate effective and appropriate policies and procedures; fourth, police officers who work on the streets and may come in contact with women and, in some cases, children who are the victims of sex trafficking or sexual exploitation. This is especially true in those American communities that have large numbers of immigrant women from both the former Eastern bloc countries as well as from Asia and Central and South America; fifth, members of both nongovernmental agencies (NGOs) and governmental agencies who provide physical, psychological and economic support to the many thousands of victims of sex trafficking; lastly, federal, state or local legislators who may wish to implement laws to expand the authority of law enforcement officials and others to deal more effectively with sex trafficking in their communities.

This book has been organized based upon the international variations of sex trafficking. These include sex trafficking in North America and South America, Europe, Asia, Australia and Africa. Although there is a great deal of similarity between sex trafficking in women and children in these various parts of the world, there are certain aspects that are idiosyncratic to them as both receiver and sender countries. Their similarities and dissimilarities are discussed in great detail within the research papers presented in this book. We have also devoted an entire section to child sex tourism focusing on those parts of the world where this problem is endemic and have set forth the ways in which it can and is being combated.

KEY TERMS

Normally when key terms are incorporated into an edited volume they are inserted either after each research paper or in the back of the book. However the editors have made a decision to place them up front because it is easier and more convenient for the reader to become familiar with these "key terms" prior to reading each of the papers or for that matter having to constantly go to the back of the research paper or the back of the book to check the key terms. It is strongly recommended that readers become familiar with the key terms before they start to read this book.

Abolitionism – This arose as a specific response to the Contagious Diseases Act enacted in England in the 1880s which epitomized the regulationist approach to the control of prostitution through medical supervision. The Abolitionists wanted not only to abolish prostitution but also aimed to cleanse society of vice through a repressive program focusing on the sexual behavior of young people.

All China Women's Federation (ACWF) – This group has a number of ongoing prevention and education projects in affected provinces in China.

Broken in – This is a term used for young girls, often virgins, who are repeatedly raped and beaten in order to intimidate and coerce them into becoming compliant prostitutes.

Butlerite Feminists – This group was named after Josephine Butler who famously led a feminist campaign to abolish prostitution in England in the 1880s. The Butlerites opposed the then view of prostitutes as fallen women or sexual deviants and placed the blame for prostitution squarely on the shoulders of unbridled male lust. They viewed prostitutes as victims who should be rehabilitated rather than policed and punished.

C3 Visas – This is a 90-day visitor's visa. Many women, especially those who go to Korea, overstay the time allotted on their visas and as a result are then working illegally.

Cadena Case – This is a case in which a Mexican crime family trafficked 25-40 Mexican women and girls into the United States between 1996 and 1997 and forced them into prostitution, working primarily in migrant camp farm worker communities throughout Florida.

Canada's Immigration and Refugee Protection Act (IRPA) – This is a law which prescribes fines for human trafficking of up to $1 million and imprisonment for up to life. The IRPA also allows victims to make a claim for refugee protection in order to apply for permanent status.

Canadian Aboriginal Girls – These are indigenous girls, many of whom belong to the First Nations, Inuit and Métis tribes.

Canadian Stop The Traffic Coalition – This is a group which initiated communication with the Royal Canadian Mounted Police (RCMP) and local police to establish an action plan on how to best deal with human trafficking. The plan was then submitted to Parliament.

Child Sex Tourism – This is tourism organized with the primary purpose of facilitating the commercial sexual relations of an adult with a child.

Chinese Triads – These are Chinese organized crime groups heavily involved in human smuggling.

Coalition Against Trafficking in Women (CATW) – Founded by Kathleen Barry it is one of the largest and most influential international anti trafficking organizations. It takes a neo-abolitionists' view of prostitution and descends from the late 19th century Butlerites who considered prostitution as violence against women.

Comfort Women – A term used by the Japanese army, when they occupied Korea up to 1945, to describe Korean women they forced into sexual slavery to service Japanese soldiers.

Commercial Sex Act – This term means any sex act for which anything of value is given or received by any person.

COYOTE (Cast Off Your Old Tired Ethics) – This is a pro-prostitution lobby group in the United States which favors decriminalizing prostitution and has been promoting its ideas since the early 1980s.

The Daughters Education Program (DEP) – This is a group in Thailand that provides alternative education programs including leadership and skills training for girls at risk who may come from families of former prostitutes, broken homes, or families with substance abuse problems.

Debt Bondage – This is the status or condition of a debtor arising from a pledge by the debtor of his or her personal services or those of a person under his or her control as a security for debt.

Deceptive Recruiting – This is deceiving a person for the purpose of sexual servitude, debt bondage or other forms of sexual exploitation.

Domestic Trafficking – This is sex trafficking within the borders of a country and recognition that the tactics used by procurers and pimps are the same. The women are recruited and transported within the same country.

"Drinkie Girl" – This is a slang name given by American military personnel to the foreign women in South Korea who work in clubs which are often located in close proximity to American military bases. The name is a reference to the drinking system that operates in all clubs. Under this system, customers buy the women's time in the club with purchase of a drink for her. Each drink costs the customer between $10 and $20 with the expectation of having sex with her.

Employment Agencies Network – This includes domestic servants, babysitters, travel escorts and artists, dancers, singers, etc.

End Child Prostitution in Asian Tourism (ECPAT) – This is one of the first groups organized to seek the end of the sex trade in children. It monitors the child sex trade around the world.

Entertainment Network – This includes shopping malls, nightclubs, bars, restaurants, motels, beach tents, fast food restaurants, show houses, samba gatherings, brothels and massage parlors.

E6 Entertainer Visa – Many Filipina women arrive in South Korea on these visas. They are recruited as overseas performing artists (OPA) and they are required to prove they have entertainer skills before they are granted authorized entry into other countries to work in the entertainment industry.

European Women's Lobby (EWL) – This group maintains the primary view of prostitution as violence and sexual slavery. The victim stance taken by this abolitionist group is in contrast to the sex workers' rights perspective that was concerned with women's agency.

Fashion Market Network – This includes modeling agencies (photography, videos and movies) and provides traffickers with great access to particularly attractive or appealing women and girls.

Fautor – In modern usage the term means patron, supporter, or abettor (a.k.a. Johns). It usually refers to men who frequent, use, and pay for sexual services of other persons (usually women).

Forced Prostitution – This refers to women or girls who are compelled to engage in sexual acts with strangers in exchange for commodities with the compulsion emanating from either physical violence and threats to their lives or bodily integrity or those of their families, emotional and physical coercion based on their indebtedness to the smugglers and procurers and/or their presence in a foreign country without legal status and any support network.

Gabfai Theater Group – This is an innovative program established in Chiang Mai, Thailand in 1966 and has reached over 136,000 people since then. The theater group travels to high risk areas involving communities in various projects, performances and workshops using drama and related activities to teach, inspire discussion and address problems including the empowerment of people through education with regard to the issues involved in sex trafficking.

Gharwalies – These are brothel owners with whom most Nepali girls are associated.

Global Alliance Against Traffic in Women (GAATW) – A group founded in Thailand along with the Network for Sex Work Projects (NSWP) that distinguishes between forced and voluntary prostitution in support for sex work safe labor conditions.

Greater Mekong Sub-Region (GMS) – This includes the countries of Thailand and Cambodia, in particular, and are increasingly viewed as an epicenter for trafficking for both sexual and labor exploitation in Asia.

Hetaerae – A term used for foreign women who are considered exotic and erotic. This perception, in turn, has fueled the demand for their services in prostitution, further inflating the demand for trafficked women.

Human Smuggling – This relates more to immigration laws than it does to criminal statutes. There is a contractual agreement in which one person (the smuggler) agrees to take, guide, or transport another person (the smuggled human) across a national border illegally for a fee.

Human Trafficking – It can encompass two forms, namely, the trafficking of women, girls, and boys for the purpose of sexual exploitation, as well as the trafficking of males and females for labor exploitation.

Immigration and Refugee Protection Act (IRPA) – This act proscribes fines for human trafficking of up to one million dollars and imprisonment for up to life. It also allows victims to make a claim for refugee protection or to apply for permanent resident status.

International Abolitionist Federation (IAF) – This group maintains the primary view of prostitution as violence and sexual slavery.

International Catholic Migration Commission (ICMC) – This is a group that has developed a referral and shelter program for women coming from Albania, Kosovo and other Eastern European countries.

International Organizations (IOs) – These are organizations that help to formulate and implement anti-traffic programs and include: UN agencies, NATO (North Atlantic Treaty Organization), the European Union (EU), the Organization of Security and Cooperation for Europe (OSCE) and, the Council of Europe.

Kijichons – These are military camp towns in South Korea which are closed to South Korean citizens but allow US troops to enter. It is estimated that 20,000 women work in the various kijichons to provide sexual services to American military personnel.

Korea Church Women United (KCWU) – This is a religious feminist nongovernmental organization (NGO) that wrote a report on sex trafficking in US military camp town areas drawing on cases of over 40 women, including Filipinas and Russians.

Ma Mawi Wi Chi Itata Center – This Canadian group created the "Honouring the Spirit of Our Little Sisters" which is an establishment of healing centres and shelters specifically to meet the needs of trafficked girls, and adequate child welfare managed by Aboriginal organizations.

Manitoba Warriors – A Canadian Aboriginal street gang involved in sex trafficking.

Mann Act of 1910 – A law used by the police in the United States as justification to arrest prostitutes and to persecute black men for having sex with white women.

Marriage Agency Network – There are at least two types of trafficking through marriage agencies. Either the woman replies to an advertisement or she joins a sex tourism agency that also arranges marriages for foreigners.

Model State Anti-Trafficking Criminal Statute – Developed by the United States Department of Justice. It can be used by state legislatures in the United States as a model for developing their own state statutes.

Natashas – The generic name given in some parts of the world, most notably in Israel and Turkey, for women from Russia and other republics of the former Soviet Union who provide services as prostitutes.

Native Syndicate – A Canadian Aboriginal-based street gang involved in sex trafficking.

Nepali Kothas (Compounds) – This is where Nepali girls in India's red light district remain largely segregated in brothels.

Network for Sex Work Projects (NSWP) – This group maintains the primary view of prostitution as violence and sexual slavery.

Non Governmental Organizations (NGOs) – These are organizations that are neither paid by nor officially connected with any other governmental agencies, although they do work very closely with them on a variety of human trafficking and sex trafficking issues.

Organized Criminal Group – This is a structured group of three or more persons existing for a period of time and acting in concert with the aim of committing one or more serious crimes or offenses in order to obtain directly or indirectly a financial or other material benefit.

Overseas Performing Artists (OPA) – These are performing artists who are required to prove they have entertainer skills before they are granted authorized entry into other countries to work in the entertainment industry.

Palermo Protocol – Also known as the United Nations Protocol to Prevent, Suppress, and Punish Trafficking in Persons, Especially Women and Children. This protocol defines trafficking in persons to mean the recruitment, transportation, transfer, harboring or receipt of persons, by means of the threat to use force or other forms of coercion, of abduction, of fraud, of deception, of the abuse of power or of a position of vulnerability or the giving or receiving of payments or benefits to achieve the consent of the person having control over another person for the purpose of exploitation.

Perestroika – The political term used to describe the disintegration of the Soviet Union which opened borders for travel and migration and privatized trade which in turn facilitated the operation of criminal networks.

Pillow Houses – These are the cheapest brothels in Nepal, which are no more than dark claustrophobic rooms with cloth dividers hung between the beds. This is what they are known by among Nepalis.

POPPY – A group in the United Kingdom helping trafficked women to successfully integrate into British society. Managed by the EAVES Housing for Women, which is a feminist organization committed to lobbying for the abolition of prostitution, including all forms of sexual exploitation caused by male demand for commercial sex acts which in turn facilitates and increases sex trafficking.

Preferential Child Molester – A person somewhat akin to a pedophile, although the definition would also include those whose preference is for sex with post-pubertal children.

Prostitution – It is usually assumed the chief actor is a woman, but it can be a man, who sells sexual favors for money, products, or privileges.

Ramos Case – This is a case in which a family of Mexican-American labor contractors subjected migrant farm workers to involuntary servitude in Florida's agricultural fields between 2000 and 2001.

Regulationists – Those who are in favor of the state system of licensed brothels in which prostitutes are subjected to various forms of regulation such as forced medical examination and restriction on mobility. The ideology behind regulation was that of prostitution as a necessary evil.

Second Wave – One of the most common ways women are recruited from the Ukraine to come to foreign countries and engage in prostitution is through a friend or acquaintance. Once the woman has been trafficked and trapped in the sex industry she has few options.

Sexual Servitude – Defined as occurring when sexual services are provided because of force or threats and the person is not free to cease providing those services.

Sex Trafficking – A commercial sex act which is induced by force, fraud, or coercion in which the person induced to perform such an act has not attained 18 years of age or the recruitment, harboring, transportation, provision, or obtaining of a person for labor or services through use of force, fraud, or coercion for the purpose of subjection to involuntary servitude, peonage, debt bondage, or slavery.

Sex Tourism Industry – Comprised of travel agencies that arrange for hotels, health spas/resorts, and transportation where trips are arranged for men (and sometimes women) to have sex with local women and children who are provided to service this demand.

Sex Tourists – Usually men who employ prostituted women and children. They are both homosexual and heterosexual and generally choose locations that combine widespread poverty with a well developed and highly commercialized sex industry.

Sex Workers Rights Approach – In this view prostitution is seen as a viable option and a choice that women make in order to survive and should be respected and not stigmatized. The pro-rights or sex worker perspective is supported by the belief that women have the right to sexual determination, the right to work in safe labor conditions and the right to migrate for sex work wherever they choose.

Sham Marriages – These are marriages by US GIs to foreign women and is a primary method for getting the women back into the United States. Once back in the United States quickie divorces are obtained and the women are forced to work in sexually-oriented businesses such as massage parlors.

Situational Child Molesters – This is someone who does not have a sexual preference for children but engages in sex with children for varied reasons. This would include persons of poor self-esteem and coping skills as well as those who display morally or sexually indiscriminate behavior is a "why not" approach to sex.

Sonogachi Project – This is a project in India recognized by the United Nations as a model program for addressing the problems faced by sex workers such as the spread of HIV and protection of rights.

Standing Against Global Exploitation (SAGE) – Survivors of prostitution have been working with feminist activists and others in the Coalition Against Trafficking in Women to develop an international network aimed at ending men's abuse of women in prostitution.

Status of Forces Agreement (SOFA) – This is a security treaty between the United States and the Republic of Korea which has made it difficult for the Korean government to take legal action against US troops even when they have committed crimes.

Subaltern Men – Men considered to belong to a lower social class or race.

Taxi Connection – These are taxi drivers who serve a number of different functions within the broader field of trafficking. This includes serving as recruiters for traffickers by identifying potential victims, acting as the transporters of trafficked individuals, and finally, linking women or children with their customers.

Technical Education and Skills Development Authority (TESDA) – An organization that supervises the training and testing centers that determine if women sent abroad are qualified as performing artists. They are sometimes involved in bribery and deception with the issuance of E-6 Visas (Entertainer Visa).

The Tier System – The US, along with a few other western European countries, has awarded itself tier one status which represents sufficient efforts at combating trafficking. However those countries that do not demonstrate adequate means and efforts to end trafficking, as judged appropriate by the US, are ranked either as tier two or three. Most countries judged as being on tier three are then subject to sanctions by the US (except for sanctions on humanitarian aid).

Trafficked Person – This is someone who is transferred or transported across national or international borders by means of threat or coercion for the purpose of economic exploitation in prostitution, forced labor, slavery or the removal of organs.

Trafficking in Persons Report (TPR) – This is the means by which the United States government passes judgment on itself and other countries of the world regarding their commitment toward anti trafficking.

Trafficking Victims Protection Act of 2000 (TVPA) – Under the provisions of the TVPA, the United States declared the war on sex trafficking a national and international priority and has predicated US foreign aid, in part, upon compliance with the TVPA's mandate that all states undertake similar efforts. Also under the provisions of the TVPA, the US advocates the 3 Ps approach to fighting trafficking, namely, **P**revention, **P**rosecution, and **P**rotection.

Transnational Crime Coordination Center – This Center was established within the Australian Federal Police (AFP) and aims to collaborate internationally to prevent, dismantle, and investigate transnational crime and will target investigations into five key transnational crimes which include: terrorism; illicit drug trafficking; people smuggling; high tech crime; and money laundering.

Transnational Trafficking – The sex trafficking of women that involves the crossing of an international border.

Transparency International Corruption Perceptions Index (CPI) – Permits one to determine the extent to which a country tolerates trafficking in or through its territory and the extent to which it is seen to be corrupt.

Travel and the Single Male (TSM) – An American-based organization run by and for sex tourists and boasts some 5,000 members. It publishes a guidebook and sells club membership for $50 per annum.

United Nations Office for Drug Control and Crime Prevention (UNODCCP) – Emphasizes research which seeks to shed more light on the phenomenon of trafficking human beings in particular on criminal practices, roots and networks that facilitate the process and provides technical assistance projects to strengthen governmental responses to the smuggling and trafficking problem.

United Nations Protocol to Prevent, Suppress and Punish Trafficking in Persons Especially Women and Children – Commonly known as the Palermo Protocol under the provisions of TVPA the United States not only declared the war on trafficking a national/international priority, it predicated U.S. foreign aid upon compliance with the TVPA's mandate that all states undertake similar efforts.

Unemancipated Women – These are women who are characterized as poor, naïve, and unempowered in the third world or former communist countries and are perceived as being unable to act as agents in their own lives or to make an uncoerced decisions to work in the sex industry.

United States Trafficking in Persons List (TIP) – The expected standards on the TIP include: national laws prohibiting and punishing acts of trafficking, laws prescribing commensurate punishment for grave crimes (such as; trafficking involving rape, kidnapping or murder); actions sufficiently deterrent to prevent trafficking; and serious and sustained efforts to eliminate trafficking.

Universal Federation of Travel Agents Associations – This is a group that has produced a children and travel agents charter. Their pledge is to give assistance to various organizations concerned with the welfare of child victims or sex tourism to help restore the dignity, physical and mental health to such children.

WHISPER (Women Hurt in Systems of Prostitution Engaged in Revolt) – Survivors of prostitution have been working with feminist activists and others in the Coalition Against Trafficking in Women to develop an international network aimed at ending men's abuse of women in prostitution. This movement considers men's abuse of women in prostitution to constitute a form of men's sexual violence against women.

White Slavery – The procurement by force, deceit or drugs of a white woman or girl against her will for prostitution.

Women And Girls Network (WAGN) – A British feminist group that works with women who have experienced violence, and a commitment to a multicultural approach, ensuring that the experience is therapeutic for a particular woman, given her cultural background.

Women's Agency – In the context of the sex industry this means the right of a woman to voluntarily choose or not choose to engage in prostitution.

PART I

Sex Trafficking in North America and South America[*]

Sex Trafficking of Women in the United States. The study by the Coalition Against Trafficking Women is the first to research both international and domestic trafficking of women for sexual exploitation in the United States and to include primary research information from interviews with trafficked and prostituted women in the sex industry. This research paper focuses on recruiters and pimps, the methods of recruitment, methods of movement, methods of initiation, methods of control, profiles of the men who buy women for prostitution, discusses the health of women, the methods women employ for coping and resistance and recommendations for change.

Human Trafficking: Victims' Voices in Florida. To better ascertain the needs of human trafficking victims, the Florida State University Center for the Advancement of Human Rights conducted in-depth interviews in 2002-03 with 11 female survivors of trafficking in Florida. Subjects included victims of sex trafficking and domestic servitude. The qualitative research indicated that physical security, followed by basic needs, was the greatest priority for the victims. Findings also included public and commercial venues to which the women had limited access while enslaved, and media sources available to them at the time. Finally, the victims discussed encounters—and near encounters—with law enforcement that might have liberated them sooner.

Domestic Sex Trafficking of Aboriginal Girls in Canada: Issues and Implications. The current discourses on trafficking in Canada do not take into account domestic trafficking, especially of Aboriginal girls. Notwithstanding the alarmingly high numbers of missing, murdered and sexually exploited Aboriginal girls, the issue continues to be portrayed more as a problem of prostitution than of sexual exploitation or domestic trafficking. The focus of this study was to examine the issue of sexual exploitation of Aboriginal girls as identified by the grass root agencies and to conceptualize them within the trafficking framework with the purpose of distinguishing sexual exploitation from sex work. In doing so the research paper outlines the root causes that make Aboriginal girls

---

[*] The vast majority of the abstracts presented at the front of Parts I through VI were, with slight modifications, taken directly from the original research papers and were written by the author(s) of these papers.

1

vulnerable to domestic trafficking as well as to draw implications for policy analysis.

Trafficking in Women: The Canadian Perspective. In Canada trafficked women are usually discovered through police raids or when victims seek asylum. The Royal Canadian Mounted Police (RCMP) estimates 800 persons a year are trafficked into Canada. Estimates by nongovernmental organizations (NGOs) however estimate this number to be closer to 16,000. In addition there is no official collaborative effort between the Canadian government and NGOs which impedes the assessment of trafficking in Canada. In 2004 the Canadian government introduced an organized effort to battle trafficking at a national level. This was done by establishing a new federal agency, the International Departmental Working Group on Trafficking led by the Foreign Affairs and Justice Department. Their task was to coordinate the work of 14 government agencies and to develop a national strategy against human trafficking.

Defining the Problem of Trafficking: The Interplay of US Law, Donor, and NGO Engagement and the Local Context in Latin America. Efforts to combat trafficking are hindered by poor understandings of the problem. Using Latin America as a case study, this research paper identifies the definitional, sociological, and legal issues that hinder an accurate assessment of the problem. The paper focuses not upon the empirical problems of assessment, but upon issues within the compass of policy makers and advocates. The paper then describes the basic features of trafficking in Latin America and identifies efforts to address the problem, highlighting the role of the United States, and the Trafficking Victims Protection Act (TVPA).

1
SEX TRAFFICKING OF WOMEN IN THE UNITED STATES

Janice G. Raymond, *Ph.D., University of Massachusetts,*
Donna M. Hughes*, Ph.D., University of Rhode Island*
Carol J. Gomez, *BA, Project Coordinator*

Within the last decade, the trafficking of women and children for sexual exploitation has become a major concern for governments, nongovernmental agencies (NGOs) and the media. Although, the United States has been less visible as a site of transnational and domestic trafficking in women than other countries in Europe, and countries such as Japan, Canada and Australia, this situation has dramatically changed. Recent accounts about sex trafficking in the United States, mainly appearing in national and local media, indicate that trafficking for commercial sexual exploitation is a national problem, and one that is increasing in scope and magnitude. The U.S. government estimates that 50,000 women and children are trafficked each year into the United States, primarily from Latin America, countries of the former Soviet Union and Southeast Asia. This study by the Coalition Against Trafficking Women is the first to research both international and domestic trafficking of women for sexual exploitation in the United States and to include primary research information from interviews with trafficked and prostituted women in the sex industry.

Research Aims and Methods

The aim of this research was to broadly investigate the international and domestic trafficking in women in the United States. The specific goals were to:

- Document known cases and information on sex trafficking in the United States
- Establish a research framework for studying sex trafficking in the United States
- Describe the connections between the *supply* of women trafficked from abroad and within the United States to the *demand* created by the sex industries
- Describe local sex industries and their involvement in sex trafficking and prostitution
- Describe linkages between international and domestic trafficking and sex industries
- Describe regional differences in sex trafficking and sex industries in the United States

✓ Describe the social consequences of sex trafficking in terms of violence, crime, health and other human costs.

The research framework follows the path of trafficked women through their experiences in the sex industry. Interviewees were questioned about women's background before being recruited or trafficked into the sex industry, the methods used to recruit them, whether and how they were moved around while in the sex industry, how they were initiated into the roles and activities they had to carry out, how they were controlled, and how they coped with and resisted the conditions under which they lived. Interviewees were asked about the recruiters, traffickers and pimps and the men who buy women in the sex industry. They were asked about women's health and well being while in sex industry and after getting out. Interviewees were also asked about the operation of the sex industry in their region. Finally, the interviewees were asked for their recommendations for policies on trafficking and prostitution.

Five U.S. regions were selected for regional comparisons in trafficking and operation of the sex industry: Metro San Francisco, Metro New York, Northern Midwest, the Northeast and the Southeast. These cities have large sex industries that enable comparisons of geographical differences, routes of trafficking, source countries of trafficked women and the operation of the sex industry.

Target sampling was used to gather information from the most informed experts on the topic. One hundred and twenty-eight individuals were interviewed, including international (N=15) and U.S. (N=25) women who had been or are in the sex industry in the United States, law enforcement officials (N=32) who have experience and expertise in sex-industry related cases or immigration, social service workers (N=43) who provide services to women in prostitution or may come in contact with women from the sex industry, and those providing services to immigrant populations, academic researchers and investigative journalists who have studied the sex industry or trafficking of women and/or migrants, and health care workers (N=13) who provide services to women in prostitution or may come in contact with women in the sex industry.

A unique source of data was used to research these topics. Men's writings on their experiences buying women in prostitution were downloaded from the Internet. Qualitative data analysis was used to analyze men's descriptions of the operation of the sex industry and their activities and behavior inside prostitution establishments.

Major Findings

Operation of the Sex Industry
The sex businesses in the five regions investigated are prolific and diverse. Each region had elements of operation that were both similar

and unique. Sex businesses thrive in all areas—urban, suburban and rural, as well as in areas surrounding U.S. military bases. Internationally trafficked women are reported to be present in all of these diverse areas.

Some sex enterprises operate legally or are incorporated as legal. Others operate behind legal front businesses, such as restaurants or nail salons. Yet others are makeshift ventures, operating out of mobile trailers or warehouses that are converted into brothels. Many sex entrepreneurs are constantly changing not only the location, but also the venues and ways of operating the businesses.

Sex businesses are advertised in a variety of ways including in print media such as mainstream English language newspapers and periodicals, non-English community newspapers and periodicals, pornographic magazines, sex guides, the *Yellow Pages*, and billboards. The industry is further advertised through electronic media such as television advertisements and on the internet, mobile advertising such as through billboards on trucks and in informal ways using business cards, flyers, matchbooks and word of mouth.

In the Northeast reported sex businesses include street prostitution, escort services, massage parlors, health clubs, brothels in hotels, rented houses and apartments and legitimate front businesses. In Metro New York, reported sex businesses include street prostitution, strip clubs, go-go bars, peep or fantasy booth shows, massage parlors, after-hours clubs, private apartments, hotels, escort services and makeshift operations in beauty parlors, restaurants and warehouses. The Northern Midwest has high street prostitution activity, saunas, health clubs, strip clubs, bars, escort services, "chicken shacks" (dwellings used for quick prostitution transactions) and brothels in migrant farm worker camps. Metro San Francisco's sex industry includes street prostitution, strip clubs, bars, adult entertainment theatres, pornography emporiums, massage parlors, escort services, private residences and rent-by-the-hour hotels. Sex businesses reported in the Southeast include massage parlors and brothels in urban and suburban areas as well as makeshift brothels in gambling halls, houses and trailers in isolated and rural farm worker camps.

U.S. military bases, especially in the South replicate the sexual rest and recreation (R&R) areas that proliferate near military bases abroad. This infrastructure of sex clubs, brothels and massage parlors has been recreated here, with inordinate numbers of Asian women especially trafficked and exploited in the sex industries surrounding the bases.

Controllers and operators of the sex industry vary. Some sex businesses are family owned and others may be owned or backed by prominent local community members, including judges and lawyers. Others are controlled or financed by organized crime groups. The majority of law enforcement agents reported that 76-100 percent of the sex enterprises in the Northeast, Metro New York, the Southeast, and Metro

San Francisco are controlled, financed, or backed by organized crime groups. In some cases, trafficking rings supply women to sex establishments.

Organized crime groups may be highly structured organizations, run by a hierarchy of individuals and groups, with many key players, or decentralized and less organized small groups of individuals who get together for a "business venture" with no central leader. Sex enterprise owners rarely are involved in the daily or frontline operations, and may depend upon many layers of people to run the business.

Background of the Women in the Sex Industry in the United States

Men's writings from the Internet revealed large differences in racial and international proportions of women in prostitution in three regional cities. In New York City, more "Hispanic/Latina" and "Black" women were identified as compared to San Francisco, where "Asians" strongly predominate. In Minneapolis/St. Paul, race was less often mentioned and the proportions of the racial groups are equal. In San Francisco, the most frequently mentioned national groups by geographical area were largely Asian, followed by small numbers of Eastern Europeans and Central Americans. In New York City, the most frequently mentioned national groups by geographical area were South and Central American, followed equally by Asian and Eastern European national identities. In Minneapolis/St. Paul, there were no women identified by nationality. There was no mention in the men's writings of women from African countries.

The international women interviewed in this study were predominantly from the former Soviet Union (13 of 15), and over half of the U.S. women were African American (13 of 25). The majority of international (80%) and U.S. women (83%) interviewed in this study entered the sex industry before the age of 25, many of them as children. Sixty percent of the international women had been in the sex industry before entering the United States. Seventy-three percent of international women had no or very little English language proficiency while in the sex industry in the United States. The majority of international women arrived in the country on tourist visas (53%) and other legal means, while others were trafficked in with the use of fraudulent travel papers.

Recruiters, Traffickers and Pimps

Organized businesses and crime networks, such as escort services, bars, brothels, clubs, "biker gangs" and the mafia, were instrumental in recruiting the international (60%) and U.S. women (40%). U.S. servicemen have also been involved in recruiting Asian women, especially from Korea, Vietnam and Japan into the sex industry in the United States. Often the servicemen marry prostituted women around military bases abroad, bring them to the United States and pressure them into prostitution. A large number of foreign military wives become victims of domestic violence, displaced or homeless, and end up in prostitution around U.S. military bases.

The majority of international (75%) and U.S. (64%) women reported that people who recruited and/or trafficked them were connected to pimps in the sex industry. Recruiters, traffickers and pimps are involved in other criminal activity, such as fraud, extortion, migrant smuggling, theft and money laundering, in addition to trafficking and prostitution. Most trafficking organizations were small, with only one to five people involved, although there were some large (6-15 people) and very large (50-100 people) networks reported. Husbands and boyfriends acted as pimps for some of the international (20%) and U.S. (28%) women.

Methods of Recruitment

Conditions facilitating recruitment of women include economic desperation and disadvantage, lack of a sustainable income, and poverty— all of which are preyed on by recruiters, traffickers and pimps.

Reported push factors were economic and oppressive conditions in countries of origin. In some families, girls were seen as burdens and liabilities, and lack of family support, or direct family pressure or coercion, precipitated women's entrance into the sex industry. Sometimes older brothers or uncles acted as conduits for recruitment.

Traffickers and pimps recruited a significant number of international and U.S. women. Recruiters or pimps promised money and the opportunity to make a lot of money to many of the international (73%) and U.S. (33%) women. Some international women were brought into the United States through marriage to U.S. men, especially military personnel.

Some international women answered ads for jobs in the United States or responded to ads placed in "the personals." Several women entered the country independently, arranging for their own legitimate or illegitimate travel documents.

Pimps recruit young, vulnerable U.S. women in malls and clubs by befriending and creating emotional and drug or alcohol dependencies to entrap them. Pimps are also adept at preying upon women's vulnerabilities. Coercion and violence are also used.

Methods of Movement

Entry points for trafficked women into the United States are strategic sites along the U.S., Canadian and Mexican borders and international airports. These entry points for trafficking are fluid, shifting to other locations when there are crackdowns.

Many of the U.S. (62%) and international (29%) women are domestically trafficked inside the United States. These trafficking patterns are diverse with international women transported from the East to the West coast, from the South to the Northeast, and from urban to rural and rural to urban districts. Similarly, U.S. women are domestically trafficked across city, state and even national borders.

Methods of Initiation

Twenty percent of the international and 28 percent of the U.S. women had intimate relationships with the men who pimped them. They and other victims described classic dynamics of battering that evolved into pimping. Emotional and physical coercion was used to break the women's resistance to entering prostitution. Pornography was used as an "educational tool" with many (50%) of the international women. For some, stripping was the entrance point into the sex industry, after which they were constantly pressured into prostitution.

Methods of Control

Methods used to control women in the sex industry included: denying freedom of movement, isolation, controlling money, threats and intimidation, drug and alcohol dependencies, threatened exposure of pornographic films, and physical and sexual violence.

Some women were held captive and some were not free until they paid off accumulated debts. The majority of law enforcement (76%) and social service providers, advocates and researchers (71%) confirmed that a large number of women were not free to leave the sex industry

Pimps controlled most of the money and many of the international (36%), and U.S. women (76%) had money withheld from them.

Violence was an intrinsic part of the prostitution and sexual exploitation used to control and intimidate the women. Eighty-six percent of U.S. women, and 53 percent of the international women reported being physically abused by pimps and traffickers. One half of the U.S. women, and ⅓ of the international women described frequent, sometimes daily assaults. Eighty-eight percent of U.S. women and 50 percent of international women reported psychological abuse. Ninety percent of the U.S. women and 47 percent of international women reported verbal threats. Seventy percent of U.S. women and 40 percent of international women reported being sexually assaulted in prostitution at the hands of the pimps and traffickers. As evidenced from the context of interviews with women, the research team believes that these findings represent underreporting of the actual violence perpetrated, especially against international women by pimps and buyers. There may be many reasons for this underreporting including normalization or non-naming of the violence in their lives.

Women were isolated, confined and guarded to prevent them from leaving. Thirty-five percent of international women, and 64 percent of

U.S. women were held in isolation and under guard in brothels or compounds.

Men Who Buy Women for Prostitution

Many of the brothels housing international women catered to buyers in specific immigrant or migrant worker communities. Some brothels had selective entrance for men from their own ethnicity, nationality or race.

Buyers came from all ages (15-90) and socioeconomic classes. The majority of men were married.

The majority of international (82%) and U.S. (58%) women said that men expected them to comply with all their requests. Men, in their writings, confirm this. Almost half of the international and U.S. women (47% each) reported that men expected sex without condoms. Fifty percent of the international women, and 73 percent of U.S. women reported that men would pay more for sex without a condom. A significant portion of the international (29%) and U.S. (45%) women said that men became abusive if women tried to insist that they use condoms.

Buyers subjected women to physical violence (international women – 28%, U.S. women – 86%), sexual assault (international women – 36%, U.S. women – 80%) and other forms of threats and violence.

Health of Women

Although a number of studies in the medical and social science literature investigate the rates of HIV/AIDS and sexually transmitted infections (STIs) of certain populations of women in prostitution, there has been no focus on the larger health consequences to women who have been trafficked and prostituted. International and U.S. women suffered severe health consequences from the injuries caused by violence and diseases contracted while in the sex industry. Many women sustained injuries such as broken bones, bruises, and cuts requiring stitches. Almost half of the U.S. women (47%) reported head injuries. Thirty-six percent of the international women and 53 percent of the U.S. women reported mouth and teeth injuries. Fifty-six percent of the U.S. women required emergency room treatment for injuries and illnesses sustained while in the sex industry.

Most of the women contracted sexually transmitted infections while in the sex industry.

Many of the women suffered emotionally from their experiences in the sex industry. Eighty percent of international and U.S. women felt depressed. Many of the international (50%) and U.S. (41%) women felt hopeless. Almost ⅓ of the international and 64 percent of the U.S. women experienced anger and rage. Sixty-four percent of U.S. women said they had suicidal thoughts and 63 percent said they had tried to hurt or kill themselves.

Methods of Coping and Resistance

Although women were severely victimized while in the sex industry, they were not simply victims. They found many ways to cope, resist and survive the exploitation and violence. The vast majority of international (87%) and U.S. (92%) women used drugs or alcohol to cope while they were in the sex industry. Half of the women began using drugs and alcohol after they entered the sex industry to numb themselves to the trauma of unwanted sex.

Many women (international women – 50%, U.S. women – 43%) tried, sometimes multiple times, to leave the sex industry. Twenty-seven percent of the international women and 52 percent of the U.S. women said economic necessity, drug dependencies and pimps who beat, kidnapped, and/or threatened them or their children prevented them from leaving.

Interviewees' Viewpoints

Interviewees were asked their opinions on topics that are often debated, such as legalization of prostitution. Fifty percent of the international women said that prostitution should not be legalized or recognized as a form of work. The same number said they could not recommend prostitution to any other women. Sixty-seven percent of the U.S. women said prostitution should not be legalized or recognized as a form of work. Ninety-four percent said they could not recommend prostitution to other women.

When asked if women enter the sex industry voluntarily, most respondents in all groups reported that choice could only be talked about in the context of other options. Most emphasized that women who were trafficked and prostituted had few other options. Many spoke about prostitution as a final option.

Recommendations for Change

The national anti-trafficking plan of the United States recommends prevention, protection for victims and prosecution of traffickers. Our recommendations are based on the connections between prevention, protection and prosecution.

A Human Rights Definition of Trafficking

Human rights legislation against trafficking must apply to both international and U.S. women, otherwise there is a risk of stereotyping trafficking as an immigration problem, and depriving all women of recourse, remedy and redress. The definition of trafficking used to analyze data from this project was a draft international definition of trafficking from the draft *Protocol to Prevent, Suppress and Punish*

Trafficking in Persons, Especially Women and Children, supplementing the *United Nations Convention Against Transnational Organized Crime.*

> *"Trafficking in persons" shall mean the recruitment, transportation, transfer, harbouring, or receipt of persons, by the threat or use of force, by abduction, fraud, deception [inducement] coercion or the abuse of power, or b the giving or receiving of payments or benefits to achieve the consent of a person having control over another person, for the purpose of exploitation [irrespective of the consent of the person]; exploitation shall include, at a minimum, [the exploitation of prostitution or other forms of sexual exploitation], forced labour of services, slavery or practices similar to slavery [or servitude].*

In this definition, exploitation, rather than coercion, is the operative concept.

Research, legislation and enforcement strategies would benefit from a common definition of trafficking that is broad and inclusive enough to represent the reality of what happens to all women who are trafficked for purposes of sexual exploitation—across borders and within countries, into or in a country, with or without their consent, and through force, fraud, deception, or abuse of the vulnerability of a victim.

Trafficking cannot be separated from prostitution. Anti-trafficking policies and programs must address organized prostitution and domestic trafficking.

Education and Public Awareness

Creative resources need to be developed for raising public awareness about sex trafficking in both sending and receiving countries. Within sending countries, people must be made aware of the risks of trafficking. Education and public awareness campaigns about trafficking should utilize the media in immigrant communities in the United States.

Legal information should be disseminated to social service providers and advocates for immigrants and abused women, in an easy-to-understand style. Guidebooks or other information should include specific contact information for federal agencies and departments that investigate trafficking and prosecute traffickers.

Strict Penalties and Consistent, Uniform Law Enforcement

Penalties must fit the crime. Sentencing guidelines should reflect the seriousness of the crime.

Evidentiary standards need to change. Currently, prosecution of traffickers depends on testimony from victim witnesses. Videotapes or wiretaps should be allowed as evidence. Police officers should be able to serve as complainants.

Civil statutes to combat the promotion and spread of sex industries also can be used in addition to criminal prosecutions. Local ordinances that clamp down, for example, on local sex venues, should also be employed.

Jurisdictional differences within states need to be harmonized, since pimps and owners of establishments are quick to capitalize on these differences.

The Women

Trafficked women should not be treated as criminal illegal immigrants, but as victims of violence and human rights abuses.

Women in the process of emigrating to and arriving in the United States should be made cognizant of their civil and legal rights when in this country.

Trafficking victims are in a legal no-woman's land. The new "T" visa would give trafficked women residency status in the United States. This visa has been proposed for undocumented persons who have been victims of severe abuse in the United States, and who can provide material information to a crime.

The Traffickers

The burden of proof needs to be shifted to the traffickers. Legislation must not allow traffickers to use the consent of the victim as a defense against trafficking.

Sex trafficking cases, like prostitution cases, are not given priority. Police must receive the resources to investigate and prosecute trafficking kingpins—the people at the top.

Military authorities must work in concert with other government agencies, to investigate the role of U.S. military men in trafficking women into and in the United States.

The Buyers

Laws and law enforcement must address the demand side of the sex industry. It must be made more difficult for buyers to purchase women for commercial sex. Laws against buying women must be strengthened.

Specific legal measures recommended included care forfeitures/confiscations of men arrested for soliciting, publication of buyers' names in the newspapers, and more "johns schools" where first offender buyers are "educated" about the harm of prostitution to the women, the neighborhood and themselves.

Enforceable policies are needed within U.S. military contexts that enjoin U.S. military from engaging in commercial sexual exploitation at home and abroad.

Community Involvement

Community involvement is essential to prevention, prosecution and protection. Media, law enforcement and social service providers must be sensitive to the complexities of community participation in anti-trafficking campaigns, especially within immigrant communities.

Communities should not bear the resource burden alone. There should be a joint effort of government, women's and community groups to act quickly on behalf of trafficking victims and to provide long-term assistance.

Government should work with a variety of community-based groups to design and implement victim services and support networks in various regions of the country.

Coordination and Collaboration

Immigration and law enforcement agencies worldwide should coordinate efforts. A computerized database to share information would be helpful, not only at the international level, but at the local level as well.

There should be some way of tracking U.S. men who travel to the same or different countries, and return to the United States with serial foreign fiancées or wives.

More coordination and cooperation are needed between local police officers and federal law enforcement agencies and prosecutors.

Law enforcement, immigration and social service providers should collaborate and cooperate in prevention of trafficking, protection of victims, and prosecution of traffickers.

NGOs working on trafficking issues in the United States should work closely with NGOs abroad. NGOs in the women's countries should help ensure that repatriated women do not end up back in the hands of recruiters and traffickers, and that they receive assistance.

Culturally Appropriate Legal Strategies and Social Services

The criminal justice system must be made more immigrant-friendly. Many social service providers reported that the current system hampers victims from coming forward who fear deportation.

Trafficked victims should be eligible for welfare and government funding without penalty to their future immigration status.

Legal advocacy entities, receiving funds from the Legal Services Funds Corporation, should be allowed to represent trafficked victims in court.

More resources and services are needed for women in the sex industry, especially those who have been trafficked—e.g., witness protection programs, health care, housing, shelter, counseling, legal services, English-language education, job training and financial assistance.

Law enforcement officials need investigators and consultants—cultural advisors—who are familiar with the cultural environments of both victims and traffickers.

More funding from the Violence Against Women Act should be made available for research, education, training and services for trafficking victims. The Crime Victims Fund should also be used to support services and shelters for trafficked women. When assets are seized from traffickers, they should be used for victim support.

Discussion Questions

1. *What was the aim of the research in this paper?*

2. *What five regions of the United States were selected to gather information for this study?*

3. *What regional variations exist in the sex trade in the United States?*

4. *What type of people were reported by the majority of international and US women as recruiters, traffickers, and pimps?*

5. *What were the conditions of facilitating recruitment of women?*

6. *What methods of initiation were employed by the men who pimped the women?*

7. *What methods of control were employed to control the women?*

8. *What types of health problems did the trafficked women have?*

9. *What methods of coping and resistance did the women employ to resist and survive their exploitation and violence?*

10. *What recommendations were made regarding education and public awareness of the sex trafficking trade?*

Note

This document was taken in its entirety from the Executive Summary of research supported by the National Institute of Justice (NIJ) Grant 98-WT-VX-0032 in a report titled Sex Trafficking of Women in the United States: International and Domestic Trends, co-Principal Investigators, Janice G. Raymond, Ph.D., University of Massachusetts, Amherst and Donna M. Hughes, Ph.D., University of Rhode Island, Project Coordinator, Carol J. Gomez, BA, March 2001, p. 7-15.

2

HUMAN TRAFFICKING:
VICTIMS' VOICES IN FLORIDA

Terry Coonan, *JD, MDiv, Florida State University, Tallahassee, FL*

The International Labor Association has termed trafficking in persons "the underside of globalization" (U.S. Department of State, 2003). For most Americans, terms such as "sex trafficking" and "involuntary servitude" may conjure up images of Asian brothels or Third World plantations. The reality is much closer to home. The past decade in Florida witnessed some of the highest profile cases to date of human trafficking in the United States. These included the *Cadena* case, in which a Mexican crime family trafficked some 25 to 40 Mexican women and girls between 1996 and 1997 for forced prostitution, and the *Ramos* case, in which a family of Mexican American labor contractors subjected migrant farm workers to involuntary servitude in Florida's agricultural fields between 2000 and 2001.

In 2002, the Florida Department of Children and Families (DCF) Office of Refugee Resettlement awarded the Florida State University (FSU) Center for the Advancement of Human Rights a 1-year grant to assess human trafficking in Florida.[1] The resulting project had manifold objectives: (a) to hear from victims themselves about their experiences and post-emancipation needs; (b) to make policy recommendations to DCF for best practices in assisting trafficking victims; (c) to develop the groundwork for eventual protocols in the state law enforcement and social service fields for identifying and assisting trafficking victims; and (d) to make recommendations on how to coordinate a community response to trafficking in Florida.

Fundamental to all these objectives was the research task of identifying and interviewing victims of trafficking in Florida. Qualitative U.S. research focused upon victims' own experiences of human trafficking is still at a nascent stage. The State Department's annual Trafficking in Persons Report alludes to victim stories but remains opaque insofar as its sources and even methods for estimating victim numbers are concerned (U.S. Department of State, 2003). Richard's (2000) landmark study on human trafficking drew extensively on interviews with law enforcement and immigration officials. Raymond,

---

[1] The Florida DCF grant resulted in the creation of the FSU Human Trafficking Project. Professor Terry Coonan of the FSU Center for the Advancement of Human Rights and Professor Robin Perry of the FSU School of Social Work served as principal investigators of the project and Robin Hassler Thompson served as program director. The interdisciplinary project further included students from the FSU Criminology School, FSU Law School, FSU School of Social Work, and FSU School of Education.

Hughs, and Gomez (2001) interviewed both international and U.S. citizen women in their study of trafficking in the U.S. sex industry. The Protection Project's (2002) Report on Trafficking in the United States relied heavily on journalistic sources in its survey of cases nationwide. For its part, the DCF-FSU research project sought out the voices and experiences of trafficking victims themselves in making its policy recommendations. In this sense, the project was nontraditional in its research scope: It did not begin with hypotheses but rather with open questions as to how Florida can best assist victims of these egregious human rights abuses.[2]

Method of Investigation

Participants

The DCF-FSU research project was limited both in time (May 2002-May 2003) and in scope (trafficking victims already identified by Florida social service providers or law enforcement). A total of 11 women agreed to be interviewed, 10 of whom were victims in the *Cadena* sex trafficking case and 1 who was a victim of domestic servitude. The sex trafficking victims were natives of Mexico between the ages of 21 and 29. All had been between the ages of 14 and 22 when they were trafficked to Florida. The domestic servitude victim was in her 40s and from a Central American country. All 11 were native Spanish speakers, and none was fluent in English.

The trait shared by all these women was the lack of economic opportunity in their native countries. Few had completed more than junior high school, and most had begun full-time work after that. Such work included lemon picking, belt making, and domestic services such as childcare and housecleaning. Of the 11, 10 had been single at the time they were trafficked, and 1 was a widow. Two of the women had left children behind in their native countries.

The sex trafficking victims had initially been approached about participating in the project by their lawyers at the Florida Immigrant Advocacy Center (FIAC). Given the special trust that had evolved between these victims and their lawyers, the FIAC attorneys first clarified that there was no expectation on their part that the victims would participate in the research. Instead, they explained that the purpose of the study was to assist future victims of trafficking in Florida with the insights and experiences of known victims. Of the 14 victims of sex trafficking assisted by FIAC, 10 agreed to participate in the project. There was no likely inherent pattern to those who declined to

---

[2] A comprehensive list of the recommendations generated as a result of the project is contained in the report *Florida Responds to Human Trafficking*. Included are recommendations for law enforcement officials, social service providers, prosecutors, and state agencies.

participate. A lawyer from FIAC accompanied each of the 10 victims throughout their interviews. These victims comprised a discrete subject group that was *sui generis* for several reasons: The women had a common history, a shared experience of victimization, and their participation in the research was the result of purposive rather than random sampling. A Victim Advocate of a Florida County Sheriff's Office referred the case of the 11th victim (a survivor of domestic servitude) to the FSU researchers, and accompanied the victim during her interview. FSU provided each interviewee a $100 stipend for her participation.

Interview Instruments

The FSU Trafficking Team created two interview instruments: a first that was case-specific to the *Cadena* sex trafficking victims and a second that was a broader instrument applicable also to cases of forced labor and domestic servitude. The first instrument was more narrowly constructed given that much was already known of the *Cadena* victims' background and sexual exploitation from court records and media articles. Researchers devised the interview instrument in the conscious awareness that the victims had already been required to tell their stories numerous times in law enforcement and judicial fora. Findings by other investigators who have studied potential effects of interviews upon victims (Pennebaker, 1990, 1993, 1997; Walker, Newman, Koss, & Bernstein, 1997), and in particular, victims who are refugees (Dyregrov, Dyregrov, & Raundalen, 2000) or survivors of trafficking (Bales, 1999) guided the formulation of the interview questions. In order to avoid any retraumatization, the FSU questions focused not on the explicit abuses suffered by the sex trafficking victims but rather on four areas deemed important for future interventions. These areas included:

1. what level of contact the victims had during their captivity with U.S. media sources;
2. what access the victims had to U.S. public life during that time;
3. what contact, if any, the victims had with U.S. law enforcement during their enslavement; and
4. what services and benefits the victims had most needed following their emancipation.

The second interview instrument—used with the victim of domestic servitude—included additional questions about the victim's background and the types of coercion employed by traffickers against the victim. It is a more general instrument designed for interviewing victims of trafficking about whom little or nothing may be known at the outset. The research team translated both interview instruments into Spanish, using back translation to ensure equivalence. The FSU Human Subjects Committee approved both instruments and their respective consent forms.

Procedure

The basic research procedure used was that of an in-depth audio recorded interview. Given the trauma suffered by these victims and their ongoing need for security, this phase of the research project included numerous protective measures. The researchers conducted the interviews at dates, locations, and times convenient to the interviewees. The victims' true names were never recorded or used in the written transcripts of the interviews. Researchers further decided that any identifying information disclosed by the victims during the interviews would not be transcribed into any print document. As a final measure to safeguard the privacy rights of the victims, the researchers erased the interview tapes at the end of the project (May 31, 2003).

Researchers also employed certain procedures to ensure the reliability and validity of their interview findings. They taped prepilot interviews with native Spanish speakers to prepare the interviewer and to test the interview instrument for questions that might be ambiguous or confusing (with such questions then being revisited or eliminated). The researchers took particular care to eliminate leading or double negative questions. Consistent with the design theory for qualitative interviews espoused by previous proponents (Appleton, 1995), the FSU Team used open-ended questions to elicit a broad range of details and to encourage victims to respond in their own words.

The two researchers conducting the interviews were both fluent in Spanish and very familiar with the cultural background of the victims.[3] At the outset of each interview, the interviewer reassured the interviewee that she could decline to answer any question that she chose; could at any time request a break; could at any time confer off the record with her advocate; and could terminate the interview if she so chose at any time. The interviewer also reassured the interviewee that she would receive her stipend no matter how few or how many questions she chose to answer. Finally, the interviewer thanked the interviewee for her willingness to share her experiences and allow future victims of trafficking to benefit from such research.

Analysis

Following the completion of the recorded interviews, researchers transcribed the interviewees' Spanish responses verbatim. A professional translation service then translated the responses. Three members of the research team who were fluent in Spanish independently

---

[3] The interviewer for the 10 victims of sex trafficking was a bilingual female graduate student from the FSU School of Social Work. A native of Mexico for whom Spanish is a first language, she was intimately familiar with both Mexican culture and the many Mexican-Spanish colloquialisms used by the interviewees. The interviewer for the domestic servitude victim was a bilingual human rights lawyer who had worked in the victim's native Central American country, and who had 15 years of experience interviewing asylum-seekers and torture victims.

reviewed the translation for grammatical and contextual accuracy. These three researchers also independently coded the interview findings according to theme and then together created categories by which they grouped and compared the responses.

Results

The 11 interviews provided a broad range of qualitative data regarding the experiences of victims of trafficking in Florida. Without exception, all of the women identified physical security as their most overwhelming need following their liberation. The victims also identified certain media sources and a number of nexuses with the U.S. public domain to which they had access during their periods of captivity. Most surprisingly, they detailed a number of encounters, or near-encounters, with U.S. law enforcement that might have led to their earlier emancipation. Though they were not asked about the abuses they had suffered, many ventured information about their exploitation that afforded a harrowing glimpse into the world of trafficking victims.

Sex Trafficking Victims

The victims of sex trafficking had all grown up in the Veracruz area of Mexico – many of them alongside members of the Cadena family who would eventually exploit them so ruthlessly. The women had been trafficked and confined together in trailers that functioned as brothels in migrant farm worker communities throughout Florida. Their periods of captivity ranged from several months to a year, during which time their traffickers forced them to have sex with 25 to 30 men per day. Holding them in groups of 4 to 5, their traffickers moved them from one location to another at 2-week intervals. After being emancipated in November 1997 raids conducted by the FBI and U.S. Border Patrol, the women remained together in confinement at Krome INS Detention Center in Miami. When FIAC lawyers at last secured their release, they lived together for 1 year at a women's shelter while the prosecution of their traffickers remained ongoing.

The Trafficking Enterprise

The victims' contact with the traffickers invariably began with seemingly casual approaches, the recruiting most often done in the victims' hometowns by a well-dressed Mexican woman. Deceit, rather than kidnapping or brute force, was the hallmark of the recruiting strategy. None of the victims reported previous exploitation in Mexico; their vulnerability appears to have been heightened by their inability to begin to imagine the kind of exploitation they would eventually suffer. In at least two instances, relatives were complicit in the recruiting: one woman was trafficked by her cousins, and another by the daughter of her stepfather. The traffickers typically offered the young women 6-month contracts in Florida working in the Cadena family's restaurants or serving as nannies in the homes of the Cadena brothers. Such jobs proved illusory. Charging their victims approximately $2000 in smuggling fees, the traffickers ultimately coerced the victims into sexual servitude as a means of supposedly acquitting this debt. Guarded constantly by armed pimps upon their arrival in Florida, the women suffered repeated beatings, rapes, and threats against the lives of their families in Mexico.

Contact With Media Sources

The women had certain limited access to media sources during their captivity. In an apparent concession to the drudgery of the forced prostitution, the traffickers allowed almost all of them access to television. This included the *Univision* Spanish language channel, Spanish soap operas (*telenovelas*), Spanish talk shows (*Cristina and Marta Susana*), and current events programs (*Primer Impacto*). The sole English language television sources the women recounted watching were American cartoon shows – a poignant reminder that a number of them were still children at the time of their victimization. Many of the women also had access to radio, which they had recourse to in the late evening hours. They favored Spanish pop stations, and one woman recalled listening often to *Romance 106.5*. The traffickers also allowed their victims limited access to magazines, including the Spanish language version of *Cosmopolitan*, the TV Guide (*TV Notas*), and *Vanidades*.

Contact With U.S. Public Life

Despite their isolation, the victims nonetheless achieved certain minimal nexuses with U.S. public life. While always accompanied by armed pimps in their forays into the public domain, the women reported being taken to a number of commercial venues. These included supermarkets (Winn Dixie and Publix), Mexican food stores, music stores, Laundromats, pay phone booths (where the traffickers monitored the women's weekly calls home to Mexico), and Western Union offices (where the traffickers allowed the women to wire money home to their families). When being transported from one brothel to another, the women were able to use restrooms in gas stations and fast-food restaurants. These brief stops in public restrooms comprised the victims' only respite from their traffickers' otherwise relentless control.

While generally denied medical care, the women incurred emergencies that required their traffickers to allow them access to medical facilities. Such emergencies included the need for abortions, for treatment after severe beatings, and one situation in which a drunken pimp shot a female victim in the foot. In almost all such instances, one of the traffickers would accompany the woman to the medical facility and identify himself as her husband. In scenes reminiscent of domestic violence episodes, the trafficker would tell the medical staff that the woman had been injured in a fall or an accidental mishap. Frequently the medical staff spoke no Spanish and so the traffickers were allowed to "translate" for the victim.

Somewhat surprisingly, the women also reported visiting certain recreational venues, though always in the presence of armed traffickers. In one instance, an armed trafficker took several of the women to a public beach for a day. The women in another brothel persuaded their pimps to take them to a nightclub; the pimps complied but forbade the women from leaving their table or interacting with anyone else. The women's only unguarded moment proved to be when they were allowed to visit the restroom. Sadly, this brief respite yielded only an offer from a Spanish-speaking female bartender for the women to escape and work as prostitutes under her own supervision. This encounter was consistent with others in which neighbors or store employees identified the women as prostitutes but not as victims of trafficking.

Arguably the most significant means of access to the U.S. public that the women had was in the sexual commerce they were forced to transact. Even here, the trafficking operation by design mitigated the chance that contact with a large group of "johns" could lead to relationships or to rescue. Moving the women repeatedly from one brothel to another precluded both possibilities and left the victims in perennial uncertainty of their location. Moreover, the fact that the traffickers sought to restrict their clientele to migrant farm workers – many of whom were illegal themselves, spoke almost no English, and would be little inclined to contact U.S. law enforcement – further insulated the illegal operation and isolated its victims. Even so, sympathetic "johns" were a repeated occurrence. Some left without demanding sex once apprised of the involuntary nature of the service. Others attempted to arrange escape attempts, though such attempts invariably failed due to the constant presence of the armed traffickers or the fear that they had inculcated in their victims. The interviews further revealed that not all the clients had been the stereotypical migrant farm workers—also included in their number were businessmen and an engineer.

Contact With U.S. Law Enforcement

Equally surprising was the number of encounters—or "near-encounters"—that the sex trafficking victims had with U.S. law enforcement during their period of captivity. Local law enforcement officials on several occasions chanced upon the victims and their traffickers in the trailer brothels. At times this was in response to neighbors' suspicions that drug trafficking was occurring; in at least several instances such visits were the result of phone calls from sympathetic clients. In almost every case, because of the physical isolation of the trailers and cell phone warnings from lookouts, the traffickers were able to hide the condoms, weapons, and financial records that were evidence of their criminal enterprise. As had been the case with so many of the health care personnel, few of the law enforcement officers spoke Spanish. Typically the traffickers were left to translate for the police, and they invariably identified the women as their girlfriends or wives. One encounter with potential law enforcement liberators left the women particularly disheartened. Several of the victims had learned from watching *Primer Impacto* that dialing 911 would bring emergency assistance. Finding a telephone buried in a bedroom closet, the women plugged it in, hurriedly dialed 911, but encountered an operator who spoke no Spanish. Afraid they would be caught, they hung up and hid the phone. Tracking the call, emergency personnel arrived at the trailer shortly thereafter. The traffickers insisted that there was no phone in the trailer and that no one had called. The responding officer spoke no Spanish, and the traffickers persuaded him that it had been a false alarm. Fearful that their pimps would discover the source of the emergency call, the women decided it was too futile and too dangerous to call 911.

Victim Needs

Without exception, each of the sex trafficking victims emphasized that physical protection from their traffickers was their overwhelming need after they had been liberated. Next were immediate survival needs: housing, food, and medical services. Each of the women interviewed expressed great satisfaction with the living arrangements made for them at a local women's shelter where they remained for almost a year after their release from INS detention. It was in this ambience that the women encountered a balance of both physical security and autonomy, and they recounted positive experiences of group living. The women also gave very high marks to their social workers and the FIAC lawyers who had advocated on their behalf. Notwithstanding such support, many of the victims acknowledged ongoing struggles with depression and nightmares. Even after the passage of 6 years, most still felt a sense of guilt and shame. One woman persisted in referring to herself as "illegal" even after her advocate reminded her that she now has legal immigration status. Another woman reflected how she now needs to behave well ("necesito portarme bien") as if she were somehow responsible for the acts her traffickers forced her to perform. Curiously, almost all the women acknowledged a need for counseling and psychological support services, but few have sought out such help despite its ready availability. Almost all the women spoke rather of the need *to forget* what had been done to them. Significantly, all the women spoke of their need during their captivity to be informed that they had legal rights in the United States despite their irregular immigration status.

Domestic Servitude Victim

The profile of the domestic servitude victim was distinct from that of the sex trafficking victims. In her 40s, she was considerably older than the *Cadena* victims and was the beneficiary of more education (she had completed some university studies in her native Central American country). In addition, she had owned her own business, though it was the failure of that business that led her to seek employment in the United States. Widowed and faced with mounting debt, she believed that domestic work in Florida might afford her the financial stability that eluded her in her homeland.

The Trafficking Enterprise

The victim in this case sought the help of a female friend who worked in an employment agency. The friend informed her of a house-keeper position in the Florida home of a Latin American businessman and his wife. The Florida couple promised the victim work as a live-in maid with a monthly salary of $400. The victim secured a tourist visa and the traffickers paid her airfare. Met by the businessman upon her arrival in Miami Airport, her work began the next day. She quickly discovered that she was a slave in his lavish South Florida home. Forced to work 70+ hours a week, she became responsible for all the child care and cleaning in the house. While her traffickers took care never to hit her physically, they subjected her to constant verbal abuse, and the male trafficker threatened that he could "disappear" her as he had done to others. The traffickers confiscated her passport, monitored her phone calls home, and kept her confined in their large house where security cameras observed her every move. After the traffickers deducted what they claimed she owed them for travel expenses, she earned less than a dollar an hour. Her servitude lasted for 6 months until she escaped.

Contact With Media Sources

The victim in this case had almost no contact with media sources. She was allowed access only to English-language television, which her traffickers knew she could not understand.

Contact With U.S. Public Life

The victim's only access to public life consisted of Sunday church services that her traffickers allowed her to attend locally. Even this public access was narrowly circumscribed: the traffickers required the woman to write down the name, address, telephone number, Social Security number, and driver's license number of each church member with whom she associated.

Contact With U.S. Law Enforcement

In this case, the traffickers deterred contact with law enforcement by a simple hoax. Showing the victim pictures of their son in his Florida law enforcement uniform, they informed her that he took care of their law enforcement "needs," and could deport her at any time (a subsequent investigation revealed that the son had no knowledge of or complicity in the trafficking scheme).

Victim Needs

The victim finally escaped with the assistance of her fellow church members. Infuriated, the traffickers retaliated by destroying the victim's immigration documents and the few possessions she had left behind. As a consequence, the victim urgently needed shelter, clothing, food, and medical attention. She secured work authorization through provisions of the Trafficking Victims Protection Act of 2000 (TVPA), but still needs English language and job skill training. As did the other victims interviewed, she identified physical safety as her greatest preoccupation.

Discussion

The interviews with trafficking victims revealed a group of women who have survived tremendous human rights violations but who have proven surprisingly resilient. Nevertheless, it is clear that the psychological scars of their victimization are deep and lasting. While their captivity may have been induced by severe physical abuse, it was the women's isolation and fear that likewise limited their freedom of movement and their ability to escape. This phenomenon perhaps underscores the importance of provisions in the TVPA that recognize that psychological forms of coercion may at times be more constraining than physical ones. Notably, many of the sex trafficking victims also alluded to the stigma that remained as a result of having been incarcerated by U.S. law enforcement.[4] Detained initially with their traffickers, many did not even self-identify as victims when first liberated. Again, provisions of the TVPA that recognize trafficking victims as beneficiaries rather than violators of U.S. law appear critical for better assisting such victims in the future.

While investigators found it somewhat perplexing that the victims have shown little inclination to utilize job training or psychological support services that are available to them, this pattern conforms to findings of previous researchers (Vega, Kolody, Aguilar-Gaxiola, & Catalano, 1999) regarding general underutilization of mental health care services by immigrants. The trafficking victims' reluctance may in part be culturally conditioned: They expressed very low expectations of government assistance due to their perceptions of government in their native countries. This suggests that U.S. social service providers may need to be especially proactive in assisting survivors of trafficking, perhaps even accompanying them to appointments with mental health care officials.

Even the circumscribed contacts of the trafficking victims with media sources indicate that public service announcements for victims

---

[4] The *Cadena* case was prosecuted prior to the enactment of the Trafficking Victim Protection Act of 2000, and the sex trafficking victims were detained for several months before attorneys from the Florida Immigrant Advocacy Center arrange for their release. The prior law in effect at that time did not clearly identify trafficking victims as beneficiaries rather than violators of U.S. law.

may prove a viable means of informing them of their rights. Magazines, television channels, and radio stations that offer programming in Spanish or other languages would seem optimal for such announcements. Similar announcements could be posted as fliers or tearaway sheets in supermarkets, ethnic food stores, and the stalls of women's restrooms in public venues.

Finally, the research reveals that most often it is local law enforcement officials who will encounter trafficking victims in the field. Therefore, it is incumbent upon U.S. law enforcement to develop better foreign language capabilities, as well as training for field officers to discern evidence of human trafficking in their jurisdictions.

One area for future research is the development of clinical as well as longitudinal studies of trafficking victims' needs. The FSU study was policy-oriented rather than clinical in nature, and it dealt moreover with victims whose traumatization had occurred in the recent past (1 to 6 years). Human trafficking, rather than a single event in time, is more accurately a continuum of human rights violations suffered by victims. The long-term effects of human trafficking remain to be determined, perhaps by clinical investigations that will illuminate the etiology of victims' trauma as well as the sequelae likely to be experienced over time.

Discussion Questions

1. *What was the one trait shared by all of the women in the Cadena sex trafficking case?*

2. *Given the trauma suffered by these victims and their ongoing need for security the research phase of interviewing these victims had numerous protective measures. What were they?*

3. *What type of contact did the victims have with U.S. public life?*

4. *What were the overwhelming needs of the women after they were liberated?*

References

Appleton, J.V. (1995). Analyzing qualitative interview data: Addressing issues of validity and reliability. *Journal of Advanced Nursing, 22,* 993-997.

Bales, K. (1999). *Disposable people. New slavery in the global economy* (Appendix 1: Slavery research questions). Berkeley and Los Angeles: University of California Press.

Dyregrov, K., Dyregrov, A., & Raundalen, M. (2000). Refugee families' experience of research participation. *Journal of Traumatic Stress, 13,* 413-426.

Pennebaker, J.W. (1990). *Opening up. The healing power of confiding in others.* New York: William Morrow.

Pennebaker, J.W. (1993). Putting stress into words: Health, linguistic, and therapeutic implications. *Behavior Research and Therapy, 31*, 539-548.

Pennebaker, J.W. (1997). *Opening up. The healing power of expressing emotions.* New York: Guilford Press.

Protection Project. (2002) *Human rights report on trafficking of persons, especially women and children: United States Country Report.* Retrieved August 28, 2003, from http://209.190.246.239/ver2/cr/us.pdf.

Raymond, J.G., Hughs, D.M., & Gomez, C.J. (2001) *Sex trafficking of women in the United States: International and domestic trends.* New York: Coalition Against Trafficking in Women.

Richard, A.O. (2000). International trafficking in women to the United States: A contemporary manifestation of slavery and organized crime [Monograph]. *Center for the Study of Intelligence.*

U.S. Department of State (2003). *Trafficking in persons report June 2003.* Washington, DC: Author.

Vega, W.A., Kolody, B., Aguilar-Gaxiola, S., & Catalano, R. (1999). Gaps in service utilization by Mexican Americans with mental health problems. *American Journal of Psychiatry, 156*, 928-934.

Walker, E.A., Newman, E., Koss, M., & Bernstein, D. (1997). Does the study of victimization revictimize the victims? *General Hospital Psychiatry, 19*, 403-410.

Acknowledgments
The findings and recommendations of the Florida State University Human Trafficking Project are contained in its report *Florida Responds to Human Trafficking*, available on the website of the Center for the Advancement of Human Rights, http://cahr.fsu.edu. Some of the findings referred to in this article are noted and discussed in Chapter 2 of the FSU report entitled "Trafficking Cases in Florida: Victims and Perpetrators." The FSU Human Trafficking Project Team is grateful to the statewide members of the FSU Human Trafficking Working Group, whose law enforcement and social service expertise informed both the project and its final report. Finally, the project team thanks the Florida survivors of trafficking whose voices were the substance and reason for our research. It is their pain and their resilience that suffuses our findings.

Offprints
Requests for offprints should be directed to Terry Coonan, JD, MDiv, FSU Center for the Advancement of Human Rights, 426 W. Jefferson St., Tallahassee, FL 32301. E-mail: tcoonan@admin.fsu.edu.

3

DOMESTIC SEX TRAFFICKING OF ABORIGINAL GIRLS IN CANADA: ISSUES AND IMPLICATIONS

Anupriya Sethi, MSW, MBA

Introduction

General Trends

Human trafficking has received growing attention in recent years, both in Canada and worldwide, especially in the wake of increased focus on nation States' security and tightening the borders (Oxman-Martinez, Hanley, Gomez, 2005). The discourses on sex trafficking of women and girls in Canada continue to highlight international trafficking thus positioning Canada more as a transit and destination country than an origin country. Notwithstanding the fact that 500 Aboriginal[1] girls and women (and maybe more) have gone missing over the past thirty years (Amnesty International, 2004), domestic trafficking has not received the attention it deserves. Instead of being contextualized in a trafficking framework, sexual exploitation of Aboriginal girls is portrayed and understood as a problem of prostitution or sex work.

Similarly, despite the wide-ranging and often complex problems facing Aboriginal peoples today, policies continue to be dominated by a limited range of issues like health, violence, poverty and the criminal justice system (Stout & Kipling, 1998). This, coupled with the tendency in policy decisions to analyze one issue at a time as against a holistic approach, limits, if not excludes, the examination of linkages with the sexual exploitation of Aboriginal girls in Canada.

Significance, Purpose and Limitations of Study

The focus of this study is to first identify key issues in domestic trafficking of Aboriginal girls, and outline implications for policy formulation and implementation at various levels of the Canadian government- federal, provincial and territorial, second is to highlight the issues, as identified by the grass root agencies working with trafficked girls, and to contextualize them within the trafficking framework in order to distinguish sexual exploitation from sex work. The study begins by outlining the definition of trafficking, which will form the basis of

---

[1] Throughout this document, the terms "First Nations", "Indigenous", "Aboriginal" and "Native" peoples have been used interchangeably. While these terms can include all peoples of Aboriginal ancestry, it is essential to note that First Nations are identified as a distinct group with unique legal status. Within Canada, Aboriginal peoples are constitutionally recognized as Inuit, Métis and First Nations.

subsequent discussion and analysis in the paper. The next section examines the root causes that make Aboriginal girls vulnerable to sex trafficking, and the exploitation and manipulation they face in the trafficking process. Recommendations for policy research and analysis are discussed in the final section.

Although this paper brings forth some key issues in the domestic trafficking of Aboriginal girls today, it is a preliminary study restricted in its scope and application. The primary limitation of this research is that it is based on the feedback and input of NGOs working with trafficked girls in Canada and does not necessarily reflect the views of the trafficked girls themselves. This is because all interviews with the key informants of this research were done over the phone due to constraints of mobility and time, but for the exception of a roundtable held in Vancouver, BC. Hence, it was considered inappropriate, unethical and impractical to interview sexually exploited girls over the phone. Another limitation is that the paper makes reference to all Aboriginal girls rather than making a distinction between First Nations, Inuit and Métis girls whose issues and realities could be similar and yet different. The limited data available on domestic trafficking combined with the small sample size made it difficult to identify the issues specific to each Aboriginal community. Finally, due to its limited scope, the paper does not necessarily draw linkages between domestic and international trafficking.

Furthermore, it is essential to note that the study focuses primarily on the sexual exploitation of Aboriginal girls and not Aboriginal women. While some issues are common to both women and girls, there are significant differences regarding the concepts, policies and laws that are applicable to each group. Therefore, to maintain clarity and keeping in view the fact that Aboriginal women are being initiated into sex trafficking at an increasingly younger age (Assistant Deputy Ministers' Committee, 2001), the focus of this study is Aboriginal girls.

Methodology

Considering the limited information available on domestic trafficking of Aboriginal girls in Canada, the methodology adopted for this study was twofold. The first phase involved conducting interviews and discussions with key informants from NGOs, women's organizations and other community-based groups or individuals dealing with the issue of sexual exploitation in Canada.[2] A total of 18 key informants participated in the study. Five key informants were interviewed over the phone from four regions-Quebec[1], Prairies & NW Territories[2], Ontario[1],

---

[2] The data for this study was generated as part of the author's work with Status of Women Canada in Ottawa. However, this paper expresses the views of the author and does not represent the official policy or opinion of Status of Women Canada or the Government of Canada.

Atlantic[1]. In BC, a one-day roundtable was organized in Vancouver on 7th July 2006, which was attended by thirteen representatives from different community groups.

While the majority of the key informants were front line workers, some were researchers and program coordinators, and a couple of them were the manager or director of the organizations providing services to sexually exploited women. Few key informants, now working as service providers, identified themselves as trafficked into sex trade in the past. The mandate of the key informants' organizations ranged from providing drop-in services to outreach, counseling, research, advocacy and/or a combination of these services. The interviews with the key informants were semi-structured and lasted for about 45 minutes to an hour.

The questions and discussions with the key informants covered three main areas—First, participants were asked about the mandate and clientele of their organization, and their experiences of working with sexually exploited girls. Second, informants outlined the root causes of sex trafficking, the methods traffickers use to maintain control and dominance over the girls, and the role of racism in the sexual exploitation of Aboriginal girls. Finally, the informants were asked to comment on the existing policies and programs to address domestic trafficking of Aboriginal girls and make suggestions, both at the policy and grass root level, to address the issue.

The second phase of the project involved analyzing the information gathered from the discussions and consultations with key informants, and substantiating it with published research in the form of journal articles, reports, government documents and other related materials.

Overview

Definition of Trafficking

This paper draws upon the trafficking definition of the United Nations Protocol to Prevent, Suppress, and Punish Trafficking in Persons, especially Women and Children, supplementing the United Nations Convention Against Transnational Organized Crime.

> "Trafficking in Persons shall mean the recruitment, transportation, transfer, harboring, or receipt of persons, by means of threat or use of force or other forms of coercion, of abduction or fraud, of deception, of the abuse of power of a position of vulnerability or of the giving or receiving of payment or benefits to achieve the consent of a person having control over other persons, for the purpose of exploitation. Exploitation shall include, at a minimum, the exploitation of the prostitution of others

or other forms of sexual exploitation, forced labor or services, slavery or practices similar to slavery, servitude
or the removal of organs" (United Nations Crime and
Justice Information Network, 2000).

As outlined in this definition, trafficking comprises use of threat,
force, deception, fraud, abduction, use of authority and giving payment
to achieve consent for the purpose of exploitation, including sexual
exploitation. The element of 'consent' in the trafficking definition is
usually misunderstood thus conflating sexual exploitation with sex work.
It is often argued that a person who consents to engage in prostitution
cannot be considered trafficked thereby suggesting that only coercion or
force should form an integral part of the trafficking definition. However,
it is essential to recognize that consent does not necessarily suggest an
informed choice. As one key informant remarked, 'it is rare that
Aboriginal girls or women of color experience sex work. They are often
trafficked for power and control, and coerced into prostitution for their
survival needs'. Therefore, this paper would consider all those
circumstances, which are elaborated in root causes, that lead to the
sexual exploitation of girls as part of trafficking.

Scope of Domestic Trafficking

There is no national level data that tracks the transient Aboriginal
population and their trafficking in sex trade. Lack of focus and/or clear
understanding of domestic trafficking since sexual exploitation is often
conflated with sex work, underground nature of the crime, and mobility
of the trafficked persons across various cities, often make it difficult to
assess the actual numbers. Moreover, majority of the cases of trafficking
go unreported as girls are scared to take action against their traffickers[3],
resulting in the data on trafficked persons being partial, varied and
debatable.

In the absence of actual figures on domestic sex trafficking in
Canada, a look at the number of Aboriginal girls in prostitution can help
throw some light on the extent of the issue. First Nations girls are over
represented in prostitution with an especially high number of youth
ranging from 14% - 60% across various regions in Canada (Assistant
Deputy Ministers' Committee, 2001). National data in Canada reveals
that 75% of Aboriginal girls under the age of 18 have experienced sexual
abuse, 50% are under 14, and almost 25% are younger than 7 years of
age (Correctional Service of Canada, cited in McIvor and Nahanee,
1998). In Vancouver alone, 60% of sexually exploited youth are
Aboriginal (Urban Native Youth Association, 2002). One key informant

---

[3] Several factors explain the reluctance of girls to take action against their traffickers.
Some of these include life threats to trafficked girls and their families, condition of
confinement, fear of penalization, and lack of safe houses, shelters and other resources.

reported that children as young as 9 are sexually exploited in Saskatoon and the average age of being forced into prostitution is 11 or 12.

Although the limited data available on sexual exploitation focuses primarily on urban centers like Vancouver, Toronto, and Montreal, it does not imply that the issue is less chronic in smaller cities and rural Aboriginal communities. Only that it is not widely known or acknowledged (Blackstock, Clarke, Cullen, D'Hondt, and Formsma, 2004).

Pattern of Domestic Trafficking

Domestic sex trafficking of Aboriginal girls in Canada has various forms. It can be familial-based, i.e., family members forcing other members to take part in sex trade. For instance, there are communities in the North wherein First Nations girls are sexually exploited and initiated into prostitution by their male and female relatives—brother, father, grandfather or an uncle (Lynne, 1998). Many key informants identified familial-based sex trafficking as poverty-driven and inter-generational or cyclical resulting from the residual impact of colonization and residential schools. Another type of sex trafficking is organized (gang related) and sophisticated in the form of escort services, massage parlors or dancers. One key informant referred to the hidden forms of domestic trafficking such as the existence of "trick pads"[4] in some parts of Canada.

Additionally, key informants pointed out a characteristic intrinsic to the trafficking process—the movement of trafficked Aboriginal girls that follows a pattern of city triangles across different provinces in Canada. For instance, in Saskatoon, which is in close proximity to Edmonton and Calgary, girls are moved in triangles such as Saskatoon-Edmonton-Calgary-Saskatoon and Saskatoon-Regina-Winnipeg-Saskatoon. These triangles, often interconnected, are spread across Canada. For example, once girls are trafficked into Calgary, the triangle is Calgary-Edmonton-Vancouver. Although several factors contribute to the movement of girls, an emerging trend that a key informant pointed out, is the increased trafficking of girls due to the flourishing oil rigs and mining businesses in Alberta. Significant number of men travel back and forth from Saskatchewan to northern Saskatchewan or Alberta for short periods of time to work in oil rigs or at uranium mines. In keeping with their movement, girls are increasingly being moved around and sexually exploited.

---

[4] A trick pad is a place, usually a house in a secluded area, where girls are kept against their will and are coerced to engage in prostitution. Sometimes the girls are physically kidnapped and taken to trick pads (Urban Native Youth Association, 2002).

Recruitment Methods

Coercion and deception are the underlying elements in the various methods that traffickers use to force Aboriginal girls in sex trafficking. Consultations with key informants of this research project revealed some of the ways of the recruitment of girls.

Airports

A couple of key informants identified airports as the point of recruitment in big cities like Montreal, which are witnessing a growing movement of Aboriginal girls, especially Inuit, from Northern communities. Traffickers often know someone in the community who informs them about the plans of the girls moving to the city. Upon their arrival at the airport, traffickers lure the girls under the pretext of providing a place to stay or access to resources. In the words of a key informant working as an Aboriginal outreach worker, 'Girls tend to believe in the promises of the traffickers as they are young, naïve and vulnerable in a new and big city. They are unsuspecting of the motives of the traffickers, since they belong to communities that have a culture of welcoming strangers'.

Schools

In cities like Winnipeg, Vancouver and others with high concentrations of Aboriginal peoples, traffickers are increasingly targeting schools as recruiting grounds. Traffickers entice Aboriginal girls, as young as sixth or seventh graders, on school playgrounds or on their way to school by promising them gifts, a good life style or getting them addicted to drugs (West, 2005). These girls are too young and vulnerable to understand or take action against sexual exploitation.

Bars

Several key informants discussed 'bars' as a fertile recruiting ground successfully targeted by traffickers. Young Aboriginal girls who move from reserves to big cities might go to bars to "bridge the isolation" and connect with other Aboriginal peoples, especially since community centres in many cities close early in the day. Traffickers frequent these places to befriend girls, by buying them a drink or offering to help connect with other Native peoples, and later sexually exploit them.

Boyfriends

In many cases, traffickers pose as boyfriends and seduce young girls by buying them expensive gifts and/or emotionally manipulating them. Hence, it is common for sexually exploited girls to refer to the traffickers as their boyfriends. Due to their emotional and economic dependence on

the traffickers, many girls refuse to identify themselves as sexually
exploited (Thrasher, 2005).

Girls as Recruiters

In yet another method, trafficked girls, as young as 11, are forced to
recruit other girls (Urban Native Youth Association, 2002). When young
girls approach their counterparts with dreams of a better lifestyle, it is
real and convincing. Girls working as recruiters, in most cases, have no
choice but to agree to the wishes of the trafficker due to fear or, in some
cases, to meet their survival needs. It often results in a hierarchal set up
wherein recruiters take the share of the earnings of the girls they have
recruited. As recruiters move up in the hierarchal chain, they aim to get
rid of the street work.

Dancers

Aboriginal girls, recruited as dancers at a young age, are frequently
moved across provinces for their dance shows. Over a period of time,
they lose ties with their home and community thus becoming isolated
and vulnerable. When these girls grow old, appear less attractive and
are forced out of dancing, they are sexually exploited for their survival
needs.

Internet

Traffickers are increasingly using the internet as a means to entice
young Aboriginal girls, especially in rural communities (Thrasher, 2005),
with the charm of a big city or false promises of a good job. Once these
girls are in the cities, away from their family and friends, they are
trafficked into the sex trade.

Hitchhiking

First Nations intergenerational poverty, lack of recreation and social
activities for youth on-reserve, and inadequate public transportation
facilities force young girls to hitchhike thus making them vulnerable to
sexual exploitation. The Yellow Head Highway in BC, also known as the
Highway of Tears, along which several Aboriginal girls have gone
missing or found murdered (Wilson, 2004), is a glaring example.

Root Causes

Key informants of this study identified the root causes that affect the
safety and well-being of Aboriginal girls and put them at risk of sex
trafficking. Although discussed under separate headings for the sake of
simplicity and clarity, these causes are interrelated thus forming a
vicious circle. It is important to note that while factors such as poverty,

violence, and racism surface in various discussions in existing literature and policy decisions on Aboriginal peoples, their linkages with sexual exploitation have not been fully explored (Blackstock, Clarke, Cullen, D'Hondt, and Formsma, 2004).

Legacy of Colonization and Residential Schools

The majority of the key respondents referred to the history of colonization as a fundamental factor behind the sexual exploitation of Aboriginal girls. Various aspects of colonization such as capitalism, church and the military have affected family units, language, culture and identity, economic status and parenting abilities of Aboriginal peoples (Lynne, 1998). The destruction of the social structures and family support system has rendered some communities dysfunctional thus leading to increased rates of violence, sexual abuse, substance abuse and suicide rates (Bennett & Shangreaux, 2005).

According to one key informant, sex has traditionally been considered sacred in Aboriginal culture—A gift from the creator and a way to communicate. As a result of colonization, sexual abuse was introduced to Aboriginal communities, now living with the "historic imagery of Aboriginal girls being sexually available." Due to the intergenerational effects of residential schools, men and women have not learnt the meaning of healthy sexuality and parenting resulting in many residential school survivors sexually exploiting their own children (Assistant Deputy Ministers' Committee, 2001). Girls suffering perpetual violence and abuse have no choice but to leave their communities in search of a safer place. This coupled with culturally inappropriate welfare practices and lack of adequate support systems further expose them to the risk of sex trafficking.

Lack of Awareness, Acknowledgment and Understanding of Sexual Exploitation

Sections of the Canadian society such as Aboriginal communities (Thrasher, 2005), law enforcement officials, media, policymakers, and legal system are unwilling to acknowledge domestic trafficking, especially of Aboriginal girls.

According to key informants, several factors prevent Aboriginal communities from acknowledging the sexual exploitation of their girls. These include poverty, limited resources, lack of education and understanding of the exchange of sexual favors for goods and resources as sexual exploitation and the fear of outside involvement resulting from ineffective past interventions. As one key informant remarked, 'our people have been researched to death but nothing has been done.'

Aboriginal girls in rural communities might be reluctant to talk about sexual exploitation, as sometimes they are battling with their own physical and mental health problems such as HIV/AIDS, sexually transmitted infections, depression and post traumatic stress disorder. Inadequate resources and the taboo associated with such diseases limits their capacity to advocate for ending sexual exploitation.

Limited initiative and willingness on the part of law enforcement authorities to actively deal with sex trafficking aggravates the reluctance in Aboriginal communities. One key informant mentioned a case wherein a law enforcement official, while speaking on the issue of sexual exploitation, expressed hesitation to specifically talk in the context of Aboriginal girls stating that 'they (police) do not work in the First Nations communities'. In cases, where officials do take a proactive approach to undertake research or document cases, they often lack the culturally relevant approaches or tools to address it adequately.

The lack of acknowledgment of sexual exploitation of Aboriginal girls acts a hindrance to initiating and implementing measures for addressing it. Thus, sexual exploitation continues to be viewed as or conflated with sex work. Aboriginal peoples are stereotyped as 'willing' to take up sex work and a great deal of ignorance surrounds Aboriginal culture and their living conditions.

Violence

A significant consequence of colonist government policies is the violence plaguing Aboriginal communities. Loss of cultural identity coupled with social and economic marginalization fuels violence and sexual assault (Mann, 2005). As pointed in the Aboriginal Justice Enquiry in Manitoba, violence in Aboriginal communities has reached epidemic proportions (Hamilton & Sinclair, 1991). While there are complexities in defining and contextualizing violence in Indigenous communities, suffice it to say that as a result of oppression and colonization "violence has invaded whole communities and cannot be considered a problem of a particular group or an individual household" (Jacobs, 2002 p.3). Increased family breakdown due to violence is resulting in an ever-increasing number of Aboriginal children in the welfare system. They experience culture loss and disassociation, and become extremely susceptible to sexual exploitation as a means to meet their emotional and practical needs.

The cycle of violence, which Aboriginal girls face, begins from their communities and continues into the trafficking process. Traffickers impose various forms of violence-physical, emotional, economic and sexual to initiate girls into sex trafficking and maintain control over them. Girls are forced to go with johns, not use condoms, and live in poor and unhygienic conditions. Traffickers often keep the earnings and the identification documents of girls to minimize their chances of escape, as in the absence of identification, girls have negligible or limited access to resources such as welfare services or addiction treatments.

Poverty

As Raven Bowen (2006) found in her study on domestic trafficking, poverty is a major cause of sexual exploitation. Girls are forced to move in search of survival opportunities and in the process suffer the kind of exploitation and isolation that is similar to that of international trafficking or organized crime. Poverty in Aboriginal families have reached an all time high, with 52.1% of all Aboriginal children living in extreme poverty (Ontario Federation of Indian Friendship Centres, 2000). In urban Winnipeg, Regina and Saskatoon, 80 to 90% of single Aboriginal mothers were living below the poverty level (Royal Commission on Aboriginal Peoples (RCAP), 1996). One of the main reasons for poverty among Aboriginal girls is the limited opportunity for employment and education. On-reserve unemployment is three times the national average and, in some Aboriginal communities, about 90% of the population is unemployed (McKenzie & Morrissette, 2003). High rates of unemployment coupled with limited welfare services leads to poor health, violence, cultural disintegration and increased poverty rates among Aboriginals (Bennett & Shangreaux, 2005). High level of poverty in a patriarchal society is directly related to high rate of sexual exploitation (Farley & Lynne, 2005).

Closely related to poverty is homelessness, which is another significant risk factor in sexual exploitation (Farley & Lynne, 2005). Although the population of Aboriginal peoples is growing at a rapid rate, their housing needs remain unmet. Lack of affordable housing is evident from the fact that 84% of Aboriginal households on-reserve do not have sufficient income to cover the cost of suitable and adequate housing (RCAP, 1996). In the face of extreme poverty and consequently the absence of safe and affordable housing, girls become vulnerable to sexual exploitation to meet their basic needs of food, clothing and shelter.

Isolation and Need for a Sense of Belonging

Girls experience isolation in rural Aboriginal communities due to various reasons—boredom, dysfunctional families, limited education and employment opportunities, and taboo due to HIV/AIDS, Hepatitis C and other sexually transmitted infections. Traffickers lure young girls by glamorizing life in a big city and presenting it as a way out of their communities.

The movement from reserve to big cities can be an overwhelming experience for many young girls brought up in a culture of strong family and community ties. In cities, they suffer isolation, racism and consequently low self-esteem. During the course of time, they lose contact with their communities and experience culture loss (Save the Children Canada, 2000). Many girls go to bars to overcome their isolation and end up being recruited by traffickers. Limited knowledge and availability of resources to Aboriginal peoples off-reserve further puts the young girls at risk.

Once forced into sex trade, Aboriginal girls continue to suffer sexual exploitation and turn "to street communities, drugs, pimps and dealers to develop personal identities and an enduring sense of place and belonging" (Downe, 2003, p.47). There is a spirit of camaraderie and unity among trafficked girls, as they share the same stories and a common history. Driven by the desperate need for trust and acceptance, many Aboriginal girls find love in their traffickers who they often refer to as their boyfriends. 'It is amazing what girls can do to feel that they belong', one key informant remarked. In such a scenario, although girls consent to being sexually exploited, they do it as they have no choice or means to help them in their loneliness, marginalization and lack of support system. Hence, it is essential to recognize isolation and social exclusion as a root cause of sex trafficking, instead of viewing it as a part of voluntary sex work.

Racism

The systemic racism that Aboriginal girls face from different sections of the Canadian society—media, justice, police, law-makers, service providers and the Canadian society at large, emerged as a key factor in discussions with almost all the key informants. In addition to the inadequate representation of Aboriginal peoples in the media, the ignorance and stereotypes associated with their culture and identity marginalizes them, especially youth. Aboriginal girls are perceived as 'easily available' due to the discriminatory and sexist polices, and their unequal status in the Canadian society (Mann, 2005; Olsen 2005). A study (Gorkoff & Runner, 2003) involving 45 interviews with sexually exploited girls revealed that Aboriginal girls are at risk not just because they are female, poor and homeless but also because they suffer racism and exclusion. Thus, the sexual exploitation of Aboriginal girls is yet another form of racial discrimination.

While stressing on the lack of concern or interest toward Aboriginal girls in sex trafficking, one of the key informants mentioned a profound example wherein a large number of people attended a presentation that a local faith-based agency had organized to highlight the international trafficking of girls from Ukraine to Canada. However, the turn out of people is significantly low when such initiatives are organized for addressing trafficking of Aboriginal girls in their own city. 'People are willing to speak abut trafficking in terms of World soccer and Asian gangs but disinterested to talk about the sexual exploitation of young Aboriginal children in their own backyard', remarked the key informant. This indifference and discrimination toward the plight of Aboriginal girls reflects a NIMBY (Not-In-My-Backyard) syndrome, also known as NIMBY-ism. The NIMBY syndrome is often widespread and deep-seated, and involves intentional exclusion and inhibition of growth (Kean, 1991). In the 1996 trial of John Martin Crawford, a serial killer convicted of killing three Aboriginal girls, Warren Goulding, one of the journalists covering the trial said, "I don't get the sense the general public cares much about missing or murdered Aboriginal girls. It's all part of this indifference to the lives of Aboriginal people. They don't seem to matter as much as the white people" (Amnesty International, 2004, p.24).

Substance Use

Drug addiction "sucks Aboriginal girls in and keeps them there." Traffickers lure young girls into taking drugs and then sexually exploit them. In many cases, Aboriginal girls with no prior history of substance use, take drugs to numb the pain of shame and humiliation they experience as a result of being sexually exploited. A study by Ontario Native Women's Association (1989) found that eight out of ten Aboriginal girls have suffered some form of abuse—physical, sexual, psychological or ritual-in their communities and that these factors were associated with high rates of alcohol and drug use in these communities. Over time, the substance use develops into a chemical dependency[5], which forces girls to engage in prostitution in order to support their addiction. One key informant quoted a trafficked girl, "I have two choices—To do drugs or to die."

Role of Gangs

Gangs are playing an increasing role in the sexual exploitation of Aboriginal girls. Some of the Aboriginal-based street gangs include the Manitoba Warriors, the Native Syndicate and the Indian Posse (Turenne, 2006). One key informant observed that a number of Asian and Somali gangs have been able to recruit Aboriginal girls and traffic them into the sex trade. Recruitment of gang members takes place not only in urban centres but also on-reserves and small rural communities (Criminal Intelligence Service Canada, 2004). The average age of a female gang member ranges from 11-30 years with the majority between 14-25 years. The fastest growing street gang population consists of young children under 16 years old (Nimmo, 2001).

The reasons for young girls falling a prey to gang recruitments vary— poverty; physical, emotional and sexual abuse in their families and communities; sense of power, recognition and protection from street life; and most importantly, the need for belongingness and acceptance (Fontaine, 2006). Many young girls are attracted to gangs because they have suffered loss of cultural ties and find an alternative 'family' in the gangs (RCAP, 1996; Native Women's Association of Canada (NWAC), 2007a).

---

[5] In many cases, the chemical dependency is a gradual transition beginning from alcohol, which is easily available, to marijuana, cocaine and then crystal meth.

Most gangs thrive in drug trafficking; however, some engage in sex trafficking as well. The gang culture follows a hierarchal framework in which there are a powerful few at the top followed by the various levels of workers underneath (Nimmo, 2001). Accordingly, gang members have different status and roles. Prostitution is considered as the lowest activity in the gang and young girls, who are at the bottom of the hierarchy, are forced into prostitution to earn money for the gangs (Nimmo, 2001; Fontaine, 2005). These girls are also exploited to recruit other young girls in order to move up in the hierarchy and away from the street work.

Gaps in Service Provision

Key informants pointed toward the existence of a cycle of power, control and systemic oppression in the way services are delivered to sexually exploited girls. The narrow mandate and rigid functioning of certain agencies limits the scope and extent of services available to girls. For instance, trafficked girls usually work in the night and sleep during the day but most shelters do not accommodate this pattern (Canadian Housing and Renewal Association, 2002). Similarly, the long waiting period in service provision combined with the lack of consistent long-term funding act as deterrents for girls wanting to escape sexual exploitation. This is particularly true for the treatment of alcohol and drug addiction, which is often a difficult service to access. Healing and transition to a normal life is usually a lengthy process (Assistant Deputy Ministers' Committee, 2001), especially if a woman has been abused and exploited at a young age or for a long period. However, limited and short-term funding focused on instant results fails to take into consideration the period required for healing and is often not enough to help trafficked girls make the transition to a healthy life. As one key informant effectively summed up - 'Drugs are more easily available than counseling or other support services.'

Culturally relevant services managed by Aboriginal peoples are minimal and even more limited are the services specifically for sexually exploited Aboriginal girls (Canadian Housing and Renewal Association, 2002). For instance, many key informants pointed out the scarcity of female-only residential treatment centres and the unwillingness and/or the inability of these centres to address sexual exploitation issues. Treatment of addictions without addressing sex trafficking has limited effectiveness. Moreover, placing sexually exploited girls with other groups such as battered women may lead to bias and discrimination due to issues of class, and is usually not helpful as the problems and interventions for these groups are different from each other. Co-ed treatment centers can be unsafe for girls as older men in these centres may sexually exploit young girls (Canadian Housing and Renewal Association, 2002).

The contradictory welfare policies along with the lack of suitable alternatives for income also pose a barrier to girls wanting to exit domestic trafficking. A key informant working as an Aboriginal outreach worker discussed the problem of girls losing their housing when admitted to residential treatment centres, as welfare stops paying for it. Considering that finding a safe and affordable housing is a challenging task, such policies may uproot girls and make them further vulnerable to trafficking. Similarly, in the absence of apprenticeship programs, the employment opportunities for Aboriginal girls are limited especially since they have little or no education due to their trafficking at a young age. The gaps and barriers in service provision frustrate Aboriginal girls who often find it difficult to sustain their fight against sexual exploitation, which seems to be "the only thing normal and working."

Discriminatory Policies and Legislations

Several policies and legislations continue to marginalize Aboriginal peoples, especially girls. For instance, in the absence of clear policies around matrimonial property rights, Aboriginal girls are forced to leave their homes when marriages break up. The shortage of alternative housing services on-reserves and in rural communities forces girls to move to cities where they live in poverty thus becoming highly susceptible to sex trafficking. Similarly, Section 67 and Bill C-31 of the Canadian Human Rights Act discriminate against Aboriginal girls and their descendants, and negatively impact their rights and chances of a respectful life (NWAC, 2006).

Section 67 of the Canadian Human Rights Act provides that nothing in the Act affects any provision of the Indian Act, thus prohibiting Aboriginal peoples from lodging a complaint against the federal or the Native government. Such a provision perpetuates the oppression that status Indian girls face in their communities and leaves them without any protection that is available to other Canadian girls (Native Women's Association of Canada, 2007b). Despite amendments to the Indian Act, Section 6 in Bill C-31 translates into a loss of status after two consecutive generations of girls have married with non-registered partners and it is anticipated that by 2060, there will be no Aboriginal people with Indian Status (Mann, 2005). The benefits that Aboriginal girls are entitled to under registered status are of great importance since they remain the primary care givers in the family. Some of these benefits include access to Indian and Northern Affairs Canada's programs, national-level services, non-insured health payment and tax benefits in addition to non-tangible benefits such as identification with their culture and community (Mann, 2005). The denial of these benefits may further isolate Aboriginal girls making them an easy target for traffickers.

Policy Recommendations

Based on the analysis of the root causes that make Aboriginal girls vulnerable to sex trafficking and the factors that contribute to their ongoing exploitation in sex trade, the key informants of this study made the following policy recommendations:

Acknowledgment and Recognition
Sexual Exploitation - A trafficking and human rights issue:
The first step in addressing domestic trafficking of Aboriginal girls is to acknowledge the seriousness of the problem. Countries like Canada are increasingly under pressure to tighten their borders and undertake measures on the prosecution aspect of human trafficking, especially in the wake of US Trafficking in Persons (TIP) report. The over emphasis on criminalizing the movement of people across borders has shifted the focus away from trafficking as a human rights issue. Moreover, the discourses in transnational trafficking in Canada do not include domestic trafficking of Aboriginal girls within and across provinces. It is erroneous and unjust to consider domestic trafficking as less serious than transnational trafficking because the issues of control, isolation and exploitation that girls face at the hands of traffickers are severe irrespective of whether it is cross-cultural or cross-border (Bowen, 2006).

Honor Indigenous Knowledge
There is a serious need to recognize and honor Indigenous knowledge (Stout & Kipling, 1998) by engaging "Aboriginal people as knowledge-keepers." Awareness and education programs are effective when implemented through participatory, interactive and inclusive processes that acknowledge the lived experiences of Indigenous peoples. A significant amount of research has been done on Aboriginal communities. While continuing further research in unexplored areas, the critical knowledge that already exists needs to be utilized and acted upon. The already identified gaps such as homelessness, poverty and unemployment demand action, as against further research and deliberations.

Recognize Diversity among Aboriginal Peoples
Although larger systemic problems like poverty and the impact of colonization are common to several Aboriginal communities, there are issues that are typical of each community. As pointed out by a key informant, 'saying someone is an Aboriginal is like saying someone is a European meaning that there are many groups, territories, languages, etc. of Aboriginal peoples.' Policy making should take into account this diversity, as there is no one pan-Aboriginal identity. Formulating and implementing a blanket policy meant to address the issues of all Aboriginal communities has limited effectiveness and sometimes perpetuates the already existing problems in different communities.

Collaboration

Establish a National Level Strategy for Domestic Trafficking

Due to the lack of understanding or acknowledgment of domestic trafficking, there is no national level strategy to address, both the immediate causes and the larger systematic issues, which lead to the sexual exploitation of Aboriginal girls. Key informants expressed frustration at the disconnect that exists among the various levels of the government and other agencies like law enforcement, justice, health care and child welfare. Considering that the issues identified in domestic trafficking fall under the mandate of various agencies, standardized protocols and guidelines are essential to bring together initiatives of different stakeholders. A uniform approach shall help in sharing information and ideas, increasing awareness about domestic trafficking, and enabling different agencies to work toward common goals.

Bridge the Policy-Practice Gap

Many participants pointed out the existing policy-practice disconnect reflected in the policy decisions. Although both the grass root agencies and policy makers are experts in their respective areas, the communication gap between them is rather unproductive. A limited, if not negligible, understanding of the other side often creates and widens the gap between what is required and what ends up being delivered thus leading to quick fix solutions rather than addressing the fundamental problems.

Input from communities, women's groups and grass root agencies in the policy-making processes can help ensure an informed decision-making. Furthermore, it is crucial to engage in a dialogue with the trafficked Aboriginal girls regarding various social policy issues that affect them since their input is based on lived experiences. At the same time, it is important to ensure that these girls do not end up being a poster child. The story of one girl should not be regarded as a blanket experience of all sexually exploited girls, because each has their own struggles and disadvantages. There is a wealth of knowledge and community experience at the grass root level, which should be validated and fed into the social policies.

Alliance Between Aboriginals and Non-aboriginals

The success of non-Aboriginals in forming productive alliances with Aboriginals has been limited. A key informant observed that at one extreme is the lack of concern or a hands-off approach toward Aboriginal issues and on the other extreme is the fear of recolonizing Aboriginal peoples. The informant emphasized that the guarded approach on the part of non-Aboriginals is equally unhelpful, as it further isolates

Aboriginal girls who end up fighting for their rights in isolation. Non-Aboriginals will have to learn to be good allies by supporting and collaborating with Aboriginals populations in a way that gives Aboriginal girls the power and right to determine what is best for them.

Funding and Resources

Preventive Rather than a Reactionary Approach

One key informant remarked that traditionally Aboriginal peoples view life as a cycle of seven generations. The wisdom from the past three generations is used to guide the present, which is the fourth generation, and lay the foundation for the future three generations. The understanding of this vision is not reflected in social policies today, which focus on immediate and reactionary measures instead of combining it with long term prevention strategies.

Funding and services should be directed toward prevention programs like educating and mobilizing young girls in Aboriginal communities, raising awareness regarding the dangers of sex trafficking, and increasing collaboration between urban Aboriginals and communities on-reserve so that girls do not lose touch with their culture and homes. In addition to focusing on young girls vulnerable to sex trafficking, prevention strategies should focus on girls who have exited sexual exploitation to prevent them from being retrafficked.[6] Funding should be granted for longer periods, as prevention work usually involves implementing a long-term strategy, which does not necessarily deliver quick results measurable in numbers.

Culturally Relevant Services

Aboriginal girls should have access to culturally relevant services that move beyond crisis intervention and are long enough to help them make a successful transition to a safe and healthy life. Key areas in service provision should include culture specific safe transitional housing for sexually exploited girls and their children similar to the program "Honouring the Spirit of Our Little Sisters" created by Ma Mawi Wi Chi Itata Centre in Winnipeg (see endnote no. 6), establishment of healing centres and shelters specifically to meet the needs of trafficked girls, and adequate child welfare managed by Aboriginal organizations. The

---

[6] For instance, Ma Mawi Wi Chi Itata Centre in Winnipeg, Manitoba, was instrumental in developing a safe house for sexually exploited Aboriginal girls in Winnipeg, aged 13-17, through the development of an advisory committee consisting of experiential victims of sexual exploitation who were consulted in planning the details of the site. The home called "Honouring the Spirit of Our Little Sisters" is for Aboriginal girls who have been sexually exploited. They are referred to this program from Child and Family Services and can stay as long as they want. The girls voluntary choose to be involved in the program and its location is kept hidden to protect its clients (Kotyk, 2003).

existing welfare services should be made more accessible. For instance, increased access to programs like income security, flexible curfew times in shelters, follow-up support, and reduced wait times in treatment centres. Similarly, harm reduction should be recognized as a useful measure for the health and safety of sexually exploited girls. Services like needles, food, condoms, and education regarding HIV/AIDS and other sexually transmitted diseases should be readily available.

Capacity Building of NGOs

Funding arrangements with NGOs should be flexible, adequate and long-term, especially for macro issues like domestic trafficking of girls. Key informants mentioned situations wherein agencies have to modify and, in some cases, reframe their mandates to fit the funding require-ments. The excessive focus on the outcome of the funded initiatives affects the kind and extent of services that NGOs are able to offer to sexually exploited girls. The evaluation guidelines often make it difficult for NGOs working with vulnerable groups to demonstrate and quantify the work done at the ground level. Similarly, inconsistency in grants leads to NGOs devoting considerable time, energy and resources in arranging funds for their projects. The tight funding also leads to a high rate of employee turnover, as wages are limited and people are hired on a contract basis. A high turnover affects the efficiency of the NGOs' projects, which require building long-term partnerships with stake-holders.

Additionally, more resources and opportunities are needed to enhance communication and collaboration among different NGOs in order to enable them to coordinate their efforts against domestic trafficking – an issue which cuts across regions, instead of being confined to a specific area. The competitiveness for funding often leads to organizations working against each other rather than working with each other. Considering that a strong united voice is paramount to advocating for a social policy change, the funding arrangements should recognize the power dynamics and ensure that the role of NGOs as advocates for social justice remains unaffected.

Capacity Building in Aboriginal Communities

Resources are needed for Aboriginal communities to support them in dealing with their challenges and problems. Aboriginal women are rather alone in their work against sexual exploitation of girls, especially on-reserves, where they face resistance from various sections like chiefs and counsels who refuse to admit that the problem has reached epidemic proportions (Save the Children Canada, 2000). Girls in Aboriginal Communities should be mobilized and encouraged to take up the leadership role and teach their future generations to value both men and women.

Elders have a wealth of experience which they can share with youth to guide them through their curiosities, questions and dilemmas. Aboriginal youth should be provided an environment that facilitates an open dialogue with both their peers and elders. Similarly, there is a need for better role-models for young Aboriginal girls. A key informant spoke of a case wherein an Aboriginal girl, who had grown up in a city, came to live on-reserve. Just by being confident in her approach toward men, she subtly taught other Aboriginal youth the meaning of self-pride.

Schools and community service providers should be proactively engaged to decrease the dropout rates of young children. Measures such as family support, counseling, homework clubs and culturally appropriate classes need to be in place to support children and keep them in the education system thus reducing their vulnerability to trafficking (Urban Native Youth Association, 2002). Resources should also be directed toward transportation, recreation facilities, awareness campaigns and apprenticeship programs in Aboriginal communities.

Legislative Reforms

Matrimonial Property Law needs to be reviewed, in consultation and partnership with Aboriginal peoples, to ensure that Aboriginal girls living on-reserve have equal property rights as those living off-reserve. Policy and legislative changes are also required in Bill C-31 to remove the residual gender discrimination against Aboriginal girls and their descendants, and rectify the loss of status under the Indian Act (NWAC, 2006). Similarly, Section 67 of the Canadian Human Rights Act should be repealed and a parallel human rights system be established in consultation with Aboriginal representatives to ensure that Aboriginal girls have access to remedies for violations of their economic, social and cultural rights (NWAC, 2006).

Conclusion

Key informants of this study identified significant issues and implications in the domestic sex trafficking of Aboriginal girls in Canada. However, the root causes and recommendations highlighted in this paper need further examination and analysis to better inform the future initiatives in domestic trafficking in Canada. As a starting point, it is of utmost importance to determine the actual number of girls that are domestically trafficked in Canada including smaller cities and rural areas. Further research should also include other groups such as immigrant girls, visible minorities, Aboriginal boys or two-spirited youth. Although many root causes and recommendations in this report could be generalized to other groups as well, there are subtle differences in each group which need to be explored for a thorough analysis. Additionally, there needs to be focus on addressing the role of men in Aboriginal communities. National level initiatives catering specifically to the abuse and trauma that men have suffered as a result of colonization are limited. Domestic trafficking of girls will continue to be a self perpetuating phenomenon and the efforts to heal girls might not yield the desired results so long as the role of their abusers remains unaddressed.

As observed in the Aboriginal Justice Enquiry of Manitoba, "Aboriginal women and their children suffer tremendously as victims in contemporary Canadian society. They are the victims of racism, of sexism and of unconscionable levels of domestic violence" (Hamilton & Sinclair, 1991). Instead of conveniently labeling domestic trafficking of Aboriginal girls as 'sex work', the holistic approach to dealing with it should begin by an acknowledgment of the problem from the various sections of the Canadian society. As recommended in the Article 4 of the Convention on the Elimination of All Forms of Discrimination against Women, state parties should recognize some groups of women as particularly vulnerable to sexual exploitation including Aboriginal women (Lynne, 2005). The fundamental issues that put Aboriginal girls in a disadvantageous situations today underline the importance of recognizing and addressing their sexual exploitation as integral to the dialogue on trafficking within Canada.

Bio

Anupriya Sethi is Canadian Commonwealth Scholar from India with two Masters degrees—a Masters in Social Work (MSW) from Carleton University in Ottawa and a Masters in Business Administration (MBA) from India. Her research interests include human trafficking, organ donation and organ trafficking, women's health, gender equality and Aboriginal child welfare. Anupriya has authored reports on 'Trafficking of Women and Girls in Canada: A Health Perspective' and 'Demystifying the Urban Legend: The Reality of Organ Trafficking' and co-authored a report on 'Reconciliation: Looking Back, Reaching Forward, Indigenous Peoples and Child welfare'. She has also written articles on social policy and gender equality issues such as dowry harassment, domestic violence and family mediation. During her academic and professional career, Anupriya has won several scholarships, awards and distinctions including a Canadian Commonwealth Scholarship awarded by the Government of Canada, two full scholarships under the Department for International Development Shared Scholarship Scheme from the Government of United Kingdom and a Government of India National Scholarship. Prior to coming to Canada, Anupriya has worked as a Family Counsellor in India. Anupriya is currently working as a Policy Analyst with the Labour Program of the Human Resources and Social Development Canada.

Discussion Questions

1. *What are the various forms of domestic sex trafficking of aboriginal girls in Canada?*

2. *What are the underlying elements in the various methods that traffickers use to force aboriginal girls into the sex trade?*

3. *What are some of the most common locations from which aboriginal girls are recruited?*

4. *What are some of the root causes that put aboriginal girls at risk of sexual trafficking?*

5. *What key policy recommendations were made in this study to make aboriginal girls less vulnerable to the sex trade?*

References

Amnesty International Canada. (2004). *Canada: Stolen Sisters-A Human Rights Response to Discrimination and Violence Against Indigenous Women in Canada.* Ottawa: Amnesty International.

Assistant Deputy Ministers' Committee on Prostitution and the Sexual Exploitation of Youth. (2001). *Sexual Exploitation of Youth in British Columbia.* Victoria: Ministry of Attorney General, Ministry for Children and Families, and Ministry of Health and Ministry Responsible for Seniors.

Bennett, M. & Shangreaux, C. (2005). Applying Maslow's Hierarchy Theory. *The First Peoples Child and Family Review,* 2(1), 89-116.

Blackstock, C., Clarke, S., Cullen, J., D'Hondt, J., and Formsma, J. (2004). Chapter Eight: Sexual Exploitation. In *Keeping the Promise The Convention on the Rights of the Child and the Lived Experiences of First Nations Children and Youth,* pp. 182-196. Ottawa, ON: First Nations Child & Family Caring Society of Canada. Retrieved on 10 August 2007 from http://www.fncaringsociety.ca/docs/KeepingThePromise.pdf.

Bowen, R. (2006). *From the Curb: Sex Workers' Perspectives on Violence and Domestic Trafficking.* Vancouver: British Columbia Coalition of Experiential Women.

Canadian Housing and Renewal Association with Novac, S., Serge, L., Eberle, M., & Brown, J. (2002). *On Her Own: Young Women and Homelessness in*

Canada. Ottawa: Status of Women Canada. Retrieved on 1 August 2007 from http://www.swc-cfc.gc.ca/ bpus /bpuspr/0662318986/ 2003030662318986_e.pdf.

Criminal Intelligence Service Canada (CSIC). (2004). *2004 Annual Report on Organized Crime in Canada.* Ottawa: Criminal Intelligence Service Canada.

Downe, P with 'Ashley-Mika.' (2003). "The People We Think We Are": The Social Identities of Girls Involved in Prostitution. In K. Gorkoff & J. Runner (Eds.), *Being Heard. The Experiences of Young Women in Prostitution.* Winnipeg, MB: Fernwood Publishing and RESOLVE (Research and Education for Solutions to Violence and Abuse).

Gorkoff, K. & Runner, J. (2003). 'Introduction: Children and Youth Exploited Through Prostitution'. In K. Gorkoff & J. Runner (Eds.). *Being Heard. The Experiences of Young Women in Prostitution.* Winnipeg, MB: Fernwood Publishing and RESOLVE (Research and Education for Solutions to Violence and Abuse).

Farley, M. & Lynne, J. (2005). Prostitution of Indigenous Women: Sex Inequality and the Colonization of Canada's First Nations Women. *Fourth World Journal,* 6(1), 1-29.

Fontaine, N. (2005). Surviving Colonization: Anishinaabe Ikwe and Gang Participation. In Gillian Balfour and Elizabeth Cormack (Eds.), *Criminalizing Women: Gender and (In)justice in Neoliberal Times.* Winnipeg, MB: Fernwood Publishing.

Hamilton, A. & Sinclair, C. (1991). *Report of the Aboriginal Justice Enquiry of Manitoba.* Winnipeg: Aboriginal Justice Enquiry of Manitoba.

Jacobs, B. (2002). *Native Women's Association of Canada's Submission to the United Nations Special Rapporteur Investigating the Violations of Indigenous Human Rights.* Ottawa: Native Women's Association of Canada.

Kean, T.H. (1991). *"Not in My Backyard": Removing Barriers to Affordable Housing. Report to President Bush and Secretary Kemp. Advisory Commission on Regulatory Barriers to Affordable Housing.* Washington: United States Department of Housing and Urban Development.

Kotyk, R. (13 November, 2003). A place to call home: New safe house for sexually exploited youth tries to empower its residents. *The Manitoban.* Retrieved on 10 August 2007 from http://themanitoban.com/2003-2004/1119/ne_03.html.

Lynne, J. (2005). *Prostitution of First Nations Women in Canada.* Retrieved on 12 March 2007 from http://sisyphe.org/article.php3?id_article=1803.

Lynne, J. (1998). *Colonialism and the Sexual Exploitation of Canada's First Nations Women.* Paper presented at the American Psychological Association 106th Annual Convention, San Francisco, California, August 17, 1998.

Mann, M. M. (2005). *Aboriginal Women: An Issues Backgrounder.* Ottawa: Status of Women Canada.

McIvor, S. D. & Nahanee, T. A. (1998). 'Aboriginal Women: Invisible Victims of Violence.' In Bonnycastle, K. & Rigakos, G.S (Eds.), *Unsettling Truths: Battered Women, Policy, Politics, and Contemporary Research in Canada*, pp. 63-69. Vancouver, BC: Collective Press.

McKenzie, B. & Morrissette, V. (2003). Social Work Practice with Canadians of Aboriginal Background: Guidelines for Respectful Social Work. *Envision: The Manitoba Journal of Child Welfare*, 2, 13-39.

Native Women's Association of Canada (NWAC).(2007a). *Aboriginal Women and Gangs: An Issue Paper prepared for the National Aboriginal Women's Summit at Corner Brook, NL*. Ottawa: Native Women's Association of Canada. Retrieved on 6 August 2007 from http://www.nwac-hq.org/en/documents/nwac-gangs.pdf.

Native Women's Association of Canada (NWAC). (2007b). *Repeal of Section 67: An Issue Paper prepared for the National Aboriginal Women's Summit at Corner Brook, NL*. Ottawa: Native Women's Association of Canada. Retrieved on 6 August 2007 from http://www.nwac-hq.org/en/documents/nwac-repeal-of-s67-jun1607.pdf.

Native Women's Association of Canada (NWAC).(2006). *Native Women's Association of Canada's Report in Response to Canada's Fourth and Fifth Reports on the International Covenant on Economic, Social and Cultural Rights covering the period of September 1999- December 2004*. Ottawa: The Author.

Nimmo, M. (2001). *The "Invisible" Gang Members: A Report on Female Gang Association in Winnipeg*. Manitoba: Canadian Centre for Policy Alternatives.

Olsen, S. (2005). *Just Ask Us: A Conversation with First Nations Teenage Moms*. Winlaw, BC: Sononis Press.

Ontario Federation of Indian Friendship Centres (OFIFC). (2000). *Urban Aboriginal Child Poverty: A Status Report on Aboriginal Children and their Families in Ontario*. Toronto: OFIFC

Ontario Native Women's Association. (1989). *Breaking Free: A Proposal for Change to Aboriginal Family Violence*. Thunder Bay: Ontario Native Women's Association.

Oxman-Martinez, J., Hanley, J., & Gomez, F. (2005). 'Canadian Policy on Human Trafficking: A Four Year Analysis'. *International Migration*, 43(4), 7-29.

Royal Commission on Aboriginal Peoples (RCAP). (1996). Report of the Royal Commission on Aboriginal Peoples. Ottawa: Minister of Supply and Services Canada.

Save the Children Canada. (2000). *Sacred lives: Canadian Aboriginal children and youth speak out about sexual exploitation*. National Aboriginal Consultation Project. Ottawa: The Author.

Stout, M. D. & Kipling, G. D. (1998). *Aboriginal Women in Canada: Strategic Research Directions for Policy Development*. Ottawa: Status of Women Canada.. Retrieved on 18 March 2007 from http://www.swc-cfc.gc.ca/pubs/pubspr/index_e.html.

Thrasher, P. (2005). *'Child Sexual Exploitation, Port Alberni, B.C.'*. B.C: Port Alberni Women's Resources Society.

Turenne, P. (5 June, 2006). 'Drugs and Violence, the Common Thread'. *Edmonton Sun*.

United Nations Crime and Justice Information Network. (2000). *United Nations Protocol to Prevent, Suppress, and Punish Trafficking in Persons, especially Women and Children, Supplementing the United Nations Convention Against Transnational Organized Crime*. Retrieved on 30 March 2007 from http://www.uncjin.org/Documents/Conventions/dcatoc/final_documents_2/convention_%20traff_eng.pdf.

Urban Native Youth Association. (2002). *Full Circle*. Vancouver: Urban Native Youth Association.

West, J. (2005). 'Pimps and Drug Traffickers Target First Nations School Girls'. *First Nations Drum*, Summer 2005. Retrieved on 1 April 2007 from http://www.firstnations drum.com/Sum2005/WomGirls.htm.

Wilson, D. (November 2004). 'The Lonely Road of Matty Wilson'. The United Church Observer Magazine. Retrieved on 7 August 2007 from http://www.ucobserver. org. /archives/nov04_cvst.shtml.

This research paper was originally published in First Peoples Child and Family Review, Vol. 3, No. 3, pp. 55-71.

4

TRAFFICKING IN WOMEN: THE CANADIAN PERSPECTIVE

Donna E. Stewart, *Women's Health Program, University Health Network Professor, University of Toronto*

Olga Gajic-Veljanoski,*Women's Health Program, University Health Network, Department of Health Policy, Management and Evaluation, University of Toronto*

Trafficking in human beings is an international crime, an undesirable by-product of globalization that generates annual profits of US$5-$7 billion. Trafficking of women for sexual exploitation is the industry's major component. In 2000, the United Nations (UN) acknowledged the magnitude of this criminal activity with the creation of a protocol to combat the problem (a summary is available at www.unode.org/unode/en/trafficking_protocol.html).

Trafficking entails the denial of human rights, including the right to health. It is essential for physicians to know its extent and the health problems likely to be found in this exploited population.

The Scope of the Problem

Because of its covert nature, trafficking is very difficult to quantify. Any official numbers obtained from police or court records are undoubtedly underestimates whose magnitude is unknown. Some sources indicate that more than 4 million girls and women are sold worldwide into forced prostitution, slavery or forced marriage. The US government suggests smaller numbers for global trafficking (600,000-800,000) and estimates yearly trafficking into the United States at 14,500 to 17,500 people, 80% of whom are female[1].

In Canada, trafficked captives are usually discovered through police raids or when victims seek asylum. This likely represents but a fraction of this activity. The Royal Canadian Mounted Police (RCMP)[2] estimates that 800 persons are trafficked into Canada per year; estimates by nongovernmental organizations (NGOs), however, run to as many as

---

[1] *Trafficking in persons report*. Washington: US Department of State; 2003 and 2004. Available: www.state.gov/g/tip/rls/tiprpt/2003 and www.state.gov/g/tip/rls/tiprpt/2004 (accessed 2005 May 17).

[2] RCMP. Human trafficking. Feature focus in: RCMP, ed. *Environmental scans*. Ottawa: Strategic Policy and Planning Branch, Royal Canadian Mounted Police; 2004. Available: www.rcmp.ca/enviro/2004/scan2004_h_e.htm (accessed 2005 May 17).

16,000.[3] There is no official collaboration between the Canadian government and NGOs, which impedes the assessment of trafficking in this country.

As problematic as statistics on criminal activities may be, part of the differences in the estimates may also be due to confusion between smuggling and trafficking—although people choosing to be smuggled can later become trafficked if their freedom is restricted at their destination.

The Health Problems

Women who have been trafficked are at increased risk for a range of physical and mental health problems (Box 1). Research on this population is extremely difficult. Victims are usually vulnerable, often young and single (or single mothers), from poorer educational and socio-economic backgrounds, although some cases involving highly educated older women have been described. Most victims are either unable or afraid to ask for legal help because of past or present abusive situations, fear of retaliation, language barriers, or expectations of deportation and criminal charges. At present, the UN has made the provision of citizenship status to trafficked victims optional, as it could encourage trafficking and illegal migration.

The Situation in Canada

Canada is both a destination and a transit country for victims trafficked from Eastern Europe, China, Southeast Asia and Latin America.[4] Women come here as visitors, family-class immigrants, temporary work migrants (e.g., working as dancers or strippers) or refugees. After false promises of substantial earnings and bogus jobs as nannies, housekeepers, waitresses, exotic dancers or sex workers, the women may end up working in appallingly abusive conditions, exploited as prostitutes working up to 18 hours a day for 7 days a week, until they repay enormous so-called travel debts to regain passports confiscated by their captors or employers.[5]

A 2003 US report on human trafficking[6] found little Canadian data and described Canada as lacking a national strategy on trafficking, making little effort to prosecute traffickers, giving victims no assistance or protection, and frequently deporting or charging them as criminals. The report therefore downgraded Canada from the (top) rating of a tier 1 country to one of the 75 tier 2 countries,[7] which include Albania,

---

[3] Hughes DM, Sporcic, LJ, Mendelsohn NZ, Chirgwin V. *The factbook on global sexual exploitation.* Coalition Against Trafficking in Women, 1999.
Available: www.uri.edu/artsci/wms/hughes/factbook.htm (accessed 2005 May 17).

[4] *Trafficking in persons report.*

[5] RCMP. Human Trafficking.

[6] *Trafficking in persons report.*

[7] Ibid.

Angola and Bangladesh. Until 2004, Canada focused its efforts mostly on prevention, with strict migration rules and by contributing to anti-trafficking funds in source countries.[8]

Other developed countries have invested substantially in combating trafficking both domestically and worldwide. For example, the US enacted 2 laws specific to trafficking and established a government office to monitor and combat human trafficking and prepare annual reports on the global status of the problem. It endowed $10-$20 million in grants and victim assistance programs, and organized a hotline for helping trafficked victims and for reporting potential trafficking cases. European countries imposed specific laws to prosecute traffickers, formed national anti-trafficking police units, invested in national and international trafficking prevention programs and organized national victim-protection programs for shelter, social, medical and legal assistance[9] (see the online table at www.cmaj.ca/cgi/content/full/173/1/25/DC1 for an illustrative comparison of the Netherlands, United States and Canada).

The slow pace of Canadian anti-trafficking initiatives is illustrated by the protracted interval between signing the UN protocol in 2000 and ratifying it in May 2002. Some projects such as Project Almonzo in Toronto, a joint effort of immigration, police, social-work and licensing bodies established in 1999 to help trafficked women both in crisis situations and to prepare them for other lines of work, ran out of funds in 2000 and came to an end. Several studies identified frameworks of trafficking specific to Canada and proposed immigration and other policy changes. However, information about the impact or implementation of the proposed policies is sparse.

Substantial efforts have been made by some NGOs, such as the Canadian StopTheTrafficking Coalition, which initiated communication with the RCMP and local police, established an action plan on how to deal with human trafficking and submitted it to Parliament (Feb 2004) as a draft private members bill (Act Against Human Trafficking).

Since 2002, Canada's Immigration and Refugee Protection Act (IRPA) prescribes fines for human trafficking of up to $1 million and imprisonment for up to life. IRPA also allows victims to make a claim for refugee protection or to apply for permanent-resident status. The RCMP have reported[10] no cases prosecuted under IRPA, but the Department of Foreign Affairs have documented 19 cases of trafficking arraigned under the Criminal Code. Ironically, women who have been criminally charged (e.g., for illegal immigration or prostitution) are ineligible for refugee status.

In 2004, the Canadian government introduced an organized effort to battle trafficking at a national level: it established a new federal agency, the Interdepartmental Working Group on Trafficking, led by the Foreign

---

[8] Ibid.

[9] *Trafficking in persons report.*

[10] RCMP. Human Trafficking.

Affairs and Justice departments, to coordinate the work of 14 government agencies and to develop a national strategy against human trafficking. Although this is a step in the right direction, effective measures have yet to be demonstrated.

Canada still seems to be focused more on criminal and educational approaches (tight border and visa control, criminal prosecution, advertising on Web sites of the dangers of trafficking) than on human rights such as victims' assistance, protection and right to health. It is vital to implement a system to monitor the problem, along with multi-disciplinary programs with measurable outcomes. These programs will require health care, social, legal and police personnel specifically trained to recognize all aspects of human trafficking and to assist victims with appropriate health, educational, social and legal services.

Box 1: Physical and psychological health risks faced by women who are trafficked

- Food and sleep deprivation
- Repeated rape
- Physical injury such as bruising, broken bones or teeth, mouth injuries, cuts, burns
- Emotional manipulation, including threats, blackmail
- Persistent sexual exploitation, social marginalization
- Sexually transmitted diseases and unwanted pregnancies from unsafe sexual practices such as condom refusal
- Forced or unsafe abortions
- Absence of gynecologic care and HIV testing
- Anxiety, post-traumatic stress disorder, depression, suicidality
- Somaticized symptoms and other sequelae of abuse (e.g., headaches, back and body aches, dizziness, nausea, vision disturbances)
- Inability to recuperate and integrate into society.

This article has been peer reviewed.

Acknowledgments: We are grateful to all individuals from non-governmental and governmental agencies (such as the Department of Foreign Affairs and International Trade) who provided valuable information related to trafficking in Canada, specifically the Canadian StopTheTrafficking Coalition and the Help Us Help The Children Anti-Trafficking Initiative.

Discussion Questions

1. *What is the scope of the human trafficking problem in Canada?*

2. *What are the physical and psychological health risks faced by women who are trafficked?*

5

DEFINING THE PROBLEM OF TRAFFICKING: THE INTERPLAY OF US LAW, DONOR, AND NGO ENGAGEMENT AND THE LOCAL CONTEXT IN LATIN AMERICA

David E. Guinn, Executive Director of the International Human Rights Institute at DePaul University College of Law.

Guinn, David E., Defining the Problem of Trafficking: The Interplay of US Law, Donor, and NGO Engagement and the Local Context in Latin America. Human Rights Quarterly 30:1 (2008), pp. 119-145 ©2008 The Johns Hopkins University Press. Reprinted with permission of The Johns Hopkins University Press.

Introduction

Criminal trafficking and slavery is, all acknowledge, a significant and long-standing problem. This is as true in Latin America as throughout the rest of the world. As early as 1928, the League of Nations identified the trafficking of women and children for purposes of commercial sexual exploitation as a significant problem within the region. Based on a three-year global study of sex trafficking, researchers noted that "Latin America is the traffic market of the world."[1] While current estimates suggest that South and Southeast Asia and the former Soviet Union respectively represent the largest sources of trafficking victims, trafficking appears to be growing in Latin America and the Caribbean.[2]

Trafficking has received enormous attention since the late 1990s,[3] driven in particular by the US initiatives under the Trafficking Victims Protection Act of 2000 (TVPA),[4] and its subsequent reauthorizations in

---

[1] H. Wilson Harris, Human Merchandise: A study of International Traffic in Women 187 (1928).

[2] Clare Ribando, *Trafficking in Person in Latin America and the Caribbean, in* CRS REPORT FOR CONGRESS 1, 4 (2005); International organization for migration (IOM), Exploratory Assessment of Trafficking in Persons in the Caribbean Region: The Bahamas, Barbados, Guyana, Jamaica, The Netherland Antilles, St. Lucia, Suriname 1 (2005), *available at* http://www.oas.org/atip/Caribbean%20Research%202005.pdf.

[3] *See, e.g.,* Mohamed Y. Mattar, *Trafficking in Persons: An Annotated Legal Bibliography*, 96 Law Libr. J. 669 (2004).

[4] Trafficking Victims Protection Act of 2000 §102, 22 U.S.C. §7101 (2000) [hereinafter TVPA].

2003[5] and 2005[6] and the United Nations Protocol to Prevent, Suppress and Punish Trafficking in Persons, Especially Women and Children (2000)[7] (commonly known as the Palermo Protocol). Under the TVPA, the United States not only declared the war on trafficking a national and international priority, it predicated US foreign aid, in part, upon compliance with the TVPA's mandate that all states undertake similar efforts.[8] The donor community and local and international NGOs also have aggressively worked on the problem. The media has increasingly focused on trafficking throughout the world, drawing attention to the horror of this human rights abuse. Nonetheless, trafficking remains ill-defined and efforts to combat it have floundered.

Unfortunately, the actors responsible for putting the fight against trafficking on the public agenda—the United States, the donor/NGO community, and the media—have at the same time, wittingly or unwittingly, shaped and sometimes distorted our understandings of the problem and the efforts needed to address it. These difficulties are not unique to Latin America, although this research paper will focus attention there.

In order to highlight the overall problem of trafficking, this article will begin by identifying the definitional, sociological, and legal obstacles that hinder the development of an accurate assessment of the problem. The focus will not be on the empirical problems of research and assessment, an area addressed by others more qualified to do so,[9] but rather on those issues within the compass of policy makers and advocates. The paper will then describe the basic features of trafficking in Latin America and identify efforts to address the problem, highlighting, in particular, the role played by the United States, the TVPA, and the donor/NGO community. Finally, the conclusion will suggest appropriate methods for reducing trafficking and assisting its victims.

---

[5] Trafficking Victims Protection Reauthorization Act of 2003, Pub. L. No. 108–193, 108th Cong. (2003) [hereinafter TVPRA 2003]

[6] Trafficking Victims Protection Reauthorization Act of 2005, Pub. L. No. 109–164, 109th Cong. (2005).

[7] *Protocol to Prevent, Suppress and Punish Trafficking in Persons, Especially Women and Children, Supplementing the United Nations Convention Against Transnational Organized Crime*, G.A. Res. 25, U.N. GAOR, 55th Sess., Annex II, Supp. No. 49, at 60, U.N. Doc.A/45/49 (2001) (*entered into force* 9 Sept. 2003) [hereinafter UN Protocol].

[8] TVPA, *supra* note 4, §110(d)(1).

[9] Guri Tyldum & Anette Brunovskis, *Describing the Unobserved: Methodological Challenges in Empirical Studies on Human Trafficking, in* Data and Research on Human Trafficking: A Global Survey 17 (Frank Laczko & Elzbieta Gozdziak eds., 2005).

Obstacles to Assessment

It is virtually impossible to obtain reliable data on trafficking in Latin America—or indeed anywhere else in the world. Clearly, the status of trafficking as an illegal enterprise plays a part in this difficulty; however, reasonably reliable statistics can be found about many aspects of other organized crime. Nor is it adequate to blame the region, with its lack of resources and sophistication, though those play a part. For example, even the United States with all of the resources available to it has trouble acquiring reliable data, as the number of trafficking victims has drastically fallen from the 1999 Central Intelligence Agency estimates of 45,000 – 50,000 victims to current estimates of 14,500 – 17,500 victims.[10]

The real obstacles to assessment are structural and systemic, inherent in the very nature of the problem of trafficking. Factors that impeded the collection and analysis of data in this area include basic controversies over the definition of the crime, sociological factors inhibiting data collection, and legal and logistical obstructions.

A. *Definitional Controversies*

Trafficking and slavery has long been recognized throughout Latin America and has received regional and international condemnation.[11]

---

[10] Some researchers believe these figures to be merely best "guesstimates." Elzbieta M. Gozdziak & Elizabeth A. Collett, *Research on Human Trafficking in North America: A Review of the Literature, in* Data and Research on Human Trafficking, *supra* note 9, at 99, 108.

[11] The international community has repeatedly condemned forced slavery, violence against women, and other trafficking elements, through declarations, treaties, resolutions, and United Nations reports, including the Universal Declaration of Human Rights, *adopted* 10 Dec. 1948, G.A. Res. 217A (III), U.N. GAOR, 3rd Sess. (Resolutions, pt. 1), at 71, U.N. Doc. A/810 (1948), *reprinted in* 43 Am. J. Int'l L. 127 (Supp. 1949); Fourth World Conference on Women: Action for Equality, Development, and Peace, Beijing Declaration and Platform for Action, *adopted* 17 May 1995, U.N. GAOR, 12th Sess., U.N. Doc. A/CONF.177/20, *reprinted in* Report of the Fourth World Conference on Women (1995) (recommended to the UN General Assembly by the Committee on the Status of Women on 7 Oct. 1995); International Covenant on Civil and Political Rights, *adopted* 16 Dec. 1966, G.A. Res. 2200 (XXI), U.N. GAOR, 21st Sess., Supp. No. 16, U.N. Doc. A/6316 (1966), 999 U.N.T.S. 171 (*entered into force* 23 Mar. 1976); Convention Against Torture and Other Cruel, Inhuman or Degrading Treatment or Punishment, *adopted* 10 Dec. 1984, G.A. Res. 39/46, U.N. GAOR, 39th Sess., Supp. No. 51, U.N. Doc. A/39/51 (1985) (*entered into force* 26 June 1987), *reprinted in* 23 I.L.M. 1027 (1984), *substantive changes noted in* 24 I.L.M. 535 (1985); Conference on Security and Co-operation in Europe: Document of the Moscow Meeting of the Conference on the Human Dimension, *adopted* 3 Oct. 1991, *reprinted in* 30 I.L.M. 1670 (1991); Supplementary Convention on the Abolition of Slavery, Slave Trade and Institutions and Practices Similar to Slavery, *adopted* 7 Sept. 1956, Economic and Social Council, Res. 608 (XXI), (*entered into force* 30 Apr. 1957); American Declaration on the Rights and Duties of Man, *signed* 2 May 1948, OEA/Ser.L/V/II.71, at 17 (1988); ILO

With the adoption of the TVPA in 2000, the United States further promoted international efforts to address trafficking. Many felt that the adoption of the Palermo Protocol on Trafficking would further advance the effort by providing a comprehensive definition of the problem upon which all could agree. Clearly, in order to attack trafficking as a crime on an international level, all of the countries of the region needed a common statutory definition. Palermo could provide a legal basis for a common crime. As one way of satisfying the demand by the United States that countries demonstrate their commitment to prohibiting trafficking, eighteen of the twenty-three Latin American countries have adopted the protocol; while two others have signed but not ratified. The number of signatories gives the Palermo definition legal standing throughout the region.[12] Specifically, the Palermo Protocol provides that:

> "Trafficking in persons" shall mean the recruitment, transportation, transfer, harbouring or receipt of persons, by means of the threat or use of force or other forms of coercion, of abduction, of fraud, of deception, of the abuse of power or of a position of vulnerability or of the giving or receiving payments or benefits to achieve the consent of a person having control over another person, for the purpose of exploitation.[13]

Thus, the signing nations have agreed to prohibit both sex trafficking and labor trafficking.

While this definition resolved a number of disputes within the field as to what qualifies as trafficking, two features remain problematic. First, the Palermo Protocol assumes that trafficking involves the movement of persons from one state to another. Research clearly indicates, however, that trafficking can occur within individual countries and that often being trafficked in-country may be the first step to joining the larger stream of international trafficking.[14] Second, the Palermo Protocol is part of the larger United Nations Convention on Transnational Organized Crime. While it is true that many organized crime groups are active in trafficking, significant parts of the trafficking networks are the products of ad hoc activities of individuals and small groups.[15]

Convention No. 105 concerning the Abolition of Forced Labor (1957).

[12] *See* Table 1.

[13] UN Protocol, *supra* note 7, art. 3(a).

[14] *See* In Modern Bondage: Sex Trafficking in the Americas (David E. Guinn & Elissa Steglich eds., 2003); Study on Trafficking in Women, Children and Adolescents for Commercial Sexual Exploitation in brazil (Maria Lucia Leal & Maria de Fatima Leal eds., 2003).

[15] David A. Feingold, *Human Trafficking*, For. Pol., Sept.–Oct. 2005, at 26, 28.

DEFINING THE PROBLEM OF TRAFFICKING: THE INTERPLAY OF US LAW, DONOR, AND NGO ENGAGEMENT AND THE LOCAL CONTEXT IN LATIN AMERICA

61

In theory, these definitional issues could prove problematic within the overall effort of assessment. However, demonstrating the power of US influence, analysts and countries in the region have generally attempted to comply with the US definition of trafficking, which both include in-country trafficking and does not require evidence of the involvement of organized crime. Nonetheless, even this apparent consensus masks a deeper failure to establish an effective means of studying and identifying the problem of trafficking.

The working elements of the US-influenced definition include: (1) the individual being subjected to; (2) forced or coerced into; (3) a situation of unlawful exploitation.[16] This clearly covers any type of trafficking for sexual exploitation or labor exploitation/slavery. However, in practice, the operational understanding of trafficking includes three types: child trafficking; trafficking in women for purposes of sexual exploitation; and trafficking for purposes of labor exploitation/slavery. This three-point categorization in large part grows out of the fact that outrage over the over the sexual exploitation of trafficked women, and especially children,[17] has provided the initial and primary political impetus to attack trafficking within the region. Specifically, beginning in the 1990s, NGOs and intergovernmental organizations mobilized to work against the commercial sexual exploitation of children and youth, i.e., trafficking for pornography, sex tourism, and prostitution. This resulted in a series of international events including: the Fourth World Conference on Women in Beijing (1995); the Seminar Against the Sexual Exploitation of Children and Adolescents in the Americas, held in Brasilia (1996); the UN Convention Against Transnational Organized Crime in Palermo (2000), and the First and Second World Congresses Against the Commercial Sexual Exploitation of Children, held in Stockholm (1996) and Yokohama (2001). Indeed, it appears that this newest effort to address the trafficking of women emerged as simply an extension to the concern over children and adolescents, while concerns over forced labor subsequently emerged as an ancillary to the two concerns over sexual exploitation.

These three operational categories are not treated equally, consequently, assessing the issue of trafficking as a whole suffers from this disparate treatment. Moreover, each embodies certain internal conflicts on how particular countries treat the problem, and this can affect data collection and analysis.

---

[16] *See* U.S. Department of State, Trafficking in Persons Report, *available at http://www. state.gov/g/tip/rls/tiprpt/.*

[17] Children are not only protected under the terms of the Palermo Protocol, but also the Optional Protocol to the Convention on the Rights of the Child on the Sale of Children, Child Prostitution, and Child Pornography, G.A. Res. 54/263, Annex II, 54 U.N. GAOR Supp. (No. 49) at 6, U.N. Doc. A/RES/54/49, Vol. III (2000), (*entered into force* 18 Jan. 2002.)

B. Child Trafficking

Out of all forms of trafficking, child trafficking receives the greatest attention and condemnation. Countries that provide practically no programs to combat the trafficking of women or trafficking for labor exploitation nonetheless make some effort to prevent child trafficking, especially trafficking for purposes of sexual exploitation as reported in the US Trafficking in Persons (TIP) Report.[18] Trafficking in children most frequently tends to be reported as trafficking for purposes of sexual exploitation in association with sex tourism.[19] Other forms of trafficking include using children as panhandlers, news agents, garbage recyclers (i.e., those who sort through the public dumps for recyclable materials), domestic help (especially in Haiti),[20] mining, agriculture,[21] illegal adoption (particularly in Costa Rica and the Dominican Republic),[22] and child soldiers (in Columbia).[23]

Trafficking in children primarily involves in-country exploitation, and in the case of sexual exploitation, may be categorized as trafficking even where the child remains in residence with their parents or close relatives.[24] This characterization of child trafficking as almost exclusively in-country rather than international, however, most likely rests on biased data. Because trafficking in children attracts far greater attention and penalties, traffickers often lie about the victims' ages, force the victims to lie about their ages, and provide victims with forged identity papers.[25] Moreover, a significant difficulty in identifying child trafficking in Latin America arises from the wide discrepancy in the legal age of consent for females in these countries, which averages from

---

[18] The situations in Jamaica, Nicaragua, and Uruguay are examples listed in the TIP Report. U.S. Department of State, 2005 Trafficking in Persons Report 7 (June 2005) [hereinafter 2005 TIP Report].

[19] Examples of countries that report in this manner include: Brazil, Costa Rica, and the Dominican Republic. *See, e.g.*, 2005 TIP Report, *supra* note 18, at 72, 87, 156.

[20] *See* Ribando, *supra* note 2, at 5.\

[21] For example, Bolivia has trafficking for mining and Brazil has trafficking for agriculture. *See, e.g.*, 2005 TIP Report *supra* note 18, at 68, 71.

[22] *Secretariat Report, Implementation of the Protocol to Prevent, Suppress and Punish Trafficking in Persons, Especially Women and Children, supplementing the United Nations Convention against Transnational Organized Crime* (2005) CTOC/COP/2005/3, 10 [hereinafter CTOC Report].

[23] 2005 TIP Report *supra* note 18, at 85.

[24] Zoila Gonzalez de Innocenti, Oficina Internacional del Trabajo, Programa Internacional Para La Erradicación del Trabajo Infantil (OIT/IPEC), Explotación Sexual Comercial de Niñas y Adolescentes: Una Evaluación Rápida (2002), *available at* http://www.oit.org. pe/ipec/documentos/explotacion_sexual_comercial_de_ninas_y_adolescentes_paragua.pdf.

[25] In Modern Bondage, *supra* note 14, at 65.

DEFINING THE PROBLEM OF TRAFFICKING: THE INTERPLAY OF US LAW, DONOR, AND NGO ENGAGEMENT AND THE LOCAL CONTEXT IN LATIN AMERICA

63

fourteen years of age,[26] to eighteen-year-old age of consent provided in the Palermo Protocol.

C. Trafficking in Women for Purposes of Sexual Exploitation

As previously noted, trafficking in women for purposes of sexual exploitation was recognized within the region as early as 1928 and the topic received significant international attention throughout the twentieth century.[27] This category exists separately from labor exploitation for two reasons. First, it reflects the US resistance to labeling prostitution as a legitimate form of sexwork. The US government and many activists within the United States, favor broadening the definition of trafficking in persons to include prostitution as a prohibited form of sexual exploitation, with the element of force or coercion being implicit in the act itself. They argue that all forms of prostitution are inherently acts of violence against women in which there is no possibility for voluntary consent.[28] Moreover, US government officials argue that: "Where prostitution is legalized or tolerated, there is greater demand for human trafficking victims and nearly always an increase in the number of women and children trafficked into sex slavery."[29] In order to promote this approach, the United States has gone so far as to link HIV/AIDS and anti-trafficking program assistance to groups that explicitly condemn "prostitution and sex trafficking."[30] Second, as the adage goes, "sex sells." One of the principal ways data is collected about trafficking is through media reports.[31] Inevitably, raids on brothels or other sex industry sites will receive greater media attention than other forms of labor abuse.

---

[26] See Table 1.

[27] See, e.g., Convention for the Suppression of the Traffic in Persons and of the Exploitation of the Prostitution of Others, adopted 2 Dec. 1949, G.A. Res 317 (entered into force 25 July 1951), 96 U.N.T.S. 271; Convention on the Elimination of All Forms of Discrimination Against Women, adopted 18 Dec. 1979, G.A. Res. 34/180, U.N. GAOR, 34th Sess., Supp. No. 46, U.N. Doc. A/34/46 (1980) (entered into force 3 Sept. 1981), 1249 U.N.T.S. 13, reprinted in 19 I.L.M. 33 (1980); Inter-American Convention on the Prevention, Punishment and Eradication of Violence Against Women, "Convention of Belém do Pará," adopted 9 June 1994, OAS/Ser.L.V/II.92/doc.31 rev.3 (1994) (not in force), reprinted in 33 I.L.M. 1534 (1994).

[28] See, e.g., Janice G. Raymond, Sex Trafficking is Not "Sex Work," Conscience (2005).

[29] See Ribando, supra note 2, at 19.

[30] See, e.g., United States Leadership Against HIV/AIDS, Tuberculosis, and Malaria Act of 2003 §301, 22 U.S.C. §7601 (2003); TVPRA 2003, supra note 5.

[31] See 2005 TIP Report, supra note 18, at 7.

Complicating enforcement and assessment, despite US objections to the practice, most Latin American countries have legalized prostitution.[32] In addition, given the economic situation of women who are frequently denied education and other opportunities to make a living, as well as pressure upon poverty-stricken families seeking ways to economically situate their daughters, questions arise as to the practices of marriage agencies and the possibilities of coerced or forced marriages (for examples, in El Salvador).

D. *Trafficking for Labor Exploitation*

Trafficking for purposes of labor exploitation is perhaps the most difficult and politically contentious of the three types of trafficking. When practiced domestically, except with respect to children, it is likely to be subsumed under the umbrella of labor law violations that may or may not protect the victim. Once the victim enters the international movement of trafficking, the victim simultaneously becomes an irregular or undocumented migrant. As experience has shown, it is often difficult to ascertain whether a particular case falls under the definition of trafficking in persons or smuggling of migrants, as both activities share some common elements.[33] Finally, once they reach their country of destination, they are illegal aliens, liable for prosecution as such.

In theory, advocates against trafficking in women and children for purposes of sexual exploitation (largely identified with women's rights movements) should be equally concerned with labor trafficking, as women and female children make up 56 percent of those trafficked.[34] In practice this does not appear to be the case. Thus, one finds conflicting assertions. Laura Langberg, in a review of the Organization of American States (OAS) research on trafficking, notes that while trafficking for forced labor is recognized as a serious situation in Latin America, trafficking for purposes of sexual exploitation has been perceived as a more widespread and pressing regional concern.[35] By contrast, the International Labour Organization (ILO) has reported that sex trafficking victims represent only 9 percent (113,520) of the 1.3 million people in Latin America engaged in forced labor.[36]

Further illustrating the tendency to attempt to link other concerns to the popularity of sexual trafficking, as has occurred in the case of

---

[32] In Modern Bondage, *supra* note 14, at 59.

[33] CTOC Report, *supra* note 22, at ¶¶ 37–38.

[34] ILO, Report of the Director General: A global alliance against forced labor 15 (2005), *available at* http://www.ilo.org/public/english/standards/relm/ilc/ilc93/pdf/rep-i-b.pdf.

[35] Laura Langberg, *A Review of Recent OAS Research on Human Trafficking in the Latin American and Caribbean Region, in* Data and Research on Human Trafficking, *supra* note 9, at 129, 130.

[36] ILO, *supra* note 34, at 13–14.

labor exploitation, it should be noted that a number of countries, such as Chile and Costa Rica, include trading in organs or tissue as a form of trafficking.[37] While justification exists for such a policy, it generally falls outside of most studies on trafficking and is normally reported under public health and health law related studies.[38] Moreover, whereas the affinities between trafficking in women and children for sexual exploitation and labor exploitation offer mutually informing insights over such issues as the types of traffickers and the routes used, organ trafficking necessarily involves greater levels of specialized expertise and narrower channels of distribution that bear only limited relations with the other forms of trafficking.

E. Social, Economic, and Political Concerns

If these definitional challenges were not enough, efforts to assess trafficking are further complicated by social, economic, and political concerns, which affect the collection and analysis of data. Of these forces, three specific facets emerge as critical.

First, the impetus to combat trafficking did not arise within the governments of the region. Instead, governments have been forced to respond to demands by the international community, particularly the United States, to address this problem. While indigenous NGOs have joined in supporting this international effort, from the perspective of the local government anti-trafficking programs nonetheless remain an effort adopted under a certain degree of external force or coercion. Evidence of this can be found in the practice of many governments to adopt anti-trafficking legislation modeled on the US TVPA as opposed to legislation reflecting local concerns and needs.[39] They do so because the US Department of State, in the TIP report, evaluates each country in accordance with how it complies with the requirements of the standards in the TVPA.

Second, one of the most significant factors hindering efforts to gather accurate data on the extent of trafficking and to combat its practice is a lack of resources. Clearly, too few governmental investigators (police officers, immigration officials, etc.) will limit a government's ability to identify and prosecute trafficking cases. Equally significant but less obvious, when faced with scarce resources government enforcement officials will have to make tough resource allocation decisions among a variety of deserving causes: whether to pursue drug smugglers or traffickers; violent crimes or brothel owners (in countries where

---

[37] CTOC Report, *supra* note 22, at ¶ ¶ 23, 37, 38.

[38] *See, e.g.*, Michele Goodwin, Black Markets: The Supply and Demand of Body Parts (2006).

[39] *See* Ribando, *supra* note 2, at 17.

prostitution is legal); or even whether to combat trafficking or provide education for women and girls. Adding to this resource concern, trafficking represents a significantly greater commitment of assets than other related crimes. For example, while undocumented aliens can simply be repatriated, if the alien is identified as a trafficking victim and the state fully complies with the requirements of the TVPA and Palermo Protocol, enforcement requires that the victim be offered incentives to cooperate in the prosecution; she will require living assistance and healthcare in the interim and potentially support for retraining and resettlement. In order to avoid the obligation to prosecute, government officials have an incentive to look away and fail to identify trafficking victims.

Complicating these judgments about domestic resource allocation, governments may be concerned that if they aggressively pursue accurate data, they risk being cited by the United States as having a major trafficking problem.[40] While many countries respond to a poor ranking in the TIP report based on concerns about their reputation, particularly where tourism is a major industry (e.g., Costa Rica, Jamaica), others will be driven by concerns over the possible imposition of sanctions by the United States.

Finally, our understanding of the nature of trafficking may be distorted by the resources available to address it. In particular, intergovernmental organizations (such as the Inter-American Commission of Women and the Inter-American Children's Institute of the Organization of American States), charities, and NGOs (such as Save the Children and UNICEF) focusing upon children and women are among the most active groups in the region both in terms of monitoring trafficking and providing services for victims. Insofar as they are among the primary sources of data on the problem, analysis of that data will necessarily highlight their concerns. While the ILO and the International Organization for Migration (IOM) are very active in this area, it does not appear that they have similar resources.

F. Legal and Logistical Concerns

The final challenge in assessing trafficking arises out of legal and logistical obstacles to accurate data collection. Again, three key concerns emerge. First, many countries in Latin America do not have special laws addressing trafficking. Instead, insofar as they address the problem as required under their ratification of the Palermo Protocol or the Optional Protocol to the Convention on the Rights of the Child on the Sale of

---

[40] *See, e.g.*, Human Rights Watch, U.S. State Department Trafficking Report Undercut by Lack of Analysis (June 2003), *available* at http://www.hrw.org/press/2003/06/trafficking report. htm; Frank Laczko & Marco A. Gramegna, *Developing Better Indicators of Human Trafficking*, 10 Brown J. World Aff. 179 (2003) at 179.

Children, Child Prostitution and Child Pornography (CRC Protocol),[41] they do so through statutes directed against the sexual exploitation of children (e.g., Mexico) or prohibitions against procurement (e.g., Brazil). Thus, in assessing trafficking on a regional level, it may be difficult to establish accurate equivalence among the potential criminal charges.

Second, because trafficking is a regional problem, it requires cooperation and collaboration among enforcement agencies throughout the region. This requires not only a shared understanding of how to define trafficking but also the infrastructure to support that exchange of information. In many border areas, immigration and police often do not even have phones or fax equipment capable of contacting their counterparts across the border.[42]

Finally, given the inadequacy of official records on trafficking, most assessments are based upon "open source data" (i.e., data generally available to the public in government, NGO, academic, or media reports).[43] Given the paucity of governmental data, media data often forms a potentially disproportionate resource. This type of data has the potential to induce bias toward the more newsworthy forms of trafficking, and to mislead where the nature of the crime has been obfuscated by government efforts to protect the identity of minors, or by a failure to identify the role of trafficking.

Scope of The Problem of Trafficking

Existing qualitative research provides us with a relatively clear picture of trafficking: its victims, its perpetrators, and its methods. Indeed, qualitative research exists as a methodology because it is well suited to providing a deeper and more detailed character portrait of those involved in social phenomena than other types of empirical research. Therefore, we can describe the problem in some detail.

Victims of trafficking are primarily driven by economic necessity, either for survival or the desire for a better life. Thus, trafficking follows a path not just toward the obvious destination countries of the United States, Canada, and Europe, but from poor areas to areas of relative prosperity. This includes movements from rural to urban areas, then from poorer urban areas to more prosperous areas within or outside the

---

[41] Optional Protocol to the Convention on the Rights of the Child on the Sale of Children, Child Prostitution, and Child Pornography, G.A. Res. 54/263, U.N. GAOR, 54th Sess., Annex II, U.N. Doc. A/54/49 (2000) (*entered into force* 18 Jan. 2002).

[42] In Modern Bondage, *supra* note 14, at 66.

[43] Office to Monitor and Combat Trafficking in Persons and the Bureau of Intelligence and Research, Seminar on Trafficking in Persons Research (14 Nov. 2005) [hereinafter TIP Research].

country of origin. Contributing to this economic motivation, particularly in the case of women and children, are: economic discrimination (e.g., as of 2001, women's income averaged one-third of that of men in Latin America);[44] the rising disintegration of traditional family units leaving women as the primary heads of household; sexual violence, which contributes in particular to the likelihood that women and children will be trafficked for purposes of sexual exploitation; and the loss of social support networks such as the extended family, schools, or other civil society groups.[45]

The Palermo Protocol is predicated upon the idea that trafficking involves organized crime. However, existing research demonstrates that while traditional organized crime groups such as the Russian Mafia (particularly related to trafficking into the Iberian Peninsula), the Yakuza (Japan), and drug cartels (who often combine drug trafficking with the trafficking of the individuals used to transport the drugs) are actively engaged in trafficking, significant elements within the trafficking enterprise are the result of informal relationships among individuals arising out of opportunity. For example, many women and children traveling north as part of the undocumented migration toward the United States wind up in trafficking situations through misadventure.[46] They may hitch a ride with a trucker or hire a taxi driver who takes advantage of their isolation to highjack them and sell them to the next bar or brothel owner on their route.

Finally, we know that the countries of the region can simultaneously function as source, transit, and destination countries within the trafficking regime. As noted above, because the movement of trafficking follows relative economic disparities, even poor countries can have pockets of prosperity or particular industries that draw trafficking victims. Sex trafficking closely follows migratory patterns. Moreover, trafficking does not always involve a single transfer, where the victim is recruited and immediately sent to their final destination. Particularly in sex trafficking, victims are often first trafficked in-country and are then transported through a string of intermediary stops before moving to another country.[47]

While it is possible to outline this general picture of trafficking, given the definitional, cultural, and legal difficulties outlined above, the challenge remains to find ways to quantify the problem. Most government officials (whether speaking on the record or off the record),

---

[44] Comisión Deonómica Para América Latina y el Caribe [CEPAL], Statistical Yearbook for Latin America and the Caribbean 2001, at 58 (2002).

[45] In Modern Bondage, *supra* note 14, at 29–31; Study on Trafficking, *supra* note 14, at 54–59.

[46] In Modern Bondage, *supra* note 14, at 33.

[47] *Id.* at 37–40.

Defining the Problem of Trafficking: The Interplay of US Law, Donor, and NGO Engagement and the Local Context in Latin America

69

NGOs working in the area, media reports, and academic researchers all agree that trafficking, in all its forms, is a major concern in Latin America.[48] Relative assessments suggest that Latin America is the third largest source of trafficking victims, after South and Southeast Asia, and the former Soviet Union.[49] Similarly, under the US government's assessment in the 2005 annual TIP Report, a higher percentage of countries within Latin America fell into the Tier 3 ranking (the lowest) than any other region in the world (though this situation improved significantly by the time of the 2007 TIP Report where only two Latin American and Caribbean countries remained at Tier 3).[50] Quantifying the full extent of trafficking can be extremely difficult and four possible approaches are currently used to address these challenges.

A. Legal and Undocumented Migration

First, many researchers and advocates focus upon general legal and illegal migration, where significant statistics exist. Research amply demonstrates that trafficking is closely related to illegal migration and smuggling.[51] While it may not be possible to quantify the exact percentage of illegal migration/smuggling that ends in exploitative trafficking, qualitative research suggests that it is significant.

Thus, one way to quantify the problem draws attention to statistics indicating that Latin America and the Caribbean have the highest rate of movement and out-migration in the world.[52] The movement of undocumented migrants toward the United States is escalating; US Border Patrol and other officials detained almost 1.16 million individuals in 2004 and the number of non-Mexican undocumented migrants apprehended has tripled over the last three years.[53] According to the United States, Latin America is the primary source for the estimated 14,500 to 17,500 individuals identified as being trafficked into the United States each year, though it appears that those figures may

---

[48] *Id.* at 13–16 (discussing research methodology).

[49] Ribando, *supra* note 2, at 1.

[50] This latter assessment, however merely indicates the countries failure to comply with the United States requirements regarding efforts to combat trafficking where trafficking is identified as a problem. It does not rank the significance of the problem in terms of the numbers of victims or traffickers involved.

[51] CTOP Report, *supra* note 22, at 9.

[52] *See, e.g.,* IOM, World Migration (2005); Exploratory Assessment of Trafficking *supra* note 2.

[53] Blas Nuñez-Neto, Alison Sisken & Stephen Viña, Border Security: Apprehensions of "other than Mexican" Aliens (2005); Ribando, *supra* note 2, at 1.

include victims from other parts of the world for whom Latin America is merely a transit region.[54]

Taking the implicit association between undocumented migration and trafficking one step further, researchers for the country reports on Brazil, Colombia, and the Dominican Republic in the 2005 TIP Report, estimated that 70,000 Brazilians, 45,000–50,000 Colombians, and 50,000 Dominicans were engaged in prostitution in Europe under the assumption that all or most may have been the victims of trafficking—figures that were repeated verbatim in the 2006 TIP Report. Yet, these figures have been questioned because they have not been confirmed by European police officials.[55]

To these figures we can add larger estimates provided by organizations such as the ILO, that 1.3 million people in Latin America are victims of forced labor, of whom 250,000 have been trafficked within the region.[56] It is estimated that 650,000 Haitians have been virtually enslaved in the sugar cane bateyes of the Dominican Republic.[57]

B. Prosecutions

Another way to define the scope of the problem targets prosecutions of traffickers. The TIP report adopts this approach as one way to measure not only the scope of the problem, but more importantly, the local government's efforts to combat trafficking. Thus, the 2006 TIP Report states that in 2003 there were 175 prosecutions and twenty-seven convictions in the Western Hemisphere (presumably all countries other than the United States); in 2004, 145 prosecutions and fifty-six convictions; and in 2005 there were 170 prosecutions and fifty-nine convictions.[58]

Unfortunately, it is not clear what these numbers mean. First, one would need to know whether these prosecutions involve major traffickers or other heavily involved individuals, or whether it may be one person arrested for the enslavement of an individual victim of trafficking. Second, given the definitional ambiguity noted above, these simple prosecution numbers do not tell us what type of trafficking is involved (i.e., children, or women for sexual exploitation, or labor).

---

[54] U.S. Dept. of State, 2004 Trafficking in Persons Report 23 (June 2004), *available at* http://www.state.gov/documents/organization/34158.pdf.

[55] Ribando, *supra* note 2, at 6.

[56] ILO, *supra* note 34, at 13–14.

[57] U.S. Dept. of State, Country Reports on Human Rights Practices 2004: Dominican Republic (2005), *available at* http://www.state.gov/g/drl/rls/hrrpt/2004/41758.htm.

[58] U.S. Dept. of State, 2006 Trafficking in Persons Report (June 2006), *available at* http://www.state.gov/g/tip/rls/tiprpt/2006/65986.htm.

C. Trafficking Networks or Entry Points

A third way to suggest the extent of trafficking is to identify the multiple and diverse ways in which individuals enter this criminal enterprise. It can be assumed from the variety and existence of multiple identifiable entry points that many have entered trafficking through these doorways. Illustrative of these entry points or trafficking networks are those identified in the International Human Rights Law Institute's (IHRLI) study of trafficking for purposes of sexual exploitation in Brazil.[59] This study identified different trafficking networks at both the domestic and international levels, which were roughly subdivided into seven different categories based upon their principal methods of recruitment (e.g., how they deceive the women and adolescents, etc.), and how they market the trafficking victims (e.g., marriage brokers; tour agents, etc.), or both:

(1) Entertainment network: shopping malls, nightclubs, bars, restaurants, motels, beach tents, fast food restaurants, showhouses, samba gatherings, brothels, and massage parlors. Trafficking financed by nightclubs, bar owners, and other "entertainment" sources constitute the most common type of trafficking network. According to statements provided by their informants, nightclub owners finance the girls' interstate trips, their maintenance in the destination city, and provide them with alcohol and drugs, as well as their first clients.

(2) Fashion Market Network: modeling agencies (photography, videos, and movies). Modeling agencies provide traffickers with great access to particularly attractive or appealing women and girls. Throughout the world, modeling agencies have served as a primary entry point into pornography. They have served a similar purpose for trafficking networks.

(3) Employment Agencies Network: domestic servants, babysitters, travel escorts, and artists (dancers, singers, etc.). Given the strong connection between trafficking and economic migration, employment agencies are often used as a front for recruitment.

(4) Marriage Agency Network: Among all the forms of trafficking networks, marriage agencies are the most difficult to characterize. According to a study conducted by the Center of United Marginalized Populations (CEAP) in 1997, there are at least two types of trafficking through marriage agencies: either the woman replies to an advertisement, or she joins a sex tourism

---

[59] Study on Trafficking, *supra* note 14, at 66–72.

agency that also arranges marriages for foreigners.[60] In either case, the foreign man comes to Brazil to pick up the female candidate. She often leaves the country not knowing that there is a contract between the agency and her prospective husband.[61]

(5) Tourism Industry Network: travel agencies, hotels, health spas/resorts, and tourist transportation. Tourism, especially sex tourism (where the object of the trip is to have sex with a local), fuels the demand for women and children who are trafficked to service this demand. While this is an oft-used network for domestic trafficking, it is also a destination network for international trafficking entering Brazil.

(6) The Taxi Connection: While not a network in themselves (in the sense of a complete connection between recruitment and destination) taxi drivers serve a number of different functions within the broader field of trafficking. First, taxi drivers may serve as recruiters for traffickers by identifying potential victims. This particularly arises in connection with those women who have already entered the migrant labor movement and find themselves isolated in a new environment. Second, taxi drivers often act as the transporters of trafficked individuals. Finally, taxi drivers may actually link women or children with their "johns."

(7) Recruitment Agencies for Infrastructure and Development Projects Network: recruitment for agriculture, highway and waterway construction, gold mining, and others. Large infrastructure projects and mining operations lead to massive relocations of people—most frequently men without female partners. The prostitution market, and the trafficking of women and children to service that market, develops accordingly—it follows the migratory flow, increasing and decreasing according to construction and gold mining operations. These networks are found throughout Latin America.[62]

While these divisions provide some insights, these typologies of networks are not absolute, with individual networks often interacting with or sharing features with networks categorized under a different typology.

---

[60] *Id.* at 69.

[61] *Id.* at 69.

[62] In Modern Bondage, *supra* note 14, at 37.

D. Trafficking Routes

A final way to profile the problem is to identify the number of routes and destinations for trafficking. This is illustrated by drawing upon IHRLI's Brazilian sex trafficking research. Trafficking is a complex form of trade involving the movement of significant numbers of people both from region to region within a country (Brazil) and internationally across multiple borders. This presents numerous logistical challenges for traffickers including both the physical demands of moving individuals from place to place and issues of regulatory compliance or avoidance. To answer these challenges, those involved in trafficking develop routinized practices incorporating paths of movement, methods of travel, means of addressing regulatory challenges, and so forth. For convenience, these practices can be identified collectively as trafficking routes.

Studying trafficking routes represents a particularly useful and important means to research trafficking.

First, while there is some evidence that a significant amount of international trafficking is operated by organized crime, it has also been found that trafficking routes are constituted by a less formal association of unrelated independent agents whose operations are limited to one small segment within the chain. For example, while we know that individuals are passed between internal trafficking networks within Brazil and international networks that move those individuals to foreign countries, the linkage between the two may be nothing more than that of a seller (the internal trafficker) and buyer (the individual or group responsible for introducing the trafficked person into that particular trafficking route at that particular point of contact).

Second, studying trafficking routes may provide insights as to the points of entry and potential points of vulnerability for legal and social intervention. For example, another study conducted by the IHRLI in Central America found that many women who were economic migrants followed the routes developed for illegal immigrants and became trafficking victims when they were intercepted within the illegal immigrant system and diverted into the trafficking system.[63]

Third, determining the exact numbers of individuals being trafficked is quite difficult. It is an illegal activity which has, in many cases, been shielded by governmental complicity. One possible alternative to assess the magnitude of the problem is to measure the number of routes being used for trafficking. By definition, a route involves multiple transports of individuals. Ergo, the more routes used, the more victims being trafficked to, from, or through that area.

Fourth, studying trafficking routes allows researchers to distinguish among those being trafficked. That is to say, the type of trafficking

---

[63] *Id.*, at 33.

route used and its destination often varies according to the type of person being trafficked. For example, because it is likely to be more difficult to transport them across borders, the logistics of moving children or adolescents will demand a different type of network from that of transporting adult women. Similarly, the end markets for trafficking may prefer one ethnic, racial, cultural, or age group over others. That preference would inform the network created to meet that demand.

Finally, identifying the routes followed by trafficking victims helps guide the disposition of limited governmental and nongovernmental resources to measure the movement of individuals within the trafficking system.

E. Domestic Trafficking Routes

As previously noted, one of the reasons for including the Brazil study within the research on trafficking in the Americas was that Brazil represented a major economic power in the region, covering an expansive geographic territory with a large population. Prior research had demonstrated that even within some of the smaller countries in Central America, internal trafficking could be observed in the movement of individuals from one part of the country to another for purposes of sexual exploitation.[64] This study has found that internal trafficking represents a major phenomenon within Brazil. In order to study it effectively, the country was divided into five geographic regions and routes were mapped within and between these regions.

In studying these routes and characteristics of the individuals trafficked in these routes, many features conform to expectations and the findings of prior research. In Brazil, most trafficking routes originate in rural areas and move toward the large urban centers or international border regions, which serve as either an initial point for international trafficking or as a destination for sex tourism. Similarly, routes emerge to serve dramatic changes in the economic environment created by development. For example, in the Northeast region, significant trafficking routes have developed to transport women, some of whom have been identified as Amer-Indian, to serve the railroads and gold mining zones.[65]

Methods of transporting trafficked individuals domestically reveal some interesting features that might be of use in enforcement. Specifically, while Brazil is a large country with a large navigable system of waterways, the primary method of domestic transport is overland, with taxis and trucks as the preferred vehicles, followed by cars and buses. Interestingly, the limited domestic trafficking that

---

[64] *Id.* at 40.

[65] Study on Trafficking, *supra* note 14, at 73–94.

utilizes airplanes as the method of transport is used almost exclusively to transport adolescents.[66]

Finally, as previously noted, analysis of the domestic routes reveals that adolescents are the primary subjects of domestic trafficking, followed by women. Data on child trafficking is, unfortunately, extremely limited.[67]

F. International Trafficking Routes

Researchers have identified 131 international trafficking routes to seventeen different destination countries for women and children. Here again, certain characteristics are notable. As is the case with domestic routes, those regions under the most economic stress are also the points of origin for the most international trafficking routes. However, the distribution among the regions is less disproportionate than with domestic routes. Among the destination countries, Spain is by far the most common destination country for Brazilian women. It is followed by the Netherlands, Venezuela, Italy, Portugal, Paraguay, Switzerland, United States, Germany, Suriname, Israel, Hong Kong, Bolivia, Japan, French Guiana, Peru, and Taiwan.[68]

Unlike domestic trafficking, where adolescents are among the most frequently trafficked, international routes are primarily devoted to trafficking women. However, once again, these statistics must be considered in light of the tendency of traffickers to identify older adolescents as being eighteen years of age or older.

Finally, the linkage between trafficking and organized crime appears most clearly in connection with international trafficking. For example, trafficking to Spain almost always involves the "Iberian Connection," a collaboration of a number of criminal organizations, in which the Russian Mafia appears dominant. The Russian Mafia is reported to make US $8 billion per year through its brothels in Portugal and Spain.[69]

Local and International Efforts to Address Trafficking

National and international efforts to address the problems associated with trafficking and slavery throughout the region, and indeed the world, have been primarily driven by the United States under the terms

---

[66] *Id.* at 73–79.

[67] *Id.* at 110.

[68] *Id.* at 95–110.

[69] *Id.* at 107–08.

of the TVPA and the TIP Reporting System. These efforts have been supported by NGO communities involved in these areas, especially those concerned with children's rights, women's rights, and migration. Nonetheless, advocates widely acknowledge the important role played by the United States in this effort.

US efforts have reaped significant benefits.

First, the United States has succeeded in calling national, regional, and world attention to the problem. As previously noted, the existence of a trafficking market in Latin America had been widely acknowledged throughout the twentieth century. However, the problem was not significantly addressed until the United States expressed its concern and exerted pressure on national governments within the region to find ways to combat trafficking.

Second, while trafficking may occur within a single country, the larger portion of the crime involves an international component—either the movement of victims to a place of exploitation or the movement of exploiters to a territory (e.g., sex tourism). As such, efforts to effectively address the problem require the cooperation of many countries—those whose citizens are being trafficked (the source countries), those through whom victims may be trafficked (transit countries), and the countries of destination. Thus, the United States encourages the development of consistent legal standards regarding the crimes involved and cooperation among all of the states within the region.

Third, the TVPA developed a "carrot and stick" approach to encourage countries to join the fight against trafficking. The TIP Report and foreign assistance restrictions represent the stick. The Report and its categorization of states into tiers sought to shame countries into compliance. This has been particularly true with many countries, such as the Dominican Republic and Costa Rica, who depend upon tourism as a significant component of their economies.[70] The second tool within the arsenal of "sticks" is the statutory direction that foreign assistance, including military aid, be withheld to those countries categorized in the lowest tier, Tier 3. Many have criticized the application of this part of the law due to the national security exception allowing the president to exempt a country from sanctions upon a finding of national interest. Thus, one finds that the only countries consistently being subject to the Tier 3 linked sanctions are countries such as Cuba and Venezuela, who are already considered pariah states by the US and are not receiving assistance in any event.[71]

However, in addition to these coercive tactics, the TVPA has included significant funds to be disbursed by the Office of Trafficking in Persons within the State Department to support local efforts to address

---

[70] *See* Ribando, *supra* note 2, at 19.

[71] *See* Feingold, *supra* note 15, at 30.

trafficking—the "carrots" in the US approach. In 2004, it supported over thirty-eight programs in the region (plus twenty-two in the United States) with grants totaling $16,951,000.[72] In 2005, there were thirty-three programs in the region, with grants totaling $16,482,000.[73] A significant portion of this funding has been disbursed to improve enforcement efforts (though sometimes labeled as prevention or protection) throughout Latin America, particularly through the provision of training.

The US leadership in the fight against trafficking has, however, also caused problems, both for what it requires and as an unintended consequence of flaws within its data collection methods. Data is collected by overworked political service officers within local embassies on a short deadline. As described in one interview with the author, the political officers received an extensive questionnaire with a response deadline of three weeks.[74] Because they are not experts themselves, officers are forced to draw upon the expertise of local government officials and available resources in the NGO community. Unfortunately, government officials do not always have the answers and many have political incentives to distort the information to make it more favorable to them. Meanwhile, those in the NGO community may be biased toward particular aspects of the overall problem or may be simply inadequately suited to the task. In either case, the political officers often focus upon the easiest quantifiable data, such as the existence of laws, the numbers of training sessions for officials, and the numbers of prosecutions. This in turn leads local governments to target their efforts to satisfy US requirements by emphasizing those efforts easily categorized or quantified for the TIP reports. The more troubling features of this effort are discussed here.

First, there are indications that some local governments in the region are drafting and enacting anti-trafficking laws specifically to satisfy the requirements of the TVPA rather than to meet local needs. Such laws may not address specific aspects of the local problem nor accommodate the capacity of local law enforcement to support the new laws.[75]

---

[72] *See* The U.S. Government's International Anti-Trafficking Programs Fiscal Year 2004 (The Office to Monitor and Combat Trafficking in Persons), (3 June 2005), *available at* http://www.state.gov/g/tip/rls/rpt/51687.htm#westernhemisphere.

[73] *See* United States Government Funds Obligated in Fiscal Year 2005 for Anti-Trafficking in Persons Projects (The Office to Monitor and Combat Trafficking in Persons), *available at* http://www.state.gov/g/tip/rls/fs/2006/63816/htm.

[74] Confidential Interviews with political affairs officers, Amman Jordan (2004); Rome, Italy (2004).

[75] *See* Ribando, *supra* note 2, at 17.

Second, countries emphasize easily quantifiable activities such as providing specialized training to a significant number of officials without regard to whether or not those employees actually interact with victims or traffickers.[76] Training, while necessary, does not require the sustained effort or resources needed to actually investigate or prosecute trafficking crimes or to address the social demographics that encourage trafficking. Moreover, many NGOs offer training, without significant cost to the government, offering the country a virtually cost-free means of complying with US demands.

Third, US officials have emphasized the importance of trafficking prosecutions under the TVPA.[77] When it became evident that a number of countries were reacting to this pressure by initiating prosecutions without necessarily achieving a corresponding number of convictions, the US adjusted its standards in the 2003 TVPA Reauthorization Act.[78] Nonetheless, the mere accumulation of prosecutions does not necessarily indicate the quality of the prosecutions or the significance of those being prosecuted, e.g., whether they are minor figures or major traffickers. Moreover, as previously indicated, some evidence suggests that countries may exaggerate or hold back trafficking estimates, including prosecutions, depending upon their assessment as to how such figures could adversely affect their TIP rating.[79]

Donors and the nongovernmental organizations that deliver the programs they fund, provide the secondary drive for enforcement and prevention efforts. Domestically based NGOs are widely acknowledged as a crucial force within the countries of the region, providing information, services, and marshaling domestic political support for efforts to combat trafficking.[80] Their importance is magnified by the fact that they are the primary conduit for donor funding. While obtaining donor resources is often necessary within the region, this can potentially bias the enforcement effort, skewing it to address issues of particular concern to funders, such as favoring efforts to help children or address sex trafficking—issues with strong emotional appeal to donor organizations and their supporters and funders—rather than issues of labor abuse and slavery that may be far greater in impact. This topic fragmentation by funders also impairs the effort to develop a coordinated, coherent national and regional plan for the overall anti-trafficking effort.

---

[76] In Modern Bondage, *supra* note 14, at 65.

[77] TVPA, *supra* note 4, §108(b)(1).

[78] TVPRA 2003, *supra* note 5, §6(d)(1).

[79] *See, e.g.* Human Rights Watch, *supra* note 40; Laczko & Gramegna, *supra* note 40.

[80] Study on Trafficking, *supra* note 14, at 35.

Additional international actors in the region include the Organization of American States (OAS), the Inter-American Commission of Women (CIM), and the Inter-American Development Bank. The OAS and the CIM have been actively addressing trafficking, starting with their collaboration with IHRLI in conducting the nine-country regional research project on trafficking in the Americas in 1999, funded by the United States Agency for International Development (USAID). Since that time, it has actively pursued additional research and provided significant training efforts throughout the region. The Inter-American Development Bank, in coordination with the OAS and the International Organization for Migration, initiated a working group in 2004 on anti-trafficking efforts in the region and developed technical cooperation projects for Bolivia, Columbia, El Salvador, Guyana, and Paraguay.[81]

Methods to Limit Or Eliminate Trafficking

Under the TVPA, the United States advocates the "three P approach" to fighting trafficking: Prevention, Prosecution, and Protection. The long war on drugs and arms trafficking reveals that efforts focused solely on the prosecution of the criminal traffickers will ultimately fail. Some opportunities in this area appear promising, especially in terms of attacking criminals through greater attention to money laundering, and coordinating border protection to address the range of problems from drugs, arms, terrorism, and trafficking in persons. However, emphasizing prevention and protection based upon a careful study of the characteristics of the victims and methods of exploitation promises greater rewards. Attention to the victim and practices of trafficking can reveal the limitations of some current efforts.

For example, the 2005 TIP report cites a program by Brazil to provide anti-trafficking information to all women and children at international airports and borders, warning them of the risks of trafficking and providing them with contact information for assistance in the event they fear they are being trafficked. Providing this type of information is, to a greater or lesser extent, quite popular and common throughout the region. For example, in the 2006 TIP report, Ecuador was highlighted for its efforts to place trafficking alert information in taxis and other forms of public transportation. However, two problems emerge with this approach. First, as previously noted, many women and children are initially trafficked within their country of origin. This information, while it may help them escape later, reaches them after they are already in the control of their traffickers. Second, entering into situations that place them at risk for trafficking may not be a matter of choice for these women and children, but rather one of necessity. To

---

[81] *See* Ribando, *supra* note 2, at 14.

inform them of the risks does not address the violence or desperate poverty that may initially coerce their actions.

In the long term, more important interventions must work on "push" problems—those factors that drive a person into the illegal migration/ trafficking system—and the demand elements, i.e., those that create the market for their abuse. Push concerns start with a focus on meeting fundamental economic needs. Since women and children are most vulnerable to trafficking, special attention should be given to them to address issues of economic disparity, education, gender discrimination, racial discrimination, and violence.[82] Efforts must be made to counter the deterioration in the family and address the needs of women as heads of households.

Demand, especially in terms of sex trafficking, is primarily a result of prostitution. Men need to be educated against the abuse of women through prostitution. Whether or not prostitution should be legal stands as an enormous challenge within the field. The United States takes the position that legalized prostitution creates the market into which increasing numbers of women and children are imported to exploit.[83] However, throughout much of Latin America prostitution is legal. Sex trafficking adds to the problem by increasing the market for trafficked women and children, even though child sex exploitation is illegal throughout the region. Thus, efforts to inform potential sex traffickers of potential sanctions, especially for child prostitution, such as those undertaken in Costa Rica are quite important.

Care for Victims

Meeting the needs of victims, referred to as the tactic of protection under the TVPA, falls into two categories. First, how should the victim be cared for in the country where she is being exploited? Second, how can or should repatriation be handled?

In terms of trafficking victims' assistance, some of the most effective training programs being offered within the region are those that focus on training diplomatic personnel in the recognition and care of trafficking victims.[84] Consular and diplomatic personnel from the country of origin in the country of exploitation are a natural point of contact for victims. They share the same language, culture, and citizenship. Trafficking victims, particularly those being held in isolation, are more likely to seek out their consulate or embassy than the police. Training consular officials to help the victims negotiate the laws

---

[82] Joan Fitzpatrick, *Trafficking as a Human Rights Violation: The Complex Intersection of legal Frameworks for Conceptualizing and Combating Trafficking,* 24 Mich. J. Int'l L.1143, 1165 (2003).

[83] Ribando, *supra* note 2, at 19.

[84] In Modern Bondage, supra note 14, at 74-75.

regarding trafficking in that country, along with the possible need to assist in repatriation, represents a critical effort.

The governments of states in which exploitation is taking place have certain obligations toward the victims and toward combating trafficking. For example, prosecutions of traffickers require the cooperation of victims. At a minimum, they will need to be allowed to stay in residence, in spite of their obvious undocumented status, for the duration of the prosecution and to be provided with necessary services (e.g., food, shelter, healthcare, and possible psychological counseling) for this period. Moreover, to gain cooperation, it may be necessary to provide incentives—including the potential of being granted legal residence. This, in turn will require a coherent approach not only to trafficking, but to the larger issue of undocumented migration.

In the absence of prosecution, the most common response to the capture of trafficking victims by government officials throughout the Americas is to repatriate them to their country of origin—or to the last border that they crossed. Research demonstrates that returning a victim to their country of origin without any further assistance or counseling simply results in starting the trafficking process all over again.[85] Indeed, repatriated victims of sex trafficking are often in a worse position than they were when they originally left their home countries due to social isolation arising from disapproval of their status as former prostitutes. Among all trafficking victims, children's programs appear to have received the most attention and funding. In a number of countries, children are taken into custody by the state (thus removing them from family situations that often contributed to their trafficking status), provided care, therapy, and educational training. Similar efforts need to be directed toward women as well.

Conclusion

Few people question the troubling pervasiveness of trafficking or the fact that it represents a serious abuse of human rights. However, as happens all too frequently, the legal developments intended to address the problem of trafficking have been driven by events that engaged public attention and outrage, leading to political movements for legislation shepherded along by special interest groups. In the rush to remedy the perceived wrongs, these legal actors move from identifying the problem to implementing corrective actions without engaging in the serious research and reflection necessary to accurately measure and define the problem, thereby leaving it subject to misperceptions and misunderstandings that hinder the accomplishment of their ultimate goal. The object of this research paper has been to promote the necessary reflection and identify the areas requiring further research.

---

[85] Feingold, *supra* note 15, at 30-31.

TABLE 1
Defining the Problem: Trafficking

	2005 Tier Placement	2006 Tier Placement	UN TIP Signed	Protocol Ratified(a)	ILO 182 Ratified(a)	CRC Opt. Signed	Protocol Ratified(a)	CRC Armed Signed	Conflict Ratified(a)	ILO 29	ILO 105
Argentina	Tier 2	Tier 2 (W)	X	X	X	X	X	X	X	X	X
Belize	Tier 2 (W)	Tier 3		X(a)	X	X	X	X	X	X	X
Bolivia	Tier 3	Tier 2 (W)	X		X	X	X		X(a)	X	X
Brazil	Tier 2	Tier 2 (W)	X	X	X	X	X	X	X	X	X
Chile	Tier 2	Tier 2	X	X	X	X	X	X		X	X
Columbia	Tier 1	Tier 1	X	X	X	X	X	X		X	X
Costa Rica	Tier 2	Tier 2	X	X	X	X	X	X	X	X	X
Cuba	Tier 3	Tier 3				X	X		X	X	
Dominican Rep.	Tier 2 (W)	Tier 2	X		X	X	X	X			X
Ecuador	Tier 3	Tier 2	X	X	X	X	X	X	X	X	X
El Salvador	Tier 2	Tier 2	X	X	X	X	X	X	X	X	X
Guatemala	Tier 2	Tier 2		X(a)	X	X	X	X	X	X	X
Guyana	Tier 3	Tier 2		X(a)	X					X	X
Haiti	Tier 2 (W)	Tier 2	X			X		X	X(a)	X	X
Honduras	Tier 2	Tier 2			X	X	X(a)		X(a)	X	X
Jamaica	Tier 3	Tier 2 (W)	X	X	X	X		X	X	X	X
Mexico	Tier 2 (W)	Tier 2 (W)	X	X	X	X	X	X	X	X	X
Nicaragua	Tier 2 (W)	Tier 2		X(a)	X		X(a)		X(a)	X	X
Panama	Tier 2	Tier 2	X	X	X	X	X	X	X	X	X
Paraguay	Tier 2	Tier 2	X	X	X	X	X	X	X	X	X
Peru	Tier 2 (W)	Tier 2	X	X	X	X	X	X	X	X	X
Suriname	Tier 2 (W)	Tier 2				X		X		X	X
Venezuela	Tier 3	Tier 3	X	X	X	X	X	X	X	X	X

Notes:
1. For an explanation of Tier Placement see U.S. Dept. of State, *Trafficking in Persons Report*, (June 2005); (June 2006)
2. (W) Indicates placement on the Tier 2 Watch List as opposed to Tier 2
3. (a) Indicates accession.
3. (a) Indicates accession.

Conventions and Protocols

UN TIP – United Nations Protocol to Prevent and Punish Trafficking in Persons

ILO 182 – Convention on the Worst Forms of Child Labor

CRC Optional Protocol – Optional Protocol to the Convention on the Rights of the Child (CRC) on the Sale of Children, Child Prostitution and Pornography

CRC Armed Conflict – Optional Protocol to the CRC on the Involvement of Children in Armed Conflict

ILO 29 – Conventional concerning Forced or Compulsory Labour

ILO 105 – Abolition of Forced Labor Convention

David E. Guinn is the Senior Scholar in Judicial Ethics, Education and Research at the Administrative Judicial Institute within the New York City Office of Administrative Trials and Hearings. He is a moral, political, and legal philosopher and human rights lawyer with a broad and diverse range of scholarship. He has written extensively on issues of national and international human rights, pluralism, and law, writing, co-writing and/or editing thirteen books and over sixty articles. Representative of these are: *Handbook of Bioethics and Religion* (Oxford UP, 2006), *Protecting Jerusalem's Holy Sites: Negotiating a Sacred Peace* (Cambridge, 2006), *Faith on Trial: Religious Freedom and the Theory of Deep Diversity* (Lexington Books, 2002/2006), *In Modern Bondage: Trafficking in the Americas* (Transnational, 2003), *Religion and Civil Discourse* (Park Ridge Center, 1997) and *Religion and Law in the Global Village* (McGill 1999). As Executive Director of the International Human Rights Law Institute at the DePaul University College of Law, he oversaw such projects as the Institute's work in legal education reform in Iraq and Trafficking in the Americas and taught as an adjunct professor of law. Dr. Guinn is currently working on a new book: *Constantine's Standard: Meditations on Religion, Violence, Law, Politics and a Faith to Die For.*

This article was presented at the Joint Area Centers Symposium on Criminal Trafficking and Slavery: The Dark Side of Migration, University of Illinois, Champaign, 23–25 Feb. 2006.

Discussion Questions

1   *What has the U.S. done as a result of the Trafficking Victim Protective Act (TVPA)?*

2   *What is the formal name for the Palermo Protocol?*

3   *What does the Palermo Protocol provide?*

4   *Why is there significant difficulty in identifying child trafficking in Latin America?*

5   *Efforts to assess trafficking are further complicated by social, economic and political concerns which affect the collection and analysis of data. Which three specific facts emerged in this article?*

6   *What are the legal and logistical concerns expressed in this article regarding trafficking?*

7   *There are a number of trafficking and entry points for human trafficking. What are they?*

8   *What are some of the common traffic routes in human trafficking?*

9   *What are the most common destinations for women trafficked from Brazil?*

10   *What are the major characteristics of the Iberian Connection?*

11   *What are the methods suggested to limit or eliminate trafficking?*

PART II

SEX TRAFFICKING IN EUROPE

Pathologies of Security Governance: Efforts Against Human Trafficking in Europe. The trafficking of women and girls for the purpose of sexual exploitation has reportedly been booming in Europe since the 1990s. Governments, international organizations, and private actors have addressed the causes and consequences of sex trafficking in various ways. This research paper shows that the concept of security governance helps to understand efforts against human trafficking and their shortcomings. The anti-trafficking security governance system consists of five approaches; legal measures, prosecution, protection, prevention in countries of origin, and prevention in countries of destination. Although progress has been made, the security governance system is marked by several pathologies, especially a lack of programs that prevent trafficking in countries of origin and destination, insufficient protection for trafficked persons, and deficient networks bringing together the various actors involved in anti-trafficking. To make governance against human trafficking more effective, efficient, and just, the security governance system must be better balanced and networked.

Sexual trafficking of Women: Tragic Proportions and Attempted Solutions in Albania. This research paper describes issues related to sex trafficking in Albania (one of the centers of the recruitment and transport of women from eastern Europe to other countries, especially western European) and the current efforts and challenges in addressing the problems, and implications of the practice in eastern Europe and other countries. The Albanian situation reflects both global trends and its special characteristics. Information has been drawn from area research, international news reports, and nongovernmental organizations (NGOs).

The 'Natasha' Trade: The Transnational Shadow Market of Trafficking in Women. This research paper focuses primarily on the sending country of Ukraine, now the second largest country in Europe, and currently one of the largest suppliers of women for prostitution. At the beginning of this paper, the scope of the problem of trafficking is discussed and the definition of the term trafficking is reviewed. Next, the international gray market for women is located in the globalization process and characterized as a modern day slave trade. The role of transnational crime networks in the trafficking of women is examined with a few illustrative cases. A part of this paper is also devoted to a discussion of the methods of recruitment and trafficking, and also describes how women are recruited from their hometowns and transported to sex industries in other countries. Although there are a number of ways that women are trafficked, their ultimate circumstance is entrapment in prostitution.

Loose Women or Lost Women? The Re-emergence of the Myth of White Slavery in Contemporary Discourses of Trafficking in Women. This research paper compares current concerns about "trafficking in women" with turn of the century discourses about "white slavery." It traces the emergence of narratives on "white slavery" and their re-emergence in the moral panics and boundary crises of contemporary discourse on "trafficking in women." Drawing on historical analysis and contemporary representations of sex worker migration, this paper argues that the narratives of innocent, virginal victims purveyed in the "trafficking in women" discourse are a modern version of the myth of "white slavery." This paper argues that while the myth of "trafficking in women"/"white slavery" is ostensibly about protecting women, the underlying moral concern is with the control of "loose women."

Integration of Trafficked Women in Destination Countries: Obstacles and Opportunities. The physical and psychological effects of human trafficking can be severe and long-term. Yet with appropriate support at all stages of the trafficking process women can be rehabilitated and re-integrated within society. This research paper highlights the unique needs of trafficked women and explores the work of the POPPY Project (the sole United Kingdom (UK) government-funded dedicated service for women trafficked into prostitution) in helping trafficked women integrate into UK society successfully.

6

PATHOLOGIES OF SECURITY GOVERNANCE: EFFORTS AGAINST HUMAN TRAFFICKING IN EUROPE

Cornelius Friesendorf, *Geschwister-Scholl-Institute, Ludwig-Maximilians University, Munich, Germany*

Introduction

Human trafficking ranks high on the European security agenda. Over recent years, the link between human trafficking and organized crime, fears over illegal migration, and the violent nature of trafficking have caused significant concern between policymakers and the public. This research paper examines strategies against human trafficking. It focuses on the trafficking of women and girls for the purpose of sexual exploitation, which has been at the center of the debate over trafficking. Human trafficking also encompasses the trafficking of men and boys for sexual exploitation, the trafficking of males and females for labor exploitation, the 'mail-order bride' business, the trade in children offered for adoption, and the illicit trade in human organs.

This paper also conceptualizes efforts against sex trafficking and explains their shortcomings. The concept of security governance offers valuable insights. The first part of the paper describes human trafficking and counter-efforts. The second part underlines the usefulness of the concept of security governance for analyzing counter-efforts. The third part shows that anti-trafficking efforts have evolved into a system of security governance that consists of five approaches: legal measures, prosecution, protection, prevention in countries of origin, and prevention in countries of destination. The fourth part underlines the pathologies of security governance that have hampered action against trafficking. The geographic focus is on Southeast Europe, a prominent region of origin and destination, and the European Union (EU), where many trafficked people arrive.

Human Trafficking and Counter-Efforts

The UN Protocol to Prevent, Suppress, and Punish Trafficking in Persons, Especially Women and Children was signed in December 2000 in Palermo, Italy, and entered into effect in December 2003. According to the Protocol,

"Trafficking in persons" shall mean the recruitment, transportation, transfer, harboring, or receipt of persons, by means of
the threat or use of force or other forms of coercion, of abduction,
of fraud, of deception, of the abuse of power or of a position of
vulnerability, or of the giving or receiving of payments or
benefits to achieve the consent of a person having control over
another person, for the purpose of exploitation.

Exploitation shall include, at a minimum, the exploitation of the
prostitution of others or other forms of sexual exploitation,
forced labor or services, slavery or practices similar to slavery,
servitude or the removal of organs.[1]

The Protocol also stipulates that the 'consent of the victim of
trafficking in persons to the intended exploitation set forth in paragraph
(a) of this article shall be irrelevant where any of the means set forth in
subparagraph (b) have been used'. A distinction is often made between
human smuggling and human trafficking. The latter implies a more
permanent relationship between trafficker and trafficked person and
higher risks of deception and abuse than the former. In reality, of course,
there are varying degrees of consent, and the distinction between
smuggling and trafficking is not clear-cut.

Over recent years, there have been numerous, and often sensationalist, reports on sex trafficking. Observers who describe trafficking as a
modern slave trade (see, for example, Masci, 2004) tell stories of
psychological and physical torture, rape, drugging, and murder. Such
representations present trafficking predominantly as an organized-crime
problem, neglect the social and economic conditions that lead women to
migrate, and overemphasize the naivete of 'sex slaves'. The anti-
trafficking campaign has strong moralistic undertones and has been
instrumentalized by a conservative Christian-feminist coalition in the
United States whose aim is to abolish all forms of prostitution (for
critiques, see Berman, 2003; Soderlund, 2005). Nevertheless, it is true
that many women work as prostitutes in brothels and private
apartments, 'entertainers' in bars, and "actors" in pornography films
under appalling conditions.

Trafficked people generally come from places where economic and
social difficulties make migration a popular choice. Women are often
recruited by strangers or acquaintances (often women themselves) who
promise well-paid jobs abroad. Many of those who accept the offer to
migrate have their passports taken away and receive no income at all for
their work in the sex industry, or are forced to work off bogus debts.
While some women expect to work in the sex industry when taking their

---

[1] See http://untreaty.un.org/English/notpubl/18-12-a.E.doc.

decision to migrate, few anticipate the violence and exploitation to which many trafficked persons are exposed.

Owing to the clandestine nature of human trafficking and the paucity of systematic empirical research (Laczko & Gramegna, 2003: 181), there are no precise figures, and figures that do exist vary. The US government estimates the number of people trafficked across borders at 600,000 to 800,000, of whom 80% are female and up to 50% minors (US Department of State, 2005: 6). Most victims are thought to work in the sex industry. It is estimated that human trafficking yields almost $10 billion in profits every year (US Department of State, 2005: 13–14). The International Labour Organization (2005: 10) reports that of the 12.3 million people in forced labour worldwide, 2.4 million are victims of trafficking, both internally and across borders. The industry generates annual profits of over $32 billion.

In Europe, the dimension of the problem is unclear as well. In 2003, the EU reported that Balkan criminal networks traffic around 200,000 women per year for the sex trade (Solana, 2003: 9). This figure is probably exaggerated. In Bosnia and Herzegovina, for example, only 66 people were registered as potential victims of trafficking in 2005 (State Coordinator, 2006: 30). Germany, Europe's main country of destination (UNHCR, 2005: 63), counted 642 trafficked persons for the same year (Bundeskriminalamt, 2006). To be sure, most trafficking cases go un-noticed, and perceptions about the scale of the problem vary signifi-cantly. To stay with the example of Bosnia, while the European Union Police Mission (EUPM) says that it is unlikely that a very high number of women and girls are trafficked within Bosnia, the International Organization for Migration (IOM) states that trafficking in the country has been pushed underground and that it is still a big industry.[2]

Uncertainties and exaggerations notwithstanding, the problem has been increasing in Europe since the end of the East–West conflict. The countries of the former Soviet Union, Central Europe, and Southeast Europe have become main regions of origin, transit, and also destination. Women from other world regions have been trafficked through Southeast Europe, and women from Southeast Europe, particularly from Albania, Bulgaria, Moldova, and Romania, have been trafficked to the EU. Moreover, internal trafficking in Southeast Europe has risen sharply as well. In Kosovo and Bosnia, the presence of tens of thousands of peacekeepers and other international staff has exacerbated human trafficking. The primary reason is that some 'internationals' have fueled the demand for commercial sexual services, and that some of the women providing these services have been trafficked. The response of countries contributing personnel for NATO and United Nations operations has

---

[2] Author interviews with representatives of international organizations, Sarajevo, August 2006.

initially been one of neglect and denial (Mendelson, 2005; Vandenberg, 2005: 73–74; author interview with a trafficking expert of medica mondiale, 27 October 2006, Zurich).

Over recent years, numerous actors have joined efforts against human trafficking. Besides governments, international organizations (IOs) formulate, promote, and implement anti-trafficking programs. UN agencies, NATO, the EU, the Organization for Security and Cooperation in Europe (OSCE), the Council of Europe, and others are active in anti-trafficking. Moreover, non-state actors are deeply involved. Numerous nongovernmental organizations (NGOs) promote and implement policies, and businesses participate as well.

Actors' motivations to "fight" trafficking varies. Governments are primarily concerned about links between human trafficking and other forms of crime, such as money laundering, drug trafficking, the illegal weapons trade, and document forgery, as well as the risk of profits from human trafficking financing terrorist activities. These fears are exacerbated, particularly in wealthy countries, by concerns about illegal migration. Many NGOs, in contrast, emphasize that human trafficking is a serious human rights violation, and that a focus on organized crime and illegal migration is inappropriate. International organizations play a prominent role in anti-trafficking not least because of significant funding opportunities. The same holds true for many NGOs. Last, and as mentioned above, moral outrage about sexual slavery and/or prostitution has also contributed to pushing human trafficking onto the security agenda.

There has been an increase in research on human trafficking over recent years. Authors (see Stoecker & Shelley, 2005; Haynes, 2004) often combine description (how has human trafficking evolved, and which countermeasures have been adopted?) with prescription (how can countermeasures be improved?). Unfortunately, many authors present long lists of actors and activities and arbitrarily single out presumed policy weaknesses. In other words, research on counter-trafficking is under-theorized.

International relations (IR) research, on the other hand, has not applied its theoretical and conceptual tools to human trafficking. This reflects the problem for IR of coming to terms with illicit non-state activities, which are marked by complex non-linearity and a lack of data (Friesendorf, 2005). IR scholars who do theorize human trafficking focus on criticizing the predominance of law enforcement in counter-trafficking (Berman, 2003). More theoretically informed works are needed to illuminate changing political practices and to reveal the pathologies of seemingly benign action. Security governance is a particularly promising concept.

Security Governance and Human Trafficking

One remarkable trend in international security after the end of the
East–West conflict has been the growing importance of non-state actors
pursuing criminalized activities across national borders. During the
East–West conflict, security practices and security debates focused on
military issues negotiated among a relatively small number of
decisionmakers. The trafficking of women, drugs, or diamonds is
different. More individuals and groups are involved, there is a higher
degree of transnationalism, and trade patterns are very complex. There
are thousands of human traffickers operating independently, within
relatively hierarchical groups, or as part of decentralized networks.
These traffickers exploit tens or even hundreds of thousands of women
and girls, often in cross-border operations that violate countries'
sovereignty. The causes of human trafficking are multifaceted, and so
are the consequences. Negotiating and implementing arms control
agreements was (and is) not easy, but negotiating and implementing
adequate responses to human trafficking is even more difficult.

How can efforts against human trafficking be conceptualized and
their shortcomings explained? The concept of security governance is
particularly useful. According to Elke Krahmann, who has played a
central role in developing the concept, security governance relates to the
emergence of governance in general: 'Governance denotes the structures
and processes which enable a set of public and private actors to
coordinate their independent needs and interests through the making
and implementation of binding policy decisions in the absence of a
central political authority' (Krahmann, 2003: 11).

This definition refers to two elements that characterize efforts
against human trafficking: the limits of hierarchical government and the
participation of private actors in governance. Traditional national
hierarchical decisionmaking and implementation structures are unable
to reduce the transnational trafficking of people or goods. To address
human trafficking and other illicit activities of non-state actors,
governments have to step up transnational cooperation, work together
with NGOs and private businesses, and act within and alongside
international organizations. Efforts against human trafficking are thus
a prime example of the paradigmatic shift from government to
governance (Czempiel & Rosenau, 1992) and, more specifically, security
governance. The functional need to address the various causes and
consequences of human trafficking effectively, efficiently, and justly, as
well as institutional and ideological dynamics (some of which were
mentioned above), have led to the incremental creation of a complex
security governance system against human trafficking.

But what are the criteria for successful security governance against criminalized activities such as human trafficking, with success defined in terms of crime reduction? It is not enough to say that anti-trafficking efforts must be non-hierarchical and include non-state actors. It is important to specify what replaces hierarchy, and how the public and private actors constituting a security governance system are interlinked.

Three criteria can be derived from the theoretical literature on governance and networks and the empirical literature examining past and present strategies against criminalized non-state activities. The first criterion pertains to the need for transnational cooperation among various actors; the second to the need for well-balanced governance arrangements reflecting the nature of the problem that is to be addressed; and the third to the need for networks among actors pursuing any one governance approach (such as transnational law enforcement networks), as well as networks between actors pursuing different approaches (such as networks between police and human rights NGOs).

First, for security governance to be successful, and for crime transgressing national borders to be reduced, states must intensively cooperate with one another. However, transnational governance is not about one unitary state cooperating with another unitary state. Rather, fostering flexible forms of governance requires states to disaggregate into their functionally differentiated parts, as emphasized by Anne-Marie Slaughter (2004). On criminal matters, police officials, border guards, customs officers, prosecutors, judges, and intelligence agents cooperate with their foreign counterparts. Police forces of various countries, for example, were already exchanging information during the 19th century and before. Since the end of the East–West conflict, and particularly after 9/11, transnational police cooperation has been intensifying dramatically (Andreas & Nadelmann, 2006).

The complexity, and indeed messiness, of security governance is further enhanced by the presence of international organizations, NGOs, and private businesses in governance arrangements. States, even when disaggregated, can only do so much against complex security problems. They must draw on the expertise and material resources of IOs and private actors (Caparini, 2006). Reducing the risk that violent conflict erupts or re-erupts hinges stable economy, and thus on private investments. Private companies must therefore be drawn into conflict prevention, post-conflict reconstruction, and peace building efforts (Wenger & Möckli, 2003). With regard to human trafficking, women's rights groups are better suited to support victims of trafficking than police forces, who know much more about arresting criminals than about the needs of trafficked persons.

The **second** of the three criteria for successful security governance identified above pertains to policy strategies (in contrast, criteria 1 and

3 pertain more to the institutional structure of the governance system).[3]
Security governance must reflect the nature of the problem. The more
complex the problem, the more multifaceted must be the governance
system. If a problem is caused not only by the greed of criminals but also
by poverty, the success of governance depends on poverty reduction. 'If
governance is to be effective, it needs to be strategic. Any chance of real
success requires an integrated comprehensive approach' (Williams &
Baudin-O'Hayon, 2003: 142). Equally important, security governance
must balance the different approaches constituting the governance
system in order to ensure that the causes and consequences of a problem
are properly addressed. 'Soft' policy elements must be more than tokens
to prevent strategies from being overly repressive, and thus ineffective
(for an analysis of unbalanced post-conflict reconstruction efforts, see
Law, 2006).

The **third** criterion for successful security governance pertains to
networks among and between actors constituting the governance system.
Networks are core elements of security governance.[4] They are
decentralized arrangements in which multiple actors (nodes) sharing an
interest in a specific issue area are dispersed and loosely connected.
Exchange can be formal and institutionalized, but is more often informal
and voluntary (Eilstrup-Sangiovanni, 2005: 7; Krahmann, 2005: 25).
Networks are often associated with 'dark networks' (Raab & Milward,
2003) – that is, illicit structures that benefit from new information
technologies and other features of globalization. Human trafficking is
largely a networked activity, with various trafficking groups reducing
operational risks through decentralized action. Although the structure
of trafficking networks differs, most lack a center of gravity, such as a
boss that can be arrested. And, even if one network is dismantled,
another one will replace it.

The networked structure of human trafficking forces governments
to adopt flexible, functionally differentiated forms of cooperation
themselves. 'It takes networks to fight networks' (Arquilla & Ronfeldt,
2001: 15). Anti-trafficking networks can have hierarchical features, as
is the case when one government, on a ministry, agency, NGO, or
international organization takes the lead in addressing a specific cause
or consequence of trafficking. However, horizontal networks are at least
as important as vertical ones, if not more so, since they bring together

---

[3] I thank a reviewer for suggesting the use of a distinction between institutional structure
and policy strategy.

[4] Elke Krahmann (2005) argues that governance and network analyses pose and answer
different questions. However, examining the achievements and shortcomings of anti-
trafficking efforts necessitates looking both at the transformation of security policymaking
(the governance aspect) and the relations and interactions between different actors
constituting the governance system (the network aspect).

a host of different actors operating across borders (Krahmann, 2005: 24) who would be generally unwilling to accept the lead of any one actor.

Indeed, for security governance to work, it is vital that there are networks not only among actors pursuing the same governance approach (such as police, border guards, and prosecutors, all of whom pursue a law enforcement and criminal justice approach), but also between actors pursuing different approaches (such as networks between the police focusing on the prosecution of traffickers and NGOs focusing on the protection of trafficked persons). Peace building efforts, for example, have often suffered from insufficient networking between the security and development communities (see Krause & Jütersonke, 2005). Networks are thus needed among actors with a similar outlook and between actors with a different outlook.

More generally, and no matter whether networks are hierarchical or decentralized, or how many actors they include: networking must not be obstructed by red tape, the failure to exchange information, and zero-sum games between networked actors.

Hence, successful security governance against human trafficking depends on intense transnational cooperation among specialized state agencies, and on the participation of international organizations, NGOs, and private businesses in policymaking and implementation. Moreover, security governance must be multifaceted, and there must be a balance between different policy approaches in order to address the various causes and consequences of trafficking. Last, networks are needed among and between actors constituting the security governance system. Has the anti-trafficking governance system met these requirements for effective, efficient, and just action? The next two sections show that, although some progress has been made, several pathologies have hampered, and continue to hamper, efforts against human trafficking.

The Anti-Trafficking Security Governance System

Since the late 1990s, a host of actors have joined the 'fight' against sex trafficking. Counter-efforts have focused particularly on Southeast Europe, where numerous anti-trafficking programs have been implemented. Main reasons for this are the embarrassing implication of peacekeepers in human trafficking and the perceived need to combat organized crime in Southeast Europe as a precondition for peace and democracy in the region and for crime reduction in the EU. Table 1 provides an overview of governance approaches, activities, and dominant actors.

Table 1: Governance Against Human Trafficking in Europe

Governance Approach	Activity	Dominant Actors
Legal measures	• Criminalization of trafficking • Harmonization of laws	IOs Governments NGOs
Prosecution	• Arrest of traffickers • Zero-tolerance policies • Asset seizure and forfeiture • Capacity-building • Creation of databases • Witness protection programs • Border controls • Anti-corruption efforts	Governments IOs International authorities
Protection	• Identification of trafficked persons • Hotline services • Sheltering and counseling • Medical and psychological support • Reintegration of trafficked persons • Private-sector programs	IOs NGOs Governments Businesses
Prevention in countries of origin	• Awareness campaigns • Empowering high-risk groups • Measures against discrimination • Assisting migrant workers • Research on traffickers • Development policy	IOs NGOs Governments
Prevention in countries of destination	• Migration policy • Awareness campaigns • Prostitution policies • Private-sector programs	Governments NGOs Businesses

The terms prosecution, protection, and prevention are commonly used in the literature on human trafficking ('the three Ps'). The table adds legal measures to the three Ps. The adoption of new laws and the harmonization of existing ones provide the legal basis for prosecution, protection, and prevention. Moreover, the table distinguishes between prevention in countries of origin and destination. After all, prevention of trafficking in Germany by way of assisting immigrants is different from prevention of trafficking in Moldova by way of assisting would-be emigrants.

Two caveats are in order. First, the analysis brackets anti-trafficking efforts in transit countries. Second, the five governance approaches, which complement each other, are ideal-types with significant overlap, for example between protection and prevention: The reintegration of trafficked persons into their home communities reduces the likelihood of re-trafficking and thus has a preventive effect. Hotlines not only help trafficked persons, but also inform potential victims about migration risks and opportunities. And the identification of a trafficked person has a preventive effect if achieved before that person is forced to work in the sex industry, that is, during the migration process.

The first approach pertains to legal measures. Over recent years, European countries have included human trafficking as a criminal offense in their penal codes and, to some extent, harmonized their anti-trafficking laws. IOs are at the forefront of setting new legislative standards, such as the 2000 UN Protocol, the 2005 Council of Europe Convention on Action against Trafficking in Human Beings, various acts of EU institutions, and the OSCE Action Plan to Combat Trafficking in Human Beings. NGOs have played a prominent role in promoting many of these initiatives.

Prosecution has a central position in the anti-trafficking governance system. The UN Protocol, which is relatively strong on law enforcement and weak on human rights protection, has served as a catalyst for coercive initiatives on the regional, national, and local levels. Prosecution includes the arrest of traffickers and those who condone trafficking; the adoption and implementation of zero-tolerance policies intended to prevent peacekeepers from purchasing sexual services;[5] the seizure and forfeiture of traffickers' assets; security-sector capacity-building; the collection and exchange of information about traffickers; the use of victims as witnesses in trials; reinforced borders; and efforts against corruption. While prosecution is the traditional prerogative of government agencies, IOs have become increasingly involved as well. The United Nations Office on Drugs and Crime (UNODC) and IOM, for example, help to train judicial and law enforcement institutions.

The third approach of the anti-trafficking governance system focuses on the protection of trafficked persons. IOs, governments, and various NGOs identify trafficked persons; establish hotlines; provide trafficked

---

[5] On NATO's zero tolerance policy, see http://www.nato.int/issues/trafficking/index.html (accessed 24 May 2006).

persons with safe housing, legal and professional advice, medical assistance, and psychological support; and reintegrate trafficked persons into their home communities (or, if return is not an option, help them find a new place). Reintegration can be achieved through grants and loans for setting up businesses; schooling and training; and family support. NGOs do most of the work on the ground. They receive project-specific funding from governments and international organizations such as the IOM, which became the lead agency for return and reintegration within the framework of the Stability Pact for South Eastern Europe. Businesses are involved as well. Airlines and bus companies, for example, are being 'deputized' to help detect trafficked people through stricter controls of travelers. The hospitality and tourism industries have been asked to regulate themselves by increasing the awareness of tourists and business travelers on trafficking. In addition, some hotels provide high-risk groups with professional skills (Baumeister & Maley, 2005).

Prevention in countries of origin, the fourth governance approach, is one of the most multifaceted. IOs, NGOs, and governments raise awareness about the risks of accepting dubious migration and job offers; empower high-risk groups such as Roma, orphans, or women with a history of family violence; mitigate gender, ethnic, or religious discrimination; and inform those who decide to migrate about bureaucratic procedures and their rights. Moreover, research into the causes and consequences of trafficking is crucial for devising and implementing effective policies. Last, and most important, effective prevention implies an improvement of the social and economic conditions that lead people to take risky migration decisions. Development-oriented efforts against trafficking must improve educational, medical, and social infrastructures, and create viable employment opportunities, particularly for women and minorities. Here, businesses have a role to play. They can teach people skills for which there is a need on the labour market.

The last approach aims at prevention in countries of destination. Governments can reduce the risk of women being recruited by traffickers by offering them legal migration and employment opportunities. Women from Southeast Europe who want to work in the EU need visas, work permits, and residency permits so as not to have to rely on criminals who offer migration, accommodation, and employment services. Governments can also legalize the presence of foreign victims of trafficking. Moreover, awareness campaigns that inform clients of prostitutes about trafficking can help reduce the demand for trafficked persons and, thus, traffickers' profits. Prostitution policies may also have an impact on demand, as shown further below. Main protagonists of prevention are governments, because migration and prostitution policies are national prerogatives. However, NGOs are active in demand-reduction efforts through awareness campaigns. Businesses play a role as well. For example, entertain-

ment companies should ensure that 'cabaret' dancers from Southeast
Europe are not forced into prostitution.

Does the current anti-trafficking governance system meet the three
criteria for successful security governance outlined above? The first
criterion has largely been met: states have disaggregated into their
functionally differentiated parts, and these parts, or state agencies, have
stepped up transnational cooperation. Moreover, international organizations and private actors participate in anti-trafficking. But, with regard
to the other two criteria, developments over recent years have been less
promising.

Table 2: Pathologies of Governance Against Human Trafficking in Europe

Governance approach	Activity	Dominant actors
Legal measures	Advanced	• Lack of adequate legislation in some countries • Many non-binding guidelines
Prosecution	Relatively advanced	• Arrest and deportation of trafficked persons • Lenient sentences for traffickers • Reluctance of military to do police work • Trafficking has been driven underground • Red tape and corruption
Protection	Developing	• Short-term funding priorities • Governments donate to 'their' NGOs • Deficient witness-protection programs • Deficient reintegration programs • Lack of networked cooperation
Prevention in countries of origin	Neglected	• Deficient awareness-raising campaigns • Lessons learned not documented or shared • Development decoupled from anti-trafficking
Prevention in countries of destination	Contested	• Few migration and job opportunities • Reinforced borders benefit traffickers • Insufficient demand-reduction efforts • No 'perfect' prostitution policy

Pathologies of the Anti-Trafficking Security Governance System

Security governance against human trafficking does not fully meet the second and third criteria for successful governance. As Table 2 shows, counter-trafficking efforts have been suffering from serious short-comings.

Legal Measures

Over recent years, some approaches have evolved faster than others. Legal responses to trafficking are by now at an advanced stage. Some legal loopholes remain, and some regulatory efforts suffer from the non-binding nature of many international agreements. However, most European countries have adopted legislation against human trafficking. Interestingly, Southeast European states generally have better laws against trafficking than old EU member-states in Western Europe, since the adoption of new laws in the criminal field is now a central precondition for becoming a member of the EU.

Prosecution

Prosecution is relatively advanced, with significant progress made over recent years. To be sure, law enforcement and criminal justice responses to trafficking are far from perfect. Often, trafficked women have been, and continue to be, arrested and deported for having violated migration and/or prostitution laws, which obviously makes them reluctant to testify against traffickers. In other cases, police, following bar raids, have referred only those women to shelters who agree to become witnesses for the prosecution, or have demanded unconditional access to shelters (Limanowska, 2005a: 28). On paper, the UN Protocol and other agreements emphasize the need to orient law enforcement pressure against the traffickers, but in practice police have taken a more non-discriminatory approach (Haynes, 2004). Suspicion among victims is nurtured also by the fact that convicted traffickers often receive relatively lenient sentences (UNHCR, 2005), not least because courts perceive human trafficking as a less serious form of crime than the trade in drugs or weapons.

The reluctance of the military to engage in law enforcement has been another obstacle for firm action against traffickers. In recent years, the 16,000-strong Kosovo Force (KFOR) has been reluctant to support efforts of the United Nations Mission in Kosovo (UNMIK) against organized crime.[6] The 5,500-strong European Union Force (EUFOR) in Bosnia has similarly limited its role to law enforcement support.[7] This division of

---

[6] Statement of a former commander of KFOR in Geneva, 5 October 2005.

[7] Statement of a former commander of EUFOR in Geneva, 24 January 2006.

labor could be justified on the grounds that military forces lack law enforcement expertise, and military-style law enforcement poses problems of accountability and legitimacy. However, it comes at a cost: Police in Southeast Europe often do not have the manpower and technology to attack the more sophisticated and violent trafficking networks. In Bosnia, a senior police official in the Ministry of Interior said that four of his inspectors tasked with fighting organized crime had to share one computer—which was broken.[8]

When police do act, they push the industry underground. While trafficking had been fairly visible in some parts of Southeast Europe in the 1990s, traffickers have since become much more cautious. They have switched from brothels to private apartments, from land lines to mobile phones, and from international to internal trafficking (Europol, 2006; author interviews with senior police officers in Macedonia, Kosovo, and Bosnia, July–August 2006). These trends go hand in hand with a drop in the number of reported cases of trafficking, both in Southeast Europe and in the EU. Governments tend to cite this drop as an indicator of policy success, but it merely reflects the transformation of the trafficking industry. Another problem is that transnational cooperation on criminal matters suffers from red tape and corruption, which means that traffickers are sometimes not arrested or convicted (see the country reports in UNHCR, 2005).

However, despite the fact that traffickers have mastered the network structure much better than their enemies, the prosecution of traffickers has picked up momentum over recent years. Indeed, prosecution is now one of the most advanced governance approaches. The dominance of this approach over protection and prevention is indicated by the strong position of ministries of the interior in national anti-trafficking arrangements (Limanowska, 2005b: 3). EU policies in Southeast Europe further underline the hegemonic role of law enforcement and criminal justice. The European Commission (2005: 3) calls for 'a coordinated policy response notably in the area of freedom, security and justice, external relations, development cooperation, social affairs and employment, gender equality and non-discrimination'. However, there is little evidence that the EU has pursued holistic policies that integrate the various EU policy instruments in a balanced way. Trafficking is framed predominantly as an issue of justice and home affairs; capacity-building, the buzzword of EU policy in the region, has meant little more than strengthening security agencies, particularly through the CARDS program (Community Assistance for Reconstruction, Development, and Stabilization). To be sure, EU institutions and EU member-states have financed protection and prevention programs as well. However, the bulk of funds have been destined for law enforcement and criminal justice (Lindstrom, 2004: 51).

---

[8] Author interview, Sarajevo, 29 August 2006.

Protection

The protection of victims is relatively advanced in some respects, yet remains deficient in others. The popularity of anti-trafficking action has led to the creation of numerous shelters for trafficked women in Southeast Europe, but funding for other programs has been reduced, such as for programs assisting victims of domestic violence.[9] Such short-term donor policies are counter-productive, since domestic violence is one of the factors pushing women to take risky migration decisions. Further problems are the short duration of many anti-trafficking programs and government support for 'willing contractor' NGOs whose spending decisions and implementation practices governments can control (Limanowska, 2005b: 53).

Moreover, witness programs do not afford women sufficient incentives and protection to testify against traffickers (El-Cherkeh et al., 2004: 23–24). In Germany, for example, requirements on the cooperation of women with prosecutors are excessive. Women are offered a 'reflection period' of only four weeks, during which they have to decide whether they want to testify against traffickers to obtain a temporary residence permit—a rather short period given that some women have been traumatized. NGOs are not afforded the right to refuse to give evidence in court, making these NGOs an unreliable partner for women who have broken migration or prostitution laws. And, since there is generally only one recovery center for trafficked women per German state, women have reason to fear reprisals by traffickers (Deutscher Bundestag, 2006). The obvious consequence of a lack of protection is that few trafficked people agree to become witnesses for the prosecution.

Another major shortcoming of protection is a lack of sustainable reintegration programs. In Southeast Europe, there is not enough funding to provide trafficked persons with the security, psychological and medical help, economic support, skills training, and job counseling needed to avoid retrafficking.[10] Also, many women refuse the assistance offered to them because they fear collusion between state agencies and traffickers, or deportation to the country or community they had wanted to get away from.

A further pathology of victim protection (and of other approaches) is a lack of networking. As outlined above, for security governance to work, actors constituting the governance system must be networked. In anti-trafficking, stakeholders have often proven unable or unwilling to properly coordinate their work (Kanics et al., 2005: 66–67). Cooperation problems are apparent among actors pursuing the same security

---

[9] Author interviews with social service providers in Bulgaria, Macedonia, Kosovo, and Bosnia, July–August 2006.

[10] Author interviews with NGO representatives in Southeast Europe, September 2005 and July–August 2006.

governance approach and between actors pursuing different security governance approaches. The director of a women's rights NGO in Bulgaria, talking about the challenges of effective and efficient networking, likens the anti-trafficking system to a 'jungle'.[11]

For example, there has been, and continues to be, a lack of cooperation among EU donor countries, who simply inform each other about their policy priorities in Southeast Europe.[12] Similarly, cooperation among NGOs protecting trafficked persons has proven problematic in Southeast Europe and the EU owing to a lack of funding that would allow NGOs to organize regular meetings on the local, national, and international levels in order to agree on common strategies and their implementation (El-Cherkeh et al., 2004: 98). Further, international organizations do not represent a unified front against trafficking: 'Every agency has carved out its own little turf.'[13] While a division of labor potentially mitigates agency rivalries, a senior IO official said that the 'terrible competition' for funding in the field of anti-trafficking is unlike anything he saw in other policy fields.[14] Moreover, deficient networking between IOs and local NGOs, and among large international and small local NGOs, translates into a lack of local ownership, depriving projects of vital local expertise.[15] Finally, relations between the security sector and NGOs have improved significantly over recent years, but still suffer from mutual suspicions and the frequent failure to exchange information.

Prevention in Countries of Origin

The fourth governance approach, the prevention of trafficking in countries of origin, has been neglected over recent years. Prevention has not evolved much beyond awareness-raising campaigns informing people about trafficking, despite doubts over the effectiveness of awareness campaigns. Worse, campaigns can be counterproductive. Some campaigns in Southeast Europe have been perceived as anti-migration campaigns that instrumentalize trafficking in order to reduce migration to the EU (Limanowska, 2005b: 21–22). In Albania, shock tactics employed in campaigns have led some families to forbid their daughters to leave the house (Dottridge, 2006: 51). Moreover, campaigns are implemented in an ad hoc and uncoordinated manner. In Kosovo, one anti-trafficking campaign begun in late 2005 was followed, a few weeks

---

[11] Author interview, Sofia, 5 July 2006.

[12] Author interview with the ambassador of an EU member-state, Tetovo, Macedonia, 25 July 2006.

[13] Author interview with an official of the United Nations Office of the High Commissioner for Human Rights (OHCHR), Geneva, 4 April 2006.

[14] Author interview, Geneva, 8 March 2006.

[15] Author interview with NGO representative, Sofia, 6 July 2006.

later, by another campaign, to the surprise of almost everyone involved in anti-trafficking in Kosovo.[16] Moreover, lessons learned from campaigns have generally not been documented and shared.

Yet these problems pale when compared to the lack of development-oriented anti-trafficking programs. Economic and social root causes of trafficking include unemployment, poverty, discriminatory practices, a lack of access to education and medical services, and domestic violence. In Southeast Europe, these problems have been caused or aggravated by war, reckless privatization, and structural adjustment programs that have exacerbated the 'feminization of poverty'. Few programs in Southeast Europe so far have systematically addressed the economic and social root causes that push women to seek a better life abroad. The main reason for this has been a lack of donor interest in development-oriented prevention programs proposed by international organizations (Limanowska, 2005b: 9), as well the neglect of a labour-market perspective. While Southeast Europe counts numerous development initiatives, they generally lack anti-trafficking components—which means that economic development helps potential victims of trafficking only coincidentally. Moreover, skills training programs were rarely based on sound research identifying labour market needs. To make matters worse, agencies promoting gender equality, the rights of children, social support, and efforts against HIV/AIDS have not systematically mainstreamed anti-trafficking components within their activities.

This neglect of prevention in countries of origin reflects the enormous challenge of development in Southeast Europe, but also the predominance of law enforcement, which results from the political priority of reducing unwanted migration. Under the banner of anti-trafficking programs, funds have often been destined to create databases of migrants, reinforce borders, and strengthen law enforcement agencies.[17]

Prevention in Countries of Destination

The fifth security governance approach focuses on prevention as well, but in countries of destination. This approach is highly contested, since counter-trafficking demands a rethinking of migration and labor policies. Traffickers have been benefitting from a lack of legal migration and employment opportunities that EU countries offer to non-EU citizens. Anti-trafficking policies that grant visas, residency, and work permits to potential or actual victims of trafficking would reduce trafficking. The lifting of visa restrictions for Romanians by the EU in 2002, for example, was followed by a drop in the number of assisted Romanian victims of trafficking (El-Cherkeh et al., 2004: 51). However,

---

[16] Author interviews with representatives of international organizations, NGOs, and the Ministry of Justice,Prishtina, late July–early August 2006.

[17] Author interview with trafficking expert, Sarajevo, 15 and 30 August 2006.

negative perceptions of migrants prevent the systematic embracing of this strategy. Over the 1990s, policymakers and the general public have increasingly securitized' migration (Huysmans, 2000). Irregular migrants, and particularly migrants working in the sex industry, are seen as transgressors of migration and prostitution laws, as well as violators of norms of decency. This helps to explain the frequent arrest of trafficked persons by the police, who generally represent conservative, male segments of society.

The negative image of migrant prostitutes means that EU countries extend residence permits to trafficked persons only for short periods, and only if they testify against traffickers (Goodey, 2003: 169), a practice that has not been substantially altered over recent years.[18] An OHCHR official confirmed that there is a lack of political will to use the migration lever for empowering trafficked persons: the OHCHR largely failed in its attempts to introduce legal migration and residence provisions into the 2005 Council of Europe Convention on Action Against Human Trafficking.[19]

The securitization of migration has led to the reinforcement of 'Fortress Europe'. Yet, more border guards and the use of sophisticated technology actually benefit illicit entrepreneurs. They force migrants to seek help from smugglers, who may turn out to be traffickers (see International Crisis Group, 2005). Moreover, stronger borders are not a panacea for identifying trafficked persons: During the migration process, many women are not aware that they are being trafficked, and thus do not want to be detected. Slipping information leaflets containing hotline numbers into the passports of potential victims at borders addresses this problem, yet is an intervention that comes relatively late during the trafficking circuit. Prevention should commence earlier.

Prevention, in countries of both origin and destination, also suffers from insufficient demand reduction. The implementation of prohibition regimes is particularly difficult when there is a resilient demand for goods or services (Nadelmann, 1990). This is the case with sexual services. There are still not enough awareness campaigns informing potential or actual buyers of sexual services about human trafficking (Howe, 2005: 99).

A major reason for the lack of demand-oriented awareness campaigns is that such campaigns are inextricably linked to prostitution policies. The debate over prostitution is an ideological minefield, a fact that limits the ability of international organizations to address clients of prostitutes.[20] Prostitution laws differ widely across Europe, and there are few signs of harmonization. Countries such as Germany, the

---

[18] Author interview with a deputy of the Bavarian parliament, Tutzing, 29 October 2006.

[19] Author interview, Geneva, 14 March 2006.

[20] Author interview with a senior IO official, Geneva, 8 March 2006.

Netherlands, and Switzerland have regulated or partially legalized the purchasing and selling of sexual services, hoping that the registration of prostitutes would empower women vis-à-vis pimps or bar owners. Women's rights groups defending legalization argue that criminalizing prostitution deprives women of their agency—that is, their ability to freely decide what to do with their bodies. These groups speak of sex workers instead of survivors. Other countries such as France favor an abolitionist prostitution policy. Abolitionist governments and NGOs decry the commodification of female bodies through prostitution. As an adviser to the Swedish government writes, 'males who use women and girls in prostitution are sexual predators and rapists' (Ekberg, 2002: 8).

Even if one does not accept the mantra of abolitionists that prostitution is inevitably about rape and exploitation, and that the distinction between consensual prostitution and coerced trafficking is a false one, it may well be the case that prostitution regimes influence trafficking patterns. It is not clear which prostitution policy is best suited to reduce trafficking, but there are indications that the legalization of prostitution is not a panacea against trafficking. As shown in Germany after the introduction in 2002 of a law that legalizes prostitution, many prostitutes do not register and sign work contracts with brothel owners, not least because they do not want to pay the relatively high social security contributions and taxes (Holm, 2005). Moreover, foreign prostitutes, who constitute the majority of people working in the sex industry, are not eligible to register, since they do not have residency and work permits. Pimps and brothel owners continue to exploit these women. And, even if legalization leads to better working conditions for registered prostitutes, these prostitutes might stay in the business longer. Traffickers would continue to make money, because of constant client demand for young women and girls.[21] Hence, legalization might not break the link between organized crime and the sex industry, but rather strengthen it, encourage the growth of the sex industry, and increase trafficking (Bindel & Kelly, 2003: 13–15; Hughes, 2000: 646–648). Yet, the criminalization of prostitution is not a smart option either. The US example illustrates the negative effects of law enforcement pressure on women, who have been victimized by pimps, clients, and the police (Weitzer, 1999).

Sweden has adopted an innovative, and hotly debated, policy: In 1999, the government legalized the selling of sexual services and criminalized the purchase of such services. According to the Swedish government, this strategy was followed by a reduction in sex trafficking to Sweden (e-mail to the author from Madeleine Elgemyr, Swedish Ministry of Industry, Employment and Communications, 7 March 2006; Bindel & Kelly, 2003: 25, 29). The government argues that, instead of

---

[21] I thank Louise Shelley for mentioning this point to me.

pushing the industry underground, the law has created an anti-prostitution climate and has made the country unattractive to traffickers.

However, evidence that the policy has reduced trafficking is sketchy,
and the Swedish model is unpopular in other EU countries—as
illustrated by the German government's tolerance toward prostitution
during the 2006 Football World Cup, which has drawn acid comment
from abolitionists (Neuwirth, 2006). While there is a trend to criminalize
demand for services provided by trafficked persons, implementing this
policy is difficult. In many cases, proving that a client knew that a
prostitute was trafficked is impossible.

The discussion above shows that counter-trafficking efforts have not
fully met the second criterion for successful security governance. While
the anti-trafficking security governance system does encompass various
approaches, these are not properly balanced. Few initiatives have
addressed the economic and social root causes of trafficking, or reduced
the demand for trafficked women, and trafficked persons have not
received sufficient protection. The hegemony of prosecution indicates the
perception of trafficking as an organized crime and migration problem.
Anti-trafficking policies are 'skewed and imbalanced, focus too much on
law enforcement, and are marked by wrong attitudes of cops'.[22]

Moreover, shortcomings have also been detected with regard to the
third criterion, which stipulates networking as a precondition for
successful security governance. Networked relations are relatively
smooth among some actors, especially between law enforcement and
criminal justice institutions. However, anti-trafficking networks still
have many weaknesses, especially those networks bringing together
different types of actors pursuing different governance approaches.

Conclusion

History shows the inadequacy of coercive strategies against complex
social problems. The late 19th and early 20th century saw a reduction
in the number of women trafficked from Europe to the USA for
prostitution. Although international agreements against the transatlantic 'White Slave Trade' mitigated the trade, contingent conditions such
as the equalization of the sex ratio in the USA were more important
(Nadelmann, 1990: 513–516). In the second half of the 20th century, law
enforcement within the USA had not abolished prostitution, but instead
harmed prostitutes (Weitzer, 1999). Similarly, despite its decade-old
military-style 'war on drugs', the USA has not reduced illicit drug
supplies. Instead, coercion has coincided with a worldwide growth of the
drug industry, and exacerbated corruption and human rights abuses
(Friesendorf, 2005). Most US drug policymakers regard illicit drug
supplies primarily as a criminal and not a socio-economic problem.

---

[22] Interview with a senior OHCHR official, Geneva 4 April 2006.

Although sex trafficking would continue even if counter-efforts found a balance between prosecution, protection, and prevention, a better governance system would reduce trafficking. Governance must be more preventive. In countries of origin, counter-trafficking must reduce poverty and discrimination. In countries of destination, progress against trafficking requires a rethinking of narrow-minded migration policies. Extending migration and employment opportunities to people who risk being trafficked would not only help these people, but also rejuvenate an aging Western Europe. Destination countries must devise better strategies for reducing the demand for trafficked women both through awareness campaigns and through the systematic, unideological evaluation of the impact of different prostitution regimes on trafficking patterns.

In addition to more balanced security governance, there is a need for better networked governance. While criminal networks are fast and flexible, the same cannot be said about anti-trafficking networks. Red tape, corruption, competition for funding, different agency mandates and world views, institutional inertia, and the frequent turnover of personnel (successful networking hinges on good personal relationships) hamper effective networking among and between the stakeholders involved in counter-trafficking. To be sure, networking has improved. Helga Konrad, the OSCE's first Special Representative for anti-trafficking, fostered cooperation in order to move away from separate projects toward concerted action. In the framework of the Alliance Against Trafficking in Persons established in July 2004, she convened regular meetings at the political and expert level. In Southeast Europe, the OSCE established National Referral Mechanisms (NRMs), which are intended to ensure that governments protect and promote the human rights of trafficked persons and prosecute traffickers. NRMs bring together various national stakeholders who negotiate adequate and flexible responses to trafficking. Hence, NRMs cut across the different approaches constituting the anti-trafficking governance system.

This positive example notwithstanding, it is unlikely that networked anti-trafficking efforts will greatly improve in the near future. The failure to acknowledge that the success of one's own approach partially depends on the success of other approaches continues to hamper progress. There is no trade-off, for example, between law enforcement and protection: the closer police work together with NGOs in protecting trafficked persons, the higher the chances of successfully prosecuting traffickers. The fact that, in 2005, only about half of all European countries have instituted interagency cooperation mechanisms against human trafficking (UNHCR, 2005: 8) indicates the bureaucratic and political obstacles to effective networking.

Strategies against human trafficking are a prime example of a major change in international relations: the change from government to governance. Government is unable to cope with this complex challenge. Well-calibrated and networked security governance is the only viable option, but the travails and pathologies of anti-trafficking efforts underline that the shift from government to governance is not smooth.

Cornelius Friesendorf is a postdoctoral researcher at the University of Munich, where he is writing a book on security governance in Bosnia and Herzegovina. Publications include US Foreign Policy and the War on Drugs: Displacing the Cocaine and Heroin Industry (Routledge, 2007). Earlier versions of this article were presented at conferences in London, Berlin, and Ljubljana. For helpful comments or fruitful discussions, the author would like to thank J. Peter Burgess, Helga Konrad, Barbara Limanowska, Angela Paul, Susan Penksa, Johanna Willems, the reviewers, and the interviewees (who would like to remain anonymous). The author also thanks the Volkswagen Foundation for financing his fieldwork in Southeast Europe. E-mail: friesendorf@gsi.uni-muenchen.de.

Discussion Questions

1 *What do the letters IOs and NGOs stand for?*

2 *What do IOs do within the context of human trafficking?*

3 *What do NGOs do within the context of human trafficking?*

4 *What does the term "security governance" mean within the context of human trafficking?*

5 *Three criteria can be derived from the theoretical literature on governance and networks and the empirical literature examining past and present against criminalized non-state activities. What are they?*

6 *What five approaches have been suggested to combat human trafficking within the context of the anti-trafficking governance systems?*

7 *What are some of the shortcomings of counter trafficking efforts?*

8 *Sweden has adopted an innovative and hotly debated policy on the subject of sexual trafficking. What is this policy?*

References

Andreas, Peter & Ethan A. Nadelmann, 2006. Policing the Globe: Criminalization and Crime Control in International Relations. New York & Oxford: Oxford University Press.

Arquilla, John & David Ronfeldt, eds, 2001. Networks and Netwars: The Future of Terror, Crime, and Militancy. Santa Monica, CA: RAND.

Baumeister, Sebastian & Susie Maley, 2005. 'The Role of the Private Sector in Developing Youth Careers', in Sector Project Against Trafficking in Women, eds, Challenging Trafficking in Persons: Theoretical Debate & Practical Approaches. Baden-Baden: Nomos (81–85).

Berman, Jacqueline, 2003. '(Un)popular Strangers and Crises (Un)bounded: Discourses of Sex Trafficking, the European Political Community and the Panicked State of the Modern State', European Journal of International Relations 9(1): 37–86.

Bindel, Julie & Liz Kelly, 2003. A Critical Examination of Responses to Prostitution in Four Countries: Victoria, Australia; Ireland; the Netherlands; and Sweden. London: Child and Woman Abuse Studies Union, London Metropolitan University.

Bundeskriminalamt, 2006. Lagebild Menschenhandel 2005 [Situation Report Human Trafficking 2005]. Wiesbaden.

Caparini, Marina, 2006. 'Applying a Security Governance Perspective to the Privatisation of Security', in Alan Bryden & Marina Caparini, eds, Private Actors and Security Governance. Vienna & Berlin: LIT (264–282).

Czempiel, Ernst-Otto & James N. Rosenau, eds, 1992. Governance Without Government: Order and Change in World Politics. Cambridge: Cambridge University Press.

Deutscher Bundestag, 2006. 'Menschenhandel bekämpfen – Opferrechte weiter ausbauen' [Fighting Human Trafficking: Strengthening Victims' Rights], Antrag der Fraktion Bündnis 90/Die Grünen, Drucksache, 16/1125, 4 April.

Dottridge, Mike, 2006. Action To Prevent Child Trafficking in South Eastern Europe: A Preliminary Assessment. Geneva: UNICEF/Terre des Hommes.

Eilstrup-Sangiovanni, Mette, 2005. 'Transnational Networks and New Security Threats', Cambridge Review of International Affairs 18(1): 7–13.

Ekberg, Gunilla, 2002. 'The International Debate About Prostitution and Trafficking in Women: Refuting the Arguments', paper presented at the Seminar on the Effects of Legalisation of Prostitution Activities, Stockholm, 5–6 November; available at www.regeringen.se/content/1/c4/22/84/0647d25a.pdf.

El-Cherkeh, Tanja; Elena Stirbu, Sebastian Lazaroiu & Dragos Radu, 2004. EU-Enlargement, Migration and Trafficking in Women: The Case of South Eastern Europe, Report 247. Hamburg: Hamburg Institute of International Economics.

European Commission, 2005. 'Fighting Trafficking in Human Beings: An Integrated Approach and Proposals for an Action Plan', Communication to the European Parliament and the Council, Brussels, 18 October, COM (2005) 514 final.

Europol, 2006. 'Trafficking of Human Beings for Sexual Exploitation in the EU: A Europol Perspective', Factsheet, Brussels; available at www.europol.eu. int/publications/SeriousCrimeOverviews/2005/THB_factsheet.pdf.

Friesendorf, Cornelius, 2005. 'Squeezing the Balloon? U.S. Air Interdiction and the Restructuring of the South American Cocaine Industry in the 1990s', Crime, Law & Social Change 44(1): 35–78.

Goodey, Jo, 2003. 'Recognising Organized Crime's Victims: The Case of Sex Trafficking in the EU', in Adam Edwards & Peter Gill, eds, Transnational Organized Crime: Perspectives on Global Security. London & New York: Routledge (157–173).

Haynes, Dina F., 2004. 'Used, Abused, Arrested and Deported: Extending Immigration Benefits To Protect the Victims of Trafficking and To Secure the Prosecution of Traffickers', Human Rights Quarterly 26(2): 221–272.

Holm, Carsten, 2005. 'Luftnummer im Puff' [Legislation Flops in Red-Light District], Der Spiegel, 5 February.

Howe, Christiane, 2005. 'Non-Discriminatory Approaches To Address Clients in Prostitution', in Sector Project Against Trafficking in Women, eds, Challenging Trafficking in Persons: Theoretical Debate & Practical Approaches. Baden-Baden: Nomos (98–103).

Hughes, Donna M., 2000. 'The "Natasha" Trade: The Transnational Shadow Market of Trafficking in Women', Journal of International Affairs 53(2): 625–651.

Huysmans, Jef, 2000. 'The European Union and the Securitization of Migration', Journal of Common Market Studies 38(5): 751–777.

International Crisis Group, 2005. EU Visas and the Western Balkans, Europe Report No. 168. Brussels: ICG.

International Labour Organization (ILO), 2005. A Global Alliance Against Forced Labour: Global Report Under the Follow-Up to the ILO Declaration on Fundamental Principles and Rights at Work. Geneva: ILO.

Kanics, Jyothi; Gabriele Reiter & Bärbel Heide Uhl, 2005. 'Trafficking in Human Beings –A Threat Under Control? Taking Stock Four Years After Major International Efforts Started', Helsinki Monitor 16(1): 53–67.

Krahmann, Elke, 2003. 'Conceptualizing Security Governance', Cooperation and Conflict 38(1): 5–26.

Krahmann, Elke, 2005. 'Security Governance and Networks: New Theoretical
Perspectives in Transatlantic Security', Cambridge Review of International
Affairs 18(1): 15–30.

Krause, Keith & Oliver Jütersonke, 2005. 'Peace, Security and Development in
Post-Conflict Environments', Security Dialogue 36(4): 447–462.

Laczko, Frank & Marco A. Gramegna, 2003. 'Developing Better Indicators of
Human Trafficking', Brown Journal of World Affairs 10(1): 179–194.

Law, David M., 2006. The Post-Conflict Security Sector, Policy Paper No. 14.
Geneva: Geneva Centre for the Democratic Control of Armed Forces.

Limanowska, Barbara, 2005a. 'The Victim-Perspective – A Neglected
Dimension', in Sector Project Against Trafficking in Women, eds,
Challenging Trafficking in Persons: Theoretical Debate & Practical
Approaches. Baden-Baden: Nomos (27–31).

Limanowska, Barbara, 2005b. Trafficking in Human Beings in South Eastern
Europe. Belgrade: UNICEF/UNOHCHR/OSCE-ODIHR; available at
www.unicef.org/ceecis/Trafficking.Report.2005.pdf.

Lindstrom, Nicole, 2004. 'Regional Sex Trafficking in the Balkans:
Transnational Networks in an Enlarged Europe', Problems of Post-
Communism 51(3): 45–52.

Masci, David, 2004. 'Human Trafficking and Slavery', CQ Researcher 14(12).

Mendelson, Sarah E., 2005. Barracks and Brothels: Peacekeepers and Human
Trafficking in the Balkans. Washington, DC: Center for Strategic and
International Studies.

Nadelmann, Ethan A., 1990. 'Global Prohibition Regimes: The Evolution of
Norms in International Society', International Organization 44(4): 479–526.

Neuwirth, Jessica, 2006, 'The World Cup and the Johns: Sex Trafficking and
Prostitution', International Herald Tribune, 11 April.

Raab, Jörg & Brinton H. Milward, 2003. 'Dark Networks as Problems', Journal
of Public Administration Research & Theory 13(4): 413–439.

Slaughter, Anne-Marie, 2004, A New World Order. Princeton, NJ & Oxford:
Princeton University Press.

Soderlund, Gretchen, 2005. 'Running from the Rescuers: New U.S. Crusades
Against Sex Trafficking and the Rhetoric of Abolition', NWSA Journal 17(3):
64–87.

Solana, Javier, 2003. A Secure Europe in a Better World – European Security
Strategy. Paris: European Union Institute for Security Studies.

State Coordinator, 2006. Report on Trafficking in Human Beings and Illegal
Migration in Bosnia and Herzegovina. Sarajevo: State Coordinator for

Combating Trafficking in Human Beings and Illegal Migration in Bosnia and Herzegovina.

Stoecker, Sally & Louise Shelley, eds, 2005. Human Traffic and Transnational Crime: Eurasian and American Perspectives. Lanham, MD: Rowman & Littlefield.

UNHCR, 2005. Combatting Human Trafficking: Overview of UNHCR Anti-Trafficking Activities in Europe. Geneva: Bureau for Europe Policy Unit, United Nations High Commissioner for Refugees.

US Department of State, 2005. Trafficking in Persons Report. Washington, DC: US Department of State.

Vandenberg, Martina E. 2005. 'Trafficking in Armed and Post-Conflict Situations', in Sector Project Against Trafficking in Women, eds, Challenging Trafficking in Persons: Theoretical Debate & Practical Approaches. Baden-Baden: Nomos (69–75).

Weitzer, Ronald, 1999. 'Prostitution Control in America: Rethinking Public Policy', Crime, Law & Social Change 33(1): 83–102.

Wenger, Andreas & Daniel Möckli, 2003. Conflict Prevention: The Untapped Potential of the Business Sector. Boulder, CO: Lynne Rienner.

Williams, Phil & Gregory Baudin-O'Hayon, 2003. 'Global Governance, Transnational Organized Crime and Money Laundering', in David Held & Anthony McGrew, eds, Governing Globalization: Power Authority and Global Governance. Cambridge: Polity (127–144).

Note: Reprinted with permission of SAGE.

7

SEXUAL TRAFFICKING OF WOMEN: TRAGIC PROPORTIONS AND ATTEMPTED SOLUTIONS IN ALBANIA

Mary P. Van Hook, *School of Social Work, University of Central Florida, Orlando, FL*
Eglantina Gjermeni, *Lecturer in the Social Work Department, University of Tirana, Tirana, Albania and Director of the Women's Center of Tirana*
Edlira Haxhiymeri, *Prefect of Tirana District, and former Director of the Social Work Department, University of Tirana, Tirana, Albania*

Poverty and reduced status place women at increased risk in the world of sexual trafficking, a nether-land of fear, violence, and emotional and physical degradation. Forced into prostitution under a variety of circumstances, many young women are trapped in their own and other countries and face threats of violence or death if they try to escape (Boudreaux, 2001; Burrell, 2002; Crane, 2001; DeStefano, 2001; Hope, 2000; LaCava and Nanetti, 2000; Ryan and Hall, 2001; Smith, 2002; US Senate Subcommittee on Near East and South Asian Affairs, 2000; Watts and Zimmerman, 2002; Wood, 2000). With no accurate count of the women involved, United Nations figures estimate that 3 million people are trafficked each year, and the numbers are rising (Crane, 2001; Watts and Zimmerman, 2002). A 2000 report indicated that approximately 45,000–50,000 women and children are trafficked annually into the United States, primarily from Latin America, Russia and the newly independent states of eastern Europe (US Senate Subcommittee, 2000). The UN, the US State Department and other international organizations are recognizing that sexual human trafficking is part of the major problem of the evil of involuntary servitude involving sexual and other forms of slavery that include trafficking between countries or bondage inside countries (US State Department, 2005).

As a result of the social and economic upheavals accompanying the fall of communism and various regional wars, sexual trafficking has grown dramatically in the eastern European countries formerly part of the Soviet sphere of influence. Indeed, eastern Europe is identified as the largest source of women being trafficked for prostitution (Watts and Zimmerman, 2002). This has robbed entire villages and towns in Albania, Moldova, southern Bulgaria and Romania of their young women (Smith, 2002).

Recently there has been increasing attention to the problem of sexual trafficking in the mental-health (Farley, 2003) and policy literature (Lederer, 2001). This research paper describes issues related to sexual trafficking, especially in Albania (one of the centers of the recruitment and transport of women from eastern Europe to other countries, especially western Europe) (Smith, 2002; US Government, 2001), the current efforts and challenges in addressing the problems, and implications for practice in eastern Europe and other countries. The Albanian situation reflects both global trends and its special characteristics. Information has been drawn from area research, international news reports, non-governmental organizations (NGOs), United States and Albanian government documents, presentations and the experience of the authors.

The Albanian Context

While it is impossible to know exactly how many Albanian women are involved in sexual trafficking, Save the Children recently estimated that 30,000 Albanian women were sex slaves abroad (out of a national population basis of about 3,900,000) (Vickers and Pettifer, 1997). A 1997 study by Useful to Albanian Women (an Albanian NGO) indicated about 10,000 young Albanian women were prostitutes in Italy and Greece, with many other young women in other countries (LaCava and Nanetti, 2000). Similarly to global trends that women from poorer countries are either enticed or coerced into prostitution in wealthier countries (Ryan and Hall, 2001), young Albanian women are often enticed with the promise of working in restaurants or caring for children or older adults in Greece or Italy but are then forced to become prostitutes.

Albania, one of the most repressive and isolated communist countries of eastern Europe until the fall of communism in 1991, was also one of the poorest European countries and heavily rural. On the downfall of communism Albania suffered from serious internal divisions based on ancient family and clan alliances, distrust toward outsiders and state authority, and unrealistic expectations about external support. The 1997 collapse of a pyramid scheme that enticed millions of Albanians into investing and losing their life savings further contributed to a period of violent anarchy that has had a lasting adverse impact on the infrastructure, the social fabric of society and international investment. Despite the establishment of some degree of law and order, the economic picture remains bleak as the government tries to cope with the residue of a rigidly centralized planning system, outmoded factories and the attempt to introduce privatization (UNDP, 2000; LaCava and Nanetti, 2000; Olsen, 2000).

Poverty and Sexual Trafficking in Albania

Poverty is a global risk factor, and Albania demonstrates the tragic interplay between poverty and gender issues that heightens women's vulnerability. The response to poverty and hopelessness about the future has been massive emigration from the rural to urban areas and other countries, especially western Europe. Many men have sought work in other countries and most Albanian families have a family member working in Greece or Italy (Kule et al., 2002; LaCava and Nanetti, 2000; Olsen, 2000). This migration has reduced educational and marital opportunities.

Decimated rural communities cannot support secondary education. The school system has also been hurt by lack of teachers, especially in the rural areas, and the devastation that occurred during the period of economic chaos. Many young women do not receive a secondary education because parents are reluctant to send daughters to distant schools because of realistic fears they will be abducted and forced into prostitution (Albanian and Spanish Red Cross, 2001; LaCava and Nanetti, 2000; Olsen, 2000).

The departure of large numbers of men has meant a drastic decline in the number of males who can marry the young women. Parents fear that their daughters will not find a man to marry and anxiously seek husbands for them. Young men promise that engagement and marriage will be a route out of poverty and instead use this as a ruse to trap young women into prostitution (LaCava and Nanetti, 2000).

Massive unemployment in the rural areas has contributed to family poverty generally and has especially reduced economic opportunities for women. The decline or disappearance of agricultural cooperatives, the main form of employment in the villages, creates joblessness for women and cuts them off from opportunities to support their families and gain economic power. Such women are especially vulnerable to deceitful promises of a better life (Miria et al., 2000; Council of Ministers of the Republic of Albania 2001), and this too reflects global trends (Ryan and Hall, 2001; Watts and Zimmerman, 2002).

Poverty and the reduction of legitimate economic opportunities have contributed to a widespread and powerful criminal network engaged in drug and sexual trafficking by Albanians in Albania and the rest of Europe. Sexual trafficking has become a lucrative business (Council of Ministers of the Republic of Albania, 2001; LaCava and Nanetti, 2000; Post, 1998; Vickers and Pettifer, 1997).

Gender Patterns and Sexual Trafficking

Although laws give women equal rights with men, implementation has been limited and traditional patriarchal customs continue to devalue women, especially in the rural areas (Van Hook et al., 2000). Rural young women live in a social context in which obedience to husbands and male relatives is unquestioned (Olsen, 2000). When a young man promises the desperately poor family that he will marry the daughter and provide her with a better life, many family members make these arrangements for their daughters who then have little recourse (LaCava and Nanetti, 2000). The strong betrothal tradition according to which parents can arrange binding marriage engagements also makes it difficult for young women not to concur with them or to leave these arrangements. As a result many young women are trapped into prostitution by men posing as boyfriends. They are further trapped by fear of violence toward themselves or their families and their unwillingness to disgrace their families (Boudreaux, 2001; Council of Ministers of the Republic of Albania, 2001; Olsen, 2000; Smith, 2002). Compounding the situation are women's low expectations and fatalism about their future (LaCava and Nanetti, 2000) and a history of women learning to endure as a way of coping with extremely difficult life circumstances, especially in rural areas (Post, 1998).

With the state powerless to create order, people in northern Albania have turned to the earlier tradition of the code of kanun. The misuse of this traditional code has placed women at greater risk of false promises of marriage, subsequent kidnapping and sale into prostitution by powerful men in the community (Schwandner-Sievers, 2000).

Women face many difficulties when escaping prostitution and returning to their communities. They are realistically fearful of violence and of being retrafficked back by the Albanian mafia that is well connected with organized crime in western countries. As illegal residents in other countries they have no legal protection (Burrell, 2002; Crane, 2001; Vickers and Pettifer, 1997). They often have little hope for a good life back in Albania. Having been labeled a prostitute, they will not be viewed as marriageable. They are too embarrassed to return and fear their families and communities will not accept them. Some young women who returned have committed suicide or have been killed by their father or brother because the labeling and stigma from the community were so unbearable. For some women, it means a return to a situation of domestic violence. Their lives as prostitutes have also left them with emotional and physical scars. Unprotected sex has placed them at risk for AIDS and other forms of sexually transmitted diseases.

The International Context

Beginning in the metropolises of Greece, Italy and the UK, eastern European sexual trafficking has spread to other European metropolitan centers (Dettmer, 2001; The Economist, 2001). Albanians run 70 percent of the brothels in central London and three-quarters of the women working in them are from eastern Europe. An estimated 140,000 foreign women are brought to the UK's vice trade, mostly from Albania, Latvia and Ukraine (Burrell, 2002). Greece has a booming trade in sexual trafficking (Smith, 2002). Half of the Albanian women in sexual slavery are estimated to be in Italy (Boudreaux, 2001). Lack of official interest and policies that deport these young women before their traffickers can be prosecuted have made it difficult to identify the extent and to take action. Lack of efforts to reduce demand is also problematic (Burrell, 2002; Dettmer, 2001). Albanian pimps in these countries are described as particularly cruel in their torture of the women (Boudreaux, 2001; Smith, 2002).

Response to the Problem

After an initial period of denial of the seriousness of the sexual trafficking, the Albanian government began to recognize the problem in response to pressure from the European Union and the UN. Together with other governments and NGOs, especially neighboring Italy, the government has responded through various efforts in the three areas identified by the US Senate Subcommittee: prosecution and enforcement against the traffickers, prevention of trafficking, and protection of and assistance to its victims (US Senate Sub-committee, 2000), with some apparent reduction in the numbers of people involved (Aronowitz, 2003).

The Albanian government created a high-level coalition of governmental officials representing various ministries and NGOs to develop a national strategy that incorporated these three elements. A strategy approved by Parliament in December 2001 included action steps and a budget to implement the activities with a deadline of September 2004 (Aronowitz, 2003).

The activities included:

- research on trafficking;
- services to protect trafficked persons, including shelters to be managed by NGOs;
- reintegration programs for trafficked persons;
- general campaign on prevention and raising awareness supported by the Ministry of Education, including anti-HIV/AIDS education;
- education of women and children about protection against trafficking and exploitation;
- improvement of social and economic conditions for women;
- measures to prosecute and punish traffickers, including changes to legal regulations and better law enforcement;
- strengthening control of national borders.

Legal Reform

Albanian legislation has identified a specific crime, 'the trafficking of human beings', and the punishment is quite severe (Council of Ministers of the Republic of Albania, 2001). Unfortunately police corruption and lack of successful prosecution reduce the effectiveness of these laws (Aronowitz, 2003; US Government, 2001).

Italy, prompted by the increasing number of murders caused by sexual trafficking, has taken an important lead in legally opposing forced prostitution (Boudreaux, 2001; Sydney Morning Herald, 2001). It has passed strict legislation against trafficking. It has also passed laws that protect the women and give female victims the protection of a potentially renewable six-month legal residency, even if they do not denounce their traffickers. Unfortunately, women in many other countries are required to denounce their trafficker and are frequently repatriated to Albania or their native country (Crane, 2001). English policy immediately deports women before they have given evidence against the trafficker. Women are then often met at the airport and returned to the sex trade (Burrell, 2002).

Educational Efforts

The Women's Center in Tirana, with help from the German Embassy in Tirana and funding from the German Ministry of Foreign Affairs, implemented a series of educational prevention efforts. They published and distributed about 3000 copies of leaflets to educate middle- and high-school students and the general public about the existence of the problem. They created posters with a short story and a message on it, for example, about a woman promised paradise in Italy who instead finds a nightmare. Posters were put in bus stations, embassies and in middle and high schools. Drawing upon the expertise of various professionals, they broadcast six radio programs describing the nature, cause and consequences of the problem and ways to prevent it. People could call in and speak to experts.

The center collaborated with Albanian journalists to create a TV documentary called 'Life sold on the sidewalks'. They collected data, and interviewed victims as well as representatives of governmental institutions in Albania, Italy and Greece, to describe the nature of the problem and the actions of the state and society to prevent it, including the role of the family, the media, the NGOs and education. The interviews with the victims were also collected in a booklet and distributed to the students and teachers in the high schools and other organizations (Women's Center, 2000).

Shelter and Reintegration Services

Albanian NGOs led by women have provided shelters to offer reintegration and a support network. Save the Children and USAID supported a shelter administered by Women's Hearth in Vlora. The women are screened by the United Nations High Commissioner for Refugees (UNHCR) at the shelter and those willing to return home are referred to the International Organization of Migration (IOM) in Tirana. The shelters provide counseling, vocational training and assistance with finding jobs. The challenge of integrating victims of prostitution remains especially in the rural areas (Olsen, 2000). The International Catholic Migration Commission (ICMC) developed a referral and shelter program for women coming from Albania and Kosovo and other eastern European countries. Upon learning about a woman from the Albanian police, the center caseworker meets with the woman to determine if she wants to escape from her trafficker and return home. She is then referred to a shelter in Tirana where she receives counseling and medical attention. Through help from the governments of Canada, Sweden and USAID, she receives her board and lodging. The caseworker and the woman establish a plan for reintegration to identify the services needed to return home and reestablish her life there. Partners at the IOM work with the relevant embassies to provide documentation and tickets. Despite efforts to keep the location of the shelter a secret to protect women from traffickers, the center has received threats and has had to call upon the Albanian police for protection (Patterson, 2000).

Italy has also taken the lead in creating shelters. New Wings, funded by the Roman Catholic Church and the Italian government, serves as a model approach. Women receive shelter and protection and are enabled to work while going through the legal process. The center also addresses the problem through economic development in the home country, especially in Moldava and Ukraine (Crane, 2001). These efforts are risky because the men involved in the Albanian mafia do not want centers to interfere with their lucrative business (Crane, 2001; Olsen, 2000).

Lessons and Challenges

The experience in Albania and other countries points out some important lessons and challenges in addressing this complex problem. Planning and implementing these efforts requires continuing partnerships among social workers, NGOs and governmental entities, both domestically and internationally.

The international nature of sexual trafficking requires that efforts in one country are joined with efforts from social workers, other advocates for women and human rights, and organizations in other countries. Without coordination, women are subject to revictimization.

Legal issues are essential to protect the rights of women, punish the traffickers and enable women to seek help from the authorities without fear of deportation or lack of protection. Legal changes must be paired with adequate implementation that guards against corruption and lack of training and resources (Aronowitz, 2003). Such issues require continuous monitoring and advocacy by social workers and their colleagues in the fields of women's issues and human rights.

Efforts to improve the economic situation of communities and families are essential. Addressing poverty for women is a priority. Social workers are challenged to be part of broad social efforts in economic development. There is a big need in Albania for development projects instead of only emergency projects. These provide employment opportunities for women and increase their chances of a normal life. Programs that encourage women to start small businesses, including providing them with micro credit loans with low interest for a long period of time, are needed.

With rural young women at heightened risk, communicating with rural residents is both especially important and challenging. The rural patriarchal culture that limits the decision-making ability of young women poses continuing problems. Prevention efforts need to be directed toward educating families, especially men, about the presence and criminal nature of sexual trafficking and ways to protect their daughters.

Reintegration services are essential and involve a complex array of services: psychological counseling to address the trauma and economic and social skills for economic support. Women might need help in renting small apartments (perhaps in other towns than their home village), with finding jobs, and with credit for small businesses to begin their new lives. Based on research, the dramatic lack of control that these women have experienced may place them at greater risk of depression (Regehr et al., 1999). Finding ways to empower women to take control over their lives is important. Traumatized women need the opportunity to share with others their experiences and feelings, as they feel ready to do, as part of the healing process (Van Soest, 1997). The role of shelter staff can be especially crucial because community attitudes can make acceptance back into the community problematic. Addressing the community barriers to acceptance is an important challenge, especially given the 'familism' that organizes Albanian society (and many other developing countries) and the vulnerability of women lacking male protection (LaCava and Nanetti, 2000). The potential danger faced by shelter staff means that the risks of vicarious trauma experienced by workers exposed on a regular basis to the horrors faced by these women (Figley, 1995; White, 1998) are accentuated by their own personal risks.

Prevention efforts aimed at the populations at greatest risk and the general public require key partnerships including the media, NGOs and governmental organizations locally and internationally. The educational system can strengthen the education of women, equip them with the skills needed to support themselves economically, acknowledge the rights of women and educate specifically about sexual trafficking. In Albania, the IOM signed a Memorandum of Understanding with the

Ministry of Education regarding the inclusion of the topic of sexual trafficking in the school curricula. The media can help raise awareness of the problem and report cases of criminal prosecution.

Sadly, the poverty that places women at risk also poses ongoing problems for providing the stable resource base needed to establish and maintain programs.

Conclusion

The tragedy of sexual trafficking affects thousands of women in Albania and other countries. Poverty, gender patterns and social events contribute to vulnerability. Efforts to prevent the problem and to respond to victims of trafficking require social work partnerships to address legal, economic and family issues and to meet the needs of women traumatized by their experience.

Discussion Questions

1 *Why are many Albanian families reluctant to send their daughters to distant schools for education?*

2 *What have been the implications of the departure of large numbers of men from Albania?*

3 *What difficulties do many Albanian women face when they escape from prostitution and return to their communities?*

4 *What role do the Albanians play in human trafficking in various parts of Europe?*

References

Albanian and Spanish Red Cross (2001) 'Children and Youth at Risk'. Albanian Red Cross/Spanish Red Cross (November). Tirana.

Aronowitz, A. (2003) Anti-Trafficking Programs in Albania. Washington, DC: Management Systems International (18 February).

Boudreaux, R. (2001) 'Journal into Sex Slavery', Los Angeles Times (17 August): A1.

Burrell, I. (2002) 'Police Ignore Vice Trade from Eastern Europe', The Independent (London) (23 January): 10.

Council of Ministers of the Republic of Albania (2001) 'National Strategy to Combat Illegal Trafficking in Human Beings' (7 December). Tirana.

Crane, K. (2001) 'Italian Haven Offers Hope to Trafficked Women', The Christian Science Monitor (1 November): 7.

DeStefano, A. (2001) 'Smuggled for Sex', Newsday (New York) (13 March): A06.

Dettmer, Jamie (2001) 'Heroin and Sex Trade Fuel Albania Nationalism', Insight on the News (13 August) 17, 30,13.

The Economist (2001) 'So Hopeless', issue no. 8227(359) (23–9 June): 52.

Farley, M. (2003) Prostitution, Trafficking, and Traumatic Stress. Binghamton, NY: Haworth Maltreatment and Trauma Press.

Figley, Charles (1995) Compassion Fatigue: Coping with Secondary Traumatic Stress Disorder in Those Who Treat the Traumatized. New York: Brunner/Mazel.

The Hearth (2001) Through the Trafficking in Women: Realized by the Psychosocial-Social Center (July–August). Vlora, Albania: The Hearth.

Hope, Kerin (2000) 'Europe: Trafficking in Women Plan', Financial Times (London) (3 July): 8.

Kule, Dhori, Ahmet Mancellari, Harry Papapanagos, Stefan Qirici and Peter Sanfey (2002) 'The Causes and Consequences of Albanian Emigration During Transition: Evidence from Micro Data', International Migration Review 36(1) (Spring): 229–40.

LaCava, G. and R. Nanetti, eds (2000) 'Albania: Filling the Vulnerability Gap'. World Bank Technical Paper No. 460, Europe and Central Asia Environmentally Sustainable Development Series. Washington, DC: World Bank.

Lederer, L. (2001) Human Rights Report on Trafficking of Women and Children. Protection Report. Baltimore, MD: Johns Hopkins University Press.

Miria, S., M. Bello and B. Bodinaku (2000) 'Survey on Violence Against Women and Children in Rural Areas of Lezha District April 2000'. Counseling Center for Abused Women in Tirana.

Olsen, Neil (2000) Albania: An Oxfam country Profile, Part 1, Page 1. London: Oxfam.

Patterson, Ken (2000) 'Women Rescued from Forced Prostitution', Migration World Magazine 28(4) (May): 17.

Post, Susan E. Pritchett (1998) Women in Modern Albania: Firsthand Accounts of Culture and Conditions from over 200 Interviews. Jefferson, NC: McFarland and Co.

Regehr, Cheryl, Susan Caldwell and Karen Jansen (1999) 'Perceptions of Control and Long-term Recovery from Rape', American Journal of Orthopsychiatry 69(1) (January): 110–15.

Ryan, Chris and C. Hall (2001) Sex Tourism: Marginal People and Liminalities. London: Routledge.

Schwandner-Sievers, Stephanie (2000) 'Kinship, Family, and Regional
Differentiation in Albania', in G. LaCava and R. Nanetti (eds) 'Albania:
Filling the Vulnerability Gap', World Bank Technical Paper No. 460,
Europe and Central Asia Environmentally Sustainable Development Series,
pp. 73–8. Washington, DC: World Bank.

Smith, Helen (2002) 'Trade in Sex Rocks Greece', Sunday Herald (10 February):
41.

Sydney Morning Herald (2001) 'A Living Hell: Europe's Sex Trade Network' (4
June): 13.

United Nations Development Programme (UNDP) (2000) Albanian Human
Development Report. New York: UNDP.

US Government (2001) Albania. Country Reports on Human Rights 2000.
Washington, DC: Government Printer.

US Senate Subcommittee on Near Eastern and South Asian Affairs, Committee
on Foreign Relations (2000) International Trafficking in Women and
Children. 22 February. Washington, DC: Government Printer.

US State Department (2005) 'Trafficking in Persons Report'. Released by the
Office to Monitor and Combat Trafficking in Persons. Available online at:
http://www.state/gov/g/tip/rls/tiprpt/2005/46606.htm

Van Hook, M., E. Haxhiymeri and E. Gjermeni (2000) 'Responding to Gender
Violence in Albania', International Social Work 43(3): 351–63.

Van Soest, D. (1997) The Global Crisis of Violence: Common Problems,
Universal Causes, Shared Solutions. Washington, DC: NASW Press.

Vickers, Miranda and James Pettifer (1997) Albania: From Anarchy to Balkan
Identity. New York: New York University Press;

Watts, Charlotte and Cathy Zimmerman (2002) 'Violence Against Women:
Global Scope and Magnitude', Lancet 359: 1232–7.

White, Geoffrey (1998) 'Trauma Treatment Training for Bosnian and Croatian
Mental Health Workers', American Journal of Orthopsychiatry 68(1)
(January): 58–62.

Women's Center (2000) Annual Report. Tirana.

Wood, Nicholas (2000) 'Kosovan Sex Slave Ring Is Smashed', Guardian (18
November): 21.

Note: Reprinted with permission of SAGE.

8

THE "NATASHA" TRADE: THE TRANSNATIONAL SHADOW MARKET OF TRAFFICKING IN WOMEN

Donna M. Hughes, *University of Rhode Island*

> *"Can people really buy and sell women and get away with it? Sometimes I sit here and ask myself if that really happened to me, if it can really happen at all."*
> – A Ukrainian woman who was trafficked, beaten, raped and used in the sex industry in Israel. After a police raid, she was put in prison, awaiting deportation.[1]

Introduction

Trafficking in women for the purpose of sexual exploitation is a multibillion dollar shadow market.[2] Women are trafficked to, from, and through every region in the world using methods that have become new forms of slavery.[3] The value of the global trade in women as commodities for sex industries is estimated to be between seven and twelve billion dollars annually.[4] This trade in women is a highly profitable enterprise with relatively low risk compared to trades in drugs or arms. The moneymakers are transnational networks of traffickers and pimps that prey on the dreams of women seeking employment and opportunities for the future. The activities of these networks threaten the well being and status of women as well as the social, political and economic well being and stability of nations where they operate.

The transnational trade in women is based on supply and demand from sending and receiving countries. Countries with large sex indus-

---

[1] Michael Specter, "Traffickers' New Cargo: Naïve Slavic Women," *New York Times*, 11 January 1998.

[2] Trafficking for purposes of sexual exploitation often includes girls under the age of consent. The percentage of victims of trafficking who are under age is not known, although raids on brothels frequently find girls as well as women. In this paper, I talk about trafficking in women, but it is assumed that many of the victims are under age girls.

[3] Donna M. Hughes, Laura Joy Sporcic and Nadine Mendelsohn, *Factbook on Global Sexual Exploitation* (Kingston, Rhode Island: The Coalition Against Trafficking in Women, 1999), http://www.uri.edu/artsci/wms/hughes/catw/factbook.htm; Dorchen Leidholdt, "Prostitution: A Contemporary Form of Slavery," Presentation at United Nations Working Group on Contemporary Forms of Slavery, Geneva, Switzerland, May 1998, http://www.uri.edu/artsci/wms/hughes/catw/slavery.htm

[4] "UN official warns of rise of new slaves of prostitutes," *Xinhua*, 21 September 1999.

tries create the demand and are the receiving countries, while countries where traffickers easily recruit women are the sending countries. For decades the primary sending countries were Asian countries, such as Thailand and the Philippines. The collapse of the Soviet Union opened up a pool of millions of women from whom traffickers can recruit. Now, former Soviet republics, such as Ukraine, Belarus, Latvia and Russia, have become major sending countries for women trafficked into sex industries all over the world. In the sex industry markets today, the most popular and valuable women are from Ukraine and Russia.[5]

This paper focuses primarily on the sending country of Ukraine, now the second largest country in Europe, and currently, one of the largest suppliers of women for prostitution. Although a comprehensive understanding of trafficking from the former Soviet republics is lacking, more research on trafficking in women and advocacy for trafficked women has been done by nongovernmental organizations in Ukraine than the other primary sending countries from that region.

At the beginning of the paper the scope of the problem of trafficking is discussed and the definition of the term trafficking is reviewed. Next, the international shadow market for women is located in the globalization process and characterized as a modern day slave trade. The role of transnational crime networks in the trafficking of women is examined with a few illustrative cases. A section on the methods of recruitment and trafficking describes how women are recruited from their hometowns and transported to sex industries in other countries. Although there are a number of ways that women are trafficked, their ultimate circumstance is entrapment in prostitution. How women are controlled and why it is so difficult for them to escape is described. The next section focuses on who is profiting from this slave trade and how official corruption and collaboration with organized crime networks facilitates and protects the traffickers. Some people suggest that prostitution and trafficking are shadow economies that enable unemployed women to earn a living. The idea that women and communities may benefit from the shadow market of trafficking in women is examined. This section describes who profits from trafficking in women. Although the problem of trafficking in women in gaining more attention, when the causes of trafficking are examined, the gendered dimension of the supply and, especially, the demand are frequently left out of the analysis. The section on the gendered supply and demand challenges a frequent assumption that poverty is the most important factor in determining which countries will become sending countries. The last section takes a closer look at the demand side of the dynamics of supply and demand from sending and receiving countries. The legalization of prostitution and brothels is examined and old and new legal remedies that address the demand are discussed.

---

[5] Specter, *New York Times.*

Numbers of Trafficked Women

It is difficult to know how many women have been trafficked for the purpose of sexual exploitation.[6] The trade is secretive, the women are silenced, the traffickers are dangerous, and not many agencies are counting. In examining trafficking from countries of the former Soviet Union, they are referred to as "Russian" or "Eastern European" without further information on the specific country. Also, the word "trafficking" does not have a universal usage, resulting in different numbers of women being counted depending on the definition used. In writing and analyzing trafficking in women, I use a definition of trafficking that I think includes the essential elements to be considered in trafficking of women for the purpose of sexual exploitation.[7]

> Trafficking is any practice that involves moving people within and across local or national borders for the purpose of sexual exploitation. Trafficking may be the result of force, coercion, manipulation, deception, abuse of authority, initial consent, family pressure, past and present family and community violence, economic deprivation, or other conditions of inequality for women and children.[8]

This definition recognizes that trafficking of women for the purpose of sexual exploitation occurs within the borders of a country as well as across international borders, as women are sometimes recruited and exploited in local sex industries before they are trafficked transnationally. This definition accepts that trafficking occurs even if the woman consents, which is consistent with the 1949 United Nations Convention for the Suppression of Traffic in Persons and of the Exploitation of the Prostitution of Others.[9] Narrower definitions of trafficking require acts of violence or coercion against the victim before trafficking is said to occur. According to estimates from the United Nations, one quarter of the four million people trafficked each year are exploited in sex industries. In the last decade, hundreds of thousands of

---

[6] Sexual exploitation is a practice by which a person achieves sexual gratification, financial gain or advancement through the abuse or exploitation of a person's sexuality by abrogating that person's human right to dignity, equality, autonomy, and physical and mental well-being; i.e. trafficking, prostitution, prostitution tourism, mail-order-bride trade, pornography, stripping, battering, incest, rape and sexual harassment.

[7] Human trafficking occurs for purposes other than sexual exploitation, such as for labor in sweat shops and as domestic servants and agricultural workers and children for adoption, but this paper will focus on trafficking of women and girls for the sex industry.

[8] This definition of trafficking was modified slightly from that put forth by the international non-governmental organization, the Coalition Against Trafficking in Women.

[9] The text and signatories of the 1949 Convention can be viewed at http://www.uri.edu/dignity/49conven.htm

women have been trafficked from Central and Eastern Europe and the republics of the former Soviet Union into prostitution throughout the world. In the European Union, there are an estimated half a million Central and Eastern European women in prostitution.[10] A criminal investigation in Germany in 1998 found that 87.5 percent of the women trafficked into Germany were from Eastern Europe. Seventeen percent were from Poland, 14 percent from Ukraine, 12 percent from Czech Republic and 8 percent from the Russian Federation.[11]

In 1998, the Ukrainian Ministry of Interior estimated that 400,000 Ukrainian women were trafficked during the previous decade; other sources, such as nongovernmental organizations, thought the number was higher.[12] The International Organization for Migration estimated that between 1991 and 1998, 500,000 Ukrainian women had been trafficked to the West.[13] Popular destination countries for women from Ukraine include: Turkey, Greece, Cyprus, Italy, Spain, Yugoslavia, Bosnia and Herzegovina, Hungary, Czech Republic, Croatia, Germany, United Arab Emirates, Syria, China, the Netherlands, Canada and Japan.[14] According to a Ukrainian diplomatic source there are 6,000 Ukrainian women in prostitution in Turkey, 3,000 in Greece, and 1000 in Yugoslavia.[15] Ukrainian women are the largest group of foreign women in prostitution in Turkey[16] and the second largest group of foreign women in prostitution outside the U.S. military bases in Korea.[17]

Similarly, as a result of trafficking, Russian women are in prostitution in over 50 countries.[18] In some parts of the world, such as Israel and Turkey, women from Russia and other republics of the former Soviet Union are so prevalent, that prostitutes are called "Natashas."[19]

---

[10] Roland-Pierre Paringaux, "Prostitution take a turn for the West," *Le Monde*, 24 May 1998.

[11] "Most of foreign prostitutes in Germany come from Eastern Europe," *Itar-Tass*, 15 November 1999.

[12] International Organization for Migration, *Information Campaign Against Trafficking in Women from Ukraine-Research Report* (Geneva, Switzerland: International Organization for Migration, July 1998).

[13] Chris Bird, "100,000 Ukrainians slaves of West's sex industry," *Reuters*, 6 July 1998.

[14] Kateryna Levchenko, *Combat of Trafficking in Women and Forced Prostitution: Ukraine, Country Report* (Vienna: Ludwig Boltzmann Institute of Human Rights, September 1999).

[15] "Ukraine cracks down on sexual slavery," *Newsline* Vol. 2, No. 71. Part II (Prague, Czech Republic: Radio Free Europe/Radio Liberty, 14 April 1998).

[16] "Ukraine film warns of forcible prostitution abroad," *Russia Today*, 1 July 1998.

[17] Personal communication from Jean Enriquez, Coalition Against Trafficking in Women-Asia Pacific, Manilla, the Philippines, 17 November 1999.

[18] MiraMed Institute, "Who is trafficking CIS women?" *Preliminary Survey Report on Sexual Trafficking in the CIS*. Moscow: MiraMed Institute, June 1999).

[19] Martina Vandenberg, "The Invisible Woman," *Moscow Times*, 8 October 1997, p. 8.

A Modern Day Slave Trade: The International Shadow Market for Women

The growth of shadow economies and transnational criminal networks in newly independent states are negative manifestations of globalization, arising from expanding economic, political and social transnational linkages that are increasingly beyond local and state control. An important component of globalization is the transnational linkages created by migration. Members of organized crime rings establish contacts with willing collaborators in diaspora communities throughout the world and work within migrating populations to build transnational criminal networks. Increased migration also serves as a cover for traffickers in transporting women to destinations in the sex industry.

Privatization and liberalization of markets have created wider and more open marketplaces throughout the world. Another important component of globalization, computer communication technologies have enabled the increased volume and complexity of international financial transactions, which increases opportunities for transnational crime and decreases the probability of detection and apprehension. This technological aspect of globalization enables the money gained through illegal activities, like trafficking in women, to be transferred and laundered.

In the former Soviet Union, the shadow economy began long before the collapse of the communism. The state economy didn't supply the general population with the goods and services they needed or wanted. For decades, a shadow economy operated to meet those demands. There is even evidence that shortages were planned, so as to benefit those controlling and profiting from the shadow economy.[20]

When the political and economic system weakened and collapsed, existing organizations leaped to fill the vacuum. Following the end of a government run economy, privatization enabled previously illegal markets of the shadow economy to operate legally and expand, but they retained the same methods of doing business based on corruption and protection schemes. As independent states emerged from the former Soviet Union they lacked organized and efficient regulatory agencies to hinder the growth and activities of crime networks. When the state system was no longer able to pay the salaries of many employees, they joined the criminal networks.[21] In Ukraine, people who were no longer able to support themselves with one salary or weren't being paid for long periods of time, sought additional work. The only jobs available were in

---

[20] William H. Webster, *Russian Organized Crime-Global Organized Crime Project* (Washington D.C.: Center for Strategic and International Studies, 1997), pp. 26-32.

[21] Todd S. Fogelsong and Peter H. Solomon, Crime, *Criminal Justice and Criminology in Post-Soviet Ukraine - A Report* (Washington, D.C.: National Institute of Justice, August 30, 1999).

the newly emerging privatized, criminal businesses. By 1995, the shadow economy accounted for 50 percent of the GDP.[22] The result has been a criminalization of the economy in general and expansion of organized criminal networks.

Transnational trafficking of women is a new type of crime in the republics of the former Soviet Union. This activity first started in the Soviet Union during perestroika, when restrictions on international travel were eased. The disintegration of the Soviet Union opened borders for travel, migration and privatized trade, all of which facilitated the operations of criminal networks. Sex industries in receiving countries create a demand for women that transnational crime networks from the newly independent states organized to fill with relatively low risk and high profits for the networks. Trafficking exists to meet the demand for women, who are used in brothels, massage parlors, bars and stretches of streets and highways where women are sold to men in prostitution. Ukraine, especially, has become a major source of young women for the international sex markets.[23] Hundreds of victims of trafficking have recounted their experiences to nongovernmental organizations, reporters and police. Although there are individual variations, there are similar themes of manipulation and violence from the traffickers and further persecution by the police.

> Irina, aged 18, responded to an advertisement in a Kyiv, Ukraine newspaper for a training course in Berlin in 1996. With a fake passport, she traveled to Berlin, Germany where she was told that the school had closed. She was sent on to Brussels, Belgium for a job. When she arrived, she was told she needed to repay a debt of US$10,000 and would have to earn the money in prostitution. Her passport was confiscated, and she was threatened, beaten and raped. When she didn't earn enough money, she was sold to a Belgium pimp who operated in Rue d'Aarschot in the Brussel's red light district. When she managed to escape through the assistance of police, she was arrested because she had no legal documentation. A medical exam verified the abuse she had suffered, such as cigarette burns all over her body.[24]
>
> Lena, aged 21, was recruited by a woman who said her daughter was working in Greece and making a lot of money. When Lena arrived in Greece, her passport had been taken away and she was put into a small room in a brothel guarded by two

---

[22] Taras Kuzio, *Ukraine Under Kuchma-Political Reform, Economic Transformation, and Security Policy in Independent* Ukraine (New York: St. Martin's Press, 1997), p. 152.

[23] Bird, *Reuters*

[24] Paringaux, *Le Monde*

dogs. She was sold in prostitution each night from nine in the evening until six in the morning. When she escaped and returned to Mykolayiv she had US$55.00.[25]

Tatyana, aged 20, is from a small town in Lugansk Oblast in Eastern Ukraine. She could not find a job there because the economy is very poor and the factories are closed. A friend of her mother told her that rich families in the United Arab Emirates were hiring housemaids and she could earn US$4000 a month there. However, when she arrived in the United Arab Emirates, her passport was taken away and she was sold to a brothel for US$7,000 and forced into prostitution to repay the purchase and travel costs to the owner. When she managed to escape and went to the police for help, she was arrested and sentenced to three years in prison for working in a brothel.[26]

Transnational crime networks take advantage of patterns of migration to traffic women. An example is the increased migration and trafficking of women from the former Soviet Union to Israel. After 1989, Soviet Jews started immigrating to Israel, resulting in 800,000 new immigrants to Israel. Russian and Ukrainian traffickers used this cover to bring 10,000 women into Israel for the sex industry. The sex industry in Israel has since grown into a US$450 million a year industry, which is dependent on trafficked women from Eastern Europe.[27] Professor Menachem Amir of Hebrew University, an expert on organized crime in Israel, estimates that 70 percent of the women in prostitution in Tel Aviv are from the former Soviet republics.[28] Moreover, according to Israel's report to CEDAW (Convention for the Elimination of All Forms of Discrimination Against Women) Report, more than 95 percent of the women deported from Israel for illegal prostitution are repatriated to the former Soviet Union.[29] From 1995-1997, Israel deported 1500 Russian and Ukrainian women.[30]

In Israel, a Russian or Ukrainian woman earns the pimp who controls her between US$50,000 and $100,000 per year. The women are enslaved and get to keep little, if any, of the money. Often, their only

---

[25] Bird, *Reuters*

[26] Narcisa Escaler, "Statement at the United States-European Union Transatlantic Seminar to Prevent Trafficking in Women," Lviv, Ukraine, 9-10 July 1998.

[27] "Israel prostitution ring targeted," *AP Online*, 23 December 1998.

[28] Israel Women's Network, *Trafficking of Women to Israel and Forced Prostitution* (Jerusalem), November 1997.

[29] Ibid.

[30] Specter, *New York Times*.

way out of the sex industry is a police raid, which results in deportation.[31] Women are held in debt bondage in which they must repay their purchase price, travel expenses and all other expenses charged to them, which can be considerable, before they are allowed to leave. A woman may be sold from one pimp to another at which time her debt to be repaid starts all over again. There are indications that pimps, working in collaboration with officials, tip-off police on the whereabouts of women just about the time the women have earned enough money to leave, resulting in the women being arrested and deported and the pimps keeping all the money.[32] A number of trafficking rings have been uncovered which reveal the tactics, financial rewards and transnational reach of traffickers.

In March 1999 in Sevastopol, Crimea, Ukraine, two men and a woman, using the firm "Sight" as a cover, were arrested for selling 200 Ukrainian women and girls, aged 13 to 25, for the sex industry in Turkey, Greece and Cyprus. The traffickers were intercepted as they attempted to send more women to Turkey by ship. The traffickers received US$2000 for each woman. The women were held in debt bondage until they repaid their expenses. If they complained, their debt was tripled.[33]

In Poland, where approximately 70 percent of the Ukrainian women are working under duress in the sex industry, a prostitution ring, called Agencija Tovazhyshka, controls three to ten women. Guards travel with the women and watch them at all times. The women are sold from one agency to another for DM2,000 to 5,000 and each time the woman incurs the debt that must be repaid.[34]

In August 1999 police arrested three people in Chernihiv Oblast, Ukraine for trafficking women to Hungary. They had previously sold 16 women to Italian and Spanish brothels for US$800 each.[35]

---

[31] "A modern form of slavery," *Jerusalem Post*, 13 January 1998.

[32] Israel Women's Network, "Trafficking in women to Israel and forced prostitution," *Refuge* 17 (November1998): 26-32.

[33] "Ukrainian police arrest sex trade gang," *Newsline* Vol. 3, No. 54, Part II (Prague, Czech Republic: Radio Free Europe/Radio Liberty, 18 March 1999). Regional Security Office, U.S. Embassy, Kyiv, Ukraine, *Crime Digest*, March 1999, http://www.usemb.kiev.ua/rso/CrimeDigest9903.html

[34] Regional Security Office, U.S. Embassy, Kyiv, Ukraine, *Crime Digest*, January 1999, http://www.usemb.kiev.ua/rso/CrimeDigest9901.html

[35] Regional Security Office, U.S. Embassy, Kyiv, Ukraine. *Crime Digest*, August 1999, http://www.usemb.kiev.ua/rso/CrimeDigest9908.html.

In September 1999, a woman psychology teacher from Cherkasy, Ukraine was charged with being head of an international trafficking ring that sold young Ukrainian women into the sex industry in the United Arab Emirates. Along with criminals from Kazakhstan, Syria and the United Arab Emirates, the gang promised 30 young women jobs as dancers, waitresses or domestic servants, then sold them to buyers in the sex industry.[36]

Methods of Recruitment and Trafficking

Sex industries use up women, physically and emotionally, necessitating fresh supplies of women on a regular basis, which keeps the recruitment and trafficking of women so profitable. Recruiters, traffickers and pimps who engage in trafficking in women for the purpose of sexual exploitation have developed common methods of operation. One method of recruitment is advertisements in newspapers offering lucrative job opportunities in foreign countries for low skilled jobs, such as waitresses and nannies. Some advertisements promise good salaries to young, attractive women who will work as dancers and hostesses. An inspection of newspapers in Ukraine showed that each contained five to 20 suspicious advertisements.[37] Women are recruited through social events and auditions, such as photo sessions. The process is usually complex, with detailed deception calculated to reassure the women that the employment opportunity is genuine.[38] It is estimated that 20 percent of trafficked women are recruited through media advertisements.

Another method of recruitment is "marriage agencies," sometimes called mail-order-bride agencies or international introduction services. According to the International Organization for Migration, all mail-order-bride agencies with women from the republics of the former Soviet Union are under the control of organized crime networks.[39] Many of these agencies operate on the Internet.[40] Recruiters use "marriage agencies" as a way to contact women who are eager to travel or emigrate. This route into the sex industry can take several forms. The recruiters may be traffickers or work directly with traffickers. The woman may meet with a man who promises marriage at a later date. The man may

---

[36] "Ukrainian teacher held over sex ring allegations," *Reuters*, 24 September 1999.

[37] Levchenko, *Combat of Trafficking*

[38] MiraMed Institute, *Preliminary Survey Report*

[39] International Organization for Migration.

[40] Donna M. Hughes, "Sex tours via the Internet." *Agenda: A Journal about Women and Gender* 28 (1996): 71-76.

use the woman himself for a short period of time, then coerce her into making pornography and later sell her to the sex industry, or he may directly deliver the woman to a brothel.

Some traffickers use the woman's legal documents and tourist visas to legally enter the destination countries. The women may be put on a circuit by pimps in which they are moved from country to country on legal tourist visas or entertainers' visas. Other times, the woman is given false documents. In this case, the woman is even more vulnerable after she arrives in the destination country because she is there illegally. If police discover her, she is arrested and deported.

The most common way women are recruited in Ukraine is through a friend or acquaintance, who gains the woman's confidence. An increasing phenomenon is called "the second wave," in which trafficked women return home to recruit other women. Once a woman has been trafficked and trapped in the sex industry, she has few options. Escape may be difficult. Since women get to keep little of the money they earn, they often have little to show for their experiences abroad. Also, because of the stigma attached to women in prostitution, they often face discrimination at home. One of the few means of escaping the brutality of being forced to have unwanted sex each day with multiple men is to move from victim to perpetrator. To do this, women who have been trafficked return home to recruit new victims.[41] According to one report, for instance, in Ukraine, 70 percent of pimps are women.[42] A recruiter gets from US$200 to $5,000 for each woman recruited.[43]

Sometimes women are recruited in groups. In one case, women from Lviv, Ukraine were offered housekeeping jobs in the Czech Republic. The traffickers took their passports when they crossed the border. Upon their arrival in the Czech Republic, they were sold for US$300-$700 each to a pimp who forced them into prostitution on the Czech-German highway.[44]

Entrapment of Women in Prostitution

Whatever the recruitment method, the majority of women do not expect the sexual exploitation and violence that awaits them. Aleksandr Strokanov from Interpol-Ukraine estimated that 75 percent of the

---

[41] Ibid.

[42] "Ukrainian women - victims of sex industry," *Itar-Tass*, 30 June 1998.

[43] Lily Hyde and Marina Denisenko, "Modern-day slavery traps local women," Kyiv Post, 9 October 1997.

[44] Lily Hyde and Marina Denisenko, "Modern-day slavery traps local women," *Kyiv Post*, 9 October 1997.

women do not realize they will be forced into prostitution.[45] After the woman has reached the destination country, the trafficker or pimp will tell her that she is not going to work as a waitress, nanny, or whatever more agreeable opportunity was offered, but will be in prostitution. The methods used to control women once they reach the destination country include: confiscation of travel documents, violence, threats to harm family members and debt bondage.

Even when women know they will be in prostitution, their expectations are usually far from the reality. One woman, who knew she would have to engage in prostitution, thought it would be like in the film "Pretty Woman," where one man would support her.[46] The women don't realize the lack of control they will have, the level of the violence used against them, and what small percentage of the money they will receive. In one case, a friend introduced a Ukrainian woman to a pimp, who told her she could make US$2000 a month in a club in the Netherlands where prostitution was optional, but not required. When she arrived in the Netherlands, she was told that prostitution was a requirement and no man could be refused. When she protested, she was raped. She was forced to engage in prostitution seven days a week for three months before she paid off the debt. She feared trying to escape because the pimp knew where to find her at home in Ukraine. When she left she only got 50 percent of what she had been told she had earned.[47]

Even women who voluntarily travel to engage in prostitution do not anticipate the level of manipulation, deception and coercion to which they will be subjected. According to Narcisa Escaler, Deputy Director General of the International Organization for Migration:

> "...the question of the voluntariness of the movement of trafficked migrants merits particular attention. For many migrants who are eager to escape poverty to escape or political or social insecurity, and who are unaware or unmindful of the pitfalls of irregular migration...But, in many instances, trafficked migrants are lured by false promises, misled by misinformation concerning migration regulations, or driven by economic despair or large scale violence. In such cases, the migrant's freedom of choice is so seriously impaired that the "voluntariness" of the transaction must be questioned."[48]

---

[45] Ibid.

[46] Ibid.

[47] Ibid.

[48] Escaler, Statement

The networks that traffic women are modern day slave traders. There are even aspects of trafficking in women—such as auctions—that are reminiscent of the 18th and 19th century African slave trade. In Milan, Italy in December 1997, police uncovered a gang that was holding auctions of trafficked women from the former Soviet Union. The women were stripped partially naked, displayed and sold for an average price of US$1000.[49] Traffickers and pimps use extreme violence to control their women and territory. In Italy, police report that one woman in prostitution is murdered each month.[50] Women are mutilated and murdered as warnings to competing traffickers and pimps and as punishment for refusing to engage in prostitution. In two reported cases, women who resisted were killed as an example to other women. In Istanbul, Turkey, two Ukrainian women were thrown off a balcony and killed, while six of their Russian friends watched. In Serbia, a Ukrainian woman who resisted was beheaded in public.[51]

Levels of violence and discrimination against women trafficked into prostitution are extreme. Trafficked women get little sympathy or assistance once they are under the control of traffickers and pimps, either from the general public or social service agencies. In receiving countries, they are treated as criminals, either as prostitutes or illegal immigrants. When they are discovered, often in police raids, they are arrested or jailed pending deportation. Almost no services exist that address the needs of victims of trafficking who are suffering from trauma, poor health, and physical injuries.

Assistance to victims is hampered by the lack of recognition of the harm to trafficked and prostituted women.[52] Studies on the health of women in the sex industry indicate that many women have serious health problems and are exposed to life-threatening risks. Women suffer from infectious diseases, sexually transmitted diseases, injuries from violence, drug and alcohol addictions, depression and other mental health problems as a result of trauma.[53]

---

[49] Specter, *New York Times.*

[50] Ibid.

[51] Ibid.

[52] Norma Hotaling, "Making the harm visible," in *Making the Harm Visible-Global Sexual Exploitation of Women and Girls, Speaking Out and Providing Services,* eds. Donna M. Hughes and Claire M. Roche (Kingston, Rhode Island: Coalition Against Trafficking in Women, 1999): 227-232. Melissa Farley and Howard Barkan, "Prostitution, violence against women and posttraumatic stress disorder," *Women and Health,* 27 (1998): 37-49. Melissa Farley, Isin Baral, Merab Kiremire and Ufuz Sezgin, "Prostitution in five countries: Violence and posttraumatic stress disorder," *Feminism and Psychology,* 8 (1998): 405-426.

[53] Ruth Parriott, *Health Experiences of Twin Cities Women Used in Prostitution: Survey Findings and Recommendations,* May 1994.

Many people view the women as complicit in the trafficking, as immoral or as workers—a wide span of perspectives, all of which ignore the harm to the victims. An investigation on trafficking and prostitution in the Czech Republic found that people had little sympathy for victims of trafficking and assumed they were getting rich.

> "It is typical for the Czech post-communist society that it is totally indifferent to the destiny of these victims. Our investiga-tion...confirms that the brothels operating in small towns and villages in the frontier zones are considered as a 'tax for capitalism' by local inhabitants. Practically nobody is interested in the living conditions of most Ukrainian, Russian and Bulgarian women. This commonplace [sic] is nourished even by the media which present prostitution mostly as a highly 'profitable profession.'...NGOs which deal with the problems of trafficking in women and their slavery status are considered 'too feministic.'"[54]

Societies and institutions still hold patriarchal attitudes toward women in prostitution, which blame the victims for crimes committed against them. Officials often minimize or deny the severity of the problem, the violence and coercion used in trafficking and the harm to victims. According to Gennadi Lepenko, Chief of Interpol-Kyiv, Ukraine, "Women's groups want to blow this all out of proportion. Perhaps this was a problem a few years ago. But it's under control now."[55] Advocates for trafficked women report that officials' acceptance of prostitution and trafficking exacerbate the problem. According to Kateryna Levchenko, Coordinator of La Strada-Ukraine, "Complacency on the part of government and law enforcement officials is as much to blame as financial difficulties. Our government bodies cannot understand that it is very, very important for women."[56] Some government officials may be collaborators in trafficking networks. Investigations by the Global Survival Network documented the involvement of government officials in the trafficking of women from Russia.[57] Of course, male officials themselves may be buyers of women in prostitution, resulting in lack of empathy for victims of trafficking and prostitution.

---

[54] Stanislava Hybnerová and Harald Scheu, *Combat of Trafficking in Women and Forced Prostitution-Czech Republic Country Report* (Vienna, Austria: Ludwig Boltzmann Institute of Human Rights, September 1999), p.8.

[55] Specter, *New York Times*.

[56] Lily Hyde, "Women's groups battle sex slavery," *Kyiv Post*, 23 January 1998.

[57] Global Survival Network, *Crime and Servitude* (Washington, D.C.: Global Survival Network, 1998).

Profit and Corruption

Once a woman is under the control of a trafficker or pimp, she can be exploited to make a large profit. Pimps can make five to 20 times as much from a woman as they paid for her.[58] Research by the International Organization for Migration indicates that trafficked women receive little of the money, but the profits for traffickers are enormous. In a case study of women trafficked into Germany, they found that each time a man buys a woman in prostitution, he pays DM30-50, but the woman gets to keep almost nothing. First, the trafficker or recruiter requires payment of US$3,000 - $30,000 for her travel expenses and her purchase price. Then she must pay for her room and board in the brothel, which can be as much as DM280 a day, the pimp's fees, compulsory lawyer's fees, doctor's fees, and sometimes, private living expenses. In the end, the woman often is in debt.[59] Even after a woman has paid off her debt, she must turn over 50 to 75 percent of her earnings to pimps.[60] In numerous documented cases of trafficking, the pimps earn large profits, while the woman receives a small portion of the proceeds.

> A Ukrainian woman in a massage parlor owned by a Russian in Silver Spring, Maryland, USA was allowed to keep only 30 percent of the US$70 price for a massage. If she wanted more money, she had to perform sexual services for tips.[61]
>
> During a three-month stay in Germany on a tourist visa, a woman will make $20,000 for a pimp, according to German police. An Eastern European woman will earn more than that for a pimp or trafficker in Japan, where Eastern European women are considered exotic.[62]
>
> Oksana Ryniekska, a Ukrainian doctor, operated a brothel with non-English speaking women from Eastern Europe in Essex, UK for eight months before she was arrested. During that time she made more than GBP130,000 (US$210,000).[63]

Mikhail Lebed, Chief of Criminal Investigations for the Ukrainian Ministry of the Interior said, "It is a human tragedy, but also, frankly, a national crisis. Gangsters make more from these women in a week

---

[58] Levchenko, *Combat of Trafficking.*

[59] International Organization for Migration, *Information Campaign.*

[60] Levchenko, *Combat of Trafficking.*

[61] Hyde and Denisenko, *Kyiv Post.*

[62] Paringaux, *Le Monde.*

[63] "Doctor who ran brothel is jailed," *The Herald* (UK), 4 October 1999.

than we have in our law-enforcement budget for the whole year."[64] The money made from the sexual exploitation and often enslavement of trafficked women enriches transnational criminal networks. Trafficking in women has arguably the highest profit margin and lowest risk of almost any type of illegal activity. According to Michael Platzer, United Nations Center for International Crime Prevention, "There's a lot of talk about drugs, but it's the white slave trade that earns the biggest money for criminal groups in Eastern Europe."[65]

Corruption of officials through bribes and even collaboration of officials in criminal networks enables traffickers to operate in communities and states. Officials in key positions and at many levels use their authority to provide protection to criminal activities. During a two-year investigation of trafficking in women from Russia, the Global Survival Network found evidence of government collaboration in the Interior Ministry, the Federal Security Service and the Ministry of Foreign Affairs.[66] As the influence of criminal networks deepens, the corruption goes beyond an act of occasionally ignoring illegal activity to providing protection by blocking legislation that would hinder the activities of the groups. As law enforcement personnel and government officials become more corrupt and members of the crime groups gain more influence, the line between the state and the criminal networks starts to blur. This merging of criminal networks and the government seems to have occurred in many of the states that have emerged from the Soviet Union.[67] Under these circumstances it is difficult to intervene in the succession of corruption, collaboration, crime and profit.

Kateryna Levchenko from La Strada-Ukraine made the following comment about the criminal networks' interests in creating and maintaining an environment favorable to trafficking in women:

> "...the main part of income from this criminal business is obtained by foreign criminal organizations that are the ones interested in preservation of the current situation. They do not want any improvements in the status of Ukrainian women or in Ukrainian economy as a whole. The scale of this illegal business, huge monthly and annual turnovers, merging with certain power structures (first of all, the police) in the countries of

---

[64] Hyde, *Kyiv Post*, 23 January 1998.

[65] Paringaux, *Le Monde*.

[66] Vladimir Isachenkov, "Soviet women slavery flourishes," *AP Online*, 6 November 1997.

[67] Brunon Holyst, "Organized crime in Eastern Europe and its implications for the security of the Western world," in *Organized Crime-Uncertainties and Dilemmas*, eds. Stanley Einstein and Menachem Amir (Chicago, Illinois: The Office of International Criminal Justice, 1999): 67-93.

Central and Eastern Europe, make it a real national security issue."[68]

The cooperation of criminals and corrupt government officials in the trafficking in women ensures that traffickers can operate with little or no interference, leaving women vulnerable to whatever treatment and exploitation is profitable for traffickers and the sex industry.

Impact on Communities

Trafficking in women as a shadow economy does not bring financial prosperity to local communities. The women often end up with nothing, or any money they earn comes at great cost to their health, emotional well being and standing in the community. The money made by the criminal networks does not stay in poor communities or countries, but is laundered through bank accounts of criminal bosses in financial centers, such United States, Western European countries or in offshore accounts.[69] Transnational money laundering schemes often include proceeds from trafficking in women.

In Israel, for instance, organized crime groups from the former Soviet Union, collectively referred to as "Russian" organized crime groups, have invested profits from trafficking in women, along with other activities, into legitimate businesses. Israel is considered a "safe haven" for illegal profits because money laundering there is fairly easy. In 1995, it was reported that between 2.5 and 4 billion dollars had been invested in banks and 600 million in real estate.[70]

Moreover, trafficking in women has been found to be part of broader transnational criminal schemes. In August 1999, a money-laundering scheme was uncovered in the Bank of New York, USA. From early 1998 until mid-1999, US$10 billion dollars had been laundered through the bank. The account belonged to known Ukrainian-born crime boss Semion Mogilevich, who the FBI and Israeli intelligence reported was involved in prostitution, weapons and drug trafficking and investment scams. According to one source, Mogilevich headed a large prostitution ring that operated in the Black and White Nightclubs in Prague, Poland and Budapest, Hungary.[71] Mogilevich's crime network, called the Red Mafia,

---

[68] Levchenko, *Combat of Trafficking.*

[69] Ernesto U Savona, "The organizational framework of European crime in the globalization process" (Tokyo, Japan: 108th International Seminar on Current Problems in the Combat of Organized Crime, 27 February 1998). Accessed at http://www.jus.unitn.it/transcrime/papers/wp20.html

[70] Menachem Amir, "Organized crime in Israel," in *Organized Crime-Uncertainties and Dilemmas*, eds. Stanley Einstein and Manachem Amir (Chicago, Illinois: Office of International Criminal Justice, 1999): 231-248.

[71] "Les nouvelles mafias d'Europe de l'Est," *Marianne en ligne*, 5 December 1997. Accessed at http://www.marianne-en-ligne.fr/12-05-97/dessus-b.htm

operated in Ukraine, Hungary, the Czech Republic and the United States.[72]

Cases such as these demonstrate that most of the money made from illegal operations, such as trafficking in women, does not make its way back to the community. The money goes to the top where crime bosses make enormous profits. The "dirty money" is laundered into clean money after which it can be used to buy legitimate businesses and properties.

Gendered Supply and Demand

Trafficking and prostitution are highly gendered systems that result from structural inequality between women and men on a world scale.[73] Men create the demand and women are the supply.[74] In this gendered system of supply and demand, little or no attention is paid to the legitimacy of the demand. The ultimate consumers of trafficked and prostituted women are men who use them for entertainment, sexual gratification, and acts of violence. Victims and advocacy groups for survivors of prostitution compare the dynamics of prostitution to battering and sexual assault. Survivors often recount their experiences spent in sex industries as being abusive, degrading, and harmful to their health and well being.[75]

The most crucial factor in determining where trafficking will occur is the activity of traffickers. Poverty, unemployment, inflation, war and lack of a promising future are compelling factors that facilitate the ease with which traffickers recruit women, but they are not the cause of trafficking. Many regions of the world are poor and chaotic, but not every region becomes a major supplier of women trafficked into the sex industry. Traffickers take advantage of poverty, unemployment and a desire to emigrate to recruit and traffic women into sex industries. Women, in large numbers, do not make their way across borders to enter prostitution, nor do they traffic themselves or organize themselves en masse to travel internationally to enter prostitution. Women do not

---

[72] Jaroslav Koshiw, "A native son and the Bank of New York scandal," *Kyiv Post*, 26 August 1999.

[73] Kathleen Barry, *Female Sexual Slavery* (New York: New York University Press, 1979); Kathleen Barry. *The Prostitution of Sexuality* (New York: New York University Press, 1995).

[74] This dynamic is the case for heterosexual prostitution. Exceptions are gay prostitution, men's sexual abuse of boys, the occasional sexual abuse of children by women and the almost non-existent prostitution of men by women.

[75] Norma Hotaling, "What happens to women in prostitution in the United States," in *Making the Harm Visible-Global Sexual Exploitation of Women and Girls, Speaking Out and Providing Services*, eds. Donna M. Hughes and Claire M. Roche (Kingston, Rhode Island: Coalition Against Trafficking in Women, 1999): 239-251.

voluntarily put themselves in situations where they are exploited, beaten, raped and enslaved. Without recruiters, traffickers and pimps, trafficking in women would not exist. According to Michele Hirsch, a barrister in Brussels in her report to the Council of Europe:

> "Poverty does not automatically and in every case lead to traffic in human beings and in fact only creates the necessary conditions....Trafficking will appear only when criminal elements take advantage of this desire to emigrate to entice people, particularly women, to the West under false pretences."[76]

More than 120 million people in Eastern Europe earn less that US$4 per day.[77] Where old Soviet economic systems have been disrupted or discarded, there has been economic contraction and hyperinflation, which has wiped out people's savings and security. In Ukraine, over 60 percent of the unemployed are women, and of those who have lost their job since 1991, more than 80 percent are women. The average salary in Ukraine is about US$30 a month, but in many small towns, it is only half that.[78]

Women's NGOs report that the economic hard times has lead to a depression of women's psychological state with loss of self-esteem and hope for the future. Women accept unlikely offers of employment in unskilled jobs at high salaries with the resignation that "it cannot be worse" than their present lives.[79] Recruiters for the sex industry target the most economically depressed areas. According to an estimate by a Ukrainian women's NGO, one-third of unemployed young women get involved in illegal sex businesses.[80]

There also tends to be a paucity of information about the problem in sending countries. MiraMed, an anti-trafficking NGO, asserts that there has been a "relative media blackout" on the subject of trafficking in women, which has left women without information about what is happening to women who have gone abroad.[81]

The International Organization for Migration (IOM) conducted a survey of 1,189 women and girls, aged 15 to 35, in ten urban regions of Ukraine. The purpose was to assess women's attitudes and intentions

---

[76] Michele Hirsch, *Plan of Action Against Traffic in Women and Forced Prostitution* (Strasbourg: Council of Europe, 1996).

[77] United Nations Development Program, *Human Development Report, 1997* (New York: Oxford University Press, 1997).

[78] International Organization for Migration, *Information Campaign*, pp. 9-11.

[79] Levchenko, *Combat of Trafficking*.

[80] Ibid.

[81] MiraMed Institute, *Preliminary Survey Report*.

toward migration. The IOM concluded that 40 percent of the women in Ukraine are at risk of becoming victims of trafficking mainly due to their interest in emigrating or seeking employment abroad. Although many young women are eager to travel to seek jobs, prostitution was viewed as absolutely unacceptable. When asked if "a job in the sex industry" was an "acceptable job abroad," none of the women and girls in any age group (Ages 15-17, 18-19, 20-24, 25-15) said yes. When asked if being a "dancer" or "stripper" was an "acceptable job abroad," however, all of the girls aged 15-17 indicated that it was, while none of the older women said yes.[82]

These findings indicate that when accurate naming of activities, such as "job in the sex industry" occurs, rather than the use of euphemisms, such as "hostess" or "entertainer," women are not interested in these "jobs."

Legal Factors and the Demand for Trafficked Women

Although trafficked women can be found almost anywhere, even in quite unexpected places, the destinations for most trafficked women are countries and cities where there are large sex industry centers and where prostitution is legalized or widely tolerated. Trafficking exists to meet the demand for women to be used in the sex industry. Although some women may appear to voluntarily enter prostitution, this number could never meet the demand. If prostitution were a desirable, rewarding, lucrative job, traffickers would not have to deceive, coerce and enslave women to get them into and keep them in the sex industry.

Most approaches to the problem of trafficking have focused on the sending countries. In countries of the former Soviet Union there have been prevention education projects aimed at potential victims of trafficking and nongovernmental organizations have established hotlines for victims of trafficking or women seeking accurate information about the risks of accepting job offers abroad. Less attention has been focused on curtailing the demand created in receiving countries. For example, in Summer 1998, I participated in the Training Program to Combat Trafficking of Women from Ukraine in which twenty Ukrainian representatives from government ministries, law enforcement, social services, media and nongovernmental organizations came to the United States for training on trafficking in women. The site of the conference was New Jersey where hundreds of Ukrainian women have been trafficking into strip clubs and massage parlors. A Special Agent from the United States Department of Justice, Immigration and

---

[82] International Organization for Migration, "Slavic women trafficked into slavery," *Trafficking in Migrants Quarterly Bulletin* (Geneva, Switzerland: International Organization for Migration, June 1998).

Naturalization service told the Ukrainian audience, "This is your problem that you are going to have to solve. Like drugs you have to get at the root of the problem, which is overseas."[83] He located the problem of trafficking of women in the sending country of Ukraine, even though there had been little action against the traffickers and pimps in the receiving country-the United States-or the demand made by the illegal sex industry.

The most popular destinations for trafficked women are countries where prostitution is legal such as the Netherlands and Germany. The Dutch Foundation Against Trafficking in Women (STV) surveyed women in the sex industry in the Netherlands and found they came from 32 countries. In 1994, in the Netherlands, 70 percent of the trafficked women were from Central and Eastern European countries.[84] A survey of women from Central and Eastern Europe found that 80 percent of the women had their passports confiscated, were kept in isolation and forced to work long hours for no pay and were physically and emotionally abused by pimps, traffickers and male buyers.[85]

In the Netherlands, in 1995, more women in prostitution were from Ukraine than any other foreign country and in 1996 they ranked second.[86] According to Dr. Gerben Bruinsma of the University of Leiden, 33 percent of the 25,000 women in prostitution in the Netherlands are from Ukraine, and three percent are from Russia. Most of these women are in conditions of slavery.[87]

In Germany, prostitution is legal for citizens of the European Union, but illegal for non-European Union citizens. Therefore, while it is legal for men to engage in prostitution and for pimps to run brothels, trafficked women are doubly victimized, first by being victims of trafficking and second for being foreign citizens. An estimated one quarter of the 200,000 to 400,000 women in prostitution in Germany are from Eastern Europe.[88] Another source estimates that 80 percent of the

---

[83] Personal notes from "Training Program to Combat Trafficking of Women from Ukraine," July 1998.

[84] International Organization for Migration, *Trafficking and Prostitution: The Growing Exploitation of Migrant Women from Central and Eastern Europe* (Geneva, Switzerland: International Organization for Migration, May 1995), http://www.iom.ch/IOM/ Publica tions/books_studies_surveys/MIP_traff_women_eng.htm

[85] Hyde and Denisenko, *Kyiv Post.*

[86] Ibid.

[87] Louise Shelley, "Human Trafficking: Defining the Problem," *Organized Crime Watch - Russia* Vol. 1, No. 2, February 1999 (Washington, DC: Center for the Study of Transnational Crime and Corruption at American University).

[88] Irena Omelaniuk and Ginette Baerten, "Trafficking in women from Central and Eastern Europe - Focus on Germany," in *Migration in Central and Eastern Europe, 1999 Review.* (Vienna: International Organization for Migration and International Center for Migration Policy Development, March 1999).

trafficked women in Germany are from Central and Eastern Europe and CIS countries. The German Family Ministry reported that 1500 trafficked women were caught by police in 1997. Ninety-five percent were deported.[89]

Legalization of prostitution, pimping and brothels causes an increase in trafficking in women to meet the demand created by a legalized sex industry. There is also evidence from Australia that legalized prostitution and brothels resulted in a "significant rise in organized crime"[90] and an increase in trafficking and enslavement of women.[91]

Legalized prostitution makes it difficult to hold traffickers accountable for their activities. Trijntje Kootstra, from La Strada, said that traffickers evade prosecution by claiming the women knew what they were getting into and that prosecutors generally have a hard time establishing the line between voluntary and forced prostitution.[92] When prostitution is legal, the prosecution's case depends on proving that the woman did not consent. Considering how vulnerable the women are in these slave-like circumstances and that women often do initially consent to traveling or even being in prostitution, it makes the case much more difficult to prove. According to Michael Platzer, Head of Operations for the United Nation's Center for International Crime Prevention, "The laws help the gangsters. Prostitution is semi-legal in many places and that makes enforcement tricky. In most cases' punishment is very light."[93] In the Plan of Action Against Traffic in Women and Forced Prostitution for the Council of Europe, Michele Hirsch stated, "where only forced prostitution is illegal; inability to prove constraint has repeatedly led to international procurers being acquitted by the courts."[94]

The trafficking of women for purposes of sexual exploitation is not a new phenomenon and international laws were drafted and ratified in the earlier half of this century. In 1949, the United Nations General Assembly passed the Convention for the Suppression of Traffic in Persons and of the Exploitation of the Prostitution of Others. The convention states that "prostitution and the accompanying evil of the traffic in persons for the purpose of prostitution are incompatible with the dignity and worth of the human person and endanger the welfare of

---

[89] International Organization for Migration, *Information Campaign*.

[90] Andreas Schloenhardt, *Organized Crime and the Business of Migrant Trafficking-An Economic Analysis* (Canberra: Australian Institute of Criminology, 10 November 1999).

[91] Debra Way, "Number of sex slaves in Australia quadruples," *Australian Associated Press*, 9 December 1999.

[92] Hyde, *Kyiv Post*, 23 January 1998.

[93] Specter, *New York Times*.

[94] Hirsch, *Plan of Action*.

the individual, the family and the community."[95] Ukraine is a signature of the 1949 Convention (1954), along with Latvia (1992), Belarus (1956), and the Russian Federation (1954).[96] The 1949 Convention states that consent of the trafficked person is irrelevant to the prosecution of the exploiter.[97] The 1949 Convention was not widely ratified and did not create a monitoring body, so there has been no ongoing evaluation of its implementation or effectiveness. In 1998 at the United Nations Commission on the Status of Women, the World Federation of the Ukrainian Women's Organizations and World Movement of Mothers called for governments to work toward suppressing the trafficking of women and girls and implementing the 1949 Convention.[98]

Currently, the 1949 Convention is under strong attack by those who favor legalized prostitution and "consensual trafficking." The trend toward legalization of the sex industry and narrower definitions of trafficking which require proof of coercion or force will make the conviction of traffickers very difficult and will greatly benefit transnational criminal networks.

Another approach to ending trafficking is to intervene in the demand for women to be used in prostitution. In 1998, Sweden passed a law on violence against women that created a new offense—"gross violation of a woman's integrity." Prostitution was included as a type of violence against women. As of January 1, 1999, the "purchase of sexual services" was prohibited, punishable by fines and/or imprisonment up to six months. The Swedish government was clear that this new offense marked Sweden's attitude toward prostitution as an "undesirable social phenomenon" and an act of violence against women.[99] The new offense of gross violation of a woman's integrity and the prohibition on purchase of sexual services aims to eliminate acts of violence that stand in the way of equality for women.

---

[95] Convention for the Suppression of the Traffic in Persons and of the Exploitation of the Prostitution of Others, http://www.uri.edu/dignity/49conven.htm

[96] Status of Ratification, Convention for the Suppression of the Traffic in Persons and of the Exploitation of the Prostitution of Others, http://www.un.org/Depts/Treaty/final /ts2/newfiles/past_boo/vii_boo/vii_boo/vii11.html

[97] Ibid.

[98] "Statement submitted by the World Federation of the Ukrainian Women's Organizations and World Movement of Mothers, non-governmental organizations in special consultative status with the Economic and Social Council," Commission on the Status of Women, Forty-second session, 2-13 March 1999. The statement was also signed by Zona International, the National Council on Family Relations, the International Union of Family Organizations, the World Union of Catholic Women's Organizations, the Women's International Democratic Federation, the International Health Awareness Network, the International Federation on Ageing, World Information Transfer, the International Alliance on Women, and the Global Alliance for Women's Health.

[99] Violence Against Women, *Kvinnofrid*, http://www.kvinnofrid.gov.se/regeringen/ faktaeng.htm

Sweden's approach recognizes the harm done to women under conditions of sexual exploitation. Their approach starts from the premise that women have the right to dignity, integrity and equality. This new law is the first that aims to protect women from violence by holding men accountable and thereby addressing the demand for women to be trafficked for prostitution. There are indications that Norway is also considering this approach as a way to combat the trafficking of women for sexual exploitation.[100]

Conclusion

In the Soviet Union, a shadow economy, often controlled by government officials, existed for decades to meet the needs of the people for goods and services. When the Soviet Union collapsed, the shadow economy networks expanded to become transnational criminal networks that increasingly operate beyond the reach of law enforcement in any one state, and more ominously, operate in cooperation with law enforcement and government officials in some states. One of the commodities that is in great demand and Ukraine, and other republics of the Soviet Union, have in great supply, are women who were eager to travel and look for opportunities abroad. The trafficking of women for purposes of sexual exploitation has become a highly profitable shadow market for organized crime networks. The lucrative trade in women garners billions of dollars for criminals, who use the money to enrich themselves and buy influence to further their activities. Although organized crime networks have benefitted, trafficking in women is not a shadow economy that has brought prosperity to local communities. The growth in number and size of organized crime networks has become a threat to the safety of citizens and to legitimate economic, social, and political institutions.

Trafficking in women is a modern day slave trade that is consuming increasing numbers of women, especially from Ukraine and other republics of the former Soviet Union. The existence of recruitment and enslavement of women for purposes of sexual exploitation threatens the status of women throughout the world. There can be no true democracy in any country if half the population can be viewed as potential commodities to be recruited, bought, sold and enslaved.

Most analyses of trafficking in women focus on the supply side in the sending countries, with economic factors assumed to be the primary cause of trafficking. A more complete understanding of trafficking in women is achieved by also examining the demand for trafficked women in sex industries in receiving countries and the essential role played by organized crime networks in committing serious crimes against women. In addition, the gendered nature of the dynamics of the supply and

---

[100] Personal communication with non-governmental organizations in Norway.

demand has to be examined. It cannot be ignored that women are the sole victims in trafficking in women for prostitution and men are the sole players in creating the demand for women in prostitution.

Legalization of prostitution is sometimes thought to be a solution to trafficking in women, but evidence seems to show that legalized sex industries actually result in increased trafficking to meet the demand for women to be used in the legal sex industries. Increased activity of organized crime networks also accompanies increases in trafficking.

Legal remedies that address the demand side of trafficking have been passed at the international level at the United Nations and the national level in Sweden. The older 1949 United Nations Convention for the Suppression of the Traffic in Persons and the Exploitation of the Prostitution of Others has not been widely ratified and lacks a monitoring body, so it has had limited impact against the transnational trafficking of women. The newly defined type of violence against women and crime in Sweden "the purchase of sexual services" has only been in place for one year and its effectiveness is yet to be evaluated.

Trafficking in women for the purpose of sexual exploitation has become such a large and severe crisis for the well being of women and the security and stability of some states that interventions are needed at all levels and points in the trafficking process. This modern slave trade is a shadow market that benefits only criminals.

Acknowledgments

The following people provided thoughtful comments on this paper: Lesley Rimmel, Assistant Professor of History, Oklahoma State University, USA; Dianne Post, Attorney, American Bar Association Central and Eastern European Legal Initiative, Moscow, Russia; John Picarelli, Analyst, Veridian-Pacific Sierra Research; Mary Layne, Associate, Abt Associates, USA; and Victoria Marinelli, community activist.

Biography

Donna M. Hughes holds the Eleanor M. and Oscar M. Carlson Endowed Chair and is the Director of Women's Studies at the University of Rhode Island. She has been involved in community work, education and research on violence against women and sexual exploitation for fifteen years. Currently, she is conducting research on trafficking in women into the United States and is a member of the U.S. National Institute of Justice and Ukrainian Academy of Law Ukrainian-US Research Partnership, where she is researching trafficking in women from Ukraine.

Discussion Questions

1   *What is the estimated dollar value of the global trade in women as commodities for sex industry?*

2   *How was trafficking defined in the article?*

3   *How many women is it estimated were trafficked from the Ukraine and in what countries were they working?*

4   *What were the effects of perestroika on transnational trafficking of women?*

5   *What methods are used in the recruitment of trafficking of women?*

6   *What are examples of the types of health problems and emotional trauma many of the women face once they have been forced into prostitution?*

7   *What type of profits do traffickers and pimps make from prostitution?*

8   *What happens to the money made by the criminal network?*

9   *What are the most crucial factors in determining where trafficking will occur?*

9

LOOSE WOMEN OR LOST WOMEN?
THE RE-EMERGENCE OF THE MYTH OF
WHITE SLAVERY IN CONTEMPORARY
DISCOURSES OF TRAFFICKING IN WOMEN

Jo Doezema, Ph.D.

Introduction

The campaign against "trafficking in women" has gained increasing
momentum worldwide, but in particular among feminists in Europe and
the United States, in the last two decades. This current campaign is not
the first time that the international community has become concerned
with the fate of young women abroad. Modem concerns with prostitution
and "trafficking in women" have historical precedent in the anti white-
slavery campaigns that occurred at the turn of the century. Feminist
organisations played key roles in both past and present campaigns.
While current concerns are focused on the exploitation of third world/
non-western women by both non-western and western men, concerns
then were with the abduction of European women for prostitution in
South America, Africa or "the Orient" by non-western men or other
subalterns. Yet, though the geographical direction of the "traffic" has
seemingly switched, much of the rhetoric accompanying the campaigns
sounds remarkably similar. Then as now, the paradigmatic image is that
of a young and naive innocent lured or deceived by evil traffickers into
a life of sordid horror from which escape is nearly impossible.

The mythical nature of this paradigm of the "white slave" has been
demonstrated by historians. Similarly, recent research indicates that
today's stereotypical "trafficking victim" bears as little resemblance to
women migrating for work in the sex industry as did her historical
counterpart, the "white slave." The majority of "trafficking victims" are
aware that the jobs offered them are in the sex industry, but are lied to
about the conditions they will work under. Yet policies to eradicate
"trafficking" continue to be based on the notion of the "innocent,"
unwilling victim, and often combine efforts designed to protect
"innocent" women with those designed to punish "bad" women: i.e.,
prostitutes.

In this article, I examine how narratives of "white slavery" and
"trafficking in women" function as cultural myths, constructing
particular conceptions of migration for the sex industry. The myths
around "white slavery" were grounded in the perceived need to regulate

female sexuality under the guise of protecting women. They were indicative of deeper fears and uncertainties concerning national identity, women's increasing desire for autonomy, foreigners, immigrants and colonial peoples. To a certain extent, these fears and anxieties are mirrored in contemporary accounts of "trafficking in women." My intent is to lay the two sets of discourses, as it were next to each other, and compare them, to evaluate to what extent "trafficking in women" can be seen as a retelling of the myth of "white slavery" in a modern form.

Until recently, very little examination of the modern anti-trafficking movement from a discourse perspective has been done: that is, a critical examination of the ideology, organisation, and strategies of the anti-trafficking movement.[1] The "white slavery" campaign, in contrast, has been studied by feminist and non-feminist historians alike (Bristow, 1977, 1982; Connelly, 1980; Walkowitz, 1980; Rosen, 1982; Gibson, 1986; Corbin, 1990; Grittner, 1990; Guy, 1991; Irwin, 1996; Fisher, 1997; Haveman 1998).

The sheer volume of material, in the forms of reports, books, academic papers, newspaper articles, videos, Internet sites, and national and international legislation, concerning "trafficking in women" is vast, and attempts to synthesize or analyze it nearly non-existent. This article is not intended to provide a definite conclusion to the analysis of "trafficking in women" as cultural myth, but rather to begin the discussion. I have chosen to focus on a number of key documents, including reports from anti-trafficking and human rights organisations, newspaper reports, and recent national and international policy documents. There is some danger in basing an analysis on a limited amount of material. Nonetheless, I have chosen documents that I believe give a picture of the current debate. My aim is to identify certain general themes common to both "white slavery" and "trafficking" narratives. As a consequence of this method, differences in discourses, for example those produced in different regions, have not been investigated. In the first section, a brief history of the anti-white slavery movement is given, and the core elements of the "white slavery" myth are set out. The re-emergence of these core elements in the "trafficking in women" discourse is examined in section two. In the final section, an analysis of the deeper fears and anxieties about sexuality, the role of women, class, and race underlying the myth is made.

The Cultural Myth of White Slavery

It is difficult to define "white slavery," as the term meant different things to different social actors, depending on their geographic and/or ideological location. The discourse on "white slavery" was never mono-

---

[1] Some beginning analyses have been made, see Doezema, 1995, 1998; Cbapkis, 1997; Kempadoo, 1998a; Lyons, 1999; Murray, 1998; Pike, 1999.

lithic, nor was it inherently consistent. For some reformers, "white slavery" came to mean all prostitution, others saw "white slavery" and prostitution as distinct but related phenomena (Malvery and Willis, 1912). Others distinguished between movement within a country for prostitution (not white slavery) and international trade (white slavery) (Corbin, 1990, p. 294). Nonetheless, it is possible to establish some elements in perceptions of white slavery that were common to almost all interpreters of the phenomenon (examined later). "White slavery" came to mean the procurement, by force, deceit, or drugs, of a white woman or girl against her will, for prostitution.[2],[3]

The extent of the "white slave panic" in Europe and the United States has been extensively documented (Bristow, 1977, 1982; Connelly, 1980; Walkowitz, 1980; Rosen, 1982; Gibson, 1986; Corbin, 1990; Grittner, 1990; Guy, 1991; Fisher, 1997; Haveman, 1998). There were organisations worldwide devoted to its eradication; it received extensive coverage in the world's media; was the subject of numerous novels, plays, and films; and led to a number of international conferences, new national laws, and a series of international agreements.[4]

From the time they were produced to the present time, the narratives of the "white slave trade" have been accepted as literal truth by many, including many feminists (Irwin, 1996, p. 4). However, a number of contemporary historians question the actual extent of the "white slave trade." Their research suggests that the actual number of cases of "white slavery," as defined earlier, was very low (Walkowitz, 1980; Bristow, 1982; Rosen, 1982; Corbin, 1990; Guy, 1991).[5] Seen from

---

[2] Men were not considered victims of the "white slave trade," though the U.S. Immigration Commission Report of 1914 noted that young men were being imported from Europe for "unnatural practices." This was a reference to the supposed European perversion of homosexuality and the threat of its importation to the U.S. (Grittner 1990, 1991). In today's discourse on "trafficking in women," very little mention is made of men being trafficked, Campaigns that focus specifically on child prostitution, in contrast, often highlight the presence of boys, reflecting an anti-gay bias.

[3] Grittner defines the American myth of white slavery as "the enslavement of white women or girls by means or coercion, tricks or drugs by a non-white or non-Anglo-Saxon man for purposes of sexual exploitation" (1990, p. 5). My definition differs slightly: while the non-white, non-Anglo-Saxon character of the white slaver was often a feature of white slavery reports, it was not always so, particularly in Europe, where the "otherness" of the white slaver was also established by making him a "foreigner" or from a different class than that of the reformer. I have also avoided the use of the term "sexual exploitation" as it is both ambiguous and introduces a concept with no currency at the time of the panic.

[4] The International Agreement for the Suppression of the White Slave Trade, 1904; the International Convention for the Suppression of the White Slave Trade 1910; and the International Convention for the Suppression of the Traffic in Woman and Children, 1921.

[5] As Grittner (1990) notes, Rosen (1982) takes a rather contradictory position--though she concludes that the actual number of cases of white slavery were very few, she also devotes an entire chapter to establishing that white slavery existed, quoting many of the sources

this perspective, the narratives of "white slavery" become something other than factual accounts of women's experiences. Rather, "white slavery" becomes a metaphor for a number of fears and anxieties in turn of the century European and American society.

Grittner, in his analysis of the anti-white slavery campaign in America, introduces the idea of "white slavery" as a cultural myth. According to Grittner, a myth does not simply imply something that is "false," but is rather a collective belief that simplifies reality (1990, p. 7). Grittner explains his conception of myth as follows:

> As an uncritically accepted collective belief, a myth can help explain the world and justify social institutions and actions . . . When it is repeated in similar form from generation to generation, a myth discloses a moral content, carrying its own meaning, secreting its own values. The power of myth lies in the totality of explanation. Rough edges of experience can be rounded off. Looked at structurally, a cultural myth is a discourse, "a set of narrative formulas that acquire through specifiable historical action a significant ideological charge" (Slokin cited in Grittner 1990, p. 7).

This view of "white slavery" as cultural myth can go some way toward accounting for its persistence and power, even if very few actual cases of "white slavery" existed. After setting the historical context in which the "white slavery" debates took place, I make use of Grittner's idea of the mythical nature of white slavery to explore the construction of and impact of "white slavery" narratives in Europe and America.

Regulation, Abolition, and Feminism

The campaign against "white slavery" needs to be seen in the context of the European and American nineteenth century discourses on prostitution. Two competing views can be distinguished: that of the "regulationists" and that of the "abolitionists." "Regulation" refers to the state system of licensed brothels, in which prostitutes were subjected to various forms of regulation, such as forced medical examinations and restrictions on mobility. The ideology behind "regulation" was that of prostitution as a "necessary evil." Pre-Victorian regulation of prostitution was based on the religious/moral notion of the prostitute as a "fallen woman" (Guy, 1991, p. 13). In the Victorian age, new rationale was found for regulation in the "science of sexuality" (Foucault cited in Walkowitz, 1980, p. 40) in which the prostitute was constructed as a sexual deviant and spreader of disease (Walkowitz, 1980, p. 40).

"Abolitionism" arose as a specific response to the Contagious Diseases (CD) Acts enacted in England in 1864, 1866, and 1869, which

---

discredited by other historians such as Connelly (1980) and Grittner (1990).

epitomised the regulationist approach to the control of prostitution through medical supervision.[6] Under the acts, any woman who was suspected of prostitution could be detained by the police and forced to undergo an internal examination. Josephine Butler famously led a feminist campaign to abolish the acts, which were repealed in 1886. Butlerite feminists opposed the then-current views of the prostitute as "fallen woman" or "sexual deviant"; placing the blame for prostitution squarely on the shoulders of unbridled male lust. Prostitutes were seen as victims who should be rescued or rehabilitated, rather than policed and punished. Feminists in Butler's repeal movement objected to the CD Acts for what they saw as official state recognition of the "double standard" of sexual behaviour for men and women. They also objected to the way the CD Acts gave the state additional powers to police and control the lives of women, especially working class women.[7] The feminist abolitionist campaigners were joined in the campaign against the CD Acts by "social purity" reformers. Social purity reformers, many of them male, wanted not only to abolish prostitution, but also aimed to cleanse society of vice through a repressive programme focusing on, in particular, the sexual behaviour of young people (Coote 1910, 5).

From Abolition to "White Slavery"

As European women began to migrate to other countries in search of work, stories of "white slavery" began to circulate (Guy 1992, p. 203). A number of highly publicized "exposes" of the traffic served to generate widespread public attention for the issue (Grittner, 1990, p. 41). As Grittner remarks, social purity reformers "soon discovered the rhetorical power that 'white slavery' had on their middle-class audience" (Grittner, 1990, p. 41). Butlerite feminists supported the social purist campaign against "white slavery," as they believed that the system of licensed brothels abroad furthered the traffic in women (Walkowitz, 1980; Gibson, 1986). They also supported the social purists' agenda of a single standard of chastity for both sexes and shared their concern with youthful sexuality (Bristow, 1977; Walkowitz, 1980). Eventually, the abolitionist campaign was eclipsed by the campaign for social purity, as the emotive issue of "white slavery" succeeded in whipping up public concern to a fever pitch.

The repressive nature of the social purity campaign was recognised and condemned by some feminists of the time. Theresa Billington-Grieg (1913) published an article in the English Review in which she argued that feminist anti-white slavery activists had "provided arms and

---

[6] The term "abolition" was derived from the campaigns against African slavery. For an examination of the links between this movement and the campaign against "white slavery," see Irwin (1996).

[7] See Walkowitz (1980) for an in-depth analyses of feminism and the repeal of the CD Acts.

ammunition for the enemy of women's emancipation" (p. 446). Josephine Butler publicly condemned the repressive aspects of the social-purity movement, but many of her erstwhile followers joined the ranks of the social purists (Walkowitz, 1980, p. 252). In other European countries and the United States as well, feminists initiated or became involved in the drive to abolish prostitution and "white slavery." And, as in England, these campaigns were increasingly dominated by repressive moralists, as alliances were forged with religious and social purity organisations (Gibson, 1986; Grittner, 1990; Haveman, 1998).

From "Fallen Woman" to "White Slave": Perceptions of the "Victim"

An essential aspect of the abolitionist campaign against "white slavery" was to create public sympathy for the victims. Neither the pre-Victorian "fallen women" nor the Victorian "sexual deviant" was an ideal construct to elicit public sympathy. Only by removing all responsibility for her own condition could the prostitute be constructed as a victim to appeal to the sympathies of the middle-class reformers, thereby generating public support for the end goal of abolition. The "white slave" image as used by abolitionists broke down the old separation between "voluntary" sinful and/or deviant prostitutes and "involuntary" prostitutes. By constructing all prostitutes as victims, it removed the justification for regulation (Wallcovitz, 1980; Grittner, 1990)

The "innocence" of the victim was established through a variety of rhetorical devices: by stressing her youth/virginity; her whiteness; and her unwillingness to be a prostitute. The "innocence" of the victim also served as a perfect foil for the "evil trafficker"; simplifying the reality of prostitution and female migration to a melodramatic formula of victim and villain (Gibson, 1986; Corbin, 1990; Grittner, 1990).

The Maiden Sacrifice

Deceit, force, and/or drugging featured heavily in the accounts of "white slavery." Some accounts reported women and girls kidnapped outright, others focused on "deceit," with violence entering in after the "victim" became aware of what was expected of her, to ensure compliance and prevent escape. This process was referred to as being "broken in" (NVA, 1910, p. 15).

The horror of the supposed trade in "white slaves" was magnified by stressing the youth of the victim. As Walkowitz (1980) points out, by the time the English abolitionists had seized on "white slavery" as an issue, the image of the "victim" was several years younger than in earlier decades. The two extremely emotive issues of "white slavery" and "child prostitution" were linked, as exemplified in W.T. Stead's "The Maiden Tribute to Modern Babylon" published in the Pall Mall Gazette in 1885. In this fantastically sensational series, he claimed to provide investigative evidence of hundreds of young English girls deceived, coerced, and/or drugged into prostitution and accused poor parents of selling their daughters to "white slave traders" (Stead cited in Fisher, 1997, pp. 130-2). In other countries, as well, the extreme youth of the victim was stressed in campaigns against "white slavery." According to Corbin, in French accounts,

> The victim is always young—even very young, hardly past childhood—considered a virgin even when her innocence is not self-evident (1990, p. 291).

In the U.S., the primary narrative motif was that of the "innocent country girl" lured to the dangerous and corrupt city (Grittner, 1990, P. 62), a theme with resonance in Europe as well (Bristow, 1982, p. 24).

Linked to the youth of the victim was her "purity" and virginity. The image of "innocence debauched" has a particularly strong and prurient content. As Corbin notes:

> [it was] the martyrdom of virginity . . . not the fact of women being sold, but the idea of the virgin ravished that aroused its rather salacious disapproval (1990, p. 277).

The titles of books and newspaper articles attest to the fascination with the despoiling of youthful purity: Stead's "The Maiden Tribute to Modern Babylon" (see earlier) conjures up images of virgin sacrifice, as did constant comparisons in French newspapers to the myth of Greek girls sacrificed to the Minatour (Corbin, 1990, p. 291).

Another recurring motif related to the narrative devices of sacrifice, youth and virginity, was that of disease, in particular syphilis, and death. As a member of the Argentinean Societe de Protection et de Secours aux Femmes expressed it:

And what is the end of their career? When their health is broken down, their bodies utterly ruined, their minds poisoned and dulled, they are thrust out into the streets to perish there, unless some hospital ward opens its door to them. What else could happen to them? (NYA, 1910, p. 18)

As Grittner remarks of this rhetorical repetition:

> The emphasis on inevitability of disease, degradation, and death, and the totality of the slave experience, led to the inescapable conclusion that women were helpless victims (1990, P. 68).

Blacks, Foreigners, Immigrants and Jews: Perceptions of the "White Slaver"

The image of the migrant prostitute as "white slave" fit into racist conceptions of Americans and Europeans. For many Europeans, as Guy points out,

> It was inconceivable that their female compatriots would willingly submit to sexual commerce with foreign, racially varied men. In one way or another, these women must have been trapped and victimised. So European women in foreign bordellos were construed as "white slaves" rather than common prostitutes (1992, p. 203).

Accounts of the day stressed the "whiteness," equated with purity, of the victim:

> The traditional Western connotation that whiteness equals purity and blackness equals depravity nourished in a myth that appealed to the moral and prurient natures of its audience (Grittner, 1990, p. 131).

Only white women were considered "victims"; for example, campaigners against the "white slave trade" from Britain to Argentina were not concerned about the situation of native-born prostitutes (Guy, 1991, P. 24), nor were American reformers concerned about non-Anglo Saxon prostitutes (Grittner, 1990, p. 56).[8]

The "white slave" had as her necessary opposite the "non-white slaver." "Non-whiteness" was usually literally represented, but also figuratively, with "otherness" from the social group conducting the campaign serving as a marker of "non-whiteness." The very name "white slavery" is racist, implying as it does that slavery of white women was of a different, and worse, sort than "black" slavery. In America, in particular, this contrast was explicitly used to downplay the black slavery experience (Grittner, 1990). In both Europe and the United States "foreigners," especially immigrants, were targeted as responsible for the traffic. Jews, in particular, were seen as responsible (NVA, 1910; Bristow, 1982; Grittner, 1990; Guy, 1991).[9] According to Bristow, the term "white slavery" first appeared in 1839, in an anti-Semitic context (1982, p. 34).

---

[8] Some American social purity groups drew attention to the presence of Chinese women in California brothels, but this merely served to reinforce the notion of depraved habits of Chinese men, who were the supposed "slavers" (Grittner, 1990).

[9] Bristow (1982) details the anti-Semitism of the anti-white-slavery campaign.

Consequences of the Campaign

The original, emancipatory thrust of the abolitionist movement, dedicated as it was to decreasing state control over poor women, ironically evolved to support a "social purity" agenda that would give the state new repressive powers over women and subaltern men. The campaign against white slavery led to the adoption of the Criminal Law Amendment Act of 1885 in Britain that was used against prostitutes and working class women, rather than "white slavers" (Walkowitz, 1980). In the U.S., the Mann Act of 1910 was used by police as an excuse to arrest prostitutes and persecute black men (Grittner, 1990, pp. 96-102). Greece fought "white slavery" by passing legislation in 1912 forbidding women under twenty-one to travel abroad without a special permit (Bristow, 1977, p. 178).

After 1914, when migration from Europe effectively halted due to WWI, the anti-white slavery campaign lost momentum. Currently, the issue of women being forcibly transported to the sex industry is once again the subject of a massive international campaign. In the next section, I examine the emergence of the current campaign against "trafficking in women," and compare its discursive structure to that of "white slavery."

From "White Slavery" to "Trafficking in Women"

The re-emergence of "white slavery," now called "trafficking in women" as a political issue for feminists, human rights organisations, religious groups, and others, and its reappearance on national and international political agendas can be dated from the beginning of the 1980s.[10] While originally the focus was on the "traffic" from Latin America and Asia to western Europe, increasingly, it is on women from Russia, the Newly Independent States (NIS), and Eastern Europe being "trafficked" to Western Europe, the United States, and Asia (GSN, 1997; Wijers and Lap-Chew, 1997). There is also an increasing focus on inter-regional "traffic" such as from Nepal to India (HRW, 1995), and Burma to Thailand (HRW, 1995), and rural to urban "trafficking" within one country (Wijers and Lap-Chew, 1997).

Modern accounts of "trafficking in women" vie with "white slavery" stories in their use of sensational descriptions and emotive language,

---

[10] Current anti-trafficking campaigns often include "trafficking" for purposes other than prostitution, such as for domestic service or marriage, among their concerns. However, it is the issue of "trafficking" for prostitution that continues to receive the most emphasis and get the most publicity. Widening the scope of anti-trafficking campaigns, can, but does not necessarily, help campaigners to break out of the straightjacket imposed by myth. See pages 31-32.

though the "victims" are no longer white, western European or American women, but women from the third-world or the former Eastern bloc.

> Trafficking Cinderella features gut wrenching testimonies of broken dreams, withered illusions, rape and humiliation from six Eastern European girls sold as prostitutes throughout the world. This film was made on behalf of all these lost girls; confused by the crumbling post-communist reality they became an easy prey for pimps, procurers and sex-traffickers.[11]

> Think of it. You're a young girl brought from Burma, you have been kidnapped or bought. You're terrified...if you haven't already been raped along the way (or sometimes even if you have) you're immediately brought to the "Room of the Unveiling of the Virgin." There you are raped continuously—until you can no longer pass for a virgin. Then you are put to work (Mirkenson, 1994, p. 1).

It is possible to see in these stories the re-working of several of the motifs identified in the first section: innocence; youth and virginity; deception and violence. If "white slavery" has been shown to be a cultural myth with repressive consequences for women, especially prostitutes, and subaltern men, what are the implications of this for the current campaign against "trafficking in women"?

Evidence of "Trafficking in Women"

In analyzing the mythical nature of the "trafficking in women" discourse, I do not mean to imply that any accounts of "trafficking," including those referred to in this article, are "false." Women who travel for work in the sex industry are often lied to about the conditions they will work under, and in a number of cases are subjected to violence and/or find themselves working in slavery-like conditions. Some women are also lied to about the type of work they will be doing (GSN, 1997; Wijers and Lap-Chew, 1997). The repetition of the discursive foundations of "white slavery" do, however, lead to the question: does the campaign against "trafficking in women" revolve around a relatively few number of cases that conform to the stereotype of the innocent girl lured or abducted into the sex industry? A systematic investigation of reports and statistics of "trafficking in women," similar to those undertaken by chroniclers of the white slavery panic, has yet to be done. However, there are a number of reasons to question the reliability of evidence of "trafficking in women."

---

[11] Publicity flyer for the documentary "Trafficking Cinderella," directed by Mira Niagolova, distributed at the Transnational Training Seminar on Trafficking in Women, June 20-24, Budapest; italics added.

First, evidence of "trafficking" is often based on unrevealed or unverifiable sources. The Global Alliance Against Trafficking in Women (GAATW), who undertook a year and a half-long investigation into "trafficking in women" internationally at the request of the UN Special Rapporteur on Violence Against Women, stated that finding reliable statistics on the extent of trafficking in women was virtually impossible. According to GAATW, this was due to "factors including" a lack of systematic research, the lack of a "precise, consistent and unambiguous definition of the phenomena [of 'trafficking in women']" and the illegality or criminal nature of prostitution and "trafficking" (Wijers and Lap-Chew, 1997, p. 15).

Second, as the writers of the GAATW report note, when statistics are available, they usually refer to the number of migrant or domestic sex workers, rather than cases of "trafficking" (Wijers and Lap-Chew, 1997, p. 15). Statistics on "white slavery" to Buenos Aires were based on the numbers and nationalities of registered prostitutes (Guy, 1991, p. 7). In a striking parallel, a Global Survival Network (GSN) report (1997) uses the rise in numbers of Russian, Eastern European, and MS women in the sex industry in western Europe and the U.S. as evidence of "trafficking" (pp. 5, 7). But even these figures are not to be trusted: Kempadoo notes (1998a, p. 15) the extreme variations in estimates of numbers of prostitutes in Asia: estimates for the city of Bombay alone range from 100,000 to 600,000. As she remarks:

> To any conscientious social scientist, such discrepancies should be cause for extreme suspicion of the reliability of the research, yet when it comes to sex work and prostitution, few eyebrows are raised and the figures are easily bandied about without question (1998a, p. 15).

Third, and most significant, there are emerging indications that it is sex workers, rather than "coerced innocents" that form the majority of this "traffic." GAATW, whose report is based for a large part on responses of organisations that work directly with "trafficking victims," found that the majority of "trafficking" cases involve women who know they are going to work in the sex industry, but are lied to about the conditions they will work under, such as the amount of money they will receive, or the amount of debt they have to repay (Wijers and Lap-Chew, 1997, p. 99). They also conclude that abduction for purposes of "trafficking" into the sex industry is rare (p. 195). GSN (1997) relates the testimonies of a number of women who had been sex workers before their migration and who were lied to about working conditions, rather than the nature of the work. Research by the Foundation for Women in Thailand concluded that the largest group of Thai migrants working in the sex industry in Japan had previously worked in the sex industry in

Bangkok (Skrobanek, 1997, p. 49). Watenabe (1998), who worked as a
bar girl herself in Japan in the course of her research into Thai women
migrating to the Japanese sex industry, found that the majority of sex
workers she interviewed were aware of the nature of the work on offer.
Other research, such as that by Brockett and Murray (1994) in
Australia, Anarfi (1998) in Ghana, Kempadoo (1998) in the Caribbean,
the Centro de Orientacion Integral, COIN, (1998) in the Dominican
Republic, and the Salomon Alapitvany Foundation in Hungary (1998)[12]
indicates that women seeking to migrate are not so easily "duped" or
"deceived," and are often aware that most jobs on offer are in the sex
industry.

Feminism, Neo-Abolitionism and "Trafficking in Women"

The modern feminist anti-trafficking campaign is split along
ideological lines on their views of prostitution. One side is represented
by the "neo-abolitionists," whose most important text is Kathleen Barry's
Female Sexual Slavery (1979). The organisation founded by Barry, the
Coalition Against Trafficking in Women (CATW) is one of the largest
and most influential international anti-trafficking organisations. The
neo-abolitionist view of prostitution, as the name suggests, descends
from the turn of the century Butlerites (see section one). Prostitution is
considered violence against women and defined as "sexual exploitation":
"prostitution victimizes all women, justifies the sale of any woman, and
reduces all women to sex" (CATW, 1998. p. 2). According to this definition, there can be no such thing as "voluntary" prostitution, as all
prostitution is a violation of human rights, and "trafficking in women"
is taken to mean any migration for prostitution (CATW, 1998).

The second position in the feminist campaign against "trafficking"
is one that makes a distinction between "trafficking in women" and
"forced prostitution" on the one hand, and "voluntary prostitution" on
the other. GAATW is the primary exponent of this position. According
to GAATW,

> Traffic in persons and forced prostitution are manifestations of
> violence against women and the rejection of these practices,
> which are a violation of the right to self-determination, must
> hold within itself the respect for the self-determination of adult
> persons who are voluntarily engaged in prostitution (GAATW,
> 1994, par. 111.1).

In adopting this position on prostitution, GAATW and other feminists were heavily influenced by the sex worker rights' movement,

---

[12] Presented at the Transnational Training Seminar on Trafficking in Women, June 20-24,
1998, Budapest.

whose contemporary organisation began in the mid-1970s.[13],[14] Sex workers themselves are a completely new entry to the debates about their livelihood: in the "white slavery" debates, prostitutes' voices are notably absent.

The Reconstruction of "Innocence"

The archetypical "white slave," as I have shown, was suitable for public sympathy (and delectable tabloid fodder) because of her youth and innocence. This "innocent victim," over 100 years older but not a day wiser, makes her reappearance in contemporary "trafficking" stories. As in white slavery narratives, her "innocence" is established in a number of ways: through stressing her lack of knowledge of or unwillingness to accede to her fate; her youth-equated with sexual unawareness and thus purity; and/or her poverty.

Abducted, Lured or Deceived

In the typical "trafficking" narrative, the village girl or girl from the third world or the former Eastern Block is abducted or "lured" to the city/the west by promises of well-paid jobs or marriage:

> Seeking financial security, many women are lured by traffickers' false promises of a better life and lucrative jobs abroad (Wellstone and Feinstein, 1998).
> Jewelleries (sic), money, fancy clothes and Hindi movies are luring girls to the cold city of neon lights away from the warm lap of the cool mountains (Kathmandu Post, 27-10-1997).

As explained earlier, there is some recognition that the majority of "trafficking" cases for prostitution involve women who are aware that they are going to work in the sex industry but are unaware of the conditions under which they will work. How does the deceived sex worker fit into the myth of innocence in peril? In the first instance, she would seem to radically contradict the construction of the innocent victim. However, a closer reading indicates that this potentially myth-busting perception is coated with a dusting of victimisation to make it

---

[13] For documentation of the sex worker rights movement see P. Alexander and F. Delacoste (eds.) 1987. Sex Work: Writings by Women in the Sex Industry. Pittsburgh, PA: Cleis Press; G. Pheterson (ed.) 1989. A Vindication of the Rights of Whores. Seattle, WA: Seal Press; W. Chapkis, 1997. Live Sex Acts: Women Performing Erotic Labor. New York: Routledge; Kempadoo and Doezema, 1998.

[14] Sex worker rights' activists are increasingly wary of the split between "victims of trafficking/forced prostitution" and "voluntary prostitution." Too often, the distinction is interpreted in such a way as to deny sex workers' rights, as in the regulationist reasoning: "innocent girls" need protecting, "bad women" who chose prostitution deserve all they get (Doezema, 1995, 1998; Murray, 1998; Wijers, 1998).

more palatable. The sex worker who is a "trafficking victim" is rendered innocent by the ritual invocation of her poverty and desperation.

Susie is the face of contemporary poverty. That her job as a debt-bonded sex-worker is the best economic option available to her is a metaphor for most of the world's women, whose grinding impoverishment in the Third World is accelerating (Matheson, 1994, p. 1).

Who could blame a mother for "turning to prostitution" to feed her children?

I would not argue that poverty and a lack of economic opportunities do not influence a woman's decision to become a sex worker. (Of course, this begs the question of why all poor women don't choose sex work). I am interested here in the rhetorical use of "poverty" to push the sex worker into the mythical mold of deceived innocence.

Youth and Virginity

As with white slavery narratives, the "innocence" of the victim is further established by emphasising her youth and virginity. The sensationalist use of the highly emotive and sexually charged image of "despoiled virginity" plays on prurient fascination at the same time as it whips up public indignation.

> Nations struggle to address the problem [of "trafficking"]— yet the practice continues—actually increases, with younger and younger girls being sought for this lucrative business (Captive Daughters, 1998, p. 1).

> Actually to call most of them women is a misnomer, for often they are young girls, ages 10-15. Some have not even reached the age of menstruation, many have no idea what sex is (Mirkenson, 1994, p. 1).

Blurring the distinction between child and adult helps fix the image of the "trafficking" victim as young and helpless. A UNICEF report states that the majority of "girls" "trafficked" from Burma to Thailand "are between 12 and 25 years old" (UNICEF, 1995, p. 38). No indication is given as to what percentage of these "girls" is actually under 18. A particularly manipulative attempt to link the issues of "child" and "prostitution" in an emotive way is evident in a photo-series included in the GSN report (1997). The caption reads:

> "Sveta," a 15-year-old Muscovite, works as a prostitute. Here we see her picking up a Russian policeman. Below, at home, she brushes her doll's hair (GSN, 1997, p. 9).

Violence and Death

The victimisation of the "trafficked woman" is reinforced through the repetition of stories of horrific violence. According to a Ukrainian parliamentarian:

> Many Ukrainian women seeking jobs abroad "are raped, beaten and drugged" while being coerced into being prostitutes (quoted in Radio Free Europe/Radio Liberty, 14-04-98).

The term "broken in," familiar from accounts of "white slavery," also makes a reappearance:

> Most girls and women start out in these cheap brothels, where they are "broken in" through a process of rapes and beatings (HRW, 1995, p. 232).[15]

As in "white slavery" narratives, the emphasis on violence serves to underscore the complete victimisation of the woman: the more violence, the more helpless and truly victim she is (Grittner, 1990, p. 68). It also presents a popular sexual fantasy in a culturally acceptable manner. Headlines such as "$1m Trade in Sex Slaves" (The Australian, 23-02-98), "The Selling of Innocents" (Kathmandu Post 10-27-97), "Sex Slaves: Fodder for Flesh Factories" (Toronto Sun 05-10-98) sell titillation under the cover of concern.

Just as the "white slave" was doomed to misery, disease, and death as a result of her loss of virtue, today's "victim of trafficking" shares the same inevitable fate:

> From desperate mothers to sex masters, they do not experience anything but humiliation, diseases, and death (Seraphini, 1998, p. 2).

> A woman tries to stand up, saunters [sic] and falls back . . . She doesn't say anything . . . can't say it . . . the words don't come out. She's embarrassed. She's sick. She's a sex worker (Kathmandu Post, 27-10-97).

The above quote is particularly striking in light of the AIDS pandemic: the "white slave" was condemned to syphilis, her modem counterpart to AIDS.

---

[15] See page 8.

Innocent Victims Versus Guilty Whores

The effect of these motifs of deception, abduction, youth/virginity, and violence is to render the victim unquestionably "innocent." Desperately poor, deceived or abducted, drugged or beaten into compliance, with a blameless sexual past, she could not have "chosen" to be a prostitute.

> Maya Tamang . . . was a victim of ignorance, poverty, and the greed of an unscrupulous relative who sold her to a brothel in Bombay . . . Her story is not much different from hundreds of similar horror stories surrounding once beautiful and innocent young Nepali girls (Peoples Review, 25-01-96, 7).
>
> It happens every single day . . . throughout the world, where selling naive and desperate young women into sexual bondage has become one of the fastest-growing criminal enterprises in the robust global economy (New York Times 11-01-98).

"Innocent," "naive," and "desperate" in these accounts are code for "non-prostitute." The construction of a "victim" who will appeal to the public and the policy makers demand that she be sexually blameless. This is illustrated by a journalist's perceptive reaction to reports of a Toronto "sex slave" ring:

> The day they were arrested, last fall, they were the darlings of the media and a favourite porn fantasy, all wrapped up in one righteous story of salvation: 22 victims of "sex trafficking" liberated from their debasement in Toronto's suburbs by a carefully planned police raid. Everywhere . . . they were droolingly described as "sex slaves," conjuring up a vision of exotic but helpless beauties. A day or two later, police revealed that the 22 women, mostly Thai or Malaysian, had willingly come to Canada to ply their trade; wiretaps caught them boasting, long distance, about the amount of money they were earning. Public opinion did an instant about-face. Now the women were hardened delinquents, illegal immigrants, tawdry, dismissable, selling their bodies of their own free will. Phew! No need to fret about their fate (Toronto Star 19-04-98).

As with the public outcry against "white slavery," the real concern for public and policy-makers is not with protecting women in the sex industry, but with preventing "innocent" women from becoming prostitutes, and keeping "dirty" foreign prostitutes from infecting the nation (Doezema, 1998; Wijers, 1998). A "guilty" prostitute is not considered a possible "victim of trafficking": as expressed by a delegate at a recent conference on trafficking: "How can I distinguish an innocent victim from a sex worker?" (Wijers, 1998, p. 11).[16] Thus, women who knowingly migrate to work in the sex industry and who may encounter exploitation and abuse, are not considered to have a legitimate claim to the same sorts of human rights protections demanded for "trafficking victims" (Doezema, 1998; Wijers, 1998). This is a reflection of the earlier regulationist reasoning: "innocent girls" need protecting, "bad women" who chose prostitution deserve all they get (Doezema 1995, 1998; Murray 1998; Wijers 1998).

The "Colonial Gaze"

The overt racism in the "white slavery" campaigns is largely absent from anti-trafficking campaigns. However, an implicit racism is still evident in western anti-trafficking campaigns.[17] It finds its expression most fully in the construction of the non-western "trafficking victim," while in "white slavery," it was most evident in the view of the foreign "white slaver." Modern accounts do however, to some extent, have a racist interpretation of the causes of contemporary "trafficking" as explored later. It is a complex mix, for western countries and western men are also blamed, as trafficking is linked to western development policies, western clients, and sex tourists (Wijers and Lap-Chew, 1997).

Unemancipated Women

Pictured as poor, naive, and "unempowered," women from the third world or former communist countries are perceived as unable to act as agents in their own lives or to make an uncoerced decision to work in the sex industry (Doezema, 1995; Murray, 1998).

> The Los Angeles activist wants to shed a different kind of light on the allure of this and other large American cities to young girls-from back country and backward countries alike (The Christian Science Monitor, 12-03-98).

> Many, in their naivete, believed that nothing bad could happen to them in rich and comfortable countries such as Switzerland, Germany, and the United States (GSN, 1997, p. 1).

Presenting "non-western" women as helpless, childlike creatures is both a result of and perpetuates what Chandra Mohanty has identified as the "colonial gaze" of western feminists:

---

[16] See note 12.

[17] The nature of racism and class bias in trafficking narratives that originate in the "third world" or in former communist countries is beyond the scope of this paper. See Lyons (1999) for an analysis of the Orientalist nature of the anti-trafficking discourse in Asia. Pike (1999) examines the intersections between the discourses of AIDS, prostitution and "trafficking in women" in Nepal.

Third world women as a group or category are automatically and necessarily defined as: religious (read 'not progressive'), family oriented (read 'traditional'), legal minors (read 'they-are-still-not-conscious-of-their-rights), illiterate (read 'ignorant'), [and] domestic (read 'backward') (1988, p. 22).

This tendency is particularly pronounced in the works of "neo-abolitionist" feminists like Kathleen Barry. Kamala Kempadoo analyses the racism inherent in Barry's 1995 book The Prostitution of Sexuality: The Global Exploitation of Women:

She [Barry] constructs a hierarchy of stages of patriarchal and economic development, situating the trafficking in women in the first stage that "prevails in pre-industrial and feudal societies that are primarily agricultural and where women are excluded from the public sphere" and where women, she states, are the exclusive property of men . . . At the other end of the scale she places the "post-industrial, developed societies" where "women achieve the potential for economic independence" (Kempadoo, 1998a, p. 11).

This perception reinforces the assumption "that people in the third world have just not evolved to the extent that the west has" (Mohanty, 1988, p. 22).

The Trafficker
Western development policies and western "sex tourists" are blamed for being at least partially responsible for "trafficking in women" (Mirkenson, 1994; IMADR, 1998; Wijers and Lap-Chew, 1997). However, as in "white slavery" accounts, to western eyes, the "traffickers" themselves are seen to be foreigners. According to Cheryl Harrison of GAATW/Canada, media reports of the "trafficking" of 14 Thai women to a Toronto brothel painted Asians as criminals (GAATW Bulletin, March, 1998, p. 5). Usually the "traffickers" are portrayed as mafia-like "foreign criminal gangs," often working in collusion with "corrupt" (read—they can't manage their own affairs) third world/post-communist governments (HRW, 1995, pp. 196-273; GSN, 1997, pp. 33-46).

The other "villains" to whom the finger is repeatedly pointed as the cause of "white slavery" are third world villagers who reportedly sell their daughters to "traffickers."

People sell their daughters because they are poor and materialistic--they might want a television, good clothes (Worker for the French organisation Action for Women in Danger (AFESIP) quoted in Reuters 25-02-98).

The Myth Re-Told

From tales of deceived innocence to reports of the poor selling their daughters, contemporary accounts of "trafficking in women" make use of the many discursive foundations of the "white slavery" myth. Similarly, the consequences of the "anti-trafficking" campaign are proving to be disastrous for women, especially sex workers. Increasingly, countries are restricting women's migration possibilities, and policing and deporting sex workers. These consequences, and the assumptions, fears, and anxieties underlying the structure of the "white slavery/trafficking in women" myth are examined in the next section.

Moral Panics and Boundary Crises

Below, I explore the ways in which the myths of "white slavery" and "trafficking in women" both reinforce and are reinforced by fears and anxieties about women's sexuality and independence, and of "foreigners" and migrants. There are other fears and anxieties that are important but beyond the scope of this paper to address, including the link between "trafficking in women" discourses and a wider repressive moral agenda, particularly around child sexuality; and the intersections between discourses of disease—syphilis and AIDS—and "white slavery" and "trafficking in women."

Behind the Myth

The trigger for the "white slavery" panic was the huge increase in migration between 1860 and the outbreak of the First World War, of which women formed a large part. The campaign against "white slavery" coincided with the mass migration of thousands of women from Europe and Russia to the Americas, South Africa, other parts of Europe, and Asia (Bristow, 1982; Guy, 1992). This increase was facilitated by the colonialism of the "Pax Britannia," which made travel from the "centre" to the "periphery" a possibility for millions of working class people. It was also facilitated by new technology, especially the steamship and telegraph (Bristow, 1977, p. 177).

Another factor contributing to the widespread panic was the calculated use of the emotions generated by images of "white slaves" to garner support for the repression of prostitution (Walkowitz, 1980; Gibson, 1986; Corbin, 1990; Grittner, 1990). Because of the lurid nature and sensationalism of "white slavery," it gained more support than abolitionism ever could:

> Transformation of an individual concern into a "public problem" and onto the political agenda is never easy, but the

ability to tie an issue to symbolically charged language can
improve its chances of success (Grittner 1990, p. 7).

But behind these material/political realities, other, deeper fears
underlay the "white slavery" panic. Grittner, in his analysis of the
American myth of white slavery, describes it in terms of a "moral panic"
as defined by Stan Cohen:

> Societies appear to be subject, every now and then, to
> periods of moral panic. A condition, episode, person or group of
> persons emerges to become defined as a threat to societal values
> and interests; its nature is presented in a stylised and
> stereotypical fashion by the mass media; the moral barricades
> are manned by editors, bishops, politicians and other right-
> thinking people; socially accredited experts pronounce their
> diagnosis and solutions; ways of coping are evolved or (more
> often) reverted to . . . sometimes the panic is passed over and is
> forgotten, except in folklore and collective memory; at other
> times it has more serious and long-lasting repercussions and
> might produce such changes as those in legal and social policy or
> even in the way society conceives itself (Cohen cited in Grittner,
> 1990, p. 64).

While the discourse on "white slavery" ostensibly was about the
protection of women from (male) violence, to a large extent, the welfare
of the "white slaves" was peripheral to the discourse. A supposed threat
to women's safety served as a marker of and metaphor for other fears,
among them fear of women's growing independence, the breakdown of
the family, and loss of national identity through the influx of
immigrants.

Female Migration and Sexual Danger

As in "white slavery" campaigns, the "trigger" for the "anti-
trafficking" campaigns is actual female, and especially prostitute,
migration. A 1996 International Organisation for Migration (IOM) report
noted the "feminisation" of international labour migration (cited in
Kempadoo, 1998a, p. 15), and the nearly half of the migrants worldwide
are women (Wijers and Lap-Chew, 1997, p. 44). Recent studies indicate
that sex workers are increasingly mobile (Skrobanek, 1997; Watenabe,
1998; Brockett and Murray. 1994; Brussa, 1998).

What is behind the new wave of migration by women? In contemporary analysis of "trafficking," the changing economic situation for
women in former communist and third world countries is presented as
a "push" factor for "trafficking," as the west's development policies and
the chaotic post-communist economies are seen to leave women with

little choice other than to accept malafide offers of employment else-where (GSN, 1997; HRW, 1995).

> Each day, thousands of women and girls are lured into the international sex trade with promises of a better life and a lucrative job abroad. These false promises are especially appealing to the scores of unemployed and underemployed women struggling to survive in impoverished regions and in societies facing post-communist transition (GSN, 1997, III).

Analysed in this way, female migration is seen in exclusively negative terms, a desperate flight from intolerable conditions, with no agency credited to the woman. Wijers contrasts this with views of male migration:

> Whereas men [who migrate] tend to be viewed as active, adventurous, brave and deserving of admiration, for the same behaviour women are pictured as passive, foolish and naive, deserving either rescue or punishment (1998, p. 12).

Other analysts, such as GAATW, stress that the increase in female migration, including migration for sex work, is in part due to women seeking increased autonomy and economic independence (Wijers and Lap-Chew, 1997, p. 43). Watenabe, referring to her interviews with Thai sex workers in Japan, writes that "According to Lak, Sai, and Meow, sex work assured them of freedom from marriage and men" (1998, p. 120). While economic motives often predominate, for many, sex work is seen as a route to amassing capital or ensuring later economic independence, rather than as a last resort from dire poverty. Anarfi (1998) found that Ghanaian sex workers who migrate to Cote d'Ivoire hoped to gain enough capital to buy houses or set up as market traders. Kempadoo observes that for women in the Caribbean:

> It is not always clear that it is due to abject poverty, or lack of other skills and possibilities that women turn to this particular income-generating activity (1998b, p. 128).

Rather, sex work is one of a number of "sources of livelihood" utilised by these women (Kempadoo, 1998b, p. 128).

During the "white slavery" era, the "moral panic" was in part provoked by the desire of women for increased independence. Accounts of white slavery served as "cautionary tales" for women and girls (Guy, 1991, p. 6), with a message of sexual peril as the inevitable fate of women who leave the protection of the family. As Guy observes:

Fears of white slavery in Buenos Aires were directly linked to European disapproval of female migration. Racism, nationalism, and religious bigotry fueled anxieties. Men could safely travel abroad, but unescorted women faced sexual danger (1991, p. 7).

This disapproval was linked to insecurities about urbanisation and the appeal of city life to single women seeking independence, and the perceived disintegration of family, exacerbated by rapid processes of industrialisation (Bristow, 1982; Grittner, 1990). During the "white slavery" panic, leaflets and posters at railway stations were produced to warn girls off venturing abroad or to the city (Coote, 1910). Today, prevention efforts also concentrate on warning women of the sexual dangers of life away from home and hearth. Numerous videos and pamphlets directed at "vulnerable" young women are produced by anti-trafficking organisations, portraying in graphic detail the likely fate of those who dare to migrate.

Women's independence was, and is, seen as a threat to the stability of the family and by extension, of the nation. Contemporary efforts to stop trafficking draw on underlying moral values of feminine dependence and the ideal role of women in the family. Sometimes this is made explicit, as in the International Movement Against All Forms of Discrimination and Racism's (IMADR) report for the UN Working Group on Contemporary Forms of Slavery. Referring to state policies that support the export of female labour, the report says:

> State sponsored export of labour to foreign countries places increasing numbers of women at risk for sexual exploitation. Additional negative aspects . . . are linked to erosion of the family. Prolonged separation of husbands and wives can lead to divorce. Children left unattended and unguided may lapse into juvenile delinquency or fall victim to traffickers and paedophiles (IMADR, 1998, p. 15).

More often, however, it is implicit. Most anti-trafficking campaigns target the west's development policies as a cause of "trafficking," pointing out that women bear the brunt of poverty in the third world/former communist states. They also stress the need to develop more economic opportunities for women in the third world and in former communist countries. NGOs in "trafficking origin" countries accuse governments of failing to direct development efforts at rural areas, forcing women to migrate to the city or abroad in search of work (India Abroad 06-06-97). But these laudable aims link all too easily into fears about women running wild away from family supervision.

Maintaining Boundaries

The perceived sexual threat to women travelling abroad is linked to women's role as bearers of their families', and the nation's honour. Grittner analyses the "moral panic" around white slavery in terms of Kai Ericson's notion of a "boundary crisis"; in times of cultural stress, a community "draws a symbolic set of parenthesis" around certain human behaviour, limiting the range of acceptable action (Ericson cited in Grittner, 1990, p. 7). According to Grittner, white slavery was part of a larger boundary crisis in America involving "women, sexuality, and the family" (1990, p. 8).

The notion of "boundary crisis" is particularly pertinent when looking at the role of women in a community. Drawing from her earlier work, Nira Yuval-Davis (1997) analyzes the intersections between discourses of nation and gender at four levels: women as biological reproducers of the nation; women's role in cultural construction of nations; gender relations, citizenship and difference; and the gendered character of the military and of wars. It is at the second level, that of women's role in the cultural construction of nations, that a link can be made between Grittner's use of the concept of a "boundary crisis" and constructions of gender/state relations in discourses of "white slavery" and "trafficking in women." According to Yuval-Davis:

> Women especially are often required to carry this 'burden of representation', as they are constructed as the symbolic bearers of collectivities' identity and honour, both personally and collectively... Women, in their 'proper' behaviour, their 'proper' clothing, embody the line which signifies the collectivities' boundaries (1997, pp. 45-46).

Donna Guy (1991) drawing on the earlier configuration of gender/ state relations in Anthias and Yuval-Davis (1989), signals this link as well:

> The central issue that united anti-white slavery campaigns in Europe and Argentina was the way unacceptable female sexual conduct defined the behaviour of the family, the good citizen, and ultimately national or religious honor . . . Rather than reflecting a completely verifiable reality, white slavery was the construction of a set of discourses about family reform, the role of women's work in modernizing societies, and the gendered construction of politics (1991, p. 35).

Today, laws and practices link national honour and female sexuality, particularly in so-called "countries of origin." The Third City Mission, campaigning against trafficking of Nigerian and West African women, advocates for a return to the traditional values of pride in female virginity.[18] In Romania, police officers have started targeting suspected sex workers in response to reports of Romanian women being trafficked:

> The women are told that for the protection of Romania's international reputation they will be denied travel documents and that they must surrender their passports or be prepared to be arrested and imprisoned for any number of fabricated offences relating to domestic prostitution.[19]

As national honour is dependent on women's sexual purity, "impure" women forfeit the right to protection by the state. Prostitutes have for centuries been subject to laws which give them fewer rights than even the limited ones granted "good" women (Walkowitz, 1980; Guy, 1991, 1992). Emigrant women are expected to carry the nation's honour abroad: when "impure" women travel, they can be under no illusion of protection. Not surprisingly, then, a woman's "virtue" is at the heart of state laws and practices against "trafficking." In Germany, the penalty for trafficking is reduced when a woman knows she is going to be a prostitute or is deemed "not far from being a prostitute." Other countries, including Columbia, Uganda, Canada, Japan, and Brazil have similar provisions (Wijers and Lap-Chew, 1997, pp. 128-130). When cases of trafficking are brought to court, defence lawyers attempt to discredit the victim by focusing on her sexual history:

> The fact that a woman's alleged character and sexual history is relevant in deciding whether or not she can be a victim of trafficking exemplifies the widespread and deep-rooted notion that only "decent," that is "innocent" or "chaste," women can claim protection against violence, rape, or abuse (Wijers 1998, 11).

The policies of many so-called "trafficking destination countries" reflect another aspect of "boundaries": the fear of the racial/cultural "other." During the white slavery panic, people in the United States felt under threat from waves of immigrants (Grittner, 1990). In Europe, the perceived threat from socialism and the proletariat threatened the cultural hegemony of the middle class (Walkowitz, 1980). Today, in Western Europe and in the United States, there is a growing feeling that "the community" is under threat by the importation of new cultural norms through immigration. The worsening economic situation for many countries, and the growing polarity between rich and poor countries, has

---

[18] Third City Mission, personal correspondence (1998).

[19] Salomon Alapitvany Foundation, personal correspondence (1998).

led inhabitants of rich countries to feel that they are under threat from hordes of "economic migrants" out to grab what they can.

Yuval-Davis analyses the backlash to multiculturalism in the west in terms of the desire for the re-establishment of a cultural identity perceived to be under threat (1997, pp. 55–64). Grittner (1990) and Stoler (1987) demonstrate that it is precisely in these times of crisis, when community identities are threatened, that the policing of boundaries becomes paramount. These boundaries are laid out along class, race and gender lines, with sexual behaviour as a crucial marker of community inclusion or exclusion. Stoler analyses how concern over protection of white women increased in times of perceived crises of colonial control, and argues that "sexual control . . . was . . . a fundamental class and racial marker implicated in a wider set of relations of power" (1987, p. 366).[20]

During the "white slavery" era, restricting immigration was seen as a solution to the problem:

> By blaming foreign villains, native-born Americans affirmed the basic purity of the nation and simplified the solutions to white slavery and vice: immigration should be restricted and undesirable aliens deported (Grittner, 1990, p. 130).

Today's policies differ little in form or intent. A recent paper on European anti-trafficking legislation is entitled, with knowing irony, "Keep your women home" (Wijers, 1998). Once again, measures to protect "innocent" women are being used to counter the supposed threat to society posed by "bad" women and racial/cultural "others." Repressive immigration measures enacted to stop "trafficking" include limiting the number of visas issued to women from "origin" countries, increased policing of borders and high penalties for illegal migrants and those who facilitate their entry or stay (Wijers, 1998). For example, in Macao, the government has decided to combat "trafficking" by refusing to issue visas to Russian women (GSN, 7); in Australia, 67 illegal sex workers had been deported between July 1997, and February 1998 (The Australian, 23-02-98).

Beyond "Trafficking"

In line with their views on sex work, GAATW has been attempting to alter the paradigmatic view of the "trafficking victim." As mentioned above, they stress that the majority of women who end up in

---

[20] Stoler (1989) and Yuval-Davis (1997) analyse the myth of the rape of white women by black men, a myth also archetypical in the U.S. (see Grittner, 1990 as an example of a sexual/racial demonisation of the "other"). Like "white slavery" and "trafficking," the myth of black men raping white women was based on a nearly non-existent number of cases, and served the same function of boundary making.

"trafficking" situations are, or know they will be sex workers (Wijers and Lap-Chew, 1990, p. 99). They also broaden the focus of "trafficking in women" to include domestic labour and marriage, and link it to larger issues of labour migration and the lack of informal-sector labour regulation.

The reality of female labour migration for the sex industry and other industries is complex, messy, and resists easy explanations and solutions. It certainly has very little to do with the stereotypical interpretation of "trafficking in women." Myth, on the other hand, is persistent precisely because it reduces complex phenomena to simple causes and clear-cut solutions: the victim and the villain (Grittner, 1990; Irwin, 1996).

The myth of trafficking both creates and limits the discursive space around which these issues can be aired. The term "trafficking in women" is laden with mythical resonance, and when an organisation like GAATW uses the term, it is not the complexity of women's work and migration that is pictured in the mind of the listener/reader, but the "erotic-pathetic" sex slave (Murray, 1998, p. 60). The strategy of continuing to use the term "trafficking in women" to get publicity and funding, a defence often used by feminist organisations who recognise the inaccuracy and damaging effects of the stereotype,[21] uses the discursive space created by the trafficking myth. However, attempts to combat the myth while using the terminology of trafficking are doomed by the limits to the discursive space imposed by the myth. Each repetition to the effect that "trafficking in women" is a huge problem serves merely to reinforce the myth that campaigners are also attempting to break down, thus turning this into a futile effort.

This damaging effect of continuing to view female labour migration for the sex industry through the lens of "trafficking in women" has been recognised by sex worker rights activists (NSWP, 1999; Doezema, 1998; Murray, 1998; PROS et al., 1995), and by some anti-trafficking activists, such as Marian Wijers of GAATW:

> Moreover, given the history of the use of anti-trafficking measures to police and punish female migrants and female sex workers and to restrict their freedom of movement rather than to protect them from violence and abuse, serious doubts are raised as to appropriateness of the existing anti-trafficking framework (Wijers, 1998, p. 26).

As a consequence, the search is on to find a new framework to cover human rights and labour abuses in female migration, both within and

---

[21] In discussions at two recent conferences on "trafficking in women": The European NGO Conference on Trafficking in Women, Noordwijkerhoudt, 5-7 April 1997 and the Transnational Training Seminar on Trafficking in Women, June 20-24, Budapest.

between countries, for work in the sex industry, as well as other informal labour sectors (Leigh and Wijers, 1998).

An essential element in this new framework is the improvement of the legal and social position of sex workers. Sex workers' organisations have long argued that viewing prostitution as work is a necessary first step in protecting the rights of women and men involved in the sex industry.[22] The social stigma and legal restrictions surrounding prostitution mean that women and men in the sex industry are denied the legal protection granted others as citizens and as workers. Many of the problems described by anti-trafficking campaigners, including debt bondage, illegal confinement, coercion in the process of migration, deception, and extortion are, in fact, covered by existing international and national labour and human rights standards, yet are not applied in the case of the sex industry (Bindman and Doezema, 1997). The inclusion of women's and men's work in prostitution and other informal labour sectors in existing labour and human rights mechanisms offers the most in terms of ensuring the rights of those involved (Bindman and Doezema, 1997; Wijers and Lap-Chew, 1997; Haveman, 1998; Wijers, 1998).

Rather than new laws that target "guilty" women at the expense of "innocent" ones, that restrict women's ability to migrate and are based more on states' interests in controlling immigration and women's sexuality, policies towards "trafficking" must be based on the recognition of women's and migrant's rights, among them:

> women's rights to control their own body, life, work and specifically, to migrate, to decide for themselves whether or not to work in prostitution and under what circumstances, and to be free from violence and constraint (Wijers and Lap-Chew, 1997, p. 208).

Conclusion

The repetition of core elements of the "white slavery" myth in accounts of "trafficking in women": innocence deceived, youthful virginity despoiled, the motifs of disease and death, the depraved black/Jewish/foreign trafficker, point in the direction of a new telling of an old myth. "Trafficking in women" is the re-telling of the myth of "white slavery" in a modern form, a new "moral panic" arising in the context of "boundary crises" involving fears of loss of community identity. In the west, communities feel under threat through immigration and multiculturalism; in the third world, communities worry about the perceived threat to tradition by encroaching western values; while in former communist countries, stress is caused by the difficult transition from communism to market economies. All over the world,

---

[22] See note 13.

communities are caught up in identity crises in the face of displacement, mass migration, and globalisation. The myth of "trafficking in women" is one manifestation of attempts to re-establish community identity, in which race, sexuality, and women's autonomy are used as markers and metaphors of crucial boundaries. Thus, while incidents reported in accounts of "trafficking" may be "true," they may be at the same time mythical, to the extent that the events are (re) constructed in such a way as to conform to the framework established by the myth.

In the face of the often horrific reports of violence that occur when women migrate for work in the sex industry, it may seem an unaffordable luxury to step outside and examine "trafficking in women" as a discourse, rather than to campaign for policies to stop it. Yet the consequences of failing to recognise the fears and anxieties that underpin the myth of "trafficking" are severe. One of the most damaging effects of the myth is the "spin" it puts on the experiences of women who migrate for work in the sex industry. Migration for the sex industry is, for some women, a way of expanding life choices and livelihood strategies. Insisting on viewing these women as victims means denying that they can have agency in their own lives. To the myth of the white slave's innocence has been added the "third world difference" (Mohanty, 1988, p. 22) of supposed ignorance, faithfulness to tradition, and sexual backwardness.

The myth of "white slavery"/"trafficking in women" is ostensibly about protecting women, yet the underlying moral concerns are with controlling them. Policies adopted to stop "trafficking" that are based on the mythical notion of the "coerced innocent" and the "evil foreign trafficker" serve to reinforce the construction of state/gender relations that determine that women's purity and dependence are essential to family well being and national honour. Once it is recognised that debt bondage and other slavery-like practices, when they occur, are actually problems for women who are already sex workers or who plan to be, it is impossible to get around the fact that these are abuses of sex workers' rights. However, this is unpalatable to many in anti-trafficking campaigns and in governments: it is one thing to save "innocent victims of trafficking"; quite another to recognise that "guilty" sex workers deserve respect for their rights as workers, as women, and as migrants.

Women who migrate for the sex industry can only be freed from violations of their human fights if they are first freed of their mythical constraints. They must no longer be used as the canvas upon which societies' fears and anxieties are projected; be defined no longer as innocent, sexless, "non-adults" or as the oppressed sex of backward countries; but as agents endowed with the ability to think, to act and to resist.

An earlier version of this paper was presented at the International Studies Association Convention, Washington D.C., February 16-20, 1999, and is available on-line at www.walnet.org/NSWP.

Jo Doezema is a Ph.D. Candidate at the Institute of Development Studies, University of Sussex, Brighton BN1 9RE, UK.

Discussion Questions

1   *There are two competing views of white slavery namely regulationists and abolitionists. What are the differences?*

2   *Why did the feminist Josephine Butler campaign to abolish the Contagious Disease Acts, which were eventually repealed in 1886?*

3   *What type of individuals were a part of the "social purity" reform movement and what did they want to accomplish?*

4   *Why did the Butlerite feminists support the social purist campaign against white slavery?*

5   *The "innocence" of the victim of prostitution was established through a variety of rhetorical devices. What were they?*

6   *There are a number of reasons to question the reality of evidence of "trafficking of women." What are they?*

References

Anarfi, J.K. 1998. "Ghanaian Women and Prostitution in Cote d'Ivoire," in K. Kempadoo and J. Doezema (eds.), Global Sex Workers: Rights, Resistance and Redefinition. New York and London: Routledge.

Barry, K. 1979. Female Sexual Slavery. New York: Avon.

Barry, K. 1995. The Prostitution of Sexuality: The Global Exploitation of Women. New York: New York University Press.

Billington-Grieg, T. 1913. "The Truth about White Slavery," English Review (June): 435-446.

Bindman, J. with Doezema, J. 1997. Redefining Prostitution as Sex Work on the International Agenda. London: Anti-Slavery International and the Network of Sex Work Projects.

Bristow, E.J. 1977. Vice and Vigilance: Purity Movements in Britain since 1700. Dublin: Gill and Macmillan; Rowman and Littlefield.

Bristow, E.J. 1982. Prostitution and Prejudice: The Jewish Fight against White Slavery 1870-1939. Oxford: Clarendon Press.

Brockett, L. and A. Murray. 1994. "Thai Sex Workers in Sydney," in R. Perkins et al. (eds.), Sex Work and Sex Workers in Australia. Sydney: University of New South Wales Press.

Brussa, L. 1998. "The TAMPEP Project in Western Europe," in K. Kempadoo and J. Doezema (eds.), Global Sex Workers: Rights, Resistance and Redefinition. New York and London: Routledge.

Captive Daughters. 1998. Statement at GABRIELA Speakout. Columbia University, March 8, 1998, at www.captive.org.

Centro de Orientacion Intergral (COIN) 1994. La Industria del Sexo por Dentro. Santo Domingo: COIN.

Chapkis, W. 1997. Live Sex Acts: Woman Performing Erotic Labor. London: Cassell.

Coalition Against Trafficking in Women (CATW). Philosophy of the Coalition Against Trafficking in Women, at www.uri.edu/artci/wms/hughs/catw.

Connelly, M.T. 1980. The Response to Prostitution in the Progressive Era. Chapel Hill, NC: University of North Carolina Press.

Coote, W.A. 1910. A Vision and Its Fulfilment. London: The National Vigilance Association.

Corbin, A. 1990. Women for Hire: Prostitution and Sexuality in France after 1850. Translated by Alan Sheridan. Cambridge, MA: Harvard University Press.

Doezema, J. 1995. "Choice in Prostitution," in Conference Book: Changing Faces of Prostitution. Helsinki 3-5 May. Helsinki: Unioni, The League of Finnish Feminists.

Doezema, J. 1998. "Forced to Choose: Beyond the Voluntary v. Forced Prostitution Dichotomy," in K. Kempadoo and J. Doezema (eds.), Global Sex Workers: Rights, Resistance and Redefinition. New York and London: Routledge.

Fisher, T. 1997. Prostitution and the Victorians. New York: St. Martins Press.

GAATW. 1994. "A proposal to replace the Convention for the Suppression of the Traffic in Persons and of the Exploitation of the Prostitution of Others." Utrecht: GAATW

Gibson, M. 1986. Prostitution and the State in Italy 1860-1915. New Brunswick, NJ: Rutgers University Press.

Global Survival Network (GSN). 1997. Crime and Servitude. Washington, D.C.: GSN.

Grittner, F.K. 1990. White Slavery: Myth, Ideology and American Law. New York and London: Garland.

Guy, D.J. 1991. Sex and Danger in Buenos Aires: Prostitution, Family and Nation in Argentina. Lincoln, Nebraska and London: University of Nebraska Press.

Guy, D.J. 1992. "'White Slavery,' Citizenship and Nationality in Argentina," in A. Parker et al. (eds.), Nationalisms and Sexualities. London: Routledge.

Haveman, R. 1998. Voorwaarden voor strafbaarstelling van Vrouwenhandel. Doctoral Thesis, University of Utrecht. Utrecht: Gouda Quint.

Human Rights Watch (HRW). 1995. Human Rights Watch Global Report on Women's Human Rights. New York: Human Rights Watch.

International Movement against All Forms of Discrimination and Racism (IMADR). 1998. Strengthening the International Regime to Eliminate the Traffic in Persons and the Exploitation of the Prostitution of Others. Tokyo: IMADR.

Irwin, M.A. 1996 "'White Slavery' as Metaphor: Anatomy of a Moral Panic." The History Journal vol. 5.

Kempadoo, K. 1998a. "Introduction: Globalising Sex Workers' Rights," in K. Kempadoo and J. Doezema (eds.), Global Sex Workers: Rights, Resistance and Redefinition. New York and London: Routledge.

Kempadoo, K. 1998b. "The Migrant Tightrope: Experiences from the Caribbean," in K. Kempadoo and J. Doezema (eds.), Global Sex Workers: Rights, Resistance and Redefinition. New York and London: Routledge.

Leigh, C. and M. Weijers. 1998. Statement on Trafficking, Stigmatisation and Strategies for Alliances, prepared for the Transnational Training Seminar on Trafficking in Women, June 20-24, 1998, Budapest.

Lyons, Harriet D. 1999. "The Representation of Trafficking in Persons in Asia: Orientalism and Other Perils" Re/productions, Issue #2, Spring.www.hsph.harvard.edu/Organisations/Healthnet/Sasia/repro2/orientalism.

Malvery, O. and W.N. Willis. 1912. The White Slave Market. London: Stanley Paul and Co.

Matheson, A. 1994. "Trafficking in Asian Sex Workers." Green Left Weekly, no. 26, p. 1.

Mirkenson, J. 1994. "Red Light, Green Light: The Global Trafficking of Women." Breakthrough (Spring) at www.captive.org.

Mohanty, C. 1988. "Under Western Eyes: Feminist Scholarship and Colonial Discourses." Feminist Review 30:3-28.

Murray, A. 1998. "Debt Bondage and Trafficking: Don't Believe the Hype," in K. Kempadoo and J. Doezema (eds.), Global Sex Workers: Rights, Resistance and Redefinition. New York and London: Routledge.

Network of Sex Work Projects (NSWP). 1999. "Commentary On The Draft Protocol To Combat International Trafficking In Women And Children Supplementary To The Draft Convention On Transnational Organized Crime," at www.walnet.org/NSWP.

Pike, L. 1999. "Innocence, Danger and Desire: Representations of Sex Workers in Nepal" Re/productions, Issue #2, Spring. www.hsph.harvard.edu/ Organisations/Healthnet/Sasia/repro2/orientalism.

Prostitutes Rights Organisation for Sex Workers (PROS), et al. 1995. Alleged Trafficking of Asian Sex Workers in Australia. Sydney: PROS et al. discussion paper for Beijing.

Rosen, R. 1982. The Lost Sisterhood: Prostitution in America, 1900-1918. Baltimore and London: John Hopkins University Press.

Seraphini, M. 1998. "Why Not Call it Sexual Slavery." Captive Daughters Pioneer Columnist, www.captive.org.

Skrobanek, S. et al. 1997. The Traffic in Women: Human Realities of the International Sex Trade. London: Zed

Stoler, A.L. 1989. "Making Empire Respectable: The Politics of Race and Sexual Morality in 20th Century Colonial Cultures." American Ethnologist 16:4 pp. 634-660.

The National Vigilance Association (NVA). 1910. The White Slave Traffic. London: M.A.P.

UNICEF. 1995. Trafficking of Women and Children in Myanmar: A Situation Analysis. New York: UNICEF

Walkowitz, J. 1980. Prostitution and Victorian Society: Women, Class and the State. Cambridge: Cambridge University Press.

Watenabe, S. 1998. "From Thailand to Japan: Migrant Sex Workers As Autonomous Subjects," in K. Kempadoo and J. Doezema (eds.), Global Sex Workers: Rights, Resistance and Redefinition. New York and London: Routledge.

Wijers, M. and L. Lap-Chew. 1997. Trafficking in Women, Forced Labour and Slavery-Like Practices in Marriage, Domestic Labour and Prostitution, Utrecht and Bangkok: The Foundation Against Trafficking in Women (STV)/The Global Alliance Against Trafficking in Women (GAATW).

Wijers, M. 1998. "Keep Your Women Home: European Policies on Trafficking in Women." Unpublished manuscript.

Wellstone P. and D. Feinstein, U.S. Senators. 1998. Letter to Senate colleagues asking support for legislation against trafficking in women, March 5.

Yuval-Davis, N. 1997. Gender and Nation. London: Sage Publications.

Yuval-Davis, N. and F. Anthias. 1989. Woman-Nation-State. London: Macmillan.

10

INTEGRATION OF TRAFFICKED WOMEN IN DESTINATION COUNTRIES: OBSTACLES AND OPPORTUNITIES

Sarah Stephen-Smith, *POPPY Project, London, United Kingdom*

Introduction

'Integration' refers to a:

> *long-term and multi-faceted process that is not completed until the individual becomes an active member of the economic, cultural and political life of a country and perceives that s/he has oriented and is accepted* (Gaunt et al, 1999).

To victims of trafficking, 'integration' often refers to the resettlement stage, when women are helped to rebuild their lives and live independently without the need for ongoing professional support. For some women, this involves returning to their country of origin and a context and social environment they know well and feel comfortable in; for others, it requires a fresh start in their country of destination. This article will explore the work of a service provider, POPPY, in the UK in helping trafficked women successfully integrate into British society. POPPY is managed by Eaves Housing for Women, a feminist organisation which is committed to lobbying for the abolition of prostitution, including all forms of sexual exploitation caused by male demand for commercial sex acts which in turn facilitates and increases sex trafficking. The services division has been funded since March 2003 by the Home Office (Victims and Confidence Unit). This article is not intended to provide a blueprint for integration of victims of trafficking, but to offer suggestions and guidance based on POPPY's many years of experience.

Resettlement of Trafficked Women in the United Kingdom

The physical and psychological effects of human trafficking can be severe and long-term (Zimmerman *et al*, 2006). A recent multi-country study on trafficking and health identified key health issues that are direct effects of trafficking, including physical damage, mental health problems, damage to sexual health caused by experienced violence. Nearly three in five women (57%) reported suffering more than 12 different physical

185

symptoms when they entered care, including headaches, dizzy spells, back pain, stomach/abdominal pain, fatigue and memory problems. Nearly seven in ten still had headaches after more than 90 days in care; 56% of women reported symptom levels suggestive of post-traumatic stress disorder (PTSD) on entering care.

Trafficked women's anxiety, depression and hostility levels are extremely high—in the top 10th percentile of the norm for the whole female population; 38% report suicidal thoughts, and 95% report feeling depressed. More than 60% of women report pelvic pain, vaginal discharge and gynecological infections on entering care. Most women report that they were sometimes made to have sex without a condom and 17% report having had at least one abortion during the trafficking. Many express concern about their fertility and future ability to have children. Physical or sexual violence while in the trafficking situation was reported by nearly all women (95%). Respondents described violence such as being kicked, burnt with cigarettes, punched in the face, choked with wire and having a gun held to their head. Yet with appropriate support trafficked women can be rehabilitated and re-integrated within society.

A 2003 study from the London School of Hygiene and Tropical Medicine (Zimmerman *et al*, 2003), which looked at the many service needs of trafficked women, highlighted how factors such as language, cultural differences, discrimination and stigmatisation affected the study participants and their uptake of services. According to Zimmerman (2003), these factors also have potential health consequences for women.

For example, limited adaptation to social and cultural norms, and language limitations, can lead to a deterioration of health and alienation from available health services. Similarly, limited quality of care due to discrimination, language and cultural differences can result in potentially dangerous self-medication due to an inability to afford health-promoting products and activities. Public discrimination and stigmatisation related to gender, ethnicity, social position, form of labour frequently result in an increased physical and psychological dependence on abusers or exploitative employers. Women's use of clandestine movements and high mobility also has an impact on women, and often leads to loneliness and other negative mental health outcomes.

The factors which make it difficult for women to access services, including lack of sufficient resources and restrictions due to the criteria for services, are the same for all women working in the sex industry, regardless of whether they have engaged in 'forced' or 'voluntary' prostitution (POPPY adopts an abolitionist perspective on prostitution, and therefore views all prostitution as sexual exploitation. It follows that the issue of 'choice' is regarded as irrelevant—Raymond, 1998.) In order to limit these negative effects, the report recommended that statutory bodies should increase funding for key service provision components, such as medical care, housing, psychological support, and educational and occupational training to assist the women's integration. At the time the report was written, there were no established services for trafficked women in the UK. [1]

Eaves began working with women trafficked for the purposes of sexual exploitation in January 2001, when a woman was referred to the Project after appearing in a Channel 4 (UK television channel) documentary about the sex industry (her placement with us was partly funded by a grant from Channel 4) A further four trafficked women were accommodated by Eaves between 2001 and 2003, when the Home Office decided to fund a six-month pilot project administered by Eaves. These four women ranged in age from 18 to 21, and came to the UK from Albania, Sierra Leone, Romania and Thailand. Three of these women wished to remain in the UK, and one decided to return home almost immediately, which was facilitated by Eaves in partnership with the International Organisation for Migration (IOM).

Four years on, the POPPY Project, which also functions as a London-based research and development unit specializing in counter-trafficking and existing prostitution work, remains the sole government-funded provider of supported housing and complex services for women trafficked into the UK for sexual exploitation. There is currently only one faith-based organisation (FBO) officially providing accommodation and support to trafficked women in the UK: CHASTE, which has 18 beds in a number of safe houses in Cambridgeshire. However, organisations such as the Salvation Army receive periodic referrals of trafficked victims. The role of FBOs in shaping trafficking policy is significant. The recent Home Office publication of responses to its consultation entitled *Tackling Human Trafficking* revealed that half (n=89) of more than 200 respondents approaching were from FBOs. In other countries, such as Italy, Catholic FBOs are original actors in the modern fight against sex trafficking and are well established in providing services to trafficked victims.

The POPPY Project has housed and supported a total of 140 women since March 2003. Of these 35 women have been successfully re-integrated since the resettlement service was established in September 2005. The resettlement process is focused on supporting trafficked women to develop the skills, confidence and resources to move on from the POPPY Project and live independently, whether in the UK or in their country of origin. The following section provides an overview of the resettlement services that the POPPY Project provides to victims of trafficking, from the first point of contact through to the end of the resettlement process.

Meeting Women's Needs: Support Provided by the POPPY Project

In 2006, the Home Office granted funding to POPPY for the creation of a 24/7 outreach team, tasked with identifying and approaching women involved in the sex industry who might be victims of trafficking. In conjunction with proactive work, strategies are being developed to create accessible, appropriate and safe exit strategies for trafficked women trapped in prostitution. Partners include the police, immigration and sexual health outreach projects. Services include advice/advocacy, crisis intervention, signposting to other services, safety planning, short-term crisis intervention support, training and capacity building with external agencies, awareness raising/lobbying and onward referrals.

Article 12 of the Council of Europe Convention (CAHTEH) requires states to provide support and rehabilitation to trafficking victims, including housing, counseling, medical services, financial support and information concerning their legal rights and the service available to them. The UK became the 34th signatory to the Convention on the 23rd March 2007. The Government now needs to take all necessary steps to implement the Convention prior to ratification. The aim is for the Inter-Departmental Ministerial Group on Human Trafficking to considering preliminary implementation plans later this year.

In addition to the specific services outlined in this article, all women supported by the POPPY Project have access to a number of specialist services, including specialist counseling, free personal safety training, and kick boxing and yoga sessions. For counseling, POPPY has established a service level agreement with the Women and Girls Network. The WAGN has a feminist model of working with women who have experienced violence, and a commitment to a multicultural approach, ensuring that the experience is therapeutic for a particular woman, given her cultural background. WAGN also agreed to offer flexibility in the service offered to each woman, for example holding trauma, or safely allowing women to release their emotions at the pace they are able to. They have also agreed to vary the frequency of sessions to meet each woman's needs and circumstances.

Safety training was provided by the London School of Personal Safety with the back-up of two support workers from the pilot project. The sessions enabled women to reflect on their experiences and how they had affected their feelings and actions around personal safety. In some cases this has led to the women not feeling able to go out alone (meaning that workers had to accompany them to all appointments) or not wanting to go out in the evenings. This had contributed to women feeling as though they continued to have very restricted lives. The course enabled women to learn new strategies and to feel more self-assured and regain a sense of control over their lives. We hope to be able to offer this course again in the future—subject to funding.

Other services include induction sessions covering topics such as diversity and equal opportunities, sexual health and relationships, cooking healthy meals on a budget, welfare benefits, keeping healthy and reducing stress. Services available to all women during the first four weeks are short-term accommodation, food/subsistence allowance, interpretation and translation services, health assessment, general support, information about the implication of assisting the authorities—including further support available—information on the research element of the Project, and liaison with Police and Immigration.

The resettlement process is complemented by the work achieved through assessment, key-working and multi-agency partnership working, as carried out b the POPPY senior support workers. While the resettlement support provided by the POPPY Project is tailored to each individual woman and takes personal circumstances and experiences into account, the assistance described below has generally been found to be of particular relevance to victims of trafficking. It is also important to recognise that some women supported by the POPPY Project have limited entitlements in the UK due to their nationality and/or immigration status. These limitations affect the resettlement options available to POPPY service users and, in turn, the resettlement support that the POPPY Project is able to offer.

Stage One: Crisis Intervention

Women arriving at the Project often have difficulties in forming trusting relationships because in the process of being trafficked they were often deceived by somebody they had reason to trust such as a boyfriend or a relative (Stephen-Smith, 2007). This distrust can also extend to those who offer assistance or help, including immigration authorities and law enforcement officials, who victims often believe will either prosecute or deport victims as a result of their seeking help (Dickson, 2004). (Trafficked women are routinely deported, despite the levels of abuse and trauma they have experienced in the UK, and without access to victim support services.)

The first priority of a service provider is to make women feel safe and to establish a supportive relationship between each woman and the support worker responsible for her. POPPY support workers are trained in motivational interviewing techniques which enable them to support women to make their own choices about change and recovery/their future. They are also experts in working with vulnerable women in a supportive but empowering way.

Women are provided with a 'reflection period' on entering the project, which lasts for four weeks. This provides women with a space in which to access their options and make a proper assessment of their needs and the risks to them should they decide to co-operate with the police and/or return home. Research carried out by Zimmerman and colleagues (2006) on the physical and psychological health consequences of trafficked women found that it took up to 90 days after entering a post-trafficking support programme for women to show significant reduction in their reported levels of depression, anxiety and hostility. Within the first 14 days, 70% of women reported experiencing 10 or more mental health symptoms. By 28 days, this figure had fallen to 52%, which is why it is vital that women are offered a period of reflection of at least 28 days to enable them to make informed decisions about their future. Women reported similar reductions in their levels of anxiety and hostility.

Although women trafficked from EU member countries have automatic rights to remain in the UK, these rights are forfeited if they are classed as illegal entrants, and they are liable to be detained. Women who wish to remain in the UK and whose country of origin is not one of the EU accession countries (or those who asylum application is already under way and whose solicitor is not sufficiently knowledgeable about human trafficking) are referred to one of the Project's highly experienced solicitors, who will help prepare their application for asylum. The success rate of women on the POPPY Project is six times as high as the acceptance rate of asylum appeals overall, which the Project believes is due, in part, to the high quality of legal advice women receive (Richards et al, 2007). Where women want to return to their home country, arrangements can be made with organisations working in countries of origin, such as IOM, to arrange their return. The POPPY Project works closely with these agencies once women have returned to their countries of origin, providing training and capacity building and sharing best practice. These organisations can assist in the woman's re-integration and minimise the risk of re-trafficking.

Stage Two: Meeting Ongoing Needs

During the second stage, which usually lasts for up to 12 months, women supported by POPPY are helped to move from the Project into permanent or supported accommodation. The women are housed in rooms in shared houses and flats across London. The rooms are fully locked and the homes are fully furnished. Bedding, towels and basic toiletries are provided. Women who arrive with little or no clothing are also provided with up to £50 worth of clothing vouchers.

The Project continues to help women with their applications for asylum, or with return to their home country through the Voluntary Assisted Returns Programme (VARRP) where appropriate. Women who have exhausted all applications for leave to remain in the UK will normally be referred to the International Organisation for Migration (IOM) London, but they may choose to return to their country of origin without involving IOM London. If this is the case, the POPPY Project will aim to identify an NGO which may be able to offer support, subject to the woman's agreement.

Women's support needs and readiness for resettlement are reviewed every three months with their dedicated support worker, in one of their weekly keywork sessions. Interpretation is provided by arrangement for keywork sessions, appointments with doctors, police and so on where required. Only female interpreters are used. English (ESOL) classes are compulsory for all women on Stage Two support, unless they are proficient in English, in which case alternative vocational courses would be identified. With even a basic understanding of English, women are more likely to feel confident in dealing with authorities. This can help with criminal proceedings, as the women may be more confident in assisting. A working knowledge of English will also clearly help women to find work and integrate socially. Whether in countries of origin or destination, women need to build new social networks around themselves, for example to find new friends, and participate in new activities.

Stage Three: Toward Independence

Resettlement or integration is the final stage. Once women reach this stage they are allowed to remain on the Project for up to 12 months. During this period, the Project helps women prepare for independent living and provides a variety of support services, including the following.

Education and Training

Victims of trafficking may need to further their school or university education or participate in vocational training in order to find employment. While many trafficked women have low levels of education, some individuals have valuable qualifications—58% of trafficked women surveyed by the POPPY Project had completed high school, 17% had completed primary school, 9% had attended university and 1% had no previous education at all (Stephen-Smith, 2007). Thirteen women on the Project have entered either part-time or full-time study. POPPY also has the capacity to support women to gain conversion qualifications, allowing them to practice their profession in the UK.

Employment Assistance

The POPPY Project recognises that mainstream employment may not be an option for all POPPY service users, given their ongoing support needs, potential language barriers and lack of relevant experience. For women who are eligible to work and for whom it is considered appropriate, the Project provides help in preparing their curriculum vitae, attending job interviews and securing volunteer placements. To date, five women have found full-time employment since leaving the

Project, and a further four have undertaken work placements. Women who exit the POPPY Project through employment will be entitled to ongoing resettlement support. European Union nationals are helped to register with the Worker's Registration Scheme (WRS), in order to seek employment and finance alternative accommodation.

Financial Assistance

Women's entitlement to benefits depends on their status in the UK. Until women find work, they need assistance with applying for the relevant welfare benefits and entitlements, including Job Seeker's Allowance, Income Support, Housing Benefit and National Asylum Support Service (NASS) payments. Once women have been employed under the WRS for a period of 12 continuous months (with less than 30 days spent not working), they will normally be entitled to work-related benefits, such as Housing Benefit, Council Tax Benefit and Working Tax Credit. Women who are EU nationals but not from one of the accession countries and who have been employed for six months will normally be entitled to work-related benefits, such as Housing Benefit, Council Tax Benefit and Working Tax Credit. POPPY will also provide financial support to women from the EU who are preparing for work, until they are ready for self-sufficiency.

Supported Housing

At the same time as securing employment, women are helped to sustain a tenancy. The support worker can refer the woman to supported housing, the homeless persons unit (HPU), rent deposit schemes, Housing Benefit accepted schemes, NASS, and advice and advocacy regarding suitable accommodation. A woman who has a pending application for asylum or leave to remain in the UK, is ready for resettlement, and has stayed with the POPPY Project for 16 weeks or more will normally be referred to NASS. Women who are referred to NASS will be entitled to ongoing resettlement support from the POPPY Project. Other women on the project have moved into independent housing, for example, have moved in with friends or private rented accommodation and have used their own initiative.

A woman who has been granted refugee status or leave to remain in the UK and is ready for resettlement will be offered the option of transferring to Eaves' Supported Housing. The option of transferring to Eaves' Supported Housing is also available to women who have the right to remain in the UK, are able to demonstrate clearly that they can meet the cost of Eaves' accommodation without recourse to welfare benefits (such as EU nationals), and are ready for resettlement. A woman who has been granted refugee status or leave to remain in the UK and is ready for resettlement may choose not to transfer to Eaves' Supported Housing. In such a case, the resettlement worker will help to identify alternative appropriate accommodation in the Resettlement Support

Plan. In certain circumstances, a transfer to Eaves Supported Housing may not be appropriate. This may be the case when a woman has exceptionally high ongoing support needs or very low support needs. In such a case, the resettlement worker will help identify alternative appropriate accommodations in the Resettlement Support Plan.

Conclusion

Whether in countries of origin or destination, trafficked women need help to rebuild their lives and live independently. Specialist service providers, such as the POPPY Project, play a central role in helping trafficked women's successful integration, both in the UK and in countries of origin. As well as practical, social, economic, cultural and linguistic barriers to accessing services, trafficked women also face personal security risks, risks associated with being a refugee, ongoing isolation and exclusion, immediate and longer-term mental and physical health consequences, as well as the risk of re-trafficking (Zimmerman *et al.*, 2003). Yet with appropriate specialist support, trafficked women can overcome these barriers and function in society again.

POPPY adopts the definition of trafficking as set out in Article 1 of the Council of Europe Convention, which itself follows Article 1 of the UK Protocol to Prevent, Suppress and Punish Trafficking in Persons, especially Women and Children (known as the Palermo Protocol). *'Trafficking in human beings' shall mean the recruitment, transportation, transfer, harbouring or receipt of persons by means of the threat or use of force or other forms of coercion, of abduction, of fraud, of deception, of the abuse of power or of a position of vulnerability or of the giving or receiving of payments or benefits to achieve the consent of a person having control over another person for the purpose of exploitation. Exploitation shall include, at a minimum, the exploitation of the prostitution of others or other forms of sexual exploitation, forced labour or services, slavery or practices similar to slavery, servitude or the removal of organs*

Discussion Questions

1   *In a recent multi-country study on trafficking a number of health issues were linked to the direct effect of trafficking. What were they?*

2   *What is the position of POPPY on prostitution?*

3   *What services are provided by POPPY to women who have been trafficked?*

4   *What types of special services have been provided POPPY to trafficked women?*

5   *What are the three phases of the resettlement process?*

References

Dickson S (2001) *Sex in the City: Mapping Commercial Sex across London.* POPPY Project, London. Available at: www.eaveslwomen.co.uk/POPPY_Project/Documents/Recent_Reports/Sex%20in%20the%20City.pdf.

Dubourg R & Prichard S (Eds) 2007. *Organised Crime Revenues, economic and social costs, and criminal assets available for seizure.* London: Home Office.

Gaunt S *et al* (Eds) (1999) *Good Practice Guide on the Integration of Refugees in the European Union.* The European Council on Refugees & Exiles (ECRE) ECRE Task Force.

Raymond J (1998). *Legitimating Prostitution as Sex Work: UN Labour Organisation (ILO) calls for recognition of the sex industry.* Available at www.hartford.hpw.com /archives/26/119.html.

Richards S, Steel M & Singer D (2006). *Hope Betrayed: An analysis of women victims of trafficking and their claims for asylum.* London: POPPY Project.

Stephen-Smith S (2007). (forthcoming) *When Women Are Trafficked.* London: POPPY Project.

Zimmerman C, Hossain M, Yun K *et al* (2006) *Stolen Smiles: The physical and psychological health consequences of women and adolescents trafficked in Europe.* London: LSHTM.

Zimmerman C, Yun K, Schvab, I *et al* (2003) *The Health Risks and Consequences of Trafficking in Women and Adolescents. Findings from a European study.* London: School of Hygiene & Tropical Medicine (LSHTM).

PART III

SEX TRAFFICKING IN ASIA, AUSTRALIA AND AFRICA

Modern-Day Comfort Women: The US Military, Transnational Crime, and the Trafficking of Women. The trafficking of women has been a lucrative moneymaker for transnational organized crime networks, ranking third, behind drugs and arms, in criminal earnings. The U.S. military bases in South Korea were found to form a hub for the transnational trafficking of women from the Asia Pacific and Eurasia to South Korea and the United States. This study examined three types of trafficking connected to U.S. military bases in South Korea: domestic trafficking of Korean women to clubs around the military bases in South Korea; transnational trafficking of women to clubs around the military bases in South Korea; and transnational trafficking of women from South Korea to massage parlors in the United States.

Foreign Women Trafficked to United States Military Areas in South Korea: Trafficking Processes and Victim Profiles in a Different Context. This research paper details the specific circumstances of foreign women sex trafficked to American military base areas (camp towns) in South Korea, focusing particularly on Fillipinas. The paper suggests that the process and patterns of trafficking to Korea, including the victim profiles and their migration trajectories, differ in several important respects from those put forward under prevailing stereotypes of trafficking victims, which is based largely on selected findings about trafficking in South Asia and the Greater Mekong Sub-Region (GMS). The departures presented by the Korean context point to the need to recognize differences as well as commonalities in the characteristics of sex trafficking throughout the region and the need to draw more fully on a range of trafficking sites beyond the more often discussed South Asia and GMS in extending our understanding of trafficking.

Life Histories and Survival Strategies Amongst Sexually Trafficked Girls in Nepal. Many girls involved in sex work in Asia do so because they are compelled by economic circumstances and social inequality. Some enter sex work voluntarily. Others do so by force or deception, sometimes involving migration across international borders. Nepalese girls involved in sex work via trafficking are the focus of this research paper, which aims at increasing our understanding of the context of sex trafficking, the methods and means of trafficking, the living conditions in brothels and survival strategies among trafficked girls. Girls trafficked from Nepal to India are typically unmarried, illiterate and very young. Key routes to sex trafficking include employment-induced migration to urban areas, deception (through false marriage or visits) and abduction. Past initiatives alone are inadequate as they ignore the importance of empowerment of women in the migration process and skill development in community re-integration.

Human Trafficking in China. The trade of women and girls for sexual exploitation is a clear trafficking challenge for the Chinese. Although prostitution is illegal, the problem of the burgeoning illicit sex industry creates a vulnerability for sex trafficking. Women and children are trafficked into the country from North Korea, Vietnam, Burma, Mongolia and Thailand. Chinese women are also trafficked abroad for sexual exploitation. However China has engaged with the U.S. government and international and nongovernmental organizations to work on anti-trafficking initiatives. China recently hosted a Children's Forum in Beijing, in which they brought child representatives from across the country to discuss measures to prevent vulnerable youth from being trafficked and to increase protection and prevention.

Law Enforcement Responses to Trafficking in Persons: Challenges and Emerging Good Practice. In recent years the Australian Government has committed significant resources to combating trafficking in persons. Within this larger anti-trafficking effort, the community sector, law enforcement, prosecutors, health professionals and members of the community all have an important role to play. As each sector comes to terms with the reality of trafficking in Australia, it is important that emerging challenges and possible solutions are identified. This research paper focuses on the challenges that may confront law enforcement officials in any country in their efforts to detect trafficking, identify victims, investigate offenses and contribute to the successful prosecution of offenders. Drawing on international experience, this paper identifies some examples of emerging good practices that can help to overcome these challenges, and contribute to the effectiveness of the larger criminal justice responses to trafficking.

Trafficking and the Sex Industry: From Impunity to Protection. This research paper provides an overview of the global trade in trafficking of women into the sex industry in Australia. It sets out the regulatory challenges posed by transnational crimes of this nature; discusses some of the difficulties in reaching consensus on the extent of the problem in Australia; explains the confusion between people trafficking and people smuggling; analyses existing criminal and migration law and practice; and suggests reasons why, to date, there have been no prosecutions of traffickers under the Commonwealth Criminal Code. The analysis is informed by domestic and international research and recent developments in international law that provide an internationally agreed upon definition of people trafficking. The paper refers briefly to strategies adopted in the US and in Europe to combat this crime.

Human Trafficking in Australia: The Challenge of Responding to Suspicious Activities. This research paper relates to the Australian government's community awareness campaign, as part of the *Action Plan to Eradicate Trafficking in Persons*, in response to evidence of human trafficking in Australia. The authors explore the challenges that are likely to be encountered during the implementation of the campaign using empirical data from two Victorian studies, the first of which explored community awareness of trafficking and the second of which examined Victoria Police and local government's responses to trafficking. The authors conclude there are significant barriers to both the community and authorities in identifying suspicious activities and acting on reports from the community. In addition, institutional challenges faced by Victoria police and local government in dealing with referred information appropriately will jeopardize the success of the initiative.

Corruption and Human Trafficking: The Nigerian Case. This research paper discusses the interrelationship between corruption and human trafficking in Nigeria. In countries like Nigeria corruption has adversely affected governance and the larger social structure. Government's ability to provide vital services such as water, sanitation, health care, education, etc., is usually severely constrained. This generally leads to a retardation of economic development and to the deterioration of whatever public infrastructure has been put in place. The paper concludes that in Nigeria unbridled corruption has led to bad governance in spite of the various legislations put into place to check corruption, whether under military or civil rule.

11

MODERN-DAY COMFORT WOMEN: THE U.S. MILITARY, TRANSNATIONAL CRIME, AND THE TRAFFICKING OF WOMEN

Donna M. Hughes, Ph.D., *University of Rhode Island*
Katherine Y. Chon, Sc.B. and Derek P. Ellerman, Sc.B, co-founders of the *Polaris Project*

The trafficking of women is a lucrative moneymaker for transnational organized crime networks, ranking third, behind drugs and arms, in criminal earnings. The present study provides evidence that as of the year 2002, U.S. military basses in the Republic of Korea (commonly known as South Korea) formed an international hub for trafficking of women for prostitution and related forms of sexual exploitation. The trafficker recruited and transported women to meet the demand largely created by U.S. military personnel and civilian men in South Korea and the United States. In some cases, the U.S. servicemen themselves are traffickers working with Asian organized crime networks.

This study, conducted in 2002, examined three types of trafficking that were connected to U.S. military bases in South Korea: domestic trafficking of Korean women to clubs around the military bases in South Korea, transnational trafficking of women to clubs around the military bases in South Korea, and transnational trafficking of women from South Korea to massage parlors in the United States. Although the three types of trafficking will be discussed separately, in reality, they sometimes overlap. For example, in one case a Korean woman was the victim of multiple acts of trafficking: She was abducted at age 14 from her village in South Korea, and was repeatedly raped and exploited by soldiers of the South Korean army. An American soldier brought her to the United States through a sham marriage, where she was then trafficked within the United States on a massage parlor circuit (Gallagher, 1995).

Method

Terms and Definitions

For the purpose of this paper, the definition of "trafficking" is based on the U.S. Victims of Trafficking and Violence Protection Act of 2000. "Sex trafficking means the recruitment, harboring, transportation, provision, or obtaining of a person for the purpose of a commercial sex act." A commercial sex act is defined as "any sex act on account of which anything of value is given to or received by any person." For criminal charges to be brought against perpetrators, their activities must meet the criteria of "severe form of trafficking in persons," which is "sex trafficking in which a commercial sex act is induced by force, fraud, or coercion, or in which the person induced to perform such act has not attained 18 years of age." Coercion is defined as: "(A) threats of serious harm to or physical restraint against any person; (B) any scheme, plan, or pattern intended to cause a person to believe that failure to perform an act would result in serious harm to or physical restraint against any person; or (C) the abuse or threatened abuse of the legal process." "Transnational trafficking" is used to mean sex trafficking of women that involves the crossing of an international border. "Domestic trafficking" is used to mean sex trafficking within the borders of a country in recognition that the tactic s used by procurers and pimps are the same when women are recruited and transported within the same country. Often, as in the case of massage parlors, the women are used on regional and national circuits, which should be recognized as a form of domestic trafficking.

In discussing the sites of prostitution in the U.S., the term "massage parlor" is used, although the establishments are also known by other euphemisms such as "spas," "modeling studios," and "hostess bars."

Sources of Data

Prior to the initiation of this research, no studies on the trafficking of women to Korea had been conducted or completed.[1] Similarly, there were no research studies on the trafficking of women from Korea, or trafficking of Korean women that involved U.S. servicemen. There have been several studies on the use of Korean women for prostitution by U.S. servicemen, but the focus was not on trafficking. Korean and other Asian nongovernmental organizations (NGOs) have documented the transnational and domestic trafficking of women associated with U.S. military personnel, but they were not research reports. Because of the lack of previous research, the paper relied on NGO reports and media stories from the U.S., South Korea, and the Philippines.

For this research report, the authors conducted 36 interviews using open-ended questions with social service providers, activist organizations, law enforcement officials, reporters, and a researcher in the U.S. and South Korea. The interviews included 19 law enforcement officials, 10 social service providers and/or activist organizations, 6 reporters, and 1 researcher. All interviews were conducted by telephone in August, September, and October 2002.

---

[1] While the research for this paper was underway, the International Organization for Migration released its report "Women Trafficked for U.S. Military Bases – IOM Report," September 3, 2002.

Results

U.S. Military in Republic of Korea and Violence Against Women

The United States has had troops in South Korea for almost six decades, starting in 1945 following World War II.[2] Today, there are 100 U.S. military bases throughout South Korea with 37,000 troops.

From the 1950s to 1970s, the United States Forces in Korea (USFK) and the Republic of Korea cooperatively agreed to set up "rest and relaxation" centers for U.S. troops. The purpose was to provide entertainment and improve the morale of the troops. The kijichon (military camp towns) around the U.S. military bases that resulted from this policy is closed to South Korea citizens and allow only U.S. troops and those who provide services to enter. Although prostitution is officially illegal in South Korea, the sex industry around the U.S. military bases thrives with an estimated 20,000 women in the *kijichon* (Kim, 1997). Most of the clubs or bars in the *kijichon* have rooms upstairs for prostitution (McMichael, 2002a; Moon, 1997).

The abuse and exploitation of Korean women for "rest and relaxation" by soldiers preceded the arrival of U.S. troops. The Japanese army used Korean women for sexual slavery during World War II (Howard, 1995; Hicks, 1995). At the time, the women were euphemistically referred to as "comfort women," and although that term is no longer used, a number of Asian women's nongovernmental organizations (NGOs) characterize the ongoing trafficking and sexual exploitation of Korean and Philippine women by U.S. military troops as a continuation of the same practice. In fact, several sources say that some of the original "comfort women" used by the Japanese army were in turn used by U.S. troops following the defeat of Japan (Kim, 1997). The experiences of the women are similar; except now, the U.S. troops refer to them by other euphemistic and derogatory terms, such as "guest relations officer," "bar girls," "hostesses," "entertainers," and "juicy girls" (Donato, 2002; Demick, 2002; Kim, 1997).

During the almost six decades that U.S. troops have been stationed in South Korea they have committed many crimes in the Korean communities (Ahn, n.d.). One group gathered crime reports and found that from 1945 to 1999, servicemen committed over 10,000 crimes (National Campaign for the Eradication of Crimes by U.S. Troops in South Korea, 1999). In 1992, the brutal rape and murder of Yoon Keum Yi, a prostitute, by a U.S. serviceman, generated public outrage about crimes committed by U.S. troops (Kim, 1997; Kirk, Cornell & Okazawa-

---

[2] For a detailed account of U.S. and Korean relations and their tacit accommodation of U.S. servicemen with women for sex, see Katherine H.S. Moon. *Sex Among Allies: Military Prostitution in the U.S.-Korea Relations.* New York: Columbia University Press, 1997.

Rey, 2000). More recent crimes include the stabbing murder of Si-Sun Li near a U.S. military base in 1998 and the beating death of a 31-year-old bar waitress by two American soldiers in 2000. In both cases, the men said they got angry because the women refused to have sex with them (Associated Press, 1998; Associated Press, 2000).

The Status of Forces Agreement (SOFA), a security treaty, between the U.S. and Republic of Korea makes it difficult for Koreans to take legal action against U.S. troops, even when they have committed crimes (Moon, 1997). Created during the Cold War era, the U.S. was able to "negotiate separate and often unequal security treaties with each of its Asian allies," providing few favorable provisions for countries like the Republic of Korea (Cornwell and Wells, 1999). While the Republic of Korea has some legal jurisdiction over crimes committed by U.S. troops, a clause in SOFA's article 22 states that South Korea must give "sympathetic consideration" for any request made by the U.S. to waive its rights unless the case is considered of "particular importance" (Moon, 1997; "Activists intensify SOFA," 2002). According to the National Campaign for the Eradication of Crime by U.S. Troops in Korea, the U.S. military is responsible for disciplining their troops, but frequently, when crimes are committed, the men are just moved to another post (Kirk & Okazawa-Rey; n.d.). In 1999, only 3.6 percent of all crimes committed by U.S. servicemen were brought to trial by the South Korean government (Young Koreans United, 2000). In the climate of tolerance for crimes committed by U.S. troops, prostitution and trafficking for prostitution are among the most tolerated.

Domestic Trafficking of Korean Women for U.S. Military Personnel

According to one estimate, over one million Korean women have been used in prostitution by U.S. troops since the end of World War II (Moon, 1997). One man, formerly stationed at the Osan Air Base described the contemporary kijichon locale and prostitution in the following way:

> Outside the front gate of our air base is a town called song-tan [sic]. There is a strip of bars along this street...about 25 bars. Men go to these bars to see the 'juicy girls.' "...when a man sees [see] a girl that he likes, he calls her over, or sometimes one of the old ladies that work at the bar just brings a girl to the man. He then buys her a 'juicy' (a small glass of juice or alcohol) for about $10. sometimes they just talk, or sometimes he gropes her, but many times the talk negotiate [sic] a 'barfine' ... money paid to the owner of the bar so that the girl can go out for the evening 'bar hopping,' or to a hotel to have sex" (Anonymous , email, May 2001).

Korean girls and women become vulnerable to recruiters after they have been abandoned by families or run away from home because of abuse. They usually have limited job skills and few options for work. They are domestically trafficked from various regions of South Korea for kijichon prostitution outside U.S. bases. Korean women are recruited into prostitution by employment agencies that play a central role in domestic trafficking (Yu, n.d.). Young women who run away from home are often searched for by employment agencies. When the girl or woman is found, the cost to trace her is charged to her as a debt that she then has to repay (Yu, n.d.). Also, Korean women enter prostitution as a way to pay off credit card debt without knowing the conditions and violence they will face. According to one agency, "We hear many cases of those who started out making quick money to pay off credit card debts but ended up in situations they didn't know existed" (Go, IOM-Seoul, personal communication, September, 2002).

Once Korean women are in prostitution, they quickly accumulate more debt. Pimps manipulate the women into incurring debts, so that they will not be able to leave. Women are charged for rent, food, furniture, clothes, and medical expenses; so often, the longer the woman is in prostitution, the larger is her debt. One former bar woman said her debt accrued for 25 years while she was being used in the kijichon. Over this period of time, she had to pay for 25 abortions because she said she could not "bring another life into this world if he/she has a life like mine" (Kirk, 1995). According to the representative of United Voice for the Eradication of Prostitution in Korea (Hansori):

> Every day a woman has to pay her pimp the money from three customers. If she fails to pay, it is added to her debt. A woman is sold from one place to another every one to two months, and the agency fee that the employer pays the employment agency is added to her debt. [One woman] started with no debts, but at the end of eight years in prostitution, her debt increased to over 20 million won (over US$20,000) (Yu, n.d.).

The pervasive tactic for recruiting and coercing Korean women into prostitution is through the creation and manipulation of debts. These debts are then used to control the women and keep them in prostitution, often for years.

Transnational Trafficking of Women to South Korea

In the last decade, the economic conditions have improved for South Korea, offering women more opportunities than in the past. Consequently, foreign women are increasingly replacing the Korean women in prostitution around the U.S. bases. Women from the Philippines, the Russian Federation, Bolivia, Peru, Mongolia, China, Bangladesh, Kyrgyzstan, and Uzbekistan have been trafficked into South Korea (Jhoty, 2001; McMichael, 2002a; Lhagvasuren, 2001). According to the International Organization for Migration in Seoul, 5,000 women have been trafficked into South Korea, mostly Russians and Filipinas, who are replacing the Koreans (Capdevila, 2002a; Go, IOM-Seoul, personal communication, September 2002). For example, in one kijichon area with 40 clubs, of the 301 women in prostitution, 107 were Korean, 149 were Philippine, and 45 were Russian (Union of Women's Social Organizations in the Kyonggi-do Province, n.d.).

For decades, Filipina women have been used in prostitution by U.S. troops around the large military bases in the Philippines, but those bases closed in the 1990s. The closing of the U.S. military bases, as well as the Asian economic crisis led to high unemployment, especially among women in the Philippines where only 46.8 percent of women are employed compared to 85.7 percent of men (Enriquez, n.d.). The Philippine government supports and facilitates the overseas employment of Filipinos because it helps solve their unemployment problem, and the workers abroad send home money to support families, helping to alleviate poverty (Enriquez, n.d.). Because the Philippines is a source of unskilled workers for South Korea, there are a number of agencies and schemes that recruit and facilitate the travel and work of Filipinos in South Korea (Enriquez, n.d.). Traffickers work within this system. Recruiters who work for foreign employers travel around the countryside offering poor young women opportunities for work abroad, often giving parents advance payments on their daughters' wages (Cruz, 2002). As thousands of Filipinas go abroad expecting to find work, many are now in circumstances of sexual exploitation by US troops in South Korea similar to those they were in when the U.S. military bases were in the Philippines.

The presence of Filipinas around the U.S. bases in South Korea was noted as early as 1987, but in recent years, the numbers have been increasing (Enriquez, n.d.). In 1994, there were approximately 250 Filipinas in prostitution around the U.S. military bases in South Korea. By 1997, the number increased to 1,365, and by 2002, the number rose to 3,000 (Donato, 2002). Traffickers target particular communities for recruiting women for prostitution abroad, such as those displaced in Central Luzon due to the eruption of the Mt. Pinatubo volcano and closure of the U.S. bases (Enriquez, n.d.). The women are mostly young, with high school or less education, coming from the rural areas and from poor families (Enriquez, n.d.). Many Filipinas are recruited by agencies that require the women to pay placement fees to secure good jobs for them (Donato, 2002). Instead of the jobs promised, the women are met at the airport and taken to bars or clubs around U.S. military bases (Donato, 2002).

In other cases, many Filipina women arrive in South Korea on E-6 entertainer visas and/or false documents (Go, IOM-Seoul, personal com-

munication, September, 2002). They are recruited as Overseas Performing Artists (OPA), for which they are required to prove they have
entertainer skills before they are granted authorized entry into other
countries to work in the entertainment industry ("Filipino Women
Hired," 2002). There are indications that the Technical Education and
Skills Development Authority (TESDA), which supervises the training
and testing centers that determine if the women sent abroad are
qualified as performing artists, is involved in bribery and deception with
the issuance of E-6 visas (Cruz, 2002). Recruiters either bribe the
authorities at the testing centers or send in skilled doubles to perform
in order to get the needed certification for the woman to be able to go
abroad on an entertainer visa (Cruz, 2002). When the woman arrives at
the destination abroad, she is in the country legally as an entertainer
with heavy debts owed to her employer, but with no true artistic skills.
She is then forced into prostitution.

According to the Korean Immigration Bureau of the Ministry of
Justice, the number of people entering South Korea on E-6 entertainment visas has climbed steadily: 2,150 in 1998, 4,486 in 1999, and 7,044
in 2000 (Jhoty, 2001). According to one report, the Korea Special
Tourism Association, an association made up of 189 club owners near the
kijichon areas, was the chief contractor for holders of the E-6 visas
(Capdevila, 2002b). The Association began lobbying the government to
bring in foreign women to work in the nightclubs in 1996. The president
of the Association claimed that their organization plays an important
role in preventing GI harassment of Korean women and in strengthening
U.S.–South Korea relations: "If it hadn't been for us, there would be
sexual violations, maybe rapes. We are contributing to United States
and Korean relations in our own way, and nobody appreciates it"
(Demick, 2002). This claim is the same one used by the Japanese during
World War II: Providing "comfort women" to the Japanese troops would
prevent them from raping or harassing the local women.

Many women overstay the E-6 visas or work illegally on 90-day
visitor's visas, known as C-3 visas (Jhoty, 2001). According to a
spokesperson at the Ministry for Gender Equality, more women are
trafficked through C-3 visas than E-6 visas. For example, in 2001, 1,500
Filipina and 3,518 Russian women entered on E-6 visas, while 6,675
Filipinas and 11,633 Russian entered on C-3 visas (Sung, 2001). A
Ministry spokesperson said it is difficult to locate the holders of the C-3
visas after the visas expire because they are issued without strict
passport inspection (Sung, 2001). If the women escape from the
traffickers or pimps, they are considered illegal immigrants, sent to
immigrant detention centers, and deported (Jhoty, 2001).

The collapse of the Soviet Union has created conditions in which tens
of thousands of women from former Soviet countries are going abroad
looking for work (Hughes, Forthcoming). Many of the Russian women

held professional jobs at home before going to South Korea with false passports (Capdevila, 2002b). Between January 2000 and March 2001, approximately 6,000 Russian women entered Korea through Busan port and Gimpo airport (Jhoty, 2001). In 2000, 3,064 Russians entered South Korea on E-6 visas, 2,927 of them women (Jhoty, 2001). Less is known about the Russian or Russian-speaking women who are used in prostitution around the bases. The lack of information is due to fewer NGOs collecting information and documenting the women's experiences. Russian officials have repeatedly refused to comment on the situation (Jhoty). According to an IOM-Seoul representative, there are more Russian women in prostitution in South Korea than Philippine women, but there are more Filipinas in kijichon prostitution because they speak English, which is in demand around the U.S. bases (Go, IOM-Seoul, personal communication, September, 2002).

Organized crime groups have taken advantage of the economic difficulties faced by women. In January 2000, a network involving Russian organized crime and Koreans was broken up in Seoul. The Russian group supplied the women and received $1000 per month for each woman they supplied. The Koreans operated a job placement agency, through which they had trafficked over 50 Russian women into South Korea during the previous year ("10 arrested," 2000).

There is evidence that although the Philippines and countries of the former Soviet Union are geographically, linguistically, and culturally distant, the same traffickers are at work in the recruitment and enslavement of women. Several years ago, Kim Kyong-Su was investigated by the Yong-San District police for "importing 1,093 foreign women, from the Philippines and Russia, to work as entertainers near the U.S. military camp." He was suspected of being paid recruiting fees by 234 club-bar owners to provide women for their use. He and two accomplices were charged with illegal recruitment and forging documents (Enriquez, n.d.).

After women arrive in South Korea, some are forced into prostitution right away; others are worn down by pressure and inability to pay their debts unless they engage in prostitution. In the beginning, the women are only required to sit with men and push drinks, but they make no money. They soon discover that the only way to make money and pay their debts is through prostitution (McMichael, 2002a).

Recent investigations found that the women "are all indentured servants, modern-day sexual slaves. ... These Filipino girls say they're locked in the bar every night" (Merriman, 2002). Another investigative report found that every woman interviewed inside and outside the clubs, with the exception of some in Seoul, said they were trafficked (McMichael, 2002a). The journal of a 22-year-old Filipina detailed how she and other trafficking victims were locked in their rooms, had their passports and travel documents confiscated, threatened with violence, prohibited to make phone calls, and were given less than $10 a week for food (Demick, 2002). In some housing for the women, video cameras are mounted over the doors to monitor their movement. Women are usually allotted only a short period of freedom, such as a half hour per day (McMichael, 2002a). One reporter found that the women were "[s]ometimes packed into one room with six or more women, they often survive on little more than ramyeon (noodles) and are forced to work, even when ill" (Jhoty, 2001). These detainment conditions led to five foreign women dying in a fire in a Gunsan brothel in 2000. In early 2002, a similar fire broke out in a Gunsan pub, and 12 women died because they were prevented from escaping by barred exits (Lee, 2002). According to a member of the U.S. Air Force who was stationed at Osan Air Base:

> [M]ost have a contract for one year. They supposedly get paid $300-$350 per month. But their wages are held by their owners for 3 to 4 months to pay for the airline ticket and other expenses. they usually work from 7 p.m. to 1 or 2 a.m. 7 days a week. they are usually confined to their quarters from 2 a.m. to noon the next day. this is to make sure the girl is not prostituting herself without the owner getting his cut. because of the long nights that these girls put in, they often turn to shabu (that is the name for the drug speed here in the orient) to keep themselves awake and looking happy. (Anonymous, email, May 2001).

In an exposé, TV reporter Merriman filmed U.S. military police patrolling and protecting the bars and brothels where U.S. servicemen use trafficked women for prostitution. The military officers acknowledge on camera that they know the women are trafficked, but that it was their job to protect the bars and brothels to ensure the safety of US servicemen (Merriman, 2002). One soldier stationed at Camp Casey remarked, "You know something is wrong when the girls are asking you to buy them bread. They can't leave the clubs. They barely feed them" (Demick, 2002). A different report documented the good relations between the bar owners, pimps, and military police (McMichael, 2002a). U.S. soldiers said that the club-bar owners buy the women at auctions and must earn large sums of money before they are given their passports and freedom (Merriman, 2002).

When the women come to the attention of the Korean government, the most usual response is deportation. The Korean government defends their treatment of women as illegal aliens, not as victims, because they allegedly voluntarily engage in prostitution and make money (Jhoty, 2001). In 2001, in an international assessment of countries' efforts to combat trafficking, the U.S. State Department ranked South Korea on tier 3 (the lowest rating) because South Korea did not comply with minimum standards and had made no efforts to comply. The Trafficking in Persons Report stated that Korea was a country of origin and transit for trafficked persons. Teresa Oh from the Korean NGO Saewoomtuh criticized the report because it failed to recognize that South Korea was also a destination country for trafficked women and children (Jhoty, 2001). Other Korean NGOs demanded that the "U.S. shares the blame for Korea's problem of prostitution and human rafficking," referring to the significant role the U.S. military plays in creating the demand for trafficked women (Kim, n.d.).

Trafficking Korean Women to the United States

Asian and Asian-American organized crime networks operate transnationally within and between South Korea and the U.S. One of their activities is operating massage parlors throughout the U.S. that use Korean women for prostitution. The trafficking networks use some of the same methods migrant smugglers use to get women into the U.S., including: uninspected entry, meaning the women are smuggled into the U.S. across the borders with Mexico or Canada without passing through immigration control points, the use of counterfeit documents, and entry on student or tourist visas. Another route that is routinely used by traffickers involves marriage to U.S. military personnel. In some cases, traffickers pay servicemen to bring Korean women into the U.S. through sham marriages. In other cases, traffickers and pimps target Korean women who are abandoned or divorced by U.S. military personnel.

Korean-American gangs that are known to be involved in prostitution are the Korean Fuk Ching, the Green Dragons, the Korean Killers and Korean Power. The gangs also engage in international drug trafficking, extortion, home invasions of Korean immigrants, and gambling (McGarvey, 2002).

Law enforcement officials describe the nationwide network of massage parlors as having a "layered business structure" (Doucette, 2002a), and "hierarchy" (Sergeant Jim Lalone, Waterford Township Police, Michigan, personal communication, August 30, 2002). One law enforcement officer described one network that was headquartered in Houston with links to Seoul, "The mamasans in the massage parlors [in the network around the country] send the money to Houston and Dallas, and they send it back to Korea. ... Someone is running these rings. They are routing the women. ... Someone is keeping track... There is a hierarchy" (interview, August 30, 2002). An indication of a well-organized network is the efficiency and quickness with which massage parlors reopen after a raid. Usually, the massage parlors reopen within days or weeks of a police raid (New York law enforcement officer, personal communication, September 2002; Michael Mendez, Vice Unit, Dallas Police Department, Texas, September 5, 2002; Doucette, 2002b). In some cases, if the climate becomes too hostile, the pimps move to another location before reopening.

U.S. Military Personnel as Traffickers

A high proportion of the Korean women used in the massage parlors in the U.S. were originally married to U.S. servicemen. According to one INS agent, "I don't recall ever having interviewed a Korean prostitute in this country that was not in the country as a result of being married to an American serviceman" (Goldman, 2002). A social service provider in New York City stated that the majority of women from massage parlors that she sees were previously married to U.S. military servicemen (Rainbow Center, personal communication, October 17, 2002).

For women in prostitution around the military bases in South Korea, it is difficult to escape the stigmatization of society. Their only hope of getting out of prostitution and emigrating to the U.S. is to marry a US serviceman (Moon, 1997, p. 4). Even the trafficked women from the Philippines say their dream is to marry an American man who will buy their freedom (Merriman, 2002). In some cases, U.S. men pay off the women's debt to the pimp to free them (Kim, 1997). In one case, a U.S. serviceman helped a trafficked woman escape by contacting a known anti-trafficking activist in Seoul (McMichael, 2002b).

In the 1980s, Army statisticians reported that the decade produced 25,000 marriages between Korean women and U.S. soldiers, at a rate of about 3,500 a year (Henican, 1989). Although many of these marriages may start off with good intention, 80 percent of marriages between Korean women and U.S. servicemen end in divorce (Moon, 1997, p.35). The women may have poor job or language skills, and are often victims of domestic violence or abandoned by their American husbands (Rainbow Center, personal communication, October 17, 2002). Isolated from both Korean and American communities, they have few options but to return to prostitution (Kim, 1997; Raymond, Hughes & Gomez, 2001). Traffickers or pimps often target women who were married or recently divorced from U.S. servicemen with attractive job offers. Korean women owners or recruiters for massage parlors are familiar with cultural practices and family obligations that could be used to pressure women into earning money. For example, the madams look for Korean women who were formerly married to U.S. servicemen and are trying to survive economically on three to four part-time jobs. She tells them they can make more money working part-time in the massage parlor. According to a former law enforcement officer who worked on prostitution and massage parlor cases for ten years: "There were Korean women who were predators, recruiting other women into the business....They knew where to push the buttons" (Former New York law enforcement officer, personal communication, October 15, 2002).

In some cases, the marriages between Korean women and U.S. servicemen were never intended to be legitimate; they were a way to bring the women into the U.S. The woman may have cooperated in a sham marriage in order to get into the U.S. in the hope of finding a better life. In other cases, her new husband served as a trafficker, working with an Asian crime network in deceiving the woman. Victims often say that their "husbands" sold them to massage parlors after their arrival in the United States (Unidentified woman, Fox on The Record, 2002; Kim, 1997). According to a former law enforcement official in New York City, women may be coerced into the sham marriages by Korean/Korean-American gangs to repay a debt (Former New York law enforcement officer, personal communication, October 15, 2002). Korean-American gangs obtain young women for prostitution through connections to organized crime groups in South Korea, and use sham marriages to American military servicemen to get the women into the US; they are then turned over to the Korean-American gangs that run massage parlors. Some of the young women may have been abducted from villages in South Korea and forced into sham marriages (McGarvey, 2002)

After gathering information from numerous massage parlor raids around the country, law enforcement officials name "sham marriages" with "GIs" as one of the primary methods that traffickers use to get women into the U.S. (Doucette, 2002c).

In Houston, police who issued licenses to work in "sexually oriented businesses" identified two general groups of Korean women in the area massage parlors. The women in one group speak no English and need an interpreter to assist them with the application. These women have Korean family names on their passports, but the passports are not stamped as they should be if they passed through official immigration control points when leaving Korea or entering the U.S. There is another group of Korean women who can speak more English and have American last names, indicating that they have been married to an American man (Sergeant Tim Cox, Vice Division, Houston Police Department, personal communication, September 12, 2002).

According to a police officer who was involved in raids on Korean massage parlors in the Midwest, the network that operates in his area is run by a Korean organized crime network based in Seoul, and relies on U.S. military personnel to bring Korean women into the U.S. The women are usually young and attractive: Some are as young as 18, most are in their early 20s, but a few are in their 50s:

> The men are paid by the Korean mob that is based in Seoul. They are paid $1500 to marry the Korean woman. In San Francisco, the divorce is already arranged as soon as he gets her into the country. Then he gets another $1500 ... Black military personnel are involved .... Don't know why that is, but 90 percent of the men are black. A few white guys, and never a Hispanic man. (Interview, August 30, 2002).

According to Police Chief William Dwyer who was involved in closing Korean massage parlors in Farmington Hills, Michigan in the mid-1980s:

> We learned servicemen had married some of the defendants in the case and brought them over here for a certain amount of money—$5,000 to $10,000 .... It was a slavery thing. They divorced them once they were here and [the women] went to work for a Korean crime cartel who had them actually living inside these places (Martindale, 2000).

According to a representative of the Army's Criminal Investigation Division, "soldiers are seldom punished even when sham marriages are suspected" (Henican, 1989). Other police sources indicate that this pattern continued through the 1990s (Gillerman & Goodrich, 1997). In 1993, police obtained specific information on a member of the U.S. Navy who delivered a Korean woman to a massage parlor in Oakland County, Michigan. One of the women, who had just been delivered to the brothel two weeks before the raid, was willing to talk to the police and tell them that her "husband" had taken her to the brothel, then left her there. According to the Oakland County prosecutor: "She was his wife, officially. He was paid to bring her here. He was in town less than 24 hours. He then left for Norfolk, Virginia" (interview August 30, 2002).

Marriage certificates to American men enable women to obtain additional pieces of identification, which makes it more difficult to detect the activity of the traffickers. According to one officer involved in the raid of a club with Korean women in Rhode Island:

> They were Korean women, with Americanized names. We checked on their legal status with INS—and they all cleared ... they had IDs, driver's licenses .... What happens is they would marry American servicemen and then get divorced. (Raymond, Hughes & Gomez, 2001).

Transnational trafficking networks have several ways to get women into the US for use in massage parlors, one of which is to use US military personnel. According to one law enforcement officer, "The military is the key! I've never seen it any other way" (Sergeant Jim Lalone, Waterford Township Police, Michigan, personal communication, August 30, 2002). Different transnational crime groups may use different methods, which probably change over time as other opportunities for supplying women arise, but at least some of them make heavy use of U.S. military personnel as couriers, making them traffickers by law.

Massage Parlor Circuits

Crime groups usually manage a string of massage parlors around the country. Sometimes Korean women who were formerly prostitutes own the individual massage parlors (Former New York law enforcement officer, personal communication, October 15, 2002). Women are rotated from place to place, in order to supply "fresh faces" for the men (Merriman, 2002). According to one police officer, "They women are there just a short time and then move on to the next location ... They move from one big city to the next" (interview, September 5, 2002).

One network of Korean massage parlors has a circuit around the Midwest and southeast. The string of massage parlors runs across the southern seaboard, up the eastern seaboard and across the Midwest. According to a law enforcement officer who has been involved in raiding a number of the massage parlors in Michigan:

> They start the women off in Houston and Dallas. Then they take them east along the southern seaboard. Then they go onto Florida, Georgia, from there, to Ohio, Michigan. We have 3 to 4 towns they are in here: Grand Rapids, Flint, Waterford, and Saginaw. They move them around in vehicles; they never fly. The women spend one month in each place, then move on to the next. They want fresh faces. (interview, August 30, 2002).

What happens to women in the massage parlors was described as "horrible, unbelievably terrible" by an NGO representative (Frank Barnaba, Paul and Lisa Program, personal communication, September, 2002). Throughout the country, sources report that women live under similar conditions in most locations. The women have few possessions and live in the massage parlors, usually sleeping on the floor (Merriman, 2002). According to one law enforcement official who was involved in several raids:

> When we raided the spa, we found that the women's sleeping quarters upstairs .... This apartment ... was not furnished at all ... there were blankets and sleeping bags all over the place. Almost like a communal type living. Next to the sleeping bag, was a cosmetic bag, handbag. The women slept there, made a small space for themselves next to their sleeping bags .... I was think they get moved a lot. So this is temporary living situation. How they were living was definitely made for easy mobility. If they closed overnight, they could just pack up and throw everything into a van and just go. (Raymond et al. 2001).

The women seldom leave the premises and are required to work all the time.

They don't have access to a vehicle. We've never seen cars parked in the vicinity to indicate that these women are independent to drive out when they please. We've also never observed these women ever venture outside of the premises. I believe that the managers feed, clothe them as they see fit. If they do go out, it is probably an organized outing in the company van.... These women were not just walking out the door. (Raymond, Hughes & Gomez, 2001).

Women are required to work to pay off debts. Even daily expenses for travel and living expenses, referred to as papkap or "rice money," are added to the women's debt. In one case in Royal Oak, Michigan, the prosecutor said that in Korea the women's family members were living under threat or she was being used to pay off a family debt (Charles Semchena, Royal Oak, Michigan Attorney's Office, personal communication, September 4, 2002). In another case in Rhode Island, the women had to work 16 to 18 hours per day to repay their $10,000 debt for travel to the U.S. A police officer noted that one of the women had cigarette burns on her arm. The club owner provided housing and food for the women, but did not pay them. Any money they made came from tips, which required the women to engage in prostitution (Rockoff, 1998).

Some women in the massage parlors are subjected to high rates of violence. In one case in Washington, D.C., a man killed a woman by stabbing her 23 times in the face, neck, chest, arms, and hands (U.S. Attorney's Office, July 17, 2001). A researcher who has done studies on massage parlors in connection to AIDS commented on the level of violence and coercion the women are subjected to:

I'm aware that many of these women are abused by clients and by their employers. They are required to have sex with several men on a daily basis, and are indebted to their employers. Some are required to pay off debts. Some are under contract for their work, and must work a certain amount of time and [earn] money to meet the requirements of their contract. (Tooru Nemoto, Center for AIDS Prevention Studies, University of California—San Francisco, personal communication, October 11, 2002).

The crime networks have many ways of preventing the women from leaving. The women believe that if they can make enough money to pay their debt, they will be able to leave and look for other opportunities. This keeps them compliant. According to an officer in the Houston Vice Division, "They save their money to pay their debt. Then just about the time their debt is paid, someone breaks into the massage parlor and steals their money." The women are told they have to continue working to pay their debt.

In other situations, drugs were used to control the women. A former law enforcement officer commented:

> The prevalence of crack and cocaine was a device that a lot of madams used to create some level of obligation. Girls would get addicted to the stuff. Even if there was no original debt going into the situation, debt was incurred by purchasing narcotics. It would be done informally, while they were waiting for customers. They did it because others did it. (interview, October 15, 2002).

A representative from the Rainbow Center who provides assistance for women from massage parlors in New York City said that many of women had been physically and verbally abused and have problems with substance abuse.

Official Corruption and Trafficking of Women

There is widespread official complicity and corruption in the trafficking of women for prostitution. Traditionally, organized crime groups strive to corrupt officials in order to conduct their activities. Transnational trafficking of women is dependent on crossing borders and obtaining the necessary travel and identity documents, so involvement of corrupt officials, who take bribes or assist in providing authentic documents, is crucial to successful operations. Because prostitution is often viewed as a "victimless crime," police and other officials are more willing to cooperate with the pimps and traffickers.

In South Korea, police are often complicit in the control of the women by returning escaping women to the bar owners (McMichael, 2002a). Teresa Oh, a social worker who assists women in prostitution reported that, "If a Russian or Filipina girl runs away, and the club owner calls the police, the police will go get her-and she will be abused when she's brought back" (McMichael, 2002a). Senior Superintendent Kim Kang-ja, Director of the Women and Juvenile Division of the Korean National Police Agency, cites widespread corruption or tolerance of prostitution in clubs around the U.S. bases. She said that "almost all" of the South Korean police and officials responsible for enforcing prostitution laws accept bribes (McMichael, 2002a). She added that if the South Korean law banning consorting with prostitutes was tightly enforced "almost all U.S. soldiers would be arrested. Korean police should arrest them, or hand them to the American officers. But it's not actually taking place. Nobody is controlling them" (McMichael, 2002a).

In the U.S., a nationwide investigation into Asian American organized crime exposed how corrupt police officers protect and assist the operation of Korean prostitution rings. Presently, as part of a nationwide crackdown on Asian-American organized crime involving Korean massage parlors, a Sunnyvale, California police officer stands accused of accepting gifts, cash, and sex in exchange for police information and protection for two Korean "hostess bars." In addition, he helped the owners of the club track down women who escaped before paying their debt. On one occasion, he traveled with the owner of the club to Hawaii to threaten a woman with jail or deportation if she did not pay the owner money (Stites, Cronk, & Pittman, 2002).

Several law enforcement officials who were interviewed noted suspicious patterns in the identity documents that the Korean women in the massage parlors had when a raid took place. One officer noticed that although the women had what appeared to be authentic passports, they were not stamped which would be required if the women had passed through immigration control (Sergeant Tim Cox, Vice Division, Houston Police Department, personal communication, September 12, 2002). Another official noted that most of the women had driver's licenses issued for the same place (Prosecutor, Oakland County, Michigan, personal communication, August 30, 2002). These irregularities or suspicious patterns seem to indicate that corrupt officials may be involved in assisting the traffickers or massage parlor crime groups in getting identity documents for the women.

U.S. Military, Government, and Federal Law Enforcement Response

When confronted with evidence of U.S. troops using women for prostitution and women being trafficked for prostitution in South Korea, the Department of Defense has two standard responses. The first is to say that engaging in prostitution is a violation of US Military Code of Conduct, thereby stating that they have an official policy against it and that men who engage in prostitution are in violation of the rules. The Department of Defense's second response is to say it is prevented from taking action in South Korean civilian criminal activity because it would violate South Korea's sovereignty (McMichael, 2002a).

According to a man formerly stationed at the Osan Air Base, South Korea:

> I also believe that the Korean government and the United States Forces Korea (USFK) knows what is going on and does very little to stop it. The USFK has the military authority to make these place "off-limits" but doesn't unless they find out that prostitution is going on in an establishment. Then they usually make that establishment "off-limits" for a while then it gets taken off their list of "off-limit establishments" and they're back in business again. Prostitution is prohibited to military personnel by the military uniform code of justice but it goes on (Anonymous, email, May 2001).

The U.S. State Department is on record saying that U.S. soldiers should not engage in prostitution. Nancy Ely-Raphel, former head of the Office to Combat Trafficking in Persons said, "There's a zero-tolerance policy on the part of our military toward prostitution and toward frequenting brothels. So the military can do a lot about it" (McMichael, 2002c). Yet, in a report released by Saewoomtuh, a South Korean NGO providing services to military base prostitutes, eighty-four percent of male U.S. military personnel admitted to being with a prostitute (Kim, 2000).

In the spring and summer 2002, exposés on the exploitation of trafficked women around U.S. military bases in South Korea were aired by several news agencies. The reports showed that military police were aware of the activities and patrolled the bars. In response, a number of U.S. Congressmen wrote a letter to Secretary of Defense Donald Rumsfeld requesting an investigation. Army Secretary Thomas E. White responded that military police "do not regulate, protect, or support Korean businesses or enterprises in any way" (McMichael, 2002a). Further investigation is underway, and there may be Congressional hearings on this topic in the future.

The trafficking of Korean women for prostitution in the U.S. is not a new phenomenon, and in the past has received periodic federal attention. In 1986, the Senate Permanent Subcommittee on Investigations reported on U.S. servicemen's involvement in bringing Korean women into the U.S. for use in massage parlor prostitution circuits. They identified a pattern of Asian/Asian-American organized crime groups using sham marriages to get women into the U.S. According to Dan Rinzel, the chief Republican counsel to the subcommittee nearly all the women entered the U.S. "by visas obtained through fraudulent marriages to American GIs stationed in Korea" (Yeager, 1994).

In summer 2002, a crackdown by federal agents on Asian organized crime in the U.S. revealed both the scope of the massage parlor networks and the progress that needs to be made by U.S. authorities in effectively countering trafficking. Eighty-seven warrants were served in California, Michigan, Kentucky, Nevada, Tennessee, Connecticut, Ohio, North Carolina, Texas, Georgia, Pennsylvania, and Virginia (Associated Press, 2002a). The investigation was initiated five years before when one of the massage parlor operators tried to bribe public officials, including a judge (Associated Press, 2002b).

This series of cases was investigated from the framework of organized crime, which focused on the crimes of money laundering and bribery, not trafficking in women. Initial comments by FBI and local police that appeared in newspaper stories indicated these women were in classic trafficking conditions: the women were recruited in South Korea and provided visas by brokers; if visas could not be arranged, the women were flown into Mexico and smuggled across the border; the women were brought to the U.S. under false pretenses; the women were obligated to repay debts for travel and living expenses by engaging in prostitution; and the women lived in the massage parlors and were only allowed to leave for short periods of time (Mickle & Palmer, 2002; Associated Press, 2002a; Associated Press, 2002b). While initial investigations by the FBI did not find any evidence of trafficking, screening for trafficking may have failed due to intimidation of the victims by organized crime groups, cultural barriers in communication, and lack of follow-up by law enforcement. One FBI official involved with the case believes that trafficking was probably present, and cited lack of prioritization by the FBI as the reason why the screening may have failed and no follow-up was planned (FBI agent, Michigan, personal communication, August 10, 2002). Calls to newspaper reporters in the towns where arrests were made indicated that just days after the raids and arrests, the massage parlors were open again (Ken Palmer, reporter, Flint Journal, personal communication, August 7, 2002).

Local Law Enforcement Response

Although a few smaller municipalities have worked vigorously to close massage parlors because of their unpopularity in the community, in larger cities, there is little enforcement of laws concerning massage parlors or the establishments reopen within a few days of a raid (Michael Mendez, Vice Unit, Dallas Police Department, personal communication, September 5, 2002). Reasons given for lack of enforcement range from massage parlors being a lower priority than other types of prostitution or organized crime, lack of personnel and resources due to decrease in size of vice units, and legal challenges to ordinances regulating massage parlors (Sergeant Jim Lalone, Waterford Township Police, Michigan, personal communication, August 30, 2002; Keith Haight, Vice Unit, Los Angeles Police Department, personal communication, September 5, 2002; Sergeant Tim Cox, Vice Division, Houston Police Department, personal communication, September 12, 2002).

Law enforcement personnel in the United States are generally unaware that Korean women in massage parlors are potential victims of trafficking. The women are usually treated as criminals, as in Flushing, New York, where the women were arrested or in Providence, Rhode Island, where one victim with cigarette burns was arrested and deported. Many police recognize the slavery-like conditions under which the women work, but are unaware of the concept of trafficking in persons as a human rights violation and the legal status of a trafficking victim. Women's possession of U.S. drivers' licenses or other documents makes victimization harder to recognize. Prosecution of the victims further victimizes the women, and shields the traffickers from being held accountable under US anti-trafficking law.

Conclusion

The U.S. military bases in South Korea form a hub for the transnational trafficking of women from the Asia-Pacific and Eurasia to South Korea and the United States. Over the past six decades, U.S. troops have used an estimated million Korean women in prostitution. During the 1990s, increasing numbers of women from the Asia-Pacific and Eurasia, particularly the Philippines and Russia, were trafficked into bars and brothels around the military bases in South Korea. From South Korea, women are trafficked, frequently by U.S. servicemen, to the United States where they are used in prostitution on massage parlor circuits. Asian, Russian, and Korean-American organized crime groups cooperate with each other to run the trafficking networks. The number of different groups or gangs that are involved, how they are interlinked, or cooperate is unknown. They exist to make money by supplying women to meet the demand for prostitution by U.S. military personnel in South Korea and men in the United States.

A significant number of Korean women in massage parlors in the U.S. are former wives of U.S. servicemen. Some of the marriages are legitimate, but after being abandoned or divorced, Korean women are vulnerable to being recruited for the massage parlor circuit. In other cases, the marriage was a sham arranged by organized crime networks as a method to get Korean women into the U.S.

The widespread tolerance of prostitution in bars around the U.S. bases in South Korea and the massage parlors around the U.S. has fueled the demand for women, resulting in increased trafficking of women. In South Korea, if there are too many negative incidents relating to prostitution in the bars, they are listed as off-limits to the troops for a certain period of time; later the ban is lifted. In the U.S., a few smaller communities have permanently closed massage parlors, but in most large cities, there is little investigation or effective enforcement of laws. Most of the massage parlors reopen within days of police raids.

In both South Korea and the United States, some members of the military, police, and social service agencies recognize the abusive, exploitive, and often slavery-like conditions under which the women live. Yet, the women are still usually treated as criminals, instead of victims. In South Korea, the foreign women are deported. In the U.S., with a few exceptions, most police raids on massage parlors focus on arresting the women.

Discussion Questions

1   *What three types of trafficking were studied in this article?*

2   *What is a "kijichon?"*

3   *What are some of the common names used by US troops for "comfort women?"*

4   *Why did the Philippine government support and facilitate the overseas employment of their citizens?*

5   *What arguments were presented by the Korea Special Tourism Association as to how prostitution provided protection from G.I. harassment of Korean women?*

6   *Law enforcement officials describe the nationwide network of massage parlors in the United States as having a "layered business structure." What does this mean?*

7   *What was the explanation provided as to why 80 percent of all marriages between U.S. servicemen and Korean women ended in divorce?*

8   *What was the primary reason for sham marriages to G.I.s?*

9   *Since it is a violation of the U.S. Military Code of Conduct for American service personnel to use the services of a prostitute how come the violation is almost never be enforced or prosecuted?*

10 *What reasons were cited by American law enforcement agencies for the lack of enforcement of massage parlors which were often used as fronts for prostitution?*

References

10 arrested in connection with Russian prostitutes. (2000, January 6). The Korea Herald.

"Activists intensify SOFA revision efforts." (2002, August 6). Korea Times.

Ahn, I.S. (n.d.). Violations of Human Rights against Korean Women and Children by the United States Forces in Korea (USFK): Mighty Army, Great Father-TheUSFK and Prostitution in Korea. Retrieved from Korea Church Women United Web site: http://maria.peacenet.or.kr/il.htm.

Associated Press. (2002a, July 24). FBI, IRS raid massage parlors in Asian crime crackdown. Associated Press.

Associated Press. (2002b, July 28). FBI busts national prostitution, bribery and money laundering enterprises. Associated Press.

Associated Press. (2000, April 29). Murder suspect captured in Korea. Associated Press.

Associated Press. (1998, February 28). Court upholds prison for U.S. soldier. AP Online.

Capdevila, G. (2002a, September 5). Korea's new "comfort women." Asia Times.

Capdevila, G. (2002b). Women Trafficked for U.S. Military Bases (International Organization for Migration).

Cornwell, R. and Wells, A. (1999). Deploying Insecurity. Peace Review 11(3), 409-414.

Cruz, N.H, (2002, July 22). Government sending women to prostitution abroad. Daily Inquirer (Philippines).

Demick, B. (2002, September 26). Off-base behavior in Korea: By allowing GIs to patronize certain clubs, the U.S. military is seen as condoning the trafficking of foreign women for prostitution. Los Angeles Times.

Donato, A.E. (2002, March 3). Trafficking of Pinays going on in Mindanao, S. Korea: NGO. Manila Times.

Doucette, J.H. (2002a, June 24). Fuji Spa a satellite of illicit sex circuit. Times Herald Record.

Doucette, J.H. (2002b, June 24). Goshen massage parlor reopens. Times Herald Record.

Doucette, J.H. (2002c, June 18). Another raid at Goshen spa lead to six arrests. Times Herald Record.

Enriquez, J. (n.d.). Filipinas in prostitution around U.S. military bases in Korea: A recurring nightmare. The Coalition Against Trafficking in Women – Asia Pacific.

Filipino women hired to provide sex to U.S. troops. (2002, March 4). The Straits Times (Singapore).

Gallagher, M. (1995, April 7). Prostitution ring traps South Koreans. USA Today.

Gillerman M.& Goodrich, R. (1997, June 6). Police link raids, illegal immigration: Seven charged with prostitution at massage parlors in Collinsville. St. Louis Post Dispatch.

Goldman, J. (2002, June 11). Fox On The Record.

Henecan, E. (1989, March 19). Rubbing city the wrong way: Korean massage parlors. *New York Newsday*, p. 7.

Hicks, G. (1995). The comfort women: Japan's brutal regime of enforced prostitution in the Second World War. New York: W.W. Norton.

Howard, K. (Ed.). (1995). True stories of the Korean comfort women: Testimonies compiled by the Korean Council for Women Drafted for Military Sexual Slavery by Japan. London: Cassell.

Hughes, D.M. (Forthcoming). Supplying women for the sex industry: Trafficking women from the Russian Federation. Sexualities in Postcommunism.

Jhoty, B. (2001, November 2). Trapped in modern slavery: Sex trafficking turns Russian women into Korean pawns. The Korea Herald.

Kim, H.S. (2000). The Problems Facing Women and Children at Kijichon in Korea. (Saewoomtuh report, p. 30).

Kim, H.S. (1997). The Problems Faced by Women and Children in Korean GI Towns (Presentation at the International Conference, Okinawa). Retrieved from: http://maria.peacenet.or.kr/i3.htm

Kim, H.S. (n.d.) Commentary: A backward country when it comes to human trafficking. Retrieved from: http://www.womensnews.co.kr/ewnews/enews15.htm

Kirk, G., Cornwell, R., & Okazawa-Rey, M. (2000). Women and the U.S. military in East Asia. Foreign Policy in Focus, 4(9).

Kirk, G. & Okazawa-Rey, M. (n.d.) East Asia-U.S. women's network against U.S. militarism in South Korea. Retrieved from: http://www.apcip.org/women'snetwork/skorea.htm.

Kirk, G. (1995). Speaking out: Militarized prostitution in South Korea. A Journal about Women, 40(6).

Lee, J. (2002, February 2). Victims of Gunsan pub fire were locked in by owner. Korea Herald.

Lhagvasuren, N. (2001, August 21). Waking up to a new reality. Transitions Online.

Martindale, M. (2000, September 6). Police raids shut down illegal massage shops-Storefronts concealed sex services in Oakland. The Detroit News.

McGarvey, B. (2002, August 22-28). Silent threat. Philadelphia CityPaper.net. Retrieved from: http://citypaper.net/articles/2002-08-22/cb2.shtml

McMichael, W. H. (2002a, August 12). Sex slaves. Navy Times.

McMichael, W. H. (2002b, August 12). Soldier drew the line, helped free a girl. Navy Times.

McMichael, W. H. (2002c, August 12). MP's watch clubs closely, but some say military looks the other way. Navy Times.

Merriman, T. (2002, June 11). Fox On the Record.

Mickle, B. & Palmer, K. (2002, July 24). $300,000 seized during massage parlor raids. Flint Journal.

Moon, K.H.S. (1997). Sex Among Allies: Military Prostitution in U.S.-Korea Relations. New York: Columbia University Press.

National Campaign for the Eradication of Crimes by U.S. Troops in Korea. (1999). The never ending history of pain: American military crimes. Seoul: Kaema-sowon.

Polaris Project. (2002, October). Unpublished research.

Prosecution combats brothels near U.S. bases. (2002, October 11). Korea Times.

Protesters' voices heard. (2002, December 14). Korea Now. Retrieved from: http://kn.koreaherald.co.kr/SITE/data/html_dir/2002/12/14/ 200212140007.asp

Raymond, J. G., Hughes, D. M., and Gomez, C. J. (2001, March) Sex trafficking of women in the United States: International and Domestic Trends. Coalition Against Trafficking in Women.

Rockoff, J. D. (1998, November 24). Police allege club was a brothel. The Providence Journal.

Stites, R., Cronk, M., & Pittman, R. (2002, July 24). Officer charged in sex racket. Mercury News.

Sung, T. K. (2001, October 15). Prostitutes use visitors visas to enter Korea. Korea Times.

Union of Women's Social Organizations in the Kyonggi-do Province. Retrieved from: http://my.netian.com/~wintry/chapter1e.htm.

Yeager, H. (1994, January 12). 'Very organized operation' gets Korean women into U.S. brothels. States News Service.

Young Koreans United of USA. (2000). National campaign to revise SOFA. Retrieved from: http://www. ykusa.org/english/peace/sofa.html.

Yu, T.H. (n.d.) Sex work in South Korea. Retrieved from: http://www.amrc. org.hk/arch/3309.htm.

12

FOREIGN WOMEN TRAFFICKED TO UNITED STATES MILITARY AREAS IN SOUTH KOREA: TRAFFICKING PROCESSES AND VICTIM PROFILES IN A DIFFERENT CONTEXT

Sallie Yea, Ph.D., *Charles Sturt University*

Introduction

South Korea (hereafter Korea), along with some other sex trafficking destination countries in the Asia-Pacific region such as Hong Kong, Japan and Australia, represents a different context for sex trafficking from the commonly cited cases of South Asia and the Greater Mekong Sub-Region (GMS) that appear in both academic literatures (*see*, for example, Skrobanek et al., 1997, Phongpaichit, 1999; Frederick and Kelly, 2000; AFESIP, 2005) and governmental and nongovernmental reports (see, for example, Asia Watch/Women's Rights Project, 1993; Caouette and Saito, 1999; IOM, 1998; CWDA, 1996; Human Rights Watch, 1995). The departures presented by these other contexts, including Korea, point to the need to recognize differences as well as commonalities in the nature and characteristics of sex trafficking throughout the region and the need to draw more fully on a range of trafficking sites beyond the commonly discussed South Asia and GMS in extending our knowledge of sex trafficking and ability to respond with appropriate actions.

The GMS—Thailand and Cambodia in particular—are increasingly viewed as an epicenter for trafficking for both sexual and labor exploitation in Asia. India and Pakistan, on the other hand, are the major destinations for a burgeoning South Asian trafficking trade involving Nepal and Bangladesh as primary source countries. It is estimated, for example, that over 5,000 girls and young women have been trafficked from Nepal to Pakistan and from Nepal to India over the past 10 years. The rate continues at 200-400 victims per month, a figure which is still considered to be a fairly accurate estimate today (Human Rights Watch, 1995). In Southeast Asia, some estimate that, at a minimum, between 200,000 and 250,000 women and children are trafficked annually (IOM, 2000). These disturbing statistical patterns, coupled with dramatic horror stories of victims' experiences, have lead to a higher level of concern to these two sub-regions than some other areas in Asia.

Nonetheless, some commentators have already begun to problematize the discursive construction of sex trafficking victims and operations based on evidence largely from these two sub-regions to reveal the powerful operation of an emerging "trafficking myth." Frederick (2005: 127), for example, describes the trafficking myth and its consequences in the following way:

[T]he trafficking "myth" is a typifying narrative of the trafficking episode. The myth serves several purposes: it is the "consensus description" of a typical trafficking episode around which the discourse revolves; it encapsulates the issues for the media, public, governments, and donors, and—in the absence of a firm body of knowledge—it is the basis upon which some, but not all, anti-trafficking interventions are determined.

In Korea, very little was written on sex trafficking until 2000 when a religious-feminist NGO based in Seoul, the Korea Church Women United (KCWU), wrote a report on sex trafficking in US military camp town areas, drawing on cases of over 40 women, including Filipinas and Russians (KCWU, 2000). Despite the in-depth information available in this report, the bulk of information that has appeared since its publication has reinforced a pervasive "sex slave" stereotype (for exceptions, see Yea, 2004; Cheng, 2002; KCWU, 2002). This sex slave persona mistakenly draws on elements of the broader trafficking myth in the GMS and South Asia. Recent international and local media attention (Fox Television, 2002; MacIntyre, 2002; McMichael, 2002; *Hangyure Magazine*, 13 November 2000; SBS Television, 2002) on the plight of the women in Korea has come to dominate discussions and responses to sex trafficking in Korea. This media attention began in April 2002, when a Fox Television report on the women was aired nationally in the United States. This report included secretly filmed footage of conversations by the reporter with US soldiers in the clubs in one US military camp town near the North Korean border.

After the Fox Television report was aired, a series of English-language newspaper and magazine articles began to appear in major forums, such as *Time Magazine* (Asian Edition), the *Air Force Times* and the *L.A. Times*. These articles reinforced the image established by the Fox Television report of the women as sex slaves. Take the following excerpt from a feature article by Donald MacIntyre in *Time Magazine* (5 August 2002), for example:

Rosie Danan found out just how bad [Club Y was] the week she started working there in late 1999, at the age of 16. Back home in Manila, a recruiting agency had promised Danan the job would require her merely to serve drinks and chat with customers. After she arrived in Korea—on a false passport— Club Y's mama-san took her papers away and told her the rules: she would be serving up her body as well as booze. She would get no days off for the first three months. And later she could earn days off only if she sold enough drink and sex. She would live in a room above the club and, unless she was with the mama-san,

Foreign Women Trafficked to United States Military Areas in South   **225**
Korea: Trafficking Processes and Victim Profiles in a
Different Context

would not be allowed outside except for three minutes a day to make a phone call. The penalty for coming back late: $8 a minute.

The horror story of Danan is typical of the style in which the women's cases were being reported and reflect elements of the broader trafficking stereotype in the region, including being a minor (16 years of age), forced sex, forced confinement and withdrawal of documents.

The remainder of this paper attempts to interrogate this sex slave image as it exists in Korea. I begin with an overview of some of the commonly discussed characteristics of sex trafficking in the Asian region, particularly relating to the much cited GMS and South Asian subregions that collectively help form the "trafficking myth." This is followed by a brief background to the history of militarized prostitution and sex trafficking in South Korea. The rest of the paper examines four major ways in which the Korean context presents departures from the sex trafficking myth and thwarts the emerging "sex slave" image of women trafficked for prostitution in that context. These include: the migration trajectories and motivations of victims to migrate; the processes of recruitment and conditions under which migration takes place; the processes and strategies by which brothel and club owners force and coerce women into undertaking prostitution and other sexual services; and structural and other characteristics of the destination (particularly the profiles of customers, the level of development in Korea and so on) which greatly affect the mode and circumstances of victims' exit from trafficking situations and type of repatriation/reintegration processes after trafficking.

The Sex Trafficking Myth in Asia

Sex trafficking of women and girls in Asia, both internally and trans-nationally, has become an issue of significant concern in international migration, transnational crime, international development and human/women's (and children's) rights over the past decade. The number of trafficked persons continues to escalate reaching up to five million in 2004 (United Nations Office on Drugs and Crime, 2004), generating up to US$5-7 billion annually in illicit profits for criminal syndicates (www.uri.edu/artic/wms/hughs/catw, accessed on 3 April 2005). Four major types of human trafficking have been recognized by the United Nations Protocol to Prevent, Suppress and Punish Trafficking in Persons, Especially Women and Children (hereafter the UN Trafficking Protocol); forced labor, slavery, trafficking for organ removal, and sex trafficking. To date, sex trafficking has accounted for approximately 90 percent of global trafficking cases detected. Major transnational governance bodies, national governments and local and international NGOs have called for concerted research and action to document and combat all forms of human trafficking but, given its predominance in scale and documentation of cases, particular attention has focused on sex trafficking. Yet, despite this call for research and documentation, very little *in-depth* research has to date been available, despite the plethora of reports, commentaries and general overviews being produced. This has created the milieu in which trafficking myths have been able to take hold.

Although the elements that together constitute such a myth have been described at length elsewhere (*see*, for example, Frederick, 2005) a brief description nonetheless helps us understand its influence over policy and ways of viewing and interacting with trafficking victims and survivors. Notwithstanding minor variations, the myth as it is circulated in the Asian region contains two basic intertwining elements: first, a typical trafficking victim profile; and second, a typical trafficking scenario (including a description of the mode of recruitment, movement to the destination, conditions of "work" once deployed, processes of exit from trafficking situations and trajectories of victims after exit).

First, the typical sex trafficking victim in Asia is described as young (often prepubescent or in the early stages of puberty), female, innocent, and helpless in the sense of being unable to influence or alter the conditions of her situation. Doezema (2000) and others (Murray, 1998; Kempadoo and Doezema, 1998) have begun to raise concerns about the constellation of these images of innocence, backwardness/ignorance and helplessness. They rightly suggest that these images are often based on considerations of a narrow range of cases that can nonetheless serve to create a powerful stereotype of the "third world trafficking victim" that is used as the primary basis for policy interventions.

In Korea, thanks largely to media portrayals, this typical trafficking victim has also become well established in discussions of sex trafficking. The *Air Force Times* (15 August 2002), for example, perpetuated this image in an article titled, "Sex Slaves and the US Military" stating that, "At a time when the U.S. State Department and the United Nations labor to combat the international trafficking of women, the U.S. military supports a *flourishing trade in sex slaves* [italics added] in South Korea. Hundreds of trafficked women, mostly from former Soviet bloc countries and the Philippines are forced by local bar owners to work as prostitutes in bars that cater to American servicemen." What constitutes a sex slave is not examined in this or other articles which draw their strength precisely from their lack of specificity. Yet we know from the sex slave stereotype already prevalent in the region that such a label implies a complete lack of agency or ability of the victim to negotiate and/or transform their situation. It implies situations of physical confinement/ imprisonment of innocents who are duped and forced into the provision of sexual services for no recompense. In Korea, however, the vast majority of victims are not underage, are not "backward" in the sense of being economically marginal or having limited formal education, and are not helpless in their situations, often exerting considerable agency to resist and negotiate the circumstances of their trafficking to the extent possible.

Apart from a typical sex trafficking victim, the trafficking myth also contains a typical trafficking scenario which outlines the stages in the trafficking process and conditions at the trafficking destination. Frederick (2005) has identified three stages of the sex trafficking process which have become subject to the trafficking myth: the transportation stage, the situation at the destination and withdrawal from the destination. The image of victim transportation established under this myth involves the victim being moved through porous land borders with no documents and where border guards or authorities are complicit in the process. While this is a common scenario for many countries with landed borders in Asia (such as in the GMS and South Asian sub-regions), it does not encapsulate the experiences of victims who are transported across borders legally (and therefore with falsified documents) and via other modes of transport where they may be subjected to scrutiny by immigration authorities at the points of exit and entry. These other transportation scenarios are not given much discursive space under the trafficking myth.

Another important area of trafficking myth that can be contested in the case of Korea is the situation at the destination. The dominant and enduring image established under the trafficking myth is, as Frederick (2005) points out, modeled on the "cages" of Mumbai, where girls are locked in cages, forced to service upwards of 20 clients a day, are subject to extreme forms of violence and torture, and are often HIV positive. Again, while some of these elements may be present for some victims, the circumstances described under the myth cannot be taken as representative of the broad spectrum of different circumstances that characterize the situations of victims once they reach the destination. This includes cases where victims are not always or necessarily physically confined (and may instead be subject to various forms of psychological control and dependency), where there may be a variety of forms of sexual labor involved, rather than penetrative sex alone (such as oral and anal sex, genital massage, lap dancing, strip dancing and so on), and where customers may not reach upwards of 20 per day but may be closer to five or less or, on some days, none. Further, in some contexts, including Korea, condom use is common and is enforced to the extent possible by the club owners and managers as well as the victims themselves. Unwanted pregnancies and the incidence of sexually transmitted infections and HIV/AIDs are therefore dramatically reduced in these contexts.

Finally, the trafficking myth describes a clear mode of exit (with-drawal) of the victim from the trafficking situation. Under the with-drawal scenario the victim is rescued by some well-intentioned NGO or benevolent policing or immigration authority. As Frederick (2005:134) rightly points out one of the reasons for the prevalence of this scenario is that, "it casts NGOs and police as dramatic heroes, and provides the illusion, particularly for the public and donors that something is being done." As we will see below, in Korea very few victims are "rescued" and most withdraw from trafficking situations through the assertion of their own agency where no NGO or other organization is involved. The main reasons this alternative scenario is so commonplace is because victims wish to remain in the trafficking destination of Korea in order to fulfill the original goals of their migration that were denied to them when they become trafficked.

In sum, it is necessary to question the trafficking myth in Asia for its accuracy and to look at the precise way the experiences of different migration contexts can act to contest some its main tenets, such as the profiles of victims, the transportation scenario, the circumstances at the destination and the mode of exit from the trafficking situation. Effective counter-trafficking policy requires that these complexities and differences be taken into account. We now turn to Korea to explore some of these complexities and examine the ways they confound the myth that has emerged to define our understandings of this problem in the Asian region.

Militarized Prostitution and Sex Trafficking in South Korea

Immediately after World War II, the United States military presence expanded rapidly in Asia in order to contain the threat of communist expansion in the region. Japan, South Korea, Thailand, the Philippines and numerous other states played host to United States military personnel either permanently stationed or on rest and recreation leave. In every Asian country where US soldiers have been based a highly systematized sex industry catering to them has also emerged (*see* Enloe, 1989). Until the mid-1990s in Korea such an industry relied exclusively on the sexual labor of Korean women. Filipinas and Russians began to enter Korea as "entertainers" to work in the US military camp town clubs as recently as 1995.[1] The increasing use of foreign women in the camp town clubs and bars can be explained by the far greater profit

---

[1] As KCWU (1999) noted, in 1997 there was a large protest in "America Town," the US military camp town outside Kunsan, North Cholla Province. This protest involved Korean camp town hostesses and prostitutes rallying against the increasing numbers of foreign women working in the clubs who were taking over their customers.

margins for club owners.[2] The greater profitability of foreign women is intimately linked to their "foreignness," which produces a situation of heightened vulnerability for the women, and thus the possibility of greater exploitation. Most of the foreign women in the clubs do not, for example, have unlimited freedom of movement and, virtually without exception, their salaries, passports and alien registration cards are withheld so that they do not run away. In addition, part or all of the women's salaries are normally withheld as an additional incentive to supplement their incomes through their sexual labor, and to keep the women from running away. Unlike their salaries, the money made from their sexual labor and drink sales is normally paid to the women in cash on a regular basis (usually either weekly or monthly). The women rely on this money for their daily living expenses. Recruitment agencies in Korea and the Philippines also make large sums of money from the deployment of foreign women to Korea, a sector that would not exist if Korean women continued to constitute the mainstay of the camp town's prostitution business.

Although the Korean War ended in 1953, approximately 37,000 United States military personnel remain in South Korea to defend the nation against the possible threat of an invasion from communist North Korea. There are currently 99 military bases and installations in South Korea, and several of the larger ones have an associated "camp town" [kijich'on in Korean]. Camp towns may be defined as areas in the immediate proximity of the base that are oriented predominantly to the entertainment, leisure and consumption needs of the US military personnel therein.[3] In most camp towns the streetscape is dominated by businesses with signage in English and goods and services catering to American tastes, including bars, clubs and brothels.

---

[2] The rise in the use of foreign women in the US camp town areas is also, I believe, linked to a prolonged history of anti-Americanism in Korea. In May 1995, just prior to the arrival of the first foreign women into the camp towns, a fight broke out at a Seoul subway station between a group of US GIs and Korean men. The incident was the subject of intense media attention and public debate for several months afterwards, and was followed by other, similar incidents. Until the arrival of foreign women onto the camp town scene a strong and repeated thread running through the discourse of anti-Americanism was the violation of Korean women by US military personnel. Thus, the entry of foreign women has acted to diffuse this particular tension in US-Korea relations somewhat.

[3] In early 2002, the United States Forces Korea (USFK) announced that it was planning to hand back over some of the land currently occupied by US military bases in Korea with several smaller bases being merged with larger ones. In addition, this plan received further impetus with the US occupation of Iraq and the increasing need for a larger US military presence there, a large proportion of which is likely to come from troops currently deployed in South Korea. This implies that there will be fewer camp towns, but they will most likely be of a much larger scale.

The five largest military camp towns in Korea are located in It'aewon (Seoul), Kunsan (North Cholla Province), Tongducheon (Kyunggi Province), Songtan (Kyunggi Province) and Uijongbu (Kyunggi Province). The presence of United States military personnel is far more pronounced in these areas than are Korean nationals, and indeed some camp town areas have been designated as "Korean Special Tourist Districts" by the Korean Special Tourism Association (KSTA), thus demarcating these spaces as open only to foreigners (as they offer tax-free liquor). Tongducheon and Songtan—the two sites for this study—both became Special Tourism Districts in 1997. All of the members of the KSTA are bar or club owners in these camp towns. In fact, the former National President of the KSTA, Kim Kyung Soo, owns a club and a promotion agency in Tongducheon's camp town whilst the current National President owns clubs in Songtan.[4]

Filipinas (and Russians) began to be sent to Korea as "entertainers" in the camp town entertainment establishments in 1995. In 2002, according to the National Statistics Office figures, approximately 1,599 Filipinas and 3,518 Russian women entered Korea on E-6 visas, which together comprise sixty percent of the total entertainers that entered Korea for that year, reflecting a similar pattern to that of Japan (*see* Ballescas, 1992 and Matsui, 1995 for background discussions on Filipina entertainers in Japan). Although it is difficult to ascertain the precise numbers of foreign women deployed in the camp towns, based on numbers of official and unofficial entrants, as well as counts of women made in clubs, one may safely estimate that there are at least 5,000 at any one time for all camp town areas. The numbers of Russian women are similar to those of Filipinas, although it appears that many more Russian women work in Korea prostitution districts, rather than US military camp towns.[5] A study published in December 2001 by one of the nongovernment organizations (NGOs) addressing camp town prostitution issues in Korea counted the number of foreign women (Russian and Filipinas) in Tongducheon camp town area alone at over 1,000 (Saewoomt'uh, 2001:132).

---

[4] On 22 August 1999, Kim Kyung Soo and three others were charged with placing foreign women in drinking establishments for the purpose of prostitution. It was reported in the media at the time that, "Kim Kyung Soo... worked with agents and brokers beginning in July 1996 to recruit 1093 Russian and Filipino women... They collected over W160,000,000 as payment from 234 club owners" (*Hankyurye Sinmun*, 22 August 1999). On 24 August, the charges against Kim were, however, dropped due to insufficient evidence that Kim forced the girls to prostitute themselves and deprived them of their salary.

[5] One of the main reasons for this pattern of migrant geography is the preference of US GIs for Filipinas since their English is normally much better than that of the Russian women. In the absence of comprehensive research on the situations of Russian entertainers, much of the information surrounding their experiences is, to date, based on speculation and casual observations.

To date there have been a few empirical studies (KCWU, 1999 and 2002; Cheng, 2002; Korean Sociology Association, 2003; Yea, 2004) and two background reports (Saewoomt'uh, 2001; Lee, 2002) written on this issue. This paper is concerned with the experiences of Filipinas trafficked as entertainers in the US military camp town clubs in Korea. The discussion in this paper is based on research with ninety women in total. All participants completed an in-depth questionnaire which focused on a range of issues including processes of recruitment and migration to Korea, women's financial and work situation, experiences of abuse and violence in their work, and their health and welfare. In addition, twenty-five of these women also agreed to participate in an in-depth, semi-structured interview in which subjects of customers, boyfriends, life before migration and in Korea, and women's future plans were discussed. Only five of the participants were still working in the clubs at the time of their participation, while the remainder had run away from the club in which they were employed (either recently, that is within a month of being interviewed, or within the previous year). These women were met either in shelters, in private residences where they were hiding/living or in factories where they were working after running away. The paper also draws on information gained from interviews with other Filipinas conducted as part of other studies and/or official investigations and complaints against bar owners, including interviews with eleven Filipinas who were rescued from a club in June 2002 and this researcher's informal interactions and discussions with over 200 other Filipinas who chose not to formally participate in the study. The fieldwork for the research was carried out over a period of 16 months from June 2003 to October 2004.

Some of the participants who continued to reside in Korea after running away from the clubs were interviewed more than once, and additional informal discussions in person or over the telephone were regularly held (every week or second week). This minimized the likelihood of the research presenting a "snapshot" of participants' experiences in Korea and their broader lives. Ongoing and more intensive relationships with these participants also provided a means of responding to Kelly's (2002:8) call for trafficking researchers to, "... think seriously about these issues [of approach and methodology], experimenting with methods and approaches explicitly designed to counteract barriers to disclosure and discovery." More extensive relationships over a sustained period of time with participants enabled a greater degree of trust and rapport between us so that participants were generally willing to disclose much more intimate aspects of their experiences. Other participants, including those who were still working in the clubs and those who had run away from the clubs and returned within a few days to the Philippines, were normally interviewed only once. Pseudonyms are used when referring to the women interviewed as part of this study.

Filipina participants were between the ages of seventeen and thirty; however, the majority of women were in their early to mid-twenties. Fourteen participants were still working in the clubs at the time they were interviewed, while the remaining 76 were interviewed after running away (either at a shelter, factory, or private dwelling where they were hiding). Although participants were drawn from a range of different areas in the Philippines, the majority were from Mindanao, Laguna, Bulacan, Manila and Quezon City. For most, Korea represented their first experience to go abroad for work, but some of the women had also been to Japan, Malaysia or Saipan previously to work as entertainers. Half of the participants were single mothers and many had separated from their Filipino boyfriends or husbands prior to their migration to Korea.

Processes of Migration and Motivations to Migrate

This section of the paper examines two important and overlapping areas in which the sex trafficking myth is contested in the case of Korea: recruitment of victims and motivations of victims to migrate. There are three main ways in which sex trafficking victims become vulnerable to trafficking situations according to whether or not they are intentional migrants: as a result of vulnerable circumstances outside their immediate control where there is no intention to migrate; as a result of reluctant migration, where there is an intent to migrate but this derives not form the intending migrant her/himself; or as a result of attempts to assert agency in actively seeking migration opportunities by the intending migrant that may inadvertently lead to their being exposed to trafficking. The first situation applies to some victims in some other trafficking source countries in Asia (for example, Nepal, Vietnam and Cambodia) where women and, more usually girls, are physically abducted, sold by relatives or sent away with recruiters by relatives for what they believe to be other, legitimate forms of paid employment (*see* Rushing, this issue). Under such conditions the victim herself is not motivated to migrate through independent decision-making and is not seeking opportunities to do so. In the Philippines, however, the vast majority of women who are trafficked transnationally have made a conscious decision to migrate abroad for work. Allowing for the recognition of this distinction between voluntary/motivated and non-voluntary/non-motivated migrants enables us to focus on uncovering the characteristics of women trafficked through voluntary migration, rather than focusing on the first scenario where the victim is abducted, sold or physically removed. In particular, focusing on willing migrants enables us to recognize the important role of *recruitment strategies* in the trafficking process and to uncover some of the *motivations* for potential victims to migrate, particular motivations that extend beyond the much cited factor of poverty.

Promotion Agencies, Recruitment and Contracts

The UN Trafficking Protocol identifies four different ways in which potential trafficking victims may be recruited. According to the Protocol, "Trafficking in persons means the recruitment, transportation, purchase, sale, transfer, harboring or receipt of persons: 1. by threat or use of violence, abduction, force, fraud, deception or coercion (including the abuse of authority), or debt bondage for the purpose of: 2. placing or holding such persons, whether for pay or not, in forced labor or slavery-like practices, in a community other than the one in which such a person lived at the time of other original act described" (UN,2000). Thus, recruitment may be by force or the use of violence, by abduction, by fraud or deception or by coercion. Where women and girls are physically abducted, forced, sold or purchased, there are generally very simplistic or non-existent recruitment strategies. Recruitment strategies in such circumstances are largely redundant since victims can be secured without the need for employing such means. However, where trafficking of women and girls involves the movement of victims through their initial consent—as in the case of the Filipinas trafficked to Korea—it becomes necessary to invoke often sophisticated recruitment strategies. This is particularly the case where transnational movement of victims is difficult because of the restrictive nature of immigration policies and strict border controls in the destination countries.[6] Recruitment strategies are an important, but often under-explored characteristic of the trafficking process in many source countries in the Asian region. Although there is usually some discussion of recruitment strategies in many trafficking reports for the region, they often fail to engage deeply with the complexities of different types of recruitment strategies, the role of women's and girls' agency in the process, and key arrangements through which deception is assured.

---

[6] Prior to 2001 most women came to Korea via Hong Kong or Bangkok, where they received their E-6 visas for Korea. None of the women who came to Korea this way personally appeared at the Korean Embassy to apply for their E-6 visa; their promotion manager performed this task. In 2001 it became clear that promotion agencies were utilizing the Korean Embassies in Hong Kong and Bangkok s a means of facilitating the entry of Filipinas and Russians into Korea on E-6 visas, even where they were clearly not professional entertainers. After this was recognized agencies no longer used these routes to bring women into Korea. Of those arriving since late 2001, all the women interviewed for this study stated they came directly to Korea. This indicates the ability of agencies to respond quickly to changing circumstances for the movement of women to Korea. Before late 2001, women tended to come in large groups; thereafter, respondents said they traveled in smaller groups (2-6) persons, especially if they are dancers who usually perform in troupes, or alone, as in the cases of women entering as singers.

In the Philippines, women and girls falsely and deceptively recruited to work as entertainers abroad fall broadly into four different groups:

1. those who have no previous experience working in clubs as strippers, erotic dancers or prostitutes and think they are migrating for other work, such as being a waitress or hostess;
2. those who have previous experience working in the entertainment sector as professional singers and dancers and think they are going abroad for work in this profession;
3. those who have worked in clubs previously as professional strippers and/or prostitutes, who may have a good idea that they will be performing prostitution-related work but are nonetheless still deceived about the conditions of both the work and other aspects of their migration; and
4. women who have migrated previously to work as "entertainers" in other countries, including Japan, and understand that their work and working conditions will be similar to those of previous migration experiences, including being a hostess, but not necessarily being a prostitute.

Recruitment strategies will often vary slightly according to which of these groups a woman falls under, but common to all four groups is the high level of *deception* involved in the way women are recruited. For the women who participated in this research, none had engaged in prostitution previously in their home countries, and only one had previously been employed as an erotic dancer in a club in Manila. Twenty-five of the participants stated that they were professionally trained singers and nine said they were professional cabaret dancers, while the remainder, as stated above, were students, unemployed or unskilled/low skilled workers in other sectors before coming to Korea as entertainers.

The variations in recruitment for these four different groups of women relate largely to the level of knowledge they have about the nature of their work duties in Korea prior to migration. For women who are professional entertainers (singers or dancers), they normally expect that their jobs will be as a professional entertainer in Korea in which they will perform each evening according to conditions agreed to in their contracts. Angel (26 years old), for example, was working in a club as a singer in the Philippines, when her Filipina boss introduced her to Kim Kyung Soo, an infamous club and promotion agency owner in Tongducheon (*see* footnote 4), who makes regular trips to the Philippines to select women to bring to Korea. Angel said:

> Kim Dyong Soo in P (Club P)—my owner—he always goes to the Philippines. I think my work here (in Korea) is a good job. You know, singer—like that. But I get here Monday night and I

see Club P and I say, "Where [is] the singer here?" They say, "No singer here, just drinkie girl," like that.[7] And my boss said, "You practice dance," and I have no choice, because, you know, I'm here already. My boss Jimmy (Kim Kyung Soo's son), he fight me. I'm shocked because I want a job as singer. I have no choice because the Korean doesn't speak English much and my English [is] no good. He (Kim Kyung Soo) lied to me.

None of the women interviewed for this study had a desire to work in Korea specifically and, in fact, many of the women had expected to be sent to Japan, rather than Korea. Korea entered the women's migration decisions as a possible destination usually in the context of their inability to secure an entertainer's visa for Japan. Most commonly, the women are convinced to go to Korea because it is relatively easy compared to Japan. The women need normally only wait two weeks before they can depart, compared with Japan where it can sometimes take several months in order to obtain the necessary documentation. The relative ease of getting a visa for Korea as compared with Japan often made this an attractive alternative for women intending to migrate as entertainers. In addition, recruiters and managers often tell the women that Korea was similar to, or better than Japan, so that women's knowledge of Korea could come to be constructed through their prior knowledge or imaginings about Japan. This was clearly the case for Lenny (28 years old):

> I have a cousin in Japan who is an entertainer and so I became interested in becoming an entertainer because of that. My cousin said she would help me get my ARB [Artist Record Book] and go to Japan. So I studied for two months at the promotion agency before passing my ARB as a singer. But then I waited two years after getting my ARB to go to Japan! My cousin didn't really help me like she promised. So then my promoter said maybe I should try Korea instead.

For those who are not professional entertainers, they are normally given a job description which includes entertaining customers by taking their order for drinks and sitting or dancing with them and chatting to them, or serving drinks:

---

[7] "Drinkie girl" is the slang name GIs give to the foreign women who work in the clubs. The name is a reference to the drink system that operates in all the clubs. Under this system customers buy women's time in the club through the purchase of a drink for her. Each drink costs the customer between US$10-20.

> The contract said we would be a waitress, entertain and talk
> and like that. But when we get here in Korea we have to sit
> down on their (customers') laps, lap dance, VIP[8] and going out on
> bar fine—only sometimes VIP and bar fine. But we need the
> money 'cause they don't pay us the salary.   — Jenny, 26 years old

Before deceptive explanations about work to be performed in Korea
can be made by promotion agencies in the Philippines, women must first
appear at an agency. There are thousands of both registered and unregistered promotion agencies in the Philippines and over 200 counterpart agencies in South Korea. There are three common processes by
which women contact a promotion agency. The first is for recruitment
agents to go to provinces and approach women and tell them that they
can help them go abroad. This strategy is normally utilized for women
who have had no previous experience working in clubs or as professional
entertainers. Rae (18 years old), for example, learned about working in
Korea through such a recruiter:

> This Korean woman came to my house where I was living in
> Manila one day. I was asleep when she knocked on the door. I
> answered it and she said to me, "Do you want to go to another
> country? It's fast. Just a couple of weeks and you can go." This
> woman, she spoke very good Tagalog but she's Korean. I thought
> it sounded like a good idea and easy to make money. So I went
> to the agency, which was on the ninth floor of this building in
> Santa Cruz (in Manila).

The second common method of recruitment is for a person directly
known to the woman to suggest she go to Korea. This could include
friends, relatives or talent managers (the latter being agencies that train
women to be professional entertainers and assist them in passing their
Artist Record Book examinations in exchange for a fee). One participant
in this study, Cheryl (24 years old) said that she heard from a friend
about working in Korea. Cheryl's friend had said something like, "It's
easy to go to Korea. It only takes two weeks. The work is easy. You just
serve drinks and dance with guys." Cheryl's friend had not been to
Korea, but this is what she had heard. Indeed, such narratives of Korea
as an easy place to make a lot of money, as a place that is (compara-
tively) easy to go to, and as a place where the work to be performed is
very clearly expressed as serving drinks, chatting to and dancing with
customers, are circulated widely amongst women who wish to migrate
abroad to work. Normally, the women will go to a specific agency in the
Philippines that is recommended by the recruiter or a friend/relative.
Finally, women are recruited through print advertisements that

---

[8] *See* p. 515 for a brief description of VIP rooms.

circulate either in the media (for example, newspapers) or on signboards and walls on the street. These advertisements are posted by both talent agencies and promotion agencies.

Once registered with a promotion agency, most of the women will have an "audition" and, on this basis, the selection of women to go abroad is made. Seventy-one (88 percent) of the participants in this research had an "audition" for placement in Korea. Sometimes the club owners or the counterpart Korean promotion agencies will themselves travel to the Philippines to attend the auditions and meet the women. What the women have to do in an audition varies. Some women perform (sing or dance) while others simply stand on stage. Without exception all women who had an audition stated that they had to wear a "sexy costume" for the audition, which revealed parts of their bodies. Some women stated that the club owners from Korea or the Korean promoters would "touch their body," including their breasts and "check their body of stretch marks" at the audition. The importance of the auditions lies in the fact that it is a key site in which deception about the nature of work to be performed in Korea occurs, since women do not perform strip shows or lap dances or sexy dance wearing a bra and g-string in the context of the audition. Ally (28 years old) stated that in her case:

> I found out about working in Korea from a friend. My friend said, "I know about entertainers in Korea. You must apply Ashman promotions." I applied for Japan but it is difficult and a long time, and one friend said, "To Korea is quick." I had an audition in the Philippines before coming to Korea (in June) and then I received the visa in August. At the audition they just said, "You will belong to Shield Club," then they took my photograph. That's all I had to do.

The auditions commonly take place in one of three locations: a business in the Philippines (usually a club or restaurant) owned by a Korean; a talent or promotion agency; or a hotel or nondescript office space. All the Filipinas in this study had their auditions in the Philippines.

Women's contracts are the other major way in which they are deceived about their work and conditions in Korea. Only 13 (16 percent) of the participants in this study held a copy of their employment contract and none of the women—whether they held a copy of their contract or not—had seen a copy of their contract translated into Tagalog or English. Sixty-eight (85 percent) of the participants stated that they were both not doing the work they had agreed to in their contracts and that other parts of their contracts were not being fulfilled (including salary, living conditions, freedom of movement and so on). A further five

(6 percent) of the participants stated that they were not doing the work they had agreed to in their contract, but were receiving all their agreed to salary. The other seven (8 percent) of participants stated that they were doing the work they had agreed to but other conditions of their contracts were not being upheld. Seventy-five (93 percent) of the participants were thus subject to labor, sexual and financial exploitation. The women's contracts stipulated that each woman would receive a salary of normally between US$380 and US$500 per month. All the women who participated in this study knew what their monthly salary was supposed to be in Korea – whether they had seen this written in their contract or had this explained to them verbally.

Vulnerability to Sex Trafficking and Victim's Motivations to Migrate

The second way in which the trafficking myth is confounded by the experiences of victims sex trafficked to Korea is in the arena of victim motivations to migrate. As I have argued elsewhere (Yea, 2004:2) "In existing studies of women trafficked for prostitution the causes of trafficking tend to be located in women's circumstances prior to migration. These circumstances are normally limited to a few key push and pull factors that reinforce stereotypical understandings of these women as, for example, trapped by a combination of poverty and familial obligations." To some extent these typical motivations were also evident for women trafficked to Korea. Only three of the participants in my research in Korea, for example, stated that they did not view migration to Korea as an opportunity to escape poverty and lack of employment opportunities back in their home countries. More specifically, the two most common motivations for the women to migrate were: first, to repatriate money to support dependents (including children, parents and other relatives); second, to earn money to pursue higher education or establish a business upon their return to the Philippines.

> I came to Korea on a fake passport to work when I was 16. I've got four younger brothers and two children. I had my first baby when I was 13 years old and then another one a couple of years later. My mother's not working, so she takes cares of my babies. My father abandoned us a few years ago. I'm the oldest and I'm the head of the family now, so I send my entire salary home to pay for everything for my two babies and my brothers. But I don't send enough because the club always cheat us our salary.   — Valerie, 18 years old

Low wage levels and unemployment, even for those women with professional qualifications, compared to the high cost of living in the Philippines provided an important incentive for women to migrate to

Korea. These women sought variously to attempt to fulfill familial obligations or save money to start a business or pay for their own education upon their return home.

However, other factors were also evident in many women's migration decisions. It is these other factors that have, to date, received relatively little attention in emerging trafficking discourses. In particular, many of my participants recounted situations of family dissolution as a central reason for migrating. Women variously experienced domestic violence, repressive family regimes and strict parents, or a failed relationship with a husband or partner. Thus, while many women were poor, they stated they would still not have considered migrating *if* their family or personal/emotional circumstances were improved. Take the experiences of Eve (26 years old) and Cheryl (24 years old) for example.[9] Eve has two daughters of five and seven years of age, respectively. She stated that she came to Korea to support her daughters, who live with her sister back in the Philippines. The Filipino father of her children is her real husband, but they separated because he became a drug addict and is currently serving a prison term in the Philippines.

Cheryl is from Manila, where her parents still live with her two younger sisters and her seven-year-old daughter. She came to Korea in April 2001 and worked in a club in Tokari for fifteen months before she ran away with the assistance of her GI boyfriend and a Filipino priest in Seoul. In the Philippines Cheryl was an exotic dancer. She did not engage in prostitution in the Philippines and considered herself to be a professional dancer. Cheryl broke up with the father of her two children in 1999 because he was a drug addict and would physically abuse her regularly. He beat her so badly on one occasion just before they broke up that she phoned the police and had him arrested. Her son is still with her ex-partner, which means she is forced to maintain contact with him. Unfortunately, for Cheryl she became involved with another Filipino man, a dentist, only a few weeks before she came to Korea. She revealed that he was also a drug addict and he beat her up so badly that she still had deep bruises on her body a month later when she arrived in Korea. Cheryl's immediate pre-migration experiences represented an extreme instance of a longer-term pattern of abuse she experienced with her two Filipino partners. Her decision to go abroad was driven by the wish to distance herself, physically and emotionally, from these men. Cheryl was making good money as an erotic dancer in the Philippines and was only marginally influenced by the desire to earn more money by working

---

[9] See also Yea (2004) for further discussion of the connection between women's pre-migration experiences of violence and familial dissolution and decisions to migrate abroad.

abroad. Other women whose partners were drug addicts or alcoholics tended to also reflect the patterns of abuse Cheryl described.

Honey's (21 years old) pre-migration experience is also typical of many of the women in this study. She dropped out of college after 3.5 years toward a Bachelor of Science in Elementary Education. She said she dropped out because, "My mom is strict because one guy wants to marry me and my mom worried. She said, 'You can marry if finish studying,' but the guy always follow me." The college was six hours from Honey's home, so Honey dropped out because her mother did not want her seeing that man any more and could not keep a watch on her from so far away. After that she went to work in an electronics factory and then a garment factory, where she would check faults in clothes. It was when she was working at the electronics factory that she decided to go to a talent agency and apply for an ARB to work abroad. In April 2001 she went to the talent manager's house in Laguna and stayed there training for her ARB as a dancer for five months. She passed her ARB in September 2001, but then waited for one year to get the visa to go to Japan. She said, "I think this is just wasting time. But the talent manager said, "Don't go back to study in case the visa comes." Instead of returning to study she went to work in the garment factory and moved out of the talent manager's house. Because the visa process for Japan was so slow Honey's talent manager said to her that she should go to Korea instead.

In contrast to the typical scenario described under the currently dominant trafficking discourse, where women and girls are pushed to migrate domestically or abroad for work or are sold, abducted or sent away to work by family or agents, Filipinas trafficked to Korea are normally active economic agents seeking migration opportunities who make the decision to migrate independently. Further, they are motivated by a range of different and often overlapping circumstances that often sit outside the familial obligations and poverty nexus discussed in much of the current literature. Different types of sex trafficking victims can be identified according to this basic distinction around whether or not victims are "intentional" (independent and autonomous) or "unwitting" (pushed, obliged, abducted, sold) migrants. Most studies of South Asia and the GMS focus on unwitting migrants, allowing the multifarious characteristics of those who are intentional migrants to remain little explored.[10]

Conditions at the Destination

This section of the paper examines two characteristics of sex trafficking once the victim reaches the destination: debt bondage and the trajectories of victims after they exit trafficking situations.

---

[10] For an exception, *see* Liz Kelly (2001) who identifies five different types of trafficking victims, but largely based on European evidence.

Debt Bondage, Economic Insecurity and Coerced Prostitution

For women trafficked to Korea debt bondage is a universally employed strategy by traffickers for the purpose of maintaining control and
exerting "ownership" over victims. Most of the participants in this
research did not pay for all or part of their migration costs to come to
Korea. This included 24 (30 percent) participants who paid only part of
their costs and 44 (55 percent) who paid none of their costs (the other
nine participants were unsure about the costs, usually because they had
never been paid since arriving in Korea and were not sure if all or part
of their salaries was going to pay their migration debt). Where the costs
of a woman's migration were paid in part or full by someone else, this
person was normally the promotion agency in Korea and/or in the
Philippines. The most common situation was one in which women would
pay for the costs of their pictorial (which was given to the promotion
agency in the Philippines for their use in placing a woman in Korea),
their passport (if they did not already have a passport), their medical
check up and, in some cases, their visa. The promotion agents normally
pay for the women's round trip airfares to Korea and often loan them
money to purchase costumes, other clothes and make-up for their first
few weeks in Korea before they have income. In order to repay these
migration costs and personal expenses the women normally have to pay
an agency fee to their promoter, the exact amount of which is often not
disclosed to the women and can be arbitrarily altered by the promoter.
Thus, all the costs for a woman's migration that are borne by the
promotion agents are added to a woman's migration debt, usually at a
highly inflated figure. Women must normally pay these costs out of their
salaries once in Korea. The amount and terms of repayment are
arbitrarily imposed and can be altered at any time at the discretion of
the promotion manager.

The women's contracts stipulate that they will receive a salary of
normally between US$380 and US$500 per month. However, in most
clubs part or all of the women's salaries are withheld from them as a
disincentive for the women to run away and to coerce them into engaging
in the provision of sexual services. In addition, many of the women
interviewed for this study indicated that their Korean manager kept a
percentage of their monthly salaries (normally 25 percent) as his fee or
to pay off the woman's migration debt. Hence, when other costs, such as
agency fee, food, costumes and makeup are deducted, the actual salary
of the women is normally less than US$300 per month, which is well
below the minimum wage in Korea (KRW474,600 or US$410 per month).

Because the women normally receive less money that has been
agreed to in their contracts, in order to have a constant source of cash

income, they must generate money through a drink sales system[11] and by engaging in the provision of sexual services at the clubs. Thus, even though many of the women are normally not physically forced to engage in the provision of sexual services, as in the case put forward for many sex trafficking victims in the GMS and South Asian subregions, a powerful form of economic coercion related to their tenuous financial situation presents an important factor pushing women into prostitution. Women who "chose" not to provide sexual services for customers say that they have no money in Korea.

In addition to the drink system, the women are coerced into generating some cash income through prostitution, which normally occurs through one of two arrangements. The first arrangement is a bar fine, which consists of a fee (fine) paid by a customer to the mama-san (female Korean bar manager) or club owner. The amount of this fine will vary according to how long the customer intends to take the women out of the club. The actual amount of the bar fine varies depending on the club—the bar fine for taking a woman for overnight (6-7 hours) would be around US$150-300. Some clubs have prostitution in the club itself in "VIP rooms," which are usually either located off the main area of the club or upstairs in private rooms. Sex in the VIP room or upstairs in the club would normally cost between US$20-50. As with the income generated from the purchase of drinks, the women normally get 10-20 percent of this money. Some clubs also offer customers other sexual services, including blow jobs (oral sex) and hand jobs (genital massage) which usually incur a cost of between US$20-40.

Customers, Exiting Trafficking and Repatriation/ Reintegration

The majority of victims come to Korea on one-year contracts, which means they need to renew their visa after six months—E-6 visas are only valid for a six-month period. Only two of the women who participated in this research "chose" to continue working in the clubs once their initial contracts had expired, although many wished to remain in Korea to seek alternative employment, usually in a factory or phone card shop.

---

[11] The drink system entails a woman having a customer buy her a drink for which she receives a percentage from the club owner. A drink for a woman normally costs between US$10-20 and, as an unwritten rule allows the customer to spend between 15-25 minutes with the woman, after which the customer must buy her another drink. In some of the worst clubs, drinks are more expensive (up to US$20). In these clubs the women are expected to do more with the customer, such as touch his genitals and let him touch her anywhere he wants. From the purchase of drinks the women get between KRW1,000-2,000 (less than US$3), or between 10-20 percent of the money; the rest goes to the club owner. Behind the bar there is normally a book in which a record of how many drinks each woman sells in a week/month is kept. The women are paid the money for their drink sales on either a daily, weekly or monthly basis in cash. In some of the clubs a drink quota is enforced, under which the women are expected to generate an extraordinarily high number of drink sales per month.

Foreign Women Trafficked to United States Military Areas in South   **243**
   Korea: Trafficking Processes and Victim Profiles in a
   Different Context

Sometimes women are sent home to the Philippines before their contracts are finished because they either become pregnant as a result of liaisons with customers or contract sexually transmitted infections or are identified as troublemakers (meaning they actively resist their exploitation and encourage other victims to also resist) by their managers. Others pay the bar owner or manager a fee (around US$500) so that they may finish their contracts earlier and return to their home country. Others still run away from the clubs and continue to reside in Korea as unauthorized migrants, usually becoming employed as factory workers or marrying their GI boyfriends. For many of the women an E-6 visa represented a tool allowing them to legally migrate to another country for work or possible marriage so that the job of "entertainer" assumed less importance than migrating overseas, after which numerous other opportunities could have presented themselves.[12] In this sense these women can be considered "gambler migrants" (Areliguer, 2002).

Filipinas are constantly running away from the club in which they are employed. During one three-month period (July to September 2002), I documented 25 cases of Filipinas who ran away from their clubs in one area (Tongducheon, north of Seoul), as well as another 20 hearsay cases. Under a human rights perspective, women's motivations for running away from the clubs are tied to the abusive and, sometimes, dangerous conditions they endure in their workplace. Such conditions include those documented above in relation to the nature of their work, their living situations (limited freedom of movement, rudimentary accommodation and so on) and the poor financial remuneration for the work they perform. Certainly, these considerations are evident amongst women I spoke to during the course of this research. Rae (18 years old) and Cheryl (23 years old), for example, ran away because they were coerced into having sex on average two or three times a day in the clubs where they worked, were subject to verbal and physical abuse by both customers and the mama-sans and papa-sans, and had virtually no personal freedoms. Rae had attempted to escape three times previously (including one attempt two days after she arrived in the club) before she was eventually successful three months after her arrival in the club.

Choices made by women after they run away relate to their future personal and financial security. Being positioned as trafficked enter-

---

[12] Some women strategize about their choices before they leave the Philippines for Korea. In these cases women will often run away from the clubs where they are working shortly after arriving in Korea to pursue a relationship (in the hope of eventual marriage) with a GI or a job in a factory. The latter option is seen as a more "respectful" and financially rewarding employment choice in Korea, but visas for unskilled factory/industrial positions are incredibly difficult for Filipinas to obtain directly and legally. That running away from clubs is invariably construed by media reports as an outcome of the abhorrent conditions in the clubs merely underscores the failure of media constructions of these women's experiences in ways that appreciate their negotiations and strategizing of their choices.

tainers *in Korea* produces a range of possibilities including factory work and marriage with their customers-cum-boyfriends that affect women's post-trafficking experiences.[13] Very rarely do victims rely on NGOs or state authorities to assist them in this process. They exert agency in their post-trafficking futures, the majority of which involve remaining in Korea rather than returning to their home country where they often face the same conditions as they did prior to their migration.

Conclusion: Trafficking in Korea vs. Trafficking in the GMS and South Asia

The cases presented in this paper allow us to draw some insights into the complexity in patterns and processes of trafficking in the Asian region that work toward an unraveling of the current prevalent trafficking myth. A large proportion of the reports and studies of women and children trafficked for prostitution in Asia focus on regions where trafficking exhibits particular, common characteristics in processes of recruitment and migration, experiences in destinations countries and mode and consequences of exit from trafficking situations. For example, in discussions of trafficking in the GMS and South Asia common patterns of recruitment, such as selling of girls by parents or other relatives, physical abduction, and trafficking in the context of migration for other work such as for domestic service, are common occurrences. In these cases, migration itself normally operates through informal networks of traffickers who move victims illegally across or within borders. This is particularly the case where countries share land borders that easily facilitates movement. Thus, women and girls in these sites exercise extremely limited agency in their migration decisions and choices and often do not have a plan to migrate abroad for work at all. The experiences of these victims of trafficking whilst in destination countries are usually characterized by severe physical confinement/ imprisonment, and where prostitution involving penetrative sex is the major, and often only, service performed by the victim. Victims are often depicted as girls and younger women, with considerably fewer being over eighteen years old at the time they are trafficked.

These types of trafficking patterns and processes common to South Asia and the GMS are, however, not the defining characteristics of the trafficking of Filipinas into Korea. In particular, Filipinas trafficked to Korea normally enter the country through legal channels, primarily an E-6, or "entertainer's" visa. This has several implications for the processes of trafficking. First, legal migration for work normally involves

---

[13] The large numbers of women who run away from clubs are a group worthy of separate consideration, as their experiences, needs and circumstances differ, often markedly, from the women who remain in the clubs. Discussion of these "runaway" women is taken up more fully in Yea (2004).

the use of deception, rather than force or coercion, in the migration process. As the Filipina participants in this study revealed, they were always complicit in their migration until they reached the destination in Korea, believing that their work did not involve prostitution, or that prostitution was optional. False or vague job descriptions, misleading contracts, and processes that reinforced the illusion of legitimacy in the nature of their work, such as auditions as entertainers in the Philippines and written contracts, were the primary means of establishing and maintaining deceit until the destination was reached.

Once in Korea some working and living conditions present parallels with other trafficking contexts in Asia, including South Asia and the GMS, such as long working hours with few breaks, substandard living conditions, deprivation of food and sleep, forced confinement in the place of work/residence and physical, sexual and psychological violence. Some conditions differ, however, primarily as a result of the presence of a legally binding contract agreed to and signed both by the women and their managers/promoters. The existence of this contract (including breaches in work performed, remuneration, conditions, benefits, over-time and free time/days off). Such claims pursued both in and out of court by support organizations, can often carry considerable compen-sation payouts to victims which would be difficult to realize without the existence of a contract. These payouts send a range of messages to traffickers, particularly club owners and managers/promoters, including signals that their operations are being monitored and scrutinized, that they can be subject to legal redress for breach of contractual arrange-ments and, more fundamentally, that violating foreign women's human rights can result in loss of income (as women run away) and loss of profits (as traffickers are forced to pay out considerable sums of money in the form of compensation claims). Contracts, in this sense, can be utilized by trafficking victims and their advocates as a means by which to seek redress and gain a certain sense of empowerment as punitive action is taken against traffickers.

The existence of a contract also dictates the specific nature of the entry of victims into prostitution and other roles in the sex industry in Korea. The low salary or withholding of part or all of salary is the main tool by which women are coerced into supplementing their finances through prostitution and other sexual services. Thus, women are rarely physically forced into prostitution as is commonly described in current trafficking discourses, but rather "consensually coerced" through financial exploitation. This indicates the need to explore the precise ways in which debt bondage operates in various trafficking situations and to warn against assuming that debt bondage is simply an inflated migration debt that keeps the victim in a trafficking situation. In addition, women are not normally subject to rape as part of the process of induction and normalization into prostitution in Korea that is a common element described in a typical trafficking scenario. Rather, isolation, including physical confinement, monitoring of free time, refusal to allow women to hold cell phones and so on, acted as the primary means by which women became resigned to their circumstances and lead to the adoption amongst many of a fatalistic attitude that was the prelude to their induction into prostitution. These strategies enable traffickers to lower women's self esteem and normalize them to their circumstances.

The fact that victims in Korea are complicit in their migration until they reach their destination also offers a significant departure from the migration patterns of the majority of trafficking victims in South Asia and the GMS. It affects the way women enter prostitution in Korea, as discussed above, and also the range of options and choices open to women after they exit from trafficking situations. As the women in this study indicated, they came to Korea for a variety of reasons that revolved around constructing opportunities for a better life, either through money they hoped to earn in Korea, possible marriage to a customer and on-migration to another country, and continued residence in a transnational field where other employment and personal opportunities may have been present. This has meant that many Filipinas trafficked to Korea for prostitution wish to remain in Korea in a post-trafficking situation (that is, after they have run away from the club where they worked or a customer/boyfriend has paid their contract so they may leave the club). This growing number of women requires a range of support services – some of which will differ quite markedly from those offered to women who are repatriated or return to their home country after being trafficked.

The Korean government carried out a relatively comprehensive research project in late 2003 to investigate the actual situation of foreign women trafficked to Korea's "entertainment" sector. Following the release of this report and extensive lobbying by Korean anti-prostitution and feminist activists, there were several policy recommendations and legislative action. These actions include a new anti-prostitution law introduced in September 2004 which was intended to better protect victims of forced prostitution (both Korean and foreign). The law deals more harshly with brothel operators and sex trade arrangers, as well as customers, whilst simultaneously adopting a progressive stance toward victims. Victims would no longer be punished for selling sex. Under the previous law, which was introduced in 1948, both victims and employers were subject to punishment, which discouraged reporting by victims who would also be subject to punitive actions. Under the new law brothel operators will receive up to 10 years prison or KRW100 million (US$87,000) in fines; a person caught arranging prostitution will receive a maximum prison term of seven years or up to KRW70 million in fines; and customers will be either sentenced to prison terms or community service. Thus, the law has the potential to address human trafficking directly by clearly defining a victim of prostitution as someone who is forced to have sex with a customer to pay back debts. In addition to the new anti-prostitution law has been the introduction in late 2003 of human trafficking offences, which are designed to take punitive action against anyone who falsely recruits, deploys or offers for sale foreign women's sexual services in Korea.

The legislation is nonetheless infused with elements of the trafficking myth, despite the fact that the sex trafficking situation in Korea is markedly different from the conditions that gave rise to the stereotypical victim purported under the myth. In particular, virtually no support services for victims who exit trafficking through the exertion of their own agency are available in Korea. Further, women who are "caught" by immigration authorities or police are still arbitrarily detained and deported as unauthorized migrants without a full investigation of their situation. Finally, punitive action against traffickers does not specify details of compensation for debt bonded and financially exploited victims, who are sent back to their home countries with the same limited resources and facing the same circumstances that motivated them to migrate in the first place. Thus, newly introduced state interventions continue to see victims as lacking agency, wishing to be repatriated home, and with no desire to migrate abroad again, despite nearly always returning to the same situation as they left.

I wish to thank the women who participated in this research for their willingness to share with me stories about their lives and experiences in Korea. I also wish to thank Father Glenn Jaron for introducing me to many of the women who participated in this research, and for inviting me to join the community of the Archdiocesan Pastoral Center for Filipino Migrants of Seoul. Finally, I acknowledge the financial and organizational support afforded to me by the Korea Church Women United and the Archdiocesan Pastoral Center for Filipino Migrants of Seoul, which made this research possible.

Discussion Questions

1   *What geographical areas are considered the epicenter of Asian trafficking and what are the major destinations?*

2   *How is a typical sex trafficking victim in Asia characterized?*

3   *What are the characterizations of the prostitutes in Korea?*

4   *Until the mid 1990s the sexual services provided to American military personnel were the exclusive domain of Korean women. But this started to change in 1995. Why?*

5   *In the Philippines women and girls falsely and deceptively are recruited to work as entertainers abroad fall into four different groups. What are these groups?*

6   *What is the drink system?*

7   *In what ways do some Filipino women strategize about their choices before they leave the Philippines for Korea?*

8   *What are some of the more common trafficking patterns for Filipino women to Korea?*

References

Asia Watch/Women's Rights Project. 1993 *A Modern Form of Slavery: Trafficking of Burmese Women and Children into Brothels in Thailand*. New York: Human Rights Watch.

Bak, J.H. and S. Chang. 1999 "Filipino Entertainers in US Military Camp towns of Korea." Paper presented at the YMCA Seminar on Asian Network of Trafficking in Women, Seoul, 6-8 May.

Ballescas, M.R.P. 1992 *Filipina Entertainers in Japan: An Introduction*. Quezon City: The Foundation for Nationalist Studies.

Cambodian Women's Development Agency (CWDA). 1996 *Selling Noodles: The Traffic in Women and Children in Cambodia*. Phnom Penh: CWDA.

Caouette, Therese and Yuriko Saito. 1999 *To Japan and Back: Thai Women Recount their Experiences*. Geneva: International Organization for Migration.

Coalition Against Trafficking of Women, Asia-Pacific (CATW-AP). 2002 *Coalition Asia-Pacific Report*, 6(1), March.

Demick, B. 2002 "Tongduch'on, South Korea," *L.A. Times*, 26 November, p. 3.

Doezema, Jo. 2000 "Loose Women or Lost Women? The Re-emergence of the Myth of White Slavery in Contemporary Discourses of Trafficking in Women," *Gender Issues*, Winter: 23-50.

Frederick, J. 2005 "The Myth of Nepal-to-India Sex Trafficking: Its Creation, Its Maintenance, and Its Influence on Anti-Trafficking Discourse." In *Trafficking and Prostitution Reconsidered: New Perspectives on Migration, Sex Work and Human Rights*. Edited by K. Kempadoo, Boulder: Paradigm Publishers.

Hangyurye Sinum (Hangyurye Newspaper). 2000 "Downfall of Filipino Women's Rights," 13 November.

_____ 1999 "Suspected Foreign Women Camouflage Jobs," 24 August.

Human Rights Watch. 1995 *Rape for Profit: Trafficking of Nepali Girls and Women to Indian Brothels.* New York: Human Rights Watch.

International Organization for Migration (IOM). 1998 *Paths of Exploitation: Studies on the Trafficking of Women and Children between Cambodia, Thailand and Viet Nam.* Geneva: IOM.

Kelly, L. 2005 "From Rhetoric to Curiosity: Urgent Questions from the UK about Responses to Trafficking in Women," *Asian Women* (Special Issue on Sex Trafficking), Spring: 21-35.

_____. 2002 "Journeys of Jeopardy: A Commentary on Current Research on Trafficking of Women and Children for Sexual Exploitation Within Europe." Paper presented at the EU/IOM European Conference on Preventing and Combating Trafficking in Human Beings: A Global Challenge for the 21st Century, Geneva, 16 September.

Kemmis, S. and R. McTaggart, eds. 1988 *The Action Research Planner.* Melbourne: Deakin University Press.

Kempadoo, K., ed. 2005 *Trafficking and Prostitution Reconsidered: New Perspectives on Migration, Sex Work and Human Rights.* Boulder: Paradigm Publishers.

Kempadoo, K. and J. Doezema, eds. 1998 *Global Sex Workers: Rights, Resistance, and Redefinition.* New York and London: Routledge.

Kim, E.H. and C. Choi. 1998 *Dangerous Women, Gender and Korean Nationalism.* New York: Routledge.

Kim, H.S. 1998 "Yanggongju as an Allegory of the Nation: Images of Working Class Women in Popular and Radical Texts." In *Dangerous Women: Gender and Korean Nationalism.* Edited by E.H. Kim and C. Choi. New York: Routledge.

Korea Church Women United (KCWU). 2002 *Fieldwork Report on Trafficked Women in Korea.* Seoul: KCWU.

_____. 1999 *Fieldwork Report on Trafficked Women in Korea.* Seoul: KCWU.

Korean National Statistics Office. 2003 Statistics Database, http://kosis.nso.go.kr/ accessed on 20 April 2004.

Korean Sociology Association. 2003 *Report on Foreign Women in Korea's "Entertainment" Sector*, Commissioned Report for the Ministry of Gender Equality, Korean Sociology Association, Seoul, South Korea.

Lee, June J.H. 2002 *A Review of Date on Trafficking in the Republic of Korea.* Geneva: International Organization for Migration.

MacIntyre, D. 2002 "Base Instincts," *Time Magazine* (Asian Edition), 160(5). Also available at http://www.time.com/time/search/article/0,8599,3338999,00.html

McMichael, W.H. 2002 "Sex Slaves," *Air Force Times*, 12 August.

Matsui, Y. 1993 "The Plight of Asian Migrant Women Working in Japan's Sex Industry." In *Japanese Women: New Feminist Perspectives on the Past, Present and Future.* Edited by Fujimura-Fanselow and A. Kameda. New York: The Feminist Press.

Ministry of Justice. 1999 *Departure and Arrival Control Year Book Series.* Seoul: Ministry of Justice.

Moon, K. 1994 *Sex among Allies: Military Prostitution in U.S.-Korea Relations.* New York: Columbia University Press.

Murray, Alison. 1998 "Debt-Bondage and Trafficking: Don't Believe the Hype." In *Global Sex Workers: Rights, Resistance and Redefinition.* Edited by K. Kempadoo and J. Doezema. New York and London: Routledge.

Phongpaichit, Pasuk. 1999 "Trafficking in People in Thailand." In *Illegal Migration and Commercial Sex: The New Slave Trade.* Edited by Phil Williams. London and Portland: Frank Cass Publishers.

Saewoomt'uh [Sprouting Land NGO]. 2000 *Kyunggi-doGiyokSungmaemae Silt'aeChosamitchChungch'aektaeanYungu* [Kyunggi-do Province Human Trafficking Investigation and Policy Research Report Seoul: Saewoomt'uh.

Takagi, J.T. and H.J. Park. 1999 *The Women Outside* (documentary video), National Asian American Television Association.

United Nations (UN). 2000 "Integration of the Human Rights of Women and the Gender Perspectives." Report of the special Rapporteur on violence against women, its causes and consequences. Ms. Radhika Coomawaraswamy, on trafficking in women, women's migration and violence against women, submitted in accordance with Commission on Human Rights resolution 1997/44.E/CN.4/2000/68; 29 February 2000.

Wijers, M. 1998 "Women, Labor, and Migration. The Position of Trafficked Women and Support Strategies." In *Global Sex Workers: Rights, Resistance and Redefinition.* Edited by K. Kempadoo and J. Doezema. New York and London: Routledge.

Yea, Sallie. 2004 "Runaway Brides: Anxieties of Identity amongst Trafficked Filipinas in South Korea," *Singapore Journal of Tropical Geography*, 25(2): 180-197.

13

LIFE HISTORIES AND SURVIVAL STRATEGIES AMONGST SEXUALLY TRAFFICKED GIRLS IN NEPAL

Padam Simkhada, Ph.D., *Department of Public Health, University of Aberdeen, Aberdeen, UK*

Introduction

The United Nations Protocol on Trafficking in Persons (UN 2000) recognises human trafficking as a modern form of slavery and forced labour that relies on coercion, fraud or abduction. Trafficking in persons, especially women and children, is globally prevalent and a major international health and human rights concern. Globally, it is estimated that between 700,000 (US Department of State, 2001) and four million (UNFPA 2000) people are trafficked each year, the large differential in estimated numbers reflecting the difficulty in obtaining accurate data. Asia is seen as the most vulnerable region for human trafficking because of its huge population, growing urbanisation, lack of sustainable livelihoods and poverty (Asha-Nepal, 2006; Huda, 2006; Kamala Kampado and others 2005).

India is a major destination country for sex-trafficked girls (Human Rights Watch 1995; US Department of State 2005) with large numbers of Nepalese, Bangladeshi and rural Indian females trafficked to Indian cities, particularly Mumbai (Bombay) (Nair, 2004). There is no accurate figure of the numbers trafficked; the International Labour Organization (ILO) estimates that 12,000 women and children are trafficked every year from Nepal (ILO/IPEC, 2002), whilst some nongovernmental organisations (NGOs) give estimates as high as 30,000. Over 200,000 Nepali girls are working in the sex industry in India (O'Dea, 1993).

There is a dearth of quantitative data on trafficking, partly because it is illegal, but also because existing data sources are not fully utilised. Much existing information about sex trafficking in Nepal is collated in NGO publications (viz. ABC Nepal 1998; Ghimire, 2001), presenting anecdotal case studies, newspaper reports and commentary from anti-trafficking agencies. There exist a limited number of unpublished reports on trafficking in the South Asia region (Huntington, 2002; Khatri, 2002) but these focus on policy analysis rather than reporting empirical research. Limited research has been published using data from Nepalese trafficked girls themselves on the characteristics of trafficking including its spatial context, their lives in brothels and the complex issues surrounding community reintegration upon return to Nepal (Asha-Nepal 2006; Hennink and Simkhada, 2004). There is also a worrying gap in information about the transit of girls through Nepal and India, and trading in girls once in India.

Trafficking has been identified as a priority issue in Nepal since the early 1990s and many NGOs, community-based organisations and Government Ministries have developed social, cultural and economic programmes to address it. However, the lack of communication and coordination, duplication and competition amongst NGOs limits opportunities for good practice (Asha-Nepal 2006). Many preventive activities in Nepal are financed by donors willing only to support activities with specific objectives over a limited period of time. The international donor community has increased funding for related social issues, including women's and child welfare issues, bonded labour and human rights. There remains a need for conceptual clarity on the context and process of sex trafficking.

Many girls who become involved in sex work in Nepal do so because they are compelled by economic circumstances and social inequality. Some enter sex work voluntarily, others do so by force or deception, potentially involving migration across international borders. Nepalese girls who become involved in sex work via trafficking are the focus of this article. The overall aim of this study was to increase our understanding of the context of girl trafficking from Nepal to India for sex work. More specific objectives were to investigate: (i) the context of trafficking; (ii) the methods and means of trafficking; (iii) living conditions in brothels; and (iv) survival strategies amongst trafficked girls. In-depth qualitative interviews were used to identify the context and survival strategies of the study population. This was most appropriate given the exploratory nature of this research amongst an understudied population subgroup (Pope and Mays, 2006) and to provide rich, in-depth information about the experiences of individuals (DiCicco-Bloom and Crabtree, 2006). Young girls who have been trafficked for sex work are a hidden population, largely due to its illegal nature. Employers of trafficked girls may keep them hidden from public view and limit contacts with outsiders. Trafficked girls may not identify themselves as such through fear of reprisals from their employers, fear of social stigma from involvement in sex work or their HIV-positive status or from their activities being revealed to family members. Therefore, identifying trafficked girls and obtaining access to them for interviews is problematic. It is only once these trafficked girls have been identified through health workers, judicial institutions, NGOs and aid organisations that they can be identified. Any interview with trafficked girls is therefore likely to be 'retrospective', accessing formerly trafficked girls in transit homes, rehabilitation centres or in their communities of origin after return. The target population for this research was therefore girls trafficked to India and subsequently returned to Nepal.

Seven in-depth interviews with key informants were conducted to pr-ovide a broader understanding of the context surrounding trafficking in Nepal and to discuss access issues. These informants included directors of NGOs working on trafficking issues, coordinators of rehabilitation centres for trafficked girls and health workers whose clientele include former trafficked girls. The second stage of data collection involved in-depth interviews with 42 girls trafficked to India for sex work but who had since returned to Nepal. Respondents were identified through several methods of purposive (non-random) sampling. Researchers worked through relevant NGOs, women's organisations and health services in Nepal which also legitimised the research, helping to foster trust between researchers and respondents. In addition, respondents were recruited through 'snowballing'. Interviews were conducted be-tween 2001 and 2003, focusing on family background, the process of traf-ficking, work and conditions in Indian brothels, the process of return to Nepal and survival strategies for the future. All interviews were conducted in Nepali, tape-recorded and fully transcribed. The textual data were analysed using thematic analysis, identifying issues, experi-ences and processes from individual case studies. Themes were then analysed across the whole data set to build a comprehensive picture of collective experience. Ethical approval was obtained from rehabilitation centres and verbal informed consent was obtained from all respondents.

Research Findings

Characteristics of Trafficked Girls
Table 1 shows the socio-demographic characteristics of interviewed girls. Trafficked girls are thus typically unmarried, non-literate and very young, the majority being trafficked before the age of 18 years. The youngest was 12 years, none older than 25 years. More than one-third of respondents were married at the time of trafficking. The predominant ethnic group of girls was Mongoloid or Dalit (untouchable) but other ethnic groups were represented.

Ways of Trafficking and Recruitment Tactics
Traffickers used a variety of means to draw girls into the sex trade. The four key tactics of sex trafficking identified included: (i) employ-ment-induced migration via a broker; (ii) deception, through false marriage; (iii) visits offer; and (iv) force, through abduction (Table 2). The majority of respondents (55%) were trafficked through false job promises.

Table 1: Socio-demographic Characteristics of Respondents
(n = 42)

Grouping	#	%
Ethnicity		
Brahmin/Chhetri	21	9
Mongoloids (Gurung,Magar, Rai, Tamang)	36	15
Dalit (untouchable)	26	11
Others	17	7
Religion		
Hindu	74	31
Buddhist	21	9
Others	5	2
Marital status at the time of trafficking		
Unmarried	62	26
Married	36	15
Other (D/W/S)	2	1
Age at the time of trafficking		
Below 15 years	31	13
16-18 years	55	23
Above 19 years	14	6
Education status at the time of trafficking		
Non-literate	86	36
Primary/non-formal education	12	5
Secondary education	2	1
Current education status		
Non-literate	33	14
Primary/non-formal education	50	21
Secondary education	17	7

D, divorced; W, widowed; S, separated

False Promises of Jobs

Jobs in carpet factories, providing Nepal's most important export, were the most common offer reported. Children from poor rural hill families are recruited from their villages and sold or apprenticed to factory owners. Brokers working within the carpet factories select likely girls, enticing them into leaving the factory with offers of better jobs elsewhere, a relatively easy task since many carpet workers are themselves caught in debt bondage where they receive no wages. The brokers arrange for their transport to India, frequently with friends' and family members' complicity.

When Dolma was 14, her stepfather took her from their village to Kathmandu, where his friend got her a job in a carpet factory. A few months later, a young male co-worker, introduced to Dolma as her 'nephew', suggested they leave the factory and go to Kakarbhitta, a town on the Indian border, where, he claimed, working conditions were better and they could earn more. Dolma agreed, and was taken out of the factory by her stepfather, her stepfather's friend and this young man. After 6 days' travelling by bus and train, they arrived in Mumbai and he sold her there.

In addition to factory recruitment, false offers of employment in other Indian and Nepali cities emerged as common forms of enticement. Sometimes older men promise girls employment in the city. Sabitri, another trafficked girl, reported that:

Table 2:   Route to Sex Trafficking, Traffickers, Destination and Mode of Exit from Indian Brothels (n = 42)

	#	%
Major motivating means		
False promises of jobs	54.8	23
Fraudulent marriage	19.0	8
Offer of visit/movie/holiday	14.3	6
Force and other	11.9	5
Traffickers		
Relatives	35.7	15
Known but not relatives	42.9	18
Unknown person	21.4	5
Destination		
Mumbai	78.6	33
Delhi	11.9	5
Calcutta/other Indian cities	9.8	4
Mode of exit		
Rescued	73.8	31
Escaped	16.7	7
Released by owner/self-return	9.5	4

In addition to factory recruitment, false offers of employment in other Indian and Nepali cities emerged as common forms of enticement. Sometimes older men promise girls employment in the city. Sabitri, another trafficked girl, reported that:

... one day I heard there was another factory nearby, paying higher wages than the factory I was currently working at. I went to the other factory to ask them if they had a job for me. 'You're in luck' said the manager, 'I need someone to accompany me and my wife to Hetauda, to collect wools for weaving. It will pay very well'. I immediately agreed and took this job. I did not think anything strange about it, especially since I would be travelling with his young wife. After a long journey I found myself in Mumbai where I was sold for Rs 40 000 by the manager.

In many cases the broker works from inside the factory, selects a girl, convinces her to go with him and then takes her to the border and sells her. When Tara was 12 years old, she was taken to Kathmandu to weave carpets in a carpet factory. She worked in two carpet factories for 5 years.

... I met a boy while I was working in factory and we became very close.... He told me that he would get me a good job. When he mentioned that I could earn a lot more money I instantly agreed to go with him. After 3 days we reached a big hotel in a new city. 'Why am I here?' I asked. 'You are going to do some cooking and cleaning work', he replied. A little while later they told me he had sold me.

Some girls, wanting to be independent, went to urban city for jobs and also ended up in Indian brothels.

Fraudulent Marriage

Fraudulent marriage offers are another common ruse employed by recruiters. In some cases, traffickers actually go through a marriage ceremony. In others, the marriage offer itself is enough to lure a woman away from home. The girl is given either a false promise of marrying the dalal (broker) who pretends to have settled down in India or she is told about a wealthy future husband, whom the dalal provides. Radha was one such victim. She readily agreed to marry an unknown person because of her family problem.

When I was fifteen ... I was married to a farmer. I lived with my husband for about one year and then returned to my mother's home. My husband came to collect me and my mother insisted I went with him. I had become pregnant. I could not work well, my husband did not treat me kindly, so again I returned back to my mother, where I gave birth to a son. My husband did not come to find me even though he knew that he had a son, so I stayed with my mother. When my son was four years old I heard that my husband had remarried. On the day of

Shivaratri (Hindu festival) I went to the river to light a candle, where I met one of my relatives from my village who was with a few other men. My relatives introduced me to one and asked me if I would marry him. I didn't take the offer seriously. 'I can't get married', I replied, 'I have a son. Besides, I hardly know that man'. But my relative kept insisting. 'Come on' she replied. 'At least think about it. He lives in Hetauda and is a great person. You should not worry about your son'. I did think about it and the idea of remarrying gave me hope that perhaps happy days would come again. I agreed and I went with him. He took me to the restaurant and after this I cannot remember anything. When I awoke I found myself in the world of brothels. I had been sold for Rs 30 000 [about $450).

Visit Offer

In many cases a girl is lured by the trafficker or his agent, often a local young man who works in Kathmandu. After enough trust is established, she is then offered a lucrative job in Mumbai as a maidservant, even as an actress, or she is told about an opportunity to set up a small business. In most people's minds, Mumbai stands for glamour, movies and prosperity, golden chances and escape from miserable lives. Priya's story is typical of this kind of trafficking. It indicates that not only poor girls, but also middle class girls are trafficked.

... My brothers used to worry about me and I used to quarrel with them. All my family would scold me, telling me to study harder but I did not listen. Even when they yelled at me I would just ignore them because I did not want to be a teacher, I was interested to be an actress...To be a good actress, you don't need to study and you don't need to go to school...One day, my friend Sita, her husband and I went to watch the movies together. After, they asked me if I would go to India with them. I couldn't refuse their request, as I wanted to be an actress. I also felt indebted to them for always welcoming me into their house. We spent three days travelling. Eventually we reached our destination—Bombay. At first we stayed at the Amar hotel but were soon taken to another place, where the women were decorated with expensive jewellery, clothes and scents. There we met a fat lady who Sita's husband introduced to us as a film director. She seemed very kind and generous...Sita's husband told the 'film director' to let us rest and said that he would come back after he had been shopping. He never returned. Later we were told that it was a brothel and we had been sold for Rs 60 000.

Recruiters sometime seduce young girls by posing as potential boyfriends, pretending they are interested in the young girl, wanting to know her better. Recruiters ask the girl's names, addresses and people they know. When the girls become comfortable with the poseurs, the recruiters offer to treat them at restaurants nearby. As the recruiters gain the girls' trust, they ask the girls to accompany them on a visit to a relative in another town, or attend a party in towns nearby. In many cases the girl elopes with her new 'friend' without even telling her parents. Twenty-one-year-old Ujeli told us that:

> ... my parents are agricultural labourers in the hills. I was able to attend school up to class 4, but then had to join my parents working on the fields, so I left school. At the age of 15, I went with a friend to watch a movie and met a young man called Kancha Lama with whom I became friendly. After some time he suggested going to a bigger southern town to buy cheap cloth with which to start my own small business. I went with him without asking my parents. Instead, he took me to India.

Abductions
Simple abductions also occur, although they are less common than cases of deceit. Some girls mentioned that they, or other girls in the brothels where they worked, had been drugged by their abductors. Girls who are abducted are often drugged before a journey during which they are sold to brothel owners in India.

> I was taken to India by neighbours, a mother and daughter, whom I knew quite well. They told me they had to go to a market far away to pick up something and asked me to come along. A taxi was waiting for them. They travelled a long way. It was very late when they finally arrived in Badi Bazaar. They got another taxi and arrived at a village house like my own. I was put in a room and the door was locked. A woman called Asa told me the woman she came with had gone out and would be back later, but she never came back. After three nights, I pleaded with her to let me go. I was told 'No, you have been sold and have to work. All Nepali girls have to work'.

Traffickers
In many cases family members, uncles, cousins and stepfathers also act as trafficking agents. Of the girls interviewed, 15 were trafficked to India with the help of family members or relatives. Likewise, 18 were trafficked by known persons but not relatives, and nine were trafficked by unknown persons. Traffickers are most typically men in their twenties or thirties or women in their thirties and forties who have

travelled to the city several times, knowing hotels to stay in and brokers to contact. Traffickers frequently work in groups of two or more. Male and female traffickers are sometimes referred to as dalals and dalali (commission agents) who are either employed by a brothel owner directly, or operate more or less independently. In either case, to stay in business, they need the patronage of local bosses and the protection afforded by police bribes.

Women who are already in the sex trade and have graduated to the level of brothel-keepers, managers or even owners travel through their own and neighbouring districts in search of young girls. The following story encapsulates the essence of the dream of success and glamour that these women symbolise to the simple village girls. Female traffickers are referred to as didi or phupu didi (literally, paternal aunt) or sathi (best friend). Local women who have returned from India are also employed as recruiters. Usually these didis return to the villages to participate in local festivals and to recruit girls to take back to the cities. These women are well placed to identify potential trafficking victims because they know local girls and their families.

> After 2 years of my marriage, my husband brought a co-wife who gave birth to a son. I was then completely rejected from them. In the meantime, a woman who had came home for vacation promised me and my three other friends good jobs. We ran away with her and she took us to Calcutta. But instead of giving us good jobs she sold us to different brothels.

Not all dalals work independently. An unknown number are connected to different networks that operate on various levels and size of organisations. Some syndicates include government officials, border policemen and politicians.

Life in the Brothels

Nepali girls in India's red-light areas remain largely segregated in brothels located in what are known as Nepali kothas (compounds). The concentrations of Nepali vary between cities, but appear to be highest in the Mumbai neighbourhood of Kamathipura. Brothels vary by size, physical configuration, ethnicity of sex workers and price. Most Nepali girls are associated with gharwalies (brothel owner). Depending upon the gharwali, the number of girls and women per brothel ranges from 5–10 to 150–200, with an average of 90–100 girls and women per brothel. In all cases, movement outside the brothels is strictly controlled, inmates being subjected to both psychological and physical abuse. The cheapest brothels, no more than dark, claustrophobic rooms with cloth dividers hung between the beds, are known among Nepali as pillow houses. Certain lanes are known particularly as Nepali gallis [street].

The living conditions of Nepali girls in all brothels are very poor. A social worker familiar with the Indian brothel system told us:

> There are several grades of sex workers, based on beauty, hard work, 'talent'. The tops are call girls. Then comes 'bungalow' which is a higher grade, then 'pillow house' which is the lowest. Most girls start in pillow house and work up if they do well ... some girls receive training, how to approach customers, languages. During training, girls are beaten and locked in a room like a jail ... until they stop fighting. At first a girl gets two or three clients a day, then it escalates ...

All interviewed girls had no previous experiences of sex work, and no intention of engaging in this trade. Jamuna recounted her early days in a brothel:

> When I entered the brothel I saw many girls who looked younger than 20 years of age. I did not know what they were supposed to do. They looked very strange to me. I had never seen girls wearing so much make-up and bright red lipstick. Their clothes were different too. They all had on very short skirts with lots of jewellery. They were not typical Nepali girls. The brothel-keeper told me to take a bath, get make-up and put on clean clothes. 'What is my job?' I asked. 'What's going on?' 'You will do what I tell you' said the brothel-keeper, 'you will find out in a few hours.' 'I don't want to stay here' I replied ... The brothel-keeper laughed and walked away. I looked at the others for help. 'There's no way out' they said 'you're going to be a prostitute'.

Sarmila recounted her terrible experiences in the brothel,

> ... on my first day, a fat man came to my room. He had paid a large amount of money to rob me of my virginity. I locked myself in the bathroom but the brothel-keeper came and made me open the door. Again the fat man came into my room. I pleaded with him and eventually he left, giving me Rs 10 .... The next day, however, a young boy came and I lost my virginity ...

Every girl said that the brothel owner or manager forced her to work by invoking her supposed indebtedness. A girl's earnings depend on the type of brothel in which she is employed, her age, appearance and the nature of the sex acts she is compelled to perform. Although most business is conducted in the brothel, and is charged by the minute or hour, customers can pay extra to take women outside. A girl may be sent to a client's house or a hotel for the night. If a customer buys a woman's services for a longer period, her debt resumes upon her return. One customer paid a large amount of money and kept a woman in his home for 2 weeks. He returned her to the brothel, where she worked to repay the remaining debt.

None of the girls knew much about the monetary arrangements between the brothel owner, the agents and their families. But later on all were frequently reminded that they had to work to pay off their debts, and many were threatened for not earning enough. Some of the girls had a vague understanding that they would have to work for a specific length of time to pay off the debt, and that there was an agreed-upon amount of payment given then. Very occasionally, brothel owners might treat a girl more kindly, buying her clothes or giving her treats. This was rare though; with few exceptions, girls were unable to communicate with anyone outside the brothel; some were even forbidden to take Nepali clients in case the latter helped girls escape. Even conversation with customers was sometimes forbidden:

> Only girls who pay off their 'loan', have gone on a holiday to their village and come back, are allowed to leave the brothel alone.

Very few of the interviewees were in occasional communication with their families. One girl found a customer who was willing to send word to her family.

> A Nepali man I met in the brothel wrote a letter to my family telling them what had happened to me ... after few months my brother went to Bombay to see me there, but he was not allowed to do so. My family then brought charges against that trafficker and brothel. I was sent back to Nepal with the help of social workers.

Besides being compelled to serve customers, brothel owners sometimes forced sex workers to perform personal housework or childcare chores.

Return and Reintegration into Community

Three major processes were involved in returning home. Girls are rescued, escape and released or self-returned (see Table 2). The majority were rescued by police and/or social workers. A few escaped on their own or with the help of other people. Only four girls were released by a brothel owner and/or self-returned (with the brothel owner's consent). Mainly, girls were being rescued and put into an Indian rehabilitation centre before returning to Nepal, or were then shifted to a Nepalese rehabilitation centre before returning to their family.

It is illegal for girls below 18 years to work in a brothel in India. Brothel-keepers always ask young girls to say that their age is more than 18 years if police raid the brothel. Some girls were able to escape from brothels with the help of others. Neela escaped with the help of her regular customer. When a girl is too old to attract customers, she is released from the brothel. Some are thrown out when they are tested HIV positive, others only when they have full-blown AIDS. Sometimes girls were allowed to come back to Nepal for a short time. Some of those girls do go back to Indian brothels and some stay in Nepal. Kanchi was sold by a family member but after working for 5 years, she was able to return to Nepal. A small number of girls accepted their lives in the brothels and became brothel owners themselves.

Many trafficked girls spend some time in a rehabilitation centre in Nepal after exiting brothels in India. Rehabilitation centres are typically run by NGOs and provide health and social assistance to returned trafficked girls. In addition, girls are provided with literacy and skill-building classes to assist them to integrate back into their communities. However, these girls reported enormous problems in returning to community life, in particular reporting high levels of social stigma directed at trafficked girls. Frequently, not only society at large but also parents condemn their daughters morally, and repudiate them. They are fully aware that society looks down on them and therefore offers no hope for a dignified life. One girl mentioned:

> I do not want to go back to my home. I would rather prefer to stay at a rehabilitation shelter and continue my studies.

A common phrase cited by a number of respondents captured the social values surrounding girls involved in sex work:

> Ke garne chori cheli dimma jastai hunchha, ekchoti futepachhi, futyo, futyo. [What to do? Unmarried girls are like eggs, once broken you cannot join them.]

If girls who return home have managed to earn money, they are more easily accepted back into their communities, and may eventually marry. Those who escape the brothels before paying off their debts, who return without money, or who are sick and cannot work, are shunned by their families and communities. Many return to India.

Conclusions

The key routes to sex trafficking include employment-induced migration to urban areas, deception (through false marriage or visits) and abduction. Current findings underline the role of poverty in the sex trafficking of Nepali girls, with over half reporting being lured by traffickers through promises of economic opportunity. The predisposing factor of poverty has been previously highlighted regarding trafficking both within South Asia and in other regions worldwide (Huda, 2006; Okonofua et al., 2004; Woolman and Bishop, 2006). At the local level, trafficking stems from deep-rooted processes of gender discrimination, a lack of female education, the ignorance and naivete of rural populations, poverty and lack of economic opportunities in rural areas with the consequent marginalisation of particular social groups. Wider factors include the low social status of the girl child, corruption of officials, an open 1500 km border with India, lax law and weak enforcement machinery, and local political apathy (Acharya, 1998; Asha-Nepal 2006; Asia Foundation and Population Council, 2001; Friedmann, 1996). These local level processes are in turn shaped by macro-level economic and social forces that are changing the way markets operate and the kind of labour that is required. None of this explains why some communities are more affected than others, however.

It is very hard to answer the question of how many girls were actually tricked or forced into the trade or how many went into the business of their own free will, because it is not clear where the dividing line is between choice and compulsion. As O'Dea (1993) noticed, the expression 'own free will' seems out of place in this context. The influence of poverty, family pressure, caste and gender discrimination has to be taken into account. Mere resignation due to lack of a viable alternative may seem a rational response. In the Nepali context, 'voluntary prostitution' is often considered a paradoxical term. However, it does not serve the reality of trafficked girls to fit their cases to a dichotomous system that only admits voluntary or forced prostitution. There are too many forces at work to decide.

Nepali girls are expected to work hard in the household. Studies indicate that to get rid of the poverty-stricken economy of the household, women and girls are always in search of economic opportunities within and outside the country (UNICEF 2006). The female crude economic activity rate in Nepal, reported over three censuses, is far lower than in men (Shtrestha and Panta, 1995). Migration is playing an increasingly important part in Nepal's economy and social structure. As these factors lead to an increase in migration, more girls are found to be trafficked in the process, a finding consistent with earlier research (Asha-Nepal 2006; Asia Foundation and Population Council, 2001; Rajbhandari, 1997). Many misconceptions or over-simplifications of the underlying causes of migration obscure the resources available to trafficked persons or their resiliency. For example, poverty is often cited as the reason for migration or accepting employment conditions of debt bondage, despite the common occurrence of migrants actually paying for transportation or transit services.

In Nepal, high-level decision makers, lawmakers and politicians at the local level are often accused of being the protector of the traffickers. Many commentators blame the lack of legal enforcement arguing that policies are sound in Nepal but not their implementation and that political commitment is required to implement public policies. Political leaders and higher authorities in bureaucracy are accused of releasing the arrested traffickers from custody and taking political and monetary benefits from them or having associations with brothel-keepers (Friedmann, 1996; Rajbhandari and Rajbhandari, 1997; Thapa 1990). Malpractice in political and administrative levels in both places of origin (Nepal) and destination (India) of trafficking were reported by both victims and key informants in this study. Much Nepali and Indian literature has mentioned the hardships experienced and the poor economic structure of the household that leads girls to being vulnerable to trafficking and to their involvement in prostitution. Case studies (ABC Nepal 1998; Rajbhandari and Rajbhandari, 1997) indicate that poor economic conditions are the most common factors identified by the girls. However, the possibility of their involvement in other sectors of economy is not detailed. Girls, once trafficked and forced to be in sex work, often accept their fate later, because there are no options or alternatives left.

The root causes of trafficking are thus multiple and complex. However, this study suggests that both trafficking and migration operate primarily through personal connections and social networks (such as an aunt who returns to the village and takes her niece back to the city), and through unregistered brokers who may or may not be strangers to the locality. Girls voice opinions like... my sister worked there before, so I went there..., which further underline the significance of social networks in the sex trade.

Debt bondage, prohibited under The U.N. Supplementary Convention on the Abolition of Slavery, the Slave Trade and Institutions and Practices Similar to Slavery, is defined as a situation in which debtors pledge their personal services against a debt they owe, but the person to whom they owe it fails to deduct the value of their services from the debt, or the length and nature of those services are not respectively limited and defined. The debt bondage which supports the trafficking nexus is also tantamount to forced labour. Slavery and forced labour are prohibited under Nepali and Indian laws. India enacted the Bonded Labour System (Abolition) Act in 1976, which outlaws all forms of bonded and slave labour. In addition, Article 374 of the Indian Penal Code makes it a crime to compel unlawfully any person to labour against his / her will (Human Rights Watch 1995). Regardless of the victims' origins, their reports of abuse in Indian brothels are remarkably consistent, indicating conditions of slavery and servitude which contravene Indian law (ILO / IPEC 1998).

It is still not known how many trafficked persons return without NGO assistance and what type of reintegration strategies they employ. There is some evidence in this study that some girls decide to settle in urban areas, setting up small businesses or, if they are sex workers, staying in the sex trade directly or indirectly as madams or brokers. At the same time, this study also noted that girls from communities where sex work is a common practice may find it easier to return home where they may marry and/or set up small businesses. Further research into coping and livelihood strategies employed by trafficked girls would assist in the development of more effective reintegration strategies. Society has traditional values that degrade brothel returnees, but brothel returnees also have a psychological stigma that makes them hesitate to face common people. It should not be implied that the brothel girls do not want to go back home; however, social norms and the possible reaction of the home community have become obstacles to restore them to normal life.

How then should we respond? The existence of specific and clearly defined networks of trafficking has implications both in terms of efficient use of resources and in terms of the effectiveness of the activities. In addition, the messages from NGOs in the form of leaflets are likely to be futile for the illiterate populations amongst whom they are distributed. Movement in and out of coercive and exploitative circumstances is a dynamic process that is well recognised in irregular migration, smuggling and trafficking. Interventions that intercept trafficking at its outcome point, rather than at the time or place when it first occurs, draw attention to the problem of identifying when movement within or between countries becomes exploitative and not voluntary, and could serve to protect an individual's right to migrate. A human rights analysis draws attention to the promotion of equality and non-discriminatory migration.

There is an overemphasis in the literature at present on legal responses. The legal response to trafficking, either through international conventions or state-sponsored regulations, can never be a complete response or a solution. Indeed, an over-reliance on legal mechanisms can produce results that are counterproductive. When laws are created to be as broadly encompassing as possible, an overgeneralisation occurs that actually restricts the application of the law, reducing its impact. Legal measures to restrict trafficking that lack specificity in terms of gender and age have been shown to mischaracterise the harm done by trafficking, and actually compound restrictions on the movement and employment of younger girls instead of protecting these rights (Huntington, 2002). Additionally, a rescued or escaped girl's rehabilitation efforts require a positive reflection of the society toward her for the rest of her life. In some cases, the hiding of brothel returnees would not be helpful, nor create general social acceptance. Traditional values and norms are hindrances to rehabilitation efforts. Social reintegration becomes much more painful for the person once involved in sex work and rehabilitated later, which may force girls to stay in the sex trade even if they return to Nepal; a significant proportion of girls have indeed reported their unwillingness to go back home after becoming sex workers. NGOs working against girl trafficking tend to focus only on the group of girls trafficked in the most exploitative way and publicise this picture. Existing interventions hardly cover the family-based trafficking which the present study has identified. Partial truths, from whatever side, do not help the issue and caution is required in assessing the situation; intervention strategies may otherwise be wasted. This study also highlights the role of violence in sex trafficking. Gender-based mistreatment in families appears often to contribute to girls' vulnerability to sex trafficking.

Significantly, the majority of trafficking victims reported being transported indirectly via carpet factories, representing a critical intervention opportunity. With appropriate training, carpet factory owners may be able to separate safely potential traffickers from victims, determine the true nature of the relationship, and secure victims' safety. Cultural factors may partially explain why such experiences place females at risk for trafficking. Nepali girls experiencing disruption via abuse or abandonment by their husbands often face extreme community ostracisation (UNICEF 2006). Families of such girls are also subject to stigmatisation and, therefore, may be reluctant to offer support or shelter based on fears of additional negative consequences for their status within the community, including marriageability of unmarried family members (Goel, 2005). Similarly, whilst traditional cultural norms associate sons with economic and social advantage, daughters are conversely constructed as burdens, particularly regarding dowry (Fikree and Pasha, 2004). Extended family members may be unwilling or unable to assume the costs of providing for unmarried / widowed females.

The study shows that stronger policy and strategy along with political commitment remain critical. There is a compelling need for interventions that actually empower women and girls in migration rather than seeking merely to protect them. The interaction of poverty and gender-based mistreatment of women and girls in families heightens the risk of sex trafficking. Prevention efforts should work to improve economic opportunities and security for impoverished women and girls, educate communities regarding the tactics and identities of traffickers, as well as promote structural interventions to reduce trafficking.

Acknowledgments

The fieldwork for this study was supported by Small Grants from the Simon Population Trust and the UK Department for International Development Knowledge Programme, Opportunities and Choices, based at the University of Southampton. The authors would also like to acknowledge the valuable support and co-operation of the Nepal NGOs which provided access to data and assisted with respondent recruitment. All names cited are fictitious to preserve anonymity.

Discussion Questions

1   *What types of girls are most often trafficked to India?*

2   *What ways were employed as a means to draw girls into the sex trade?*

3   *What three major processes were involved in returning the girls home?*

References

ABC Nepal. 1998. Life in Hell: The True Stories of Girls Rescued from Indian Brothels. ABC Nepal: Kathmandu.

Acharya U. 1998. Trafficking in Children and the Exploitation in Prostitution and Other Intolerable Forms of Child Labour in Nepal: Nepal Country Report. ILO-IPEC: Kathmandu.

Asha-Nepal. 2006. A Sense of Direction: The Trafficking of Women and Children from Nepal. Asha-Nepal: Kathmandu.

Asia Foundation and Population Council. 2001. Prevention of Trafficking and the Care and Support of Trafficked Persons: In the Context of an Emerging HIV / AIDS Epidemic in Nepal. The Asia Foundation and Horizons Project Population Council / Creative Press: Kathmandu.

DiCicco-Bloom B, Crabtree BF. 2006. Making sense of qualitative research. Medical Education 40: 314– 321.

Fikree FF, Pasha O. 2004. Role of gender in health disparity: the South Asian context. BMJ 328: 823–826.

Friedmann J. 1996. Rethinking poverty: empowerment and citizen rights. International Social Science Journal 148: 161–172.

Ghimire D. 2001. Prevention, Care, Rehabilitation and Reintegration of Rescued Girls (ABC's Experience). Paper presented at the Technical Consultative Meeting on Anti-trafficking Programmes in South Asia, September.

Goel R. 2005. Sita's Trousseau: restorative justice, domestic violence, and South Asian culture. Violence Against Women 11: 639–665.

Hennink M, Simkhada P. 2004. Sex trafficking in Nepal: context and process. Asian Pacific Migration Journal 13: 305–338.

Huda S. 2006. 'Sex trafficking in South Asia'. International Journal of Gynaecology and Obstetrics 94: 374–381.

Human Rights Watch. 1995. Rape for Profit: Trafficking of Nepali Girls and Women to Indian Brothels. Human Rights Watch: New York.

Huntington D. 2002. Anti-Trafficking Program in South Asia: Appropriate Activities, Indicators and Evaluation Methodologies. Summary Report of a Technical Consultative Meeting. Population Council: New Delhi.

ILO/IPEC. 1998. Trafficking in Children for Labour Exploitation, including Sexual Exploitation in South Asia: Synthesis Paper. ILO / IPEC South Asian Sub-Regional Consultation: Kathmandu (Unpublished).

ILO/IPEC. 2002. Internal Trafficking Among Children and Youth Engaged in Prostitution. International Labour Organisation / International Programme on the Elimination of Child Labour: Kathmandu.

Kamala K, Sanghera J, Pattainhaik B. eds. 2005. Trafficking and Prostitution Reconsidered: New Perspectives on Migration, Sex Work and Human Rights. Boulder: Paradigm.

Khatri N. 2002. Nepal: The Problems of Trafficking in Women and Children. Paper Presented at the 7th Annual Meeting of the Asia Pacific Forum for National Human Rights Institutions, 11–13 November, New Delhi.

Nair PM. 2004. A Report on Trafficking of Women and Children in India: 2002–2003, Vol. 1. UNIFEM, ISS, NHRC: New Delhi.

O'Dea P. 1993. Gender Exploitation and Violence: The Market in Women, Girls and Sex in Nepal: An Overview of the Situation and a Review of the Literature. UNICEF: Kathmandu.

Okonofua FE, Ogbomwan SM, Alutu AN, Kufre O, Eghosa A. 2004. Knowledge, attitudes and experiences of sex trafficking by young women in Benin City, South–South Nigeria. Social Science and Medicine 59: 1315–1327.

Pope C, Mays N. 2006. Qualitative methods in health research. BMJ 311: 182–184.

Rajbhandari R. 1997. Present Status of Nepali Prostitutes in Bombay. WOREC: Kathmandu.

Rajbhandari R, Rajbhandari B. 1997. Girl Trafficking: Hidden Grief in the Himalayas. WOREC: Kathmandu.

Shtrestha P, Panta P. 1995. Economically Active Population. Population Monograph of Nepal. Central Bureau of Statistics: Kathmandu; 205–238.

Thapa P. 1990. Keti bechbikhan: Lukeko Aparadh (Trade of Girls: A Hidden Crime) in Ghimire Durga. (ed). Chelibetiko Abaidh Vyapar: Yasaka vivid Paksha (Illegal trade of girls: Its various aspects). ABC Nepal, Kathmandu; 21–25.

UN. 2000. Protocol to Prevent, Suppress and Punish Trafficking in Persons, Especially Women and Children. Supplementing the UN Convention against Transnational Organized Crime, Annex II. United Nations Doc A / 55 / 383, United Nations: New York.

UNFPA. 2000. State of the World's Population. UN Fund for Population Activities: New York.

UNICEF. 2006. Situation of Women and Children in Nepal. The United Nations Children's Fund: Kathmandu.

US Department of State. 2001. Victims of Trafficking and Violence Protection Act 2000: Trafficking in Persons Report. July. US Department of State: Washington DC.

US (2005) Trafficking in Persons Report. US Department of State: Washington DC.

Woolman S, Bishop M. 2006. State as pimp: sexual slavery in South Africa. Development South Africa 23: 385–400.

14
HUMAN TRAFFICKING IN CHINA

Mark P. Lagon, Ph.D., *Department of State, Director, Office to Monitor and Combat Trafficking in Persons*

Although Chinese law prohibits forced and compulsory labor, including by children, serious problems of forced labor exist.[1] For this reason, the People's Republic of China (PRC), a source, transit and destination country, has sustained a Tier 2 Watch List ranking for three consecutive years. Though Chinese men and women are trafficked abroad for forced labor and sexual exploitation, the majority of trafficking in China is internal.

Early this summer, reports emerged of over one thousand farmers, teenagers and children, including some who were mentally handicapped, forced to work for little or no pay in scorching brick kilns, enduring beatings and confinement in worse than prison-like conditions. This was a form of modern day slavery that shocked not only the international community, but prompted an outcry between Chinese citizens and a forceful reaction from the authorities.

In response, the Chinese government organized a joint task force to investigate and punish forced labor practices. By mid-August, the joint task force reported that it had inspected 277,000 brick kilns and other small-scale enterprises nationwide, and had rescued 1,340 workers from forced labor conditions, including 367 mentally handicapped workers and an undisclosed number of children. In connection with the crackdown, Chinese authorities arrested 147 individuals for such crimes as using child labor and physically assaulting workers, with sentences of up to five years in prison. At least four county-level government officials were charged with dereliction of duty, and at least one brick kiln foreman was sentenced to death, one trafficker sentenced to life in prison, and one brick kiln owner sentenced to nine years in prison.

The trade of women and girls for sexual exploitation is another clear trafficking challenge for the Chinese government. Although prostitution is illegal, the burgeoning illicit sex industry creates a vulnerability for sex trafficking. Women and children are trafficked into the country from North Korea, Vietnam, Burma, Mongolia, and Thailand. Chinese women are also trafficked abroad for sexual exploitation. The government's main challenges in this area include their punishment of victims, poor victim protection services, and lack of transparency in criminal law

---

[1] This is an excerpt of a speech presented to the Congressional Human Rights Caucus Briefing, Washington, D.C., October 31, 2007.

enforcement by not fully disclosing what the government is doing to enforce laws against trafficking in people.

The All-China Women's Federation (ACWF) and nongovernmental organizations have a number of ongoing prevention and education projects in affected provinces. In the past five years, China has established transfer, training and recovery centers for trafficking victims in four provinces, and has assisted more than 1,000 trafficked women and children. ACWF works closely with law enforcement agencies and border officials to raise their awareness of the problem of trafficking.

In addition, the International Labor Organization (ILO) has recently begun a new project to work closely with the China Enterprise Confederation to educate entrepreneurs, owners, and managers of various enterprises that in the past have been linked to trafficking, such as hotels, karaoke bars, restaurants, bars, and massage parlors.

North Korean women crossing the border are generally most vulnerable to trafficking given their illegal status in China and their inability to return home. Conditions in the Democratic Peoples Republic of Korea (DPRK) drive many North Koreans to seek a way out of the country, putting them at risk of becoming trafficking victims. The trend of North Korean women trafficked into and within China for forced marriage is well documented by nongovernment organizations and international organizations. A potential factor, among others, in the trafficking of brides is the gender imbalance caused by China's one-child policy. All agree that neither the PRC nor the DPRK is doing enough to prevent or punish the practice of forced marriage. Nongovernment organizations and international organizations find it difficult to work independently in the PRC, so little assistance reaches this vulnerable group.

A core principle of an effective anti-trafficking strategy is the protection of victims. Unfortunately, China classifies North Korean refugees as "economic migrants" and forcibly returns them to the DPRK where, in all likelihood, they will be severely punished or even executed for escaping. The PRC stands by this policy, and has shown no resolve in treating North Korean victims in line with international agreements to which it is a signatory. China's poor transparency and the political sensitivity of the issue hamper our efforts to effectively advocate for change on this issue.

Nevertheless, China has engaged with the US government and international and nongovernmental organizations to work on other anti-trafficking initiatives, and has made some progress. China recently hosted a Children's Forum in Beijing, a joint project sponsored by the ILO and organized by the ACWF that brought child representatives from across the country to discuss measures to prevent vulnerable youth from being trafficked and to increase protection and prevention. They drafted a document of recommendations that were presented at the COMMIT Second Ministerial in Beijing in December 2007. COMMIT, a regional anti-trafficking initiative, has been given positive assessments from the

United Nations Interagency Project on Human Trafficking (UNIAP)'s regional technical leadership. Prior to the Second Ministerial, the anti-trafficking unit of China's Ministry of Public Security is expected to release a long-awaited National Action Plan on Trafficking.

Ultimately, however, China's persistent challenges with human trafficking are intimately related to overall questions of rule of law and good governance. A vibrant and healthy democracy affords full dignity and rights for women, prostituted people, and foreign migrants. A free society recognizes the critical role of civil society cooperation with government. We have seen here at home that nongovernment organizations are critical in our efforts to identify victims of trafficking and ultimately to assist them. Governments must hold exploiters including recruiters, pimps, employers, and complicit officials to fullest account, most notably with harsh sentencing.

As the world takes an increasingly close look at China's human rights record, we should remember to keep issues of forced labor and sexual exploitation in mind as part of the equation.

Discussion Questions

1   *Where do most women trafficked into China come from?*

2   *Why are North Korean women crossing the border into China generally more vulnerable to trafficking?*

15

LAW ENFORCEMENT RESPONSES TO TRAFFICKING IN PERSONS: CHALLENGES AND EMERGING GOOD PRACTICES

Fiona David, Consultant to the Australian Institute of Criminology

Since the entry into force of the UN Trafficking Protocol in 2003, 115 countries, including Australia, have agreed to a set of key legal obligations relating to trafficking. These include obligations to:

- criminalise trafficking and provide appropriate penalties
- extradite or prosecute traffickers
- actively identify victims
- diligently investigate and prosecute traffickers
- assist and protect victims
- refrain from detaining and prosecuting victims
- provide adequate and appropriate remedies to victims of trafficking
- provide special measures for children
- work towards preventing trafficking
- cooperate across borders (Gallagher 2007: 2).

Having agreed on the legal framework, the next challenge for countries is to convert these legal obligations into practical outcomes. The translation of law into practice is rarely easy, particularly for a crime as complex as trafficking. Experience in Australia and overseas confirms that enacting appropriate criminal laws is just the first step. Greater challenges lie in giving full effect to these laws, while recognizing the special rights and needs of victims of trafficking.

Drawing on the international literature, this paper seeks to identify some of the practical challenges that are likely to confront law enforcement officials in their efforts to:

- detect trafficking and identify victims of trafficking
- investigate trafficking cases
- contribute towards effective prosecution of those accused of trafficking.

Many of these challenges are interrelated, and reflect both the nature of trafficking and the impact of the crime on victims of trafficking. This paper provides an overview of some of the strategies developed in response to these challenges. These strategies take account of the particular nature of the crime type and recognise the need to protect and support victims of crime.

Why Is it So Hard for Law Enforcement to Detect and Investigate Trafficking?

Unlike many crimes, trafficking is not a single, static 'even'. It is a process that can involve multiple offenders and crime sites across several jurisdictions, ultimately leading to exploitation of the victim (ICMPD 2003: 87). Many investigations will be conducted in the country of destination where the exploitation is perpetrated. However, important evidence such as information about deceptive recruitment practices may be located in the country of origin or transit. Investigators in the country need to work closely with law enforcement officials in other countries to exchange information, and possibly also to secure evidence and extradite offenders.

The international legal definition of trafficking is complex, and incorporates a number of concepts that need to be clearly defined such as coercion, exercise of control over another, and exploitation. Many countries are still coming to terms with how best to translate these concepts into national law. Gaps in coverage, confusion or lack of clarity in legal frameworks will affect law enforcement.

Unlike simplistic stereotypes about sex slavery, trafficking cases can be complex and subtle. Victims of trafficking may or may not hold legitimate visas and they may or may not be located in the sex industry. Some cases might involve victims being controlled through violence and physical confinement but in other cases, coercion and control might be exercised through far more subtle means, such as:

- threats to turn victims over to the authorities, with threats of imprisonment or deportation and an ever increasing 'debt' that still has to be paid off
- threats of violence or other harm, including to family
- social, cultural and physical isolation that results in effective dependence.

As a result of these and other complexities, the line between willing work and the criminal exploitation involved in trafficking can be difficult to locate and even harder to prove.

Victims of trafficking may not report their experiences to law enforcement agencies. European research found that law enforcement officials were most likely to come into contact with victims of trafficking through indirect means, such as referrals from NGOs, immigration raids, or law enforcement activity around prostitution. The least common means of contact was for women to approach officials voluntarily and directly as victims of crime (Zimmerman et al. 2003: 72). The implication is that law enforcement cannot simply react to crime reports. It will need to work closely with a range of agencies, including NGOs, and be ready to recognise trafficking in a range of contexts.

Deterrents to victims of trafficking reporting their experiences include fear of reprisals from traffickers, the political and social pressures that work against undocumented and sex workers reporting abuse, the victims seeing the situation as their own fault or believing that they have committed a crime, fear of deportation and fear of law enforcement acting in collusion with the traffickers (Zimmerman et al. 2003: 72). Many migrants and members of minority communities do not trust law enforcement. They perceive it as a threat rather than a source of help (Anti-Slavery International 2005: 21).

Some victims of trafficking will not want to cooperate. They may not self-identify as victims, seeing themselves instead as people who have had back luck. In these instances, and intervention may be seen more as an oppressive interference than a rescue from an exploitative situation (Anti-Slavery 2005: 19; Zimmerman et al. 2003: 72).

A lack of cooperation can also be related to the impact of the crime on victims themselves. A victim of trafficking may have experienced severe and persistent abuse and trauma. The health impacts of this can be devastating, resulting in symptoms similar to those observed in victims of other types of chronic abuse and trauma, such as domestic violence, repeated sexual abuse and torture (ICMPD 2003: 28-30; Zimmerman et al. 2003: 23-24). Trauma can fundamentally affect a person's psychological state and behaviour, and recall and perception of events. For example, a person who has experienced a traumatic even might depersonalise the experience and come to regard it as having happened to someone else, suffer from an altered sense of time and impairment of memory, or suffer from fragmentation of perception, feeling, consciousness and memory (ICMPD 2006: 28-29, 2003: 28; Zimmerman et al. 2006: 21).

While clearly the largest impact is on the victim of crime, trauma also affects the efforts of law enforcement. For example, victims of trauma may say they do not remember key events or situations, deny that key events took place, appear to consent or agree to their situation, display a high level of apathy or indifference about their situation, or be overtly hostile, refuse to cooperate and avoid release (ICMPD 2003: 28-30). These behaviours can indicate a deliberate, rational decision not to cooperate with law enforcement. However, they might indicate that an individual is suffering from trauma and is in need of professional support and assistance (ICMPD 2003: 28-30; Zimmerman et al. 2006: 4).

The impact of fear, the victim's personal situation and trauma can play out in a number of ways in an investigation. For example, some victims may seek to change or correct their version of events over time. This may reflect the fact that they have very little recall of what happened, and their memory may improve over time. This can easily be misread as a lack of truthfulness or credibility (Zimmerman et al. 2006: 22). Other victims may have full recall of what happened but hesitate to tell their story to complete strangers, particularly foreign law enforcement officials. This scenario presents law enforcement with practical difficulties. Consistency in statements, and the related issue of credibility of witnesses, have a considerable impact on whether prosecutions (Lievore 2004: 1). Inconsistency in witness statements can be used to attack the credibility of a witness in court, and undermine their evidence.

Law enforcement also has to work within the reality that many victims will not want to participate in an investigation if it means appearing in court as a prosecution witness. This can involve waiting several years for a case to get to court, then being subjected to intrusive and hostile questioning, which can be very stressful and potentially dangerous to the victim and/or family and friends.

Efforts to Respond to These Challenges

Law enforcement agencies have been developing approaches and methods to improve the effectiveness of their response to trafficking. Many approaches are new and few have been evaluated (Putt 2007). Nonetheless, it is possible to identify a number of emerging good practices that:

- have been developed in response to clearly identified problems
- have been developed through extensive consultation with a wide range of people working in the field
- balance the rights of victims with the interest of criminal justice system
- reflect the interconnected nature of all actors in the response.

Law Enforcement Approaches That Respect the Rights of Victims

Internationally, there is strong support for the argument that supporting the rights and needs of all victims of trafficking is not only humane, it supports the criminal justice response. If the criminal justice system wants to secure the evidence of victims (who cannot be compelled to testify), it must establish their trust and address their genuine needs and fears so that:

- victims are willing to cooperate with the criminal justice system
- victims are able to cooperate with the criminal justice system

- the victim support sector feels able to cooperate with the criminal justice system (ICMPD 2003: 53).

Far from undermining the criminal justice response to trafficking, a victim-centered approach is a vital part of ensuring the effectiveness of the criminal justice response (Anti-Slavery International 2005: 11; EC 2004: 119; Pearson 2002: 35; WHO 2003: 3).

Studies of the health impacts of trafficking on victims support this approach. A recent European study of 207 female victims found that it took at least 90 days for their mental health symptoms to start to reduce once they escaped their traffickers. Even at this point, their symptoms remained problematic, to the extent that they inhibited women from re-engaging in normal daily activities (Zimmerman et al. 2006: 17).

These health impacts have implications for law enforcement. If a law enforcement official seeks to interview a victim too early in the process, or if they push too hard during an interview, they may result in an uncooperative or traumatised informant who cannot recall what happened, or who gives two or more conflicting versions of events. Accordingly, it is important to ensure that victims have sufficient time to stabilise after their experience, begin the process of recovery, and consider the range of options available to them, before being asked to make important decisions such as whether to participate in a criminal justice process. This is often referred to as a reflection or stabilization period (ICMPD 2003: 68; Pearson 2002: 41; Zimmerman et al. 2003: 5). This necessarily involves a high level of coordination and cooperation between victim support agencies and law enforcement (EC 2004: 105).

Effective Cooperation Between Law Enforcement and NGOs

Holmes argues that law enforcement should accept its dependence on NGOs for the following reasons:

- because of endemic lack of trust in law enforcement, it is NGO personnel that are able to build relationships of trust with trafficking victims
- high-grade intelligence critical to the successful identification and investigation of traffickers is likely to be provided to NGOs and not police
- NGOs have the specialist skills and experience to treat, counsel and accommodate the victims whom investigators wish to convert to witnesses.

Similarly, NGOs should accept their dependence on law enforcement for:

- the legal powers and resources to respond to requests to remove victims from exploitative situations
- referral of trafficked victims to NGOs
- protection to victims and NGO personnel (Holmes 2002: 5-6).

Having accepted this interdependency, strategies based on mutual recognition and respect are developed to ensure effective cooperation. For cooperation to succeed, victim supporters must feel confident that they will be able to fully meet their duty of care to victims, and support those who participate in the criminal justice process. Similarly, law enforcement must feel confident it can trust and work effectively with victim supporters (ICMPD 2003: 50-54).

One way of clarifying roles and responsibilities is through the formulation of protocols, such as memoranda of understanding (MOUs) (ASEAN 2006: 79; Clawson 2003: 31; ICMPD 2003: 50-54), a strategy used effectively in other contexts for many years. For example, many police services already have MOUs with providers of sexual assault or domestic violence services. Negotiating and implementing an MOU can enhance cooperation and clarity between police and victim support services in addressing issues such as:

- objectives underpinning cooperation
- division of roles and responsibilities
- standard operating procedures, for example, around referral
- information sharing and confidentiality
- strategies for regular communication between the parties.

MOUs also give the parties an objective frame of reference, against which to measure progress and resolve difficulties.

Specialists and Local Law Enforcement Responses

Many countries have established specialist units to investigate trafficking cases. Benefits to this approach include:

- consolidation of resources, including expertise and experience
- a focal point that can build strong working relationships with other key agencies, including law enforcement in other jurisdiction
- capacity to develop, test and refine appropriate and effective standard operating procedures and training.

Specialist units focused on a narrower range of crime types are likely to have in increased capacity to undertake proactive or intelligence-led policing—rather than simply responding to crime reports. They can build strong working relationships with units in other countries. This is likely to improve the flow of intelligence and facilitate the processes involved in mutual assistance and extradition (ASEAN 2006: 77-78).

Example: Technique for victim identification

The regional standard for anti-trafficking police training in south eastern Europe sets out a three-part process for which victim identification arises from insufficient knowledge and analysis of facts. Any potential trafficking situation needs to be considered from at least three angles-the law, the criminal and the victim. Specifically:

- How do the facts of the situation compare to the legal concept of trafficking?
- What did the criminal intend to do with the victim?
- What are the circumstances of the victim?

Information to answer these questions should be gathered in three ways:

- consideration of the surrounding circumstances, such as:

  o age, gender and nationality of the victim
  o control over the documentation
  o last location of the victim before coming to the attention of law enforcement
  o evidence of abuse
  o circumstances leading to the referral
  o assessment of the referring agency
  o current local knowledge about methods of operation of traffickers

- assessment interview with the victim, ideally in the presence of a trained psychological counselor
- consideration of additional corroborative material.

According to the standard, it is only once all of this information has been gathered and analyzed that it is possible to decide whether the victim has been trafficked, smuggled or is an independent economic immigrant.

Source: ICMPD 2003: 61-67

While specialist units may be at the centre of many trafficking investigations, it is essential that local or frontline law enforcement officials know how to identify and respond to trafficking. They know the local area, have local contacts, and are best placed to identify what is out of the ordinary in a way that specialist units cannot. Accordingly, it is vital that frontline officials know how to:

- quickly and accurately identify victims and perpetrators
- identify, preserve and collect evidence
- ensure victims are removed to safety and receive immediate assistance and support.

It is important that there are clear lines of communication around roles between specialist unit and front police. This will require the development and implementation of standard operating procedures, supported by training (ASEAN 2006: 85).

Because of the complexity of trafficking investigations, it is vital that law enforcement develops policies and procedures to guide the conduct of both reactive and proactive investigations. For example, the regional standard for anti trafficking police training in south eastern Europe (ICMPD 2003) includes a number of detailed policies and procedures for law enforcement officials in relation to:

- risk assessment
- processes for victim identification
- obtaining the victim-witness evidence
- scene preservation and evidence gathering
- counter-trafficking intelligence

The standard was developed by a group including the Police Department Unit at the Organization for Security and Co-operation in Europe, the Austrian Federal Police Directorate, Federal Criminal Investigation Unit and Ministry of Interior, and General Police Directorate Croatia, in addition to ICMPD and NGOs. The training program was tested and validated in a number of pilot sessions (ICMPD 2003: 3).

Investigations That Build a Broad Base of Evidence

The evidence of the victim-witness will generally be crucial to the success of any trafficking prosecution. Also, the victim's participation in the prosecution is an important part of ensuring access to justice. Nonetheless, experience from sexual assault prosecutions confirms that the most difficult cases to prosecute are those where it is 'her word against his' (Lievore 2004: 3). Similar considerations apply to trafficking prosecutions, where it is very likely that the evidence of the victim-witness will be called into question particularly through attacks on their credibility. Accordingly, law enforcement faces the challenge of building a broad base of evidence that includes, but is not limited to, the victim's testimony (ICMPD 2004: 122). This will need to include evidence that supports the testimony of the victim-witness (corroboration) and that anticipates and undermines any defenses likely to be put forward by the defendant (Lievore 2004: 3).

Law enforcement will need to draw on the full range of powers and resources available, including search and seizure, phone intercepts, surveillance, financial investigations and the use of forensics.

For example, several law enforcement training programs note the importance of conducting financial investigations as part of larger trafficking investigations (EC 2004: 126; ICMPD 2004: 115-117; UNODC 2006: 76). Investigation of financial transactions can help build up a better picture of the network, and thereby target investigations more strategically. Evidence from financial investigations can also for an important part of a prosecution case. For example, financial transactions have the capacity to:

- place a suspect at a given location and time
- establish who paid for items such as visas, accommodation, advertising, travel and daily necessities
- establish the existence of relationships between individuals
- demonstrate a gap between legitimate earnings and actual expenditure.

Evidence of financial transactions is usually in the form of documents that are difficult to rebut. The same evidence can then be used to form the basis of post-conviction confiscation of property (ICMPD 2004: 115-117).

Some law enforcement agencies have gone further by adopting proactive approaches to detecting and investigating trafficking. The objective of a proactive approach is to investigate, arrest and prosecute traffickers without having to rely on the cooperation and testimony of the victim. The intention is not to disenfranchise victims but to respond to the fact that a victim's testimony will not always be forthcoming or available. It relies on intelligence gathering, human and technical surveillance, undercover deployments and standard investigative techniques. This approach was developed by the UK Metropolitan Police, and has been incorporated into police training around the world (ICMPD 2004: 102; Kelly & Regan 2000: 33).

Supporting Victims as Witnesses

Police generally have limited or no control over the conduct of prosecutions. However, they continue to play an important role in prosecutions by taking part as witnesses. They can also help to ensure that victims of trafficking are properly supported and protected as witnesses in prosecutions. Internationally, relevant strategies include:

- ensuring victims are kept up to date about progress of court cases, particularly if the accused is about to be released (EC 2004: 112; OSCE 2004: 99-103; Pearson 2002: 52)

- provision of police protection, ranging from simple measures such as escorts to and from court, provision of mobile phones or panic buttons through to formal police witness protection programs (OSCE 2004: 99; Pearson 2002: 52).

In many cases, law enforcement agencies will have built up close relationships with the victims of trafficking and can advise the prosecution on working effectively with the victim of trafficking as a witness.

Conclusion

The entry into force of the UN Trafficking Protocol represented a major step forward in the flight against trafficking. In response, many countries have implemented criminal laws against trafficking. However, experience confirms that the introduction of criminal laws is just the first step towards an effective criminal justice response to trafficking. There are many practical challenges for the agencies responsible for implementing and enforcing the anti-trafficking laws, including law enforcement.

As individual countries and regions come to terms with the challenges, it is important that lessons learnt are collected, documented and shared. Emerging responses need to be tested and evaluated, so that is it possible to know their impact and effectiveness. This will make a significant contribution towards the larger effort of securing justice for victims, and ending the impunity of traffickers.

Acknowledgments

Funding for this project is provided through the Women's Safety Agenda, an Australian Government initiative administered by the Office for Women.

Fiona David is an expert consultant engaged by the Australian Institute of Criminology (AIC) to work on trafficking in people

Discussion Questions

1   *Since the entry into force by the U.N. trafficking protocol in 2003, 115 countries including Australia have agreed to a set of key legal obligations relating to trafficking. What do these obligations include?*

2   *Why is it so hard for law enforcement to detect and investigate trafficking?*

3   *In what ways can the lack of cooperation by the victim be related to the impact of the crime on them?*

4   *The impact of fear on the victim, the victim's personal situation and trauma can play out in a number of ways. What are they?*

References

URLs were correct in November 2007

Anti-Slavery International 2005. *Protocol for identification and assistance to trafficked persons* and *Training kit*. London: Anti-Slavery International

Association of South East Asian Nations (ASEAN) 2006 *ASEAN responses to trafficking in persons: ending impunity for traffickers and securing justice for victims*. Jakarta: ASEAN

Clawson H et al. 2003. *Needs assessment for service providers and trafficking victims*. Washington DC: National Institute of Justice

European Commission (EC) Experts Group on Trafficking in Human Beings 2004. *Report of the Experts Group on Trafficking in Human Beings*. Brussels: EC

Gallagher A 2007. The law and politics of human trafficking. Presentation at the Centre for International Justice and Governance, ANU, Canberra, 10 May

Holmes P 2002. Law enforcement cooperation with non government organisations, with reference to protection of victims and victims as witnesses. Paper to Conference on Prevention of and Fighting Against Trafficking in Human Beings with a Particular Focus on Enhancing Cooperation in the Process of European Enlargement, Brussels, September

International Centre for Migration Policy Development (ICMPD) 2006. *Anti-trafficking training material for judges and prosecutors in EU member states and accession and candidate countries (handbook).* Vienna: ICMPD

ICMPD 2004. *Regional standard for anti-trafficking training for judges and prosecutors in south eastern Europe.* Vienna: ICMPD

ICMPD 2003. *Regional standard for anti-trafficking police training in south eastern Europe.* Vienna: ICMPD

Kelly L & Regan L 2000. *Stopping trafficking: exploring the extent of, and responses to, trafficking in women for sexual exploitation in the UK.* Home Office police research series no. 125. London: Home Office. http://www.homeoffice.gov.uk/rds/progpdfs/fprs125.pdf

Lievore D 2004. Victim credibility in adult sexual assault cases. *Trends & issues in crime and criminal justice* no. 288. http://www.aic.gov.au/publications/tandi2288.html

Organization for Security and Co-operation in Europe (OSCE) 2004. *National referral mechanism, joining efforts to protect the rights of trafficked persons.* Vienna: OSCE

Pearson E 2002. *Human traffic, human rights.* London: Anti-Slavery International

Putt J 2007. Human trafficking to Australia: a research challenge. *Trends & issues in crime and criminal justice* no. 338. http://www.aic.gov.au/publications/tandi2/ tandi338.html

United Nations Office of Drugs and Crime (UNODC) 2006. *Toolkit to combat trafficking in persons, global programme against trafficking in human beings.* Vienna: UNODC. http://www.unodc.org/pdf/Trafficking_toolkit Oct06.pdf

World Health Organization (WHO) 2003. *WHO ethical and safety recommendations for interviewing trafficked women.* Geneva: WHO

Zimmerman C et al. 2006. *Stolen smiles: a summary report on the physical and psychological health consequences of women and adolescents trafficked in Europe.* London: London School of Hygiene and Tropical Medicine

Zimmerman C et al. 2003. *The health risks and consequences of trafficking in women and adolescents: findings from a European study.* London: London School of Hygiene and Tropical Medicine.

16
TRAFFICKING AND THE SEX INDUSTRY: FROM IMPUNITY TO PROTECTION

Dr. Kerry Carrington, *Social Policy Group*
Jane Hearn, *Law and Bills Digest Group*

Trafficking Sexual Labour: A Trans-national Crime

The globalisation of the world economy has provided new and lucrative opportunities for criminal entrepreneurs to be relatively free from detection and prosecution.[1] With the compression of time and distance, alongside the rapid development of information technologies, criminal syndicates operate in a global village cris-crossing national borders.[2] Yet the majority of the policy and legislative instruments and resources for responding, prosecuting and preventing crime tend to be limited by the boundaries of nation states. As such, single countries are strategically disadvantaged in curbing trans-national crimes involving fraud, money laundering, tax evasion, drug importation, firearms smuggling, terrorism, sex tourism, cyber-crime, people trafficking and the like. By operating outside the boundaries of the legal regulation of nation states, trans-national crime syndicates have been effective in evading law enforcement activities.[3] Consequently their regulation poses a particularly difficult challenge for the 21st century.[4]

There is, however, an increasing recognition that a more effective response to combating trans-national crime requires international and regional cooperation. A series of UN treaties, regional agreements and memoranda of understanding (MOU) has been signed by Australia as a critical step toward cooperating in an international environment to combat trans-national crime.[5] Additionally a Trans-national Crime

---

[1] Mark Findlay, *The Globalisation of Crime*, Cambridge University Press, Cambridge, 1999.

[2] ibid., pp. 23.

[3] ibid., p. 3.

[4] Peter Grabosky, 'Crime in a shrinking world', *Current Issues in Criminal Justice*, no. 83, Australian Institute of Criminology, Canberra, 1998; Peter Grabosky and Russell Smith, *Crime in the Digital Age: Controlling Telecommunications and Cyberspace Illegalities*, Federation Press, Leichhardt, 1998.

[5] Such as the United Nations Convention Against Transnational Organized Crime; the Protocol Against the Smuggling of Migrants by Land, Sea an Air; regional agreements in the Asia Pacific region to cooperate to combat people smuggling and trafficking (see for details, Phillip Ruddock, MP, *Press Release*, 'Agreement Signed with Thailand on Fighting

Coordination Centre was established within the Australian Federal Police (AFP) in December 2002.[6] The centre aims to collaborate internationally to prevent, dismantle and investigate trans-national crime and will target investigations into five key trans-national crimes: terrorism, illicit drug trafficking, people smuggling, high tech crime and money laundering. There is no mention of the trafficking of women and children as a priority.[7]

Typically, trafficking is confused with smuggling when viewed simply as an illegal immigration issue or threat to national security and not as a human rights violation. Both people smuggling and trafficking are trans-national crimes that may *at times* involve organised crime syndicates in the illegal cross-border movement of people.[8] However, it is inaccurate to use these overlapping but distinct concepts as inter-changeable terms. People trafficking into the sex industry involves the movement of people for the purpose of exploitation. It entails the violation of the human rights of trafficked victims, generally recruited from the poorest parts of the world and deceived, lured or abducted into servitude.

Unlike highly organised people smuggling operations, not all of those involved in people trafficking conform to the stereotype of organised criminality.[9] As trans-national crime is organised around profit, a diverse array of loose knit criminal organisations or individuals may simply work together opportunistically motivated by material gain.[10] Husbands, boyfriends, acquaintances, or family members may recruit and trade women into the international prostitution industry for profit, to repay debts or to support a family.[11] This makes the trafficking of

---

Illegal Immigration', 6 June 2001; Alexander Downer, MP, *Press Release*, 'The AustraliaIndonesia Ministerial Forum', 11 March 2003; Alexander Downer, MP, *Press Release*, 'Appointment of the Ambassador for People Smuggling', 28 February 2002). Additionally the AFP has signed a Memorandum of Understanding signed with the Indonesian International Police. The MOU provides a framework for bilateral collaboration in preventing, investigating and dismantling trans-national crime. (For details see Chris Ellison, *Media Release*, 'Indonesia and Australia Working Together to Combat Transnational Crime', 14 June 2002).

[6] For an explanation of the Centre's role and priorities see Senator Chris Ellison, Minister for Justice and Customs, *Press Release*, 11 December 2002.

[7] For a list of the priorities targeted by the new Transnational Crime Co-ordination Centre see AFP, *Australian Federal Police Counter Terrorism Measures* web site last modified, 23 April 2003.

[8] Alice Leuchtag, 'Human Rights, Sex Trafficking and Prostitution', *The Humanist*, vol. 63, no. 10, 2003, p. 12. Janice Raymond, 'The new UN Trafficking Protocol', *Women's Studies International Forum*, vol. 25, no. 5, 2002, p. 493.

[9] Mark Findlay, op. cit., p. 127.

[10] ibid.

[11] Janice Raymond, op. cit., p. 493.

women and children a more complex problem than the more organised smuggling of people for profit.

Size and Extent of Trafficking into the Sex Industry

International Picture

Due to the illicit nature of people trafficking, the number of women and children trafficked for commercial sex work is impossible to quantify. However, national and international sources agree that the global trade has increased substantially over the last decade.[12] People are trafficked to work as low-paid illegal labourers, domestic servants, or into various forms of sexual exploitation in the lucrative international commercial sex industry. The United Nations has estimated that trafficking in the global sex industry generates a US$5 billion to US$7 billion profit annually.[13]

In any market there are demand and supply forces at work. Some argue that the commercialisation of sex on the Internet and satellite television have increased the demand for women and children from the developing world to be trafficked into these new sexual entertainment industries in the western world.[14] Rather than organised criminal syndicates being at the centre of the growth of trafficking in women and children, according to some experts, the key players in the international sex industry in the 21st century are more likely to be entrepreneurs operating in a liberalised global market.[15] These entrepreneurs offer products in high demand by consumers prepared to pay substantial sums of money for the commercial sex services they offer.[16]

On the supply side, the rise in displaced persons during the 1990s and decreasing opportunity for regular migration are other factors contributing to the international growth of people trafficking. Refugee camps for displaced persons provide a ready pool of vulnerable women

---

[12] Peter Mameli, 'Stopping the Illegal Trafficking of Human Beings', *Crime, Law & Social Change*, no. 38, 2002, p. 67; Ian Taylor and Ruth Jamieson, 'Sex Trafficking and the Mainstream of Market Culture', *Crime, Law & Social Change*, vol. 32, 1999, p. 257; Donna Hughes, 'Humanitarian Sexploitation', *The Weekly Standard,* Washington, 24 February 2003; Susan Thorbek and Bandana Pattanaik (eds), *Transnational Prostitution: Changing Patterns in a Global Context*, Zed Books, London, 2002, p. 1; Linda Meaker, 'A social response to transnational prostitution in Queensland, Australia', in Susan Thorbek and Bandana Pattanaik, (eds), *Transnational Prostitution: Changing Patterns in a Global Context*, Zed Books, London, 2002, p. 57.

[13] Alice Leuchtag, op. cit., 2003, p. 12.

[14] Mary Sullivan and Sheila Jeffreys, 'Legalisation: The Australian Experience', *Violence Against Women*, vol. 8, no. 9, 2002, p. 1145.

[15] Ian Taylor and Ruth Jamieson, op. cit., p. 274.

[16] Mary Sullivan and Sheila Jeffreys, op. cit., p. 1145.

and children to be recruited into the global sex industry.[17] According to the United Nations High Commissioner for Refugees (UNHCR) there are currently 19, 783 100 persons of concern in the world. For a large number of displaced women and children, this displacement 'ends in sexual exploitation and debt bondage'.[18]

Estimates of the number of people trafficked around the world annually for sexual exploitation and other forms of exploitation vary from 700,000 to 4 million.[19] In Europe the figure has been put at somewhere between 200,000 and 500,000 women and children.[20] In any one year it is estimated that around 50,000 women and children are trafficked into the United States, by lure, force, deception or coercion to work in the commercial sex industry.[21] Many believe they are migrating across international borders to work as domestic workers, waitresses, or models for the fashion industry not the sex industry. Some women aware they are going to work as sex workers, are deceived about the conditions of work and find themselves in debt bondage, servitude or slavery.

Australian Estimates

In Australia, the high and continuing demand for young Asian sex workers, in excess of local supply, creates a market opportunity for traffickers in women and children from countries like Thailand, Philippines, China and Cambodia.[22] Australian brothels advertising exotic, oriental and Asian women are not hard to find in the on-line Yellow Pages directory giving some indication of the demand for their sexual services.[23] According to one authoritative estimate, the Australian trafficking industry nets approximately A\$1 million per week to the organisers of the trade.[24]

---

[17] Ian Taylor and Ruth Jamieson, op. cit., p. 263.

[18] Jenna Shearer Demir, 'The trafficking of women for sexual exploitation: a gender-based and well-founded fear of persecution?', *New Issues in Refugee Research, Working Paper No.* 80, European School of Advanced Studies in International Cooperation and Development, Pavia, Italy, 2003.

[19] US Department of State, *Trafficking in Persons Report*, Report Home Page, Released by the Office to Monitor and Combat Trafficking in Persons, United States, 5 June 2002.

[20] Ian Taylor and Ruth Jamison, op. cit., p. 257.

[21] Sean Murphy, 'International trafficking in persons, especially women and children', *The American Journal of International Law*, vol. 95, no. 2, 2001, p. 408.

[22] Lind Meaker, op. cit. pp. 623.

[23] For example, Exotic Asian & Oriental Models & Escorts, WA; Asian House, NSW; AAAA Asian Erotica; WA; A Taste of the Orient, WA; A1 Asian Escorts, WA; A Touch of the Orient, Vic; Bankstown Asian, NSW; Exotic Babes Escorts, WA; Exotic Studio, ACT: Exotic Erotic Ball, Vic; and Pilipino Princess Escorts, WA.

[24] Senator Ian Macdonald, Criminal Code Amendment (Slavery and Sexual Servitude) Bill 1999, Second Reading Speech, Senate, *Hansard*, 24 March 1999.

In 1995, the Joint Standing Committee on Foreign Affairs, Defence and Trade, was told that at any one time there might be 200 Asian prostitutes working in Australia who had been trafficked here by organised criminals suspected of being linked to drug trafficking.[25] In the same year, Chris Payne, the head of Australian Federal Police (AFP) investigation into sex trafficking, estimated that up to 500 trafficked women were working illegally in Sydney at any given time.[26]

In 1996 the then Department of Immigration and Ethnic Affairs (DIEA) produced a *Report into Trafficking of Women into the Australian Sex Industry*.[27] While it accurately reports that the number of non-citizens working in the sex industry is 'unknown and estimates vary considerably' it presents a contradictory picture of the nature of trafficking into the sex industry in Australia.[28] The contradiction arises mainly from a lack of clarity around the definition of crimes involving trafficking. For, on the one hand, the report states there is 'no evidence' of women being coerced against their will to work in the Australian sex industry, yet acknowledges on the other that a 14-year-old Thai girl located in a brothel during a compliance inspection, was returned to Thailand. That report is now out of date and of doubtful value, relying as it does on a very narrow and apparently confused definition of trafficking.[29]

Nevertheless, in 1999, in the second reading speech for the Criminal Code Amendment (Slavery and Sexual Servitude) Bill 1999, Senator Ian Macdonald remarked that: 'intelligence from Australian and overseas sources confirms that the problem is a significant one for Australia'.[30] He noted that the AFP had received information relating to 14 cases over the previous eighteen months, and that the National Crime Authority (NCA) was aware of 25 women being trafficked into Australia between 1992 and 1996, one of whom was allegedly a 13-year-old girl brought to Australia to pay her father's debt.

Senator Vanstone, then Minister for Justice and Customs and responsible for the development of the Bill, clearly regarded the issue as an important one for Australia and has made similar statements about

---

[25] Joint Standing Committee on Foreign Affairs, Defence and Trade, *Human Rights and Progress Toward Democracy in Burma*, AGPS, Canberra, 1995, p. 52.

[26] Mary Sullivan and Sheila Jeffreys, op. cit., p. 1145.

[27] Department of Immigration and Ethnic Affairs, *Trafficking of Women into Australian Sex Industry: A Discussion Paper,* Investigations and Liaison Section, Canberra, 1996.

[28] ibid., p. 8.

[29] DIEA, 1966, op. cit. p. 12.

[30] Senator Ian Macdonald, Criminal Code Amendment (Slavery and Sexual Servitude) Bill 1999, Second Reading Speech, Senate, *Hansard*, 24 March 1999.

the significance of the problem.[31] More recently, however, Senator Ellison, the current Minister for Justice and Customs, has stated that there is no evidence of any large scale problem within Australia.[32]

By contrast, Kathleen Maltzahn, coordinator of Project Respect, an organisation that promotes the rights of trafficked sex workers, has claimed that approximately 1000 women are trafficked into the country each year.[33] Phillip Ruddock, the Minister for Immigration and Multicultural and Indigenous Affairs (DIMIA), has disputed the credibility of this claim:

> It is not a credible suggestion that hundreds or thousands of people are being trafficked unwillingly into the industry and have escaped detection over many years While I do not diminish the concerns on trafficking, the actual complaints from individuals do not match the level of claims being made the claims being made about the wide extent of trafficking cannot be substantiated.[34]

According to the Minister, since July 2002, only four women have made complaints about trafficking, 'that is they stated they were brought to Australia under false pretences by unscrupulous individuals for the express purpose of forcing them into a form of sexual slavery'.[35] These contradictory assessments arise partly from the lack of accurate statistical data and point to a need for independent research which can provide an up-to-date national picture drawing on an array of reliable sources. The under-reporting of crime is a common problem. This is especially the case for crimes of sexual violence.[36] Under-reporting is likely to be compounded for people trafficking offences where the victim may fear reprisal and may also be engaged in illegal activity. These problems led the Australian Institute of Criminology to conclude

---

[31] Senator Vanstone, *7.30 Report*, ABC Television, 5 January 1999.

[32] Senator Chris Ellison, Justice and Customs Minister, reply to Senator Linda Kirk, Senate, *Legal and Constitutional Legislation Committee*, Attorney-General's Portfolio: Australian Federal Police, 10 February 2002.

[33] Elisabeth Wynhausen, 'One-Way Traffic of Sex Slave Trade', *The Weekend Australian*, 22 March 2003.

[34] The Hon. Phillip Ruddock, MP, *Ministerial Press Release*, 1 April 2003.

[35] ibid.

[36] Studies have consistently shown that sexual violence is heavily under-reported, although estimates of the level of under-reporting vary. See: Jenny Bargen and Elaine Fishwick, *Sexual Assault Law Reform*, Office of the Status of Women, AGPS, Canberra, 1995; NSW Standing Committee on Social Issues, *Sexual Violence: the Hidden Crime*, NSW Legislative Council, Sydney, 1993; Bree Cook, Fiona David and Anna Grant, *Sexual Violence in Australia*, Research and Public Policy Series, no. 3, Australian Institute of Criminology, Canberra, 2001.

that the limited statistical data available on trafficking provides 'very few insights into the incidence of trafficking' in Australia.[37] In the absence of any reliable statistical data, it is not surprising that a number of widely varying estimates have been proffered drawing on an array of sources. Rough estimates of people trafficking into the sex industry are usually extrapolated from secondary sources such as NGO surveys, and estimates given by police investigators, sex workers or other professionals with local knowledge of the sex industry. Some of these methods may inflate the extent of the problem. By contrast it is probable that the Government's reliance on the actual number of complaints significantly understates the problem. Relying on cases identified by compliance staff is also problematic as DIMIA appears to be relying still on a very narrow definition of trafficking which we discuss below.

The Nature of the Problem in Australia Consent, Trafficking and Servitude

The difficulty of analysing the nature and extent of the problem in Australia is driven in part by the use of differing definitions of trafficking and whether illegal migration is linked with the related crimes of slavery and sexual servitude. The prevailing emphasis on border control also makes coherent discussion of the issue difficult, with the terms 'trafficking' and 'smuggling' used incorrectly as interchangeable terms.

Comments by Phillip Ruddock, Minister for Immigration and Multicultural and Indigenous Affairs have defended the DIMIA policy of detaining and deporting illegal immigrant sex workers. In this context he stated that 'there have been some misleading assumptions with reports on trafficking confusing those who come to Australia willing to work in the sex industry, after agreeing to pay organisers for the arrangements'.[38] If the implication is that women who consent to cross borders to work in the sex industry can never be trafficking victims, then this too is questionable. While this is true for women who migrate freely and have control over their situation many women who believe they are migrating (legally or illegally to work in the sex industry) nevertheless find themselves victims of sexual servitude and slavery and other forms of exploitation such as debt bondage. Their initial consent to cross borders is irrelevant to whether or not they are in fact victimised by traffickers once in Australia.[39]

---

[37] In a report prepared by Fiona David, *Human Smuggling and Trafficking: An Overview of the Response at the Federal Level*, Australian Institute of Criminology, Canberra, 2000, p. 10.

[38] The Hon. Phillip Ruddock, MP, quoted in Natalie O'Brien and Elisabeth Wynhausen, 'Officials ignored sex slave's offer of help', *The Australian*, 2 April 2003; also see DIEA, 1996, op. cit., p. 17 for a similar definition of trafficking.

[39] Jennifer Norberry, 'Criminal Code Amendment (Slavery and Sexual Servitude) Bill 1999', *Bills Digest*, no. 167, Department of Parliamentary Library, 1999.

In 1999, in a second reading speech of the Bill introducing the new laws of sexual servitude and slavery, Senator Macdonald recognised the nature of the problem, noting that women being recruited to work in the sex industry in Australia, 'are usually unaware of the conditions under which they will be required to work'.[40] He continued:

> The reports I have received paint an ugly picture. For example, once in Australia recruits are often placed under heavy security and their movements strictly controlled. Those that are fortunate enough to live away from the brothel premises frequently find that they are driven by guards to and from work and not free to go elsewhere. Others live and work almost entirely at the brothel. The recruits are rarely allowed time off work and have little or no control over how many clients they service a day. Many are not free to reject a client or to determine the conditions on which they service them. Unsafe sexual practices are regularly imposed on them and as a consequence they live under the constant fear of contracting HIV and other sexually transmitted diseases. Their passports and other travel documents are frequently taken from them and transgressions are often met with intimidation, violence and threats to harm them or their family or to report them to immigration authorities.[41]

Many discover that the debts incurred to their agent or sponsor to arrange transport, travel documentation, accommodation and passports, are much higher than originally believed. Senator Macdonald put the figure between $40,000 and $50,000, noting that 'in many cases the recruits are detected by authorities and deported back home before they receive any payment for services'.[42]

A recent Queensland study also found that illegal migrant women working under a contract arrangement had to provide sexual services to between 500 and 700 clients to repay this debt, before being free to leave the brothel or earn money independently.[43] An earlier Sydney study found that 80 per cent of immigrant sex workers were from Thailand, and that 90 per cent were working off debts to the brokers who organised their passage and placement.[44] During the period of debt bondage, these

---

[40] Senator Ian Macdonald, Criminal Code Amendment (Slavery and Sexual Servitude) Bill 1999, second reading speech, Senate, *Hansard*, 24 March 1999.

[41] ibid.

[42] ibid.

[43] Linda Meaker, op. cit. p. 61.

[44] L. Brockett and A. Murray, 'Thai Sex Workers in Sydney', in Roberta Perkins et al. (eds), *Sex Work and Sex Workers In Australia*, UNSW Press, Kensington, 1994.

women are particularly susceptible to slavery and sexual servitude. Subservience to traffickers or their associates is typically maintained through debt-bondage, threats and abuse, passport confiscation, and threats of reprisal to the trafficked person's family.

The Commonwealth offence of sexual servitude may be committed regardless of whether women who migrate to work in the sex industry consent to do so. Yet it appears that those who do consent have been pre-judged and automatically disqualified as legitimate victims of these offences. This thinking harks back to the false distinctions that used to be applied to distinguish between deserving and undeserving victims in sexual assault cases.[45] It is also out of step with the new Trafficking Protocol to which we now turn.

The UN Protocol to Prevent, Suppress and Punish Trafficking in Persons

Australia has been an active participant in the development of a new UN Convention Against Transnational Organized Crime and its three supplementary protocols dealing with people smuggling, people trafficking and trafficking in illicit firearms. Together these new treaties provide a comprehensive legal framework to guide national governments' response to organised crime and to facilitate greater international cooperation between States.

The UN Protocol to Prevent, Suppress and Punish Trafficking in Persons, Especially Women and Children (Trafficking Protocol) was adopted by resolution A/RES/55/25 of 15 November 2000 at the 55th session of the UN General Assembly. The Trafficking Protocol opened for signature with the Convention and the other two protocols at a high level diplomatic conference in Palermo, Italy, on 13 December 2000. The Convention and its protocols enter into force as international law, 90 days after the 40th instrument of ratification has been deposited.[46] The Trafficking Protocol represents a significant international attempt to conceptualise trafficking, define trafficking in international law and provide a template for international cooperation to address the global problem.[47] Australia signed the Convention on 13 December 2000, the Smuggling Protocol on 21 December 2001 but its signature of the People

---

[45] Carol Smart, *Feminism and the Power of Law*, Routledge, London, 1989; Alison Young, 'The Waste Land of Law, the Wordless Song of the Rape Victim', *Melbourne University Law Review*, vol. 22, no. 2, pp. 44265.

[46] As at 8 May 2003, the Convention had 147 signatures and 37 parties. The Trafficking Protocol had 117 signatories and 26 parties. Signatories to the UN Convention against Transnational Crime and its Protocols, web page, last updated 8 May 2003.

[47] Barbara Sullivan, 'Trafficking in Women: Feminism and New International Law', *International Journal of Politics*, vol. 5, no. 1, pp. 6791.

Trafficking Protocol was delayed until 11 December 2002.[48] None of the instruments has yet been ratified by Australia.[49]

Under the Trafficking Protocol trafficking in persons is defined as 'the recruitment, transportation, transfer, harbouring or receipt of persons, by means of the threat or use of force or other forms of coercion, of abduction, of fraud, of deception, of the abuse of power or of a position of vulnerability or of the giving or receiving of payments of benefits to achieve the consent of a person having control over another person, for the purpose of exploitation'.[50] Exploitation is not limited to sexual exploitation but, at a minimum, includes the exploitation of the prostitution of others or other forms of sexual exploitation, forced labour or services, slavery or practices similar to slavery and servitude (art. 3). There is nothing in the definition that limits deception to the nature of the work. Thus a woman who consents to work in the sex industry but is deceived about the conditions is in fact trafficked for the purpose of sexual servitude.

The issue of consent and the link between the definition of trafficking and prostitution was a controversial subject during negotiations on the draft text. Some parties wanted the definition of trafficking to include the phrase 'irrespective of the consent of the person'.[51] While others who support voluntary migration for sex work argued that such a broad definition would include those who choose to move to work in the sex industry, broadening the scope of the protocol beyond the problem. A compromise was struck with the definition including a qualification that consent is not relevant where the threat of use of force or other forms of coercion, abduction, fraud, deception or abuse of power were used the purposes of exploitation.[52] The breadth of the definition was

---

[48] The Hon. Alexander Downer, MP, Senator Chris Ellison and The Hon. Phillip Ruddock, MP, *Joint Media Release*, 12 December 2002.

[49] The ratification of the international instruments is subject to the domestic treaty making process. Under these procedures the Commonwealth Government is required to consult with state and territory governments and other relevant stakeholders. Before moving to ratification it is normal practice for the Attorney-General's Department to conduct a review of existing domestic law and to pass necessary legislation to ensure compliance with Australia's treaty obligations before ratification which makes the treaty binding on Australia.

[50] The definition of trafficking does not require the cross-border movement of the victim and therefore people who are trafficked domestically are also protected subject to article 3 of the main Convention that requires the crime to be trans-national in nature and involves an organised criminal group.

[51] Ann Gallagher, op. cit. p. 986.

[52] ibid.

intended to ensure that all victims of trafficking are recognised and protected, not only those where force or coercion can be proved.[53]

Importantly, State parties to the Protocol have recognised that effective action to prevent and combat people trafficking requires a comprehensive international approach in countries of origin, transit and destination that combines both the punishment of traffickers and the protection of victims.[54] To this end States that ratify the Protocol make a commitment to criminalise people trafficking (as defined in the treaty), provide witness protection and special assistance to trafficked persons, paying special attention to the women and children, and to prevent re-victimisation of trafficked persons. In short, the prosecution of traffickers and protection of victims are seen as mutually reinforcing goals to achieve the overall aim of combating trafficking in the short and long term. But as the ensuing analysis indicates the existing law falls short of meeting these new internationally agreed standards in relation to people trafficking.

Domestic Law

Australian lawmakers have gone some way to addressing the problem of trafficking for the purpose of sexual servitude and slavery but it is arguable that existing law does not yet reflect fully the new internationally agreed standards set out by the Trafficking Protocol.

First, there is no separate offence of 'people trafficking' in the Commonwealth Criminal Code. Instead, in 1999 the offences of slavery, sexual servitude and deceptive recruiting were introduced by the Commonwealth's Criminal Code Amendment (Slavery and Sexual Servitude) Act 2000. These new offences were intended to target traffickers and address the problem of international trafficking of people.[55] The Act was the Commonwealth's part of a proposed package of uniform commonwealth, state and territory offences to deal with the problem and apply where an international element is present.[56] The definitions of slavery and servitude are based on earlier international

---

[53] Where a child, namely a person under 18 years, is involved, consent or the means that consent is obtained are irrelevant (art. 3(c)). The recruitment, transportation, transfer, harbouring or receipt of a child for the purpose of exploitation is sufficient alone to bring the conduct within the definition.

[54] Trafficking Protocol, Preambular paragraph 1 and operative article 1.

[55] See section 270.5 Jurisdictional requirement.

[56] The Commonwealth offences are limited to cases where there is an international element and state and territory governments are left with the responsibility of dealing with trafficking into slavery and sexual servitude that takes place wholly within Australia. To date NSW, ACT, Northern Territory and South Australia have introduced complementary provisions. WA has a bill before Parliament. See Second Reading Speech, Criminal Code Amendment (Slavery and Sexual Servitude) Bill 1999, 24 March 1999, Senate, *Hansard*, p. 3075.

treaties from the 1920s and 1950s which predate the recent developments in international criminal law.[57] As such they are not entirely in step with recent developments, nor do they really address the nature of the problem in Australia.[58]

Under the Commonwealth Criminal Code, 'slavery' is defined as occurring when ownership rights are exercised over another person and can arise from a debt incurred or contract entered into by the enslaved person (s. 270.1). It is not enough that the contract or debt is exploitative or oppressive alone, it must place that person in a condition where a power of ownership is exercised over him or her (s. 270.1). Slave trading also includes 'exercising control or direction over or providing finance for' the trade (s. 270.2). According to Senator Macdonald, the definition was intended to catch 'those who lie at the heart of the trade: the organisers, managers and financiers'.[59]

'Sexual servitude' is defined as occurring when sexual services are provided because of force or threats and the person is not free to cease providing those services (s. 270.4). Importantly, the definition of threat includes not only threat of force but also the threat of deportation recognising that women without valid visas are at risk of constant threat of deportation by their agents, pimps or brothel owners.[60] The offence applies where, as a matter of fact, the woman is held in servitude regardless of her original consent to sex work.

However, the additional offence of 'deceptive recruiting', intended to target traffickers, is limited to deception about the nature of the work and does not capture the situation where women agree to work in the sex industry but are deliberately deceived about the conditions of work (s. 270.7). Deceiving a person for the purpose of sexual servitude, debt bondage or other forms of sexual exploitation is therefore not covered. There is however the offence of 'causing a person to enter into or remain in sexual servitude' which is available (s. 270.6 (1)). Of course this offence is also limited to sexual servitude and depends on proof of causation. And a person who conducts a business that involves the sexual servitude of another, namely, the managers, financiers and organisers, are also captured by s. 270.6 (2). Again these provisions go some way toward addressing traffickers, but it is arguable that they are not entirely in step with the Trafficking Protocol.

---

[57] 1926 International Convention to Suppress the Slave Trade and Slavery and its 1953 protocol and the 1956 Supplementary Convention on the Abolition of Slavery, the Slave Trade and Institutions and Practices similar to Slavery.

[58] See Sandi Kerr, *The Trafficking of Women into Australia as Sex Workers*, unpublished Masters manuscript, ANU, Law Faculty, 2002, p. 36.

[59] Second Reading Speech, Criminal Code Amendment (Slavery and Sexual Servitude) Bill 1999, 24 March 1999, Senate, *Hansard*, p. 3075.

[60] Linda Meaker, op. cit., p. 60.

Prosecutions for Slavery and Sexual Servitude

The only known case of a conviction related to trafficking in Australia is that of Gary Glasner prosecuted under Victorian law before the Commonwealth offences came into effect. This brothel keeper was convicted of importing and imprisoning around 20 Thai women. The women were barred up in the Clifton Hotel until they repaid their debt to him for sponsoring their illegal entry into Australia through the provision of sexual services.[61] He received a fine of $31,000 and a suspended sentence.[62] We understand that Criminal Justice Visas were used in this case to bring witnesses back into the country:

> We regard sex slavery and bondage as abhorrent. We brought in laws to make sure that people could be specifically prosecuted for these offences.[63]

Despite the Minister's reassurance, to date there have been no Commonwealth prosecutions for the offences of slavery or sexual servitude.[64] In March 2003, a Senate Estimates Committee was informed that the AFP had undertaken 13 investigations into offences related to sexual servitude, that three were still under way, but that none had led to a prosecution.[65] The Federal Minister for Justice and Customs, Senator Ellison explained that:

> This is due in part to the reluctance of potential witnesses, many of whom are in the country illegally, to testify.[66]

According to media sources even when potential witnesses offer to assist, they are still swiftly deported.[67] Noi, a Thai woman recently

---

[61] Elisabeth Wynhausen, 'One-Way Traffic of Sex Slave Trade', *The Weekend Australian*, 22 March 2003; Mary Sullivan and Sheila Jeffreys, op. cit., p. 1146.

[62] Rebecca Tailby, 'Organised Crime and People Smuggling/Trafficking to Australia', *Trends and Issues in Crime and Criminal Justice*, no. 208, Australian Institute of Criminology, May 2001, p. 6.

[63] The Hon. Minister Phillip Ruddock interviewed on *Meet the Press*, Sunday 20 April 2003.

[64] See also the Annual Reports for the Commonwealth Department of Public Prosecutions for 2001 and 2002.

[65] Senator Ellison, Question Without Notice, Immigration: Ms Puangthong Simaplee, Senate, *Hansard*, 24 March 2003.

[66] ibid.

[67] Natalie O'Brien and Elizabeth Wynhausen, 'Officials ignored sex slave's offer of help', *The Australian*, 2 April 2003; Elisabeth Wynhausen and Natalie O'Brien, 'Sex slave witness set to be deported', *The Australian*, 17 April 2003; Elisabeth Wynhausen, Natalie

deported following a raid for illegal immigrants in a Melbourne brothel, has alleged that DIMIA officers were not interested in her offer to help apprehend the traffickers who had locked her in a brothel, refusing to release her until she repaid a $50,000 debt by doing 750 jobs.[68] This allegation is disturbing as, on the available facts, if accurate, the case appears to meet the definition of sexual servitude. She was only in detention a few days before being deported. Wing, another Thai woman, currently in detention at the time of writing, has made a similar allegation.[69] DIMIA has in the past openly acknowledged that as the mandatory detention provisions of the Migration Act requires the detention and removal of unlawful non-citizens as soon as practical, 'there is little effective opportunity for such a person to remain in Australia to give evidence at the trial'.[70]

Compliance actions by immigration officers bring them into frequent contact with a significant number of potential witnesses to, and victims of slavery and sexual servitude offences. For instance, from July 2002 to February 2003, 'immigration compliance staff located 134 people working illegally in the sex industry'.[71] From 1998 to 2000 387 non-lawful citizens were picked up during immigration compliance actions.[72] The contact is usually brief because, as confirmed by a senior DIMIA executive before a Senate Estimates Committee, 'people who are located working unlawfully in the community generally leave Australia promptly'.[73] In defence of this policy, DIMIA has argued that 'it has never been easy to obtain information on the organizers and the couriers in the illegal sex trade as sex workers are either fearful of reprisals against themselves or their families, or possibly may wish to use the organization again'.[74] This begs the question whether Australia is discharging its duty to protect victims of trafficking from further

---

O'Brien, and Elizabeth Coleman, 'No visa for sex slave whistleblower', *The Australian,* 21 April 2003.

[68] Natalie O'Brien and Elisabeth Wynhausen, 'Officials ignored sex slave's offer of help', *The Australian,* 2 April 2003.

[69] Elisabeth Wynhausen, Natalie O'Brien, and Elizabeth Coleman, 'No visa for sex slave whistleblower', *The Australian,* 21 April 2003.

[70] DIMIA, *Protecting the Border Immigration Compliance,* Commonwealth of Australia, Canberra, 1999, p. 31.

[71] The Hon. Phillip Ruddock, MP, *Ministerial Press Release,* 1 April 2003.

[72] DIMIA, *Protecting the Border: Immigration Compliance,* Commonwealth of Australia, Canberra, 2000.

[73] Mr Moorhouse, First Assistant Secretary, Border Control and Compliance Division, DIMIA, answer to Senator Allison, Immigration and Multicultural and Indigenous Affairs portfolio, Senate, *Legal and Constitutional Legislation Committee,* 11 February 2002.

[74] DIMIA, 1999, op. cit., p. 31.

violations of their human rights. It is not a justification for prompt removal.

The unintended consequence of this policy is that foreign and local agents and brothel owners and pimps are enjoying immunity from prosecution in Australia as investigation is impossible without the cooperation and testimony of witnesses who are routinely deported. Meanwhile victims are at risk of being returned to an unsafe environment, exposed to possible re-victimisation or worse, while brothel keepers and traffickers have the added incentive to recruit again in order to recoup their losses, or maintain their profits.[75]

Mechanisms to Protect Witnesses and Support Victims

From a public policy viewpoint, there is an inextricable link between legislation criminalizing slavery and sexual servitude and the implementation of mechanisms to protect the human rights of trafficking victims.[76] We argue below that the realization of the criminal justice objectives of the legislation, to convict traffickers, requires more than the protection of witnesses, it requires the support of victims as well.

Protecting Witnesses

Under the Convention and Trafficking Protocol the State party is required to ensure the physical protection of the witnesses as well as the protection of victims from retaliation and intimidation.[77] This may include, for example, non-disclosure of the witness's identity, giving evidence by video link and relocating the person to another State.[78] These instruments also require that victims be provided with assistance for their recovery.[79] The ongoing assistance to victims must be considered as a separate issue because not all victims of trafficking will be selected by investigating and prosecuting authorities to act as witnesses in criminal prosecutions.[80] However, measures of protection

---

[75] A similar point was made by the Editor of the *Sydney Morning Herald*, almost two years ago, when he wrote, 'indeed, in the past three years, immigration raids have netted more than 600 women working illegally in Australian brothels. Shamefully, while such women have been deported, not one prosecution has been mounted against their exploiters'. (Editorial, *Sydney Morning Herald*, 8 June 2001).

[76] Jennifer Norberry, op. cit., 1999, p. 7.

[77] Article 24 Convention and Article 6 Trafficking Protocol.

[78] Articles 24.2, 24.3.

[79] Article 25 Convention, Article 6 Trafficking Protocol.

[80] Observation by the UN High Commissioner for Human Rights and the UN High Commissioner for Refugees on the Proposal for the EU Council Framework Decision on Combating Trafficking in Human Being, para 6.

and ongoing assistance work hand in hand with an effective prosecution strategy to convict traffickers.

To assist with an investigation or prosecution, potential witnesses can be temporarily retained or be allowed to re-enter Australia on a Criminal Justice Visa and in theory granted protection under the *Witness Protection Act 1994*. But these general measures are not sufficiently tailored to meet the specific needs of trafficking victims, especially of women and children. Importantly, a Criminal Justice Visa is only available to victims selected as witnesses. Even so, it is not linked to any statutory provision for witness protection or trigger any other forms of assistance. Additionally, the procedure for granting a Criminal Justice Visa is cumbersome, involving a multitude of agencies, militating against their use.

A Criminal Justice Certificate must first be granted by either the Commonwealth Attorney-General, Director of Public Prosecutions or Police Commissioner[81] before DIMIA may consider issuing the visa.[82] The process also assumes that law enforcement agencies have had sufficient time and access to potential witnesses to make a request to the relevant authorities. Media reports indicate that witnesses are routinely and promptly deported before being interviewed by law enforcement agencies.[83]

None of the 124 sex workers picked up during compliance operations by DIMIA from July 2002 to February 2003 have been granted Criminal Justice Visas to remain in Australia.[84] This lends support to the argument that this mechanism is either underutilized or is inappropriate for this purpose. While it is possible that none were victims of trafficking, this seems highly unlikely. Of the trafficking victims located by DIMIA during compliance operations it also seems implausible that none were prepared to cooperate with the AFP. The problem may be lack of referral by DIMIA to the relevant law enforcement agencies, but some media reports also claim that the AFP

---

[81] The Hon. Phillip Ruddock, MP, *Ministerial Press Release*, 1 April 2003.

[82] Mr Moorhouse, First Assistant Secretary, Border Control and Compliance Division, DIMIA, answer to Senator Allison, Immigration and Multicultural and Indigenous Affairs portfolio, Senate, *Legal and Constitutional Legislation Committee*, 11 February 2002.

[83] Natalie O'Brien and Elizabeth Wyndhausen, 'Bureaucrats ignored sex slave sting', *Weekend Australian*, 5 April 2003.

[84] From July 2002 to February 2003, DIMIA had detained 124 sex workers, of whom 109 were removed, 16 released on temporary visas and two were in detention. None were reported to the committee as having been granted a criminal justice visa. Answer to Question Taken on Notice, Additional Estimates Hearing, Immigration and Multicultural and Indigenous Affairs Portfolio, Enforcement of Immigration Law, 11 February 2003. It was reported on Lateline ABC Television, 7 May 2003, that Wing, a Thai women who had offered to assist the AFP in investigating traffickers had been issued a Criminal Justice Visa the previous day.

have 'flatly refused to investigate allegations of sexual slavery'.[85] Under the current system, DIMIA may be put in a difficult position in cases where a victim is cooperating with a criminal investigation but the AFP fails to request a Criminal Justice Visa. Under the *Migration Act 1958* DIMIA must, subject to some qualifications, deport an unlawful non-citizen as soon as reasonably practicable. The lawfulness of the detention may come into question if the process of deportation is delayed for the purpose of facilitating an investigation.

The Minister for Justice and Customs Minister, Senator Chris Ellison, has now ordered a review into the policing of sexual servitude and slavery to examine the issue of coordination between law enforcement agencies whose responsibility it is to investigate these crimes.[86] It will be important that the review examine both the deficiencies in the current law and policy and the need for more effective cross-portfolio operational protocols between the relevant departments and units.[87] All these matters need to be considered together as part of a coherent legislative and policy response that aims to meet the dual goals of prosecuting traffickers while simultaneously supporting victims.

Supporting Victims

The successful prosecution of traffickers relies on the cooperation of the victims of traffickers, who without mandated support, protection or means of redress are understandably reluctant about cooperating with law enforcement agencies. The treatment of sex workers like Noi, deported despite her offer of assistance to convict her traffickers, reveals a systemic failure to come to grips with the necessary support for trafficking victims in Australia. This case and others like it highlight the inconsistency between the strident enforcement of immigration law and Australia's domestic and international criminal justice objectives to convict traffickers. It also raises a real question about the Commonwealth's ability to meet the new standards envisaged and encouraged by the Convention and the Trafficking Protocol to provide trafficking victims with adequate support.[88]

---

[85] Natalie O'Brien and Elizabeth Wynhausen, 'AFP refused to act on trafficking', *The Australian*, 12 April 2003.

[86] Natalie O'Brien, Elisabeth Wynhausen and Kathryn Shine, 'Canberra to review sex slave policing', *The Australian*, 4 April 2003; see also comments made by The Hon. Phillip Ruddock, MP, Lateline, ABC Television, 7 May 2003.

[87] This should include reviewing the method, quality and scope of interviewing by DIMIA compliance officers.

[88] Jennifer Norberry, 'Criminal Code Amendment (Slavery and Sexual Servitude) Bill 1999', *Bills Digest,* no. 167, Department of the Parliamentary Library, 1999, provides background to the legislation. It encouraged consideration be given to amending the Migration Act to provide special status for the victims of trafficking.

The Protocol requires that State parties 'consider implementing measures' for the physical, psychological and social recovery of victims (art. 6.2). It recommends the provision of appropriate housing, counselling and information about their legal rights, medical, psychological and material assistance and access to employment, educational and training opportunities (art. 6.3).[89] To date, statutory rights to counselling, temporary accommodation or financial assistance of the kind urged under the Trafficking Protocol is entirely missing from the Australian system. Thus the role social security and family and child services departments might play in supporting victims that would in turn increase their ability to cooperate with the police, has so far been overlooked. This will need to be addressed as part of Australia's preparation for ratifying the Trafficking Protocol.

Australia's failure to support the victims of traffickers was concretely highlighted by the death of Puangthong Simaplee in Villawood Detention Centre on 26 September 2001.[90] The inquest has sparked controversy with persistent questions being asked in the Senate and its committees about the Government's handling of victims trafficked into Australia to work in the sex industry.[91]

Ms. Simaplee told immigration officials that she was trafficked into Australia in 1986 on a false Malaysian passport.[92] While the Deputy Coroner, Carl Milovanovich, was unable to confirm her history of sexual slavery, this being outside his jurisdiction, he was concerned enough to urge law enforcement authorities to address the trafficking of women into prostitution with 'vigour and appropriate resources'.[93] The Deputy Coroner found that in September 2001 immigration officers detained Ms Simaplee following a raid on a Sydney brothel in Riley Street Surry

---

[89] The Protocol's weak protection provisions have been criticised by international law experts who predict 'is likely to undermine its effectiveness as a law enforcement instrument'. Ann Gallagher, op. cit., p. 991.

[90] Deputy State Coroner, NSW, Carl Milovanovich, *Inquest into the Death of Puongtong Simaplee*, Westmead Coroners Court, 24 April 2003.

[91] For example, Senator Linda Kirk, ALP, Attorney-General's Portfolio: Attorney-General's Department, Legal and Constitutional Legislation Committee, Attorney-General's Portfolio: Australian Federal Police, Senate, 10 February 2002; Senator Joe Ludwig, ALP, Legal and Constitutional Legislation Committee, Attorney-General's Portfolio: Australian Federal Police, Senate, 10 February 2002; Senator Lyn Allison, Question Taken on Notice, Additional Estimates Hearing, Immigration and Multicultural and Indigenous Affairs Portfolio, Senate, 11 February 2003; Senator Brian Greig, Democrats, 'Question without Notice (Speech), Immigration: Ms Puangthong Simaplee', Senate, *Hansard*, 24 March 2003; Senator Brian Greig, Democrats, 'Question without Notice, Immigration: Ms Puangthong Simaplee', Senate, *Hansard*, 25 March 2003.

[92] Leoni Lamont, 'Sold at 12: nightmare ends in death', *Sydney Morning Herald*, 13 March 2002.

[93] Deputy State Coroner, NSW, Carl Milovanovich, *Inquest into the Death of Puongtong Simaplee*, Westmead Coroners Court, 24 April 2003, p. 2.

Hills.[94] Three days later she died in an observation cell while being treated by detention centre staff for heroin withdrawal.[95] The Deputy Coroner expressed concern about the adequacy of her medical care while detained in Villawood Detention Centre and recommended that consideration be given to the hospitalisation of detainees in such instances. He also recommended that DIMIA and Australian Correctional Management (ACM) facilities work with organisations like Project Respect 'which might assist in identifying, assessing and providing the appropriate medical, community and translator services to women who might be identified as being victims of trafficking.[96] Referring to the Trafficking Protocol, the Sex Discrimination Commissioner Pru Goward commented that, 'it is to be hoped that in the future this Protocol will protect the interests and needs of women like Simaplee and that her sad case is one never to be repeated'.[97]

Special Visa Class, Temporary or Permanent Stay

A possible reason for the Government's apparent hesitance to address comprehensively concerns about its level of support for trafficking victims, is that the issue inevitably raises questions about their residency status. One way of reducing the black market in trafficked sex workers is to allow them to migrate lawfully to work in the sex industry under a special visa class of entry. Alternately the business migration stream could be expanded to include the sex industry, where there is high but unmet local demand for these workers. This idea, initially suggested by sex workers organisations,[98] was recently revived in Senate by Senator Greig.[99] While many may see the idea as politically unpalatable, it would go a long way to removing the exploitative

---

[94] ibid., p. 1.

[95] ibid.

[96] ibid., p. 15.

[97] Commissioner Pru Goward, *Media Release*, Australian Human Rights and Equal Opportunity Commission, 24 April 2003.

[98] For example Sex Workers Outreach Project (SWOP), 'proposes that sex workers be given a 12 month working visa with recommendations that they contact SWOP and sexual health clinics'. SWOP Website, visited 8 May 2003.

[99] In a speech to Senate, Senator Greig stated 'I would argue that there are perhaps only two realistic responses that government has to this situation. The first would be to provide visas to those women overseas who wanted to come here as consenting adults and work lawfully in the sex industry, given that prostitution is regulated and lawful in several states Were this to happen, I believe it would effectively snuff out this black market. happen, I believe it would effectively snuff out this black market. I do not think the government is going to give that suggestion the remotest consideration; visas on those grounds are currently denied. So it seems that the only other effective way to deal this is to get tough on trafficking.' Senator Brian Greig, Question Without Notice, (Speech) Immigration: Ms Puangthong Simaplee, Senate, *Hansard,* 24 March 2003.

conditions under which women from developing countries come to Australia to work in the sex industry. Once in Australia, they would no longer be vulnerable to the actions of traffickers or pimps who require their servitude in exchange for protecting them from immigration compliance operations. Nor would they have to enter into debt bondage, for their immigration could be arranged lawfully through DIMIA.

As a signatory to the Trafficking Protocol, the Commonwealth Government is required to consider providing the victims of trafficking with temporary or permanent residency on humanitarian grounds.[100] However, the Government took the unusual step of making a declaration at the signature stage,[101] stating that nothing in the Protocol is to be seen as imposing obligations on Australia to admit or retain any person within its national borders that it does not already have such an obligation toward.[102] The statement is a clear indication of the Government's discomfort with the idea of humanitarian support for victims and it sends a clear message that it will not consider allowing temporary or permanent stay for the victims of trafficking into the sex industry. That said, neither the declaratory statement or the terms of articles 7 or 8,[103] displace Australia's obligations of *non-refoulement* under the 1951 Convention Relating to the Status of Refugees (CSR) and other international human rights treaties not to return a person to a country where they are at risk of persecution for a convention reason or otherwise at real risk of a violation of their internationally recognised human rights.[104]

Applying for recognition as a refugee on the grounds of gender persecution is one of the few options open for trafficking victims to seek lawful residency status within Australia. But while Australia is one of the few countries to have gender guidelines the likelihood of success is

---

[100] The UN Trafficking Protocol requires State signatories to 'consider adopting legislative or other measures' to allow for temporary or permanent stay and take into account humanitarian and compassionate factors when implementing its obligation under this provision (art. 7).

[101] Australia's declaration states, 'The Government of Australia hereby declares that nothing in the Protocol shall be seen to be imposing obligations on Australia to admit or retain within its borders persons in respect of whom Australia would not otherwise have an obligation to admit or retain within its borders'. Multilateral Treaties deposited with the Secretary-General of the United Nations, Trafficking Protocol, website, visited 8 May 2003.

[102] A declaratory statement is a statement of interpretation not a reservation to the treaty. It is normal practice to enter declaratory statements and reservations at the ratification stage. Consequently, it is still open for Australia to enter a reservation limiting its obligations under the treaty.

[103] Under Article 8, repatriation of the victims is to be facilitated by receiving States, but the safety of that person on return must be taken into account (art.8).

[104] International Convention on Civil and Political Rights and the Convention Against Torture and other Cruel, In human and Degrading Treatment or Punishment.

remote. In some cases a trafficking victim might qualify for another type of substantive visa, such as a student or spouse visa, but this partial approach is not adequate either. Under the Migration Act 1958 there is no onshore mechanism by which a victim could apply for a protection visa on humanitarian grounds. Under the Act an applicant must have already been rejected for a protection or other visa before the Minister can exercise his discretion.[105] The Minister's discretion to grant a protection visa on humanitarian grounds is discretionary, non-compellable and therefore removed from the scrutiny of the courts.

Developments in the US and Europe

The approach of the US and in Europe stands in stark contrast to the current situation in Australia. As part of its overall strategy to deal with the global rise in trafficking the US State Department established a Trafficking Office. This office provides the victims of traffickers with access to services including immigration concessions, shelter, social assistance, medical care, privacy and protection, and voluntary repatriation.[106]

Importantly, the US Trafficking Victims Protection Act of October 2000, created a new T visa for trafficking victims that allows for temporary residency of up to three years but may also lead to permanent residency in cases where repatriation could lead to further harm or extreme hardship.[107] This status is only available to those willing to provide information on traffickers to police and since introducing these measures the US has doubled the number of investigations and tripled the number of convictions for trafficking.[108]

The US model was possible because of a fundamental shift in the attitude toward the victims of trafficking. The shift was from stigmatizing the victim as an undeserving lawbreaker to supporting the victim with a view to actively seeking their cooperation to combat trafficking. The approach can be criticised as pressuring victims into participating in investigation but it does go a long way toward the obligations of

---

[105] Section 417 Migration Act 1958 empowers the Minister to exercise his discretion in the public interest to substitute a decision of the Refugee Review Tribunal to grant a protection visa on humanitarian grounds if deportation of the person to their country of origin or another country would expose her to a serious risk of a violation of her human rights.

[106] US Department of Justice, Fact Sheet, Accomplishment in the Fight to Prevent Trafficking in Persons, Washington, 25 February 2003.

[107] Sean Murphy, 'International trafficking in person, especially women and children', *The American Journal of International Law*, vol. 95, no. 2, p. 410.

[108] US Department of Justice, Fact Sheet, Accomplishment in the Fight to Prevent Trafficking in Persons, Washington, 25 February 2003.

protecting victims while achieving law enforcement objectives at the same time.

In Europe, Italy has adopted measures to protect trafficking victims regardless of their cooperation with police[109] and Belgium, the Netherlands and Spain provide temporary residence permits to victims although they are limited to those willing to give evidence.[110] The Italian government has since reported a significant increase in the incrimination of traffickers.[111] In other countries in Europe trafficked women may apply for residence on humanitarian grounds.

What Direction Will Australia Take?

Some Australian Parliamentarians are already on record as favouring a more comprehensive approach to the issue. In 1995 for example, the Joint Standing Committee on Foreign Affairs, Defence and Trade recommended the Australian Government put in place 'programs which would recognise Australia's responsibilities for the protection and rehabilitation of the victims of trafficking' and where this was the case, 'consider this as a factor in any application which is made for a humanitarian visa'.[112]

Upon ratification the Government may make reservations to the Trafficking Protocol to avoid or limit further the obligations to provide assistance. This would avoid the existing contradictions between the Trafficking Protocol and the Migration Act 1958. However, as victim protection is one of the stated purposes of the Trafficking Protocol and integral to combating people trafficking, such a course may be seen as defeating the primary object and purpose of signing it.[113]

A more effective approach might be to accept the Trafficking Protocol in its entirety, remove the existing declaration, and consult widely within federal and state and territory governments and law enforcement

---

[109] Article 18 Alien Law provides a six month temporary social protection residence permit with the possibility of extension for up to eighteen months.

[110] Commission of the European Communities (2002), 'Proposal for a Council Directive on the short-term residence permit issued to victims of action to facilitate illegal immigration or trafficking in human being who cooperate with the competent authorities', Brussels, Belgium, p. 5. Italian Ministry of the Interior, *Rapporto sullo stato della sicurezza in Italia*, Rome Italy, 2001 reported in, Shear Demir J., 'The Trafficking of women for sexual exploitation: a gender based and well founded fear of persecution?', *New Issues in Refugee Research, Working Paper No. 80*, UNHCR, March 2003, p. 21.

[111] Italian Ministry of the Interior, *Rapporto sullo stato della sicurezza in Italia*, Rome Italy, 2001 reported in Shear Demir J., 'The Trafficking of women for sexual exploitation: a gender based and well founded fear of persecution?', *New Issues in Refugee Research, Working Paper No. 80*, UNHCR, March 2003, p. 21.

[112] Joint Standing Committee on Defence, Foreign Affairs and Trade, op. cit., p. 53.

[113] The validity of a reservation that is inconsistent with the object and purpose of a treaty may be opposed by other State parties to the instrument and its legal effect would be put in doubt.

agencies and the non-government agencies on the development of a package of measures and operational protocols that will achieve the goals of prosecution and victim support and protection. This approach would demonstrate our commitment to the governments of South East Asia that Australia is serious about protecting their nationals and complement our proven determination to combat the related but distinct crime of people smuggling. The UN Office of the High Commissioner for Human Rights has developed a comprehensive set of Recommended Principles and Guidelines on Human Rights and Human Trafficking that could usefully inform such a process.[114] Agencies such as the Human Rights and Equal Opportunity Commission may also have a useful contribution to make, along with NGOs, the Office of Status of Women and other Government departments such as Social Security, and Family and Community Services.

Conclusion

Despite the introduction of Federal criminal laws in 1999 designed to combat trans-national trafficking of people for slavery and sexual servitude, to date there have been no prosecutions for any of these offences. The crux of the problem, identified by a variety of commentators,[115] is that women trafficked into Australia to work in the sex industry are treated as commodities for exploitation by traffickers and brothel owners and illegal immigrants by the Government.

While securing the cooperation of potential witnesses may be difficult, recent developments in the US and Europe reviewed in this paper suggest that an approach which respects the human rights of victims is more effective in achieving the interrelated goals of prosecution and protection. In light of these recent developments and Australia's forthcoming ratification of the UN Convention Against Transnational Organized Crime and its supplementary Protocol on People Trafficking, it can be argued that it is timely to commission independent and thorough research into the extent and nature of the problem in Australia and review how best to align domestic law and policy with international best practice. While the Australian Government has taken some steps in this direction, this brief has demonstrated that existing law and policy relating to the victims and witnesses of trafficking is at best patchy and is now out of step with

---

[114] Recommended Principles and Guidelines on Human Rights and Human Trafficking, Office of the United Nationals High Commissioner for Human Rights, UN, HR/PUB/02/03, Geneva, 2002.

[115] Georgio Costello, Jammed: Trafficked Women in Australia, speech presented at Project Respect's 'Stop the Traffic' Conference, Melbourne, 25 February 2002; Kathleen Maltzahn, Trafficking in Women for Prostitution, speech presented at the Australian Women Conference Conference, Canberra, 28 August 2001; Sally Moyle, Director, Sex Discrimination Unit, 'Trafficking in Women', speech presented at the Stop the Traffic Symposium: Addressing Trafficking in Women for Prostitution, RMIT, 25 February 2002; Coalition Against Trafficking in Women Australia, website, visited 6 May 2003.

internationally agreed standards. At worse, the current approach of routinely deporting potential witnesses and victims can be seen to undermine the goals of protection and prosecution, putting victims at risk with sometimes life threatening consequences, while allowing traffickers to act with impunity in Australia and abroad.

Discussion Questions

1   *According to the United Nations how much money is generated each year by the global sex industry?*

2   *What are the estimated numbers of people trafficked around the world for sexual and other forms of exploitation?*

3   *How is sexual servitude defined?*

17

HUMAN TRAFFICKING IN AUSTRALIA: THE CHALLENGE OF RESPONDING TO SUSPICIOUS ACTIVITIES

Erica Kotnik, *Youth Reproductive Health Advisor, Partners for Development, Cambodia*
Melina Czymoniewicz-Klippel, *Visiting Research Scholar, Pennsylvania State University, USA*
Elizabeth Hoba, Ph.D., *Medical Anthropologist and Senior Lecturer, School of Health and Social Development, Deakin Univ., Australia*

Introduction

Human trafficking[1] (hereinafter referred to as trafficking) is a human rights issue of grave concern that has, befittingly, received increasing global attention over recent years. In saying this, trafficking is not a new phenomenon, but rather one that 'has been part of civilization since the beginning of human history' (Bales 2005:126), dating as far back as Roman and Biblical times (Cwikel and Hoban 2005). The literature cites an abundance of 'guesstimates' with regard to the current magnitude of the problem: for example, the US Department of State, in their fourth Trafficking in Persons Report, estimates that 600,000 to 800,000 men, women, and children are trafficked across international borders each year (US Department of State 2004). Whereas, a study of trafficked women in five countries (Indonesia, the Philippines, Thailand, Venezuela, and the United States), cites global trafficking figures of between 700,000 and 4 million (Raymond 2002). However, in reality, we remain ignorant to the full extent and complexity of this heinous and intolerable crime, notwithstanding broad consensus that the scope of the problem is expanding in tandem with growing socioeconomic inequalities across and within regions and against the background of increasing illegal migration (Marshall 2005).

---

[1] According to the United Nations protocol to prevent, suppress and punish trafficking in persons, especially women and children, "trafficking in persons" refers to 'the recruitment, transportation, transfer, harbouring or receipt of persons, by means of the threat or use of force or other forms of coercion, of abduction, of fraud, of deception, of the abuse of power or of a position of vulnerability or of the giving and receiving of payments or benefits to achieve the consent of a person baying control over another person, for the purpose of exploitation. Exploitation shall include, at a minimum, the exploitation of the prostitution of others or other forms of sexual exploitation, forced labour or services, slaver)., or practices similar to slavery, servitude or the removal or organs' (United Nations 2000).

Moreover, current debate has been channeled towards the trafficking of women and girls for sexual exploitation, mainly due to the dominance of feminist voices in the global campaign against trafficking (Doezema 2000). In addition to women and girls, large numbers of men and boys are trafficked for a range of exploitative purposes including, *inter alia*, domestic labour, marriage, industrial and agricultural work, and the trade in human organs (Kempadoo et al. 2005). While this paper, along with much of the current literature, focuses on the trafficking of women into the sex industry, it is important to recognise that trafficking for sexual exploitation is pervasive, yet not the only form of trafficking existent in Australia (Project Respect 2004).

This paper draws on empirical data gathered in Melbourne from the general public, Victorian Police and local governments to provide an overview of the challenges incurred when responding to suspected trafficking-related activities in Australia. Firstly, the situation of trafficking in Australia and the Australian Government's response to trafficking is declared. Barriers to reporting, as well as institutional obstacles faced by the authorities upon receipt of pertinent information are then discussed in relation to data collected by the first and third authors. Finally, in identifying gaps in the community's awareness of the situation and the existing response system, practical recommendations are offered to improve the manner in which the prevention of trafficking is addressed at the community level.

Trafficking in the Australian Context

Trafficking in the Australian context is seriously under-researched, resulting in a paucity of accurate information on the intricacies of the problem and, until recently, apathy and lack of acknowledgment on the part of our nation's leaders of the domestic relevance of trafficking. Recent research on trafficking in Australia, both published and unpublished work, including Burn and Simmons 2005; Farr 2005; Hoban et al. 2003; Project Respect 2004, has, however, uncovered the presence of trafficked persons in this country, chiefly in the Australian sex industry.

The Australian Federal Police (AFP) consider Australia attractive to human traffickers (No author 2003a), due to its geographic proximity, to Asia, a recognized hub of trafficking (Piper 2005), and its high and continuing demand for Asian sex workers (Batros 2004). However, the clandestine and illicit nature of trafficking, reluctance of trafficked persons to cooperate with the authorities, limited coordination between government agencies and non-government organizations (NGOs), application of differing definitions of trafficking and varied methods of gathering statistics has inhibited the accurate assessment of the scope of the problem in Australia (Carrington and Hearn 2003). Figures collated from an array of secondary sources by Carrington and Hearn (ibid), for example, consider there is between four and 1000 trafficked women in the Australian sex industry at any given time.

Lack of accurate statistics aside, evidence indicates that persons are trafficked into Australia primarily from Southeast Asia (Hoban et al. 2003). The US State Department's most recent Trafficking in Persons Report corroborates these findings, listing Australia as 'a destination country for women from Southeast Asia, South Korea, and the People's Republic of China (P.R.C) who are trafficked for the purposes of sexual exploitation' (US Department of State 2006: 62). Internally, an anti-trafficking NGO identified trafficked women in Sydney, Melbourne, Canberra, Perth and Darwin, in both licensed and unlicensed brothels (Project Respect 2004). It is important to note that in Australia legislation relating to prostitution varies by state, for example, in Victoria, Western Australia and Queensland prostitution is legal and regulated by government authorities, whereas in the remaining states prostitution remains illegal.

Brockett and Murrey (1994) claim that the majority of foreign women entering Australia to work in the sex industry are transported into Australia from Southeast Asia by plane, passing through customs with the aid of a tourist visa. Evidence collected from trafficked women indicates that many traveled willingly to work in the Australian sex industry, only to find themselves trapped in conditions of debt bondage and/or sexual servitude upon arrival (US Department of State 2004; Murphy 2006). For example, trafficked women interviewed in Melbourne and Sydney by Hoban and colleagues (Hoban et al. 2003) discussed being unable to refuse clients or leave their place of residence or work, and being subjected to threats, violence, systematic rape and unprotected sex. Yet, many trafficked women do not perceive themselves as victims, rather, they perceive benefits in their situation, i.e., the opportunity to address indebtedness and economically improve their lives, and that of their families (Commonwealth of Australia 2005a).

The Australian Government's Response to Trafficking

Since the late 1990s, trafficking has slowly crept onto the political agenda of the Australian Government, with increasing knowledge of the problem and external pressure creating progressively larger ripples of action. Movement started in 1999, when the Australian Government conducted a major reform of the criminal law to introduce the Common-wealth *Criminal Code Amendment (Slavery and Sexual Servitude) Act 1999* (Commonwealth of Australia 1999). Yet, it wasn't until the death of Puongtong Simaplee, a Thai woman trafficked into sexual servitude in Australia who died in custody at Villawood Immigration Detention Centre on the 26th of September 2001 (Commonwealth of Australia

2003), that the Australian Government's failure to adequately address trafficking was publicly exposed, community and media support criticized and serious action incited.

Over the past five years, and in particular since the Coronial Inquiry into Ms Simaplee's death in April 2003 (Milovanovich 2003), the Australian Government has worked towards a series of additional policy and legislative reforms to address trafficking. In October 2003, the Australian Government demonstrated its commitment to addressing trafficking by announcing a $20 million package to combat all forms of trafficking in persons (Attorney-General's Department 2003). In January 2004, a new visa regime was introduced, including the creation of two new visa categories to provide temporary or permanent stay to trafficked persons willing to make a significant contribution to criminal investigations or prosecutions, or who face probable danger upon return to their country of origin (Burn and Simmons 2005). Later the same year, the *Australian Government's Action Plan to Eradicate Trafficking in Persons* (hereinafter referred to as the Action Plan), comprising four central elements: i) prevention; ii) detection and investigation; iii) criminal prosecution; and iv) victim support and rehabilitation, was launched (Commonwealth of Australia 2004). Most recently, the Australian Government has introduced the *Criminal Code Amendment (Trafficking in Persons Offenses) Act 2005* (Commonwealth of Australia 2005b) to include debt bondage and human trafficking related offences, and on the 15th of September 2005 ratified the United Nations Protocol to prevent, suppress and punish trafficking in persons (Attorney-General's Department 2005).

Despite these significant advances in addressing trafficking, as highlighted in a recent NGO Shadow Report on trafficked women in Australia (UNANIMA International et al. 2006), presented at the 34th Session of the Committee for the Convention on the Elimination of All Forms of Discrimination Against Women (CEDAW) in January 2006, the current response requires further strengthening. For example, the Australian Government has been criticized for assisting only trafficked persons who agree to provide evidence that will assist in investigations and prosecutions, rather than supporting all trafficked persons irrespective of their willingness or ability to collaborate with the authorities to bring about prosecutions (Burn and Simmons 2005). Furthermore, it has been strongly suggested that future advances be addressed from a gendered perspective, within the human rights framework (United Nations 2002), and by placing the victim at the centre of any response to trafficking, as advocated in the UN Recommended Principles and Guidelines on Human Rights and Human Trafficking (UNANIMA International et al. 2006). At present, responses in Australia remain couched in wider immigration, economic and border security policies.

Community Awareness

In launching its Action Plan in 2004, the Australian Government allocated significant financial resources to trafficking-specific activities, thereby allowing the establishment of a number of key initiatives, including: the establishment of a Transnational Sexual Exploitation and Trafficking Team with the AFP; the location of a Senior Migration Officer in Thailand; a comprehensive victim support program for those granted visas to remain in Australia to assist with investigations or prosecutions; reintegration assistance for trafficked persons returning to Southeast Asia; and, of particular relevance to this paper, a community awareness strategy to increase consciousness about trafficking issues within Australia (Commonwealth of Australia 2004).

The proposed community awareness strategy aims to facilitate domestic deterrence and prevention of trafficking through increased awareness of trafficking-related matters, reporting of suspicious activity and support for trafficked persons (Commonwealth of Australia 2004). The resultant campaign will comprise two streams: the first to target trafficked persons working in the sex industry in Australia as well as others who are likely to come in contact with these people, for example, other sex workers, clients and brothel owners; the second to target the media as a means of fostering informed community debate on the issue (ibid). The Attorney General's Department is overseeing the strategy, which is anticipated to take approximately 4 years and cost $400,000 (J Baker 2004, personal communication, 27 October). Despite having commissioned initial actioning of this strategy to a Melbourne-based media consultant group, in 2004, the campaign is yet to be implemented. According to the Parliamentary Joint Committee of the Australian Crime Commission:

> ... the community awareness strategy that was intended to be implemented has been very slow in its implementation. A sum of $400,000 was to be spent on the community awareness strategy to combat sex trafficking, but government consultant Open Mind Research are finding it difficult to get appointments with the targets of the advertising—the sex industry workers and their clients. Stage 1, which is to determine the focus of the strategy and identify target audiences and to develop key messages, is still where the campaign is at.[2]

Clearly, the Australian Government has encountered significant challenges in implementing its community awareness strategy: it is anticipated the evidence provided in this paper will be beneficial to the

---

[2] Mr Kerr, 5 September 2003. Hansard, p. 11.

campaign through the provision of baseline knowledge with regard to current attitudes and knowledge of trafficking amongst the Victorian community and public institutions.

Methodology

This paper presents data from two studies conducted in Melbourne between 2002 and 2004. These studies were carried out in the Cities of Yarra and Port Phillip, local government areas that are both located within close proximity to Melbourne's central business district. These sites were chosen because of the extensive media coverage in 1998 of a criminal trial of Gary Glazner, a Melbourne brothel owner: the media reported the trafficking operations of Glazner, who purchased women to work in brothels in Victoria (Ford 2001), many of which were located in the City of Port Phillip. In addition, there is a considerable presence of the sex industry in the study locations, for example, at the time of planning the second study, the City of Yarra had 16 licensed sexual service providers, which is equivalent to 20 percent of the licensed brothels in Victoria (Hoban et al. 2003). NGO's that support women in the sex industry also have anecdotal evidence of ongoing trafficking activities in both municipalities.

The first study was conducted by the first author [EK] between June and August 2004 and sought to explore community awareness of i) the local sex industry; ii) trafficking activities in the City of Yarra; and iii) community attitudes and perceptions towards women working in the sex industry, in particular trafficked women. An initial analysis of sex industry advertisements in *The Melbourne Times*, a magazine distributed weekly throughout Melbourne, and *The Yarra Leader*, a local newspaper distributed weekly throughout the City of Yarra, was conducted to locate the street addresses of licensed brothels operating in the City of Yarra. Residential streets located in close proximity to these brothels were identified using the aid of a *Melway Greater Melbourne Street Directory* (No author 2003b: 2C & 2G) and used as a starting point for data collection. Every third household on these streets was approached and the residents who opened the door were invited to complete a brief survey on their awareness, attitudes and concerns regarding trafficking in Australia and the City of Yarra. In cases where the residents declined to participate, the household on the opposite side of the street was approached. A total of 120 surveys were conducted in four suburbs of the City of Yarra (Fitzroy, Collingwood, Richmond and Clifton Hill).

Following the completion of the surveys, 10 participants were interviewed by the researcher on the basis of their age, gender, country of birth and level of knowledge of trafficking (determined from the survey) and availability to be interviewed, with the goal of obtaining a representative sample of the demographic profile of residents in the study sites. These interviews explored participants' perceptions of and attitudes towards the local sex industry, in particular foreign women working in the industry and trafficking for sexual exploitation. Interviews were conducted in residents' houses and ranged in length from 20 minutes to 1.5 hours.

The second study was conducted by the third author [EH] between May 2002 and March 2003 in conjunction with three community-based organizations: International Social Service, Good Shepherd Youth and Family Service and Project Respect, and was funded by the Myer Foundation. It explored the nature and extent of trafficking in Australia, in particular in Victoria (Hoban et al. 2003). A case study of the Cities of Port Phillip and Yarra was conducted, involving semi-structured surveys with 55 Victoria Police Region 1 (which encompasses both the City of Yarra and City of Port Phillip) regular duty uniform and criminal investigation unit (CIU) officers. Six council planning and permit personnel completed a different semi-structured survey. Participants were selected on a random basis (i.e. those working on the day the survey was conducted) and surveyed in a face-to-face manner at their place of employment by a team of trained volunteer researchers.

Additionally, interviews were conducted with six senior members of Victoria Police, 20 Commonwealth government authorities, 15 State government authorities, including council planning and permit and statutory body personnel, 15 NGO representatives and three sex industry representatives. Interviews were also conducted with 10 women who had been trafficked to Australia from Thailand for prostitution, their families and friends; however data from these interviews will not be presented here as it does not relate directly to the focus of this paper.

Survey data from both studies were analysed independently using the statistical analysis software package, SPSS 11. Univariate and bivariate analysis was undertaken to determine associations between participants' demographic variables and their knowledge of trafficking activities. Data drawn from the semi-structured interviews were analysed manually using thematic analysis. Robson's quality control check was used to establish interpretative rigor (Miles and Huberman 1994). Deakin University Human Ethics Committee granted approval to conduct the first study. The second study was monitored by a Project Reference Group, established by the three NGO's conducting the study to oversee and guide the ethical conduct of the research. While these two studies provide an opportunity to explore in-depth community knowledge, attitudes and responses to trafficking, as they focus on only two local government areas, in particular the City of Yarra, their findings cannot be generalised across Victoria or Australia.

Results

Study One

Of all survey participants, 49.2% were male and 50.8% female. Their age ranged from 18-63 years, with the highest percentage of participants (33.3%) falling within the 32 to 45 year bracket. The majority of participants were born in Australia (74.2%), spoke English as their first language (98.3%) and had resided in the City of Yarra for 1-3 years (31.7%). Thirty-three percent resided in Fitzroy, 32.5% in Collingwood, 25% in Richmond and 9.2% in Clifton Hill. The majority, of the survey sample was well educated having completed some form of tertiary education (64%), worked full-time (63%) and held professional positions (43%). These characteristics reflect those of the City of Yarra's wider population (City of Yarra 2002). However, the lack of ethnic diversity in the sample size means that these results cannot be generalised across the municipality.

The first study revealed that within the City of Yarra, awareness of prostitution was widespread; 88% of survey participants were aware of its existence within licensed brothels in the council area. Awareness, however, was limited to brothels in close proximity to residents' homes and did not extend to specific knowledge about brothel operations, size of the sex industry, or demographics of the clients patronising the brothels or women working in the sex industry. The 10 participants who were interviewed all attributed their lack of knowledge of the local sex industry to the inconspicuousness of premises and discreet nature of operations.

For most interview participants (7 out of 10), the discreetness of the local licensed brothels had resulted in the belief that legalisation had created a clean and regularly monitored sex industry. Nine out of 10 interview participants believed that women choose to engage in prostitution to make rapid financial gains to improve their lifestyle. The majority of interview participants (9 out of 10) had no knowledge of the location of unlicensed brothels in the City of Yarra and all 10 interview participants stated they would most likely be located in discreet houses or flats in geographically isolated locations with no physical markers defining them as a business.

This first study also revealed that participants had a widespread awareness of trafficking. Of those surveyed, 92% claimed to have heard about trafficking for sexual exploitation in Australia, and approximately 1 in 3 (34%) had heard of it occurring within the City of Yarra. Awareness of local trafficking was statistically related to increasing age (2 (3) = 13.6, p=.004); increasing number of years lived at current address, (2 (3) = 9.1, p=.02); completion of tertiary education (2 (1) = 7.2, p=.007; and suburb of residence (2 (3) = 11.2, p=.011), with participants in Fitzroy (49%) and Collingwood (29%) more likely to have greater awareness than

Clifton Hill (12%) and Richmond (9%), presumably due to the media's coverage of the existence of trafficked women in a Fitzroy brothel (see discussion on Club 417 later in this paper). Despite the awareness of trafficking locally, interviews with participants indicated that there was no awareness of Commonwealth legislation that addresses slavery and sexual servitude, or the Australian Government's recent anti-trafficking initiatives. All 10 interview participants said they thought trafficked women were located in unlicensed brothels only.

Of the 10 participants interviewed, six considered trafficked women to be desperate, poor and vulnerable women who had been deceived about the type of employment or conditions in which they would be required to work. The remaining four viewed trafficked women as illegal immigrants, who had previously engaged in sex work, knowingly entered the sex industry and who were not held in conditions of slavery and sexual servitude in Australia. Three of the four participants, all of whom were male, held the view that trafficked women are seeking an Australian husband in order to gain permanent residency.

The survey data shows that 48% of residents perceived trafficking to be a 'significant concern', 30% said it was a 'moderate concern', 22% said it was 'not a concern at all'. Level of concern was statistically associated to increasing age (2 (df) = 12.2, p= .05). However, when level of concern was explored during the in-depth interviews, the six participants who said they were 'significantly concerned' were not in favour of strategies to support trafficked women in the local community. Rather, five of those six participants who said they were 'significantly concerned' were not in favour of strategies to support trafficked women in the local community. Rather, five of those six participants indicated that they felt the issue was the Australian Government's problem and should be primarily addressed by tightening border security procedures at entry points, such as airports, to stop women entering Australia. Only two out of the 10 interviewees considered the local community had a responsibility in addressing trafficking. They felt that council resources should be increased, thereby allowing council officers' greater opportunities to identify trafficked women in unlicensed brothels. They also felt that residents need to have their awareness on the issue raised and increased volition to advocate for the fights of trafficked women.

Study Two

This study provided information about Victoria Police and Cities of Yarra and Port Phillip council officers' role in relation to: i) monitoring the sex industry; ii) identifying and investigating complaints and suspected trafficking-related activities; and iii) the enactment of State and Commonwealth legislation. The survey was conducted with a total of 55 Victoria Police officers: 72% were male and 18% female; and the majority, were constables (49.1%), though the ranks of sergeant (12.7%), senior constable (23.6%), senior sergeant (5.5%) and acting senior sergeant (5.5%) were also represented. Forty percent of the police officers surveyed were employed in the suburbs of Richmond, 40% in Colling-wood, and 20% in Fitzroy (in the City of Yarra). While there were no statistically significant correlations between police officers' demographic variables, ranking and knowledge of trafficking activities in their local area, we must be cognisant of the study's small sample size.

Of the 55 police officers surveyed, 34.5% said there was State legislation that addressed trafficking for sexual exploitation, 25.5% said there was no relevant legislation, and 40% said they did not know what legislation existed. Importantly, no police officers identified the *Prostitution Control Act (PCA) 1994 (Commonwealth of Australia 1994)*, the primary legislation used to regulate the Victorian sex industry, or other relevant state legislation. Thirty-one percent of police officers said there was relevant Commonwealth legislation addressing trafficking for sexual exploitation, 24% said there was not and 45% said they did not know. Importantly, no officers could name the Commonwealth *Criminal Code Amendment (Slavery and Sexual Servitude) Act 1999* (Common-wealth of Australia 1999), which was the sole Commonwealth legislation that addressed trafficking-related offences in Australia at the time of the study. During the constables' probationary training program, which runs for 20 weeks at the Police Academy in Glen Waverley in Victoria, the PCA is mentioned; however, the *Criminal Code (Slavery and Sexual Servitude) Act 1999* is not covered.

Eighty percent of Victoria Police officers surveyed were aware of the existence of trafficking in Australia. Few survey participants had collaborated with other police officers (6.9%), government agencies (17.9%) and/or community organizations (25%) on issues relating to the Victorian sex industry or trafficking-related issues. Only 33.3% of officers surveyed perceived there to be any degree of force-wide coordina-tion with respect to policing the sex industry, however, of this group the majority could not state what type of coordinated efforts were in place. When asked how they personally responded to reports of suspicious activities in their area, the majority said they refer the matter onto more senior officers in their station or to the relevant specialist units within Victoria Police, namely the Organized Crime Unit or the Asian Squad; there is no one Specialist Squad responsible for trafficking-related matters in Victoria Police. There was a widespread belief among survey participants that women who were trafficked for prostitution were more prevalent in unlicensed versus licensed brothels.

Interviews with six senior Victoria Police officers revealed that there is a dearth of information on trafficking in the organization, no force-wide statistics are kept, and there is an absence of any preventative strategies or interest in developing them i.e. trafficking was a low priority issue for Victoria Police. They also considered there was a reactive response to policing of the Victorian sex industry, in particular after the licensing of the sex industry in 1994 (Sullivan 2005), therefore limiting police officers' exposure to trafficking-related activities in the sex industry. It was felt that the current situation in the Victoria Police force is one of the main reasons why suspicious activities are rarely reported.

Interviews with local government personnel revealed a widespread understanding that trafficking-related activities occur in unlicensed as opposed to licensed brothels. Their rationale was, brothel licenses are expensive and applicants' personal and business background is scrutinised by the Business Licensing Authority (BLA) and Victoria Police, who conduct a probity check on applicants prior to issuing them with a brothel license, a process that may take more than 12 months. The local government personnel reasoned that, if traffickers wanted to earn a large sum of money quickly, they would be more likely to place a woman in an unlicensed brothel because the brothel operators have less to lose financially if they are detected. They stated that council authorities may take several weeks to investigate a claim, by which time unlicensed brothels, usually located in rented buildings, can close down at short notice and move to another council area thereby escaping punishment. All council officers interviewed had some understanding of issues surrounding trafficking of women for prostitution, but their comprehension on the subject was limited. Some had heard rumors of 'foreign women' working in unlicensed brothels in their area; however, they had no evidence to substantiate these claims. The majority considered that trafficking related to the movement of people from other countries into Australia, in particular, illegal migration, and did not include the movement of women between Australian states. No council officer spoke of the nature, characteristics or extent of exploitation that is involved in trafficking.

Interviews with council officers revealed they were fully versed with the *PCA 1994 and the Planning and Environment Act (PEA) 1987* and the criteria for granting a planning permit for a brothel. Council permit compliance officers said they checked brothels' permits annually and promptly investigate suspected illegal brothels. The council compliance officers have the most contact with the sex industry, compared to other government agencies. However, council officers reported that they were not responsible for illegal activities inside brothels, such as trafficking: their primary concern is that of the business permit. Enforcement officers claim they act on complaints by the community about licensed and unlicensed brothels, undertake investigations and proceed with action based on the findings of the investigation.

Interviews with six council enforcement officers highlighted some of the challenges of their role, for example, limited enforcement staff to monitor compliance of premises in the area, limitations of the *PCA 1994 and PEA 1987*, and the timely nature, costs and ethical issues involved in carrying out an investigation. They expressed concern and frustration at the lack of reprisal when disciplinary action is taken by the council against illegal brothels operators. There was a sense among enforcement officers that other local councils in Melbourne and Victoria Police were doing little to address the problems of the unlicensed sex industry, which enabled operators to move their business quickly if needed and continue their illegal operations unnoticed and undisturbed by local authorities. In addition, interviewees felt there was limited coordination between the local council areas, Victoria Police, the business sector, and community groups to address illegal activities in the sex industry, including trafficking.

Discussion and Recommendations

Community Awareness

Despite the widespread claim that trafficked women are predominately working in the unlicensed sex industry in Victoria, there is no empirical data that validates this claim; in fact, there is evidence to support the contrary. On 4 June 2006 in the County Court in Melbourne a jury found Wei Tang, an Australian citizen, guilty under the *Commonwealth Criminal Code Amendment (Slavery. and Sexual Servitude) Act 1999* on ten counts of slavery; five counts of possessing a slave and five counts of using a slave (field notes [EH] 5 June 2006), and was sentenced to 10 years jail with a six year non-parole period (Fiamenga 2006). Wei Tang was the owner of Club 417, a licensed brothel in the City of Yarra. The charges in this instance relate to slavery; however the evidence presented during the trial by five female complainants, all of whom were Thai nationals, outlined deceptive recruitment, which included the extent to which they were free to leave their residence and place of work, debt bondage and the confiscation of their travel or identity documents (*R v Tang Wei*).[3] These allegations are in accordance with the definition of human trafficking outlined in United Nations (UN) Trafficking Protocol (UN 2000) and the Australian Government's *Criminal Code Amendment (Trafficking in Persons Offences) Act 2005* (Commonwealth of Australia 2005b).

Data from both studies indicate that while there is widespread awareness of sexual service providers in the City. Of Yarra, and to a lesser degree the presence of trafficking-related activities in the area, the community's and authorities' knowledge on the subject was limited. Residents who lived in close proximity to brothels were more aware of the presence of the industry, in their immediate locale than those who lived further away; however, they were unable to provide specific information about the nature and characteristics of the local sex industry, women's working conditions and clientele.

---

[3] [2006] VCC637. Case No. 04-01316

Victoria Police and most council officers assumed that the licensing of the sex industry under the PCA 1994 has created a clean, regulated and well-monitored industry where women engage in prostitution legally and as an economic strategy. This is certainly true for many licensed sexual service providers in Victoria. However, as the recent criminal trial of Crown v Wei Tang demonstrated, there are several licensed brothels in Melbourne where women who are either undocumented or in breech of their visa conditions are providing sexual services (field notes [EH] 5 June 2006). The trail proceedings showed that Club 417 undertook deceptive measures to escape the impunity of the law, for example, the brothel's management was aware that Department of Immigration and Multicultural Affairs (DIMA) staff regularly conducted raids on brothels on Thursday and Friday nights. In order for 'contract' women to pay off their debt of $40-50,000 to their 'bosses', resulting in a considerable profit for the brothel owners, the brothel management went to considerable trouble to hide women who were undocumented or in breech of their visa conditions on those nights (field notes [EH] 5 June 2006). Moreover, evidence from the trials of Crown v Wei Tang and Gary Glazner in 1998 (Ford 2001), and the findings described by Hoban and colleagues (Hoban et al. 2003) for the Cities of Yarra and Port Phillip demonstrate that the licensed sex industry in Victoria is not in fact clean, regulated and well-monitored. Mr John Dickinson, the Defense Barrister in the case of Crown v Wei Tang, stated that Club 417 was no different to many other brothels in Victoria that were facing difficulties recruiting working women. Mr. Dickinson went on to say, 'all, or a vast majority of brothels attracted workers under a similar set-up' (field notes [EH] 5 June 2006). Data from the two studies discussed in this paper, and information obtained during the trial of Crown v Wei Tang places the onus on the Victoria Police force to educate their officers as to the realities of the Victorian sex industry and their role and responsibilities in terms of its regulation.

The community's assumption that trafficked women are located in unlicensed versus licensed brothels is compounded by their limited knowledge of the location and characteristics of unlicensed brothels in their area. They considered that unlicensed brothels were located in isolated pockets of the municipality, and that brothel premises had no distinctive physical markers that would allow the premise to be identified as an unlicensed sexual service provider. Yet, unlicensed brothels are commonly located in busy residential and business zones in the City of Yarra, including along busy shopping strips. However, according to local council authorities interviewed by Hoban and colleagues (2003), many unlicensed brothels share similar, distinctive markers, such as being located on or nearby a main road, having the house number painted on the front of the building (often using an over-sized font), and having blinds covering windows at the front of the premise, which are often drawn 24 hours a day. Residents' limited knowledge in this respect will undoubtedly affect their ability to locate unlicensed brothels in their area thereby inhibiting the reporting of suspicious activities.

There was a view among City of Yarra residents that foreign sex workers in general and trafficked women in particular come from poor backgrounds with few economic opportunities available to them, have 'broken into Australia' to engage in prostitution, and remain in the country illegally to earn large sums of money and gain permanent residency through marriage. Information obtained during the trial of Crown v Wei Tang supports the views held by City of Yarra residents. Judge McInerney, who resided over the case said, 'given the women's circumstances at the time of their arrival [referring to the five complainants], the women would not have been well off...They serviced 900 men in 3 months. They would only do this from a base of poverty'. Mr. Dickinson, the Defence Barrister, disagreed with Judge McInerney's statement saying, 'these women entered into contracts to make a lot of money', to which the Judge replied, "the women entered into contracts to pay off a debt, to service 900 men and pay off that debt...these women must have come from poor backgrounds to service 900 men...to do this day-in-day-out. What do you expect? Remember what X said, "I could make a lot of money and then return to Thailand. I would not have to work in the sex industry again." Mr. Dickinson replied, 'you do not know their backgrounds', to which the Judge answered, 'I am making an inference' (field notes [EH] 5 June 2006).

Data obtained during Study One and during the trial of Crown v Wei Tang demonstrates that foreign women entering Australia to work in the sex industry are stereotyped and stigmatised. Government authorities and the community fail to engage in the contextual issues that lead to women's involvement in prostitution in Australia, such as women's lived experiences prior to entering into prostitution, choices (or lack of) that influenced women's decision to come to Australia, women's under-standing of the terms and conditions of their work contract, reasons for women's migration across international borders for employment, their psycho-social and emotional well-being while on contracts in Australia, and so on. A failure to acknowledge the complex nature of trafficking, as it is experienced by women and their families, has the propensity to jeopardize women's experiences, incite racism and sexism and create apathy towards their plight. The stigma surrounding foreign women in the sex industry could potentially discourage residents from offering assistance to trafficked women and/or wrongly identifying and reporting suspicious markers of trafficking, all of which may jeopardize the success of an awareness campaign that relies on community reporting.

Community Awareness Strategy—the Way Forward

The Australian Government's proposed community awareness strategy seeks to target trafficked persons working in both the legal or illegal sex industries, and people who are likely to come into contact with them on a regular basis (Commonwealth of Australia 2004). In addition, it aims to raise awareness of trafficking issues in the general community by working with the media to communicate information regarding trafficking in a culturally appropriate and context sensitive manner (ibid). A range of initiatives will be cited to disseminate knowledge on indications of trafficking, victims' rights and available assistance and support (UNANIMA International et al. 2006). It is now evident that the planned community awareness campaign will focus exclusively on sex trafficking rather than providing education and information about trafficking more broadly.

We recommend that the community, awareness campaign provide general and State/Territory-specific information about trafficking and reporting strategies. It is the primary responsibility of the Australian Government to fund national public awareness campaigns, such as the Anti-Terrorism Campaign (Amnesty International Australia 2005); the prevention of trafficking is of significant national interest at the human rights, economic and border-security level. We recommend that the campaign be population-based and target a wide range of groups, including: the general public; key industry groups such as the sex, tourism, manufacturing and agricultural industries; labour, trade unions and migration organizations; relevant government authorities; the judiciary; community-based organizations such as Migrant Resource Centres; ethnic communities; legal centres; sexual assault centres; health professionals and schools. It should include urban, rural and remote communities. All Australians should be provided with information about the relevant Commonwealth legislation, in addition to State/Territory-specific legal information. It should not be targeted solely on sex trafficking and address the easy to access groups, such as the proposed target groups. The narrow approach of the proposed strategies ignores the scope of trafficking activities in Australia and the role and responsibilities of the general public in preventing trafficking, thereby limiting effective reporting of suspicious activities and subsequent action.

This paper, however, is interested in campaign strategies relating specifically to the prevention of trafficking of women for the Victorian sex industry. As Australian States and Territories differ in terms of prostitution legislation, regulations and enforcement, each will need to tailor their campaign strategies to suit their legislative environment. However, there are some key elements of a campaign that need to be considered for a national lobby: i) information must be factual, for example, derived from case studies in Australia and the region, such as the trial of the Crown v Wei Tang; ii) the campaign must provide culturally-sensitive analyses of trafficked women's social and cultural backgrounds and address global gender-based social and economic inequalities that ensures a ready supply of women and governs the general increase in migration among women, especially from resource-poor to resource-rich settings; and iii) women's motivations to accept work contracts coming to Australia. These issues must be addressed in a respectful, non-judgmental manner, and in a way that does not incite racist, sexist stereotypes that further stigmatise foreign women in general and foreign sex workers in particular. In addition, we recommend that the campaign speak to the following issues: i) a definition of human trafficking; ii) exploitative nature of the trafficking experience; iii) migration fraud that accompanies work contracts; iv) nature of profits gained by traffickers; v) magnitude and characteristics of trafficking operations in Australia and the region; vi) location of trafficked women in the Victorian sex industry; vii) women's working conditions, with a focus on labour rights and occupational health and safety issues; viii) legislation and regulations that apply to the Victorian sex industry; ix) roles and responsibilities of Victoria Police and local government authorities in preventing trafficking and responding to community complaints; and x) the Australian Government's initiatives that address trafficking, such as the $20 million Action Plan, which has to date received little publicity.

The campaign must also stress that trafficking is both a global and a local problem and therefore, it is the responsibility of the community to identify and report suspicious activities. Community members, particularly younger, less educated, shorter-term residents need to be encouraged to both discuss and report any suspicious activities that could be markers of trafficking. Moreover, the campaign must educate residents as to the activities they should consider suspicious and worthy of reporting. A community awareness campaign in the current political environment is impeded by the Australian Government's response to trafficking thus far; must misguided information can be traced to DIMA reports and Hansard records and ill-informed comments by senior politicians and policy makers on the issue.[4] A community awareness campaign that corrects the years of misinformation presented to the public on this issue by government departments is desperately needed and long overdue.

---

[4] For example, in 2002 the Minister for Justice and Customs, Senator Chris Ellison, commented to the Senate Legal and Constitutional Committee that, in his belief, 'slavery chains where people are traded as goods and chattels [do] not exist in Australia' (Senator Chris Ellison MP, Minister of Justice and Customs. Senate Legal and Constitutional Committee, 11 February 2003. Hansard, p. 155).

Responsibility for Action

City of Yarra residents considered that trafficking is a Commonwealth and not a State issue (residents' made no mention of local council's role), and one that requires the Commonwealth to develop strategies, in particular that relate to migration and law enforcement, to stop foreign women entering Australia to work illegally in the sex industry. Moreover, while Victoria Police officers had a partial understanding of trafficking issues, their knowledge of the relevant Commonwealth and State legislation and persons responsible for enacting it, including their own role in monitoring the local sex industry, was limited. Whereas, council authorities, who are at the front-line, and the agency, that has the most contact with the sex industry, were aware of their role and responsibilities in terms of enforcing the *PCA 1994 and the PEA 1987*, and the human and financial limitations of doing so, they have no authority to deal with illegal activities in the sex industry. Compounding this mismatch of responsibilities is the absence of collaboration between government agencies, in particular Victoria Police, AFP and DIMA officers, municipal councils, the BLA and the community sector. There is an urgent need for a systematic, coordinated and collaborative approach by these groups to develop State-wide strategies that draw on local partnership initiatives and assist in the identification of and response to illegal activities in the Victorian sex industry, such as the prevention of trafficking. In addition, government—community partnerships could play a vital role in the development, dissemination and re-enforcement of the community awareness campaign outlined above. At the time of writing this paper, Cities of Yarra and Port Phillip councils are initiating partnerships between local councils and the AFP, DIMA and the Australian Tax Office to "develop a co-ordinated response to trafficking and illegal brothels" (Murphy 2006).

For the community awareness campaign to be effective there are several actions that need to be incited in Victoria: i) the provision of training for Victoria Police, including for the educators at the Victoria Police Academy, AFP and DIMA officers, the judiciary and Department of Public Prosecution, and local government officials about trafficking, relevant Commonwealth and State legislation, and appropriate methods of responding to reports of suspicious activity, including how to respond to and support victims of violence. This training should be conducted by specialist NGO's that are informed and engaged in trafficked women's socio-cultural, legal, migration and welfare needs. Whenever possible, these NGO's should encourage women who have been trafficked into the Australian sex industry to take leadership roles in the development and delivery of such training; ii) the Victoria Police Training Academy should undergo an evaluation of their training curriculum in terms of prostitution legislation, regulations and enforcement policies and procedures. In addition, a curriculum needs to be developed that addresses the *Commonwealth Criminal Code Amendment (Trafficking in Persons Offences) Act 2005*; iii) the development of a coordinated referral system between Victoria Police, AFP, DIMA, local councils and statutory bodies such as the BLA to respond to reports of suspicious activities in the Victorian sex industry; iv) the development of a Code of Practice for Victoria Police that relates to the *Prostitution Control Act 1994, Commonwealth Criminal Code (Slavery and Sexual Servitude) Act 1999*, and the *Criminal Code Amendment (Trafficking in Persons Offences) Act 2005*, that addresses violence against women and is based on the Code of Services, 2000); v) the higher prioritisation of trafficking as a policing issue and the incorporation of regular, random checks of licensed and unlicensed brothels into the everyday practice of on-the-ground police officers and local government employees.

Conclusion

In recent years, the Australian Government has demonstrated a greater commitment to addressing the issue of trafficking. However, data from the two studies reported in this paper indicate that there remain many challenges in responding to suspicious activities at the community level. We outlined gaps within the current response system and then we made concrete recommendations for how it may be improved. Ultimately, without addressing the identified barriers to reporting and instigating a more coordinated and streamlined system that responds to reports of suspicious activity, it is unlikely that cases of trafficking will be detected and trafficked persons continue to experience gross violations of their fundamental human rights.

Discussion Questions

1   *Why do the Australian Federal Police (AFP) consider Australia attractive to human traffickers?*

2   *Where do most women trafficked to Australia come from?*

3   *What does the pattern of legal and illegal prostitution look like in Australia?*

4   *What has been the Australian government's response to sex trafficking?*

5   *For a community awareness campaign to be effective in Australia there are several actions that need to be included. What are they?*

References

No author (2003a) 'A trade in human suffering', *Platypus Magazine: The Journal of the Australian Federal Police, 80*(October): 7.

No author (2003b) *Melway Greater Melbourne Street Directory*, Melbourne, Melway Publishing Pty Ltd.

Amnesty International Australia (2005) *Fact Sheet: Anti-Terrorism Bill 2005*, Sydney, Amnesty International Australia.

Attorney-General's Department (2003) *Joint Press Release: Australian Government Announces Major Package to Combat People Trafficking*, Canberra, Commonwealth of Australia.

Attorney-General's Department (2005) *Media Release: Australia Ratifies the UN People Trafficking Protocol*, Canberra, Commonwealth of Australia.

Bales, K. (2005) *Understanding the Global Slavery. A Reader*, California, University of California Press.

Batros, D. (2004) *The Customer is Always Right: Meeting the Demands of Victorian Brothel Clients*, Honours Thesis, Melbourne, Deakin University.

Brockett, L. & Murrey, A. (1994) 'Thai sex workers in Sydney'. In P. Perkins, G. Prestage & R. Sharp (eds) *Sex Work and Sex Workers in Australia*, Sydney, University of New South Wales.

Burn, J. & Simmons, E (2005) 'Rewarding witnesses, ignoring victims: an evaluation of the new trafficking visa framework', *Immigration Review*, 24: 6-13.

Carrington, K. & Hearn, J. (2003) *Trafficking and the Sex Industry: From Impunity to Protection.* Canberra, Information and Research Services, Commonwealth of Australia.

City of Yarra (2002) *2001 City of Yarra Community Profile*, Melbourne, City of Yarra.

Commonwealth of Australia (1994). *Prostitution Control Act 1994*, Canberra, Commonwealth of Australia.

Commonwealth of Australia (1999) *Criminal Code Amendment (Slavery and Sexual Servitude) Act 1999*, Canberra, Commonwealth of Australia.

Commonwealth of Australia (2003) *Senate Official Hansard, No. 6 2003*, Canberra, Commonwealth of Australia.

Commonwealth of Australia (2004) *Australian Government's Action Plan to Eradicate Trafficking in Persons*, Canberra, Public Affairs Unit, Australian Government Attorney-General's Department.

Commonwealth of Australia (2005a) *Official Committee Hansard Joint Committee on the Australian Crime Commission*, Canberra, Commonwealth of Australia.

Commonwealth of Australia (2005b) *Criminal Code Amendment (Trafficking in Persons Offences) Act 2005*, Canberra, Commonwealth of Australia.

Cwikel, J. & Hoban, E. (2005) 'Contentious issues in research on trafficked women working in the sex industry: study design, ethics and methodology', *The Journal of Sex Research*, 42(4): 306-316.

Department of Health Services, 2000. *Standards of Practice for Victorian Centres Against Sexual Assault*. The Victorian Centres Against Sexual Assault Inc. Melbourne: Department of Health and Human Services.

Doezema, J. (2000) 'Loose women or lost women? The re-emergence of the myth of white slavery, in contemporary, discourses of trafficking in women', *Gender Issues*, 18(1): 23-51.

Farr, K. (2005). *Sex Trafficking: The Global Market in Women and Children*, New York, Worth Publishers.

Fiamenga, M. (2006) 'Woman jailed for keeping sex slaves', *The Australian*, June 9.

Ford, M. (2001) *Sex Slaves and Legal Loopholes: Exploring the Legal Framework and Federal Responses to the Trafficking of Thai 'Contract Girls' for Sexual Exploitation to Melbourne, Australia*, Melbourne Victoria University on behalf of Project Respect.

Hoban, E., Gordon, E. & Maltzahn, K. (2003) *'We've Been to War Together'*: Experiences of Trafficked Women in the Australian Social, Legal and Political System, Melbourne International Social Services, Project Respect & Good Shepherd Youth & Family Services.

Kempadoo, K., Sanghera, J. & Pattanaik, B. (eds) (2005) *Trafficking and Prostitution Reconsidered. New Perspectives on Migration, Sex Work, and Human Rights*, Boulder, Paradigm Publishers.

Marshall, P. (2005) 'Raising our own awareness: getting to grips with trafficking in persons and related problems in South-East Asia and beyond', *Asia-Pacific Population Journal*, 20(3): 143-63.

Miles, M.B. & Huberman, A.M. (1994) *Qualitative Data Analysis*, Thousand Oaks, SAGE.

Milovanovich, C. (2003) *Inquest into the Death of Puontong Simpalee. Coroner's Findings*, Sydney, Westmead Coroner's Court.

Murphy, K. Sex Slavery. *The trade that shames us*. The Melbourne Times June 14 2006 p. 8-9.

Piper, N. (2005) 'A problem by a different name? A review of research on trafficking in South-East Asia and Oceania', *International Migration*, 43(1/2): 203-233. Project Respect (2004) *One Victim of Trafficking is Too*

Many: Counting the Human Cost of Trafficking, Melbourne, Project Respect.

Raymond, J.G. (2002) *A Comparative Study of Women Trafficked in the Migration Process-Patterns, Profiles and Health Consequences of Sexual Exploitation in Five Countries (Indonesia, the Phillippines, Thailand, Venezuela and the United States)*, Massachusetts, Coalition Against Trafficking in Women.

Sullivan, M. (2005) *What Happens when Prostitution Becomes Work? An Update on Legislation of Prostitution in Australia*, Massachusetts Coalition Against Trafficking in Women Australia.

UNANIMA International, Congregarion of the Sisters of the Good Shepherd & International Presentation Association (2006) *Australian NGO Shadow Report on Trafficking Women in Australia. Submitted to the 34th Session of the Committee for the Convention on the Elimination of All Forms of Discrimination Against Women (CEDAW). Relative to the Report of the Government of Australia as a State-Party to CEDAW*, Melbourne, Congregation of the Sisters of the Good Shepherd.

United Nations (2000) *Protocol to Prevent, Suppress and Punish Trafficking in Persons, Especially Women and Children, Supplementing the United Nations Convention Against Transnational Organised Crime*, Geneva, United Nations, United Nations (2002) *Recommended Principles and Guidelines on Human Rights and Human Trafficking*, Geneva, Office of the United Nations High Commissioner for Human Rights.

U.S. Department of State (2004) *Trafficking in Persons Report 2004*, Washington DC, Department of State, United States of America.

U.S. Department of State (2006) *Trafficking in Persons Report June 2006*, Washington DC, Department of State, United States of America.

18
CORRUPTION AND HUMAN TRAFFICKING: THE NIGERIAN CASE

Osita Agbu, Ph.D.

Introduction

> "For those of you who think it cannot happen to you, I want
> to let you know that the dragnet of the traffickers is so wide that
> only God knows who is safe."

The above statement indicates that the problem under focus is enormous, more so for those who live in highly corrupt societies. Whilst corruption is a common phenomenon in human practice, human trafficking as presently practiced is a recent addition to the dictionary of global woes. Though rampant globally, corruption varies from region to region and country to country in its intensity. Human trafficking, in contrast, tends to be systematic in its occurrence, especially that its span increases as the globalization process intensifies. Though previously in existence in forms such as prostitution, child labour and domestic servitude, today, contemporary human trafficking is an organized business just as the transatlantic slave trade was with various linkages spread around the globe. Today, not only children and women are trafficked; young boys seeking greener pastures abroad also fall prey to this evil. It can safely be argued that in this age of jet-planes, cellular phone, and the Internet, there are faster means of dealing in human commodities than before. There is little doubt that globalisation has created inequalities and inequities resulting in the migration of the poor to the rich regions of the world. Hand in hand with this came the commercialization of humanity, which is akin to modern day slavery. In times past, slavery and slave trade existed in various forms: people became slaves as war captives, criminals were punished with enslavement, and in some cases individuals in impoverished circumstances sold their relatives. However, in whatever form it took, it was quickly realized by most civilizations that the practice was the basest of crimes against humanity. One would have thought that, with the immense improvements in the understanding of human nature and the environment, any form of exploitation that looks like slavery would be abhorred automatically. Alas! This is not the case, as human beings are today, prized as commodities and exchanged for money like any other article in the market.

The business of trafficking in humans is today organized loosely by groups that are also involved in weapons and narcotics, colluding with government officials in dozens of countries. There is very little doubt, that it is a lucrative business and may be one of the most difficult to combat. Its corrupting effects on governments and institutions are barely perceptible because they are a less visible than those caused by gunrunning and drug trafficking. Exploiting the poverty and the low status of women in the developing world, middlemen are able to bring together the supply and demand for cheap labour and sex in ways that would have simply been unthinkable not long ago. Evidently, globalization has not only stimulated the movement of capital, goods, and technology but also the movement of all categories of peoples from one end of the world to the other. This global development brought in its wake the loosening up of protective barriers and political boundaries which organized criminal gangs have capitalized on to perpetrate many heinous acts including human trafficking.

Though the fact of human trafficking is not difficult to understand on its own, its dimensions and categorization continue to multiply by the day. Broadly conceptualized, human trafficking include forced and child prostitution, domestic servitude, illegal and bonded labour, servile marriage, false adoption, sex tourism and entertainment, pornography, organized begging, organ harvesting, and other criminal activities.[1] Organ harvesting, sometimes referred to as organ laundering, involves the trafficking of humans for the purpose of selling their organs for money. This shows the very barbaric dimension of this crime. A Protocol on Trafficking, attached to the UN Convention Against Organized Crime, signed by 80 countries and the European Union in December 2000, formally defined trafficking as a modern form of slavery and indentured servitude, linked to organized criminal activity, money laundering, corruption and the obstruction of justice. Using broad language, this protocol defined trafficking as the recruitment, transportation, transfer, harboring, or receipt of persons using force, coercion, abduction, fraud, deception, abuse of power, or vulnerability, or the giving and receiving of payments to achieve consent of a person or having control over another person.[2] However defined, what is generally accepted is that human trafficking, whether in women or as child labor, constitutes a fundamental violation of the human person.

However, the object of this paper, is to look more closely at the linkage between corruption and human trafficking which appears to have been given very little attention until recently. The specific questions addressed in this paper include: What really is corruption and how does it relate to human trafficking or the trafficking in persons? Is there some collusion between traffickers and government agents or officials? If so, what is the nature of this collusion? And finally, what possible

---

[1] Corbin B. Lyday, The Shadow Market in Human Beings: An Anti-Corruption Perspective, Paper Presented at Transparency International's 10th International Anti-Corruption Conference, Prague, Czech Republic, October 7 – 11, 2001.

[2] Ibid., p. 4.

policy interventions could be applied to reduce or check the opportunities for corruption, which fuels the trafficking in human beings?

Corruption and the Nigerian State

To say that corruption is rampant in Nigeria is to restate the obvious. Corruption in Nigeria, as it presently manifests, should more appropriately be termed endemic or systemic. However, this is not to say that the democratically elected government of President Olusegun Obasanjo did not recognize this fact, or has done nothing about it. But in a situation in which corruption has become institutionalized, it may take nothing less than a decade to make a dent on the solid wall of bribery and corruption existing in the Nigerian society at this moment in time.

In retrospect, the political bureau established in 1987 attributed the failure of politics and governance in Nigeria basically to corruption. Also, the British Department for International Development (DFID) maintains in its "Nigeria: Country Strategy paper for the year 2000," that poverty persists in Nigeria because of the mismanagement of resources and corruption, found particularly but not exclusively in the public sector.[3] Beyond the pilfering of public funds, the amassing of fortunes by illegal or corrupt means does not seem to necessarily disturb the average Nigerian as to make him loose sleep over it. The World Bank defines corruption as:

> The abuse of public office for private gains. Public office is abused for private gain when an official accepts, solicits, or extorts a bribe. It is also abused when private agents actively offer bribes to circumvent public policies and processes for competitive advantage and profit. Public office can also be abused for personal benefit even if no bribery occurs, through patronage and nepotism, the theft of state assets or the diversion of state resources.[4]

The Asian Development Bank understood corruption as involving "the behavior on the part of officials in the public and private sectors, in which they improperly and unlawfully enrich themselves and/or those closely related to them, or induce others to do so, by misusing the position in which they are placed."

However, corruption as a phenomenon, is a global problem, and exists in varying degrees in different countries. Whereas it may be endemic in some countries like Nigeria, it could also be moderate or low in others. For instance, corruption exists to varying degrees in the United States, Britain, France, Greece, Japan and Italy. So there could

---

[3] I. Ayua (ed.) Proceedings of the National Conference on the Problems of Corruption in Nigeria, 26 – 29 March 2001, Abuja.

[4] World Bank "Helping Combat Corruption: The Role of the World Bank", 1997.

be different types of corruption ranging from petty corruption to political corruption.[5] For our purpose here, it is necessary to pay closer attention to political/bureaucratic corruption and what has been termed systemic corruption.

Political corruption in particular should be considered a very dangerous strain as it transforms power into a means not of governing for the common good but of enriching those in power and/or spreading all manner of rewards among loyal supporters at taxpayer's expense including, of course, working up dubious financial schemes. In Nigeria, we have seen the development of a vast system of institutionalized political corruption sometimes emanating from the very top and pervading all governmental institutions with perverse influence on the rest of society.[6] Political/bureaucratic corruption also involves the violation of election laws, and campaign finance regulations. It may be intrinsic to the way power is exercised and may be impossible to reduce through lawmaking alone. An extreme instance of political and/or bureaucratic corruption occurs when state institutions are infiltrated by corrupt elements and turned into instruments of individual enrichment.

Systemic corruption, sometimes also referred to as entrenched corruption, occurs where bribery, on a large or small scale is routine. It is regularly experienced when a license or a service is sought from government officials. It takes place when wrongdoing has become the norm. It differs from petty corruption in that it is not as individualized. Systemic corruption is apparent whenever the administration itself transposes the expected purposes of the organizations; forcing participants to follow what otherwise would be termed unacceptable ways and punishing those who resist and try to live up to the formal norms.[7] In this case, societal morality is almost non-existent as it had become gravely eroded as the years went by.

For Nigeria, various factors have been identified as instrumental in enthroning corrupt practices. These include, briefly, the nature of Nigeria's political economy, the weak institutions of government, a dysfunctional legal system, a culture of affluent and ostentatious living that expects much from "big men," extended family pressures, village/ethnic loyalties, and competitive ethnicity.

However, it is in terms of the effects of corruption on a society that a clearer link is established between corruption and human trafficking. In developing countries like Nigeria, corruption has adversely affected governance and the larger social structure. Government's ability to provide vital social services such as water, sanitation, healthcare, education, etc. is usually severely constrained. This generally leads to a retardation of economic development and to the deterioration of

---

[5] International Center for Economic Growth, Information Brief 6, Causes and Effects of Corruption, Nairobi, 1999.

[6] Ayua, op. cit., p. 15.

[7] International Center for Economic Growth, op. cit .

whatever public infrastructure has been put in place. Critically, it can be observed that in Nigeria, unbridled corruption has led to bad governance, in spite of the various legislations put in place to check corruption whether under military or civil rule. The Obasanjo administration has put in place an embattled institution known as the Independent Corrupt Practices and Other Related Offenses Commission (ICPC) mandated to monitor and indict corrupt public officials. This body is embattled to the extent that the upper house of the Nigerian legislature, the senate, is seeking to weaken its investigative powers.

Suffice it to say that bad governance led to very severe economic hardship on the masses. Then came the Structural Adjustment Programme (SAP) introduced in 1986 with its anti-poor conditionalities, leading to the generation of economic migrants and the phenomenon of brain drain. Amongst these economic migrants are today's trafficked women and abused children who, for want of something to eat, ignorance or greed or a combination of these, fell victims of the international process of commodification of human beings, voracious sexual perverts, and organized criminal syndicates. In a sense therefore, human trafficking is a consequence of bribery and corruption, embezzlement, looting and siphoning of public funds abroad, and fascist military rule.[8] The cumulative psychological trauma resulting from severely constrained existential conditions made some Nigerians to flee their country and fall into traps laid by unscrupulous traffickers. Efforts to address this problem should be holistic—embracing good governance, accountability and transparency. Though, a fairly common prescription, it is in the long run, the only sustainable approach to addressing this problem.

It is not that corruption has not been recognized as the "enemy within, " it is, however, that the political will to begin to tackle this problem in Nigeria has been non-existent, except for the Muhammadu Buhari/Tunde Idiagbon regime (1984-85) and the present civilian government of Olusegun Obasanjo. Past futile interventions against corruption include, the Corrupt Practices Decree of 1975; the public officer (Investigation of Assets) Decree no. 5 of 1976, supplemented by the Code of Conduct Bureau and Code of Conduct Tribunals as provided for in the 1979 Constitution; Shehu Shagari's Ethical Revolution (1979-83), with a minister of cabinet rank in charge of "national guidance"; the "war against indiscipline" campaign under the Buhari Idiagbon junta, which was to some extent the only serious intervention; and the National Committee on Corruption and other Economic Crimes under Ibrahim Babangida (1985-93). The Babangida regime also came up with the Corrupt Practices and Economic Crime Decree (Draft) of 1990. This Decree expanded the definition of corruption to encompass the private sector. It also avoided unnecessary technicalities and provided stiffer penalties. However, that government did not really take the issue of corruption seriously. It could actually be argued that corruption in

---

[8] Innocent Ebirim, "Human Trafficking: Economic Implications", New Nigerian, 25 February 2002, p. 9.

Nigeria became institutionalized during this period. Even, the Sani Abacha regime (1994-99) came up with its own anti-corruption decree: the "Indiscipline, Corrupt practices and Economic Crime (Prohibition) Decree 1994" which was largely a replica of Babangida's 1990 draft decree on "corrupt practices and economic crime."

That the country is still preoccupied with the issue of corruption today speaks to the fact that all these interventions failed. The situation also implies that law making alone cannot solve this problem. Other policy options must be explored.

Nigeria and the Global Problem of Human Trafficking

Nigeria is not the only country perpetrating human trafficking; nor is it the only country suffering from its effects. It is estimated that one to two million people are trafficked around the world every year—mostly women and children, but increasingly men and boys as well—generally for forced prostitution, agricultural bondage, or other forms of indentured servitude.[9] One estimate indicates that approximately 50,000 of those trafficked around the world are taken to the United States.[10] A conservative count of people trafficked to all parts of the globe, especially to western Europe, the Middle East, Japan, North America and Australia, in the year 2000 included 250,000 persons from southeast Asia; 150,000 from south Asia, 100,000 each from the former Soviet Union and Latin America; 75,000 from eastern Europe, and another 50,000 from Africa. An estimated 35 per cent of all trafficked persons globally constitute children under the age of consent.

Perhaps realizing that the United States is both a transit and destination country for trafficked persons, the U.S. government has been in the forefront of those seeking remedies to this crime. Their framework for attacking the problem includes: prevention through education, increasing public awareness about economic alternatives, protection for victims of trafficking, and prosecution of traffickers. In the year 2000, for example, the U.S. Congress enacted the Victims of Trafficking and Violence Protection Act, requiring the secretary of state to report to Congress each year on severe forms of trafficking around the world, and to render assistance to governments combating human trafficking on their own soil. The Act also linked trafficking with domestic violence and spelled out sanctions against those who engage in slavery and laid down procedures for victim restitution. Programs already in place aim to foster close cooperation between government and the NGOs to enhance public education and awareness programs targeted at the vulnerable groups.

Although statistics on the number of Nigerians involved, mostly as victims, vary widely, it was reported by the Nigerian Police Force and the Women Trafficking and Child Labour Eradication Foundation

---

[9] Women Aid International Press Release (http://www.womenaid.org)

[10] Ibid.

(WOTCLEF) that between March 1999 and April 2000 about 1126 women trafficked out of the country were deported from various countries. This figure excludes the dead, the maimed, and those that sneaked back into the country. It also does not include hundreds stranded in the streets of Europe and Asia.[11] Further statistics released by WOTCLEF, put the figure of trafficked Nigerian women deported as at December 2001 at about 5000.

WOTCLEF, which was founded by Amina Titi Abubakar, wife of Nigeria's vice-president, Atiku Abubakar, estimates that "an average of 4 Nigerian girls are deported every month."[12] The effect of human trafficking especially on the victims is better told than experienced. An interview with one of such victims revealed that in Italy Nigerian women forced into prostitution are compelled to have sex with anything from four to twelve men in a day. Put crudely these women, unlike drugs that are used once only, can be used repeatedly before they are ultimately discarded. For traffickers, the profits are too high, and the penalties too low, to resist the trade. Many of the women arrested and repatriated were trafficked mainly to Italy, Belgium, Holland and France. Others were known to have moved to the Arab World and the Far East in search of greener pastures but were eventually lured into prostitution. At a March 2002 seminar organized in Lagos by the International Federation of Women Lawyers (FIDA), WOTCLEF reported that there are about 20,000 Nigerian women involved in the sex industry in Italy. *The Daily Champion* of 12 July 2002 reported that 80% of foreign prostitutes in Italy were Nigerian women. (One question many Nigerians ask is how come trafficked women manage to find their way to Italy when, under normal circumstances, it is very difficult for the average Nigerian to obtain a visa to travel Italy.) Information available revealed that most of the trafficked girls were from Edo, Delta, and Lagos states with an average age range of between 15 and 35 years. It should be noted that this is normally a highly productive—in terms of economic and social labor (like mothering)—age range in all societies.

In one revealing instance, 12 prominent businessmen suspected of trafficking 13 Nigerian women for prostitution abroad were intercepted at Nigeria's Seme border with Benin. Further investigations revealed that 500 of such women were practicing prostitution in Bamako, Mali, while more than 500 others were hawking their bodies in Burkina Faso. Those behind this trade trick the young women into traveling outside the country with promises of lucrative jobs in Europe. Once they leave, their leaders compel them to go into prostitution, ostensibly to fund their journey to Europe. Many of these women never get to the promised destination but are usually abandoned midway. A report of the International Organization for Migration noted that in many cases traffickers seize their victims' travel documents and sell the women to

---

[11] Daily Times, 14 June 2001, p. 4.

[12] Daily Champion, 5 April 2001, p. 21.

brothel owners. The victims are then told that to recover their document they would have to repay the cost of their transportation and subsistence. Failed escape attempts usually end in severe confinement and physical assault, and families of those who succeed in running away can be threatened with violence. Because these women are isolated and cannot speak the local languages, they are usually vulnerable to abuse.[13]

Unfortunately, law enforcement agents in whom women should place their trust do not make things any easier. Sometimes, law enforcement officers become part of the syndicate. In Bosnia, Human Rights Watch found evidence of visa and immigration officials visiting brothels for free sexual services in exchange for ignoring the doctored documents produced by traffickers to facilitate transport through the country. In 2001, a former police officer and 50 other Nigerians were arrested in Conakry by Guinean authorities. According to the Nigerian ambassador to Guinea, Abdulkadir Sani, of the 51 detainees, 33 were young women between the ages of 18 and 20, while 17 others were men suspected of being behind the trafficking of the girls.[14] The report disclosed that 95 per cent of those being held were from Benin, Edo State and that the former police officer among them used to work for the Benin police command. Fake Guinean passport booklets, fake flight tickets, and American dollars were recovered from the 17 suspected traffickers. The human trafficking unit of the Nigerian Immigration Services identified some countries as what may be termed consumers of human trafficking. These include Italy, Saudi Arabia, Gabon, Macedonia and India. Whilst the link between procurers of victims within Nigeria and their external collaborators has not been properly established, it has been revealed that the Nigerian Police, instead of counseling and enhancing the rehabilitation of the victims, further aggravate the predicament of these women by subjecting them to persecution and extortion while they are in holding cells. This development can only be counter-productive to the efforts at curbing this crime against humanity. These point to the fact that some collusion exists between the traffickers and certain government agencies; how else could the women have successfully traversed the various borders without being detected. The volume of human trafficking correlates, I would suggest, with the level of corruption in the agencies that directly deal with immigration and organized crime.

The relationship between corruption and trafficking in humans could be measured with instruments such as Transparency International's Corruption Perceptions Index (CPI) and the United States Trafficking in Persons List (TIP). The CPI, together with TIP, permits one to determine the extent to which a country tolerates trafficking in or through its territory and the extent to which it is seen to be corrupt. The

---

[13] Ben Uzor, "Tackling Women Trafficking through constructive Engagements", Daily Times, 8 October 2001, p. 28.

[14] Yomi Odunuga, "Ex-police Chief, 50 others arrested for human trafficking" Punch, 2 August 2001, p. 3.

expected standards under TIP include (a) national laws prohibiting and punishing acts of trafficking; (b) laws prescribing commensurate punishment for "grave crimes" (such as trafficking involving rape, kidnapping or murder); (c) actions sufficiently deterrent to prevent trafficking; and (d) serious and sustained efforts to eliminate trafficking.

Nigeria was categorized in tier 2 of the Trafficking in Persons Country List for 2001 compiled by the United States government and the Transparency International. This tier lists states that do not meet minimum standards of combating human trafficking but are recognized to be making efforts to do so. Other African countries in this category include Cote d'Ivoire, Cameroun and Uganda.[15] TIP and CPI studies conducted by the U.S. government suggest strongly that corruption and trafficking are strongly related. Indeed, the US Anti-Trafficking Act flatly states: "trafficking in persons is often aided by official corruption in countries of origin, transit and destination, thereby threatening the rule of law." Basically, trafficking can be linked to state corruption through the activities or non-action of agencies of law enforcement, customs, immigration, and banking.

Efforts at Combating Human Trafficking

Besides global interventions, both Nigerian NGOs and the government are involved in efforts to combat human trafficking. Worthy of mention amongst others are the National Council of Women Societies (NCWS), FIDA, and the previously discussed WOTCLEF. The activities of the NGOs, especially WOTCLEF, go a long way in exposing the dimensions of this trade in Nigeria and bringing succor to many of the victims. Also worthy of note is the government's interest in fighting corruption on all fronts. However, it seems Nigeria's laws cannot effectively control corruption for the simple reason that they were not designed for the kind of society existing now. There are problems with the adversarial criminal justice system not the least of which are its technicalities and inadequate enforcement agencies.

For the government, tackling human trafficking means engaging corruption directly. Drawing inspiration from the Corrupt Practices and Economic Crime Draft Decree of 1990, the Obasanjo Government has put in place the legal framework encapsulated in the Corrupt Practices and other Related Offences Act, 2000, signed into law on June 13, 2000. This bill seeks to prohibit and prescribe punishment for the hydra-headed problem of corrupt practices and related offences. To this end, the Act establishes an Independent Corrupt Practices and other Related Offences Commission (ICPC).[16] The efforts of the Obasanjo government in tackling corruption, though not very satisfactory, should be recognized. Already stolen funds totaling about N84 billion as at 2001, had so far been

---

[15] Corbin B. Lyday, op. cit.

[16] Benjamin Ike, "The Corrupt Practices and other Related Offences Act", 2000, New Nigerian, 15 September 2000.

recovered from the family of the late Head of State, Sani Abacha, and returned to the Central Bank of Nigeria. This was part of the monies stolen and stashed away in foreign bank accounts by Abacha and his family members. According to the Obasanjo administration, the recovered monies will be channeled towards the funding of development projects.

It is widely believed that the present anti-corruption law, being a federal legislation, has positioned government in a better position to confront corruption generally. Keen observation also shows that most common forms of corruption are now criminal offences. Problems associated with undue technicalities and unnecessary delays during regular trials of corruption crimes are now largely eliminated because the new law stipulates that trials must be concluded within 90 working days. The new law provides for the seizure of movable and immovable property suspected to have been acquired through corrupt means and forfeiture of same following conviction. The legal framework for preventing corruption is quite adequate in its objectives, whether it will achieve its aim will, however, depend on other variables.[17] Since a realistic way to combat corruption is to reduce or eliminate opportunities for corrupt practices, one could take the risk at this juncture to say that the political will is there on the part of the government. The only way the government can convince the people of its seriousness about fighting corruption is to enforce the law in instances where corruption has been clearly established. Unfortunately, it cannot be said that the government has done this.

From the civil society, WOTCLEF initiated an "anti-trafficking bill drafting committee" in June 2000. The committee has drafted a bill that, if passed into law, will help harmonize the existing laws, prevent trafficking, prosecute traffickers, and protect the trafficked. The bill is still before the National Assembly. The foundation has also been in the forefront of advocacy aimed at educating the Nigerian public, especially vulnerable groups, about the extent of this problem and the need to check its continued rise. It has so far visited eleven states in the country and established vanguards/clubs in many secondary schools and institutions of higher education.

Concluding Remarks

By and large, we have seen that any effort at addressing the problem of human trafficking would just have to revisit the issue of corruption in high and low places especially in government bureaucracy and other relevant agencies. Personnel of these agencies have to be made to understand the implications of their actions and inactions on issues pertaining to trafficking in women and children. Quite often, we forget that corruption in the public sector is in fact induced by private sector corruption. There is a need to address corruption in both the private and public sectors.

---

[17] Ayua, op. cit., p. 40.

Set below are some useful ways of tackling corruption and human trafficking:

- Incorporating human rights and development perspectives into anti-corruption work.
- Enacting a comprehensive law that will cover most aspects of human trafficking, specify severe punishment for traffickers, rehabilitate victims, and give law enforcement officers adequate investigate tools.
- Increasing security at border posts, and adequately equipping law enforcement agencies to check the schemes of the traffickers.
- Capacity building at all levels for the eradication of human trafficking.
- Public enlightenment through regular workshops, seminars, conferences, and through print and electronic media. Schools, religious bodies, traditional institutions, and the family should be sensitized on the evils of this abominable trade.
- Education and some form of employment for the teeming youths.
- Discouraging excessive materialism and the culture of 'get rich quick'.[18]
- Ensuring proper coordination of efforts between the police and other state security services.

In short, combating human trafficking should be located within the larger context of underlying social and economic problems. Efforts aimed at remedying the low status of women—particularly the economic disadvantages they face—must be woven into a larger anti-poverty, anti-corruption framework at national and global levels.

Discussion Questions

1   *How has globalization contributed to human trafficking?*

2   *Broadly conceptualized, what does human trafficking include?*

3   *How does the world bank define corruption?*

4   *What is a conservative account of the number of people trafficked to all parts of the globe?*

5   *What are a couple of instruments that can be used to measure the relationship between corruption and trafficking in humans?*

6   *What are the useful ways of tackling corruption and human trafficking?*

---

[18] Transparency International and Key Center for Ethics, Justice and Governance, Australian National Integrity Systems Assessment, Queensland Handbook, 2001.

References

Ayua, I. (ed.). Proceedings of the National Conference on the Problems of Corruption in Nigeria, 26 – 29 March 2001, Abuja.

Daily Times, 14 June, 2001.

Daily Champion, 5 April, 2001.

Ebirim, Innocent. "Human Trafficking: Economic Implications", New Nigerian, 25 February 2002.

Ike, Benjamin. "The Corrupt Practices and other Related Offences Act", 2000, New Nigerian, 15 September, 2000.

International Center for Economic Growth, Information Brief 6, Causes and effects of Corruption, Nairobi, 1999.

Lyday, Corbin B. The Shadow Market in Human Beings: An Anti-Corruption Perspective. Paper Presented at Transparency International's 10 ¡sup¿ th International Anti-Corruption Conference, Prague, Czech Republic, October 7 – 11, 2001.

Odunuga, Yomi. "Ex-police Chief, 50 others arrested for human trafficking", Punch, 2 August, 2001, p.3.

Transparency International and Key Centre for Ethics, Justice and Governance, Australian National Integrity Systems Assessment, Queensland Handbook, 2001.

Uzor, Ben. "Tackling Women Trafficking through Constructive Engagements", Daily Times, October 8, 2001, p.28.

Women Aid International Press Release (http://www.womenaid.org).

World Bank "Helping Countries Combat Corruption: The Role of the World Bank", 1997.

PART IV

SEX TRAFFICKING –
AN INTERNATIONAL PERSPECTIVE

A Critique of the Global Trafficking Discourse and U.S. Policy.
This research paper examines the dominant discourse on trafficking in persons and the implementation of international and U.S. policy to address trafficking globally. Features of the United Nations Protocol and the Trafficking in Victims Protection Act demonstrate how trafficking frameworks currently in place contain underlying fears of migration and female sexuality. The implications of policy on the construction of third world women as "victims to be saved" through governments, National Government Organizations, feminists and the media will show how these misrepresentations only reinforce racism and dualistic simplification of a complex issue. An emphasis is place on the importance of women's agency and the possibility of multiple realities. An alternative way of thinking about human trafficking and related policy through a labor rights, migration and human rights framework is proposed.

Globalizing Sexual Exploitation: Sex Tourism and the Traffic in Women. This research paper explains that there are many forces at work in the normalization of the international sex industry. The sex industry has become immensely profitable, providing considerable resources not just to individuals and networks involved in trafficking women but to governments who have come to depend on sex industry revenue. One aspect of the industry in particular that governments have come to depend on for revenues is sex tourism. This paper presents a critical analysis of the arguments of the normalizers of the sex industrialists or their spokesperson that sex tourism or other forms of prostitution should come to be seen as a legitimate leisure industry. In this paper the author also discusses the relationship between prostitution and sexual violence, the effects of prostitution, the causes and extent of internationalization of prostitution and ways in which to end sex tourism.

Trafficking in Women: The Business Model Approach. This research paper identifies six different models of businesses in the trafficking area. Each of these models is an ideal type associated with a different national group and reflects deep historical influences, geographical realities, and the market forces that drive the trade. The models do not fit every crime group from a particular region, but they do provide a means to categorize the business of human smuggling and trafficking. The first five models address the businesses that recruit men, women, and children to be smuggled and trafficked. The sixth model applies only to a host country and not to the groups supplying trafficked women. These models apply to different regions of the world as women are trafficked from the former Soviet Union countries, China, Latin America, and Africa.

Smuggling and Trafficking in Human Beings: The Phenomenon, The Markets That Drive It and the Organizations That Promote It. This research paper defines the concepts of smuggling and trafficking in human beings and discusses the difficulty in applying the definition. The magnitude and scope of the problem is examined as well as its causes. Trafficking in human beings is analyzed as an illegal market, particularly with reference to its relationship with other illegal markets and the involvement of organized crime groups. The paper closes with an overview of situations which facilitate the practice, and current measures and recommendations to stem the tide of human smuggling and sex trafficking.

19

A CRITIQUE OF THE GLOBAL TRAFFICKING DISCOURSE AND U.S. POLICY

Moshoula Capous Desyllas, *Portland State University, School of Social Work*

A critical analysis of the discourse on trafficking in persons requires an understanding of the discursive history behind it, the feminists' debates surrounding it, and the international and U.S. policy designed to address it. Trafficking in persons is considered to be the forced, illegal movement of people across national and international borders and enslavement of those individuals in their destination country. While forced labor migration is a violation of human rights, not every case of illegal movement across borders is forced.

I will argue for a view of trafficking "as the trade and exploitation of labor under conditions of coercion and force" (Kempadoo, Sanghera, Pattanaik, 2005b, p. viii). This perspective addresses trafficking as transnational migration for labor with a focus on the unsafe working conditions of migrants and their rights as humans. I will argue that the current trafficking framework, and the resulting policy, harm both migrants and sex workers. The latter part of this analysis will critique the U.S. policy designed to 'combat' trafficking, the Trafficking of Victim Protection Act (TVPA) of 2000, and its re-authorization (TVPRA) of 2003, in order to explore the complex effects of this policy on migrants, sex workers, and other marginalized groups. This critique will demonstrate how those countries holding power and privilege have domineering policies and imperialistic frameworks and ideologies that are imposed upon the rest of the world.

This analysis utilizes a third world feminist theoretical framework along with post-modern feminist theory to critique the trafficking in persons discourse. I use the term discourse, inspired by Michel Foucault (1972), to describe the set of accepted and relevant concepts related to trafficking which have become socially legitimized as knowledge and truth within society. I challenge this understanding of truth around trafficking since it oppresses and omits the voices of migrants from the global south and sex workers. A global feminist lens that focuses on the issues of race, ethnicity and culture as they intersect with class, gender and global economics and politics will be used. Third world feminist theory examines how global economic inequalities, including colonialism and imperialism, affect the experiences of women, taking into account the intersectionalities of sex, race, ethnicity and class (Parpart, Connelly, Barriteau, 2000, p. 65). Postmodern feminism is concerned with discourse and language, in particular with "previously silenced voices, for the specificity and power of language and its relation to knowledge, context and locality" (Parpart, et. al, 2000, p. 68). It is the hegemonic position of the global North that has dominated the construction of the definition of trafficking and its subsequent policy. I will demonstrate how underlying western fears of migration and the sexuality of women have contributed to the construction of sex trafficking as a social problem that is equated with prostitution. International and U.S. policies with underlying motivations may generate more harm to migrants and others working in the sex industry and targeted under the trafficking framework.

Feminist Debates

Historically, "trafficking in persons has been equated with prostitution" (Ditmore, 2005, p. 108). The definitions of trafficking and prostitution have been informed by opposing feminists' perspectives and theoretical frameworks. The abolitionist approach asserts that prostitution is a violation of human rights, analogous to (sexual) slavery (Bindman & Doezema, 1997) and "an extreme expression of sexual violence" (Outshoorn, 2005, p. 145). The belief is that no person can truly consent to prostitution, no woman would choose to prostitute herself by free will, and a woman who engages in prostitution is a victim who requires help to escape sexual slavery (Outshoorn, 2005). This point of view applied to trafficking always involves a victim of force, coercion and/or deception. Outshoorn (2005, p. 146) asserts that from this lens the "trafficking of migrant women is always seen as against their will; they are by definition victims of trafficking. According to abolitionists, trafficking is seen to be caused by prostitution, making the best way to fight trafficking the abolition of prostitution." While the abolitionist view of prostitution, informed by radical feminist theory, is driving the current trafficking discourse and influencing U.S. policy, it is only one side of the debate.

The other major trafficking discourse is the sex workers' rights approach, which views prostitution as a viable option and a choice that women make in order to survive that should be respected, not stigmatized (Outshoorn, 2005; Chapkis, 1997). The pro-rights or sex worker perspective is supported by the belief that women have the "right to sexual determination," the right to work in safe labor conditions, and the right to migrate for sex work wherever they choose (Outshoorn, 2005, p. 145). For this group, "it is not the work as such that violates women's human rights, but the conditions of deceit, violence, debt-bondage, blackmail, deprivation of freedom of movement, etc. be it in prostitution, in domestic labor, or in the commercial marriage market" (Wijers & Van Doorninck, 2005, p.2). Some assert that women who are in these violating conditions "can be victims of trafficking, but not all women sex workers crossing borders are victims of forced prostitution" (Outshoorn, 2005, p. 147).

Defining Trafficking

Trafficking has been nationally and internationally defined through the use of ethnocentric language and western assumptions. Scholars use "trafficking" interchangeably with diverse concepts, such as: illegal immigration, modern slavery, prostitution, and the sexual exploitation of women. Trafficking definitions often fail to distinguish clearly between trafficking and voluntary consensual migration, often combining women's migratory movement with trafficking (Kapur, 2005). Furthermore, Piper (2005) asserts that trafficking has to be seen as part of the reality of migration patterns, mainly undocumented flows. Taking into account economic globalization, O'Neill (2001, p. 156) presents trafficking as "the total commoditization of human beings traded across borders, as is the case with any other good." Definitions of trafficking are highly contested among scholars, National Government Organizations (NGOs), feminists, and governments, thus posing challenges in conducting research studies, reporting statistics and making generalizations.

Historical Fears of Sexuality and Migration

The issue of trafficking came up within the international human rights discourse and took on a moral framework. The document that set the standard for the United Nations (UN) to continue further resolutions on trafficking and prostitution was the 1949 UN Convention for the Suppression of the Traffic in Persons and Exploitation of Prostitution of Others (Saunders & Soderlund, 2003), the first international instrument that dealt with trafficking as forced prostitution. Even though this was not ratified by all countries, it still served as a model for future legislation (Doezema, 2002a). The 1949 UN Convention represented an abolitionist notion of prostitution as exploitation and as being "incompatible with the dignity and worth of the human person" (Ditmore & Wijers, 2003; Saunders, 2005).

Historical patterns in the levels of public concern in the U.S. over the trafficking of women and children are linked to periods of increased immigration (Saunders & Soderlund, 2003). The historical discourse on immigration and its links to trafficking is emphasized by Pattanaik (2002, p. 218) who states that "the term which was used to describe the ensuing abuses in the process of migration was 'trafficking.'" The U.S. immigration policies in the past are known for their racist, discriminatory, and exclusionary stances, out of fear for the "other," the unwelcome foreigner.

Racism, as it relates to sex trafficking, is raised as an issue for analysis by various feminists who critique the dominant sex trafficking framework. In response to the fear of 'white slavery,' Congress passed the White Slave Traffic Act in 1910, also known as the Mann Act. This act prohibited unmarried women from crossing state lines for immoral purposes and it criminalized interracial couples (Saunders & Soderlund, 2003, pp. 3-18). Under the Mann Act, in 1914 more than 70% of the convictions of women were related to the voluntary transportation of women for prostitution or other immoral purposes (Saunders, 2005). Racist immigration laws passed in the 1920s, Immigration Act of 1924 and the Temporary Quota Act of 1921, led to strengthening U.S. borders and the restriction of migrants from Eastern and Southern Europe and Asia. The period afterward did not see trafficking on the U.S. and international agenda to such an extent or urgency as it was seen to resurface again in the 1990s (Saunders & Soderlund, 2003).

Doezema (1998, p. 44) describes how the 19th century sex slave was "a white woman, victim of the animal lusts of the dark races" and in the 21st century, the racism changed its focus to exaggerate the new sex slaves as "passive, un-emancipated women from the developing world." In the 1800s Chinese women and other women of color were viewed as overly sexual, deviant and promiscuous, as were Mexican women at the turn of the century. It was at this time that migration was on the rise so the government felt the need to create a moral fear and panic over "the other.'

A historical context of socio-political, religious, and economic perspectives in the U.S. situates the current U.S. policy within a racist, heterosexist, hegemonic framework that harms women through so-called 'protection' and continues to colonize. The different feminist perspectives of prostitution throughout history have also influenced policy and public ideas about trafficking and the need to 'protect victims.'

The Influence of NGOs on Trafficking Policy

In November of 2000, NGOs played a major role in the development of the UN Protocol to Prevent, Suppress and Punish Trafficking in Persons, Especially Women and Children. The presence of two different NGO-lobbying groups, with opposing feminist views on sex work and trafficking in persons, had the greatest influence on the UN Protocol.

One of the lobbying groups was the Human Rights Caucus, which consisted of the union of human rights groups, anti-trafficking organizations and sex worker's rights activists. This group consisted of the Global Alliance against Traffic in Women (GAATW), founded in Thailand, and the Network for Sex Work Projects (NSWP) who distinguished between forced and voluntary prostitution, in support for sex work safe labor conditions (Saunders, 2005; Outshoorn, 2005). The work of the Human

Rights Caucus and other anti-abolitionist NGOs challenged the trafficking framework and succeeded in pushing for a broader definition of trafficking into the UN Protocol. These NGOs were successful in advocating for the inclusion of men, women and children, as well as for labor and human rights for those working in other industries, such as domestic work, and agriculture (Saunders, 2005).

The opposing side consisted of feminist NGOs and feminist abolitionists such as the American-based Coalition Against Trafficking in Persons (CATW), the European Women's Lobby (EWL) and the International Abolitionist Federation (IAF). This group maintained the primary view of prostitution as violence and sexual slavery. The victim stance taken by the abolitionist group was in contrast to the sex workers rights perspective that was concerned with women's agency. In this context, women's agency relates to "whether or not women can actually choose to work in the sex industry ... and whether trafficking should be defined by the nature of the work involved or by the use of deceit and coercion" (Ditmore & Wijers, 2003, p. 82).

The UN Protocol's trafficking definition was finally agreed upon even though it allowed a certain degree of flexibility in its interpretation by the nations that signed it. The final definition of trafficking, as stated in the UN Protocol to Prevent, Suppress, and Punish Trafficking on Persons, Especially Women and Children, supplementing the United Nations Convention against Transnational Organized Crime, is stated as follows:

> **"Trafficking in persons"** shall mean the recruitment, transportation, transfer or harboring or receipt of persons, by means of the threat or use of force or other forms of coercion, of abduction, of fraud, of deception, of the abuse of power or of a position of vulnerability or of giving or receiving payments or benefits to achieve the consent of a person having control over another person, for the purposes of exploitation. Exploitation shall include, at a minimum, the exploitation of the prostitution of others or other forms of sexual exploitation, forced labour or services, slavery or practices similar to slavery, servitude or the removal of organs. (UN Protocol 2000, p. 2)

In this framing of trafficking, there is a distinction between forced and voluntary prostitution. The inclusion of force or deception as being essential to the UN Protocol trafficking definition marked an important departure from the abolitionist perspective of the 1949 Convention. The UN Protocol definition also included trafficking for the purposes other than prostitution, and the focus shifted from morality and women's sexuality to addressing working conditions and crime (Ditmore & Wijers, 2003).

Some of the language written into the UN Protocol still allowed for the transformation of rights into privileges that governments could interpret either to work for or against migrants. The ambiguous language present in the international document and the lack of strong human rights protection language was not ultimately included by government delegates (Ditmore & Wijers, 2003). The interpretation of the UN Protocol by individual nations did not prevent a nation from using a moral lens to focus on women's sexuality, playing a major role in how U.S. trafficking policy was developed.

Doezema (2002b) points out that the exclusion of prostitution from the definitions of trafficking, and broadening the focus to include other types of labor, still created the problem of categorizing migrants into "guilty" versus "innocent." Critical analysis points to the danger of distinguishing between 'innocent victims' (who are forced and coerced as deserving pity and the criminalization of those who have abused her) versus the willing "'whore' who has sacrificed her right to social protection through her degraded behavior" (Bindman & Doezema, 1997, p. 6; Doezema, 1998). There is a dichotomizing of good versus bad: between innocent women who deserve protection and guilty women who deserve the circumstances they may get into.

Shah (2004) takes this concept further by applying it to women globally. This analysis looks at how 'forced' sex workers are represented and portrayed as living in the global South, having been coerced or abducted, or having no other option but to work in the sex industry because of their dire economic conditions. Shah (2004) contrasts this image to the 'Western' sex workers of the 'global North' who symbolize privilege, immorality, and free choice to enter into the sex industry. These contrasting images serve to construct third world women as powerless victims, without agency and bound by their circumstances. This duality of guilty sex worker versus deserving migrant, along with the construction of the third-world victim, is evidenced in the development of U.S. Policy to addressing trafficking.

U.S. Trafficking Policy

The trafficking policy in the U.S. was formed and supported by religious leaders, neoconservatives, abolitionist feminists and NGOs. Michael Horowitz, a neoconservative from the Washington, D.C.-based think tank, the Hudson Institute, formed a coalition with powerful evangelicals who pressed for legislation that would become the Trafficking Victims Protection Act (TVPA) (Block, 2004). On November 6, 1999, Representative Chris Smith drafted a bill that exclusively focused on the sexual exploitation of women and girls, excluding males and trafficking for labor (Block, 2004). The TVPA (HR 3244) was passed October 6, 2000 by a 371-1 vote. The bill passed the Senate with a 95-0 vote on October 11, 2000, and signed into Public Law (106-386) by President Bill Clinton on October 28, 2000 (State Legislatures, 2005).

The U.S. Congress enacted the TVPA of 2000 with the purpose of preventing human trafficking overseas, protecting victims of trafficking, and prosecuting traffickers. The title, alone, of this U.S. policy demonstrates how the government depicts women as 'victims' to be 'rescued' and 'protected.' Mohanty (1991) affirms that media images of third world women, in this case constructed by the U.S. government, perpetuate the stereotypes of third world women as being weak and needing to be cared for. Kempadoo & Doezema (1998, p. 42) assert that the construction of a victim "perpetuates stereotypes of sex workers as passive and exploitative victims."

The TVPA has been presented in the media as a policy that 'combats' sex trafficking. The use of the word 'combat' perpetuates a language of violence and war, bringing in the necessity of masculinity to "save" the innocent, female, childlike victims from "the barbaric crime of trafficking," as stated by President George Bush in a keynote address at the First National Human Trafficking Conference in July of 2004 (U.S. Department of Justice, 2004). The use of the word 'barbaric' serves to construct the idea of the uncivilized, dark-skinned trafficker abroad who manipulates innocent women into sex trafficking.

A definition of sex trafficking, as defined by the U.S., can be found in the annual "Victims of Trafficking and Violence Protection Act of 2000: Trafficking in Persons Report" issued by the U.S. Department of State. The U.S. definition of "severe forms of trafficking in persons" is as follows:

(a) sex trafficking in which a commercial sex act is induced by force, fraud, or coercion, or in which the person induced to perform such act has not attained 18 years of age; or

(b) the recruitment, harboring, transportation, provision, or obtaining of a person for labor or services, through the use of force, fraud or coercion for the purposes of subjection to involuntary servitude, peonage, debt bondage, or slavery (U.S. Department of State, 2002).

Although not identical in their wording, the unifying elements of both the TVPA and the UN Protocol definitions of trafficking involve the illegal transportation and the sexual slavery of persons by threat or use of force or coercion. The distinction being made between 'voluntary versus forced' creates a dichotomous framework from which to look at trafficking that is limiting and simplistic. For instance, a woman may knowingly agree to work in the sex industry, thus being defined as 'voluntary', but she may not know the extreme abuse she may be faced with, that may include 'forced' acts under abusive working conditions. Binary oppositions perpetuate silent biases and assumptions, without looking at the complexity of the issue. Mohanty (1991, p. 64) asserts that dualities are ineffective when "designing strategies to combat oppressions." Only 'severe forms" of trafficking cause the enforcement provisions of the TVPA to be implemented, with "victims" bearing the burden of proof that they were coerced.

Policy Links to U.S. Imperialism

The TVPA of 2000 is composed of features that emphasize prevention, protection and prosecution. One aspect of the TVPA's prevention component includes the U.S.'s demands on other countries to take preventative measures to end sex trafficking. The U.S. has written into policy its responsibility to make yearly assessments of other countries' anti-trafficking efforts and to rank each country according to the procedures a country takes in order to 'combat' trafficking. The Office to Monitor and Combat Trafficking in Persons with the State Department has a mandate from Congress to issue annual Trafficking in Persons (TIP) reports that rates each country's progress on eliminating trafficking. Each country is judged on a 'Tier' system, and the U.S., along with a few other western European countries, has awarded itself Tier I status, which represents 'sufficient' efforts at combating trafficking. However, those countries that do not demonstrate adequate means and efforts to end trafficking, as judged appropriate by the U.S., are ranked on either Tier 2 or Tier 3. Those countries judged as being on Tier 3 are then subject to sanctions by the U.S. (except for sanctions on humanitarian aid).

Mezler (2005) has called to attention the interesting parallel between those countries that are ranked as Tier 3 countries and their poor political relations with the U.S., such as Cuba, North Korea, and Venezuela. Venezuela's Tier 3 ranking may be more about the country's refusal to acknowledge the U.S. program than with its efforts to eliminate trafficking (Mezler, 2005). Not only does the Tier system reinforce imperialist and hegemonic relations between those in power and those not in power, but it also raises additional issues related to the U.S. role within the world. Additional countries that were placed in Tier 3 and defined as sanctionable by the U.S. State Department consisted of countries who oppose U.S. imperialism, such as Iran, and countries made up of Arab or Muslim populations, such as Indonesia, United Arab Emirates, Afghanistan, Bahrain, Lebanon, Sudan, Qatar, Turkey, and Saudi Arabia (Kempadoo, 2005, p. xxi). Enloe (2000, p. xvi) highlights the unique position of the U.S. as a nation that offers itself up as "a model to be emulated" while playing the role of a term she coins as "global policeman."

Problems With the Criminalization Approach

Another large part of the U.S. law's effort aimed at prevention, includes aspects of protection and prosecution: which appear to be addressed in conjunction with one another, rather than independent of one another. This can create undesired consequences for women. The TVPA was developed to provide a means for "non-citizen victims" of trafficking found in the U.S. to apply for a special T-visa, along with other benefits and services so that they could be "protected" and offered a chance to rebuild their lives (U.S. Department of Health & Human Services, 2004). The T-visa allows "victims of severe forms of trafficking" to remain in the U.S. provided they cooperate with law enforcement and assist federal authorities in the investigation and prosecution of human trafficking cases. While this law seeks to 'protect' and 'prosecute,' it places the burden of proof on the migrant to 'prove her innocence' and 'coercion,' as well as information about the organized criminal network that is assumed to be responsible for human trafficking. This stipulation appears to be counterintuitive to what this policy supposedly stands for, to primarily "protect victims," as stated in its title. Undocumented immigrants may still be very vulnerable due to their fear of deportation and being involved within the sex industry in a country where prostitution is illegal. Kempadoo (2005, p. 29) states that "women in prostitution are subjects of criminalizing policies, laws and ideologies." According to Chapkis (2003), the T-visa appears to be designed, not so much to meet the needs of migrants who have been sex trafficked, but as a device to assist prosecutors in closing down trafficking networks. This is evidenced in the various obstacles that migrants have to go through in order to obtain a visa.

Victim protection programs are validated behind the belief that all trafficking cases are caused by organized criminal trafficking networks. These intricate criminal networks are described in research studies (Hughes, 2002; 2001b) as composed of large organized groups with roots in villages that extend to the country of destination. Corrupt political and government officials are often linked as participants in the trafficking scheme (Raymond, Hughes, & Gomez, 2001). Agustin (2005, p. 101) notes the automatic, "hypothetical" link between trafficking and large-scale criminal organizations that are "dedicated to enslaving migrants." She points out that even though governments support policy under the assumption that organized crime is behind trafficking, the UN Crime Commission's own report found limited evidence of such activity (Agustin, 2005; CICP, 2003).

Kempadoo & Doezema (1998) assert that many rely on the assumption that 'evil' traffickers are behind trafficking because it is easier to gain support for arguing to help 'victims' rather than challenge the existing framework. This also makes it easier for the 'helpers' (made up of abolitionist feminist, anti-prostitution NGOs, and governments) to take "center stage" (Agustin, 2005, p. 107). Trafficking policy"...sets up a need for feminists, NGOs and even governments to "save" every woman migrating to work...The best policy is to put on a victimized facade—which may be partially true-allowing NGO helpers to believe they are indispensable" (Agustin, 2005, p. 107). In an effort to 'save' every migrant, the experiences of individuals are generalized without consideration that the work of 'organized criminal networks' may be the combined effort of family, friends, agents, entrepreneurs and small-time delinquents who make up these 'traffickers' (Agustin, 2001, p. 3). This knowledge slightly changes the constructed, popular idea of "traffickers" and organized crime.

Using a criminal justice response to fight organized crime, combined with border control, uses "sexual harm as a justification for restraining women's movement" (Miller, 2004, p. 34). Some migrants are being punished and sent back to their countries of origin where the economic situation in the global South may be dire and insufficient for survival. In addition, a law and order model pushes illegal migration and undocumented work further underground perpetuating unsafe labor standards for migrants. Kempadoo (2001, p. 33) emphasizes the notion that "criminalization and stigmatization ensure poor working conditions," and only if prostitution can be defined as work, and sex trafficking can be thought of as labor migration, can women in the sex industry claim labor rights and insist on safe working conditions (Kempadoo & Doezema, 1998). This labor rights perspective would not only require decriminalizing prostitution, but working towards the legalization of sex work in order to ensure safer working conditions. By implementing anti-trafficking measures, governments can justify the isolation, social exclusion, stigmatization, marginalization and criminalization of sex workers and migrants (Wijers & Van Doorninck, 2005; Wijers, 2001).

Reauthorization of a Moral Agenda

On March 12, 2004, President George W. Bush spoke of a 'new enemy': sex slavery. During this speech, he introduced Sharon Cohn, director of Anti-trafficking Operations for the International Justice Mission, a Christian organization fighting to end the practice of sex slavery (Block, 2004). The Trafficking of Victims Protection Reauthorization Act (TVPRA) was signed into Public Law (108-193) by President Bush on December 19, 2003, to include enhancements related to prevention, protection and prosecution. Currently being considered is another reauthorization of the policy; the TVPRA 2005 (HR 972).

In 2003, more than $200 million was authorized by the Bush Administration through the Trafficking Victims Protection Reauthorization Act of 2003 (TVPRA), Public Law 108-193, to "combat trafficking"

(U.S. Department of Health and Human Services, 2004). This "renewed and enhanced" policy also allows the U.S. Government to fund public awareness campaigns for foreign countries and to provide funding for research on international and domestic trafficking. However, the TVPRA refuses the granting of funds to any organization that promotes, supports, or advocates the legalization or practice of prostitution. Any organizations or NGO who advocate prostitution as an employment choice are not funded, while grantees are now being asked to state their position on prostitution in writing (Block, 2004; Melzer, 2005; Ditmore, 2003). Saunders & Soderlund (2003, p. 21) describe how those programs that utilize the term "sex work" are now considered "inappropriate partners for USAID anti-trafficking grants or contracts" since they accept prostitution as employment choice. NGOs that forcibly removed women from prostitution in order to 'save' them, have been among those given funding preferences (Melzer, 2005). This demonstrates a continued lack of attention to trafficking in other industries, such as sweatshops, construction, agriculture and domestic labor.

Not only is the focus of the U.S. policy primarily on sex trafficking, but funding is also closely linked to religious ideologies allied with conservative views on prostitution. The International Justice Mission (IJM), a Christian NGO, has received millions of dollars in federal funds to work on trafficking (Mezler, 2005). This organization is known to raid brothels in India and Thailand, placing sex workers into homes and re-education programs (Mezler, 2005). Reports about IJM from other NGOs are in the form of complaints, such as IJM operates "... 'like a bull in a china shop' without regard for the mess it leaves behind" (Block, 2005). On the other hand, organizations such as the Sonagachi Project in India, who were recognized by the UN as a model program for addressing the problems faced by sex workers, such as the spread of HIV and protection of rights, are denied funding by the U.S. (Melzer, 2005; Ditmore, 2003). U.S. sex trafficking policy overtly discriminates against humanitarian organizations that don't fit the abolitionist model. The privilege and power that the U.S. has and utilizes over other countries acts to reinforce the power hierarchy and control that maintains the inequalities and neocolonial relationships between nations, between western and third world feminists, and among poor migrants. It is crucial that western policy makers, western feminists, and others in positions of privilege decenter their western power.

Colonizing Views of Third World Women

The media play a major role in the reproduction of racial stereotypes and in the construction of images that reinforce power hierarchies. Kempadoo (2001b) describes how the media portray the global sex trade as one-dimensional, where women are just "victims" of male violence, even though the issue of migratory sex work is more complex. In western culture, the dominant image of the victimized sex worker is of a "young, brown, Asian or Black woman" (Kempadoo, 2001b, p. 169). This illustration plays into the discourse by "othering women" to justify the current U.S. policy that objectifies women, by turning them into oppressed, dependent victims in need of rescue. A critical analysis of why this occurs is presented by Kempadoo (1998), who explains that the "bad girl" illustration "threatens male control and domination." This simultaneously distorts the real lived experiences of migrants (Long, 2004), assumes homogeneity and denies women their agency.

The terminology being used shows a culturally imperialistic discourse on prostitution and trafficking. The speech delivered by U.S. President Bush in July of 2004 included this perpetuation of what Mohanty (1991, p. 57) calls "the construction of third world women as a homogenous powerless group often located as implicit victims of particular socioeconomic systems." To a group of law enforcement officers and human services providers, President Bush declared, "The lives of tens of thousands of innocent women and children depend on your compassion, they depend on your determination, and they depend on your daily efforts to rescue them from misery and servitude. You are in a fight against evil, and the American people are grateful for your dedication and services." These women of the global South are also presented as victims of dire socioeconomic conditions who need to be rescued by those of the global North. However, no responsibility is taken by the global North in the perpetuation of this poverty in third world countries through their imposed SAP and transnational corporations.

bell hooks* maintains that discounting women's agency and constructing non-western women as needing to be rescued perpetuates the idea of the weak "other" and the powerful westerner, further colonizing through the use of a hegemonic framework. Western NGOs construct the 'third world woman' as a 'damaged other' to justify their "own interventionist impulses" (Doezema, 2001, p. 1). Women are infantilized in the name of protecting and 'saving' them (Agustin, 2003b, p. 8), which takes away their power and agency. Also, requiring women to participate in a criminal justice model aimed at 'catching the bad guy' traffickers calls into question whether this policy is another way of regulating and possessing control over a woman's body through the withholding of services unless women can assist in the 'war against trafficking.'

The re-inscription of western imperialism and colonialism is evidenced through the creation and implementation of trafficking policies. A more inclusive and constructive discourse is one that takes into account the variety of conditions and agency of men and trans-gender individuals, as well the perspectives of sex workers who do not

*Lack of capitals intentional

have rights as sex workers due to the illegal nature of their work. It is also crucial to hear the diverse experiences of migrants who are in a more threatened position due to their illegal status. The focus will have to shift away from associating trafficking primarily with sexual slavery and the sex industry. Agustin (2003b, p. 8) asserts, "when the subject is not a minority of women who are duped, sequestered and enslaved, we should be able to give credit where it is due to women and transsexuals, as well as men, who dare to make decisions to better their lives by leaving their homes to work abroad, no matter what kind of work they have to do."

The current U.S. government prefers repressive strategies because they are simple and in accordance with other agendas, such as immigration control, ending organized crime, imposing ideologies onto other countries, and maintaining women's morality and sexuality. By accepting the current abolitionist framework on trafficking, the multiple realities of migrants, sex workers and other groups are ignored, agency is denied, and all experiences are assumed to be the same. When western policy makers and feminists homogenize experiences and ignore contextual differences, this leads to a disregard of the historical, cultural and socio-political background of migrants.

An Alternative Framework

A more inclusive perspective that takes into account other types of work is crucial for addressing all types of oppressive working conditions. It is important to move away from a moral lens that stigmatizes and marginalizes people, and to move toward protecting migrant workers from unsafe labor conditions. Media images and reports that focus on (sex) trafficking need to be questioned and a shift in focus away from sex work will ensure that all types of unsafe working conditions are addressed. A labor rights perspective, which focuses on the human rights of workers, incorporates all of these elements to broaden the approach to trafficking. By including all forms of labor, and by defining sex work as an economic activity that is often used in combination with other types of work (Mellon, 1999), migrants and sex workers will not be stigmatized and marginalized due to the associations of being labeled as a prostitute.

In addition to a labor rights framework, a migration perspective of trafficking will also be a more constructive alternative to the current trafficking framework. It will allow for the participation of migrants in the trafficking discourse and it will take into consideration the diverse experiences and circumstances of people's lives without the necessity of labeling and identifying a person with a particular group, such as sex worker or domestic laborer (Agustin, 2002). This framework would acknowledge that labor rights of migrants are non-existent if migrants have entered into a country illegally. A migratory lens would also address immigration laws that are less punitive and more equitable to migrants. Legal restrictions on migration for labor need to be reduced so that illegal immigration isn't pushed further underground (O'Neill, 2001, p. 162).

Overall, it is important to address migrants within the framework of U.S. and international human rights law so that policies, practices and actions towards assisting persons who are trafficked and other groups who are affected, such as sex workers, can be critically examined and evaluated. It is imperative that a forum and a space exist for multiple voices and perspectives to be heard from migrants of the global South. "Transnational movements require a transnational response and analysis" (Kapur, 2005, p. 38). Western trafficking discourse and anti-trafficking policies are "binaries and stereotypes of the third world" (Kapur, 2005: Kempadoo, 2005a, p. 30). The current western trafficking discourse and related policies that reinforce colonialistic and imperialist global inequalities and power relations need to be deconstructed and challenged in order to work toward social justice and change.

A more inclusive perspective is advocated by Kempadoo (2001, p. 43) and other feminists who support "culturally specific constructions and expressions of sexuality for and by women of color." As Kempadoo (1998, p. 14) states,

> Yet in an era when women can no longer be defined exclusively as victims, where Third World women speak for themselves in various forums, where increasingly analyses have shifted focus from simple hierarchies and dichotomies to the problematization of multiple spaces, seemingly contradictory social locations and plural sites of power, it would seem that experiences, identities and struggles of women in the global sex industry cannot be neglected.

Marginalized groups have the right to speak for themselves, and as Mohanty (1991) states, the right to set their own agendas and their own experiences. She demonstrates how people in the west are setting the agenda for the rest of the world, as evidenced in the TVPRA that consists of the Tier system for monitoring international progress to prevent trafficking. A conceptual shift needs to occur to examine the multitude of experiences of migrants, so that generalizations and sensationalist depictions of women of color and sex workers that reinforce gender, culture and power structures do not drive U.S. and international policy.

Implications for Social Work

The effects of the implementation of the TVPA on social work practice and service provision and development have not yet been explored. The implementation of this policy through social service agency policies and procedures may have effects on migrants and sex workers that are unknown. The consequences of this policy on migrants who have worked in the sex industry and others who are seeking social services have also not been investigated. With the increase in social work's involvement in national efforts to assist "victims of trafficking,' it is necessary to understand the effects of this policy and the manner in which it is being implemented.

Culturally competent research and evaluation studies are needed nationally and internationally to understand the implications and effects of this policy on the welfare of those individuals who have experienced unsafe working conditions and dangerous situations. Policy and practice strategies to benefit the well-being and safety of these individuals need to be shared globally to find the best methods in which to view the phenomenon of trafficking. Collaboration on ideas and strategies for assuring safe working conditions for migrants, sex workers and all marginalized groups working in unrecognized industries are of equal importance, while cross-cultural awareness is imperative.

Since the TVPA and its re-authorization have only been in effect for a few years, there have been no studies on the implementation and effectiveness of this policy. The proposed TVPRA of 2005 will allocate more funds to support a morally driven policy that does not take into account the individuals it claims to serve. In their pursuit of social justice, social work researchers can contribute to the understanding of the effects of this policy on those most vulnerable in society.

Presenting the ambiguous definition of trafficking and its related terms provide a foundation for the varied meanings associated with the concept of trafficking. The social and historical background of the phenomenon and the feminist debates surrounding the trafficking discourse have all contributed to shaping national and international policy to address trafficking as a global problem. The trafficking discourse serves the interests of abolitionists, feminists, religious leaders and governments driven by morality and fearful of immigration. It is crucial to examine the impact of policy. This policy might not address the safety of migrants in various types of work and individuals in the sex industry, since it appears to have been created to serve the interests and problems of the state, as well as the agenda of conservative feminists. In order to examine whether the operationalization of current policy will improve the conditions of individuals, these marginalized voices need to be heard. A new framework for understanding trafficking and for addressing issues of migration, labor rights and human rights needs to be provided so that feminists, NGOs, governments and individuals directly affected by policy change can engage in productive dialogue towards change.

Discussion Questions

1   *What is the abolitionist approach to prostitution?*

2   *What is the major trafficking discourse regarding the sex workers rights approach?*

3   *What is the White Slave Traffic Act?*

4   *Who was responsible for the development and support of the U.S. Trafficking policy?*

5   *What is the purpose of the Trafficking Victims Protection Act (TVPA)?*

6   *What is the Tier system?*

7   *What is the Sonagachi Project in India?*

8   *Why does the United States government prefer repressive strategies as it relates to human trafficking?*

9   *What alternative framework was suggested by the author?*

References

Agustin, L. (2000). Working in the European sex industry: Migrant possibilities (translated from the original Spanish), OFRIM/ Suplementos, 155-72. Retrieved January 18, 2006 from: http:// www.nswp.org/pdf/AGUSTIN-WORKING.PDF

Agustin, L. (2001). Sex workers and violence against women: Utopic visions or battle of the sexes? Development, Society for International Development, 44 (3).

Agustin, L. (2002). Challenging "place": Leaving home for sex. Development, 45 (1), 110-17.

Agustin, L. (2003a). A migrant world of services, social politics: International studies in gender. State and Society, 10 (3), 377-396.

Agustin, L. (2003b). Sex, gender and migrations: Facing up to ambiguous realities. Soundings, 23, Spring.

Agustin, L. (2004). Helping women who sell sex: The construction of benevolent identities. Retrieved February 5, 2006 from: http:// www. rhizomes.net / is sue 10/agustin.htm

Agustin, L. (2005). Migrants in the mistress's house: Other voices in the "trafficking" debate. Social Politics, 12 (1), 96-117.

Bindman, J., & Doezema, J. (1997). Redefining prostitution as sex work on the international agenda. Retrieved March 20, 2006 from http://www.walnet.org/csis/papers/redefining.html

Block, J. (2004). Sex trafficking: Why the faith trade is interested in the sex trade. Conscience, Summer/Autumn.

Chapkis, W. (2003). Trafficking, migration, and the law: Protecting innocents, punishing immigrants. Gender & Society, 17(6), 923-937.

Center for International Crime Prevention Report from the UN Center for International Crime Prevention (2003). Assessing transnational organized crime: Results of a pilot survey of 40 selected transnational organized criminal groups in 16 countries, Vienna.

Demirdirek, H., & Whitehead, J. (2004). Sexual encounters, migration and desire in post-Socialist context(s). Focaal-European Journal of Anthropology, 43, 3-13.

Ditmore, M., (2003). Morality in new policies addressing trafficking and sex work. "Women working to make a difference" IWPR's Seventh International Women's Policy Research Conference, June.

Ditmore, M., (2005). Trafficking in lives: How ideology shapes policy. In K. Kempadoo, J. Sanghera, & B. Pattanaik, (Eds.) Trafficking and prostitution reconsidered: New perspectives on migration, xex work and human rights. Boulder, CO: Paradigm Publishers.

Ditmore, M. & Wijers, M. (2003). The negotiations on the UN Protocol to trafficking in persons. Retrieved February 6, 2006 from: www. nswp.org/pdf/NEMESIS.PDF

Doezema, J. (1998). Forced to choose: Beyond the voluntary v. forced prostitution dichotomy. In K. Kempadoo & J. Doezema (Eds.), Global sex workers: Rights, resistance and redefinition. New York: Routledge.

Doezema, J. (2001). Ouch! Western feminists' "wounded attachment" to the third world prostitute. Feminist Review, 67, 16-38.

Doezema, J. (2002a). Who gets to choose? Coercion, consent and the UN Trafficking Protocol. Gender and Development, 10 (1).

Doezema, J. (2002b). The ideology of trafficking. Center for Ethics and Value Inquiry Work Conference "Human Trafficking', Ghent University.

Enloe, C. (2000). Maneuvers: The international politics of militarizing women's lives. Berkeley, CA: University of California Press.

Foucault, M. (1972). The archaeology of knowledge. London: Routledge.

Hughes, D. (2002). Supplying women for the sex industry: Trafficking from the Russian Federation. Sexualities in Post-communism, 119.

Hughes, D., & Denisova, T. (2001). The transnational political criminal nexus of trafficking in women from Ukraine. Trends in Organized Crime, 6 (3-4).

Kapur, R. (2005). Travel plans: Human rights of transnational migrants, Harvard Human Rights Journal, 18, 107-138.

Kempadoo, K. (2001a). Freelancers, temporary wives, and beach boys: Researching sex-work in the Caribbean. Feminist Review, 67, 39-62.

Kempadoo, K. (2001b). Women of color and the global sex trade: Transnational feminist perspectives. Meridians: Feminism, Race, Transnationalism, 1(2), 28-51.

Kempadoo, K. (2005). Introduction: From moral panic to global justice: Changing perspectives on trafficking. In K. Kempadoo, J. Sanghera & B. Pattanaik (Eds.), Trafficking and prostitution reconsidered: New perspectives on migration, sex work, and human rights. Boulder, CO: Paradigm Publishers.

Kempadoo, K., & Doezema, J. (1998). Global sex workers: Rights, resistance, and redefinition. New York & London: Routledge.

Kempadoo, K., Sanghera, J., & Pattanaik, B. (2005). Trafficking and prostitution reconsidered: New perspectives on migration, sex work and human rights. Boulder, CO: Paradigm Publishers.

Long, L. (2004). Anthropological perspectives on the trafficking of women for sexual exploitation. International Migration, 42 (1), 531.

Melzer, E. (2005). Trafficking in politics: Bush's strong rhetoric on Sex slavery masks policy failures, (2005, March 14), In These Times. Retrieved January 3, 2006 from: http://www.inthesetimes.com/site/main/article/2007/

Miller, A. (2004). Sexuality, violence against women, and human rights: Women make demands and ladies get protection. Health and Human Rights, 7(2), 17-47.

Mohanty, C. (1991). Under Western eyes: Feminist scholarship and colonial discourses. In C. Mohanty, A. Russo & L. Torres (Eds.), Third world women and the politics of feminism. Bloomington & Indianapolis: Indiana University Press.

Musacchio, V. (2004). Migration, prostitution and trafficking in women: An overview. German Law Journal, 5 (9), 1015-1030.

O'Neill, T. (2001). "Selling girls in Kuwait": Domestic labour migration and trafficking discourse in Nepal. Anthropologica, XLIII, 153-164.

Outshoorn, J. (2005). The political debates on prostitution and trafficking of women, social politics: International studies in gender. State and Society, 12 (1), 141-155.

Parpart, J., Connelly, P., & Barriteau, E. (2000). Theoretical perspectives on gender and development, International Development Research Centre, Ontario, Canada.

Pattanaik, B. (2002). Where do we go from here? In S. Thorbek & B. Pattanaik (Eds.), Transnational prostitution: Changing patterns in global context. London, New York: Zed Books.

Piper, N. (2005). A problem by a different name? A review of research on trafficking in South-East Asia and Oceania. International Migration, 43 (1/2), 203-233.

Protocol, United Nations, (2000). Protocol to prevent, suppress and punish trafficking in persons, especially women and children, supplementing the United Nations Convention Against Transnational Organized Crime. Retrieved November 3, 2005 from: www.uncjin.org.

Raymond, J., Hughes, D., & Gomez, J. (2001). Sex trafficking of women in the United States: International and domestic trends. Coalition Against Trafficking of Women, March.

Saunders, P. (2005). Traffic violations: Determining the meaning of violence in sexual trafficking versus sex work. Journal of Interpersonal Violence, 20 (3), 343-360.

Saunders, P. & Soderlund, G. (2003). Traveling threats: Sexuality, gender and the ebb and flow of trafficking as discourse. Canadian Woman Studies, 22, 35-46.

Shah, S. (2004). Prostitution, sex work and violence: Discursive and political contexts for five texts on paid sex, 1987-2001. Gender and History, 16 (3), 794-812.

State Legislatures, (2005). Violence Against Women Act, National Conference U. S. Department of Health and Human Services, (2004). Trafficking Victims Protection Act of 2000 fact sheet: Rescue and restore victims of human trafficking.

U.S. Department of State, (2003). Victims of Trafficking and Violence Protection Act of 2000: Trafficking in persons report, Bureau of Public Affairs.

Wijers, M. (2001). Criminal, victim, social evil or working girl: Legal approaches to prostitution and their impact on sex workers. International Seminar on Prostitution in Madrid, Institute of Women.

Wijers, M., & Van Doorninck, M. (2005). What's wrong with the anti-trafficking framework? Background Paper for the "European Conference on Sex Work, Human Rights, Labour and Migration, ICRSE (International Committee on the Rights of Sex Workers in Europe). Retrieved February 15, 2006 from: http://www.sexworkeurope.org/

20
GLOBALIZING SEXUAL EXPLOITATION: SEX TOURISM AND THE TRAFFIC IN WOMEN

Sheila Jeffreys, *Department of Politics and Science, University of Melbourne*

Introduction

Today there are many forces at work in the normalization of the international sex industry (Jeffreys, 1997). The sex industry has become immensely profitable, providing considerable resources, not just to individuals and networks involved in trafficking women but to governments who have come to depend on sex industry revenue. One aspect of the industry in particular that governments have come to depend upon for revenue is sex tourism (Bishop and Robinson, 1998). It is the concern of this paper to present a critical analysis of the arguments of the normalizers, whether sex industrialists or their spokespersons, that sex tourism or other forms of prostitution should come to be seen as a legitimate leisure industry, one in which women and children are literally 'men's leisure'.

Whilst child sex tourism has come to be seen as a major concern within the tourism industry and the human rights community since the 1989 United Nations Convention on the Rights of the Child, adult sex tourism has not been regarded as unacceptable in the same way. In late November 1998 I was invited to speak at a conference organized by the European Commission entitled *First European Meeting of the Main Partners in the Fight Against Child Sex Tourism*. It was a conference embedded in the Brussels Travel Fair and aimed at the tourism industry. The centrepiece of the conference was a video clip made by the Non-government organization (NGO) Terre des Hommes with funding from Lufthansa. The clip was meant to educate potential child sex abusers on long-haul flights against abusive behaviour. The video clip showed children's toys and gave ages of 4 and 7 for the victims. This representation of child sex tourism as the abuse of very young children will limit its effectiveness. As Julia O'Connell Davidson, co-author of the ECPAT (End Child Prostitution, Pornography and Trafficking) regional reports on child sex tourism (Davidson and Taylor, 1996), pointed out the vast majority of the 'children' abused in child sex tourism are young teenage girls who are integrated into the bars and brothels of destination countries and used by situational abusers i.e. men who neither know nor care how young the girls are. Davidson and I argued that child sex tourism cannot, therefore, reasonably be effectively tackled as if it were a discrete phenomenon. It is but one aspect of adult sex tourism, which is but one form of the international prostitution industry and only a challenge to this prostitution industry would be effective in fighting child sex tourism. Other speakers at the conference did not make these connections and this could suggest that there is a belief that adult sex tourism is too established to challenge, or even a desire by some to protect the profits that accrue to tourism operators who service sex tourists.

Melissa Farley, co-author of an important paper on the damaging effects of prostitution on prostituted women (Farley and Hotaling, 1995), has recently suggested to me that the expression 'sex tourism' is a euphemism. This makes sense. The term 'prostitution tourism' is more accurate because it does not suggest fun and entertainment so much as the abuse of women, and this term will be used henceforth.

In this paper the arguments are rehearsed of feminist antiviolence theorists and prostitution on prostituted survivor organizations who make the case that men's prostitution behavior should be seen as sexual violence and a violation of women's human rights and compare them with the arguments of those who consider that prostitution should be considered legitimate work for women. The increasing internationalization of the sex industry and the way in which prostitution tourism fits into this will be described. The Philippines will be used as an example of how prostitution tourism is organized and conducted. Then the strategies towards trafficking, prostitution tourism and prostitution proposed by groups of feminists in the human rights community who take quite opposed positions are considered. In a concluding section it is argued that prostitution tourism needs to be countered through human rights mechanisms which challenge all forms of men's prostitution behavior towards women and children as sexual violence.

Prostitution is Commercial Sexual Violence

From the nineteenth century to the 1970s feminist ideas on prostitution were consistent. Prostitution was seen by feminists from Josephine Butler to Kate Millett as arising from women's subordination and as constituting the violation of women (see Jeffreys, 1985, 1997). In the late 1980s and 1990s some feminist thinkers adopted the views promoted by some prostitutes' rights organizations and industry representatives that prostitution should be seen simply as legitimate work, as 'choice' for women or even as just 'sex'. The pro-prostitution lobby group, COYOTE (Cast Off Your Old Tired Ethics), in the USA has been promoting these ideas since the early 1980s (Jeness, 1993). Feminist theorists who have taken up these ideas in recent years include Wendy Chapkis (1997) and Jill Nagle, editor of the 1997 *Whores and Other Feminists*, who explains in her introduction that she includes only contributions that are positive about prostitution because she considers prostitution to constitute 'feminism in action.'

The justifications of prostitution on the grounds that it is women's 'choice', legitimate 'work' and just 'sex' are hugely problematic (these ideas are further discussed in Jeffreys, 1997). Women's 'choice' of prostitution is socially and politically constructed out of poverty, child sexual abuse, homelessness, family obligation. Arguments as to women's 'choice' are victim-blaming, like the arguments as to why women 'stay' in violent relationships. Such arguments remove responsibility from the perpetrators and obscure the unequal power relationships involved. Arguments that prostitution is legitimate 'work', or even skilled work (Perkins and Bennett, 1985), ignore what distinguishes prostitution and other forms of direct exploitation of women's bodies so significantly from other forms of work. Prostitution and reproductive surrogacy are the only kinds of 'work' that require only that a woman's body be present: she does not have to be able to move or even be conscious. To say that prostitution is just sex is to accept that the use of the body of a woman who is dissociating to survive, with no concern for her personhood or pleasure, is what sex can reasonably be expected to be. In fact it is precisely the 'sex' of male supremacy that feminists have been seeking for 100 years to overthrow in favour of egalitarian sexual practice.

Since the late 1980s an international movement has developed which maintains a more traditional feminist understanding of prostitution and seeks to combat attempts to normalize prostitution. This movement is composed of survivors of prostitution such as those who have set up organizations in the US to help women exit prostitution and to re-educate the male abusers, such as WHISPER (Women Hurt in Systems of Prostitution Engaged in Revolt), and SAGE (Standing Against Global Exploitation). These survivors have been working with feminist activists such as Kathleen Barry and others in the Coalition Against Trafficking in Women to develop an international network aimed at ending men's abuse of women in prostitution. This movement considers men's abuse of women in prostitution to constitute a form of men's sexual violence against women.

The integral links between prostitution and violence against women have been recognized by feminist researchers for many years. In the last decade, as well as pointing out that very large percentages of prostituted women were seasoned by being sexually abused in childhood, that prostituted women suffer a great amount of rape and violence that is not paid for, including death from the men who abuse them, some feminists are asserting that prostitution constitutes sexual violence against women in and of itself. Cecilie Hoigard and Liv Finstad concluded from their research in Oslo that prostitution constituted a 'gross form of violence'. 'The impoverishment and destruction of the women's emotional lives makes it reasonable, in our eyes, to say that customers practice gross violence against prostitutes' (Hoigard and Finstad, 1992, p. 115). Fractured jaws would heal, they said, but 'Regaining self-respect and recreating an emotional life is far more difficult.' This discovery was a surprise to them. It was '*new* knowledge' and the 'most important discovery' they made in their research.

This argument is put forward very effectively in the work of Evelina Giobbe in 'Prostitution: buying the right to rape' (Giobbe, 1991). In prostitution, she argues, 'crimes against women and children become a commercial enterprise'. These crimes include child sexual abuse when a man uses a juvenile prostitute, battery when a prostituted woman is used in sadomasochistic sex scenes, and sexual harassment and rape 'When a john compels a woman to submit to his sexual demands as a condition of "employment".' According to Giobbe's analysis the exchange of money does not transform the violence of the acts involved into something else.

> The fact that a john gives money to a woman or a child for submitting to these acts does not alter the fact that he is committing child sexual abuse, rape, and battery; it merely redefines these crimes as prostitution. (Giobbe, 1991, p. 146)

She concludes that prostitution is the commerce of sexual abuse and inequality. Kathleen Barry identifies the sex that men buy in prostitution as the 'same sex they take in rape—sex that is disembodied, enacted on the bodies of women who, for the men, do not exist as human beings, and the men are always in control' (Barry, 1995, p. 36).

The male sexual behaviour involved in using women in prostitution includes several forms of male sexual violence. The basic male sexual practice carried out upon prostituted women is what can be called 'unwanted sexual intercourse'. In heterosexual relationships this term can be used to describe those experiences of sexual intercourse in which a woman complies with a man's demands without being willing but also without acknowledging to herself a lack of consent. She will not call what is done to her rape because this would signify lack of consent, though she may bitterly resent it. This experience correlates well with prostitution in which women have their bodies used in ways they cannot refuse since their livelihoods depend upon it, but which they would never tolerate otherwise. In both practices the male perpetrators inflict sexual acts upon a woman with no respect for her personhood or her pleasure.

The other most common form of sexual violence to be paid for in prostitution is sexual harassment. Sexual harassment is one of those forms of abuse that has only been given a name and recognizable form through feminism. Catharine MacKinnon has been particularly influential in turning what feminists were beginning to define as sexual harassment into something that was actionable at law in situations, such as work or education, where it could be defined as an issue of sex discrimination (MacKinnon, 1987, p. 104). The British antiviolence feminist theorist, Liz Kelly, defines sexual harassment as including 'a variable combination of visual, verbal and physical forms of abuse'. Kelly found that the work situations in which women were most likely to experience harassment were those which were most sexualized. A woman survivor of stripping describes the abusive behaviour of the audience, 'I wish I had a pound for every time I got called a slag ... some of the things they would say were *really disgusting*. They'd do things like grab hold of a girl and try and push a bottle up her' (Kelly, 1989, p. 105).

Through different areas of the sex industry a variety of forms of sexual harassment which cause distress to women are normalized by being paid for. Prostituted women have to accept a certain amount of hands on sexual harassment as part of the job. They have to accept visual harassment too, in which they are reduced to sexual objects by the dominant male stare as men select the women they will use in brothels and on the street. A French prostituted woman, explaining what it felt like to be chosen in this way in a brothel said it was 'revolting, it's sickening, it's terrible for the women' (Jaget, 1980, p. 75). Visual harassment is what is purchased by men through stripping and tabletop dancing. Verbal harassment can also be bought through the sex industry's provision of phone sex lines. These sex lines institutionalize the practice of 'obscene phone calls.'

Effects of Prostitution and Sexual Violence

Feminist scholars and activists are also starting to define prostitution as men's sexual violence because its effects upon prostituted women replicate the documented effects found in feminist work on forms of sexual violence such as rape, incest, sexual harassment and marital rape. Evelina Giobbe argues that prostitution resembles rape in the shocking similarity of its effects, as revealed in the WHISPER Oral History Project. These effects included feelings of humiliation, degradation, defilement and dirtiness. The prostituted women experienced similar difficulties in establishing intimate relationships with men. They experienced disdain and hatred towards men. They suffered negative effects on their sexuality, flashbacks and nightmares as well as lingering fears and deep emotional pain that often resembled grieving (Giobbe, 1991, p. 155). Another effect she identifies is suicide. She reports that figures from public hospitals show that 15% of all suicide victims are prostitutes and one survey of call girls revealed that 75% had attempted suicide. These effects of prostitution, she points out, do not support the idea that prostitution is a victimless crime.

Prostituted women in her study blamed themselves for the damage they suffered, assuming that they were 'not doing it right' just as battered wives routinely blame themselves for the violence they suffer. Their sense of their own valuelessness was reinforced in prostitution because of the way the men treated them. The male abusers were so determined to treat the prostituted women they were using as non-persons that they did not even notice when women were crying as they performed their tricks. The only parallel to this trauma, she suggests, is that found in victims of serious sexual abuse, rape and battery.

Feminist psychoanalysts and psychologists, such as Judith Herman, have applied the concept of post-traumatic stress disorder (PTSD), accepted by mainstream psychologists as resulting from other forms of torture and imprisonment, to incest and domestic violence (Herman, 1994). One way in which feminists are currently seeking to show that men's use of women in prostitution constitutes sexual violence is in identifying the resulting damage of long term prostitution abuse as PTSD. Melissa Farley and Norma Hotaling gave a paper on this topic at the NGO Forum of the Fourth World Conference on Women at Beijing in 1995. They explain that their objective is to provide evidence for the harm intrinsic to prostitution (Farley and Hotaling, 1995, p. 1). They consider that prostituted women, like the victims of hostage situations and torture, suffer the multiple stressors that cause post-traumatic stress disorder. They found that overall 41% of the 130 prostituted persons they surveyed met the criteria for diagnosis of PTSD. This compares with an incidence among battered women in shelters of from 45% to 84% and amongst Vietnam veterans of 15%.

The practice of dissociation which prostituted women employ to protect their sense of self from violation is so similar to the dissociation employed by sexually abused children that Judith Herman (1994) describes, that it provides good evidence that the two experiences are similarly abusive. Hoigard and Finstad asked their interviewees in some detail about the defence mechanisms they used. They wanted to know 'How do you avoid prostituting yourself when you prostitute yourself?' and considered this to be the 'fundamental question for prostitutes around the world' (Hoigard and Finstad, 1992, p. 64). Prostituted women, they explain, have worked out an ingenious, complex system to protect 'the real me, the self, the personality from being invaded and destroyed by customers' (Ibid, p. 64). As they point out, literature on prostitution which has considered these mechanisms reports remarkably similar techniques (Jaget, 1980; McLeod, 1982). The women use different methods to cut off, such as thinking about something else, using alcohol, Valium or other drugs. A young woman who phoned and had a conversation with the author in a New Zealand radio station studio, whilst being interviewed about prostitution, explained that a psychiatric nurse also employed in her brothel had taught her to form a different personality with a new name to go into and out of at will (personal communication, Sarah, April 1998). Thus she was able to see the abuse as happening to this other person and not to her. For survivors of childhood

sexual abuse and for prostitution survivors the effects of this practice are
to damage women's relationships with their bodies and with others.

Norwegian researchers Cecilie Hoigard and Liv Finstad are able to
describe the damage done to prostituted women in Oslo in considerable
detail because of the in-depth interviews they conducted with women over
a number of years. Their respondents reported destruction of their sex
lives. One woman described her experience of seeking a sexual
relationship whilst in prostitution, 'You're a piece of shit, and you make
yourself sick ... I've thrown up during sex, just started throwing up
without thinking that it's been awful. It's just happened' (Hoigard and
Finstad, 1992, p. 109). Others speak of losing the ability to orgasm and
having to fake it, they talk of feeling they have become hard and cold. One
said 'I'm only the genitals that they use' (Ibid, p. 112). They spoke of the
inability to feel anything, not necessarily because of the unpaid 'violence'
they experienced but because of the 'regular, daily tricks' (Ibid, p. 112).

Proponents of the normalization of prostitution proclaim that
prostitution can be made safe for women once the 'stigma' of prostitution
is removed and it is made respectable and accepted (Pheterson, 1996).
The state of Victoria in Australia has gone well down the road to the
normalization of prostitution through a policy of legalization of licensed
brothels. Brothel prostitution, however, does not provide a solution to
the violence of prostitution. A prostitution survivor in the Melbourne
branch of the Coalition Against Trafficking in Women demonstrated just
how violating the ordinary acts of brothel prostitution are, whilst
describing the events of a half hour booking. She explains that the
challenge is to isolate the most violating act, penetration, to the last five
minutes. Thus she seeks to delay penetration through the gift of the gab,
at which she is skilled, and through prolonging the massage stage.
Nonetheless, the massage is a problem in itself. As she sits astride a
client he will seek to swing his arms back to grab at her breasts. To
avoid this she will get down and seek to conduct the massage from a
suitable distance. The best sort of booking, she explains, is the one in
which the man is drunk and can be persuaded to fall asleep in the spa
so that no violating behaviour ensues (personal communication, October
1997). It is hard to imagine another form of occupation so violating that
the practitioner seeks at all costs not to be subjected to it. Hairdressers
are unlikely to behave in this way.

Causes and Extent of the Internationalization of Prostitution

It is a matter of considerable concern to feminist commentators such as
Kathleen Barry, that prostitution is presently being industrialized and
internationalized (Barry, 1995). In the industrialization of prostitution

women who once had a limited ability to fix their own hours and have some control over their exploitation when not under the direct control of pimps, are not becoming subject to the exploitation of big business interests. In Melbourne, for example, since the legalization of brothel prostitution in the mid-1980s, big business has moved into the sex industry. The largest Melbourne brothel, The Daily Planet, has been quoted on the Stock Exchange. Also in Melbourne, as part of the new big business prostitution, a new brothel was opened to serve the new large scale casino, called The Boardroom to indicate its respectable and corporate status and to appeal to corporate man, the brothel provides male, female and trans-sexual 'service providers'. In Asian economies, prostitution is playing a more and more significant part. A 1998 International Labour Organization report estimated that prostitution accounted for between 2 and 14% of the economy in four Asian countries, Thailand, Indonesia, Malaysia and the Philippines (Lim, 1998). In the burgeoning trade of international trafficking in women, large-scale crime networks have evolved which find it profitable to traffic women into destinations worldwide (De Stoop, 1992). These developments indicate the extent to which the individual women and boys used in prostitution are now subject to the exploitation of international capitalism.

The internationalization of prostitution is being effected through a greatly increased trafficking in women. Trafficking for prostitution is becoming a major concern of human rights organizations and feminist activists as the size of the problem and its grievous effects on the lives of women and children are becoming better known. The shape of the traffic in women differs in significant ways from the situation discovered by the League of Nations in its reports between the two world wars (League of Nations, 1927, 1933). In this period the issue of trafficking in women for prostitution had its own committee at the League through which feminists worked to outlaw men's abuse of women in prostitution in general (Jeffreys, 1997). The Report on trafficking in the East found that the traffic consisted of 'a certain movement of occidental prostitutes to the Orient' but 'hardly any in the other direction' (League of Nations, 1933, p. 21). The most serious problem of occidental women concerned Russian refugee women in North China and Manchuria.

Most of the traffic was from one Asian country to another, the largest group being Chinese women, then Japanese, Koreans, Siamese, Filipinos, Indians, Iraqis, Persians and Syrians. The industrialization and internationalization of prostitution are linked to several developments since World War Two, including prostitution tourism, which have affected both the supply of women vulnerable to being trafficked into prostitution and the degree of demand from men to use such women.

The supply of women is greatly increased by mass migration resulting from destabilizing economic development. Nelleke van der Vleuten explains that the world-wide traffic in women 'must be analyzed in terms of the structural inequality between Third World and industrialized countries' (van der Vleuten, 1991, p. 5). It is a result, she says, of the increasing internationalization of the world economy in which local communities in the Third World become an integral part of the industrialized world, becoming dependent on social change in industrialized countries. People in the Third World lose traditional resources, such as land, paid labour or other means income and a permanent subproletariat is created with the growth of slums on the outskirts of towns and an increase in child labour. The consequences are greatest for women and girls who have to take care of children and family because of tradition or the disappearance of male support. Migration from rural areas to the cities seems one of the few possible ways for these girls and women to survive.

Another force creating the supply is warfare. Civil wars have become endemic in countries released from the rule of colonialism. In Burma, for instance, Karen refugee women and girls are vulnerable to being trafficked into prostitution in Thailand (Foundation for Women, 1994). Another is the development of new market economies in socialist and formerly socialist countries. This has led to a dramatic expansion in prostitution as poverty has increased and old ways of life have been disrupted. Well-organized networks have developed to traffic women and girls into prostitution in Vietnam after the introduction of economic reforms there (Foundation for Women, 1994). The number of prostituted women in Ho Chi Minh City, for instance, has risen from 10 000 to 50 000 (Santos, 1995). In Europe too, the breakdown of communism has led to 'professional criminal organizations' trafficking in women from Russia, Poland, Bulgaria, Romania, the former Yugoslavia and the Czech and Slovak Republics (Foundation for Women, 1994). All of these forces creating the supply of women depend upon the low status of women. In countries such as Bangladesh, where the status of women is in decline, the problem is invariably heightened (Kendar, 1994, p. 8)

Military prostitution and sex tourism have increased the global demand to use women in prostitution. Massive prostitution industries have developed in response to the large US military presence in Saigon, Thailand and the Philippines (Enloe, 1983, Sturdevant and Stoltzfus, 1992). This has led to increased local prostitution and a new phenomenon has developed, which did not exist in earlier times, prostitution tourism. Prostitution tourism is a recent phenomenon. Asian women caught up in the traffic in women in the east in the interwar period did not service occidental tourists as might happen in today's sex tourism, but went to foreign countries 'in search of clients among their own countrymen abroad' (League of Nations, 1933, p. 22). Nowhere were there found 'attempts to provide exotic novelty to brothel clients by offering them women of alien races' (Ibid, p. 22).

Affluence and leisure, the ease of communications and foreign travel, the construction of foreign prostituted women as exotic and desirable in pornography and the deliberate policies of the governments of poor countries to develop prostitution tourism as a means to gain foreign exchange, have contributed to this phenomenon (Truong, 1990). The contribution of prostitution tourism to the economies of destination countries can be considerable. Ryan Bishop and Lillian Robinson, in their new book on sex tourism in Thailand, do not seek to estimate what proportion of the worth of the tourism industry is attributable specifically to prostitution tourism, but clearly consider it significant when they say that 'A $4 billion per year tourist industry is the linchpin of the modernization process called the "Thai Economic Miracle". And the linchpin of that industry is sex' (Bishop and Robinson, 1998). Prostitution tourism can be identified in rich countries too, however. It is a part of the prostitution industry in all those areas where tourists or visiting businessmen are offered women. For example, tabletop clubs are advertised at the baggage carousels in some airport.

It is possible that the outrage of western men confronted with changes in the status of women resulting from the women's liberation movement in their countries, has exacerbated the desire to use foreign women in prostitution and as mail order brides. In her interviews with British sex tourists, Julia O'Connell Davidson found, 'Almost all the sex tourists interviewed spoke with great bitterness about white women's power to deny them sexual access'(Davidson, 1994, p. 12). Currently the international organization of prostitution tourism is facilitated by the internet.

Some internet sites are dedicated to the trade in male order brides. This trade is mainly in women from Asia, particularly the Philippines, Thailand, Korea, and Sri Lanka. In the Philippines in 1988–89 there was a 94% increase in the number of Filipino women migrating as fiancés or spouses to Japanese, Australian, German, Taiwanese, British, and US destinations. In the late 1980s and 1990s there has been a growing dissemination and diversification of pornography through cable television, dial-a-porn, home video and computers. Trafficking in women on the Internet in the form of the World Sex Guide, introducing johns to where and how to purchase women and girls worldwide, conversations between johns about using women and young girls, interactive pornography where men can instruct live women through the Internet to strip and perform sexual acts, and websites devoted to buying mail-order brides and to prostitution tourism have aided the organization and global scope of the sex industry (Hughes, 1996).

Russian women are vulnerable to trafficking because of the economic destruction of Russia following the introduction of rogue capitalism. The variety of destinations and uses to which these Russian women are being put illustrates the breadth and brutality of the international sex industry. One group of Russian women are being exploited in pornography videos sold through internet outlets, usually in the USA, to users all over the world. Some appear, for instance, on bestiality pornography sites. On one such site several Russian speaking women are sexually abused in a video entitled Gorilla Wives (Coalition Against Trafficking in Women (Australia) Newsletter, No 2, 1998, p. 2). The description explains that these women are sexually penetrated by a gorilla and a chimpanzee. The only English word they use, which is 'daddy', is addressed to the gorilla. The video portrays, then, incest/ bestiality pornography. The extreme form of sexual violence involved in such videos indicates the extreme circumstances in which impoverished Russian women can now find themselves.

Trafficking in women for prostitution is a problem in all regions of the world. Both Europe and Asia have considerable industries based upon the traffic in women for prostitution. The Netherlands is one of the main destinations within Europe for the traffic, as well as being a destination for European prostitution tourism. Nelleke van der Vleuten explains that more and more non-European women are coming to work in brothels and sex-clubs in The Netherlands (van der Vleuten, 1991, p. 3). In the Netherlands the percentage of non-Europeans among prostituted women is usually 30–40% and in some places at least 60%. The estimated total of Dutch and foreign prostituted women is 20,000. Fifty per cent of windows in Amsterdam are rented out to non-European women and there are 3,000 Latin-American prostituted women in Amsterdam. Prostitution, van der Vleuten, says, has changed and taken on an international dimension. It is large-scale and highly industrialized.

The Dutch sex industry is part of the European sex market. The majority of women travel between brothels and sex clubs in different European countries. Foreign women are the lowest in the hierarchy of prostitution. They work in unsanitary conditions and are isolated both culturally and socially. They are often illegal immigrants and have no freedom of movement. Health services cannot reach them and many work without condoms for financial reasons. A Dutch government report says many women are in a 'criminal climate, where false pretexts are used to seduce women' who are 'forced into prostitution and kept there' (van der Vleuten, 1991, p. 4).

The western human rights organization, Human Rights Watch/Asia, has published two studies of the traffic in women which describe in detail aspects of the traffic in Asia (Human Rights Watch/Asia, 1994 and 1995). *A Modern Form of Slavery* looks at the traffic of Burmese women into Thailand and *Rape for Profit* at the traffic of Nepali women into India. Non-government organizations estimate Bombay's prostituted women at 100 000 of whom up to half are Nepali. Twenty per cent of Bombay's brothel population is thought to be girls under 18 and half that population may be infected with the HIV virus (Human Rights Watch, 1995, p. 1). The demand for Nepali girls, especially those with fair skin

and Mongolian features, continues to increase. The Indian Council of
Medical Research estimates the total number of prostituted women in
India at about one million, of whom 200,000 are likely to be Nepali. But
a voluntary organization that serves the country's prostituted women
estimates that there were more than eight million brothel workers and
7.5 million call girls in 1992 (Ibid, p. 1). The age of Nepali girls is
dropping partly because fear of the HIV virus causes men to demand
'clean' women. The average age of recruitment is now 10–14, which
means that some are younger than 10. The estimated number of
prostituted women in Thailand is 800,000 to two million of whom 20,000
are Burmese.

The Human Rights Watch reports explain that men's use of women
in prostitution is often a death sentence for the women because the male
abusers pass on the HIV virus. Far from prostituted women being a
source of AIDS they are the recipients of it. Medical researchers have
hypothesized that the thinner mucous membrane of the genital tract in
girls is a less efficient barrier to viruses, and that young women may
produce less of the mucus which has an immune function (Human
Rights Watch, 1995, p. 66). The men's abuse of the trafficked women
causes them to develop friction sores of the vagina. The rate of infection
is related to the number of johns via the rate of associated vaginal
abrasion. The women are not usually permitted time off for the injuries
to heal. The injuries themselves make HIV transmission easier. Condom
usage makes the friction problem worse. The majority of Burmese
women in closed Thai brothels who started out as young, 'clean' virgins,
become infected about six months after entry (Human Rights Watch,
1994, p. 128). Of the 19 Burmese women and girls interviewed by
Human Rights Watch who had been tested for HIV, fourteen were found
to be infected with the virus. The rate of infection was roughly three
times higher than among non-trafficked prostituted women in Thailand.

Trafficked women in India and Thailand are imprisoned mainly
through debt bondage, which is understood to be a human rights abuse
and a practice akin to slavery, even in customary international law. Debt
bondage is incurred when the victim's family members, 'friends' or other
persons who demand to be repaid for transport costs, receive payment
from traffickers or brothel owners. The victim is told she must work to
pay off the debt but usually has no idea how much the debt is, how much
she earns or how long she must work to pay it off. A sum which might
have been paid off in a few months' work is usually, through this ruse,
employed to keep a victim in brothels for years. Sometimes the women
and girls are simply kidnapped and sold.

Sex Tourism in the Philippines

The Philippines is an important destination for sex tourists and the
situation in this country will be used to illustrate some of the dynamics

of prostitution tourism. In 1995 I was fortunate enough to take part in an Exposure/Study Tour of sex tourism in the Philippines organized through the Centres for Philippine Concerns in Australia and women's NGOs in the Philippines, particularly Women's Education, Development, Productivity and Research Organizations (WEDPRO) and Coalition Against Trafficking in Women (CATW). The object of the fortnight's tour was to expose Australian women to the behaviour of Australian men in the organization of and participation in prostitution tourism. As the introduction to the report on the tour explains:

> ... the sex tourism industry matters. It is big, it is wealthy, and it is damaging. It thrives on the poverty of the Philippines, and on the racism and sexism that exist in Australia, New Zealand and the Philippines. It exposes women and girls to violence and humiliation, and leaves them in it, day after day, year after year, until it has no further use for them. It paints a picture of the Philippines as a nation of available, submissive women, who can be fucked, beaten, married, discarded, divorced, killed. (Distor and Hunt (eds) 1996)

Prostitution tourism in the Philippines originated in the construction of a massive sex industry to service the American military bases. This military prostitution has spawned a considerable domestic prostitution and prostitution tourism industry. The practices are perceived as chilling in their brutality. Filipino women describe what they understand as the abuse by their American johns such as the favourite practice of 'three holes' in Let the Good Times Roll (Sturdevant and Stoltzfus, 1992). This latter practice connotes the use of a woman as an object with three convenient orifices which can all be used sexually. Women and bars were advertised to Americans as threeholers. The cruelty of this practice is described by Madelin who explains that she went with an American because she was pregnant and needed money, ' "He wanted to do things to me that I didn't like, such as three holes." She fought ... "He was choking me ... I was getting weak. I was having difficulty breathing" ' (Ibid, p. 61–2). This woman was rescued because hotel employees heard the noise of the struggle. Another American behaved in a similar way: 'He turned me over and was entering my ass. I lost it then. I fought ... I had taken part in the wrestling in the bar before' (Ibid, p. 62). The Americans demanded the institution of the practice of boxing and wrestling between women in the bars. They found the spectacle of women hurting each other exciting.

Another woman, Lita, describes her first time in prostitution with an American when she was 14 and a virgin. 'I really didn't want to, but he forced me. It was very painful. He tried to undress me but I wouldn't get undressed. There was a lot of blood on my clothes' (Ibid, p. 80). Her third

American behaved in the same way, 'He had already had sex with me. His penis couldn't enter because it was too large. I cried ... He pushed my head into the pillow so I wouldn't be able to yell ... He did all kinds of things to me. I cried' (Ibid, p. 80). Glenda, aged 30, reports of her experience in being used by Americans: 'I didn't know about blow jobs and three holes... It was anal sex that made me cry' (Ibid, p. 121). When another of her 'three holes' was used it was equally distressing: 'The first time I gave a blow job, I threw up outside. I didn't know that throwing up outside is banned. I carried a small towel with me after that' (Ibid, p. 122).

The American military abandoned their bases in 1991 as a result of local opposition and the Pinatubo volcanic explosion (Santos, 1992). The US government has recently negotiated a new treaty with the Philippines which will allow for American troops to return, not to bases, but to privileged access to 22 areas for rest and recreation, and potentially prostitution. In the intervening period brutal prostitution practices were continued through an expansion in prostitution tourism.

Prostitution tourism has been promoted by the Government in the Philippines because of its profitability. Income generated from visitor arrivals in 1992 was US$1.67 billion and in 1993 was US$2.12 billion. The bulk of tourists are men (63.7%) and have a median age of 38 years (Distor and Hunt, 1996). Women and children are vulnerable to prostitution because of the extreme poverty in which they live. Seventy-five per cent of the population live below the poverty line. The minimum wage of 145 pesos a day (nearly US$5 a day) contrasts with the daily cost of living for a family of six – 244.25 pesos. The combined unemployment and underemployment rate in the country is around 40–50%.

One of the areas we visited on the tour was Angeles City. The town owes its existence to the servicing, including through prostitution, of personnel stationed at Clark Air Force Base. When the Americans withdrew there was a hiatus in the sex industry in the city which was quickly filled by Australian entrepreneurs and Australian sex tourists. At least 80% of the 152 nightclubs and other entertainment spots are owned and operated by Australians. There are no beaches or views in Angeles City, only prostitution, and almost all hotels and bars are dedicated to that end. Australians formed the largest number out of the 120,000 tourists who visited the area in 1994 (Distor and Hunt, p. 72). Agencies in Australia arrange package tours for sex tourists to the city, amongst other destinations. Australian sex tourists are between the ages of 25 and 50 years old and are mostly working class.

As the study tour report points out, the majority of the women in the bars servicing sex tourists are very young, barely teenagers. In one bar a group of such young girls sat in a corner playing cats' cradle between sets on the dancing stage. Prostitution tourism in the Philippines works through the provision of a companion for the entire holiday or/and the buying of women and girls in bars through the payment of bar fines. The bars service different socioeconomic segments of men. Those servicing

Japanese and Taiwanese sex tourists are the most expensive and luxurious. The next layer services European and Austalasian tourists. The lowest level of bar, with no sanitation, services working class Filipino men.

In the bars groups of young women sway slightly, it would be hard to call it dancing since it is performed with such reluctance and embarrassment, on a stage in underwear or bikinis. Such is the modesty of Filipino women that they are unlikely to go into the sea without a T-shirt. The distress of the undressed dancers must therefore be acute. The tourist selects a girl and asks to buy her a 'ladies drink' and she then sits with him at a table. Girls sitting with Australian and European men showed by their body language, leaning as far away as possible, how distasteful was the idea of physical contact with these men. Men who so desired could buy the woman for the night or for the day by paying a barfine to the bar cashier of which half would go to the girl.

Girls were seen exiting bars with the men, and walking on the beach or sitting in cafes with them still seeking to minimize physical contact. Women's NGOs in the Philippines, and Filipino expatriots in the countries which send prostitution tourists are determined to end the practice because it harms generations of Filipino women who are caught up in prostitution and because it harms the status of Filipino women in general. How might this be most effectively achieved?

How to End Sex Tourism?

Prostitution tourism is but one form of the international prostitution industry and can only be challenged by challenging men's right to use women in prostitution at all. But challenging prostitution is becoming more difficult as it becomes industrialized, and as governments and sex industrialists become more invested in its defense. Presently the issue of how to deal with the traffic in women and children internationally is the focus of heated debate in international fora.

In the international human rights arena the ideas of the normalizers, of pro-prostitution lobby-groups which defend prostitution have been adopted by some Dutch feminist legal theorists who argue that the only way to address the traffic in women is to recognize prostitution as work and seek a United Nations convention that will outlaw the trafficking in any persons for any kind of work if carried out by force (Klap et al., 1995). 'Free' prostitution is, in this analysis, to be separated from the issue of trafficking and seen as acceptable. This view is promoted by an organization called the Global Alliance Against Trafficking in Women (GAATW) whose views are well represented in Kempadoo and Doezema (1998). These views are positively represented in the 1998 International Labour Organisation report on prostitution in four Asian countries, *The Sex Sector*, which argues that prostitution is so important in regional economies that it should perhaps be recognized or legalized (Lim, 1998). The concentration on distinguishing between 'forced' and 'free' trafficking would be likely to make it very difficult to prosecute any trafficking in women because of the necessity to prove force (Raymond, 1995). This approach would leave prostitution tourism, and indeed the vast majority of trafficking and prostitution, untouched and lead to its more thorough integration into national and international prostitution industries.

Prostitution tourism can be effectively countered, however, by the approach put forward by the Coalition Against Trafficking in Women. This organization has drawn up, in conjunction with the United Nations Economic and Social Council, a proposed Convention Against Sexual Exploitation which defines prostitution as a violation of human rights and calls for the penalizing of the men who force any person into prostitution (see appendix to Barry, 1995).

Over the last ten years feminist human rights theorists have sought to challenge the conservative and male biased interpretation of what should be considered human rights violations so that violence against women can be recognized as violating the human rights of women (Fitzpatrick, 1994; Copelon, 1994). Celina Romany describes such violence as 'infringement of the core and basic notions of civility and citizenship' and says that it 'assaults life, dignity and personal integrity' (Romany, 1994, p. 85). Such language lifts violence against women out of the 'private' realm in which it had been disregarded as a 'domestic' issue into terms which men had been accustomed to use to refer to injuries to themselves.

Catharine MacKinnon explains that torture and inequality on the basis of sex are largely recognized as core human rights violations and asks therefore why, when these violations are combined, as in rape, battering and pornography, no violation is recognized at all (MacKinnon, 1993). Torture is seen as taking place in the public world, and at the behest of the state. It fits the traditional understanding of human rights violations as abuses by the state of men's privileges. 'Torture is regarded as politically motivated not personal; the state is involved in it' (Ibid, p. 25). MacKinnon points out that the state is implicated in husband violence because 'the cover-up, the legitimization, and the legalization of the abuse is official' (Ibid, p. 29). The state can be held responsible because it acquiesces in violence against women. This approach has enabled feminist theorists to demand that men's violence against women be taken seriously and seen as actionable under human rights documents.

The results of such feminist efforts was that in October 1993 the General Assembly of the United Nations passed a resolution adopting the Declaration on the Elimination of Violence Against Women (United Nations, 1996). The general definition of violence against women it contains fits prostitution very well:

any act of gender-based violence that results in, or is likely to result in, physical, sexual or psychological harm or suffering to women, including threats of such acts, coercion or arbitrary deprivation of liberty, whether occurring in public or in private life. (United Nations, 1996, p. 475)

However, the list of the practices understood to constitute violence against women in this document specifically excludes 'free' prostitution. Only 'trafficking in women and forced prostitution' are included. Thus the forced/free distinction bedevils this important initiative.

The proposed 'Convention Against Sexual Exploitation' from the Coalition Against Trafficking in Women and UNESCO, however, does not make this mistake. This convention would penalize violence against women and defines all of men's prostitution behaviour as violence. Sexual exploitation is defined as:

a practice by which person(s) achieve sexual gratification or financial gain or advancement through the abuse of a person's sexuality by abrogating that person's human right to dignity, equality, autonomy, and physical and mental well-being. (Barry, 1995, p. 326)

Prostitution is defined as 'the use of a woman's body as a commodity to be bought, sold, exchanged not always for money' and includes 'casual prostitution, street prostitution, prostitution sanctioned by sociocultural practices, brothels, military prostitution, development prostitution, pornography, sex tourism, and mail-order bride markets' (Ibid, p. 327).

The most controversial aspect of the convention is likely to be the penalizing of the male perpetrators or 'clients' of prostitution. There has been a very significant and promising development in 1998, in the international struggle against prostitution which made the international call to penalize the men who abuse women in prostitution seem much more realizable. The Swedish government passed legislation against the 'buying of sexual services' which penalizes all perpetrators. This is the result of many years of campaigning by women and men to gain recognition that prostitution is male sexual violence and that men must take responsibility for their abusive behaviour.

Sex or, more accurately, prostitution tourism, then, as one form of men's sexually violent behaviour in prostitution should not be seen as an acceptable leisure industry. Like all other forms of prostitution it is damaging to the women and children who are used, and damaging to the status of all women in the countries in which it takes place. Also, it conditions the male perpetrators in the practices of unwanted sexual intercourse and sexual harassment and other forms of sexual violence by enabling them to pay to inflict that violence, and thus provides a major obstacle to the feminist struggle to end sexual violence against women. Prostitution tourism needs to be challenged as a violation of women's human rights within tourism research and the tourism industry.

Discussion Questions

1   *What do WHISPER and SAGE stand for?*

2   *The integral links between prostitution and violence against women has been recognized by feminists researchers for many years. What specific examples were provided to support this position?*

3   *The male sexual behavior involved in using women in prostitution includes several forms of male sexual violence. Which ones were cited by the author?*

4   *What is the relationship between post-traumatic stress disorder (PTSD) and prostitution?*

5   *How does the practice of dissociation work in conjunction with prostituted women?*

6   *How has warfare emerged as a force in human trafficking?*

7   *What was the implied hypothetical suggestion by the author regarding the possible outrage of Western men confronted with changes in the status of women resulting from the Women's Liberation Movement in their countries and the desire to use foreign women as prostitutes and mail order brides?*

8   *Why are Russian women so vulnerable to trafficking?*

9   *The Human Rights Watch report explains that the men's use of women in prostitution is often a death sentence for the women. Why is this so?*

10 *What was the original reason for the construction of the massive sex industry in the Philippines?*

11 *How has the author suggested that sex tourism can be ended?*

References

Barry, K. (1995) *The Prostitution of Sexuality*, New York University Press, New York.

Centre for Family and Women's Studies, Hanoi (1994). Country report: Vietnam, in *Foundation for Women, Thailand*.

Bishop, R. and Robinson, L. (1998) *Night Market. Sexual Cultures and the Thai Economic Miracle*, Routledge, New York.

Chapkis, W. (1997) *Live Sex Acts. Women Performing Erotic Labour*, Routledge, New York.

Coalition Against Trafficking in Women (Australia) (1998) Newsletter, No 2. Available from CATW, PO Box 1273, North Fitzroy, VIC 3068, Australia.

Copelon, R. (1994) Intimate terror: understanding domestic violence as torture, (edited by R.J. Cook) *Human Rights of Women. National and International Perspectives*, University of Pennsylvania Press, Philadelphia.

Davidson, J. O'C. (1994) British sex tourists in Thailand, paper presented to the Women's Studies Network Annual Conference, Portsmouth, 8–10 July. Now reprinted in (*Hetero*) *Sexual Politics* (edited by M. Maynard and J. Purvis) Taylor and Francis, London.

Davidson, J. O'C. and Taylor, J. (1996). *Child Prostitution and Sex Tourism*. (6 reports) 1. Costa Rica, 2. Cuba, 3. Thailand, 4. Goa, 5. Venezuela, 6. South Africa, ECPAT International, Bangkok.

De Stoop, C. (1992). They are so sweet, Sir. *The Cruel World of Traffickers in Filipinas and Other Women*, Limitless Asia, Leuven, Belgium.

Distor, E. and Hunt, D. (eds) (1996) *Confronting Sexual Exploitation. Campaign Against Sex Tourism and Trafficking in Filipino Women*. Justice Place, 84 Park Rd, Woolloongabba, Queensland, 4102: CPC.

Enloe, C. (1983) *Does Khaki Become You? The Militarisation of Women's Lives*. Pluto Press, London.

Farley, M. and Hotaling, N. (1995) *Prostitution, Violence and Posttraumatic Stress Disorder*, NGO Forum, Fourth World Conference on Women, Beijing, 4 September.

Fitzpatrick, J. (1994) The use of international human rights norms to combat violence against women, *Human Rights of Women. National and International Perspectives*, (edited by R.J. Cook). University of Pennsylvania Press, Philadelphia.

Foundation for Women, Thailand (1994). *International Workshop on International Migration and Traffic in Women*. Chiangmai, 17–21 October. Foundation for Women, Thailand, Women's Studies Center, Chiangmai, Women and Autonomy Centre, Leiden University.

Giobbe, E. (1991). Prostitution: buying the right to rape, in Ann Wolpert Burgess (ed) *Rape and Sexual Assault III.* A Research Handbook (edited A.W. Burgers), Garland Publishing, Inc, New York.

Herman, J.L. (1994) *Trauma and Recovery.* From Domestic Abuse to Political Terror, Pandora, London.

Hoigard, C. and Finstad, L. (1992). *Backstreets. Prostitution,* Money and Love. Polity, Cambridge.

Hughes, D. (1996) Sex tours via the internet. *Agenda – Empowering Women for Gender Equity.* No 28, pp. 71–76.

Human Rights Watch/Asia (1994). *A Modern Form of Slavery,* Human Rights Watch, New York.

Human Rights Watch/Asia (1995). *Rape for Profit,* Human Rights Watch, New York.

Jaget, C. (ed.) (1980) *Prostitutes Our Life,* Falling Wall Press, Bristol, UK.

Jeffreys, S. (1997) *The Idea of Prostitution.* Spinifex Press, Melbourne.

Jeffreys, S, (1985, 1997) *The Spinster and Her Enemies.* Feminism and Sexuality 1880–1930, Pandora, London; Spinifex, Melbourne.

Jeness, V. (1993). *Making It Work. The Prostitutes' Rights Movement in Perspective.* Aldine De Gruyter, New York.

Karen Women's Organization (1994). Country report: Burma (Karen) in *Foundation for Women, Thailand* (1994).

Kelly, L. (1988, 1989). *Surviving Sexual Violence,* Polity, Cambridge, UK.

Kempadoo, K. and Doezema, J. (eds) (1998) *Global Sex Workers. Rights, Resistance, and Redefinition,* Routledge, New York.

Kendar, A.O.S. (1994). Country Report: Bangladesh, in *International Workshop on International Migration and Traffic in Women.* Chiangmai, 17–21 October. Organized by Foundation for Women, Thailand, Women's Studies Center, Chiangmai, Women and Autonomy Centre, Leiden University.

Klap, M., Klerk, Y. and Smith J. (eds) (1995) *Combating Traffic in Persons.* SIM Special No 17. Studie – en Informatiecentrum Mensenrechten, Janskerhof 16, 3512 BM, Utrecht, The Netherlands.

League of Nations (1927) *Report of the Special body of Experts on the Traffic in Women and Children.* C. 52. M. 52. 1927. IV. League of Nations, Geneva.

League of Nations (1933), *Commission of Enquiry into Traffic in Women and Children in the East. Report to the Council.* C. 26. M 26. League of Nations, Geneva.

Lim, L.L. (ed.) (1998) *The Sex Sector. The Economic and Social Bases of Prostitution in Southeast Asia,* International Labour Office, Geneva.

Mcleod, E. (1982) *Women Working: Prostitution Now*, Croom Helm, London.

MacKinnon, C.A. (1987). *Feminism Unmodified*, Harvard University Press, Cambridge, MA.

MacKinnon, C.A. (1993) On torture: a feminist perspective on human rights, in K. Mahoney and P. Mahoney. *Human Rights in the Twenty First Century. A Global Challenge* (edited by K. Mahoney and P. Mahoney) Martinus Nijhoff, Dordrecht/Boston/London.

Nagle, J. (ed.) (1997) *Whores and Other Feminists*, Routledge, New York.

Perkins, R., and Bennett, G. (1985). *Being a Prostitute*, Allen and Unwin, Sydney.

Peters, J. and Wolper, A. (eds) (1995) *Women's Rights–Human Rights*. International Feminist Perspectives, Routledge, New York.

Pheterson, G. (1996) *The Prostitution Prism*, Amsterdam University Press, Amsterdam.

Raymond, J.G. (1995). *Report to the Special Rapporteur on Violence Against Women. The United Nations, Geneva, Switzerland.* Coalition Against Traf cking in Women: P.O. box 9338, N. Amherst, MA 01059, USA.

Romany, C. (1994) State responsibility goes private: a feminist critique of the public/private distinction in international human rights law, in *Human Rights of Women. National and International Perspectives* (edited R.J. Cook), University of Pennsylvania Press, Philadelphia.

Santos, A.F. (1992) Gathering the dust: the bases issue in the Philippines, in *Let the Good Times Roll. Prostitution and the U.S. Military in Asia*, (edited by S.P. Sturdevant and B. Stoltzfus) The New Press, New York.

Santos, A.F. (1995). Picking up the pieces of women's lives: prostitution and sexual exploitation in Asia-Pacific, paper submitted to WHO May.

Sturdevant, S.P. and Stoltzfus, B. (1992). *Let the Good Times Roll. Prostitution and the U.S. Military in Asia*, The New Press, New York.

Truong, T.-D. (1990). *Sex, Money and Morality: Prostitution and Tourism in Southeast Asia*. Zed Books, London.

United Nations (1996) *The United Nations and the Advancement of Women 1945–96*, United Nations Department of Public Information, New York.

van der Vleuten, N. (1991) Survey on 'Traffic in women'. Policies and policy – research in an international context. Vena Working Paper No 91/1 Research and Documentation Centre. Women and Autonomy, Leiden University, P.O. Box 9555, 2300 Rb Leiden.

Sheila Jefferys (1999) "Globalizing Sexual Exploitation: Sex Tourism and the Traffic in Women," *Leisure Studies* 18, 179-196. Reprinted by permission of the publisher, Taylor & Francis Ltd., http://www.informaworld.com.

21
TRAFFICKING IN WOMEN:
THE BUSINESS MODEL APPROACH

Louise Shelley, Ph.D. *Director, Transnational Crime and Corruption Center*

Trafficking in women has grown significantly in the past decade. Although this has been a long-standing phenomenon in Asia, it has spread to many more areas of the world. In the wake of this growth, three categories of analysis have emerged-the gender perspective, the human rights perspective, and the market-driven perspective. All of these perspectives contribute important insights into the phenomenon.

Despite the growing analysis of this burgeoning trend, there has been very little study of the business practices of the transnational crime groups that track women. While significant market analyses of the drug trade have been done by a variety of scholars and practitioners, we have much less of an understanding of the organized crime businesses that engage in the trafficking of women.[1]

Without an understanding of the dynamics of the human trafficking trade, there is a presumption that a single model exists which applies with only variations in the size of the groups that traffic the women. Using national data as well as actual cases, this work suggests that there are significant regional and cultural differences in tracking organizations. These differences are not merely of a descriptive character but have important implications for the ways that policy makers address the problem.

Behind the egregious human rights violations of tracking lie intricate enterprises, each with business characteristics that influence the severity of the human rights violations. The business structures of the crime groups have historical roots in the respective society, but are also shaped by the contemporary conditions in the societies from which individuals are recruited and trafficked and ultimately the countries to which they are transported. The business organization and its practices affect not only the level of profits but also the way it disposes of profits and launders their proceeds. The trafficking of women involves gross violations of human rights, but certain business practices are more conducive to major human rights violations than others.

---

[1] Francisco E. Thoumi, Political Economy and Illegal Drugs in Colombia, (Boulder: Lynne Rienner, 1995); Peter Reuter, Organization of Illegal Markets: An Economic Analysis, (Washington, D.C.: U.S. Department of Justice, 1985).

Defining The Problem

According to the United Nations Protocol, "Smuggling of migrants shall mean the procurement, in order to obtain, directly or indirectly, a financial or other material benefit, of the illegal entry of a person into a State Party of which the person is not a national or permanent resident."[2] This protocol was established to address the burgeoning trade of illegal immigrants facilitated by criminals specializing in the illegal movement of people.

Trafficking involves deception, coercion, abduction, fraud, debt bondage, and abuse of power. According to the United Nations Protocol definition, "exploitation shall include sexual exploitation, forced labor or services, slavery or practices similar to slavery, servitude or the removal of organs."[3] The trafficker, through deception, threats of violence, or actual use of violence, forces the individual to work in conditions of forced labor, servitude, or debt bondage.

Growth Of Sexual Trafficking In The Last Decade

Sexual trafficking is not a new phenomenon. At the end of the nineteenth century and the beginning of the twentieth century, extensive sexual trafficking networks in Asia sent women from China to the United States and women from Eastern European to South America.[4] At that time, the practice was referred to as the "white slave trade" and led to the enactment of legislation such as the Mann Act in the United States and governmental investigations in Argentina. The Great Depression, the advent of World War II, and the rise of the Iron Curtain at the end of World War II provided many barriers to the trafficking of women. The socialist countries of Eastern Europe and the Soviet Union were effectively closed and women could not be trafficked from or across this vast territory that ranged from the Pacific Ocean to the borders of Western Europe.

The collapse of the Soviet Union combined with increased personal mobility in a global age has facilitated the growth of human trafficking in the last decade. The replacement of superpower conflicts with an increasing number of regional conflicts has compounded the problem. This has made many women in war torn areas not only destitute but also vulnerable to trafficking networks. The privatizations of state

---

[2] "Protocol Against the Smuggling of Migrants by Land, Sea and Air, Supplementing the United Nations Convention Against Transnational Organized Crime, United Nations Convention Against Transnational Organized Crime," (New York: United Nations, 2000).

[3] Protocol to Prevent, Suppress and Punish Trafficking in Persons, Especially Women and Children, Supplementing the United Nations Convention Against Transnational Organized Crime," United Nations, 2000.

[4] Howard Abadinsky, "Organized Crime" 7th ed. (Belmont: Thomson, 2003): 241.

property which have accompanied the transition from socialism have disproportionately affected women because women are left deprived of the social safety net of the socialist system and fail to gain their share in the property redistribution which has been dominated by former party officials and crime groups.[5] This has left many women susceptible to trafficking.

Therefore, the 1990s saw an enormous growth of the phenomenon in many regions of the world. Increasingly, women who are trafficked come from former socialist countries and Africa rather than from the traditional source countries in Asia.[6] Large numbers of illegal immigrants are often moved by the same organizations from countries in Asia, often from conflict regions and the Indian subcontinent.

The trade is conducted not only by small networks but is often part of a highly organized trade that delivers individuals across continents. A recent analysis by Interpol of the different telephone logs connected with Chinese smugglers in different cities in Europe revealed a very different business structure than that observed by local European law enforcement. While the police in each city thought they were observing a small smuggling organization, in fact all these groups were merely cells of a larger network that all reported back to a single major human smuggler in China. Using data provided by the U.S. law enforcement, Interpol discovered that the same crime boss ran the smuggling rings on different continents.

The current trade in human beings combines traditional actors with new actors from the former socialist states and Africa. Without effective local law enforcement, perpetrators are able to recruit almost with impunity in their home countries. Corruption of local law enforcement agencies-such as border and customs officials-facilitates cross-border trade across vast geographic regions. This allows large-scale movement from poorer countries in Asia and Africa to Western Europe and the United States.

Human Smuggling and Sex Trafficking As Businesses

Smuggling and trafficking are undeniably part of organized crime activities. The high profits, low risk of detection, and minor penalties involved have made the human trade attractive to crime groups that previously trafficked in other commodities and to new groups which have developed recently. The business operates with the complicity of profes-

---

[5] Louise I. Shelley, "The Changing Position of Women: Trafficking, Crime and Corruption," in The Legacy of State Socialism and the Future of Transformation, David Lane (ed.), (Lanham: Rowman and Littlefield, 2002): 207-222.

[6] Trafficking in Human Beings First Report of the Dutch National Rapporteur (Hague:Bureau NRM, November 2002); Federal Criminal Police (BKA), Trafficking in Human Beings 2001 (Weisbaden: BKA, 2002); Assemble Nationale, L'esclavage, en France, aujourd' Documenthui 3459, 2001.

sionals in receiving countries that knowingly provide services to the human smugglers and traffickers. The vast profits of this business allow them to develop high-level expertise just as the drug trafficking organizations have done in recent decades. This model of trade thrives not only because of the traffickers from poor and violence-ridden societies but also because of highly paid facilitators in the west. For example, a Harvard-educated lawyer was arrested recently as the facilitator for a Chinese smuggling ring.[7]

In regions of extreme conflict where peacekeepers are stationed, the peacekeepers often contribute significantly to the growth of the trafficking networks and the embedding of organized crime within the community.[8] The peacekeepers are a major revenue source for the brothel owners who keep the trafficked women. These revenues are used to neutralize law enforcement through corruption and additionally to invest in the technology, intelligence gathering, and sophisticated communications that are needed to make the human trade grow.

Many of the trafficking and smuggling organizations commenced trading only in the last fifteen years, but they have distinctive styles of operation and structure. The trade in human beings is not a uniform business and operates very differently in diverse cultural and political contexts. Traditional patterns of trade and investment shape the trade in human beings as they do the trade in "other commodities." Despite the fact that much of the trade has emerged from the former socialist world, the trade in human beings out of Albania, Russia, and China is very different. This suggests that pre-revolutionary traditions of trade, family, and historical factors may be more important in determining the trade than the common features of the socialist system.[9] Women from Eastern Europe and the former Soviet Union are particularly vulnerable because the post-socialist transition has displaced many women from their native lands. Additionally, the worldwide feminization of poverty has been particularly acute in these former socialist countries.

The demand for cheap labor and sexual services has resulted in the growth of smuggling and tracking. This conclusion is based on a wide variety of sources including reports on cases that have been initiated and investigated, the increasingly large international literature produced by

---

[7] Mark Hamblett, "Government Outlines Case Against Porges," New York Law Journal (27 September 2000):1.

[8] "Trafficking, Slavery and Peacekeeping: The Balkan Case" Conference for International Experts (Turin, Italy, 9-10 May 2002). This meeting, organized by TraCCC and United National Interregional Crime and Justice Research Institute (UNICRI), had the aim of collecting, analyzing and comparing operational suggestions on how to tackle the traffic of human beings in Peacekeeping Operations (PKO) areas, <www.unicri.it/experts_meeting.htm>.

[9] Louise I. Shelley, "Post-Communist Transitions and Illegal Movement of Peoples: Chinese Smuggling and Russian Trafficking in Women," n Annals of Scholarship, Vol. 14, No. 2, 2000: 71-84.

scholars, individual countries, and multilateral organizations such as the United Nations and the International Organization of Migration, and various human rights reports. The demographic and capital imbalance between Western Europe and the countries of Eastern Europe, Asia, and Africa has placed enormous pressure on individuals to leave their home countries, and restrictive migration policies in Western Europe limit entrance.[10] In the western hemisphere, the enormous population growth in Latin America has not been accompanied by an increase in job creation. This has produced enormous pressures for emigration, which cannot be satisfied legally.[11] Along the U.S.-Mexican border, the business of human smuggling greatly exceeds that of human trafficking in women and children. In addition, the United States receives smuggled and trafficked men, women, and children from many other regions of the world.[12]

Categorization of Trafficking Groups as Different Business Types or Criminal Enterprises

This paper identifies six different models of business operating in the trafficking area. Each of these models is an ideal type associated with a different national group and reflects deep historical influences, geographical realities, and the market forces that drive the trade. The models do not fit every crime group from a particular region, but they provide a means to categorize the business of human smuggling and trafficking. The first five models address the businesses that recruit men, women, and children to be smuggled and trafficked. The sixth model applies only to a host country and not to the groups supplying tracked women. These models apply to different regions of the world as women are trafficked from former socialist countries, China, Latin America, and Africa.

Model 1: Natural Resource Model: Post-Soviet Organized Crime

The information for this model is based on research conducted by scholars in Russia and Ukraine under the sponsorship of the Transnational Crime and Corruption Center (TraCCC). The results were published in the volumes of Torgovlye Liudmi (Trade in People), which

---

[10] EU Organised Situation Report
<http:www.europol.eu.in/index.asp?page=EUOrganisedCrimeSitRep2000>; 2000, EU O.C. Report: Trafficking in Human Beings.
www.europol.eu.int/index.asp?page=publ_ar2000#TRAFFICKING IN HUMAN BEINGS

[11] Peter Andreas, Border Crimes: Policing the U.S.-Mexico Divide, (Ithaca: Cornell University Press, 2000); Peter Andreas and Timothy Snyder, Wall Around the West: State Borders and Immigration Controls in North America and Europe, (Lanham: Rowman and Littlefield, 2000).

[12] Amy O'Neill-Richards, "International Trafficking in Women to the United States," <2000 www.cia.gov/csi/monograph/women/trafficking.pdf>.

present the research of an inter-disciplinary team who reviewed police records, interviewed trafficked individuals, and individuals involved in recruiting women to be trafficked.[13] Additional insights were obtained by TraCCC interviews with western law enforcement investigators and prosecutors who have conducted investigations of these cases in the United States and Europe.

This model pertains almost exclusively to the tracking of women. It does not reflect an integrated business but instead focuses on short-term profits with little concern for the maintenance of supply and the long-term durability of the business. Post-Soviet organized crime groups sell women as if they were a readily available natural resource such as timber or furs. In this respect this business reflects the pre-revolutionary Russian trade in natural resources and the new Russian emphasis on the sale of oil and gas.[14]

The business focuses on the recruitment of women and their sale to intermediaries who deliver them to the markets where they will "serve clients." Most often, the women are sold off to nearby trading partners-usually the most proximate crime group. This model does not maximize profits and profits are not repatriated or used for development. Instead, profits are disposed of through conspicuous consumption or are sometimes used to purchase another commodity with a rapid turnover. British law enforcement found that the profits from trade in women were used to buy rubber boots for sale in Ukraine or cars for sale in the Baltic region.

This model results in very significant violations of human rights because the traffickers have no interest in wresting long-term profits from these women and have no connections to their families. Repatriation efforts are often unsuccessful because the women are broken by the experience, and there are not adequate social support services in their home communities.

Model 2: Trade and Development Model: Chinese Traffickers

The analysis of Chinese organized crime is based on a variety of law enforcement sources apart from the academic sources and the case materials of prosecuted cases. Materials of actual investigations of the business side of Chinese organized crime have been made available to the researcher. These include economic analyses of the crime based on materials of criminal investigations. In addition, information has been obtained from Interpol's organized crime division that is now analyzing

---

[13] E.V. Tiuriukanova, and L.D. Erokhina, Torgovlia Liud'mi Sotsiokrimologicheskii analiz. (Moscow: Academia, 2002).

[14] Shelley, "Post-Communist Transitions and Illegal Movement of Peoples: Chinese Smuggling and Russian Trafficking in Women."

the relationship among different Chinese trafficking organizations operating in Europe.

This model is most applicable to the smuggling of men but is also common in the trafficking of women who represent as much as ten percent of the total human trade. Chinese and Thai trafficking operations organize their business such that it is integrated from start to finish. These operations control the smuggling at all stages- from recruitment through debt bondage and eventually to an assignment in a brothel in order to secure long-term profits. The business structure generates lucrative profits. This trade resembles other Chinese trades in that it is integrated across continents and results in significant investment capital for China.

Much of the profit is repatriated and eventually leads to further entrepreneurship throughout Thailand and southern China. Investigators can follow these cases, in part through familial links. Assets are laundered back sometimes through wire transfers but multi-millions are returned through systems of Chinese underground banking such as gold shops and other similar techniques.

The vast majority of Chinese are smuggled and trafficked into the United States, but this model is not applicable to the United States only. There is a rise of Chinese trafficking to Europe and other parts of the world. The outcome of the smuggling differs significantly based on the country to which the individual is trafficked. Smugglers of Chinese to the United States free those they smuggle after they have worked off their debt, whereas prosecutors in Italy report that the individuals remain enslaved because these individuals cannot be absorbed into the legitimate Italian economy and pay the smugglers to transport other members of their families.

This model results in less significant violations of human rights compared to Model 1 since the smugglers and traffickers have an interest in wresting long-term profits from these women and often have connections to their families. Violations may be greater in Europe than in the United States because smuggled individuals have less chance of being amnestied and integrated into the legitimate economy.

Model 3: Supermarket Model: Low Cost and High Volume U. S. – Mexican Trade

Analysis of this model is based on readings as well as interviews with American and Mexican law enforcement personnel.[15] TraCCC researchers are presently developing a new curriculum for the U.S. border patrol which will address more directly the issues of smuggling and trafficking. The trade is based on maximizing profits by moving the largest numbers of people and not charging significant sums for each individual. The smugglers may charge as little as several hundred dollars for their services.

---

[15] Andreas, 2000. op.cit..

This model is most applicable to the smuggling of men and women. The trade in women is part of a much larger trade that involves moving large numbers of people across the border at low cost. In most cases the smugglers facilitated just the cross-border trade. This trade may require multiple attempts as evidenced by the fact that 1.8 million individuals were arrested on the border in 2000. In a small percentage of cases, traffickers exploit vulnerable individuals such as a group of deaf people who were forced to peddle small items in the streets or young girls who are forced into brothels in the Cadena case.[16] Most of the "people movers" specialize, which is trade that is based on large-scale supply and existing demand.

The ongoing trade requires significant profit sharing with local Mexican border officials. The Cadena case of young women trafficked to the southeastern United States gave insight into patterns of money laundering. Millions of dollars of profits were returned to Mexico and invested in land and farms. The investment patterns of the traffickers resembled those of people who were smuggled rather than those of drug traffickers. Just as individuals smuggled to the United States return their salaries to buy land and build and improve homes, the traffickers followed the same pattern on a large scale. They could buy millions of dollars worth of farms with the enormous profits made from trafficking even a relatively small number of women.

Detection is difficult because trafficking is hidden within large scale smuggling operations. Trafficked women often serve both legal and illegal immigrants who have little contact with law enforcement.

This model results in many significant violations of human rights and even fatalities of those smuggled. Because there is little profit to be gained from each individual who is moved, smugglers are not always concerned about the safe delivery of those smuggled to their ultimate destination. At the desert region of the border area, smugglers and traffickers are obligated to provide adequate water to those crossing the border—an obligation that is not always fulfilled. Traffickers prey on the most vulnerable sectors of Mexican society, such as the deaf and minors.

Model 4: Violent Entrepreneur Model: Balkan Crime Groups

Trafficking in the Balkans has been facilitated by interviews with large numbers of law enforcement personnel in England, Belgium, Italy, the Netherlands, and Germany with the aim of learning more about the dynamics of the trafficking and smuggling in their countries. Non-governmental organizations, multilateral organizations, and journalists have been able to obtain further information on trafficking networks within their respective countries. A conference was held at United

---

[16] Louise Shelley, "Corruption and Organized Crime in Mexico in the Post-PRI Transition," *Journal of Contemporary Criminal Justice* Vol. 17, No.3, August 2001: 226.

National Interregional Crime and Justice Research Institute (UNICRI) in Italy in May 2002 in which the problem of peacekeepers and the trafficking of women was discussed with very concrete references to the organizations that specialize in the trafficking of women.[17]

This model pertains almost exclusively to the trafficking of women. It involves large numbers of women from the Balkans and those sold off to Balkan traders by crime groups from the former Soviet Union and Eastern Europe. Therefore, it controls women from their base in the Balkans through their exploitation in the brothels of Western Europe. Balkan traders in women run an integrated business and are middlemen for the groups from Eastern Europe.

This is an opportunistic model in both the source and recipient countries. The instability and civil conflict in the home region provide a large number of women who are vulnerable to trafficking. Balkan groups take over existing markets in continental Europe and Great Britain by use of force against already established organized crime groups.[18] Trafficking victims and law enforcement professionals who seek to investigate these crimes become targets of the crime groups. The direct involvement of top-level law enforcement personnel in the home country makes international investigation more difficult. The control of many women in the highly profitable sex markets of Western Europe generates very high levels of profits for the traffickers. Profits from this trade appear to be used to finance other illicit activities at home and for investments in property and trade businesses domestically and abroad. The money is returned through wire transfers and cash carried by couriers to the home country.[19]

This model results in very significant violations of human rights and terrible violence against trafficked women. Its reliance on violence in all stages of operation makes it the most serious violator of human rights. Threats to family members at home are combined with terrible physical abuse of the women.

Model 5: Traditional Slavery with Modern Technology: Trafficking out of Nigeria and West Africa

Information on this model is based on European analyses in government reports, the limited research on the topic, and interviews with law enforcement personnel from France, Italy, and the Netherlands

---

[17] "Trafficking, Slavery and Peacekeeping: The Balkan Case."

[18] "Lawless Rule Versus Rule of Law in the Balkans Special Report No.97,"Washington D.C.: U.S. Institute of Peace, (December 2002).

[19] Testimony of Jean-Michel Colombani, 25 April 2001 in Assemble Nationale, L'esclavage, en France, aujourd 'hui Document 3459, 2001: 27-37.

which receive a disproportionate share of the trafficking victims from Africa.[20]

Nigerian organized crime groups that traffic women are multi-faceted crime groups, in which the trade of women is only one part of their criminal activities. Using female recruiters who conclude contracts with girls and women by manipulating voodoo traditions, they are able to force compliance through psychological as well as physical pressure. By employing modern transport links in present-day Nigeria, traffickers are effective because they "combine the best of both modern and older worlds by allying sophisticated forms of modern technology to tribal customs."[21] By exploiting the vulnerability of uneducated women, the trade resembles traditional slavery that has been modernized for the global age.

Human rights violations are significant. Children are abandoned in recipient countries and women are pressured to work in the most physically dangerous conditions at the lowest end of the prostitution market, usually as streetwalkers exposed to the elements. Physical violence is common.

Significant financial resources are gained from this activity as seen in the tremendous rise of African trafficking, particularly to Europe, since the late 1990s. Small amounts of the profits are returned to the local operations of the crime groups and occasionally to family members of the girls and women. Much of the profits are believed to flow to other illicit activities and are laundered.[22]

Model 6: Rational Actor Model: Dutch Approach to Regulation

The rational actor model applies to the control of trafficking in a receiving country. It is based on a regulatory model that is applied to other legitimate businesses. The effectiveness of this model is predicated on legalized prostitution and brothel keeping. It also presumes that trafficked women that are often coerced and deceived may be more attractive and younger than the legal professional prostitutes who work longer and later as prostitutes.

---

[20] Obi N.I. Ebbe, "The Political-Criminal Nexus: The Nigerian Case," Trends in Organized Crime Vol. 4, No.3, 1999:29-59; Testimony of Zohra Azirou, Celine Manceau Georgina Vaz Cabral, 25 April 2001 in Assemble Nationale, L'esclavage, en France, aujourd' Testimony,hui. volume 1, Document 3459, 2001: 12-14; IOM, "Trafficking in Women tohui, Italy for Sexual Exploitation," 1996, <www.iom.int/DOCUMENTS/PUBLICATION/EN/ MIP_Italy_traff_eng.pdf>.

[21] "European Union Organised Crime Situation Report," Europol 2000 <http://www.europol.eu.int/ index.asp?page=EUOrganisedCrimeSitRep2000>.

[22] IOM, "Trafficking in Women to Italy for Sexual Exploitation," 1996. <www.iom.int/DOCUMENTS/PUBLICATION/EN/MIP_Italy_traff_eng.pdf, pp.22-23>.

The model, as employed in the Netherlands, presumes that the brothel owner is a rational businessman and seeks to maximize his profits. In response, a licensing system is established whereby the local government sets the conditions by which brothels operate. "Regular controls by multidisciplinary teams are held to check the compliance with these criteria."[23] The legalization of brothels allows the state to regulate the market. The state outlines a range of conditions which must be met in order to operate the facility, including that the brothel owner must maintain legal workers and decent conditions In case of fragrant violations, such as the keeping of trafficked women or minors, the license can be withdrawn, the brothel closes, and prosecution ensues according to criminal legislation. A woman who has been trafficked does not have a legal right to work in a Dutch brothel. Dutch policy makers that supported this legislation suggested that the financial losses incurred by the closing of brothels outweigh the potential profits which can be made by charging more for younger, or more attractive trafficked women. Subject to serious inspections of brothels by law enforcement, the owner is incentivized to only retain workers of legal age and to refrain from employing trafficked women.

The legalization of the business does not require the laundering observed in the previous models to proceed. Investigative techniques in a regulated business assume the form of inspections rather than the long term and highly expensive investigative work needed for an organized crime investigation. Violations of human rights are restricted since the business is subject to regulation.

Categorization By Profits

Profits	High	Medium	Low
Model 1	x		
Model 2	x		
Model 3		x	
Model 4	x		
Model 5	x		
Model 6		x	

---

[23] "Policy approach on Human Trafficking and Prostitution in the Netherlands," January 2003.

Categorization By Money Laundering

Model 1: Much disposed of immediately in high consumption; some invested in other illegal businesses at home, as well as investment overseas in property and trade businesses.

Model 2: Very significant capital for development, large quantities returned home primarily through underground banking system, investment in land, homes, infrastructure, hotels, and businesses.

Model 3: Capital repatriated, invested in homes, land, and farms.

Model 4: Large-scale investments overseas and in international organized crime activity; some profits returned for investment in economy through wire transfers and couriers.

Model 5: Some profits returned to trafficker's home base and to the community; much of the profits go to other illicit activities and are laundered together with proceeds of other illicit activity.

Model 6: Profits may be invested in legitimate businesses or in the entertainment sector.

Conclusions

The business of human trafficking closely resembles the trade patterns of businesses and cultures of the region where trafficking operations are based. A single generic business model cannot encompass worldwide trafficking enterprises. However, the illicit enterprise does mirror trade in legitimate commodities. The trade patterns of the diverse business models reflect patterns of trade that are centuries old. For example, the tracking out of Africa bears much in common with the slavery of the past, with local communities involved in the recruitment and foreigners helping to facilitate the trade. Russian trade resembles the trade in natural resources, and Chinese trade seeks to fuel economic development. The Chinese model is based on family ties, whereas Russia, with less historical reliance on the extended family, is more focused on the individual. Low cost cross-border smuggling has characterized the U.S.-Mexico border for over a century.

   An important correlation exists between the violation of human rights and the business models. Such a conclusion has been demonstrated throughout history. The case of African slave trade reflect the relationship between human rights and business models. The slavery that defined the Brazilian plantations of the eighteenth and nineteenth centuries was significantly different than that experienced in the United

States. The volume of trade was affected by the life expectancy of the slaves. In Brazil, where conditions were harsher, slaves had a much shorter life expectancy than in the United States, which resulted in more people being transported to Brazil as slaves. This remains true in today's sex trafficking. In countries where conditions are particularly harsh, such as in the Balkans, there is an enormous volume of women trafficked. Factors of demand affect the volume of trafficking but the treatment of the victims also affects the volume of the business. High levels of human rights violations are associated with segmented businesses in which women are passed from one set of owners to another repeatedly. Furthermore, when there is little relationship between the past and present victims of trafficking, the level of violations increases. When groups are particularly transnational, they can threaten victims' families, increasing the degree and number of potential victims.

Trafficking does not exist in a vacuum. Without corrupt law enforcement, consular officials, and cooperative lawyers this trade could not exist. The isolation and prosecution of the facilitators of trafficking both at home and abroad is as necessary as targeting the crime groups themselves.

The profits of the trafficking business are enormous. In some cases, they fuel development and support families without other means of support. Understanding that trafficking sometimes serves an economic function to parties other than the traffickers is crucial to addressing the phenomena. Trafficking cannot be combated through legal and administrative measures alone. Economic strategies to seize the assets of the traffickers and to find other financial means of support for trafficking victims and their families are key to developing a strategy to reduce trafficking.

Dr. Louise Shelley is the founder and Director of the Transnational Crime and Corruption Center (TraCCC), and a leading United States expert on organized crime and corruption in the former Soviet Union. Dr. Shelley is a Professor in the Department of Justice, Law, and Society (School of Public Affairs) and the School of International Service at American University.

Discussion Question

1   *This paper identifies six different models of business operating in the traffic areas. Describe each of these models.*

22

SMUGGLING AND TRAFFICKING IN HUMAN BEINGS: THE PHENOMENON, THE MARKETS THAT DRIVE IT AND THE ORGANISATIONS THAT PROMOTE IT[*]

Alexis A. Aronowitz, *Assistant Professor and Academic Advisor at the University College Utrecht, the Netherlands*

Introduction

The recent death of 58 Chinese nationals found suffocated in the back of a truck in Dover served as a tragic reminder of what can go drastically wrong when people use the service of illicit smugglers. It is by no means the first time that smuggled migrants have died trying to enter other countries. More than 2,000 deaths of migrants trying to enter the European Union illegally have been documented since 1993 (J. Graff, Time, 3–7–2000, pp. 24–25).[1] As the number of illegal migrants increases—the International Organization for Migration (IOM) estimates that traffickers move over four million illegal immigrants a year (cited in Kendall 1999)—the world can expect more of these tragic incidents.

In response to the increasing[2] problem of migrants being smuggled and trafficked worldwide and the growing involvement of criminal organizations in this practice, the UN Office for Drug Control and Crime Prevention (UNODCCP) launched the Global Programme Against Trafficking in Human Beings in March 1999. The twofold programme emphasises research, which seeks to shed more light on the phenomenon of trafficking in human beings, in particular on the criminal practices, routes and networks that facilitate the process, and provides technical

---

[*] All positions, statements of fact, opinion and analysis expressed in this article are those of the author. They do not necessarily represented the position or views of the United Nations Interregional Crime and Justice Research Institute or of the United States Centre for International Crime Prevention.

[1] In one tragic incident in 1996, some 200 Sri Lankan, Pakistani and Indian immigrants drowned off the coast of Italy when the ferry they were on sank after ramming the fishing vessel that had brought them to their destination after a six-week trip (McAlllister 2000). The most recent tragedy occurred on New Year's Day 2001 when a Georgian ship sank off the Turkish coast with its human cargo of illegal Pakistani, Indian and Bangladeshi immigrants locked in the hold. Ten bodies were recovered; Turkish authorities believe 40 more perished (*Time* 15-01-2001, p. 8).

[2] Various organizations (UNHCR, UN, IOM) talk about an increase in the number of persons being smuggled and trafficked. This increase – in detection – could also be due to increased law enforcement initiatives and better law enforcement co-operation.

assistance projects to strengthen governmental responses to the smuggling and trafficking problem.

Definitions

Both smuggling and trafficking are forms of irregular migration. There are as many different definitions of smuggling and trafficking as there are organisations and governments concerned with addressing the issue (Kelly and Regan 2000; IOM 2000). While they differ, there are shared, common elements. Often both smuggled and trafficked individuals leave a country of origin willingly. Additionally, as their status in the country of destination is that of an illegal alien, both smuggled and trafficked persons are at risk of being exploited.

The UN ad hoc Committee on the Elaboration of a Convention Against Transnational Organised Crime submitted proposals in January 1999 for optional protocols on the smuggling of migrants and the trafficking of human beings, in particular, women and children. The UN Convention against Transnational Organized Crime[3] was adopted by the General Assembly at its Millennium meeting in November 2000. It was opened for signature at a high-level conference in Palermo, Italy, in December 2000. It is the first legally binding UN instrument in the field of crime.[4] It must be signed and ratified by 40 countries before it comes into force. In line with the proposed definitions in the Convention and two protocols, the UN Global Programme against Trafficking in Human Beings uses the following definitions:

> **Organized criminal group** shall mean a structured group of three or more persons existing for a period of time and acting in concert with the aim of committing one or more serious crimes or offences established in accordance with this Convention,[5] in order to obtain, directly, or indirectly, a financial or other material benefit.
>
> **Smuggling of migrants** shall mean the procurement, in order to obtain, directly or indirectly, a financial or other material

---

[3] The UN Convention and both protocols can be downloaded from the Internet at: www.uncjin.org/documents/conventions/dcatoc/final_documents_2/index.htm.

[4] The new instrument spells out how countries can improve co-operation on such matters as extradition, mutual legal assistance, transfer of proceedings and joint investigations. It contains provisions for victim and witness protection and shielding legal markets from infiltration by organised criminal groups. Parties to the Treaty would also provide technical assistance to developing countries to help them take the necessary measures and upgrade their capacities for dealing with organised crime.

[5] *Serious crime* shall mean conduct constituting an offence punishable by a maximum deprivation of liberty of at least four years or a more serious penalty. *Structured group* shall mean a group that is not randomly formed for the immediate commission of an offence and that does not need to have formally defined rolls for its members, continuity of its membership or a developed structure.

benefit, of the illegal entry of a person into a State Party of which the person is not a national or a permanent resident.

Trafficking in persons shall mean the recruitment, transportation, transfer, harbouring or receipt of persons, by means of the threat or use of force or other forms of coercion, of abduction, of fraud, of deception, of the abuse of power or of a position of vulnerability or of the giving or receiving of payments or benefits to achieve the consent of a person having control over another person, for the purpose of exploitation.

Exploitation shall include, at a minimum, the exploitation of the prostitution of others or other forms of sexual exploitation, forced labour or services, slavery or practices similar to slavery, servitude or the removal of organs.[6]

There are four elements that differentiate smuggling from trafficking (Bajrektarevic 2000a, p. 16):

1. smuggled persons always travel voluntarily; trafficked persons can either begin their trip voluntarily or may have been coerced or kidnapped;
2. trafficked persons are used and exploited over a long period of time;
3. an interdependency occurs between the trafficked person and organised crime groups;
4. trafficked persons are eligible for further networking (recruitment for criminal purposes).

While the definitions appear straightforward enough, they are open to interpretation based upon the definition of deception and coercion being utilised. There is no doubt that deception is involved and victims have been trafficked in instances where young women are promised jobs as governesses or in restaurants only to find themselves forced into prostitution upon arrival in the destination country. The situation becomes a bit more obscure when an individual, as an illegal migrant, willingly accepts a position as a domestic worker and is paid less than a national would be who is registered and must pay taxes. In some cases the 'victims' are willing collaborators (Ojomo 1999); a woman is willingly smuggled to another country to knowingly work in prostitution because her wages are much higher in the destination country than in the country of origin. However, when this woman is not allowed to keep all

---

[6] The consent of a victim of trafficking in persons to the intended exploitation shall be irrelevant where any of the means set forth (in the definition) have been used. Furthermore, the recruitment, transportation, transfer, harbouring or receipt of a child for the purpose of exploitation shall be considered 'trafficking in persons' even if this does not involve any of the means set forth in the definition.

of her wages but is forced to pay a higher percentage to her traffickers, or 'buy back' her passport at an exorbitant fee, then she too is exploited and is a victim of trafficking.

There are varying degrees of 'victimisation' which can be viewed on a continuum. Complete coercion exists when victims have been abducted. Deception occurs when individuals have been promised jobs in the legitimate economy only to find themselves forced into sexual slavery. The third level involves those individuals deceived through half-truths where they are told they will be working in the 'entertainment industry' or as dancers or strippers. The fourth category involves those women who were aware, prior to departure, of their work as prostitutes but were unaware of the extent to which they would be intimidated, indebted, controlled and exploited (Kelly and Regan 2000).

Definitions with respect to countries of origin, transit and destination are more diffuse. Traditional countries of origin are being used more frequently as transit and destination countries. Some are all three (Kelly and Regan 2000). This situation is evident in the former Yugoslavian province of Kosovo where Albanian criminal gangs traditionally abducted or lured young women to Italy and further into Europe and forced them to work in brothels. With the arrival of peacekeeping missions in Kosovo, gangs began setting up brothels filled with trafficked women to provide services to the foreign peacekeepers (Kenety 2000; Stop-Traffick 2000). With the frequent rotation between countries of young women smuggled into the European Union, it is becoming more and more difficult to determine which are the transit and which are the destination countries.

There is some indication of a link between sending and receiving countries. These links are influenced by a number of factors, such as the traffickers' use of the local knowledge about key locations or weaknesses in border or migration control (IOM 2000) or the ease in crossing borders (Kelly and Regan 2000). Other determining factors are the presence and tolerance of an extensive sex industry, historical/colonial links between countries (Kelly and Regan 2000) and the existence of a large immigrant population.

Smuggled Persons And Trafficked Victims

The borders between smuggling and trafficking become blurred when migrants voluntarily use the services of smugglers only to find themselves in coercive situations and thus become the victims of traffickers. What began as a voluntary activity on the part of the migrant, who may in fact have sought out the services of the smuggler, is easily transformed to a situation of trafficking where initial consent is invalidated through the use of deception or coercion.

The major difference between these two groups of persons is the amount of money that is paid prior to departure from the country of origin. Smuggled persons pay the amount up front and upon entering the destination country have ended their journey. Trafficked persons, on the other hand, usually pay a percentage and incur a debt for the remainder of the trip. This situation creates a type of debt bondage[7] and places them at the mercy of the traffickers and in situations in which they are easily exploited.

When illegal migrants are arrested at a border or in a country without proper documentation, they are smuggled persons. The distinction between smuggled persons and trafficked victims can only be determined after the individual has arrived in the destination country, is either free to walk away from the smuggler or is placed in a situation of debt bondage and is exploited. At this point the smuggled person becomes a trafficked victim.

Backgrounds of the Victims

The backgrounds of the smuggled persons and trafficked victims differ as much as their motivation for wanting to leave their countries of origin. Many who fall prey to smugglers and traffickers are usually those most disadvantaged in their own countries: those with poor job skills or little chance of successful employment at home. They are often women and children. This pattern is clearly seen in the trafficking patterns in countries in East and Central Europe (where women are trafficked to the West for sexual exploitation) and West Africa (where children are trafficked for forced labour).

Persons fleeing war zones or political persecution may be better educated or skilled. Once they choose, however, to use the service of smugglers to illegally enter a country, their use of these illicit channels often leads to a situation of total dependence which may result in serious human rights abuses.

Trafficking for Sexual Exploitation versus Forced Labour

Trafficked individuals are subject to various forms of exploitation and forced labour. The market in which victims are forced to work influences a number of factors such as the social stigma attached to the 'trade', the visibility of the individual, and the length of time during which the operations can exist before being dismantled by the authorities.

Both types of exploitation involve serious human rights abuses.[8] It could be argued, though, that forced sexual exploitation is morally more

---

[7] For the definitive work on debt bondage and modern slavery, see Bales (1999b).

[8] In a case prosecuted in the United States, 70 Thai nationals had been held against their will, systemically abused and forced to work 20-hour shifts in a sweatshop (Richard 1999).

reprehensible and, due to the social stigma and prejudice attached to this activity, and its sometimes illegal status in the origin and destination countries, it is more difficult to gain the co-operation of victims of sexual exploitation and to later reintegrate them back into their original communities (Ateneo 1999; Ould 1999). Additionally, these victims require more emotional and psychological support.

Because of their interaction with clients, prostitutes have more contacts with those other than their exploiters. This increases the likelihood that they will seek help, escape, or come to the attention of the authorities. To prevent this from occurring, young women are often rotated between criminal groups or between cities, states or countries (Kendall 1999; Richard 1999).

Perhaps because of isolated locations and the lack of contact with clients, forced labour operations are able to survive for longer periods of time. According to the United States Department of Justice

> [...] these operations went unnoticed or were able to exist longer than trafficking operations involving the sex industry. Labour trafficking operations generally lasted from 4½ to 6½ years whereas trafficking operations for prostitution lasted from a little over a year to approximately 2½ years before being discovered. (Richard 1999, p. 3)

The illicit markets in which trafficked migrants are forced to work will be discussed in more depth below.

Magnitude of the Problem

Due to its clandestine nature, accurate statistics on the magnitude of the problem are elusive. The International Organization for Migration (IOM), which received EU 'STOP' funds to produce accurate estimates for trafficking in women across Europe came to the conclusion that "it was not possible with any level of accuracy" (Kelly and Regan 2000). In their study of the magnitude of trafficking in the United Kingdom, Kelly and Regan (2000), based on 71 known cases, extrapolate the actual figure at between 142 and 1,420 cases annually. Experts in governmental agencies and international non-governmental organisations (NGOs) estimate the number of women and children trafficked internationally at between 700,000 and 2 million annually. This figure does not include trafficking within internal borders (Richard 1999).

At a public hearing before the European Parliament in February 2000, experts from Interpol and Europol agreed that, in spite of the difficulty in collecting statistical data, trafficking was a growing phenomenon (Kenety 2000). The Dutch Immigration and Naturalisation Service (Immigratie en Naturalisatiedienst) estimates that while 30%

of asylum seekers entering Europe used the services of smugglers in 1996, the number has risen to between 60 and 70% over the past few years (Verduyn 2000). Trafficking has become a major source of both activity and income for organised criminal networks. It was estimated that in 1993, smuggling and trafficking of human beings generated gross earnings of between US$5 billion and US$7 billion dollars (Widgren 1994); some researchers think the figure reaches $12 billion (F. McAllister, Time, 3–7–2000, pp. 26–28).

As difficult as it is to measure, the magnitude of the problem is further determined by a number of other factors including the recognition of the problem, the definition used, the available resources and the investigation efforts by the police.

In terms of the definition, if one considers trafficking for the purpose of sexual exploitation, all other forms of forced labour will be excluded. Furthermore, if internal trafficking is not taken into account, the numbers will also be much smaller. In many countries such as Brazil or Togo and Benin (West Africa), internal trafficking for the purpose of labour exploitation is a serious problem and one which occurs with greater frequency than that of transnational trafficking.

There are five basic factors which point toward an increasing and expanding market in the smuggling and trafficking of human beings (Widgren 1994). The first is the sheer number of willing targets, driven by poverty and a lack of opportunity, to take chances with smugglers and traffickers to improve their lives. Secondly, border controls, particularly with reference to a number of source and transit countries were previously strictly controlled. With the dissolution of the Soviet Union and the Warsaw Pact, control systems and the democratisation of a number of African, Asian and Latin American countries, exit controls are more lax. The third—the internationalisation of the world economy and the globalisation of world markets—and fourth—advanced communication and technology and cheap and rapid air travel—factors are closely intertwined. The fifth factor is the growing involvement of organised crime in the market and the fact that, along with money-laundering, weapons smuggling and sales, and drug transports, the smuggling and trafficking in human beings is becoming a specialised branch.

Causes

(Il)legal migration and trafficking are driven by 'push' and 'pull' factors. The causes that propel people to leave their country either through legitimate or illicit channels are the same. Traditionally, countries of origin are developing nations or those in a state of transition. Migration takes place from poorer countries to wealthier, more stable states. The 'pull' of promises of a better future are powerful.

Major migration waves, both legal and illicit, are propelled by the same 'push' factors. Immigration from Russia, Central and Eastern Europe and Asia have been greatly influenced by economic crises in these areas. Regional conflicts have been the cause of migration from areas such as Kosovo, the former Yugoslavia and certain African nations. Political and religious persecution drives others from nations such as China and Russia. A rise in illegal migration facilitates trafficking as does the increasing use of temporary labour contracts (Bales 1999a). Technological and communications advances, as well as open borders which facilitate the flow of goods also facilitate the flow of people.

The root causes of migration—both licit and illicit—lay in the significant predictors of trafficking from (the push factors) and to (the pull factors) a country. Using multiple regression,[9] the research identified the following predictors, rank ordered, 'from' a country: government corruption, the country's infant mortality rate (an indication of population pressure), the proportion of the population below the age of 14, the country's food production index (an indication of poverty), population density and conflict and social unrest.

The factors predicting trafficking 'to' a country were less conclusive. While the permeability of the country's border is a strong indicator of a 'pull' factor, this concept is virtually impossible to measure. It could be argued, however, that government corruption, particularly within border control or immigration agencies, is an indication of a permeable border (Bales 1999b). Other factors, rank ordered, predicting the 'pull' of a country were: the male population over the age of 60, governmental corruption, food production, energy consumption and infant mortality (the last three taken as indicators of the economic well-being of the destination country; Bales 1999b).

Smuggling/Trafficking As An Illegal Market

Smuggling and trafficking in migrants could not have grown to such proportions if it were not supported by powerful market forces. The increased demand for migrant labour coupled with stricter entry controls or requirements and diminishing legal channels to enter destination countries

> [...] has provided unscrupulous entrepreneurs with a potential for profit. The number of persons attempting to enter a country clandestinely has given rise to a market for services such as the provision of fraudulent travel documents, transportation, guided border crossings, accommodation and job brokering. (Escaler 1998, p. 16)

---

[9] Multiple regression examines a number of factors simultaneously and calculates the independent effect of each of the factors on the dependent variable. It indicates the strength of each factor, allowing for rank ordering, or whether a factor has no predictive value.

The crime industry involves the illicit exploitation of business opportunities and is dominated by supply organisations. Criminal organisations provide illicit goods and services to markets where the profits are high (Savona et al. 1995). Transnational criminal organizations[10]

> [...] have become major player in global economic activity, and are the key players in industries such as drug production and trafficking that are global in scope and that yield profits higher than the gross national products of some developing and developed states. Their common feature is that they engage in unregulated forms of capitalist enterprise involving illicit products, illicit smuggling of licit products and the theft of licit products, or all three kinds of activity (Savona et al. 1995, p. 5).

Unlike lawful enterprises which operate within legal parameters, transnational criminal organisations circumvent legal requirements through corruption, deceit, threats, force and other evasive tactics.

Smuggling usually involves short-term monetary profit whereas trafficking usually involves long-term exploitation for economic gain (Richard 1999). The profit in smuggling is generated possibly prior to departure and during the transportation phase. In trafficking, the profit can be made prior to and during the transportation phase and is made, in particular, afterwards through the exploitation, sexual or otherwise, of the trafficked victims.

Smuggling and trafficking can be viewed as an illicit market. It is the interaction between supply and demand. In the receiving countries there is, and always will be a demand for cheap labour and sex. In countries of origin there is always a dream of a better life and the ability to support oneself and family members back home. There is never a shortage of those willing to take risks to fulfil that dream. What occurs between the supply and demand sides of the market is a complex process linking the two.

Markets Profiting from Smuggled and Trafficked Persons

One can identify three basic (il)legal markets which are profiting from smuggled and trafficked migrants. These are the legitimate or conventional market economies (restaurants, factories, farms, etc.), the legitimate domestic service economy (households which employ maids)

---

[10] Transnational criminal organisations are defined as those who have a home base in one state but that operate in one or more host states where there are favourable market opportunities. The term was coined by Phil Williams, "Transnational Criminal Organisation and International Security", *Survival*, 36(1), pp. 96-113, 1994; cited in Savona et al. (1995).

and the criminal economies of the sex industry—foremost, prostitution (Ruggiero 1996, 1997).[11]

Forced labour on farms or plantations often involve deplorable working, living and sanitary conditions (Bales 1999a). Ould (1999) reports that Haitian workers in the Dominican Republic and Brazilian workers on plantations in Para State in Amazonia (Brazil) are subjected to slave-like conditions, kept in virtual debt-bondage and are subjected to the control of soldiers and armed guards who, on the estates of Para, will beat or shoot workers who try to escape.

Across Europe, the building trade and textile industries have benefited from smuggled and trafficked migrants. A Chinese organised crime group in Milan forced dozens of immigrants, under inhumane conditions, to manufacture clothes, handbags and belts which were bought by leading companies operating in the renowned Italian fashion world.[12] Profit is reaped by the organisations which smuggle and exploit these illegal migrants. However, the legitimate economy, which often subcontracts with these smaller operations also benefits financially from the use of exploited labour. Thus, there is a symbiotic relationship between the legal and illegal economies in this type of labour market. It is estimated that in Italy, the underground economy accounts for 28% of the GDP (Business Week, 27–11–2000, pp. 57–68).

Within the domestic service economy, the employers of domestic servants profit from their exploitation. The domestic servants are often underpaid and mistreated, both psychologically and physically. The boundaries between these three markets is not always strictly drawn and it is not uncommon for those working in the legitimate economy or in domestic service to escape unbearable conditions and find themselves in the illicit prostitution or sex industry economy. Research conducted in Germany shows that many servants escape their employee-owner and drift into prostitution (Ruggiero 1996).

In the case of the illicit sex industry, Italian researchers identify three different levels of illicit prostitution: those individual entre-preneurs who are involved in small-scale activities such as running a brothel in a particular area; the second or the mid-level prostitution schemes in which women are controlled by the clandestine operations which imported them; the third and most sophisticated level involves large-scale international criminal organisations that are linked with domestic criminal organisations. The women under the control of the third group have no documentation and are kept under tight control (Pomodoro and Stefanizzi 1995). Profits in this industry are generated

---

[11] Prostitution is not an illegal activity in all countries. In the Netherlands, for example, prostitution by adult women, if voluntary, is not an offence. It is, however, a criminal offence to live off the proceeds of a prostitute, thus pimping is illegal.

[12] Information obtained from an article in the Italian newspaper *La Stampa*, 22-9-1994; cited in Ruggiero (1996, 1997).

for the traffickers as well as for the owners of the brothels in which the women are often bought and forced to work. Huge profits generated by this industry are often reinvested in the legitimate economy through money-laundering operations and thus there is once again a profit nexus between the illicit and legitimate business worlds.

The Organisation Of Smuggling And Trafficking Operations

The degree of organization within the smuggling/trafficking chain can vary dramatically. It can be as simplistic individual providing a single service—hiding migrants in the back of a truck and smuggling them across the US—Mexican border only to abandon them once in the US. Offenders trafficking Central and Eastern European women to the Netherlands were found to be organised in trafficking networks (Vocks and Nijboer 1999).[13] It can involve numerous people who provide the entire range of services[14] and be as sophisticated and complex as the international operation which smuggled 60 Chinese persons over a 4-month period from Fujian, China, through Russia, the Czech Republic, Germany, The Netherlands and on to the UK.

It has been described as a process, depending upon the complexity of the operation, involving numerous players. Smuggling operations moving large numbers of persons through numerous countries over a longer period of time are, by nature, highly organized. Bajrektarevic (2000a, pp. 19-21; 2000b, p. 6) discusses the horizontal design of smuggling and trafficking rings. The exploiting unit and re-escort unit only provide 'services' to networks dealing with trafficked persons. The management unit maintains a vertical structure and has knowledge and controls other sub-units. All other sub-units are organised horizontally and have very limited knowledge of the other sub-units.

Schloenhardt (1999, pp. 217-219), similar to Bajrektarevic, identifies a number of specific roles that individuals take on within the organisation to provide specific services. Additionally, he addresses the issue of those in the organisation responsible for the laundering of money.

- **Investors:** those who put forward funding for the operation, and oversee the entire operation. These people are unlikely to be

---

[13] A group of Pakistanis who have been smuggled from Pakistan via Turkey to Cairo, were joined by a larger group of Sri Lankans. After boarding a ship in Alexandria and reaching the Malta-Sicily channel, they were to transfer to a smaller ship—one operated by a legitimate shipping company. The ship, which could carry approximately 100 passengers floundered and sunk resulting in the death of almost 300 passengers (Ruggerio 1997).

[14] Ruggiero (1996) reports that Albanians wishing to reside in Italy are offered a 'pack-age' which includes transport and illegal entry into Italy as well as a variety of job opportunities.

known by the everyday employees of the operation, as they are sheltered by an organisational pyramid structure that protects their anonymity;

- **Recruiters:** seek out potential migrants and secure their financial commitment. These people may be members of the culture and the community from which migrants are drawn;

- **Transporters:** assist the migrants in leaving their country of origin, either by land, sea or air;

- **Corrupt Public Officials or Protectors:** may assist in obtaining travel documents, or accept bribes to enable migrants to enter/exit illegally;

- **Informers:** gather information on matters such as border surveillance, immigration and transit procedures, asylum systems, law enforcement activities;

- **Guides and Crew Members:** are responsible for moving illegal migrants from one transit point to the other or helping the migrants to enter the destination country;

- **Enforcers:** are primarily responsible for policing staff and migrants, and for maintaining order;

- **Debt-collectors:** are in the destination country to collect fees;

- **Money-launderers:** launder the proceeds of crime, disguising their origin through a series of transactions or investing them in legitimate businesses;

- **Supporting Personnel and Specialists:** may include local people at transit points who might provide accommodation and other assistance.

What evidence points toward a high degree of organisation in the trafficking of migrants? Europol (1999) provides the following indications: different nationalities are smuggled on the same transport, a great degree of organisation is needed to smuggle large numbers of persons over great distances, large amounts of money change hands, and when things go wrong, immediate legal assistance is available. A study of illegal migrants intercepted in Lithuania (Sipaviciene 2000, cited in IOM 2000) found that they had passed through an average of 3.6 transit countries and that their journey had been 'multi-modal' with an average of 4 modes of transport used. No migrant had covered the entire journey by the same means of transport.

Transnational Organised Crime Groups

Adamoli et al. (1998, p. 11) describe organised crime groups as becoming increasingly more flexible and decentralised. This flexible structure and increased co-operation with other criminal groups allows for the prompt re-organisation of illicit activities according to threats from law enforcement, demand for services and the number of competitors. The incorporation of small sub-units of criminal specialists, who provide particular services and expertise that might otherwise be outside of the scope of the criminal organisation, enables the organisation to rapidly adjust to new market opportunities.

Criminal groups are adapting to the environment, new opportunities and markets. Europol[15] reports that criminal groups are active in a number of different markets. Technological advances have facilitated criminal activities (counterfeiting and fraud) requiring less specialisation than was previously necessary and which have allowed criminals to diversify their activities. Criminal organisations have changed from large, cumbersome, hierarchical entities to smaller, more flexible, horizontal structures. These criminal groups reach informal agreements to work together and Europol reports an increase in multinational criminal groups active in the European Union (Staatscourant, 18–12–2000, p. 5). In July 2000, the Dutch police apprehended an international criminal group including 54 Iranians, 3 Iraqis, 2 Algerians and a Romanian. They were charged with drug trafficking and falsification of documents. The criminal group, in possession of 265 passports, Schengen visas and other identification papers were also believed to be involved in the smuggling of migrants.

A number of organisations have documented the involvement of organised crime groups in the smuggling and trafficking of human beings.[16] They fall on a continuum ranging from freelance criminals with ties to organised crime overseas, as is the case with Russians smuggling women into the US to work in the sex industry, to loose confederations of organized criminal entrepreneurs or enterprises, as is seen among the Asian gangs who control the trafficking of women to and in the United States (Richard 1999). At the end of the continuum are the highly structured, criminal organisations controlling the trafficking process from start to finish (as is the case with the Albanians; see Ruggiero 1996).

Interpol's General Secretariat indicates that there has been a recent change in the structure of trafficking and smuggling.

---

[15] *Europal 1999 Annual Report on Organised Crime,* cited *Staatscourant,* 18-12-2000, p. 5.

[16] These include international and national law enforcement and intelligence-gathering agencies as well as inter-governmental agencies including, but not limited to Europol, Interpol, the US State Department, the IOM, the Global Survival Network (GSN).

Whereas in the past, the sex business was in the hands of nationals with a link to suppliers of women, and those groups dealing with women used to restrict themselves mainly to the import of women, new analysis has shown that they now tend to control the whole sex business chain, including the 'voluntary' prostitution market, in order to maximise profits [...] whereas in the past the Lithuanian and Ukrainian traffickers needed to rely on the well-organised logistics and well-defined personnel structure in the countries of destination, they can now run their own exploitation business. (Kendall 1999, p. 5)

Analytical surveys generated by Interpol indicate that half of the sex business is now in the hands of non-nationals.

Exploitative Practices and Maintaining Control over their Victims

Traffickers and enforcers have characteristically been known to use excessive violence against their victims to maintain control. Less sinister practices include seizing of documents, confinement of victims to the workplace or threatening them with deportation. More threatening practices include constant monitoring of the victims' whereabouts, threats of violence against the victim and his or her family in the country of origin, actual violence to include tattooing victims, burning them with cigarettes, assault and rape (Jantsch 1998; Vocks and Nijboer 2000).

Unlike the domineering and often violence-prone practices that Albanian and other Central and Eastern European traffickers use to maintain control over their victims, this is not the case in other countries. Accused by the US government of running a global crime network that netted her more than $40 million dollars, of corrupting foreign government officials and making her a major competitor of China's Central Bank, the 'Mother of All Snakeheads' was, to the thousands of Chinese she helped smuggle into the US, the best-known and most revered figure in New York's Chinatown. She was considered a saint for 'reuniting families' (E. Barnes, Time, 31–7– 2000, pp. 40–42).

Link to Other Criminal Activities

The networks which smuggle and traffic human beings as well as the victims themselves have been linked to other criminal activities. Criminal groups involved in smuggling and trafficking have not only forced their victims into prostitution, a criminal offence in some countries, but they have also been known to coerce trafficked victims into selling drugs (Gunatilleke 1994; Richard 1999), organised begging and pick pocketing (Kendall 1999).

The criminal groups themselves develop "horizontal interdependencies" (Adamoli et al. 1998, p. 17) which refers to the connections established among different activities by the same criminal organisation and indicates a pattern of diversification. Criminal enterprises make use of the skills, routes, existing contacts and corrupt networks developed in certain markets in specific countries and expand into other illicit markets. In addition to the trafficking, smuggling and pimping of their victims, these organisations are involved in numerous criminal activities. Intelligence sources at Interpol indicate that trafficking supplements more traditional criminal activities such as vehicle theft, drug trafficking[17] (Kendall 1999), trafficking in arms (Savona et al. 1995; Jantsch 1998), and money laundering. Traffickers have been linked to physical violence, extortion for protection money or money lending to repay debts.

The United Nations Global Programme Against Trafficking In Human Beings

The Global Programme has been developed by the Centre for International Crime Prevention (CICP) and the United Nations Interregional Crime and Justice Research Institute (UNICRI). UNICRI's research programme brings to the foreground the involvement of organised crime groups in the smuggling and trafficking of human beings and the CICP's technical assistance projects promote the development of effective criminal justice responses to it. The projects consist of an integrated package of policy-oriented research and targeted technical co-operation (UNODCCP 1999). In order to fully understand the phenomenon and be able to make effective policy recommendations at the national, regional and international levels, the projects focus on countries of origin, transit and destination.

There are a number of projects, in different stages of development in four different regions of the world: Asia Pacific (Philippines), West Africa (Benin, Nigeria and Togo), Eastern Europe (Czech Republic and Poland) and South America (Brazil). The focus of the research and assessment component is to identify the modus operandi, travel routes and degree of organisation of criminal networks/organised crime groups.

One of the objectives of the Global Programme against Trafficking in Human Beings is to collect quantitative data on trafficking patterns, routes, and illegal practices during all stages of the process from recruitment and transport to settlement and forced labour in the destination country. This data, along with information collected on best practices (to include, among others, legislation, inter-agency co-

---

[17] According to Adamoli et al. (1998, p. 17), Albanian groups smuggle both drugs and aliens across the Adriatic, while Asian crime groups use the same routes to smuggle aliens across the US—Canadian border that were formally used to smuggle cigarettes.

operation, victim support services) should be made available in a database at the end of the three-year project.

Towards this purpose, UNICRI has developed a number of questionnaires and a checklist for the analysis of case files[18] which should allow for the standardisation and comparison of data. There are three standard questionnaires aimed at different audiences. One questionnaire is designed to collect information on the work of NGOs—their mandates, the clients they serve, the services they provide, and their relationship with both NGOs and governmental agencies. As NGOs have been the forerunners in the field of identifying the problems and providing services to victims, it was felt that many of the best practices could be identified within this group.

The second questionnaire seeks to gather data directly from the victims by asking them a number of questions on their experiences. The focus remains on the illegal practices and the involvement of criminals and criminal groups. This questionnaire will undergo modifications to address specific situations or cultural variables in the countries under study. The third questionnaire, aimed at government law enforcement and intelligence sources emphasises even more strongly the practices and role of organised criminal groups in the smuggling and trafficking of human beings. There is a degree of overlap between the surveys for victims and government agencies. The topics covered in the questionnaire include recruitment practices, exploitation, routes and experience during the travel, costs and debts incurred by the victim (or his or her family), the involvement of criminal groups and organised crime, connivance and corruption. The questionnaire designed to obtain information from intelligence sources delves more deeply into the smuggling/trafficking organisation's involvement into other criminal practices and the nature of criminal earnings.

Generating detailed empirical data will allow us to transcend anecdotal stories and provide us with a deeper understanding of the phenomenon, which will allow us to develop better measures to educate potential victims and punish transgressors.

Projects in the Global Programme against Trafficking in Human Beings

In order to fully understand what fuels the phenomenon of smuggling and trafficking in the different countries under study, one must also comprehend the historical, economic, cultural and political situation in the countries of origin and destination. This section focuses

---

[18] This checklist was adapted from the checklist that was developed by members of the Van Traa Commission (a parliamentary inquiry commission in the Netherlands to examine the role of police investigative methods and organised crime) and further refined by the Research and Documentation Centre at the Dutch Ministry of Justice. It was developed for the purpose of analysing case files for the Organised Crime Monitor. For more information see Kleemans et al. (1998).

on two UN projects to show the differences in the illegal markets and what sustains them.

The Case of the Philippines: An Economically Accepted Practice

The Philippines provides the world's second largest population of overseas workers. What began as a temporary solution to the unemployment problem and balance of payment in 1974, has now reached large-scale proportions and has acquired a life of its own (Go 1996). Remittances from overseas Filipino workers amounted to US$6,794,550 in 1999.[19] The Philippine government has a vested interest in keeping its citizens safely employed abroad.

Filipinos work in over 150 countries around the world. While most of the migration of women from the Philippines is for the purpose of domestic labour and marriage, a number of the women work in Japan on entertainer visas. Two excellent studies on trafficking of Filipinos to Europe (Ateneo 1999) and Japan (IOM 1997) document cases of trafficking of Filipinas for forced labour and sexual exploitation. However, preliminary interviews in both Australia and Europe during the course of this research Project[20] indicate that while Filipinos make use of 'extra-legal' smuggling routes, usually for the purpose of joining family members, the trafficking of Filipinas to Western Europe and Australia is not reaching noticeable proportions among embassy and intelligence sources. Interviews with government officials[21] in the Philippines point to the fact that the government is most concerned with the welfare of women who have been trafficked to Japan and exploited in the sex industry. There are indications that these women are falling under the control of Japanese organised crime (Heazle 1993). The Philippines Centre for Transnational Crime (PCTC) reports, however, that Japan is no longer a favourite destination for Filipino 'entertainers'

---

[19] Source: Foreign Exchange Department, Bureau of Labour and Employment Statistics. These figures include remittance from overseas Filipino workers as well as immigrants.

[20] Interviews with officers at the Australian Embassy in Manila, the Consulate General of the Philippines, Torino, Italy an investigative officer specializing in trafficking in human beings at Europol, the Hague, and an intelligence officer at the UK Immigration Service, London, point to the fact there are few cases of trafficking of Filipinos to these destinations. The situation involves more often cases of Filipinos using illegal channels to be smuggled into the country after their relatives in Western Europe or Australia have paid their passage. While there are cases of trafficking, in particular of women, from South East Asia, it involves women from other countries in the region.

[21] Interviews were held during a mission to the Philippines in September 2000 with high ranking government officials from the following departments: Bureau of Immigration, Interpol Liaison Office, National Bureau of Intelligence, Commission for Filipinos Overseas, Philippine Overseas Employment Administration and the National Police Commission.

and only half of the 150,000 entertainers remain in Japan. The other half seek employment in Canada, Nigeria, the Middle East and other countries (Cascolan 2000).

The Philippine Government has taken strict and extensive measures to protect its citizens, including mandatory, pre-travel counselling and background checks on perspective spouses. Women wanting to leave the country on an entertainment visa must undergo an audition to prove that they can perform professionally. If this is not the case, permission to leave the country is denied.

Within the framework of the UN pilot project on Coalitions against Trafficking in Human Beings in the Philippines, a coalition has been formed between 13 government agencies which, in one way or another, address the issue of foreign workers and/or smuggled or trafficked individuals. This should facilitate the government's approach to successfully addressing the problem. To collect and concentrate expertise, the Philippines Center on Transnational Crime has been created. Awareness-raising training for law enforcement officers in outlying regions is another technical assistance measure introduced through the project.

The Case of West Africa: A Culturally-Accepted, Historical Practice

There has been extensive research on the trafficking of children for labour exploitation in West Africa (see Kekeh 1997; UNICEF 1998, 2000; ESAM 1998, 1999; Entraide Universitaire Mondiale du Canada 1999; Bazzi-Veil 2000; Verbeet 2000). The CICP/UNICRI project in West Africa focuses on the countries of Benin, Nigeria and Togo.

In West Africa, movement of persons, placement of children outside of the home and trafficking within the borders of a country are fairly common practices although, due to the stark differences in the economies of some of the Western African nations, trans-border trafficking occurs as well.

In the countries of Benin and Togo, trafficking predominantly involves children for the purpose of labour exploitation as domestic servants[22] (female children) and on farms and plantations (male children). This movement can be attributed to social, economic and historical factors. Historically, the West African region has been characterised by patterns of migration. Children have taken part in these migratory practices. Children are introduced to work at very young ages. Through this work they are taught social values. Furthermore, the life and education of a child is the responsibility of the extended family. It is not uncommon for children to grow up in the family of relatives, or third persons, if these persons are living in better circumstances and can thus provide the child with better educational and work opportunities.

---

[22] In Togo, girls are (trafficked and) placed to work as domestic servants in order to prepare them for married life and to gain their dowry (Verbeet 2000).

In part, the voluntary placement of children (which often leads to their trafficking) is driven by poverty, in part by the desire to provide a better life for their children (Verbeet 2000).

The trafficking of children may take a number of forms (Entraide Universitaire Mondiale du Canada 1999). The child can be sold outright by his or her parents for a small amount of money (which may range from CFA 10,000 to CFA 100,000 depending on the country where the transaction takes place); the child may be placed with the creditor of the family as reimbursement; the child may be promised a job and may in fact work but usually under exploitative conditions and the mediator usually collects the child's salary; lastly, the child may be given by the parents to an individual who promises to provide the child with either a good education or job training. The child receives neither and is usually forced into working on a plantation or as a maid, a 'load carrier'[23] or street vendor.

Interviews with NGOs, government officials and even trafficked children (while on mission to Benin and Togo in September and November 2000) paints a tragic picture of parents willingly giving their children to strangers who come to the village with promises of providing the children with an education and a job. The author had the opportunity to interview a nine-year-old Beninese female child who had been brought by her sister at the age of six to work as a domestic helper in a Nigerian household. After three years, the child escaped and was being assisted by the Consulate General of the Republic of Benin to repatriate her. She could not remember her native dialect and had difficulties speaking French; she could, however, speak the Yoruba dialect that she learned in the Nigerian household. Two Togolese boys were interviewed during one of the missions. Their parents had sent them to another West African country to learn a trade. Instead, they were exploited for three years and then dismissed with not even enough money to pay their transportation back to Togo. While some children want to leave, enticed by promises of bicycles or small radios, the majority of them are too young and inexperienced to make a rational decision. The younger children are involuntarily sent by their parents, in the false belief that they are helping their child who is often subjected to years of hard work and exploitation in foreign countries.

The situation in Nigeria differs somewhat from that in the other two countries under study. While Nigeria serves as a destination country for children being trafficked from Togo and Benin, it is also a source country. While Nigerian children are trafficked in the sub-region for labour exploitation, young girls and women are also being trafficked not

---

[23] 'Load carrier' is the name given to individuals who are paid meager amounts to carry large, heavy loads on top of their heads. Often these were women and young children.

only in the subregion but also to destinations in Europe and beyond for the purpose of sexual exploitation.[24]

Approximately 95% of the Nigerian women trafficked to Italy for the purpose of prostitution come from Benin City in Edo State, which, interestingly enough, is not the most poverty-stricken region in Nigeria. Reports abound of the use of 'ju-ju' or ritual contracts or oaths originating in Voodoo practices to ensure the women's success, prevent them from speaking out and protect the traffickers (Gramegna 1999; Aronowitz, interviews with various officials during the UN start-up mission to Nigeria, November 2000).

The governments in all three countries are aware of and concerned with the problem. Extensive research, in part conducted by local and foreign NGOs and Intergovernmental Organisations such as UNICEF, the International Labour Organisation (ILO) and the International Organisation for Migration (IOM) have called world-wide attention to the problem (the ILO study on child labour (Verbeet 2000) was conducted with the financial support of the US Department of Labour). Nigeria has signed bilateral agreements with a number of countries to repatriate its citizens and foreign governments have expressed interest in investing in both prevention and repatriation projects. NGOs in all three countries were and continue to be the forerunners in calling attention to the problem and providing shelter and awareness-raising prevention campaigns to victims or potential victims. In all three countries the NGOs work fairly closely with government agencies. One of the objectives of the UN's trafficking project is to assist in the design and development of a council involving all three countries in order to facilitate study of the problem of trafficking as a subregional problem and to assist in the repatriation and follow-up of trafficked victims between the countries.

These two examples shed some light on problems endemic to these countries or areas. The reasons which propel individuals from these countries or areas to sometimes use irregular channels to migrate, or the methods which are used to entice and traffic the individuals may differ somewhat from those which affect migrants from other parts of the world. The nature of the trafficking or the destination countries may differ. The conditions which these individuals flee from in their own countries, however, are comparable to those in other countries: extreme poverty, limited or non-existent educational and job opportunities and the hope for a better life for themselves or their children, elsewhere. The following section will examine, in more depth, the conditions which facilitate the smuggling and trafficking of human beings.

---

[24] Young unaccompanied (female) minors arrive in the Netherlands and within weeks disappear from reception centres to end up in prostitution. Italy is the main destination for adult Nigerian women entering (or being forced into) prostitution. Few countries are immune to the problem and even on the idyllic, tourist Canary Island of Tenerife, Nigerian traffickers have been running prostitution rings (*Tenerife News* 4-1-2000, p. 13).

Conditions Facilitating The Smuggling And Trafficking Of Human Beings

This section examines some of the reasons why transnational trafficking can exist and continue with little impunity. There are a number of elements facilitating smuggling and trafficking of migrants (Winer 1996). These elements are applicable, in varying degrees, to source, transit and receiving countries.

Lack of Legislation

Perhaps the most pervasive problem in many countries is the lack of legislation defining, and putting forth a sentence to punish the offence. While this is true of many countries in transition and development, they often have legislation prohibiting activities included in the trafficking process—falsification of documents, living off of the proceeds of a prostitute, kidnapping and/or transporting children across borders without the permission of the parents, and false imprisonment.

Lack of Political Will and Corruption

These two elements often go hand in hand. Corrupt government officials who profit from the practices involved in trafficking of human beings—payment for false documentation, visas, or the safe passage at border crossings—often lack the political will to commit to passing and enforcing legislation.

Lack of Capacity

Extensive, unguarded borders and weak border patrols as a result of a lack of both manpower and material resources,[25] hinder many immigration and law enforcement agencies and thus facilitate the smuggling of migrants and children.

Lack of Co-operation Both Internally and Internationally

Domestically, various agencies are concerned with the protection of individuals' rights and safety as well as the investigation of criminal activities. Co-operation between agencies does not always exist within a country. In order to address the problem of transnational trafficking, international police and justice co-operation is essential.

These factors, however, do not address the real causes which drive persons to take the risks: increased and widespread poverty, insufficient

---

[25] In Benin there are 700 kilometers of unguarded, porous borders. The agency responsible for protecting children throughout the country, the Brigade for the Protection of Minors, is comprised of only eight people. Nigeria must struggle with another set of problems as the country is constantly plagued by electricity outages and the immigration outposts often do not even have telephones, let alone computers. Such limitations greatly hamper even the most honest efforts to address the problem.

educational and training opportunities, high demand for cheap labour and sex, and ignorance of the risks and dangers involved (UNICEF 2000).

Strategies To Prevent And Fight Smuggling And Trafficking In Human Beings

Only an integrated and comprehensive approach will be effective in fighting and reducing the transnational trafficking in human beings. This approach must meet the following three-pronged test: prevention, protection and assistance to trafficked victims, and enforcement and prosecution of traffickers (Warnath 1998).

Prevention

Awareness and sensitization campaigns are important at two levels. On the one hand, it is necessary to target persons at risk of becoming trafficking victims in their countries of origin. Sensitisation campaigns are also necessary in the transit and destination countries to inform the local population of the plight of these victims. Too often the victims are criminalized because of their illegal status in the country or their involvement in prostitution. Populations in the receiving countries must be made to understand that these trafficked migrants are victims and need legal protection and social support services. Many NGOs at the local, national and international level (La Strada) as well as intergovernmental organizations (IOM) in the source countries are actively involved in awareness campaigns targeting potential victims.

Research is essential to identify individuals or groups at risk and to determine whether or not awareness-raising campaigns, assistance programmes and laws are effective. A study (Vocks and Nijboer 1999, 2000) on trafficked women from Central and Eastern Europe who were brought to the Netherlands and forced to work in prostitution shows that the majority of those interviewed were working as prostitutes in their own countries and/or at least knew that they would be working as prostitutes abroad. This, of course, has implications for awareness-raising campaigns in countries of origin, where information about the dangers of trafficking must be targeted toward the local prostitution population as well as towards other potential victims.

Economic alternatives require strengthening educational, training and job opportunities in the countries of origin. Numerous intergovernmental organizations such as UNICEF and NGOs in the countries of origin are actively involved in providing such opportunities to children and young women to prevent their departure or facilitate their return. Governments in destination countries can play a role as well. The United States through USAID participates in economic alternative programmes in source countries, including job and skills training, economic opportunity and small business development (Warnath 1998, p. 64). This programme has committed $3.1 million to developing economic alternatives for women in countries of origin (aimed at women in the Ukraine and Poland; US Department of State).

Intervention and deterrence measures (development of training material) are important to help those in consular offices, immigration, police and health care workers recognise a situation and be able to intervene to assist trafficking victims extract themselves from dangerous situations. This, however, is not sufficient but must be followed-up with assistance to the victims.

Strengthening Protection and Assistance to Victims

Victims require a variety of services. These range from financial and legal assistance to psychosocial support, and support and protection for the families in the country of origin. Should victims desire to return home, cooperation between destination and source countries is necessary in order to strengthen reintegration. Reintegration assistance must be provided to victims who chose to or are forced to return (for a description of IOM's work in this area see Escaler 1998).

Legislation should offer victims protection, particularly in situations when their life is in danger. In Italy, for instance, Article 16 allows the chief of police to grant a special residence permit whenever police operations, investigations or court proceedings, or the social services of a local administration identify situations of abuse or severe exploitation of a foreign citizen, and whenever the safety of the foreign citizen is seen to be endangered as a consequence of attempts to escape from the conditioning of a criminal organisation or of statements made during preliminary investigations or in the course of court proceedings (Giammarinaro 1998).

Efforts must be made to strengthen NGOs which are often the front line workers with victims of trafficking, particularly with migrants who fear or mistrust the police. Furthermore, a positive and strong working relationship must be established between police and NGOs if efforts to assist and protect victims and strengthen prosecutions are to be successful. As an example of a successful co-operative relationship, the German police often work closely with NGOs so that even in the investigative phase the trafficking unit co-operates with interpreters and the NGOs, who are present as early as the raid (Kangaspunta 2000). CO14 of the London Metropolitan Police Department endeavours to establish links with NGOs and embassy personnel in the countries of origin in order to facilitate the safe return of trafficked victims (Kelly and Regan 2000).

It must be remembered that victims of trafficking, even if the initial departure from the country of origin was voluntary, have often suffered unspeakable degradations and physical violence at the hands of the traffickers. Until their safety can be guaranteed in the destination country and the country of origin, should they choose to, or be forced to return, they should be given the right to remain safely in the destination country. A number of countries[26] have implemented this protection which grants victims of forced prostitution temporary resident permits.

Effective Legislation, Law Enforcement and Prosecution

First and foremost, legislation must exist prohibiting the offences of smuggling and trafficking. It must also be enforced. Governments must take the violation of this legislation seriously. According to Bales (1999b, p. 9)

> [...] a key finding (in his study) is the importance of govern-
> mental corruption in predicting trafficking. This analysis sug-
> gests that reducing corruption should be the first and most
> effective way to reduce trafficking. In other words, potential
> traffickers need to understand that their government perceives
> trafficking as a crime and that they cannot bribe their way out
> of prosecution or through the border if they commit the crime.

More research must be done on trafficking routes, the modus operandi of criminals and their organisations and the relationship that victims have with their traffickers. Law enforcement and intelligence agencies must keep abreast of new technology and the use of the Internet for recruitment purposes. Technical assistance programmes are essential to help strengthen law enforcement and criminal justice systems in developing countries and those in transition which are the countries of origin and increasingly new countries of transition and destination.

Awareness-raising and training among law enforcement officials is essential in many countries. It is of the utmost importance that cases be recognised as trafficking cases and not simply classified, for instance, as document forgery or prostitution cases. Further, expertise must be developed and these 'task forces' must be adequately staffed. Law enforcement should dedicate sufficient staffing to work with victims to ensure their protection and co-operation. It would behoove law enforcement (and prosecutors) to work more closely with NGOs. NGOs such as the Stichting Tegen Vrouwenhandel (Foundation against the Traffic of Women) in the Netherlands and PAYOKE in Belgium enable about half of the trafficked women they support to provide evidence against their exploiters (Kelly and Regan 2000).

Law enforcement should not, however, rely upon evidence and testimony supplied by trafficked victims. It is essential that agencies, in addition to taking a reactive approach (responding to a complaint) take disruptive and proactive measures to fight trafficking in human beings. When evidence is insufficient to mount a criminal investigation, disruptive measures can be taken by implementing health, safety, and

---

[26] Austria, Belgium, Germany, Italy and the Netherlands are among the countries which have implemented this regulation.

fire regulations to 'interfere' with the smooth operation of suspected businesses. Proactive approaches require intelligence gathering (such as wiretaps or surveillance) aimed at collecting enough evidence for a prosecution (Kelly and Regan 2000).

The improvement of data collection and information sharing is essential in the fight against organised trafficking schemes. This must occur at the local and national level to fight internal trafficking, and at the international level to aid in the fight against transnational trafficking operations. Furthermore, this information must be shared between law enforcement agencies in countries of origin, transit and destination.[27]

Awareness-raising, information sharing and training must also occur among consular and embassy offices in foreign countries to ensure that traffickers do not use false documents to apply for visas.[28]

Domestically, at the local and national level, interagency co-operation is needed to strengthen prosecutions (that is, the Department of Labour should assist in prosecution of cases involving forced labour).

Penalties for smuggling must be strengthened.[29] The length of the sentence which may be handed down upon conviction, determines, in many countries, whether or not the suspect can be held on remand. In international trafficking cases, particularly when suspects are likely to flee, it is essential that the criminal justice system is able to hold them on remand prior to trial.

Research (Slobbe and Kuipers 1999) found that an increased sentence for the smuggling of human beings in the Netherlands resulted in more cases being investigated and prosecuted in the courts than under the previous law. The increased penalty was an indication that this offence was now a priority for the criminal justice system and warranted large-scale, timely and costly investigations and prosecutions.

---

[27] Within weeks after 58 Chinese migrants were found dead in the back of a truck in Dover, law enforcement agents in various countries were able to trace the exact route taken by the smuggled victims and were able to identify part of the trafficking ring responsible for their transport and ultimate deaths.

[28] In one West African country, consular and embassy offices of many of the EU countries and the US, among others, share information on falsified documents to guarantee that smugglers and traffickers do not go 'visa hopping' (going from one embassy to the next until they find one which will issue a visa). The US embassy prints a monthly 'Anti-Fraud' bulletin and there are meetings in which embassies and consular offices exchange information on the latest 'tricks' that are being used to apply for visas.

[29]Richard (1999) makes a pleas for penalty enhancement (increasing the length of a penalty for a particular offence) if certain conditions exist, such as the trafficking of underage victims, trafficking a large number of victims, unsafe transportation or an act resulting in bodily injury or death, sexual assault, involvement in organised crime or the laundering of profits.

International Co-operation

Unless countries begin co-operating, law enforcement and criminal justice responses will continue to be ineffective. Furthermore, stringent measures in one country do not stem the flow of illegal migration or trafficking but simply displaces it. It is believed that the increase in illegal Chinese immigrants to Europe is a response to the US Government crackdown on illegal Chinese after the Golden Adventure disaster in 1993. The influx of illegal Chinese to Great Britain, is in part, attributable to Germany's 1994 law which allows migrants to be turned away along the German border before they have set foot on German soil to apply for asylum (Newsweek, 25–6–2000).

International co-operation must include, but not be limited to, the exchange of information,[30] co-ordination and harmonisation of national policies and laws, bilateral or multilateral agreements with respect to victim protection and repatriation and reintegration assistance, and extradition of criminals. More technically advanced nations should provide technical assistance to developing nations and those in transition in the fields of legislation, data collection and travel documentation. The provision of training and assistance is necessary to help eradicate corruption amongst poorly trained government officials.

Conclusions

The smuggling and trafficking of human beings, while difficult to measure in terms of the magnitude and scope, appears to be a growing phenomenon. It has been suggested that trafficking in human beings generates more profit than trafficking in drugs, because a person can be used, traded and sold numerous times. If one is caught, penalties are low compared to trafficking in drugs.

The push towards illegal migration is fueled in the source countries by severe economic conditions, ethnic wars and little future perspective. Safety and economic security in the richer countries make them attractive destinations. The patterns of illegal migration are in a constant state of flux and what were once traditional countries of origin and transition are themselves becoming countries of destination. People continue to strive towards a more positive future in other countries and there are those who will provide the illegal mechanisms to facilitate the migration. In the best case scenario, smuggled individuals become illegal migrants; in the worst they become victims of trafficking and are subjected to exploitative conditions.

The illicit migration movement can be viewed as an illegal market. The smuggling/trafficking process generates profits in its own right.

---

[30] The United States and Italy have entered into a formal agreement with respect to an exchange programme on investigation methods, statistical data and analyses of trafficking between the two countries (Sciacchitano 1999).

Further, the hidden markets, many of them (semi-)legal, profit from the use of illegal, cheap labour, thereby intersecting with the criminal(s) who smuggle and traffic illegal migrants. Individuals who employ and exploit illegal migrants range from legal 'entrepreneurs' to organised crime networks. Lastly, there is a strong link between the smuggled and trafficked persons and criminal activities as well as between the illicit markets (supported by smuggled and trafficked persons) and organised criminal activities.

Smuggled persons and trafficked 'victims' differ as do the individuals and organisations which move them. Educational and skill levels vary tremendously, as do the degree to which victims were deceived or the degree of exploitation to which they are exposed. By the same token, the criminals who smuggle and traffic them can range from individuals providing a single service to loose criminal networks to highly organised criminal operations.

The smuggling/trafficking problem is exacerbated by a number of factors to varying degrees in source, transit and destination countries, among them, lack of awareness of the problem and a common definition, insufficient or non-existent legislation, lack of, or insufficient co-operation between agencies both at the domestic and international levels.

A number of NGOs, governments and international bodies have taken measures to address the problem. The General Assembly of the United Nations has signed a Convention on transnational organised crime and two protocols on the smuggling of migrants and the trafficking of human beings. As of 15 December 2000, 123 countries have signed the Convention, 77 the Smuggling Protocol, and 80 the Trafficking Protocol. This provides governments with a common definition. Knowledge is being increased through research which is shedding light on the nature of victims and how to protect them, the effect of increased penalties, and the involvement of organised criminal networks and the routes used in the smuggling and trafficking process. Numerous conventions and conferences are placing the topic high on the national and international agenda. Countries of destination are beginning to invest in source countries. International networks of NGOs and IGOs are providing educative prevention programmes and services to victims and those at risk. And government agencies are beginning to form coalitions to address the problem at home, while international cooperation is addressing the problem at the transnational level. The United Nations, through its Global Programme against Trafficking in Human Beings will be a major contributor in assisting countries prepare for the ratification and implementation of the Convention and the protocols as well as at strengthening government responses to the smuggling and trafficking problem.

In spite of all the measures that are currently being undertaken, it will be impossible to stem the tide of illegal migration until the root causes of the problems in source countries are permanently rectified. This is a long-term commitment, but the only permanent solution to the problem.

Discussion Questions

1 *How is an organized crime group defined?*

2 *How is smuggling of migrants defined?*

3 *There are varying degrees of victimization which can be viewed on a continuum. What are they?*

4 *What is the major difference between smuggled persons and trafficked victims?*

5 *There are five basic factors which point toward an increasing and expanding market in the smuggling of trafficked human beings. What are they?*

6 *One can identify three basic legal markets which are profiting from smuggled in trafficked migrants. What are they?*

7 *There are a number of specific roles that individuals take on within the organization to provide specific services in human trafficking. What are they?*

8 *What strategies can be set forth to prevent and fight smuggling and trafficking of human beings?*

References

Adamoli, S., A. Di Nicoli, E. Savona and P. Zoffi, Organized Crime around the World. Helsinki: European Institute for Crime Prevention and Control (HEUNI), 1998.

Ateneo Human Rights Center, The Philippine–Belgian Pilot Project against Trafficking in Women. Makati City, Philippines: G/F Ateneo Professional Schools, Rockwell Center, 1999.

Aronowitz, A.A., Interviews with officials from NGOs, government agencies, Embassies and Consulates, and child victims of trafficking during start-up missions to Benin, Nigeria and Togo in September and November 2000.

Bajrektarevic, A., Trafficking in and Smuggling of Human Beings: Linkages to Organized Crime: International Legal Measures: Statement Digest. Vienna, Austria: International Centre for Migration Policy Development, 2000a.

Bajrektarevic, A., Trafficking in and Smuggling of Human Beings: Linkages to Organized Crime: International Legal Measures: Presentation Outline. Vienna, Austria: International Centre for Migration Policy Development, 2000b.

Bales, K., Disposable People. Berkeley: University of California Press, 1999a.

Bales, K., What predicts global trafficking? Paper presented at the International Conference on New Frontiers of Crime: Trafficking in Human Beings and New Forms of Slavery, Verona, 22–23 October 1999b.

Bazzi-Veil, L. and A. Ceprass, Etude sous-régionale sur le trafic des enfants à des fins d'exploitation economique en Afrique de l'Ouest et du Centre. Study presented at the Consultation sous-régionale sur le développement des stratégies de lutte contre le trafic des enfants à des fins d'exploitation du travail en Afrique de l'Ouest et du Centre, Libreville 22–24 February 2000.

Cascolan, C., The Philippine experience on trafficking in persons. Unpublished report.

Directorate for Research, Philippines Centre on Transnational Crime, 2000.

Entraide Universitaire Mondiale du Canada, Project de lutte contre le trafic des enfants au Bénin. August 1999.

ESAM, Séminaire de restitution de l'etude sur le trafic des enfants entre le Bénin et le Gabon: rapport de recherche. Lomé, 11–13 August 1999.

ESAM, Le trafic des enfant entre le Bénin et le Gabon: rapport de recherche. 1998-1999.

ESAM, Les enfants placés au Bénin: rapport de recherche. 1998.

Escaler, N., Keynote address. Report of the US–EU Trafficking in Women Seminar, L'Viv, 9–10 July, 1998, pp. 15–20. L'Viv, Ukraine, 1998.

Europol, General Situation Report 1996–1997: Illegal Immigration. The Hague, The Netherlands: Europol, File No. 2562–52, 1999.

Giammarinaro, M.G., Legislation, protection and victim assistance: Italy's recent experiences. Report of the US–EU Trafficking in Women Seminar, L'Viv, 9–10 July, 1998, pp. 33–37. L'Viv, Ukraine, 1998.

Go, S., Emigration pressures and the export of labour from the Philippines. Organization for Economic Cooperation and Development Migration

(OECDM) and the Labour Market in Asia: Prospects to the Year 2000, pp. 159–168. OECDM, 1996.

Gramegna, M., Trafficking in human beings in Sub-Saharan Africa: The case of Nigeria. Paper presented at the International Conference on New Frontiers of Crime: Trafficking in Human Beings and New Forms of Slavery, Verona, 22–23 October 1999.

Gunatilleke, G., Summary of the Report of the Rapporteur, International cooperation in fighting illegal immigration networks. IOM Seminar on International Responses to Trafficking in Migrants and the Safeguarding of Migrant Rights, Geneva, 26–28 October 1994.

Heazle, M., The allure of Japan. Far Eastern Economic Review, pp. 38–39, 14 October 1993.

International Organization for Migration (IOM), Trafficking in Women to Japan for Sexual Exploitation: A Survey on the Case of Filipino Women. Geneva, Switzerland: IOM, 1997.

International Organization for Migration (IOM), Migrant Trafficking and Human Smuggling in Europe: A Review of the Evidence with Case Studies from Hungary, Poland and Ukraine. Geneva, Switzerland: IOM, 2000.

Jantsch, H., Law enforcement: Germany's perspective. Report of the US–EU Trafficking in Women Seminar, L'Viv, 9–10 July, 1998, pp. 51–54. L'Viv, Ukraine, 1998.

Kangaspunta, K., Fact finding mission to Wiesbaden, Germany, 11 February 2000: Meeting with the Bundeskriminalamt, Trafficking in Human Beings Unit. Internal, unpublished document. Vienna, Austria: UN Centre for International Crime Prevention.

Kekeh, R.K., Le trafic des enfants au Togo: etude prospective a Lomé, Vogan et Cotonou: rapport definitif. Wao Afrique, 1997.

Kelly, L. and L. Regan, Stopping Traffic: Exploring the Extent of, and Responses to, Trafficking in Women for Sexual Exploitation in the UK. London: Home Office, Policing and Reducing Crime Unit, Research, Development and Statistics Directorate, 2000.

Kendall, R., Recent trends in international investigations of trafficking in human beings. Paper presented at the International Conference on New Frontiers of Crime: Trafficking in Human Beings and New Forms of Slavery, Verona, 22–23 October 1999.

Kenety, B., Rights-women: Trafficking of women to Europe on the increase. Terraviva, Inter Press Service, 2(67), pp. 1–3, 2000.

Kleemans, E.R., E.A.I.M. van den Berg and H.G. van de Bunt, Georganiseerde criminaliteit in Nederland. The Hague: Ministry of Justice, WODC, 1998.

Ojomo, A., Trafficking in human beings: Nigerian law enforcement perspective. Paper presented at the International Conference on New Frontiers of Crime: Trafficking in Human Beings and New Forms of Slavery, Verona, 22–23 October 1999.

Ould, D., Cross border trafficking and new forms of slavery. Paper presented at the International Conference on New Frontiers of Crime: Trafficking in Human Beings and New Forms of Slavery, Verona, 22–23 October 1999.

Pomodoro, L. and S. Stefanizzi (Eds), Traffico degli eseri umani: donne e minori: un'analisi esplorativa [Trafficking in human beings: Women and minors: An explorative analysis]. Paper presented at the conference The New Slaves: Trafficking in Women and Minors, sponsored by the Provincial Administration of Milan, Caritas Ambrosiana and the Italian Office of European Parliament, Milan, 19 October 1995.

Richard, A.O., International Trafficking in Women to the United States: A Contemporary Manifestation of Slavery and Organized Crime. Center for the Study of Intelligence, State Department Bureau of Intelligence, US State Department, 1999.

Ruggiero, V., Trafficking in human beings: Slaves in contemporary Europe. Paper presented at the Law and Society Association and Research Committee on the Sociology of Law of the International Sociological Association Joint Meetings, University of Strathclyde, Glasgow, Scotland, 10–13 July 1996.

Ruggiero, V., Criminals and service providers: Cross-national dirty economies. Crime, Law and Social Change, 28(1), pp. 27–38, 1997.

Savona, E., S. Adamoni, P. Zoffi, M. DeFeo, Organized Crime across the Border. Helsinki: European Institute of Crime Prevention and Control (HEUNI), 1995.

Schloenhardt, A., Organized crime and the business of migrant trafficking: An economic analysis. Crime, Law and Social Change, 32(3), pp. 203–233, 1999.

Sciacchitano, G., Investigative methods and international cooperation. Paper presented at the International Conference on New Frontiers of Crime: Trafficking in Human Beings and New Forms of Slavery, Verona, 22–23 October 1999.

Sipaviciene, A., New routes in trafficking of migrants: Case of Lithuania. Paper given at the International Conference International Migration Challenges for European Population, Bari, Italy, 25–27 June 2000.

Slobbe, D.F. and M.M.C. Kuipers, Verhoging van de strafmaat op mensensmokkel. Enschede: International Politie Instituut Twente, Universiteit Twente, 1999.

Stop-Traffick Listserver Archive 05/18: UN, SFOR involved in Bosnian prostitution: report. http://www.friends-partners.org/partner/stop-traffick/ 1999/0865.html; 24 May 2000.

UNICEF, Regional Office for West and Central Africa, UNICEF Experience in combating child trafficking in West and Central Africa. Unpublished paper disseminated at the Workshop on Trafficking in Human Beings, Catania, Italy, 14 December 2000.

US Department of State, International Anti-trafficking initiatives; http://www.usinfo.state.gov/topical/global/traffick/fsintl.htm (accessed 11/10/2000).

Verbeet, D., Combating the trafficking in children for labour exploitation in West and Central Africa: Draft. Working Document based on the studies of Benin, Burkina Faso, Cameroon, Cote d'Ivoire, Gabon, Ghana, Mali, Nigeria, Togo. Abijan, Cote d'Ivoire: International Labour Organisation, 2000.

Vocks, J. and J. Nijboer, Land van belofte: een onderzoek naar slachtoffers van vrouwenhandel uit Centraal- en Oost-Europa. Groningen: University of Groningen, Department of Criminology, 1999.

Vocks, J. and J. Nijboer, The promised land: A study of trafficking in women from Central and Eastern Europe to the Netherlands. European Journal on Criminal Policy and Research, 8(3), pp. 379–388, 2000.

Warnath, S., Trafficking of women and children: The future direction of United States policy. Report of the US–EU Trafficking in Women Seminar, L'Viv, 9–10 July, 1998, pp. 63–66. L'Viv, Ukraine, 1998.

Widgren, J., Multilateral co-operation to combat trafficking in migrants and the role of international organizations. Paper presented at the Seminar of the IOM on International Response to Trafficking in Migrants and the Safeguarding of Migrant Rights, Geneva, October 1994.

Winer, J., Alien smuggling: Transnational crimes versus national borders. Presentation to the Working Group on Organized Crime, National Strategy Information Center, Washington, DC, 8 October 1996.

PART V

CHILD SEX TOURISM

Sexual Exploitation of Children and International Travel and Tourism. The sexual abuse of children in developing countries by international tourists has received increasing attention recently, much of it concentrating upon the activities of pedophiles. This research paper argues that the reduction in individual and social constraints associated with tourism and international travel, and an easier access to children for sex in certain destinations, also increases the potential for 'situational' child sexual abuse to occur. It reports on a literature study of the situations in the Philippines, Sri Lanka and Thailand, which found extensive evidence of the use of children for sex by international tourists. The paper suggests that remedial action is required on three levels namely: in the tourist receiving and in sending countries and in the international arena.

Underexposed Child Sex Tourism Industry in Guatemala. With the international spotlight pointed on the child sex tourism trade in Southeast Asia, Central American countries such as Guatemala have become the new haven for child sex tourists. This morally complex human rights dilemma stems from socioeconomic disparities, cultural perceptions, government issues, and globalization. Yet the simple moral indignation at the exploitation of children is not the best guide to effective public policy. This research paper offers a series of practical short- and long-term recommendations focused on legalized child labor, a legislative reform, and nationwide awareness campaigns.

'Child Sex Tourism': An Anomalous Form of Movement? Over the past decade, public and policy concerns have increasingly been expressed about the phenomenon of 'child sex tourism', which is widely understood as an aberrant form of movement that can be cleanly demarcated from 'sex tourism; and 'tourism' more generally. This research paper critically examines that understanding, and argues that campaigns against 'child sex tourism' that fail to acknowledge its connections to and commonalities with other forms of tourism are likely to have a limited impact on the problems they set out to address, and may even have unintended consequences for local adults and children.

Halting the Trafficking of Women and Children in Thailand for the Sex Trade: Progress and Challenges. The trafficking of women and children for the sex trade is considered one of the worst and most exploitive forms of human trafficking. Thailand plays a major role globally in trafficking for the sex trade. This research paper presents estimates on the scope of human trafficking in Thailand, examines the regional and domestic context of it, explores the link between trafficking and sex work, describes what is being done to combat it, analyzes the barriers to halting it, and explores the need for more research about trafficking.

23

SEXUAL EXPLOITATION OF CHILDREN AND INTERNATIONAL TRAVEL AND TOURISM

Kevin Ireland, *Overseas Information and Research, The Save the Children Fund*

Sexual Exploitation: The International Dimension

The organized sexual exploitation of children (defined by most countries as someone under the age of 18) is a worldwide phenomenon, and one that increasingly appears to be taking on an international dimension (Andersen, 1987; Muntarbhom, 1991-93; Narvesen, 1989). Child pornography, often involving the circulation in industrialized nations of material produced in developing countries, the trafficking of children across national borders for exploitation within prostitution, the movement and sexual exploitation of female domestic workers and 'child brides' are all features of this transnational exploitation, each of which essentially involves the movement of the child or pornographic material (the 'supply') to the consumer (the 'demand').

Over the past few years, largely as a result of the international campaign to End Child Prostitution in Asian Tourism (ECPAT), more attention has been paid to that aspect of the transnational sexual exploitation of children that involves the movement of the consumers of children for sexual purposes to those locations in which they can more easily gain access to children—the sexual exploitation of children by international travellers and tourists.

The Perpetrators

Who is it that uses children sexually when travelling overseas? Much of the attention of the media and, indeed, campaigners on this subject has concentrated upon the activities of paedophiles; those with a clear and often compulsive preference for sexual activities with children. On the other hand, evidence from within countries such as the Philippines and Thailand indicates that children are present in no small number in the sexual entertainment industry, servicing foreign visitors as well as an extensive local market. The scale and nature of this use of children for sex suggests that this behaviour is not confined to committed paedophiles, especially when postpubertal children are also considered (Meyer, 1988; Srisang, 1990).

437

The distinction between 'preferential' and 'situational' child molesters (Lanning, 1987) is useful in analysing this situation. The preferential child molester is someone akin to the paedophile, although the definition would also include those whose preference is for sex with post-pubertal children. On the other hand, the situational molester does not have a true sexual preference for children but engages in sex with children for varied reasons. This would include persons of poor self-esteem and coping skills, for whom children substitute for the preferred peer sexual partner, as well as those who display morally or sexually indiscriminate behaviour—a 'why not?' approach to sex.

Finkelhor (1984) stresses the importance of social, as well as psychological factors in contributing to the propensity for child sexual abuse to occur. He proposes that the motivation of the adult to abuse children sexually may be seen as a facilitating factor, which is then constrained by internal inhibitions, external inhibitions and the resistance of the child. The findings of Briere and Runtz (1989) suggest that sexual attraction to children is not uncommon among adult males and, if extended to post-pubertal children, the sexual partnering that reinforces the value of youth in a partner (Ennew, 1986) is likely to increase significantly the numbers of those with a latent attraction to child under age sexual partners.

While internal and external inhibitions, coupled with the resistance of the child, may normally act as an effective constraint to the expression of such latent attraction, the situation for the tourist in a distant, culturally and racially different environment is radically different.

Tourism and Sexual Exploitation: A Connection

There are extensive references in tourism studies that highlight the reduction of individual and social constraints as part of the touristic experience (e.g. Crick, 1988; Wagner, 1977). When combined with a situation in which easy access is provided to children for sexual purposes, especially if this can be rationalized as a more relaxed cultural attitude to sex, then these factors provide a significantly increased potential for child sexual abuse to occur.

This link between tourism and child sexual abuse has been developed by Hiew (1993), who argues that situational conditions in tourist destinations and the state of anonymity of travellers interact with personality and cognitive factors in tourists to enhance sexual interest and reduce inhibitions to become sexually involved with children. He notes that research provides evidence of a relationship between situational factors and a variety of deviant and anti-social behaviours, through the process of 'deindividuation':

'The term refers to a feeling that one will not be held responsible for his or her behaviour. There is a loss of a person's sense of individuality and a loosening of moral restraints against deviant behaviour.' (Hiew, 1993)

This combination of factors suggests that there is something inherent in the nature of tourism to other countries and cultures that increases the potential for child sexual abuse to take place. Indeed, Ennew (1986) reports that at least two studies have suggested that men are more likely to give way to repressed paedophiliac tendencies while away from home.

There are few reliable research studies which identify the real scale or nature of the sexual exploitation of children in developing countries, and none which investigates adequately the role of the international tourist in this. However, there is sufficient evidence from organizations working with children, and from governments, to demonstrate that there is extensive and systematic sexual exploitation of children and that international tourists contribute significantly to this.

A Study of the Phillippines, Sri Lanka and Thailand

In order to establish what is-and what is not-known about the sexual exploitation of children by international tourists, the Save the Children Fund (SCF') recently commissioned a literature study on this subject (Ireland, 1993). The Philippines, Sri Lanka and Thailand were taken as example tourist receiving countries and special attention was given to tourism from the UK.

The study found that there is extensive evidence of the use of young boys for sex by adult males from the West, Australasia and other Asian countries. This appears to be the predominant feature of the sexual exploitation of children in Sri Lanka (Bond, 1980; Senevirame, 1991). While this also occurs in the Philippines (Congress of the Philippines, 1990) and Thailand (O'Grady, 1992), these countries also have an extensive sexual entertainment industry, in which girls, as well as boys, provide sexual services for foreign visitors (as well as local men). In Thailand especially, it would appear that the sexual exploitation of girls in prostitution is numerically much greater than that of boys (Skrobanek, 1990).

Tourism has been seen, in each of the countries, as an opportunity for rapid economic development, bringing in much needed foreign exchange (Richter, 1989; Senevirame, 1991). Stimulating tourism has received precedence over social policies, including the protection of children.

Various promotions and advertisements within the UK and European markets have formerly alluded, if not openly referred, to the availability of sexual entertainment in the countries studied (Ireland, 1993). There has only been very limited reference or allusion to the availability of children, although this has occurred more explicitly in some specialist, gay publications (see Aquino, 1987). Police and other sources who work with sex offenders in Britain consider that the overt promotion of the availability of children for sex is no longer an issue, as this knowledge is already widespread among paedophiles and the general public.

The sexual exploitation of children by tourists does not occur in a vacuum. Evidence from Sri Lanka is less clear, but in the Philippines and Thailand it takes place within a much more widespread exploitation of children-sexual and otherwise mew, 1992).

Poverty is an underlying cause in drawing children into sexual exploitation, but it is by no means the only factor. Disparities in wealth within the society are important, in particular the impact that this has on rural-urban migration and the consequent strain on families, traditional values and coping strategies (Hiew, 1992; Manahan, 1991; Weeramunda, 1993).

Children who live on the streets are commonly associated with sexual exploitation and prostitution, but in these countries there is more evidence of recruitment from rural areas by agents and pimps (Srisang, 1990). While there is a connection between street children and sexual exploitation/child prostitution in each of the countries, this seems to be a prominent feature in the Philippines (Abreu, 199 1).

Not only children are affected by the prostitution made but also families and communities. While some children are coerced or physically forced into sexual exploitation, without the knowledge of their parents, others are encouraged or forced to become involved by their parents, who see it as a way of supplementing family income (Abreu, 1991; Srisang, 1990).

Laws exist in each of the three countries investigated that could be used to constrain the activities of those involved in exploiting children sexually, but these laws have been implemented only minimally, especially in relation to foreign visitors. Very few foreigners have ever been convicted for the sexual abuse or exploitation of children, and in most cases *summary* deportation has been the maximum response—and this used only sparingly. Where the law has been applied, it has often been in a way that 'criminalizes' the child as an agent of prostitution rather than protects the child from sexual exploitation (Goonesekere and Abeyrame, 1986).

Governments in each of the countries investigated have recently been paying more attention to the problem of the sexual exploitation of children, with legal, administrative and political initiatives involving international cooperation.

AIDS is an enormous problem for children who are sexually exploited: they have an *extremely* high risk of being infected with *HIV*. Yet it is a sad irony that there are consistent reports that there is an increasing demand for sex with children because it is believed they are more likely to be *AIDS* free, itself a belief that appears to encourage unprotected sex (Muntarbhorn, 1991, 1992, 1993).

The trafficking of children is an integral part of organized sexual exploitation. Most often this occurs within national boundaries, children from rural areas being enticed or tricked by agents from the city, but there is also an extensive network of international trafficking (Sariola, 1986).

Remedial action is required on three levels: first, in the country in which the exploitation takes place; secondly, in the tourist originating countries; and thirdly, in the international arena. Most important of these is the first. Without effective action to address the underlying causes that lead children into sexual (and other) exploitation, and without a concerted effort to implement existing laws to constrain the activities of those who use children for sex, there can be little expectation that the scale of the problem can be reduced. Responses within tourist originating countries have included legislative change to facilitate prosecution of offenders in their country of origin and public education, although there are a number of problems to overcome if extra-territorial prosecutions for child sexual abuse are to be successful (Council of Europe, 1991; Evatt, 1992; *Humurd,* 1993).

Conclusions

The literature study confirmed that there is extensive evidence of the sexual exploitation of children, in the countries investigated, by international tourists, but failed to find conclusive proof of the hypothesis that this arises substantially from the activities of situational as well as preferential molesters of children. There is, however, much circumstantial evidence to suggest that this is the case. It was also impossible to find evidence of the extent to which tourists from the UK are involved, although details of individual cases in which the nationality of the tourist/abuser is known confirms that UK citizens are represented.

Discussion Questions

1   *Who is it that uses children sexually when traveling overseas?*

2   *What are the differences between preferential and situational child molesters?*

3   *What is the link between tourism and sexual exploitation of children?*

4   *Hiew notes that research provides evidence of a relationship between situational factors in a variety of deviant and antisocial behaviors through the process of deindividuation. What does he mean by this?*

5   *Is there any evidence to suggest that boys are also being used for sex?*

6   *Why was it suggested that there are consistent reports of increasing demands for sex with children?*

References

Abreu, L. (1991). Report presented on behalf of ECPAT Philippines to the UN ESCAP Workshop on the Promotion of Community Awareness for the Prevention of Prostitution in the ESCAP Region, in Lampang, Thailand, 20-27 August 1991. UNIESCAP, Bangkok, Thailand.

Andersen, A.G. (1987). *International Report on Child Pornography, Child Prostitution and Child Trade.* Report prepared on the authority of the Norwegian Department of Justice.

Aquino, E. (1987). Tourism and Child Prostitution in Pagsanjan (Philip pines). Rural Organisation for Development (ROAD), Pagsanjan, Laguna, the Philippines.

Bond, T. (1980). Boy Prostitution in *Sri* Lanka: *The Problems, Effects and Suggested Remedies.* Terre des Hommes, in association with Ministry of Plan Information, Colombo, Sri Lanka.

Briere, J. and Runtz, M. (1989). University males' sexual interest in children: predicting potential indices of 'pedophilia' in a nonforensic sample. *Child Abuse and Neglect,* 13, 65-75.

Congress of the Philippines (1990). Committee Report No. 1034. Submitted by the Committee on Women and Family Relations and the Committee on Local Government, 6 April, 1990.

Council of Europe (1991). *Sexual Exploitation, Pornography and Prostitution of, and Traffcking in, Children and Young Adults.* Recommendation No R (91) 11 adopted by the Committee of Ministers of the Council of Europe on 9 September, 1991 and Report.

Crick, M. (1988). Sun, sex, sights, savings and servility: representations of international tourism in the social sciences. *Criticism, Heresy and Interpretation,* 1 (1).

Ennew, J. (1986). *The Sexual Exploitation of Children.* Polity Press, Cambridge.

Evatt, E. (1992). Legal Responses to Child Prostitution and Tourism. Paper presented at the End Child Prostitution in Asian Tourism Conference, 10 November, 1992, Melbourne, Australia.

Finkelhor, D. (1984). *Sexual Abuse: New Theory and Research.* Free Press, New York.

Goonesekere, S. and Abeyratne, A. (1986). Child labour and child prostitution in Sri Lanka and the legal controls. In Report of Conference on Child Labour and Prostitution, Kuala Lumpur, 21-23 February 1986, convened by the Law Asia Human Rights Standing Committee.

Hansard (1993). 11 March 1993, Vol.220, No. 141, Cols 1084-85 (Mr Michael Jack, The Minister of State, Home Office).

Hiew, C.C. (1992). Endangered children in Thailand: third world families affected by sociwconomic changes. In Albee, G.W.. Bond, L.A. and Cook Monsey, T.V. (Eds), *Improving Children's Lives.* Sage, Newbury Park, CA, pp. 129-145.

Hiew, C.C. (1993). A Conceptual Framework to Deal With Pedophile Tourists. Paper presented to ECPAT Consultation, 11-14 May, 1993, Stuttgart, Germany.

Ireland, K. (1993). Wish You Weren't Here: The Sexual Exploitation of Children and the Connection with Tourism and International Travel. Overseas Department Working Paper No. 7, The Save the Children Fund, London.

Lanning, K. (1987). *Child Molesters:* A Behavioural Analysis. National Centre for Missing and Exploited Children, Arlington, Virginia, USA.

Manahan, B. (1991). Report presented on behalf of the Department of Social Welfare and Development, Republic of the Philippines, to the UN ESCAP Workshop on the Promotion of Community Awareness for the Prevention of Prostitution in the ESCAP Region, in Lampang, Thailand, 20-27 August, 1991. UNESCAP, Bangkok, Thailand.

Meyer, W. (1988). *Beyond the Mask: Towards a Transdisciplinary Approach to Selected Social Problems Related to the Evolution and Context of International Tourism in Thailand.* Verlag Breitenbach, Saarbrucken.

Muntarbhorn, V. (1 991 , 1992, 1993). *Sale of Children.* Annual reports of the Special Rapporteur appointed in accordance with resolution 1990/68 of the Commission of Human Rights-E/CN.4/1991/51.

Narvesen, 0. (1989). *The Sexual Exp/oitation of Children in Developing Countries.* Redd Barna (Norwegian Save the Children).

O'Grady, R. (1992). The Child and the Tourist. ECPAT, Bangkok, Thailand.

Richter, L.K. (1989). *The Politics of Tourism in Asia.* University of Hawaii Press.

Sariola, H. (1986). Child Prostitution, *Trafficking and Pornography*. Report for Defence for Children International and Central Union for Child Welfare, Finland.

Seneviratne, M. (1991). Paper presented on behalf of PEACE, Sri Lanka, to the UN ESCAP Workshop on the Promotion of Community Awareness for the Prevention of Prostitution in the ESCAP Region, in Lampang, Thailand, 20-27 August, 1991. UN/ESCAP, Bangkok, Thailand.

Skrobanek, S. (1990). Child prostitution in Thailand. *Voices of Thai* Women, Issue 4, December 1990. Foundation for Women, Bangkok.

Srisang, S.S. (1990). Tourism and child prostitution in Thailand. In *Caught in Modern Slavery: Tourism and Prostitution in Asia*. Report of the Proceedings of the Chiang Mai Consultation, May 1-5,1990. Ecumenical Coalition on Third World Tourism.

Wagner, U. (1977). Out of time and place-mass tourism and charter trips. Ethnos, 42.

Weeramunda, A.J. (1993). Report on Juvenile Delinquency and Child Prostitution in Kalutara District, commissioned by the Commissioner of Probation and Child Care Services, Colombo, Sri Lanka.

24
UNDEREXPOSED CHILD SEX TOURISM INDUSTRY IN GUATEMALA

Glenda L. Giron, *Child Rights Activist*

Introduction

One Internet site quotes a sex tourist, "When it comes to sex, it is not far from the truth to describe Guatemala as the Thailand of Central America. You only have to look in the newspapers, under the headings of 'massages' to find what you want. If you are charged more than US$50, you are being robbed."[1]

The increased level of international awareness about the prevalence of child sex tourism in Southeast Asia has forced the illicit industry to relocate to Central American countries. According to estimates provided by National Plan of Action against Sexual Exploitation of Children in Guatemala, at least fifteen thousand children suffered sexual exploitation in Guatemala in 2001.[2] Indeed, the 2002 report by the United Nations special rapporteur on the sale of children, child prostitution, and child pornography estimated two thousand minors in prostitution in Guatemala City alone.[3] Despite international public opposition to sexual exploitation of children—and legal prohibitions articulated in the United Nations Convention on the Rights of the Child[4]—the underexposed child sex tourism industry in Guatemala poses a morally complex human rights dilemma. Children are forced into the sex tourism industry to provide for their poverty-stricken families.

To understand the factors that make the child sex industry in Guatemala a complex policy dilemma, we need to identify its key players and take into account previous attempts made by the international community in countries such as Thailand and Bangladesh. Subse-

---

[1] ECPAT, "Sexual Exploitation and Trafficking of Children in Central America," ECPAT International Newsletter, 1 September 2001, http://www.ecpat.com/eng/Ecpat_inter/IRC/articles.asp?articleID=195&NewsID=24.

[2] Su Sitio.Com, "Guatemala: Destino Oculto Del Turismo Sexual," http://www.paginasdelsureste.com/printer_253.shtml.

[3] UN Commission on Human Rights, Fifth Session, 2002 Report of the Special Rapporteur on the sale of children, child prostitution and child pornography, 2002, http://www.hri.ca/fortherecord2002/documentation/commission/e-cn4-2002-88.htm.

[4] UN General Assembly, Conventions on the Rights of the Child, Resolution 44/25 (Geneva, 1989), published online via United Nations Children's Fund (UNICEF), http://www.unicef.org/crc/crc.htm.

quently, we can formulate a multilateral, comprehensive plan composed of short- and long-term recommendations that incorporates sociocultural, legislative, and economic reforms.

Key Players in the Child Sex Industry

In order to understand the magnitude of the problem and its human rights implications, one must set clear parameters to describe who is considered a child victim and who are the abusers, the duty holders, and the key NGOs involved in this predicament.

The Children

There are conflicting views about who should be considered a child and whether we should differentiate between children and adolescents. Article I of the 1989 Convention on the Rights of the Child establishes that a child is "every human being below the age of eighteen years unless under the law applicable to the child, majority is attained earlier."[5] It is important to note that under Guatemalan law, majority is also reached at age eighteen. The victims tend to be children between the ages of eight and sixteen who have been sold by their parents to traffickers or pimps. Other children, who come from the countryside, are being lured in with promises of jobs as housekeepers but are instead sent to brothels in inner cities. While most of the victims are local children, there seems to be an increasing proportion of children trafficked from other neighboring countries such as El Salvador and Honduras.

The Abusers: Customers and Suppliers

Different actors take part in the underworld industry of child sex tourism in Guatemala. The supply network is made up of not only traffickers and pimps, but also taxi drivers, managers, owners of hotels and bars, and even lawyers who falsify documents.[6] When it comes to the actual child sex tourists, there is a common misconception that the abusers are exclusively foreigners. According to a report by ECPAT International, most international child sex tourists in Guatemala are Europeans, Americans, Canadians, Japanese, and South Americans. However, internationals are not the only sex tourists in Guatemala; many are domestic.[7] In the same way, there is a tendency to believe that pedophiles are the only customers of the child sex tourism industry. Although pedophiles clearly fit the criteria of child abusers, typical male

---

[5] Ibid.

[6] Su Sitio.Com.

[7] "Sexual Exploitation and Trafficking."

tourists represent a large portion of the population of child abusers. As long as the sex partner meets the desirable physical requirements of the sex tourists, legal age of consent is not a concern. In her testimony before the Senate Foreign Relations Committee on 7 March 2002, ECPAT-USA's coordinator, Carol Smolenski, declared:

> There are other sex tourists who are not pedophiles.... These are men who wish to experiment by having children as sexual partners when they are in a situation where they believe this is acceptable behavior, for example in a foreign country, with a racial group different from their own. Or they have sex with children because they simply do not care whether their sex partner is twelve, eighteen, or twenty-five as long as that partner meets certain physical requirements that the men consider attractive.[8]

As in any other human rights issue, if there are "right bearers" (in this case, the children) there must be "duty holders." Through the Secretariat of Social Welfare, the Guatemalan government is responsible for the well-being and safety of Guatemalan children. Therefore the government of Guatemala has the obligation to implement adequate measures to combat the child sex tourism industry within its jurisdiction. If we subscribe to the idea that countries have the duty to "do no harm," we must include "sending states" (countries from which the customers hail) such as the United States, Canada, and European countries as bearers of partial responsibility.

Factors Contributing to the Child Sex Tourism Dilemma

Simply cracking down on the industry while failing to analyze the reasons that force minors into prostitution is a futile endeavor. In the case of Guatemala, these reasons include socioeconomic disparities, cultural perceptions, governance issues, and globalization.

Socioeconomic Disparities

As developing countries struggle to increase prosperity, the child sex tourism industry has emerged as a de facto tool to combat extreme poverty. Like Thailand in the early 1970s where large gaps in wealth between urban and rural communities evolved, Guatemala's current economic situation is defined by high levels of poverty, and the pressure

---

[8] Senate Committee on Foreign Relations, Convention on the Rights of the Child on the Sale of Children, Child Prostitution and Child Pornography: Hearings on Treaty Document No. 106-37B, 108th Cong., 2nd sess., 7 March 2002, http://www.ecpatusa.org/pdf/senate_testimony.pdf.

to increase revenues from services rather than agricultural production
has the potential to produce the next haven for the child sex tourism
industry. According to a recent country report by the U.K. Foreign and
Commonwealth Office, Guatemala has the world's third most unequal
wealth distribution, as measured by its Gini coefficient.[9] Although no
child should be forced, directly or indirectly, to enter the vicious cycle of
sexual exploitation for commercial means, the reality of this dilemma is
embedded in an economic framework of high demand for child sex
tourism and the readily accessible supply of economically marginalized
Guatemalan children.

Ironically, there are cases in which the abusers are seen as saviors
of impoverished communities. This was the case of Thomas Frank, an
American man accused of sexually abusing up to seventy-nine Mexican
boys.[10] Yet after having financed the installation of potable water in the
community, he was seen as the rescuer of the disadvantaged town. Even
after the abuse cases were disclosed, many residents believed that he
had done more good than harm to their community.

Cultural Perceptions

In all economic, social and political levels of the Guatemalan society,
gender perceptions are entrenched in the ideology of machismo, which
views females as sexual objects and has contributed to the societal
tolerance to exploitation of vulnerable minors, especially girls. Men are
encouraged to have sex before marriage while women are encouraged to
remain virgins until marriage, creating the demand for prostitution.
Another factor is the misleading perception that masculinity is
measured by the numbers of virgins with whom men have sex.

Machismo and other cultural beliefs deeply rooted in the idea that
men are superior to women negatively affect the self-esteem of young
girls. Even more alarming are the findings of a study conducted by Casa
Alianza activists who infiltrated the dangerous child prostitution
network in Central America. They found that many of the female minors
spoke of their exploiters in positive terms.[11] Moreover, Guatemalan
families make daughters take significant responsibility for their
economic well being. Based on these cultural practices that perpetuate
gender discrimination and inequality, sex tourists often believe that it

---

[9] UK Foreign and Commonwealth Office, "Country Profiles: Guatemala," 2004,
http://www.fco.gov.uk/servlet/Front?pagename=OpenMarket/Xcelerate/ShowPage&c=P
age&cid=1007029394365&a=KCountryProfile&aid=1020262398293.

[10] Casa Alianza, "American Accused of Sexual Abuse of Mexican Boys, Arrested in
Thailand," http://www.innocenceindanger.org/innocence/news103/news_american.htm.

[11] Casa Alianza, "Central America: Activists Infiltrate Child Sex Rings," International
Movement Against All Forms of Discrimination and Racism, 5 April 2002,
http://www.imadr.org/project/guatemala/news3.html.

is culturally acceptable to have sex with minors in developing countries such as Guatemala. They even justify their actions by arguing that they are helping these deeply impoverished children by giving them money.[12]

Governance Issues

The Guatemalan government's failure to truly recognize that the problem exists is characterized by the lack of adequate legislation to protect child exploitation, and persistent corruption among law enforcement officers is a key factor contributing to the present situation. Due to the illegal nature of this industry, estimates of the total number of victims are very difficult to establish. I argue that by using this limitation as a pretext, the Guatemalan government fails to acknowledge that the child sex exploitation industry constitutes an alarming problem. The current policies dealing with children's issues are inadequate, outdated, and paternalistic. For instance, the 1969 Children's Code in Guatemala allows judges to incarcerate children for their own protection.[13] There is no surprise that most victims choose not to report abusers since they are afraid of the police.

A central problem stems from the government's inability to stop corruption among law enforcement. It is common for sex tourists to pay police officers a mordida (bribe), a small amount of money that allows them to go home with no criminal record. Corruption also affects other branches of the government that are needed to protect children from child exploitation. In 2001, the Discipline Unit of the Guatemalan Supreme Court investigated 503 cases of wrongdoing, which resulted in fourteen judges being sanctioned, thirty-two being suspended, and four being sanctioned with the recommendation to be removed.[14] The persistent problem of corruption in the judicial system results in ineffective prosecution of child exploiters, especially child traffickers.

Even honest law enforcement officials are part of the problem. They fail to be effective due to lack of proper training and adequate knowledge of the legislation on how to deal not only with child sex tourists, pimps, and traffickers, but also the victims.

---

[12] UK Foreign and Commonwealth Office.

[13] S. Wallenberg, US Servas, "Sex Tourism," http://www.usservas.org/un_summer_2002.htm.

[14] Department of State, Bureau of Democracy, Human Rights, and Labor, "Guatemala: Country Reports on Human Rights Practices," 2003, http://www.state.gov/g/drl/rls/hrrpt/2002/18333.htm.

Globalization

Globalization has brought unprecedented levels of mobility, but also convergence in law. More countries are signing international treaties that deal with the protection of universal human rights, such as the 1989 Convention on the Rights of the Child that Guatemala has also signed and states in Article XIX:

> States Parties shall take all appropriate legislative, adminitrative, social and educational measures to protect the child from all forms of physical or mental violence, injury or abuse, neglect or negligent treatment, maltreatment or exploitation, including sexual abuse, while in the care of parent(s), legal guardian(s) or any other person who has the care of the child.[15]

Unfortunately, globalization has also produced greater economic disparity and has opened the doors to unlawful markets such as the sex child tourism industry, especially in poor, developing countries that suffer from corruption, lax enforcement of laws, and socioeconomic inequality. The Casa Alianza study collected a list of 173 direct or indirect links to Web sites on the Internet promoting child sex tourism in Central America. As Ron O'Grady puts it:

> Two of the key contributors to globalization—tourism and the Internet—have provided an unexpected bonus to child abusers, making the opportunity for child abuse more accessible. One could draw a causal relationship between the rapid expansion of globalization and the growth of child sex trade.[16]

Current Efforts by the International Community

Recently many prosperous Western countries have accepted responsibility for the acts of sexual exploitation of children committed by their citizens abroad, and they are passing laws to prosecute child sex tourists. The United States has put into effect the most stringent law of any "sending state," the 2003 Protect Act, which makes it a crime for a U.S. citizen to travel abroad for the purpose of having sex with children, punishable with fifteen to thirty years in jail.[17]

Most NGOs have taken the role of investigators, whistle-blowers, and defenders of the victims. The major NGOs in the region are Casa

---

[15] UN General Assembly.

[16] R. O'Grady, "Eradicating Pedophilia: Toward the Dehumanization of Society," Journal of International Affairs 55 (Fall 2001): 123–140.

[17] M. Hiebert, "Red Light for Sex Tourists," Far Eastern Economic Review 167 (22 April 2004): 18–19.

Alianza, the Latin American branch of the New York-based child advocacy organization Covenant House, and ECPAT International, an organization founded by the UNICEF when the child sex industry was first exposed in Southeast Asia. With the help of the international media, they have been successful in exposing abuses and helping global organizations pass international laws such as the International Labor Organization's Convention on the Worst Forms of Child Labor and the UN Convention of the Rights of the Child. The latter has revolutionized the way we used to view children as property of their parents. Now, children are endowed with inalienable rights and have the same rights as other disenfranchised minorities.[18]

Lessons from Thailand and Bangladesh

One of the turning points in the fights against the child sex tourism industry in Thailand was a 1993 Time Magazine issue. Since then, Thailand has passed laws against customers buying sex from children under fifteen. This year the United States has helped fund airport billboards warning child sex tourists of the penalties. Moreover, Thailand has received financial support for awareness campaigns, training of law enforcement bodies, and full participation of international organizations to ensure transparency and efficiency.

However, not all interventions yield positive results. With all good intentions, the United States passed the Child Deterrence Act in order to ban imports of goods made by children younger than fifteen.[19] In response to this short-sighted policy, Bangladesh dismissed thousands of child workers from their jobs, who immediately ended up in the streets, mainly working as child prostitutes. Although UNICEF eventually realized the problem and intervened, children had already been traumatized by the experience.

Words of Caution: The Larger Threat of HIV/AIDS

For policy changes to be effective, we need to ensure accountability through constant assessment of progress. On the final question of why the Guatemalan government and the international community should take all the steps necessary to fight child sex tourism, global health issues are too dangerous to be ignored. Children have a greater risk of contracting AIDS. According to a 2002 report of the Special Rapporteur on the sale of children, child prostitution, and child pornography,

---

[18] Ibid.

[19] K. Mahler, "Global Concern for Children's Rights: The World Congress Against Sexual Exploitation," International Family Planning Perspectives 23 (June 1997): 79–84.

The forced penetration of a child by a larger individual is more likely to cause injuries and bleeding by which HIV is transmitted. Children are physically weaker, less experienced and therefore less empowered to negotiate the terms of the abuse, such as an insistence on the use of a condom or refusal to be subjected to particularly violent and physically damaging sexual activity...This is particularly the case with countries in Africa, Asia, and South and Central America.[20]

Practical Short- and Long-Term Recommendations

There is no single, instant, straightforward solution to this dilemma. As such, I propose a comprehensive plan focused on economic, sociocultural, and legislative reforms and local, regional, and international participation.

Legalized Child Labor and Increased Compulsory Education

Because the severe economic desperation cannot be ignored, I propose legalized, regulated, and safe child labor as an alternative. If the main reason why Guatemalan children are facing commercial sexual exploitation is to earn money for their survival, those above the age of twelve should be allowed to work in strictly non-dangerous jobs and with full legal worker protection and benefits. To avoid labor exploitation, international organizations must oversee the program and provide reports to UNICEF.

The government must ensure that children under fifteen attend school and be allowed to work only on a part-time basis. To do this, the compulsory school level needs be raised from sixth grade to at least the ninth grade. We cannot expect children to be successful in the job market if they only complete elementary school. Possible financial sources are UNICEF, national taxes, and USAID.

Additionally, we must have a microeconomic plan in which poor families can take out small loans in order to become entrepreneurs. The World Bank must add stipulations about child sex exploitation and should give additional consideration to those countries that are willing to combat the child sex tourism industry, but have no financial means to do so.

---

[20] UN Commission on Human Rights

National Awareness Campaign and Human Rights Curriculum

In order to deal with the local demand for young girls in Guatemala, high media exposure of the horrible reality of child sex exploitation should be initiated. As in the case of Thailand, a national media campaign would educate the general public about the detrimental effects of gender discrimination and machismo. This awareness campaign could be financed with the help of the private sector in Guatemala, as well as the sending countries. To avoid misappropriation of funds, the United Nations should assign and fund ECPAT International or another appropriate international organization to oversee the program.

As a long-term approach, a human rights education curriculum should be incorporated into the Guatemalan educational system. The curriculum for both primary and secondary education should include core ideas from the UN Convention on the Rights of the Child; however, gender discrimination should be a priority at the secondary level. This subject should be explicitly taught as a single subject for at least seventy-five minutes per week. The educational campaign can be financed by national tax revenues and the national lottery as well as UNESCO.

Finally, more female participation in the political system must be encouraged, not only to address problems of discrimination and abuse previously described, but to provide positive role models for young girls.

Legislative Reform and Governmental Transparency

Current policies and laws need to be reformed in a way that protects victims and punish the abusers. The penalties for all who participate in the sexual exploitation of children should be increased, targeting first the brothel owners and child traffickers. At the same time, the practice of incarcerating rescued children must be changed. Guatemala's Secretariat of Social Welfare should be responsible for the creation and maintenance of shelters that provide psychological and educational services in key regions of Guatemala. The shelters should also provide job training, so rescued children can learn a trade and begin to earn an income.

However, simply reforming or passing laws is futile unless law enforcement officials become part of the solution. The penalties for law enforcement agents who accept bribes should be higher, while a new rewards system could acknowledge officers who demonstrate high levels of dedication and honesty. As part of the rewards system, recipients would be featured in the campaign ads against sexual exploitation of children.

As a long-term goal, the Guatemalan government needs to ensure the protection of local and foreign journalists and human rights advocates in order to guarantee freedom of expression and the collaboration between local and foreign investigative entities. The Guatemalan Ministry of Foreign Affairs must support the foreign experts and scholars who are interested in conducting research and gathering more reliable data.

Since the Guatemalan government still faces low levels of public approval regarding transparency issues, an independent judiciary body should be created in collaboration with international human rights organizations.

Globalization Can Be Part of the Solution

In an attempt to greatly diminish the foreign demand for child sex tourism, the level of international attention should be raised through an international awareness campaign focused on the travel industry to warn tourists of the penalties. As part of this campaign, brochures should be given to tourists at main ports of entry, and billboards should strategically be placed in tourist locations. Also, the creation of a hotline where the general public anonymously can report suspected cases of child sex exploitation should be a priority. Like in the case of Thailand, wealthy sending states should be responsible for paying for the campaign since it is targeted to child sex tourists from their countries.

Another long-term strategy should be international cooperation in the development of universal standards for the collection of evidence in cases of child sex exploitation in order to guarantee efficiency and accuracy. We should take advantage of the opportunity provided by globalization to create common, more effective parameters.

I concur with the vision of the World Congress against Sexual Exploitation of Children in which it was declared that child prostitution "constitutes a form of coercion and violence against children."[21] I believe that the way we treat the most vulnerable members of our society reflects who we are, and the development and well-being of children should be a primary concern to all nations. Nevertheless, policy makers must understand that when faced with this complex human rights issue, simple moral indignation is not the best guide to effective public policy. The Guatemalan government must take a realistic approach to combat the child sex tourism industry. Most child rights advocates may oppose child labor; however, when faced with a strong demand for child sex tourism and a supply of impoverished Guatemalan children, responsible societies must choose the lesser of two evils.

---

[21] "Stockholm Declaration and Agenda for Action," (outcome documents for the First World Congress Against the Commercial Exploitation of Children, Stockholm, Sweden, 27–31 August 1996), http://www.childhub.ch/webpup/csehome.

Discussion Questions

1 *What has occurred to cause the prevalence of child sex tourism to relocate to Central American countries?*

2 *Who are the key players in the child sex industry?*

3 *What are the factors contributing to the child sex tourism dilemma?*

4 *What are some of the current efforts by the international community to curb child sex tourism?*

5 *Why do the children have a greater risk of contracting AIDS than adults?*

25
'CHILD SEX TOURISM': AN ANOMALOUS FORM OF MOVEMENT?

Julia O'Connell Davidson, Ph.D., *School of Sociology & Social Policy, University of Nottingham, UK*

Introduction

In European Union and other affluent Western countries, public and policy debate on 'migration' typically focuses on those forms of migration that are viewed as a threat to national sovereignty and security, and/or to national/racial/ethnic purity. It is thus movements from poor or relatively economically disadvantaged countries to more affluent countries, from countries with predominantly black and brown populations to countries with predominantly white populations, and from Muslim to Christian countries that have received the lion's share of attention and concern, with very little interest being shown in flows of affluent, white and/or Christian persons around the world. Western tourists, gap year students, international business people, and expatriates, for example, are not usually imagined as 'migrant workers'), and while migratory flows from poor to affluent regions are widely regarded as problematic, movements from affluent to poor countries have not generally been identified as posing economic, social or political problems (see King, 2002).

One form of movement from affluent to developing countries that has been a focus of anxiety over the past decade is the phenomenon known as 'child sex tourism'. As a result of awareness raising and lobbying campaigns mounted by a number of Non-Governmental Organisations (NGOs), most particularly End Child Prostitution in Asian Tourism (ECPAT), the 1990s witnessed growing international concern about the fact that some European, North American, Japanese and Australian men travel to poor and developing countries in order to sexually abuse local children, and a number of countries introduced legislative changes to address the problem. On first inspection, increasing popular and policy interest in a problem associated with movements from affluent to developing countries might appear to represent a refreshing change from traditional approaches to 'migration', and to open up opportunities for more critical and reflexive public debate on the global inequalities that underpin all forms of population movement in the contemporary world. However, as this paper will argue, because dominant discourse on 'child sex tourism' rests on the assumption that for both moral and practical purposes, a clear boundary exists between 'child sex tourism' on the one

457

hand, and 'sex tourism' and 'tourism' on the other, and detaches all three
from their basis in global political and economic inequalities, it closes off
rather than opens up such possibilities.

Sex, Travel and 'Child Sex Tourism'

There is a strong historical association between travel, sex, race and
political domination (Nagel, 2003; Gill, 2003; Enloe, 1993; Hyam, 1990).
For centuries Africa, the Americas and Asia 'were figured in European
lore as libidinously eroticized… a *porno-tropics*… a fantastic magic
lantern of the mind onto which Europe projects its forbidden sexual
desires and fears' (McClintock, 1995, p. 22), and as Ann Laura Stoler
(1997, p. 14) notes:

> Colonial observers and participants in the imperial enter-
> prise expressed unwavering interest in the sexual interface of
> the colonial encounter. Probably no subject is discussed more
> than sex in the colonial literature and no subject more fre-
> quently invoked to foster the racist stereotype of European
> society.

Today, travel is still often associated with a quest for sexual experience with 'exotic' Others, but there is also a more general association
between travel and sex. Sex is widely understood to be part of the tourist
experience, and whether with other tourists, with local 'holiday
romances', or with sex workers, many people expect to have more sex
whilst on vacation (Oppermann 1998; Clift and Carter, 2000; Ryan and
Hall, 2001). Within this, the kind of sex they have is often more 'casual',
more risky and more risqué than the sex they would have at home.
There are European holiday destinations that are renowned for the high
level of tourist-tourist sexual interaction, and for the overtly sexualised
nature of tourism for young people in particular. Commercial sex,
including sexual entertainment such as lap dance, strip shows and live
sex shows as well as prostitution, is a feature of tourism in many tourist
destinations in both affluent and developing countries. The sex sectors
of some European and American cities (for instance, Amsterdam,
Copenhagen, Las Vegas) are tourist attractions in and of themselves,
just as the Pat Pong district of Bangkok is considered by many tourists
to be a 'must see', even if they have no intention of actually buying a
sexual service. If tourism is, to a large extent, sex, what is 'sex tourism'?
The term, though widely used, is remarkably difficult to define (Ryan,
2000, Oppermann, 1998). For some, a 'sex tourist' is a person (usually a
man) who takes an organised tour, in which the tour operator arranges
access to prostitutes along with flights, hotels, airport transfers, etc. But
this definition would exclude vast numbers of men who make their own

travel arrangements, or take 'normal' package holidays, and then proceed to avail themselves of the services of prostitutes in the tourist areas they visit. And widening the definition of a 'sex tourist' invariably leads to other problems—does the term only refer to those who travel with the explicit and conscious intention of buying sex, or does it also include those who travel for 'ordinary' reasons, but happen to buy sex one night because they are approached by a sex worker and think, perhaps through the haze of drink or drugs, 'Why not?' And what of those who enter into what they consider to be a holiday romance with a local, but also buy meals for and give gifts to their 'boyfriend' or 'girlfriend'?

Such definitional problems, alongside the fact that prostitution is not universally criminalized so that prostitution-tourism, organised or otherwise, can be quite legally pursued in some countries, make any blanket condemnation of 'sex tourism' politically controversial. But 'child sex tourism' appears to be another matter entirely. Who could fail to be appalled by the idea of Western paedophiles traveling to poor countries in order to buy experiences that are 'forbidden in their own country' (O'Grady, 1996, p. 10)? Because the campaign against 'child sex tourism' mounted by ECPAT in the 1990s presented the problem largely as one involving sexual deviants ('paedophiles' and 'child molesters') taking advantage of either weak or inadequate child protection laws or poor law enforcement in Third World countries, it was extraordinarily effective in terms of garnering international sympathy and support not just from policy makers, politicians, journalists and the general public, but also from representatives of the tourist industry and local and national tourism officials. Whilst airline executives and tour operators are hardly likely to wish to involve themselves in a campaign to impose higher moral standards on their customers than those required in law, or to try to police the consensual sexual behaviours of adults who happen to have traveled with them, they are (with some notable exceptions[1]) as likely as the next person to want to voice indignation about paedophiles.

Even commentators who in general take a rigorous and critical approach to the analysis of the sex sector have sometimes been happy to go along with sweeping claims about 'child sex tourism'. For example, Lin Lim states that:

> Child sex tourism—"tourism organized with the primary purpose of facilitating the effecting of a commercial sexual relationship with a child" (United Nations, 1995, p. 13)—is a particularly serious form of child prostitution, partly because it attracts paedophiles and also because it has been responsible for

---

[1] In 1992, a Lauda Air inflight magazine 'contained a fictitious postcard supposedly sent by a German tourist. The front showed a pre-pubescent naked child and the "message" on the back told of the erotic pleasures of the Bangkok Baby Club. There were public protests on Bangkok outside the airline office, but the airline owner, Nicky Lauda, tended to treat the whole episode as a big joke' (O'Grady, 1996, p. 60).

a palpable increase in the violation of not only young girls but also young boys (1998, p. 183).

Though perhaps unintended, the implication is that we should view the violation of young boys as *particularly* serious, and consider it somehow worse for a child prostitute to be used by a paedophile client than by a 'normal' adult. And yet Lim, like ECPAT and others who campaign against 'child sex tourism', also follows the United Nations' Convention on the Rights of the Child in defining a 'child' as a person under the age of 18. Defined as such, the majority of child prostitutes in the contemporary world are actually too old to be of interest to those who would clinically be defined as 'paedophiles' (they are aged above 13). Moreover, Lim goes on to note that 'ordinary' tourists can become situational child abusers while they are out of their own country, and to observe that the broader tourist industry is partially implicated in the tourist-related sex trade:

> Although reputable travel companies may not intentionally wish to promote sex tourism, their marketing materials often help to sustain the flow, for example, by stressing the attractions of the "nightlife" of certain resorts or by promulgating certain stereotypes of women and children in developing countries (Lim, 1998, p. 185).

There is thus a tension in her discussion of 'child sex tourism'. At one moment it appears as a particularly serious form of child prostitution primarily organized by or for paedophiles, but the next it is enmeshed in and reproduced by the ordinary tourist industry. Such uncertainty is well founded, for it is by no means clear that 'child sex tourism'— whether involving paedophiles or 'ordinary' tourists—can be meaningfully separated from 'sex tourism' or from 'tourism' more generally.

'Paedophiles who Travel Abroad' and Campaigns Against Them

Although the discourse that surrounds it is often emotive, salacious, panicky and the magnitude of the phenomenon grossly exaggerated, 'paedophile tourism' is certainly not a figment of journalists' or campaigners' imagination. It is a reality, and numerous cases have been documented in which Western men travel as tourists, or take up permanent or temporary residence in poor and developing countries in order to gain sexual access to local children (Ireland, 1993; Seabrook, 2000). The countries/regions targeted include Sri Lanka (Beddoe, 1998; Ratnapala, 1999), Goa (O'Connell Davidson and Sanchez Taylor, 1996a), Thailand (Montgomery, 1998, 2001), Cambodia (Foggo, 2002), the

Philippines (Lee-Wright, 1990), the Dominican Republic (de Moya and Garcia, 1999), Costa Rica (Aguilar, 1994). One of the most obvious explanations for this phenomenon is the fact that Westerners know that it is easier, cheaper and safer to obtain sexual access to a child in poor and developing countries than it is back home, and a key objective of campaigns against 'child sex tourism' has been to shift the perception that sex with children in poorer countries is a low-risk crime by raising awareness and encouraging the adoption of laws and policies in both receiving and sending countries that will make the prosecution of foreigners who commit sexual offenses against children abroad easier and more likely.

A first step was to put pressure on governments in receiving countries to take the issue seriously. Whilst no country ever actively promoted tourist-related child prostitution, the general phenomenon of prostitution-tourism was viewed by some governments in the 1980s and early 1990s as an inevitable, and fairly unproblematic, by-product of tourist development (Mitter, 1986; O'Connell Davidson, 1998). Part of the ECPAT campaign has been to encourage governments to recognise and condemn the sexual exploitation of children within prostitution-tourism. So, for example, in 1993, a number of political and community leaders from Thailand, Vietnam, the Philippines and other countries were asked by ECPAT to sign a statement saying: 'I oppose the prostitution of children and view with concern the growing incidence of this practice. The sexual abuse of children by foreign tourists must be ended' (O'Grady, 1996, p. 50).

Campaigners against 'child sex tourism' have also sought to identify and counteract other factors behind the relatively low risk of prosecution associated with child abuse in poor and developing countries (see Roujanavong, 1994), and have drawn attention to a lack of will to combat the problem on the part of the governments of affluent countries which send 'child sex tourists'. Campaigners pointed out, for example, that Western governments' lack of interest in crimes against 'Other' children led many sex tourist receiving countries to pursue a policy of deporting foreign nationals accused of child sexual offences rather than prosecuting them, and this, combined with the fact that offenders could often bribe their way out of trouble, meant that people who had been caught abusing children abroad could return home and continue their lives without fear of prosecution. ECPAT therefore lobbied hard and with a good deal of success for sending countries to introduce extraterritorial criminal laws that would allow states to 'penalize the sexual crimes of their nationals or residents when perpetrated against children in other countries' (Muntarbhom, 1998, p. 7). Such laws were not to be seen as a substitute for, but as a complement to, 'effective laws, policies, and law/policy enforcement in the destination countries of such exploiters' (Muntarbhom, 1998, p. 7). By 1998, 20 countries had introduced extraterritorial laws pertaining to child sex offences committed abroad, but in many of these countries, no court cases had yet been initiated. Germany, the country where most cases had not been pursued, had only prosecuted 37 people under these laws, and only six of these cases led to conviction (Muntarbhom, 1998, p. 19).

Individuals believed to profit by organising 'child sex tours' to countries where child prostitutes are more cheaply and readily available were another focus of concern in campaigns against 'child sex tourism'. Again, lobbyists often met with success. The British Government enacted legislation in 1996—Sexual Offences (Conspiracy and Incitement)—designed to 'strengthen action against those in the UK who organise sex tours or who encourage others to travel abroad for the purpose of sexually exploiting children' (Home Office, 1996, p. 10). In Australia, the Crimes (Child Sex Tourism) Amendment Act came into effect in 1994, and covered, among other things, 'those responsible for organizing overseas tours for the purpose of engaging in sexual relations or activities with minors' (Hall, 1998, p. 90).

Yet the term 'organised sex tour' is somewhat misleading. There are no 'paedophile package tour operators', garnering huge profits by chartering planes and block booking hotels in 'child sex capitals' for large numbers of individuals intent on sexually abusing small children. Although there is some evidence to suggest that organisations that support and champion paedophilia have facilitated their members travel to poor and developing countries in order to gain sexual access to children, either by providing information and advice or occasionally by more direct means, these organisations are few and far between, and in any case operate more as collectives than as large scale business enterprises. But not all 'paedophiles who travel abroad' rely on informal networks with others like themselves to provide them with access to children. Some make use of facilities that are primarily geared towards the interests of 'ordinary' sex tourists, and this draws attention to a key weakness in analyses that assume a clear line of demarcation between 'child sex tourism' and 'sex tourism' more generally.

Blurring the Boundary

Travel and the Single Male (TSM) is an American-based organisation run by and for sex tourists and boasts some 5000 members. It publishes a guidebook and sells club membership for US$50 per annum. Members receive a quarterly newsletter, discounts in some hotels and brothels, and most importantly, are provided access to the TSM internet site. This provides information on travel and prostitution in various countries around the world, access to soft-core pornographic photographs of female sex workers from those countries, two message boards and a chat room for members to swap 'sexperiences', views, 'news' and handy travel tips. The world view of TSM members typifies that of Western heterosexual men who habitually practice sex tourism to poor and developing countries, which is to say that it is profoundly misogynist, homophobic and racist (O'Connell Davidson, 1995, 1998, 2001; O'Connell Davidson and Sanchez Taylor, 1999; Seabrook, 1997).

In 1998, Jacqueline Sanchez Taylor and I interviewed several American TSM members in Boca, Chica, the Dominican Republic, as well as two expatriates whose bars, and photographs of their female bar staff, feature in the information provided on the Dominican Republic on TSM's website, and other expatriates whose names also feature in the 'chat' between members posted on the website. A group of American expatriates and sex tourists linked to TSM (one of whom was a New Jersey police officer) identified one of their cronies as having 'an obsession with virgins'. They told us that the man concerned had paid the families of eight Dominican girl children aged around eleven in order to rape them, and had shown them pornographic photographs of one of his victims. Subsequent interviews with a range of informants led us to believe that the man with 'a thing for virgins' secured access to children through an American expatriate and his Dominican wife who together run a brothel in Boca Chica catering to demand from tourist men, including TSM members (O'Connell Davidson and Sanchez Taylor, 2001). Further evidence of a link between TSM and child sex exploitation comes from postings on the message board about a man who, Ministry of Tourism officials informed us, had been deported in 1997 during a police clampdown on child prostitution that year, '*Mr D*', a French Canadian, was found to be organising the prostitution of minors from his hotel in Boca Chica. A posting from TSM's message board describes Mr. D's hotel prior to its closure and his deportation:

> many of the male guests and others from outside the hotel hang out [in the hotel bar] drinking. This as you can guess also draws the attention of the *chicas* and a number of them hang about as well. D. does not in any way discourage this as he has correctly concluded that having the girls there also keeps the guys there longer and keeps the drinks flowing... A girl... was knocking on my door literally 2 minutes after my checking in, asking if I wanted a blow job... I enjoyed my stay completely... A few girls were also staying at the hotel... They are often available for entertainment as you might expect (posted 4.9.97).

TSM is not unique, for there are many other clubs, guides and businesses catering to demand from 'normal' sex tourists (of whom more will be said below) that also facilitate paedophile tourists' sexual access to younger local children, even if those who run them are normally careful to make disclaimers about child prostitution and to ensure that their published materials contain no reference to or photographs of those under 18. Indeed, one often cited example of the successful prosecution of a 'child sex tour' operator actually involved a British man, Michael

Clarke, whose business ('Paradise Express' holidays to the Philippines) was geared to the desires of 'ordinary' sex tourists rather than paedophiles. In something of a 'sting' operation, Clarke agreed to the request of an investigative journalist and a Christian Aid worker, who were posing as paedophile tourists, for underage girls for sex. His actions were secretly filmed, which led to Clarke's arrest and trial for procuring child prostitutes and inducing others to be clients of child prostitutes. He was sentenced to sixteen years in jail, followed by deportation from the Philippines (Kane, 1998).

Though Clarke's actions are not defensible in any way, I do not think that on the basis of evidence available he can properly be described as an organiser of 'child sex tours'. He was a man attempting (and some say rather unsuccessfully) to operate a business catering to sex tourists in general, but who was apparently willing to accommodate the tastes of paedophiles when approached and asked to do so. The distinction is important if we are to see, rather than turn a blind eye to, the ways in which 'sex tourism' and 'child sex tourism' are bound up in each other, and how both are bound up in tourism more generally. And once the interconnections between 'child sex tourism', 'sex tourism' and 'tourism' are acknowledged, it becomes clear that the impact of campaigns against 'child sex tourism' may be more limited, and more ambiguous, than might first be assumed.

Travel, Sex and Inequality

Tourists have sex—commercial and non-commercial—in holiday destinations in affluent as well as poor countries. However, sites of sex tourism in developing countries can be distinguished from those in affluent countries not necessarily by the existence of a large, diverse, formally organized sex industry serving demand from tourist clients, but more particularly by the existence of a busy informal sex sector. In this later sector, local/migrant people (both adult and child) enter into a wide range of sexual-economic exchanges with tourists. For instance, there are adult and child prostitutes working either independently or under the control of a third party, soliciting custom from beaches, parks and ordinary tourist bars; there are pimps and hustlers (both adult and child) offering to procure all manner of sexual experiences for tourists; and there are individuals who may not define themselves as 'prostitutes' or 'sex workers', but who seek sexual relationships with tourists either as a means of accessing a life-style they cannot afford, or in the hopes of receiving gifts that will supplement their very low income from hotel or bar work, or because they wish to migrate to a richer country and hope to find a sponsor or marriage partner who will facilitate their migration.

Prostitute-client exchanges in the informal sector are often more open-ended and loosely specified than those which take place in the formal sector. Prices and limits to the contract are not always negotiated in advance, prostitutes may provide anything from two hours to two weeks of full access to their persons, performing non-sexual labour for the client (shopping, tidying, washing, translation, and so on) as well as sexual labour. They will also often act in ways that are taken to signify genuine affection, for instance, holding hands, kissing, walking arm in arm, sharing a bed (all things that few experienced sex workers in Western countries would do with a client). Taken together, all this means that sex tourist destinations in poor countries or regions offer the tourist not just extensive and cheap opportunities for sexual experience, but also opportunities for types of sexual experience that would not be readily available either back home or in tourist destinations in more affluent countries. This wealth of sexual opportunity leads both male and female tourists to describe such places as 'sexual paradise', 'Fantasy Island' and 'Disneyland' (O'Connell Davidson and Sanchez Taylor, 1999). But sexual Disneylands do not exist in nature. They have to be created.

There is some national and regional variation in terms of the history of such creations. In Thailand, as in several other Southeast Asian countries, a period of 'economic colonialism and militarisation in which prostitution is a formalised mechanism of dominance' has been a key stage in the development of sex tourism (Hall, 1994, p. 151; see also Truong, 1990; Bishop and Robinson, 1998). But sex tourism does not always or only involve the maintenance and development of existing large scale, highly commoditized sex industries serving foreign military personnel. It has also emerged in locations where no such sex industry existed, for instance, the Gambia (Morris-Jara, 1996) and Cuba (Fernandez, 1999).

In general, sexual Disneylands are a product of a complex set of linkages between international debt, price fluctuations in global commodity markets, economic development policy and prostitution (Kempadoo, 1999; Bishop and Robinson, 1998; Chant and McIlwaine, 1995), as well as laws and social policies adopted by individual countries (see, for example, Alexander, 1997). The International Monetary Fund agreements and World Bank structural adjustment loans, sector adjustment loans and programs loans that governments of developing countries have had little choice but to enter serve to swell the prostitution labour market, for the policy packages tied to these loans have had a devastating impact on the poor. Structural adjustment processes are widely reported to have undermined traditional forms of subsistence economies, led to high levels of unemployment, redirected subsidies away from social spending and basic commodities towards debt servicing, and often to have encouraged massive currency depreciations leading to a concomitant drop in the price of labour (Anderson and Witter, 1994; NACLA, 1997; Beddoe, 1998; Kempadoo, 1999).

Structural adjustment has created a 'surplus' labouring population, as well as driving down wages of those in work, and has thus been associated with the growth of the informal economic sector in a number of countries as ordinary people (both above and below the age of 18) desperately seek ways in which to earn a living, or supplement or substitute for impossibly low waged employment (see, for instance, Witter and Kirton, 1990; LeFranc, 1994; Safa, 1997; Black, 1995). Though sex tourism involves only a minority of local and migrant persons, expatriates and tourists in any given setting, it is nonetheless the case that prostitution and other forms of tourist-local sexual-economic exchange are amongst the wide range of activities that take place in the informal tourism economy in developing countries (for instance Phillips, 1999; Cabez, 1999; Ford and Wirawan, 2000; Sanchez Taylor, 2001; Meisch, 1995; Williams, 1999).

The economic and political position of tourists could not be more different from that of locals they come into contact with in developing countries. Even the working class, budget tourist from Britain or Germany, for instance, is in a position to spend about as much on a package holiday in Thailand or the Caribbean as most ordinary local and migrant people working in the formal or informal tourist economy will earn in a year. This means that tourists, as well as being able to afford to consume sexual services if they so choose, are in a position to freely dispense gifts and sums of money which, though negligible to them represent significant benefits to the average local person. Even the half-empty shampoo bottles, unused medicines and uneaten foodstuffs that the tourist would throw away at the end of a holiday can make an important contribution to a household that is struggling to subsist. Small wonder then, that many locals, both adult and child, seek to befriend tourists and/or to enter into sexual relationships with them.

Moreover, tourists' citizenship of politically powerful nations and their relative affluence combine to bestow upon tourists rights and freedoms that are denied to most of the locals and migrants they meet on their 'Third World' travels. Their passports allow them to cross national borders virtually at whim, and as tourists, they also enjoy a range of social, economic and cultural benefits that effectively amount to a degree of substantive citizenship far greater than that enjoyed by ordinary working class citizens of the countries they visit. A tourist can, for example, expect to be housed in accommodation that is connected to a water supply, as well as to find a range of leisure facilities geared towards his or her interests, shopping facilities to meet their desires as consumers, and so on. This is more than can be said of the average working class Jamaican, Thai, or Kenyan, for example. But tourists' privilege is not merely a reflection of their greater individual spending power. It results in large part from government spending on infrastructural development to support tourism (airports, roads, water supply, sewerage disposal, electricity and telephones), something which actually diverts money from projects that might help ordinary local people to enjoy basic social, economic and cultural rights of citizenship

(Patullo, 1996; Howard, 1999). Again, sexual relationships with tourists represent one of the few ways in which ordinary local adults and children can tap into privileges reserved for tourists and elite locals.

The tourist and the local are simultaneously brought together and separated by global inequality. Were it not for the huge disparity in terms of political and economic power between affluent and developing nations, the average Western tourist would not be in a position to take long-haul holidays to 'exotic' destinations, and those who did venture into Thailand or Sri Lanka or the Dominican Republic would not find themselves automatically positioned as the local's superior in terms of social, political and economic rights and freedoms. In a different and more equal world, long-haul tourists would find it no harder and no easier to make contact (sexual or otherwise) with local people than they find it to strike up such acquaintances with locals when they visit tourist resorts in their own country or an equally affluent country. Travel between and within affluent countries does not equip the tourist with the power to 'harm or help' the local people they come into contact with, but travel from rich to poor countries does (see Brace and O'Connell Davidson, 1996). In the 'Third World', even the 'third-rate' American/European tourist is king or queen, and whether they dream of holiday romance, or of ready opportunities for anonymous sex, or of affordable commercial sex, or of raping eleven year old girls, or just of being sweet-talked by a series of 'dusky' strangers, they are in a position to make their dreams come true. That's Disneyland.

But the global processes and national social and economic policies which bring tourists and locals face to face as profoundly unequal parties are not enough, on their own, to create the phenomenon of sex tourism. Back home, the same people often could and do find themselves face to face with individuals who are structurally positioned and socially constructed as their unequals, and yet do not necessarily feel the urge to pursue sexual contact with them. In London, Hamburg or San Francisco, for example, we rarely see ordinary, middle-aged men and women flirting with homeless teenagers who sit on the pavements begging for spare change, or inviting them out to dinner and then back home to bed. Understanding Disneyland also requires us to think about the connections between travel, sex and race, and to consider what is being consumed within tourism more generally.

The Scene and the Obscene

In a survey of 661 German men who had had sex with one or more local women or girls in Thailand, the Philippines, Kenya, Brazil and the Dominican Republic, for example, Kliebe and Wilke (1995) found that only a minority, 22%, described themselves as 'sex tourists'. As Gunther (1998, p. 71) observes, the curious phenomenon of sex tourism without

sex tourists rests on the fact that many settings of tourism-oriented
prostitution allow 'for a personal, noneconomic and self-serving
"framing"...of the tourist-prostitute relationship'. Similarly, Sanchez
Taylor's (2001) survey of 240 female tourists in the Caribbean found that
almost a third had had sex with one or more local men in the course of
their holiday. Of these, 57% acknowledged that they had 'helped' their
partner out financially or materially. Asked if they had ever used a
gigolo or male prostitute, all of them said 'No'. Such findings are partly
accounted for by the fact that the open-ended and non-contractual
nature of informal sector prostitution allows tourists to delude
themselves about the commercial basis of their sexual interactions.

But fantasies about the sexuality of the Other also play an important
role in the 'framing' of such encounters as 'not-prostitution'. Rather than
being confronted by what they understand and recognise as prostitution,
the Western tourist sees local women, men and children dancing,
drinking and smooching with tourists, and interprets this as validating
racist fantasies of the hypersexual Other (Kempadoo, 1995). The scenes
they witness in sex tourist resorts are taken as proof that different
meanings attach to sexual behaviour in the host country, that sex is
more 'natural' and 'free' amongst local people. Thus, 'open-ended' forms
of prostitution in South East Asian or Latin American/Caribbean
countries can be (mis)interpreted in such a way as to make tourists feel
chosen and desired for themselves, rather than for the contents of their
wallets (O'Connell Davidson and Sanchez Taylor, 1999; Seabrook, 1997;
Bishop and Robinson, 1998).

Awareness that local people are actually prostituting does not
necessarily prompt the reappraisal of such ideas. Instead, sex tourists
tell themselves that there are 'cultural' differences as regards
prostitution, and/or that they are not paying for sex when they give
money to a local sexual partner, but rather 'helping' her or him out.
Take, for example, the following extract from a guidebook for gay male
sex tourists to Thailand:

> Many Westerners are troubled about the idea of paying for
> a young man for his time or sex, seeing it as pure prostitution,
> but this is an oversimplification. In Thailand, as in other less-
> developed countries, you will be considered a higher-status
> person... with obligations to those less fortunate than yourself
> (Hammer, 1997, p. 18).

Jean Baudrillard's (1990, p. 55) discussion of the scene and the
obscene is useful here:

> More visible than the visible—this is the obscene. More invi-
> sible than the invisible—this is the secret. The scene is in the
> order of the visible. But...The obscene is the end of any scene...

[the] hypervisibility of things is also the imminence of their end, the sign of the apocalypse...if all enigmas are resolved, the stars go out. If everything secret is returned to the visible (and more than to the visible to obscene obviousness), if all illusion is returned to transparence, then heaven becomes indifferent to the earth.

Set in particular scenes, prostitution can appear to the tourist as quite heavenly. As has been noted, in the informal prostitution scene, the commercial basis of sexual interactions between tourists and local or migrant persons is invisible. But more than this, the gulf between each party in terms of life chances, material security, and even age, is concealed. Age means something different in a strange and 'exotic' land where children, like tropical plants, grow fast, and girls of 13 can be attracted to men of 60. 'Here a man has no age', as one expatriate in Costa Rica put it (O'Connell Davidson and Sanchez Taylor, 1996b). And last but not least, the local or migrant persons' sexual behaviour is mysterious. Even for tourists who buy explicitly commoditized sex and who recognise their behaviour as prostitute-use, the discursive construction of racial, ethnic or national difference as sexual differences means that prostitution can retain an enigmatic quality. There is something mysterious about the Other sex worker. Thus, for example, European, North American and Australian tourists marvel at Thai sex workers (unlike junkie street prostitutes or cold, hard-bitten professionals back home, they seem to be 'nice girls' who 'do it for their families' and are truly 'warm and caring') and at Brazilian and Dominican sex workers who 'seem to really enjoy the sex' (O'Connell Davidson, 1995, 1998; Kruhse Mount-Burton, 1995; Cohen, 1982).

But racism and ethnic Othering takes many forms, and its relation to sex is not always one of magical illusion, nor do all those who use prostitutes want such illusions. For some clients, the obscene is not the end but the beginning of sexual pleasure. They *want* to enter a pornutopia (see Hartsock 1983, p. 175), where women and girls are paid 'fucking machines'; or they want cheap sex, or 'dirty' sex, sex with someone they view as low and debased—sex with someone to be 'immediately devoured' rather than 'seduced', to paraphrase Baudrillard (1990, p. 59), Who better to fulfil such desires than sex workers belonging to groups that are in general socially devalued on grounds of race, ethnicity or 'caste'? All of these points hold good in relation to both paedophile and 'normal' sex tourists.

And tourists' sexual behaviour is also shaped by the discursive construction of tourist destinations as liminal spaces in which it is both possible and desirable to suspend normal routines and transgress the rules that govern daily life. This means it is not only inexpensive and convenient to engage in what Joane Nagel (2003, p. 17) terms 'ethno-sexual adventuring' and 'ethnosexual invasion' (that is, recreational sex with, or sexual abuse of, members of other ethnic groups) in tourist centres in developing countries, but also guilt-free. No matter where they come from, a great many tourists share the sentiment behind the Japanese adage 'shameless behaviour during a trip is to be scraped off one's mind' (Allison, 1994, p. 140).

Saying 'No to Child Sex Tourism!'

If 'children' are to be defined as persons under the age of 18, then it is extraordinarily difficult to sustain the idea of a clear, sharp boundary between 'child sex tourism' on the one hand, and 'sex tourism' and 'tourism' on the other. 'Ordinary' tourists who visit brothels or use street prostitutes, like 'ordinary' clients in other settings, do not necessarily care very much whether the prostitute they use is fifteen or sixteen or twenty or older, providing they fancy the look of her. The same point holds good for those tourists who find sexual partners in the informal tourist-related prostitution sector, where the bulk of child prostitution often takes place. For how are tourists to tell the exact age of the locals who proposition them, especially given that many are drunk by the time they 'pull'? The main ambition of many sex tourists—male and female—that Jacqueline Sanchez Taylor and I interviewed in Latin America and the Caribbean was to 'party' and enjoy the novel experiences of going out to bars and clubs and being surrounded by a bevy a 'lovely young ladies' or 'gorgeous young guys', all miraculously 'up for it' (O'Connell Davidson and Sanchez Taylor, 1996a,b; 2001). Such people are not paedophiles, nor do they conform to the dominant stereotype of the 'sex tourist'. They do not go to seedy brothels where women and children are visibly brutalised by brothel keepers. But they will have sex with a local fifteen year old if she or he approaches them in a disco, smiles, flirts and dances with them, and offers to come back to their room. And in the morning, if she or he asks for US$10 for the taxi fare home, they will give it, maybe with a little extra, just to be kind. They will feel no worse about this interaction, possibly better even, than they will feel about their other interactions with locals—the boys will shine their shoes, the woman or teenager who cleans their room, the small child who washes sand from their feet as they lie on a sun lounger on the beach in exchange for a few coins, the old woman who pleads with them to buy fruit from her, the little beggar child sitting on the pavement outside their hotel. The sex, like the sun, the sand, the drinking, the excess and above all the conspicuous waste (of food, energy, natural resources, and time) in places where local people cannot afford to waste anything at all is all part of the tourist experience. It is all part of the 'local colour', the 'party atmosphere', the 'exotic beach resort with a great nightlife' that tourists have been sold, not by 'organized child sex tour operators', but by big, respectable, mainstream tourism companies.

Because campaigns against 'child sex tourism' focus attention on the minority of 'deviant' tourists who travel in pursuit of sex with young children, they actually ask very little of the tourist industry. The industry can be loudly applauded for assisting with the distribution of baggage tags emblazoned with the logo 'No to child sex tourism!', for agreeing to monitor accredited members of travel agents' associations to ensure they are not advertising 'child sex tours', for being willing to show in-flight videos telling people that it is illegal and wrong to have sex with six year olds. And very few campaigners insist that the industry address questions about the derisory wages paid to hotel workers, or think about how this might contribute to their willingness to accept 'bribes' and 'tips' for turning a blind eye to the activities of tourists, or speak about the social costs of tourism, and the fact that profits from tourism are largely repatriated to affluent sending countries and so will never 'trickle down' to those who pick up tourists' litter, clean their toilets, make their beds, serve their food, and fulfill their sexual fantasies.

Saying 'No to child sex tourism' also deflects attention from the exploitation of child labour in the tourist industry more generally. As Maggie Black (1995, p. 9) comments, 'sexual exploitation is not the only hazard relating to the employment of young people' within the tourist economy, and yet 'it is the only one on which attention appears to focus'. Furthermore, as Kempadoo (1999, p. 292) observes:

> the emphasis on child prostitution as the main problem in sex tourism can be seen to quietly allow other forms of prostitution to continue to take place without hindrance, scrutiny, or attention to the human rights of women and men who provide sexual services in the tourist industry.

Worse still, it lends the cloak of legitimacy to violations of sex workers' rights (both adult and child) by police and other state actors, who have in many places responded to international pressure to end 'child sex tourism' by simply clamping down on those working in informal sector prostitution. In the Dominican Republic, for example, women and teenagers in tourist resorts were frequently rounded up by police as a response to international pressure to address the problem of 'child sex tourism' (to give an idea of the scale, 170 were arrested in a single night in a single tourist resort during one raid in 1998). Once remanded in police custody, there were no beds to sleep on, and the women and girls had no entitlement to food until such time as they were convicted. After being held in these conditions for between one and four days, they were taken to court where they were required to pay a fine in order to be released. Haitian women and teenagers were deported. Women also report having been beaten or raped by the police, as well as subject to extortion (Cabezas, 1999). This situation is not unique to the Dominican Republic. The numbers of women and teenagers who have ended up deported, or behind bars, or in 're-education', 'rehabilitation' or whatever euphemism is preferred, as a result of international concern about 'child sex tourism' far outstrips the number of Western paedophiles or men like Michael Clarke who have been similarly treated. This fact alone should, I believe, give campaigners pause for thought.

More generally, I would conclude that because campaigns against 'child sex tourism' have detached the phenomenon from its political, economic and social basis, treating it as a discrete problem that can and should be tackled primarily through better laws and stronger law enforcement, they have deflected popular and policy attention from the structural inequalities that underpin the exploitation of local children, women and men in both the sex trade and other economic sectors in the developing world. So long as they construct 'child sex tourism' in this way, such campaigns are likely to have a limited impact upon the problem they set out to address, and they will continue to miss the opportunity to challenge the dominant and enormously destructive myths that inform popular Western attitudes towards 'migration' and movement in the contemporary world.

Acknowledgments

This paper is based on a chapter from the author's book on children in the global sex trade, published by Polity Press in 2004. The support of the Economic and Social Research Council of Great Britain, which funded the author's research on sex tourism in Jamaica and the Dominican Republic, with Jacqueline Sanchez Taylor, is gratefully acknowledged (Award No: R000237625).

Discussion Questions

1 *Why do Western men sometimes take up permanent residents in poor and developing countries?*

2 *What has been done by the group End Child Prostitution in Asian Tourism (ECPAT) to deal with foreigners who perpetrate sex crimes against children in other countries?*

3 *What legal action has been taken against individuals in the United Kingdom who profit by organizing child sex tourism?*

4 *What is the purpose of the organization called Travel and the Single Male?*

5 *Why do most locals, both adult and child, seek to befriend tourists and/or enter into sexual relationships with them?*

6 *According to the author, what was the main ambition for many sex tourists?*

References

Aguilar, M. (1994) Alarma corrupcion de menores en Puntareas, Sucesos, San Jose, January 9.

Alexander, M. (1997) Erotic autonomy as politics of decolonisation: an anatomy of the feminist and state practice on the Bahama tourist economy, in M. Alexander and C. Mohanty (Eds) *Feminist Geneologies, Colonial Legacies, Democratic Futures* (London: Routledge).

Allison, A. (1994) *Nightwork: Sexuality, Pleasure and Corporate Masculinity in a Tokyo Hostess Club* (Chicago, IL: University of Chicago Press).

Anderson, P. and Witter, M. (1994) Crisis, adjustment and social change: a case study of Jamaica, in E. Le Franc (Ed.) *Consequences of Strutural Adjustment: A Review of the Jamaican Experience* (Kingston: Canoe Press).

Baudrillard, J. (1990) *Fatal Strategies* (London; Pluto).

Beddne, C. (1998) Beachboys and tourists: links in the chain of child prostitution in Sri Lanka, in M. Opperman (Ed.) *Sex Tourism and Prostitution: Aspects of Leisure, Recreation and Work* (New York: Cognizant Communications).

Black, M. (1995) *In the Twilight Zone: Child Workers in the Hotel, Tourism and Catering Industry* (Geneva: ILO).

Bishop, R. and Robinson, L. (1998) *Night Market: Sexual Cultures and the Thai Economic Miracle* (London: Routledge).

Brace, L. and O'Connell Davidson, J. (1996). Desperate debtors and counterfeit love: the Hobbesian world of the sex tourist, *Contemporary Politics*, 2(3).

Cabezas, A. (1999) Women's work is never done: sex tourism in Somia, the Dominican Republic, in K. Kempadoo (Ed.) *Sun, Sex and Gold: Tourism and Sex Work in the Caribbean* (Oxford: Rowman and Littlefield).

Chant, S. and McIlwaine, C. (1995) *Women of a Lesser Cost: Female Labour, Foreign Exchange and Philippine Development* (London: Pluto).

Clift, S. and Carter, S. (Eds) (1999) *Tourism and Sex: Culture, Commerce and Coercion* (London: Pinter).

Cohen, E. (1982) Thai girls and Parang men: the edge of ambiguity, *Annals of Tourism Research*, 9, pp. 403-428.

DeMoya, A. and Garcia, R. (1999) Three decades of male sex work in Santo Domingo, in P. Aggleton (Ed.) *Men Who Sell Sex: International Perspectives on Male Prostitution and HIV/AIDS* (London: UCL Press).

Enloe, C. (1993) *The Morning After: Sexual Politics at the End of the Cold War* (Berkeley, CA: University of California Press).

Fernandez, N. (1999) Back to the future? Women, race and tourism in Cuba, in K. Kempadoo, *Sun, Sex, and Gold: Tourism and Sex Work in the Caribbean* (Oxford: Rowman and Littlefield).

Foggo, D. (2002) It's like a sweet shop: if this girl's not right, get another, the *Telegraph*, September 15, pp. 12-13.

Ford, K. and Wirawan, D. (2000) Tourism and commercial sex in Indonesia, in S. Clift and S. Carter (Eds) *Tourism and Sex: Culture, Commerce and Coercion* (London: Pinter).

Gill, L. (2003) Consuming passions: the school of the Americas and imperial sexuality. *American Sexuality Magazine,* 1(5).

Gunther, A. (1998) Sex tourism without sex tourists, in M. Opperman (Ed.) *Sex Tourism and Prostitution: Aspects of Leisure, Recreation and Work* (New York: Cognizant Communications).

Hall, C. (1994) Nature and implications of sex tourism in South-East Asia, in V. Kinnaird and D. Hall (Eds) *Tourism: A Gender Analysis* (Chichester: John Wiley).

Hall, C. (1998) The legal and political dimensions of sex tourism: the case of Australia's child sex tourism legislation, in M. Opperman (Ed.) *Sex Tourism and Prostitution: Aspects of Leisure, Recreation and Work* (New York: Cognizant Communications).

Hammer, D. (1997) *Thai Scene* (Swaffham: Gay Men's Press).

Hartsock, N. (1985) *Money, Sex and Power* (Boston, MD: Northeastern University Press).

Home Office (1996) *Action Against the Commercial Sexual Exploitation of Children* (London: Home Office Communication Directorate).

Howard, D. (1999) *The Dominican Republic* (London: Latin America Bureau).

Hyam, R. (1990) *Empire and Sexuality: The British Experience* (Manchester: Manchester University Press).

Ireland, K. (1993) *Wish You Weren't Here* (London: Save the Children).

Kane, J. (1998) *Sold for Sex* (Aldershot: Arena).

Kempadoo, K. (1995) Prostitution, marginality and empowerment: Caribbean women in the sex trade. *Beyond Law,* 5(14).

Kempadoo, K. (Ed.) (1999) *Sun, Sex, and Gold: Tourism and Sex Work in the Caribbean* Oxford: Rowman & Littlefield).

King, M. (2002) Towards a new map of European migration, *International Journal of Population Geography*, 8, pp. 89-106.

Kleibe, D. and Wilke, M. (1995) AIDS and sex tourism: conclusions drawn from a study of the social and psychological characteristics of German sex tourists, in D. Friedrick and W. Heckmann (Eds.) *AIDS in Europe: The Behavioural Aspect, Vol. 2: Risk Behaviour and its Determinants* (Berlin: Edition Sigma).

Kruhse-Mount Burton, S. (1995) Sex tourism and traditional Australian male identity, in M. Lafabt *et al* (Eds) *International Tourism: Identity and Change* (London: Sage).

Le Franc, E. (Ed.) (1994) *Consequences of Structural Adjustment: A Review of the Jamaican Experience* (Kingston: Canoe Press).

Lee-Wright, P. (1990) *Child Slaves* (London: Earthscan).

Lim, L. (1998) *The Sex Sector: The Economic and Social Bases of Prostitution in Southeast Asia* (Geneva: International Labour Office).

McClintock, A. (1995) *Imperial Leather: Race, Gender and Sexuality in the Colonial Contest* (London: Routledge).

Meisch, L. (1995) Gringas and otavalenos: changing tourist relations, *Annals of Tourism Research*, 22(2), pp. 441-62.

Mitter, S. (1986) *Common Fate, Common Bond: Women in the Global Economy* (London: Pluto).

Montgomery, H. (1998) Children, prostitution and identity: a case study from a tourist resort in Thailand, in K. Kempadoo and J. Doezema (Eds) *Global Sex Workers* (London: Routledge).

Montgomery, H. (2001) *Modern Babylon? Prostituting Children in Thailand* (Oxford: Berghahn Books).

Morris-Jarra, M. (1996) No such thing as a cheap holiday, *Tourism in Focus*, 26, Autumn, pp. 6-7.

Muntarbhom, V. (1998) *Extraterritorial Criminal Laws against Child Sexual Exploitation* (Geneva: UNICEP).

NACLA (1997) Report on the Americas, *NACLA*, 30(5).

Nagel, J. (2003) *Race, Ethnicity and Sexuality* (Oxford: Oxford University Press).

O'Connell Davidson, J. (1995) British sex tourists in Thailand, in M. Maynard and J. Purvis (Eds.) *(Hetero)Sexual Politics* (London: Taylor & Francis).

O'Connell Davidson, J. (1998) *Prostitution, Power and Freedom* (Cambridge: Polity).

O'Connell Davidson, J. (2001) The sex tourist, the expatriate, his ex-wife and her 'other': the politics of loss, difference and desire, *Sexualities* 4(1), pp. 5-24.

O'Connell Davidson, J. and Sanchez Taylor, J. (1996a) Child prostitution and sex tourism in Goa. Research Paper. Bangkok: ECPAT.

O'Connell Davidson, J. and Sanchez Taylor, J. (1996b) Child prostitution and sex tourism in Costa Rica. Research Paper. Bangkok: ECPAT.

O'Connell Davidson, J. and Sanchez Taylor, J. (1999) Fantasy islands: exploring the demand for sex tourism, in K. Kempadoo (Ed.) *Sun, Sex and Gold: Tourism and Sex Work in the Caribbean* (Oxford: Rowman & Littlefield).

O'Connell Davidson, J. and Sanchez Taylor, J. (2001) *Children in the Sex Trade in the Caribbean* (Stockholm: Save the Children Sweden).

O'Grady, R. (1996) *The ECPAT Story: A Personal Account of the First Six Years in the Life of ECPAT* (Bangkok: ECPAT).

Opperman, M. (Ed.) (1998) *Sex Tourism and Prostitution: Aspects of Leisure, Recreation and Work* (New York: Cognizant Communications).

Patullo, P. (1996) *Last Resorts: The Cost of Tourism in the Caribbean* (London: Latin America Bureau).

Phillips, J. (1999) Tourist-oriented prostitution in Barbados: the case of the beach boy and the white female tourist, in K. Kempadoo (Ed.) *Sun, Sex and Gold: Tourism and Sex Work in the Caribbean* (Oxford: Rowman & Littlefield).

Ratnapala, N. (1999) Male sex work in Sri Lanka, in P. Aggleton (Ed.) *Men Who Sell Sex* (London: UCL).

Roujanavong, W. (1994) Thailand's image attracts the wrong people, *ECPAT Newsletter*, No. 11, December.

Ryan, C. (2000) Sex tourism: paradigms of confusion, in S. Carter and S. Clift (Eds) *Tourism and Sex Culture, Commerce and Coercion* (London: Pinter).

Ryan, C. and Hall, M. (2001) *Sex Tourism: Marginal People and Liminalities* (London: Routledge).

Safa, H. (1997) Where the big fish eat the little fish: women's work in the Free Trade Zones, Report on the Americas, *NACLA*, 30(5), pp. 31-6.

Sanchez Taylor, J. (2001) Dollars are a girl's best friend? Female tourists' sexual behaviour in the Caribbean, *Sociology*, 35(3), pp. 749-764.

Seabrook, J. (1997) *Travels in the Skin Trade: Tourism and the Sex Industry* (London: Pluto Press).

Seabrook, J. (2000) *No Hiding Place: Child Sex Tourism and the Role of Extraterritorial Legislation* (London: Zed).

Stoler, A. (1997) Carnal knowledge and imperial power, in R. Lancaster and M. di Leonardo (Eds) *The Gender Sexuality Reader* (London: Routledge).

Truong, T. (1990) *Sex, Money and Morality: Prostitution and Tourism in Southeast Asia* (London: Zed Books).

Williams, S. (1999) Commercial sexual exploitation of children in Jamaica. Unpublished Report, Caribbean Child Development Centre, School of Continuing Studies, University of the West Indies, Mona, Kingston.

Witter, M. and Kirton, C. (1990) The informal economy in Jamaica: some empirical exercises. Working Paper No. 36, Institute of Social and Economic research, University of the West Indies, Mona, Kingston.

26
HALTING THE TRAFFICKING OF WOMEN AND CHILDREN IN THAILAND FOR THE SEX TRADE: PROGRESS AND CHALLENGES

David W. Engstrom, Ph.D., Sarah A. Minas, Monica Espinoza, MSW, Loring Jones, DSW, *San Diego State University, California*

Social workers now more than ever need an international perspective (Healy, 2001) to understand the issues that are contributing to global migration, including the problem and dynamics of human trafficking. Social workers can benefit tremendously by having insight into the unique migration experiences of recent arrivals to the United States, particularly in regard to how these experiences impact the psychosocial needs of immigrants. Decision makers seeking to make global migration more humane need to know about efforts to stem the flow of human trafficking, and they need information on which interventions have worked and which have not. It is within this context that this paper about trafficking in Thailand is presented.

Trafficking in humans is increasingly a cause for alarm because it represents an assault on human rights, it is exploitative and harmful, it is illegal under international law, and it is associated with organized crime. Thailand is one target of focus in the global effort to combat the trafficking of persons. Most countries play only one role in the equation of human trafficking such as being a receiving country (United States) or a sending country (Ukraine). Thailand is unique because it is involved in three functions—it acts as a receiving country, a sending country and a transit point for victims of trafficking.

The trafficking of women and children for the sex trade is considered one of the worst and most exploitative forms of human trafficking. One-third of the world's women and children who are trafficked are from Southeast Asia (Derks, 2000), and Thailand serves as a major base of operations for traffickers. Within the region, governments, international agencies such as United Nations Children's Fund (UNICEF) and International Organization for Migration (IOM), and nongovernmental agencies have developed policies and programs to prevent and combat human trafficking, with special focus given to women and children. The prevalence of trafficking in Thailand makes it a good case study to examine the problem.

People are trafficked for a variety of reasons, most of which relate to exacting economic value from their labor. Those who are trafficked include more than just women and children. Trafficking includes the impressments of human beings for sweatshop labor, street begging, domestic work, prostitution or sex work, marriage, adoption, agriculture work, construction, armed conflicts (child soldiers), and other forms of exploitive labor or services.

This paper discusses human trafficking in Thailand, primarily for the sex trade. It presents estimates on the dimension of trafficking, examines the regional and domestic context of it, explores the link between trafficking and sex work, describes what is being done to combat it, and analyzes the barriers to halting it. Finally the paper presents a research agenda, for despite the importance of the issue, policy-makers and advocates often find themselves at a loss for information on the nature, scope, and size of problem.

Data Collection

Data collection for this paper employed the use of semistructured interviews, field observations, literature reviews, and examination of agency and government documents. Over the summer of 2003 two faculty members and two MSW student interns visited 15 anti-trafficking programs run by government (GOs) and Non-government organizations (NGOs). These agencies composed our sample frame and were initially identified through Thai experts in the field. Subsequent informants were identified through snowball sampling. Interview subjects were asked at agencies to recommend additional informants. Two MSW students interned at an anti-trafficking NGO and were participant observers in meetings and conferences between GOs, international organizations, and NGOs involved with combating trafficking in Thailand and the Mekong Region of Southeast Asia. These MSW students also conducted interviews with administrators, activists, policy makers, and experts on trafficking. Content for the interview came from a review of the literature, but questions were also developed in consultation with Thai experts. Almost all the experts were Thai who provided the students with an understanding of Thai culture that further informed their data collection. Interviews were conducted in English. Most of the informants had been educated in U.S., European, or Australian schools, and were quite proficient and comfortable in English. To honor confidentiality of sources, no names or institutional affiliations are provided. Because of the sensitivity of the information, some of the NGOs thought that if they were identified there might be negative consequences.

Interviewers kept written notes during the interviews and wrote detailed transcriptions including their observations following interviews. No attempt was made to make audio recordings since we feared it would raise confidentiality concerns. The transcripts were analyzed independently by the two faculty members in order to test reliability. This analysis consisted of identifying basic concepts and themes inductively from open-ended responses, going back and coding all responses within these categories. The analyses of the faculty members were compared and a high degree of congruence was found. The findings and conclusions of those findings were sent to a leading Thai expert for comment on their validity in a Thai context. For the most part, this expert agreed with the findings and conclusions; where there were minor disagreements, we incorporated the expert's comments into the final product.

Context Of Trafficking In Thailand

The Scale of Trafficking

Estimates are that every year at least 200,000 women and children are trafficked from Southeast Asia, and the conjecture is that anywhere from 30,000 to 50,000 of these women and children end up in the United States. Some assert that Southeast Asia is the single most important source for trafficked females to the United States (Derks, 2000). Pettman (1996) asserts that 200,000 Thai women are in Western European brothels. These data give one some idea of the scope of the problem.

The numbers of trafficked persons cited are dramatic but are, at best, rough estimates because of daunting methodological issues. Victims are often reluctant to come forward, and governments have not given high priority to data collection to document the problem (IOM, 2001). Moreover, consensus does not exist on an operational definition of trafficking. Taking a look at a category of trafficking such as prostitution, one will find that considerable differences exist between estimates. For example, "An International Labor Organization (ILO) report estimates that 200,000 to 300,000 women are trafficked for prostitution into Thailand each year. The 1998 UNICEF estimate is lower, citing about 16,000 foreign women in prostitution in Thailand, of whom a significant number are trafficked and about one-third are under 18" (The Protection Project, 2002). Such wide-ranging variations in estimates are expected, given the difficulty of obtaining accurate data on underground-illegal activity.

Definitions of trafficking found in international and national law such as the Protocol to Prevent, Suppress and Punish Trafficking in Persons, Especially Women and Children, supplementing the United Nations Convention Against Transnational Organized Crime and the U.S. Victims of Trafficking[1] and Violence Protection Act of 2000 emphasize the elements of deception, fraud, and coercion for the purpose of exploitation. Nevertheless, because it is a complex phenomenon, developing a universally agreed upon definition of trafficking has been difficult. Moreover, the debate within the field reflects honest defini-

---

[1] The United States has not ratified the UN Convention Against Transnational Organized Crime.

tional disagreements, for example, over the extent to which coercion and exploitation are necessary and whether borders need to be crossed for an activity to be labeled trafficking (Mekong Region Law Center Proceedings, 1999). The lack of a common definition contributes to the difficulty in establishing consensus on how the GOs and NGOs organizations should respond in the Mekong Region (Derks, 2000).

Consequences of Trafficking

The magnitude of the consequences of trafficking for victims is great. Trafficking most often involves the movement of people from their own communities to situations where they are isolated and dependent on those who wish to exploit them. Trafficked persons may be subject to being held in debt bondage, involuntary servitude, low or no wages, and unsafe and unregulated working conditions. A host of physical and mental health problems arise from being trafficked, such as physical injury, sexual abuse, contracting AIDS, and posttraumatic stress disorder (Bertone, 2000). Victims of trafficking often face ill treatment by public authorities who may associate them with criminal activity such as prostitution or illegal immigration. Those who return to their place of residence or country or origin may face ostracism.

Regional Disparities and Labor Flows

Thailand's relative wealth compared to most of its neighbors has resulted in considerable immigration, including substantial numbers of trafficked persons. In 2000 the $6,402 per capita income of Thailand was between 3 and 6 times greater than all other countries (Laos, Cambodia, Burma, and Vietnam) comprising the Mekong Region (United Nations Development Programme; UNDP, 2002). While each country has developed its own unique poverty measure, it is telling that using those relative measures, Thailand reports between 2 to 4 times less poverty. It is interesting to note that the UNDP rank-ordering of countries on human development suggests that the gulf between Thailand and most of its neighbors is greater than the gap between the United States (8) and Mexico (54) (UNDP, 2002).

As Thailand's economy has emerged from the economic meltdown of the late 1990s, demand for labor has increased. Immigrants are recruited to work in agriculture, construction, fishing, factories and the informal sector. Illegal immigrants represent as much as 60 percent of the migration flow into Thailand (IOM, 2000). Indeed, as employment and educational opportunities for Thais have improved, fewer Thai citizens are available (or willing) to work in some occupations such as domestic work, fishing, rice milling, garment making, and construction, creating labor shortages often filled by illegal immigrants (IOM, 2003). There is some evidence to suggest that illegal immigrants (including those trafficked) are playing a more significant role in the sex trade.

Phongpalchit, Piriyarangsan, and Treerat (1998) estimated that there were 20,000 Burmese sex workers in Thailand, representing perhaps one-tenth of all sex workers. Other research estimates that more than 40% of brothel-based sex workers in Northern Thailand were ethnic Shans from Burma (Beyrer, 2001; Beyrer, Khambonruang, Natpratan, Celentano, & Nelson, 1994). ECPAT (End Child Prostitution, Child Pornography and the Trafficking of Children for Sexual Purposes) reports that 10,000 Burmese girls and women are trafficked into Thai brothels each year (ECPAT, 2003).

The troubling political conditions of the region also serve to create and sustain migration flows to Thailand. Official estimates place the number of irregular or illegal immigrants living in Thailand at 600,000 persons; unofficial estimates place the figure at more than one million (IOM, 2000). Most illegal immigrants come from Burma, having fled the poverty and civil conflicts there, with the majority being ethnic Shan (Beyrer, 2001). The United Nations High Commission for Refugees has registered over 110,000 Burmese as persons of concern, giving a small number of them some legal status in Thailand (UNHCR, 2003). Over the past several decades, political conflicts in Laos, Cambodia, and Vietnam have produced flows of displaced persons into Thailand—though considerably less today. Nevertheless, the close cultural and ethnic links between the Isan (northeast) region of Thailand and Laos and Cambodia, and between the north of Thailand and Burma and Laos have made it relatively easy for nationals from those countries to move into Thailand. Additionally, Thailand's long and porous borders are ideal for trafficking.

Thais are trafficked within Thailand and also externally as part of global migration flows. Poverty, lack of education, and unemployment serve to push while the prospect of better opportunity and employment in urban areas such as Bangkok or the West pull Thais away from their rural villages (IOM, 2003). Domestic networks have long been established to draw Thais away from the relatively poor regions of the north and northeast (Baker, 2000). Thais are also being trafficked to Japan, Taiwan, North America, Australia, Singapore, and Western Europe (Derks, 2000; U.S. Department of State, 2002b). While Thais are trafficked for a variety of labor purposes, most attention has been drawn to the trafficking of Thai women for the purposes of sex work. A recent Human Rights Watch report estimates that over 40,000 Thai women have been trafficked for sex work to Japan (Human Rights Watch, 2000).

Sex Work and Trafficking in Thailand—How It Works

Trafficking for sex work arouses major concern in Thailand because prostitution is an illegal activity and it also carries with it a strong sense of stigma. Trafficked victims often involve the most vulnerable segments of the population: women and children (Derks, 2000; Hollingsworth, 2003).

Trafficking for the sex trade employs tactics of coercion and deception. Coercion is used to force victims into the sex trade as part of a debt bondage scheme or in the form of sexual slavery where victims are held against their will in brothels and other sex work venues, often in deplorable conditions (Skolnik & Boontinand, 1999). "Bait and switch" is a form of deception wherein victims may agree to cooperate with traffickers, thinking they will be domestic workers or entertainers but ending up in brothels. Barr reports that traffickers in the north of Thailand have employed increasingly sophisticated techniques to recruit girls from poor villages into the sex trade, emphasizing less deception and more financial incentives to their families (Barr, 1996). There is some controversy here over the extent to which parents knowingly sell their children and adult daughters to traffickers for the purpose of prostitution. Interviews with some NGOs suggest the practice is overstated and sensationalized by press accounts.

Thailand attracts disproportionate attention with regard to sex work because of its links to sex tourism and child prostitution. No reliable data exist on the number of persons trafficked to and from Thailand to work in the sex industry. Even if one takes low-end estimates, the number of child and involuntary sex workers is alarming. "Estimates of the number of children involved in Thailand's sex industry vary between 80,000 and 800,000. According to the Thai Department of Public Welfare, there are 12,000 to 18,000 children in prostitution in Thailand" (The Protection Project, 2002). One estimate claims that 35,000 women work involuntarily in brothels, and another 500,000 to 1 million women work in the sex trade under varying degrees of exploitation (Leuchtag, 2003).

The growth of the sex industry in Thailand has both international and domestic spurs. Thailand's international sex trade originated with an agreement between the Thai and U.S. governments to allow U.S. military personnel in Vietnam to use Thailand for "rest and recreation" (Leheny, 1995). Sex tourism was developed to replace GIs after the end of the Vietnam War. Developing this industry entailed reaching out to men from North America, Australia, Europe, Japan, and other prosperous Asian countries (Arnold & Bertone, 2002).

Strong domestic demand for sex workers has made the sex industry quite large. For example, even in the sexually conservative Northeast region of Thailand, researchers found that nearly half of all men had purchased sexual services (Maticka-Tyndale et al., 1997). Researchers found nearly two-thirds of recruits to the Thai Army had had sex with commercial sex workers (Jenkins et al., 1999). Other research suggests that the AIDS epidemic and the economic depression of the late 1990s reduced internal demand for sex work (Hanenberg & Rojanapithayakorn, 1998).

Thailand's Attempt To Halt Trafficking

Thai responses have included the development and implementation of a national policy for the eradication and suppression of trafficking, particularly when it involves the sexual exploitation of women and children. Efforts have focused on various social, educational, prevention, media, and legal programs. In 1999, a Memorandum of Understanding (MOU) was forged between the Thai government, police, and NGOs on the interpretation of Thai laws and policies regarding trafficking. A significant interpretation outlines that trafficked persons are to be regarded as victims, and foreign children must be accorded the same rights as Thai nationals. This is a first step in assuring protection and assistance to trafficked persons, although challenges still exist in ensuring the effective implementation of this MOU (Arnold & Bertone, 2002; Derks, 2000). After input from various agencies, this MOU was revised in 2003 to further clarify and outline procedures (Royal Thai Government, 2003).

The Thai government's action plan for policy defines prevention as the most effective measure for combating trafficking. Preventative measures include expansion of compulsory education (vocational education in particular), poverty reduction, the promotion of youth and women's social and recreational groups, the provision of nationwide public awareness campaigns about the dangers and realities of trafficking, and closer collaboration between NGOs and the government for more efficient use of resources. These efforts are aimed at internal trafficking of persons rather than foreign nationals moving through Thailand (Derks, 2000).

A few examples highlight the diverse approaches presently being undertaken to address trafficking. In an effort to alleviate the risk that certain women may have of becoming trafficked for the sex trade because they lack occupational skills, the Department of Social Welfare runs a Vocational Training Center for Women. This center, located on the outskirts of Bangkok, offers, among other things, free 6-month vocational training courses twice per year. Women between the ages of 14 and 35 live in the center while they engage in vocational training courses designed to allow them to earn sufficient income to support themselves in the future.

Gabfai Theatre Group is an innovative program that was established in Chiang Mai in 1996 and has reached over 136,000 people since that time. This theatre troupe travels to high-risk areas, involving communities in various projects, performances and workshops, using drama and related activities to teach, inspire discussion and address problems—including the empowerment and education of people with regard to the issues involved in trafficking.

Another major effort to stop trafficking is capacity-building, which includes the establishment of a Thai national ability to protect victims according to the policies established by Thai legislative mandates. Capacity-building activities focus on coordination mechanisms at various levels, including improving legislation, law enforcement, policy making, developing alternative work opportunities for those vulnerable to trafficking, and improving data gathering to better inform decision makers (Derks, 2000).

In recent years, GOs and NGOs have attempted to increase the capacity of countries comprising the Mekong Region to combat trafficking through prevention, law enforcement, and rehabilitation. Trafficking is a regional problem and can only be addressed through bilateral and multilateral efforts. The key to coalescing these efforts has been a series of international and regional conferences involving governmental and NGO representatives from the countries in the region. One of the most significant international conferences held on trafficking was sponsored by IOM in 1999, which resulted in the Bangkok declaration on Irregular Migration. The Declaration was signed by 19 Asian governments that encouraged participating countries "to pass legislation to criminalize the smuggling of and trafficking in human beings" (IOM, 1999). Additionally, national and regional conferences have used local and international expertise to identify ways in which immigration, law enforcement, and social services could increase their capacity to prevent trafficking, prosecute its organizers, and rehabilitate its victims.

The importance of placing trafficking on the public agenda cannot be emphasized enough. Largely through increased international and regional recognition of the problem, revisions to law have been made. Between 1996 and 1999, Thailand passed four laws that dealt with trafficking, the most important of which was the Measures in Prevention and Suppression of Trafficking in Women and Children Act of 1997 (Thai Ministry of Labour and Social Welfare, n.d.). Equally important, bilateral agreements are being signed that address the ways in which countries will cooperate in combating human trafficking. For example, on May 31st of 2003, Thailand and Cambodia signed a bilateral agreement on trafficking, and it is expected that other anti-trafficking agreements will soon be signed as well.

Thailand has taken an active role in providing expertise and assistance to other countries in the Mekong Region. At the same time, GOs and NGOs within Thailand have attempted to enhance Thailand's own organizational infrastructure to deal with trafficking. Within Thailand, governmental protocols have been created by various Thai ministries that specify responsibilities for suppressing trafficking and attending to victims of trafficking. The National Committee on Combating Trafficking of Women and Children regularly meets in Bangkok to discuss ways in which organizational actors can better support each others' efforts and further educate the public about the issue. Efforts are now underway to develop similar regional coalitions in Thailand to combat trafficking.

Challenges To Efforts To Halt Trafficking In The Mekong Region

Corruption

Almost all of the organizations visited identified corruption and the firmly entrenched organized crime networks in Thailand as a particular challenge when combating trafficking. Trafficking in Thailand has contributed to an illegal economy that is well integrated into the country's economic system and is protected by the country's power structure (Phongpaichit et al, 1998). According to a U.S. State Department human rights report (2000), "There continue to be credible reports that some corrupt police, military, and government officials are involved directly in trafficking or taking bribes to ignore it. Police personnel are poorly paid, and widely accustomed to taking bribes to supplement their income." This involvement fuels corruption and results in some areas of government and law enforcement having little interest in controlling trafficking or enforcing the anti-prostitution laws that have been enacted to combat this issue (Phongpaichit et al., 1998). Trafficking creates enormous profit for organized crime and corrupt government officials. Recently Chuwit Kamolvisit, an owner of many successful brothels in Bangkok, has claimed publicly that he pays over $289,000 each month in bribes to policemen (Noikorm, 2003).

The low priority given to combating trafficking by law enforcement is another barrier. At present in Thailand, law enforcement has focused almost entirely on the war on drugs. The U.S. Department of State human rights report (2000) noted, "... police officers do not view anti-trafficking as a path to advancement because their superiors do not emphasize it. Narcotics and serious crime are the preferred career concentrations, while the attitude that trafficking also qualifies as serious crime is only slowly developing." To create a situation where police actively pursue anti-trafficking efforts requires changing police perceptions. In addition, some NGO representatives felt that there may be a lack of knowledge and understanding among law enforcement about the diverse nature and extent of trafficking and effective means by which to combat it.

Citizenship

It is important to note that a particularly vulnerable group of persons within Thailand are those from the northern hill tribes, many of whom are denied the protection of Thai citizenship. Members of hill tribes without proper documentation account for approximately half the estimated 700,000 to 880,000 population (U.S. Department of State, 2001). Hill tribe people are often regarded as illegal in their land of birth. According to the United Nations Educational, Scientific, and Cultural Organization brochure "Trafficking Project (n.d.)," current estimates by the Ministry of the Interior are that 400,000 people are eligible for citizenship or permanent resident status. This brochure also states that "current research by UNESCO has shown that lack of citizenship is the single greatest factor for highland minority girls and women in Thailand to be trafficked or otherwise exploited."

Without citizenship, hill tribe people cannot own land, work, participate in politics, obtain health services, travel freely or receive publicly funded education. This social exclusion, in turn, greatly reduces their employment possibilities and, especially for women, increases their chance of being trafficked to work in the sex trade (U.S. Department of State, 2002a). According to UNESCO, "Although highland girls constitute a small percentage of the total number of sex workers, they are disproportionately represented at the worst paid and most abusive end of the spectrum."

Additionally, Thai hill tribe women and children who are trafficked and come to the attention of Thai authorities often find themselves detained as illegal immigrants. This issue has also been recognized by Human Rights Watch, which also points out that if these women are trafficked outside of Thailand, it is practically impossible for them to return, as the Thai government does not recognize their right of re-entry (Human Rights Watch, 2000). Efforts are currently under way to deal with the issue of citizenship, such as UNESCO's Highland Citizenship Registration Project.

Repatriation

The common practice of repatriating trafficked women and children to their country of origin is not without complications. Thailand has improved its handling of illegal immigrant victims of trafficking over recent years. The Memorandum of Understanding of 2003 has outlined that these women are no longer to be treated as criminals but are to be repatriated with the assistance of social services, and that there must be confirmation that there is a safe situation for them to be returned to. Many organizations expressed their concern that repatriating trafficking victims against their will is ineffectual at best and can be extremely harmful. Here the divide seems to fall between some NGOs on the one hand, which tend to wish repatriation were not always necessary, and some GOs on the other hand, which see enforcement of immigration laws as obligatory and nonnegotiable. Many NGOs see repatriation as merely one step in a cyclical process, since often the repatriated "victims" reappear in the destination country even before the person assisting them in the repatriation process returns. Some NGOs have called for the provision of rehabilitation programs to victims awaiting repatriation as one method for helping victims from other countries in overcoming their trauma ("People Smuggling," 2003).

The longstanding civil unrest in Burma, along with the well-established persecution of ethnic minorities by the Burmese government, has led some NGOs to question repatriation as the optimal way of addressing the problem of trafficking victims who are not Thai citizens.

The plight of the Shan women in Thailand illustrates the potential costs involved in repatriation. Women and children from the Shan State in Burma entered Thailand to escape poverty, violence, persecution, and torture from the military regime, including systematic rape (Shan Human Rights Foundation & Shan Women's Action Network, 2002; U.S. Department of State, 2002a). One report noted that "the estimated over 150,000 Shan refugees who have fled to Thailand following the forced relocation in Central Shan State in 1996, are denied any protection and humanitarian assistance by international aid agencies" (Shan Human Rights Foundation & Shan Women's Action Network, 2002). Shan women and children are particularly vulnerable to trafficking and other forms of exploitation (U.S. Department of State, 2001, 2002a). For these women, the cruelty of rape and torture suffered at the hands of their government is sometimes more of an evil than being trafficked to work illegally in the sex trade. The issue of repatriation comes into play when Thai authorities apprehend Shan women who are working illegally in Thailand. The standard procedure is to repatriate them back to Burma. Some NGOs argue that repatriation may mean being sent back into the hands of the military authorities who were responsible for their torture (Shan Human Rights Foundation & Shan Women's Action Network, 2002). The U.S. government has recently accused the Burmese government of "using rape as a weapon against civilian populations in the ethnic regions of the country," adding credibility to concern that repatriating Shan women and children places them in danger (U.S. Department of State, 2003).

Trafficking Versus Sex Work

Some NGOs regard the issue of trafficking as being used to bring unneeded attention on women who have voluntarily chosen to become sex workers. In their opinion, many women who are classified as trafficked have rationally decided to do sex work and do not require "rescuing." These NGOs emphasize the need to educate sex workers about practicing safe sex and to monitor the working conditions in brothels and massage parlors. Other organizations stated that they regard all those involved in the sex trade as having no element of choice and consider all sex workers as being coerced in some form or other. Most NGOs fall somewhere between these two perspectives and seek to intervene on behalf of women who are coerced at some level into the sex trade and find themselves unable to leave it because of debt-bondage or physical threats. Almost all NGOs would agree that there sometimes exists a difficulty in distinguishing between those women who choose to work in the sex trade and those who had no choice.

The issue of children being trafficked for the sex trade produces uniform consensus among NGOs that there should be no tolerance of it. Any child involved in the sex trade should be regarded as trafficked. Experts believe that child prostitution has declined in Thailand, partly as a result of NGO initiatives and prosecution of offenders. Nevertheless, it is often difficult to determine the age of workers because minors frequently lie to protect themselves.

For some NGOs it becomes hard to distinguish the victims of trafficking from those who are working in the sex industry, literally trying to survive. Some NGOs advocate for women, and others focus more on children's rights, and yet others advocate for illegal migrants. It is possible that in order to help one population, another is compromised. The solution urged by one NGO may not be regarded by another NGO as the best one. For example, one agency may feel strongly that children be rescued even if it means repatriation for some women.

Raids

At present the method that is often used to combat trafficking is the raid of a brothel. This intervention has many complications and is far from an ideal method of "rescuing victims." There are a number of issues to consider when conducting a raid.

One problem is keeping the plan to raid from those who may tip off brothel owners. In some areas, corrupt government agents are involved in trafficking or are paid to warn brothel owners of impending raids (Phongpaichit et al., 1998). NGOs report that there have been cases where brothel owners have been tipped off and cleared everyone out before the raid occurs. Keeping security tight around planning a raid has sometimes meant that very few NGOs are notified in advance and that required support systems such as social workers, interpreters, appropriate shelters and medical services may not be in place.

Often, although a raid is designed to rescue victims of trafficking, illegal immigrants who are working in a brothel voluntarily, and voluntary Thai sex workers will be caught in the net. Some NGOs suggest that letting the voluntary sex workers in a brothel know about upcoming raids may be a way for them to avoid becoming part of an operation that is not intended to involve them but invariably does. However, it is feared that the sex workers would likely inform the brothel owner, and if not, it may be difficult for them to explain their absence on the day of the raid. Others propose that voluntary sex workers choose not to work in brothels where victims of trafficking are located or else face the consequences of becoming caught and arrested in a raid. However, it is unknown how much choice these women really have about location of work.

Illegal immigrants who are voluntarily working at brothels face additional consequences of a raid. These women are subject to prosecution as illegal immigrants and perhaps deportation to a country where circumstances may be dire. Often, these women find a way to return to their work in Thailand. Some NGOs recognize these issues and are working on ways to avoid involving voluntary sex workers from being casualties of the fight against trafficking. This may include obtaining more accurate data about the makeup of a brothel before raiding and then choosing to focus on those brothels that engage in the most egregious forms of trafficking and have the most number of trafficking victims, rather than conducting raids of brothels that mostly contain voluntary sex workers. It may also include changing the criminal procedure so that prosecutions could be based on, for example, buying a trafficking victim out of the brothel and using her testimony at trial, rather than conducting a raid.

Research Needs

The most obvious need for research is for prevalence studies that would accurately count the number of trafficked persons in Thailand. UNESCO is currently working on a village-based sentinel system for tracking and analyzing the trade in girls and women from the Upper Mekong Region into Thailand. To augment that effort, research is needed to directly study those women and children who have been trafficked. Qualitative research is ideally suited to explore the processes and dynamics of trafficking and to develop the conceptual foundations for larger quantitative studies. For example, despite the focus on recruitment for human trafficking, not enough is known about the variability of recruitment strategies. Equally important, more data are necessary to better understand what happens to women and children once they are trafficked into the sex trade. Policy makers and researchers know too little about how intervention strategies such as raids affect the lives of victims of trafficking, and too little research has been done to query victims of trafficking about their needs. Finally, there is a large gap in our knowledge about what happens to victims of trafficking once they have been returned to their communities. Personal interviews and focus groups with victims of trafficking could provide insight into these issues. Qualitative research, especially if it empowers trafficking victims to shape the nature of the questions asked, can offer a voice to those who have for too long been forced into silence.

Accompanying this need is the necessity for a common definition for trafficking that could be utilized across studies. As noted earlier, differing definitions result in widely varying prevalence estimates and make it difficult to determine whether efforts to combat trafficking are producing results. There is a need for program evaluations to examine the effectiveness of the various strategies to halt trafficking and to determine the effectiveness of rehabilitation programs that emphasize vocational training to the victims of trafficking. Researchers in trafficking should consider collaborative efforts to bring together the differing perspectives and agendas of various professionals involved in combating trafficking, such as police, lawyers, social workers, economists, and policy makers, for the purpose of developing a common understanding of the problem.

Implications For Social Work

The intersection of globalization and international migration means that increasing numbers of people find themselves working outside their country of origin. Those who are trafficked are among the most vulnerable and exploited of this unprecedented flux of people. Thailand and Southeast Asia represent an important source of trafficked people to wealthy Western countries, especially to fuel the sex industry. Some citizens from the "wealthy West" travel to Thailand and Southeast Asia to procure sex from trafficked persons, most notably women and children. While directly responsible for certain features of this perverse supply and demand function, Western nations (especially the United States) have been quick to criticize countries such as Thailand for doing too little to halt trafficking, while at the same time contributing too few resources to make much of a difference. The million dollars annually granted by the U.S. to fund anti-trafficking efforts in Thailand translates into, at best, several dollars to aid each trafficking victim.

Moreover, globalization demands that social workers embrace more than just local and national perspectives but an international viewpoint as well to understand the context and dynamics of human trafficking. Trafficking in humans, especially for sexual exploitation, is such an egregious violation of human rights, human dignity, and our professional code of ethics that it compels us to approach the problem not only by tending to the trafficking victims in our communities but also working to stop it from occurring in the first place. In this area the commitment of the profession to social justice dictates that social workers advocate for ways in which U.S. resources and policies can complement and expand the capacity of countries such as Thailand to counter human trafficking. Moreover, social workers can advocate for women and children by tapping into the resources and strengths of the international social work community, and by doing so, address the problem of human trafficking on multiple fronts. This requires, at a minimum, establishing and strengthening international collaboration and networks among NGOs working in the field. Ideally, it entails coordinating policy and service between sending and receiving countries to better aid victims of human trafficking.

Social workers need to recognize that some of the thousands of trafficked women and children from Thailand and Southeast Asia will end up in the United States as our clients in emergency rooms, domestic violence shelters, mental health facilities, and child welfare systems. To intervene effectively, social workers must have knowledge about the realities of trafficking and be nonjudgmental in dealing with trafficking victims, especially those who have worked in the sex industry.

Discussion Questions

1   *What are the estimates of the number of women and children who are trafficked every year from Southeast Asia and where are most of them trafficked to?*

2   *What are the consequences of trafficking?*

3   *How does sex work and trafficking in Thailand work?*

4   *What has Thailand done to attempt to halt trafficking?*

5   *What is the difference between trafficking versus sex work?*

6   *What is the most common method used to combat trafficking in Thailand?*

7   *What are the implications of trafficking for social workers?*

References

Arnold, C. & Bertone, A. (2002, Winter). Addressing the sex trade in Thailand: Some lessons learned from NGOs part 1. *Gender Issues*, 26-51.

Baker, S. (2000). *The changing situation of child prostitution in Northern Thailand: A study of Changwat Chiang Rai.* Thailand: ECPAT International.

Barr, C. (1996). Asia's traffickers keep girls in sexual servitude. *The Christian Science Monitor: The Child Sex Trade, 88,* 11.

Bertone, C. (2000, Winter). Sexual trafficking in women. *Gender Issues*, 4-22.

Beyrer, C., Khamboonruang, C., Natpratan, C., Celentano, D., & Nelson, K.E. (1994), Incident HIV and STDs in direct and indirect commercial sex workers (CSWs) in Thailand. *Tenth International AIDS conference,* Yokohama, Japan, 7-12 August (oral presentation).

Beyrer, C. (2001). Shan women and girls and the sex industry in Southeast Asia: Political causes and human rights implications. *Social Science and Medicine, 53,* 543-550.

Derks, A. (2000). *Combating trafficking in Southeast Asia.* Geneva, Switzerland. International Organization for Migration.

ECPAT (2003). *Country profile: Myanmar.* Retrieved September 16, 2003, from http://www.ecpat.net/eng/Ecpat_inter/projects/monitoring/ online_database/index.asp.

Hanenberg, R., & Rojanapithayakorn, W. (1998). Changes in prostitution and the AIDS epidemic in Thailand. *AIDS Care, 10*(1), 69-80.

Healy, L. (2001). *International social work.* New York: Oxford University Press.

Hollingsworth, L.D. (2003). International adoption among families in the United States. *Social Work, 48,* 209-217.

Human Rights Watch. (2000, September). *Owed justice, Thai women trafficked into debt bondage in Japan.* New York: Author.

International Organization for Migration. (1999). *Bangkok declaration on irregular migration.* Retrieved September 4, 2003, from http://www.iom.int/DOCUMENTS/OFFICIALTXT/EN/Bangkok_decl.htm.

International Organization for Migration. (2000). *World Migration Report 2000.* Geneva, Switzerland: Author.

International Organization for Migration. (2001). New IOM figures on the global scale of trafficking. *Trafficking in Migrants, 23.*

International Organization for Migration. (2003). *World Migration Report 2000.* Geneva, Switzerland: Author.

Jenkins, R.A., Torugsa, K., Mason, C.J., Jamroenratana, V., Lalang, C., Nitayaphan, S., et al. (1999). HIV risk behavior patterns among young Thai men. *AIDS and Behavior, 3*(4), 335-346.

Leheny, D. (1995). A political economy of Asian sex tourism. *Annals of Tourism Research, 22*(2), 267-384.

Leuchtag, A. (2003, January/February). Human rights, sex trafficking, and prostitution. *Humanist,* 10-15.

Maticka-Tyndale, E., Elkins, D., Haswell-Elkins, M., Rujkarakorn, D., Kuyyakanond, T., & Stam, S. (1997). Contexts and patterns of men's commercial sexual partnerships in Northeast Thailand: Implications for AIDS prevention. *Social Science and Medicine, 44*(2), 199-213.

Mekong Region Law Center. (1999). *Proceedings of the 1997 Regional Conference on Trafficking of Women and Children.* Bangkok, Thailand.

Noikorn, U. (2003, August 2). *Thailand sex tycoon turns civic avenger.* Retrieved September 7, 2003, from http://www.ledger-enquirer.com/mid/ledger enquirer/news/state/6441485.htm.

People smuggling: Trafficking in north at crisis levels. (2003, January 29). *Nation.* Retrieved September 7, 2003, from http://www.nationmulti media.com/page.arcview.php3?clid=2&id=73172&usrsess=1&Keyword=

Pettman, J.J. (1996). An international economy of sex? In E. Kofman & G. Young (Eds.), *Global theory and practice* (pp. 191-208). New York: Pinter Publishing.

Phongpaichit, P., Piriyarangsan, S., & Treerat, N. (1998). *Guns, girls, gambling and ganja: Thailand's illegal economy.* Bangkok, Thailand: Silkworm Books.

The Protection Project. (2002, March). *Human rights report on trafficking in persons, especially women and children.* Washington, DC: Author.

Royal Thai Government. (2003). *Memorandum of understanding on guidelines for relevant agencies to work together in dealing with human trafficking of children and women.* Bangkok, Thailand: Author.

Shan Human Rights Foundation & Shan Women's Action Network. (2002). *License to rape: The Burmese military regime's use of sexual violence in the ongoing war in Shan State.* Retrieved September 17, 2003, from http://www.shanland.org/HR/Publication/LtoR/license_to_rape.htm.

Skolnik, L., & Boontinand, J. (1999). Traffic in women in Asia-Pacific. *Forum for Applied Research and Public Policy, 14*(1), 76-81.

Thai Ministry of Labour and Social Welfare. (n.d.). *Laws relating to prevention and combating commercial sexual exploitation and trafficking in women and children.* Bangkok, Thailand.

United Nations Development Programme. (2002). *Human development report 2002.* New York: Oxford University Press.

United Nations Educational, Scientific, and Cultural Organization. (n.d.). *Trafficking project* [Brochure]. Bangkok, Thailand: Author.

United Nations High Commissioner for Refugees. (2003, August 4). *2002 statistics on asylum-seekers, refugees, and others of concern to UNHCR.* Retrieved September 14, 2003, from http://www.unhcr.ch/cgi-bin/texis/ vtx/statistics.

U.S. Department of State. (2000). *Country reports on human rights practices for 1999.* Washington, DC. Retrieved September 17, 2003, from http://www. usis.usemb.se/human/human1999/thailand.html.

U.S. Department of State (2001). *Country reports on human rights practices for 2000.* Washington, DC. Retrieved September 12, 2003, from http://www.state.gov/g/drl/rls/hrrpt/2001/.

U.S. Department of State (2002a). *Country reports on human rights practices for 2001.* Washington, DC. Retrieved September 12, 2003 from http://www.state.gov/g/drl/ris/hrrpt/2002.

U.S. Department of State (2002b, June). *Victims of trafficking and violence protection act 2000: Trafficking in person's report.* Washington, DC: Author.

U.S. Department of State. (2003). *Fact Sheet: Rape by the Burmese military in ethnic regions.* Washington, DC. Retrieved September 15, 2003, from http://www.state.gov/g/drl/rls/16087.htm.

PART VI

THE SEX TRAFFICKER PROFILE

Meet the Traffickers. This paper discusses the kind of person who would sell another and provides a profile of such an individual. This paper discusses the various methods used to entrap girls into the life of prostitution, and the important, but unfortunate, role some corrupt law enforcement officials routinely play in facilitating the sex trafficking trade.

27

MEET THE TRAFFICKERS: WHAT KIND OF PERSON WOULD SELL ANOTHER? YOU MIGHT BE SURPRISED

Victor Malarek, *Senior Investigative Reporter for CTV, Canadian Television*

In a dusty farm village 80 miles north of Phnom Penh—the capital of Cambodia—two women sit cross-legged on a floor inside a ramshackle hut. They are transacting an important business deal and haggle for about 10 minutes before settling on the amount—2,000,000 riels, about $500.

A moment later, one of the women yells out: 'Srey!'

It's her daughter—the youngest of six children, a beaming, brown-eyed 11-year-old. Srey scurries into the hut and in a matter-of-fact tone her mother tells her that she will be accompanying her 'auntie' to the city for a short while. She is to do as she is told and she will be home in a few months.

Srey is scared. She instantly distrusts the hard-eyed, made-up lady called 'auntie'. But she obeys her mother and leaves with just the clothes on her back and her favourite rag doll.

Srey is about to enter a seedy brothel in downtown Phnom Penh—and there is not a thing she can do about it. She has no protector and no rescuer. Three days later, her face caked with mascara and ruby red lipstick, her body clad in a purple silk sarong, her virginity is sold to a portly Japanese businessman for $500. He got to use her for five days during which time he brutalized the terrified child. For the next two weeks, Srey's body was sold for $10 a customer to American, British and German paedophiles—sex tourists who care only about what their money can buy.

Then, as if someone flipped a switch, Srey's value plummeted. She was now used goods and only worth $2 a customer, mostly Cambodians and Thais. Three months later, her body racked with gonorrhea and HIV, she was sent home to die.

In a world where young women and girls are sold by the tens of thousands daily, Srey's tragic story reveals a side of trafficking that most people can never fathom—the sale of a child by her mother into the sex trade.

497

'No problem'

Most people tend to think—or want to believe—that traffickers are all thick-necked, beady-eyed thugs, members of organized crime gangs like the Albanian or Russian mob, the Italian mafia, the Japanese yakuza, Chinese triads or the Hell's Angles. But the trafficking ocean is teeming with small-time bottom-feeders who know they can make a lot of cash selling desperate, unsuspecting young women and girls to pimps and brothel owners around the globe. Luring just one person can net a trafficker anywhere from $250 to $5,000.

Traffickers use every ruse imaginable. Some even hold job fairs at high schools and universities offering exciting opportunities as nannies, maids and waitresses in foreign cities. They dispatch slick talking headhunters into towns and villages. And sadly some of the traffickers are themselves trafficked women who've been told that if they can bring in two or three fresh bodies, they will be set free.

In a spacious apartment furnished with black leather sofas and state-of-the art electronics, Ludwig Fainberg—aka: Tarzan—brags about the ease with which he was able to get young women from Russia into any Western nation. A one-time member of a notorious Russian organized crime gang in New York City, Fainberg said that he could supply women from Russia, Ukraine and Romania, 'No problem. The price is $10,000, a girl's landed. It's simple. It's easy to get access to the girls. It's a phone call. I know brokers in Moscow, St Petersburg and Kiev. I can call Moscow tomorrow and show you how easy it is. I can get 10 to 15 girls shipped to me in a week.'

Traffickers rely on threats, intimidation and beatings to control their victims. But in the case of the thousands of girls trafficked from Nigeria to work highways and truck stops in Italy, Greece and Spain, they count on something more sinister to keep them in check--juju or voodoo.

Before leaving Benin City to 'make good money braiding hair for tourists on the beaches of Italy', 16-year-old Sarah was required by her trafficker, a family friend, to visit an ohen, a priest of the indigenous religion. 'I was made to swear an oath never to say anything. The priest took some of my hair and finger nails and warned if I broke my promise, I would go mad and would suffer greatly in my next lives.'

When she arrived in Naples, Sarah was told by her Nigerian madam that she was to work as a prostitute. Two months later, she was picked up by the Italian police. Her biggest fear remains the curse of the juju taking hold of her mind and body.

Respectable Individuals

In the hustle and bustle of Odessa, Ukraine's Black Sea port, scores of boyfriends or 'pretty boys' are on the hunt, combing the discotheques for naive young women. With guile and charm the 'pretty boy' sweeps his quarry off her feet and invites her for a weekend outside the country—to Istanbul to meet his family. Within moments of her arrival, she is sold to a brothel owner.

This boyfriend approach has also been adapted by traffickers using mail-order bride agencies to ensnare victims. With countless women clinging to the fairy-tale dream of a blossoming romance and a better life in the West, the pickings are ridiculously easy.

Luan Plakici, a 26-year-old political asylum seeker from Kosovo and former interpreter for a number of London law firms specializing in immigration, quickly spotted the cash flow from trafficking. Soon after securing British citizenship, he headed for Moldova where he romanced a 16-year-old, married her and brought her back to Britain. While still on honeymoon he put her to work, servicing half a dozen clients. In the first year of their marriage, he forced his teenage bride to have two abortions, putting her back to work the day after the procedure. Plakici was eventually arrested, tried, found guilty and sentenced to 23 years in prison on seven counts of trafficking.

Rescued women and girls tell story after story of trusted people with respectable positions who have used their influence to con the unsuspecting. In one instance, a doctor who graduated from medical school in Ukraine decided to leave her native land for the greener pastures of Essex, England, to practice medicine. But the money Dr Oksana Ryniekska thought she'd make wasn't rolling in. So she devised a plan. The 26-year-old doctor became a trafficker. Instead of setting up a clinic, she set up a brothel over a dry-cleaning shop and trafficked in nine young women from her homeland. Ryniekska told her victims she would get them visas so they could learn English. But the only English they learned was the sexual terminology required to understand and service their steady stream of 'johns'. In just eight months, before being busted in an undercover sting, the doctor raked in more than $210,000. She was found guilty of trafficking, sentenced to three months in prison and then deported.

Keeping the Peace

Throughout the trafficking maze, victims routinely come up against people who should be on their side—the police. But in countries like Greece and Israel, police have become directly involved in trafficking themselves. Apart from making a lot of extra cash, the complicit cops get rewarded by the brothel owners with free sex with the young girls.

In war-ravaged Bosnia-Herzegovina, United Nations soldiers from a host of nations were brought in to bring peace and order. With the arrival of tens of thousands of peacekeepers from the US, Canada, France, Germany, Britain, Italy and Russia—the majority testosterone laden young men—the local criminal network kicked into overdrive. They turned to traffickers who began to import thousands of teenage girls from nearby Romania, Moldova and Ukraine.

The UN also brought in hundreds of police officers from a variety of nations as members of the International Police Task Force (IPTF). One of those was David Lamb, a former police officer from Philadelphia. While questioning a group of young Romanian women rescued in a brothel raid, he learned that several Romanian cops working with the IPTF were directly involved in the recruitment, trafficking, smuggling and sale of these women to local brothels. Lamb blew the whistle but instead of getting co-operation from top UN officials, he had his life threatened and his investigation killed. Lamb didn't give up. Instead, he sent an email to the IPTF command identifying five UN police officers 'linked to allegations of involvement in women trafficking'. He also pointed out that whenever investigations uncovered UN involvement, support from UN headquarters coincidently dried up. But that wasn't all.

'During investigations by my office into UN personnel involvement in women trafficking, my investigators and I experienced an astonishing cover-up attempt that seemed to extend to the highest levels of the UN headquarters,' Lamb wrote. Soon after, Lamb was sent packing and his investigation was bogged down in a sea of UN red tape.

Traffickers, and those who collude with them, really do come in all shapes, sizes and guises.

Victor Malarek is the author of The Natashas—The New Global Sex Trade, Vision 2004.

Discussion Questions

1   *Is there any evidence presented in this research paper to suggest that mothers will knowingly sell their daughters into prostitution?*

2   *What is the stereotype of the trafficker and why is it not accurate?*

3   *What are "pretty boys?"*

4   *What evidence is there that the police are complicit in trafficking?*

INDEX